S0-AXC-456

Psychophysiology
Human Behavior
and
Physiological Response
Fourth Edition

Psychophysiology
Human Behavior
and
Physiological Response
Fourth Edition

John L. Andreassi
Baruch College
City University of New York

LAWRENCE ERLBAUM ASSOCIATES, PUBLISHERS
2000   Mahwah, New Jersey   London

Copyright © 2000 by Lawrence Erlbaum Associates, Inc.
All rights reserved. No part of this book may be reproduced in any form,
by photostat, microfilm, retrieval system, or any other means, without
prior written permission of the publisher.

Lawrence Erlbaum Associates, Inc., Publishers
10 Industrial Avenue
Mahwah, NJ 07430

Cover design by Kathryn Houghtaling Lacey

Library of Congress Cataloging-in-Publication Data

Andreassi, John L.
Psychophysiology : human behavior and physiological response /
    by John L. Andreassi. — 4th ed.
        p. cm.
Includes bibliographical references and index.
ISBN 0-8058-2832-X (cloth : alk. paper) —
ISBN 0-8058-2833-8 (pbk. : alk. paper)
1. Psychophysiology. I. Title.
QP360.A53   2000
612.8—dc21

                                            99-41207
                                                 CIP

Books published by Lawrence Erlbaum Associates are printed on
acid-free paper, and their bindings are chosen for strength and durability.

Printed in the United States of America
10 9 8 7 6 5 4 3 2 1

To John, Jeanine, and Cristina

Contents

Preface

The plan of this book is to provide students with elementary information regarding the anatomy and physiology of various body systems, methods of recording the activity of these systems, and studies and concepts describing how these physiological responses have been correlated with psychological aspects of behavior. Essentially, then, I reaffirm that the goal of this fourth edition is to introduce the beginning student to the field of psychophysiology. My book provides a comprehensive introduction for those new to the area, whether they are upper-level undergraduates, graduate students, or professionals new to the field who are seeking basic information. Psychology students, and especially those in courses concerned with physiology and behavior, physiological psychology, and psychophysiology, will be users of this book. The text will also be valuable to students of behavioral medicine, psychosomatic medicine, biofeedback, biomedical engineering, and to those in other life sciences, including biology and physiology.

The field of psychophysiology continues to develop and grow at an ever increasing pace. In this fourth edition, there are both structural and content changes. There are now separate chapters on pupillography and eye movements. The chapter on eye movements has been expanded to reflect increasing interest in the eye blink and its relation to stress, and, especially, to the startle pattern. A section has been added to cover work on the eye blink component of the startle reaction as it relates to attention, emotion, and psychopathology.

The chapter on applied psychophysiology has been divided to define a division between nonclinical (e.g., detection of deception) and applications to patients in clinical settings (e.g., schizophrenia). Thus, there are now 19 chapters in this book, compared to 17 in the third edition. Another structural change is the addition of brief summaries after each major section in the book. In addition, an Appendix on laboratory safety has been included in this new edition. Part of this Appendix deals with concerns over the possible spread of infectious diseases in the psychophysiology laboratory, measures to prevent this possibility, and the other major portion concerns equipment safety.

Content changes have been made in all chapters to cover some of the newer areas of research, as well as to update findings in the traditional topics of interest. There is new information on brain waves in memory and perception (especially gamma wave activity and event-related desynchronization.) Studies of alpha brain waves and intelligence, and new information on brain imaging (positron emission tomography and functional magnetic resonance imaging) and behavior have been added. Recent research on event-related brain potentials in memory, attention, and intelligence is presented, as well as the use of brain potentials in the study of smell. New findings on patterning of facial muscle activity in emotional expressions and on central nervous system control of electrodermal activity are discussed. Other additions concern pupillary changes during processing load and heart activity changes under conditions of incentive and psychological job strain. Cardiovascular reactivity under different conditions of stress, and as a function of personality and social factors, continues as a lively topic of interest and has been extensively updated. Applications of psychophysiology to ergonomics and associated studies of vigilance, workload, and job satisfaction are considered. An update on biofeedback applications to various ailments, especially to asthma, has been accomplished along with some novel information in the area of psychoneuroimmunology (brain, behavior, and immunity). Studies bearing on conceptualizations in psychophysiology have been added as well as newer findings in environmental psychophysiology, including radiation, nicotine, and caffeine effects on brain electrophysiology. I have continued efforts to alert readers to major issues and questions early in most of the chapters.

Psychophysiology continues to be a vibrant and dynamic field. Several societies serve the professional needs of psychophysiologists by organizing meetings and publishing journals. Among these are the Society for Psychophysiological Research, which publishes *Psychophysiology*; the International Organization of Psychophysiology, responsible for the *International Journal of Psychophysiology*; the Association for Applied Psychophysiology and Biofeedback, which publishes *Applied Psychophysiology and Biofeedback*; and the Psychophysiology Society, responsible for coordination and publication of the *Journal of Psychophysiology*. Other organizations such as the Society of Behavioral Medicine, the American Psychosomatic Society, and the EEG Society also help to meet the professional needs of psychophysiologists. In addition, a new technical group of the International Ergonomics Association called Psychophysiology in Ergonomics has been formed to promote psychophysiological research and applications at the workplace. A number of universities have programs of study in basic and applied psychophisiology. Interested students can contact officials at the various societies mentioned to obtain more information.

This book is based largely on the work of psychophysiologists and other life scientists. I have been able to refer to their work that appears in scientific journals, books, technical reports, and edited handbooks of psychophysiology. There are over 1,700 references to their work, with citations conveniently presented at the end of each chapter.

Many psychophysiologists have generously supplied me with reprints of publications, and I would like to thank them at this time: Dr. Kimmo Ahlo, Dr. Michael Allen, Dr. Robert Barry, Dr. Margaret Bradley, Dr. Cornelis Brunia, Dr. John Cacioppo, Dr. John Connolly, Dr. Bruce Cuthbert, Dr. Richard Davidson, Dr. Ulf Dimberg, Dr. Blaine Ditto, Dr. Thomas Elbert, Dr. Monica Fabiani, Dr. David Friedman, Dr. M. Fredrickson, Dr. John Furedy, Dr. Susan Girdler, Dr. Eric. Granholm, Dr. Gabriele Gratton, Dr. Rita Hari, Dr. L. Hawk, Dr. Kenneth Hugdahl, Dr. William Iacono, Dr. Ray Johnson, Jr., Dr. Rathe Karrer, Dr. Thomas Kamarck, Dr. Alphonse Kok, Dr. Marta Kutas, Dr. Peter Lang, Dr. Kathleen Lawler, Dr. Kathleen Light, Dr. Paul Lehrer, Dr. William Lovallo, Dr. H. Lyytinen, Dr. Constantine Mangina, Dr. Helen Beuzeron-Mangina, Dr. Risto Naatanen, Dr. A. Papanicolaou, Dr. C. Patrick, Dr. John Polich, Dr. S. Porges, Dr, Daniel Ruchkin, Dr. Neil Schneiderman, Dr. Stuart Steinhauer, Dr. Andrew Sherwood, Dr. Joseph Tecce, Dr. Daniel Tranel, Dr. Peter Ullsperger, Dr. Dieter Vaitl, and Dr. Scott Vrana. In addition, several researchers have provided me with glossy photographs for use as figures in this new edition, and for this I express my gratitude to Drs. Peter Lang, Scott Vrana, and Eric Granholm.

Lawrence Erlbaum and Joe Petrowski of Lawrence Erlbaum Associates continue to make LEA a pleasant organization with which to work. Debra Riegert, Art Lizza, and Nadine Simms of Erlbaum helped to smooth the editorial and production process. Others who deserve special thanks are my wife Gina, and children John, Jeanine, and Cristina who continue to be a source of inspiration for me. I am proud to say that each of them has developed their own brand of scholarship. In addition, my long-time friends, Milt and Sally Adams, have provided the kind of upbeat attitude and example that helps an author through occasional bouts of adversity. Finally, there are two big brothers (George and Eugene) and one big sister (Matilda) who serve as unique role models.

—*J. L. A.*
New York
March, 1999

Copyright Information

Fig. 1.1. Copyright 1978 by Gahan Wilson. Reprinted by permission.

Fig. 2.1. From C. R. Noback and R. J. Demarest. *The Human Nervous System.* Copyright 1975, McGraw-Hill Publishing Company. Reprinted by permission.

Fig. 2.2. From C. R. Noback and R. J. Demarest. *The Human Nervous System.* Copyright 1975, McGraw-Hill Publishing Company. Reprinted by permission.

Fig. 2.3. From C. R. Noback and R. J. Demarest. *The Human Nervous System.* Copyright 1975, McGraw-Hill Publishing Company. Reprinted by permission.

Fig. 2.4. Modified from C. R. Noback and R. J. Demarest. *The Human Nervous System.* Copyright 1975, McGraw-Hill Publishing Company. Reprinted by permission.

Fig. 2.5. Modified from C. R. Noback and R. J. Demarest. *The Human Nervous System.* Copyright 1975, McGraw-Hill Publishing Company. Reprinted by permission.

Fig. 2.6. From S. P. Grossman. *Essentials of Physiological Psychology.* New York: Wiley, 1973, as taken from H. H. Jasper, "Electroencephalography" in W. Penfield & T. C. Erickson, *Epilepsy and Cerebral Localization.* Springfield: C. C. Thomas, 1941. Reprinted by permission.

Fig. 2.8. Adapted from E. Callaway. *Brain Electrical Potentials and Individual Psychological Differences.* New York: Grune & Stratton, 1975. Reprinted by permission.

Fig. 2.9. Photo by courtesy of Drs. Williamson and Kaufman of New York University, 1989.

Fig. 2.10. From Carlson, N. R. *Physiology of Behavior.* (2nd ed.) Copyright 1980, Allyn & Bacon, Inc., Redrawn with permission.

Fig. 2.11. From Carlson, N. R. *Physiology of Behavior* (2nd ed.). Copyright 1980, Allyn & Bacon, Inc., Redrawn with permission.

Fig. 4.1. Beatty, J. "Operant control of posterior theta rhythm and vigilance performance; Repeated treatments and transfer of training." In N. Birbaumer Hand. D. Kimmel (Eds.), *Biofeedback and Self-Regulation.* Copyright 1980, Lawrence Erlbaum Associates. Reprinted by permission.

Fig. 4.2. From F. Snyder and J. Scott. "The psychophsiology of sleep" in N. S. Greenfield and R. A. Sternbach (Eds.), *Handbook of Psychophysiology.* Copyright 1972 by Holt, Rinehart & Winston. Reprinted by permission of Holt, Rinehart & Winston.

Fig. 4.3. From F. E. Bloom and A. Lazerson. *Brain, Mind, and Behavior.* (2nd ed.). Copyright 1985, 1988, Educational Broadcasting Company. Reprinted by permission of W. H. Freeman & Company.

Fig. 5.1. From H. G. Vaughan, Jr. "The relationship of brain activity to scalp recordings of event-related potentials" in E. Donchin & D. B. Lindsley (Eds.), *Average Evoked Potentials.* Washington, DC: NASA, 1969. Reprinted by permission.

Fig. 5.2. Left side of figure is from J. J. Tecce. "Contingent negative variation (CNV) and psychological processes in man," *Psychological Bulletin*, 1972, 77, 73–108. Reprinted by permission. Right side of figure is adapted from H. G. Vaughan, Jr., et al. "Topography of the human motor potential," *Electroen-*

cephalography and Clinical Neurophysiology 25, 1968, Fig. 2. Reprinted by permission of the author and Elsevier Publishing.

Fig. 6.1. From Hillyard, S. A., & Hansen, J. C. "Attention: Electrophysiological Approaches." In M.G.H. Coles, S. W. Porges & E. Donchin (Eds.), *Psychophysiology: Systems, Processes, Applications.* Copyright 1986, The Guilford Press. Reprinted by permission.

Fig. 6.2. From A. F. Moskowitz et al. "Corners, receptive fields, and visually evoked cortical potentials," *Perception and Psychophysics,* 1974, 15, 325–330. Reprinted by permission.

Fig. 6.3. From J. L. Andreassi et al. "Amplitude changes in the visual evoked cortical potential with backward masking," *Electroencephalography and Clinical Neurophysiology* 1976, 41, 384–398. Reprinted by permission.

Fig. 7.1. From J. J. Tecce. "Contingent negative variation and individual differences," *Archives of General Psychiatry,* 1971, 24, 1–16. Copyright 1971, American Medical Association. Reprinted by permission.

Fig. 7.2. From W. Becker et al. "Bereitschaftspotential preceding voluntary show and rapid hand movements" in W. C. McCallum and J. R. Knott (Eds.), *The Responsive Brain.* Copyright 1976, John Wright & Sons, Ltd. Reprinted by permission.

Fig. 7.3. From S. Sutton, M. Braren, and J. Zubin. "Evoked potential correlates of stimulus uncertainty," *Science,* 1965, 150, 1187–1188. Reprinted by permission.

Fig. 7.4. From N. K. Squires et al. "Two varieties of long latency positive waves evoked by unpredictable stimuli in man," *Electroencephalography and Clinical Neurophysiology,* 1975, 38, 387–401. Reprinted by permission.

Fig. 8.1. From S. W. Jacob and C. A. Francone. *Structure and Function in Man.* Copyright 1970, W. B. Saunders Co. Reprinted by permission.

Fig. 8.2. From S. W. Jacob and C. A. Francone. *Structure and Function in Man.* Copyright 1970, W. B. Saunders Co. Reprinted by permission.

Fig. 8.3. Reprinted by permission of author and publisher from R. C. Wilcott and H. G. Beenken. "Relation of intergrated surface electromyography and muscle tension," *Perceptual and Motor Skills,* 1957, 7, 295–298.

Fig. 8.5. Adapted from J. F. Davis. *Manual of Surface Electromyography.* WADC Technical Report, 59–184, 1959. Used by permission.

Fig. 8.6. Copyright 1986, The Society for Psychophysiological Research. Reprinted by permission of the publisher and the authors from "Guidelines for human electromyographic research," by A. J. Fridlund and J. T. Cacioppo, *Psychophysiology,* 1986, 23, 567–589. (Updated diagram courtesy of Drs. Fridlund, Cacioppo and Tassinary.)

Fig. 8.7. Copyright 1993, The Society for Psychophysiological Research. Reprinted with the permission of Cambridge University Press and the author from "The psychophysiology of disgust: Differentiating negative emotional contexts with facial EMG," by S. R. Vrana, *Psychophysiology,* 1993, 30, 279–286.

Fig. 9.1. From P. H. Venables and I. Martin (Eds.). *Manual of Psychophysiological Methods.* Copyright 1967, North-Holland Publishing Co. Reprinted by permission.

Fig. 9.2. From *Essentials of Human Anatomy,* 6th ed., by Russel T. Woodburne. Copyright 1978 by Oxford Press, Inc. Reprinted by permission.

Fig. 9.3. Copyright 1967, The Society for Psychophysiology Research. Reprinted by permission of the publisher and the author from "Palmar skin resistance and sweat-gland counts in drug and non-drug states," by J. J. Juniper, Jr., D. E. Blanton, and R. A. Dykman, *Psychophysiology,* 1967, 4, 231–243.

Fig. 9.4. From P. H. Venables and M. J. Christie. "Mechanism, instrumentation, recording techniques, and quantification of responses." In W. F. Prokasy and D. C. Raskin (Eds.), *Electrodermal Activity in Psychological Research.* Copyright 1973, Academic Press. Reprinted by permission.

Fig. 10.2. From J. Beatty. "Task evoked pupillary responses, processing load, and the structure of processing resource" *Psychological Bulletin,* 1982, 91, 276–292. Reprinted by permission.

Fig. 10.3. Copyright 1996, The Society for Psychophysiological Research. Reprinted with the permission of Cambridge University Press and the author from "Pupillary responses index cognitive resource limitations," by E. Granholm, et al. *Psychophysiology,* 1996, 33, 457–461.

Fig. 11.1. From S. W. Jacob and C. A. Francone. *Structure and Function in Man.* Copyright 1970, W. B. Saunders Co. Reprinted by permission.

Fig. 11.2. From B. Shackel. "Eye movement recordings by electroculography." In P. H. Venables and I. Martin (Eds.). *Manual of Psychophysiological Methods.* Copyright 1967, North-Holland Publishing Co. Reprinted by permission.

Fig. 11.4. From B. Shackel. "Eye movement recordings by electroculography." In P. H. Venables and I. Martin (Eds.). *Manual of Psychophysiological Methods.* Copyright 1967, North-Holland Publishing Co. Reprinted by permission.

Fig. 11.5. From W. G. Iacono. "Eye movement abnormalities in schizophrenia and affective disorders." In C. W. Johnston and F. J. Pirozzolo. *Neuropsychology of Eye Movements.* Copyright 1988, Lawrence Erlbaum Associates. Reprinted by permission.

Fig. 11.6. From Yarbus, A. L. *Eye Movements and Vision.* Copyright 1967, Plenum Press. Reprinted by permission.

Fig. 11.7. From S. Coren and P. Hoenig. "Eye movements and decrement in Oppel-Kundt illusion," *Perception and Psychophysics*, 1972, 12, 224–225. Reprinted by permission.

Fig. 11.8. Copyright 1988 by the American Psychological Association. From S. R. Vrana, Spence, E. L., & Lang, P. J. "The startle probe response: A new measure of emotion?" *Journal of Abnormal Psychology*, 1988, 97, 487–491. Reprinted by permission from the authors and the American Psychological Association.

Fig. 12.1. From S. W. Jacob and C. A. Francone. *Structure and Function in Man.* Copyright 1970, W. B. Saunders Co. Reprinted by permission.

Fig. 12.2. From S. W. Jacob and C. A. Francone. *Structure and Function in Man.* Copyright 1970, W. B. Saunders Co. Reprinted by permission.

Fig. 12.3. From A. C. Guyton. *Basic Human Physiology.* Copyright 1977, W. B. Saunders Co. Reprinted by permission.

Fig. 12.7. Copyright 1973, The society for Psychophysiological Research. Reprinted by permission of the publisher and the author from "Different heart rate changes to equally intense white noise and tone," by F. K. Graham and D. A. Slaby, *Psychophysiology*, 1973, 10, 347–362.

Fig. 12.8. Copyright 1969, The Society for Psychophysiological Research. Reprinted by permission of the publisher and the author from "Cephalic vasomotor and heart rate measures of orienting and defensive reflexes," by D. C. Raskin, H. Kotses, and J. Bever, *Psychophysiology*, 1969, 6, 149–159.

Fig. 13.1. From Friedman, D. et al. "Cardiac deceleration and E- wave brain potential components in young, middle-aged and elderly adults," *International Journal of Psychophysiology*, 1990, 10, 185–190. Reprinted by permission of the author and Elsevier Science Publishers.

Fig. 14.1. From S. W. Jacob and C. A. Francone. *Structure and Function in Man.* Copyright 1970, W. B. Saunders Co. Reprinted by permission.

Fig. 14.2. From Cook, M. R. "Psychophysiology of Peripheral Vascular Changes." In P. A. Obrist, A. H. Black, J. Brener & L. V. DiCara (Eds.), *Cardiovascular Psychophysiology.* Copyright 1974, Aldine Press. Reprinted by permission.

Fig. 14.3. Copyright 1976, The Society for Psychophysiological Research. Reprinted by permission of the publisher and the author from "An improved mechanical strain gauge for recording penile circumference change," by D. R. Lewis and R. A. Bow, *Psychophysiology*, 1976, 13, 596–599.

Fig. 16.1. From D. Kurtzberg and H. G. Vaughan, Jr. "Electrophysiologic assessment of auditory and visual function in the newborn" *Clinics in Perinatology*, Vol. 12, p. 283, Philadelphia: W. B. Saunders. Reprinted by permission of the authors and publisher.

Fig. 16.2. From D. Kurtzberg and H. G. Vaughan, Jr. "Electrophysiologic assessment of auditory and visual function in the newborn" *Clinics in Perinatology*, Vol. 12, p. 288, Philadelphia: W. B. Saunders. Reprinted by permission of the authors and publisher.

Fig. 16.3. From J. F. Simpson and K. R. Magee. *Clinical Evaluation of the Nervous System.* Copyright 1973, Little, Brown Co. Reprinted by permission.

Fig. 16.4. From A. Starr and L. J. Achor. "Auditory brainstem responses in neurological disease," *Archives of Neurology*, 1975, 32, 761–768. Copyright 1975, American Medical Association. Reprinted by permission.

Fig. 16.5. From C. Shagass and M. Schwartz, "Evoked potential studies in psychiatric patients," *Annals of the New York Academy of Sciences*, 1964, 112, 526–542. Reprinted by permission of the New York Academy of Sciences.

Fig. 18.1. Copyright 1975, The Society for Psychophysiological Research. Reprinted by permission of the publisher and the author from "Some factors influencing the vasomotor response to cold pressor stimulation," by W. Lovallo and A. R. Zeiner, *Psychophysiology*, 1975, 12, 499–505.

Fig. 18.2. Reprinted from M. A. Wenger and M. Ellington. "The measurement of autonomic balance in children: Method and normative data," *Psychosomatic Medicine,* 1943, 5, 241–253. Used by permission.

Fig. 18.4. From J. D. French. "The reticular formation," *Scientific American*, May 1957, 196, 54–60. Copyright 1957 by Scientific American, Inc. All rights reserved. Reprinted by permission.

Fig. 18.5. From J. I. Lacey, 1959; obtained from R. A. Sternbach, *Principles of Psychophysiology*, New York, Academic Press, 1966. Reprinted by permission.

Fig. 19.1. Reprinted by permission from *Neuropharmacology*, A. Salamy, "The effects of alcohol on the variability of the human evoked potential."

Fig. 19.2. From C. S. Rebert et al. "Combined effects of solvents on the rat's auditory system: Styrene and trichloroethylene," *International Journal of Psychophysiology,* 1993, 14, 49–59. Reprinted by permission of the author and Elsevier Science Publishers.

Fig. 19.3. Copyright 1973 by Pergamon Press, Ltd.

1

Introduction to Psychophysiology

DEFINITIONS OF PSYCHOPHYSIOLOGY

In the first edition of this book, I wrote that "the field of psychophysiology is concerned with the measurement of physiological responses as they relate to behavior." The word *behavior* is used now, as then, in the broadest sense to include such diverse activities as sleep, problem solving, reactions to stress, learning, memory, information processing, perception, or—in short—any of the activities that psychologists are inclined to study. This characterization of the field requires some clarification. You, the reader, may ask how psychophysiology differs from the discipline traditionally known as *physiological psychology*; the answer is that it is mainly in the approach and subject matter of these areas, because the goal of understanding the physiology of behavior is the same.

Distinctions have been made between psychophysiology and physiological psychology in terms of how dependent and independent variables are used (Lykken, 1984; Stern, 1964). The *dependent* variables refer to what is actually being measured in a research project, and the *independent* variable is the aspect being manipulated. Stern and Lykken said that in psychophysiology, the dependent variables are physiological (e.g., heart rate) and the independent variables are psychological (e.g., problem solving). However, in physiological psychology the dependent variables are mainly psychological (learning, or perceptual accuracy, as examples), whereas independent variables are physiological (e.g., brain stimulation or removal of brain tissue). This distinction in terms of dependent and independent variables is useful but not entirely satisfactory to Furedy (1983), who argued that this approach does not cover the example of a physiological psychologist who records and studies changes in a single neuron while psychological stimuli are manipulated. According to Furedy's definition: "Psychophysiology is the study of psychological processes in the intact organism as a whole by means of unobtrusively measured physiological processes" (p. 13). He emphasized that a measurement made unobtrusively, as with surface electrodes, results in a more accurate picture of the behaving organism. Mangina (1983) objected to Furedy's use of the term "intact organism" because this would exclude the study of brain damaged, mentally retarded, or drug-influenced persons, and patients suffering from various psychophysiological disorders. Mangina defined psychophysiology as "the science which studies the physiology of psychic functions through the brain–body-interrelationships of the living organism in conjunction with the environment" (p. 22).

At this point, I propose a definition that attempts to integrate those previously offered: *Psychophysiology is the study of relations between psychological manipulations and resulting physiological responses, measured in the living organism, to promote understanding of the relation between mental and bodily processes.* I believe this definition can provide a useful starting point.

ACTIVITIES AND SUBJECT MATTER

A number of activities are as important to the field of psychophysiology as they are to other life sciences. These include the conduct of animal research to allow fuller understanding of basic physiological mechanisms, the development of electronic instrumentation to enable increasingly sophisticated measurements, and the testing of hypotheses that allow researchers to ask questions and obtain answers in their pursuit of knowledge.

Psychological processes studied in psychophysiology range from emotional responses, as in fear and anger, to cognitive activities, such as decision making and problem solving. The reader will find that, in this text, the word *behavior* is used broadly to encompass a variety of human activities including: learning, problem solving, sensing, perceiving, attending, sleeping, and emotional response. The physiological responses include those recorded from the brain, heart, muscles, skin, and eyes, among others. Most of the measures taken in psychophysiology can be obtained from surface areas of the body and are, therefore, considered to be noninvasive. Some of the newer techniques involve what has been termed *neuroimaging*. These include positron emission tomography (PET), functional magnetic resonance imaging (fMRI) and magnetoencephalography (MEG) (Kutas & Federmeier, 1998). The fMRI and MEG are noninvasive, but PET is minimally invasive because it involves injecting a radioactive substance into the blood stream. All of these techniques, along with the usually invasive approaches of traditional physiological psychology, are aimed at learning more about the physiological substrates of behavior. Interest in these physiological substrates has existed for centuries. In fact, this area of investigation is the modern version of what early philosophers, physicians, and scientists struggled with as the "mind–body problem." The questions revolved around the locus of those mental or spiritual events, including thoughts and feelings, that could not be easily labeled as physical activities.

There are exceptions to the noninvasive approach that characterizes most of psychophysiology. For example, some psychophysiologists have recorded directly from brain tissue of patients while they were engaged in cognitive tasks. As I stated previously, however, most studies in this area concern the behaving, intact organism, using surface recordings or other noninvasive techniques. Thus, in psychophysiology, we are able to study heart rate changes that occur in response to unexpected stimuli, or brain activity patterns recorded while an individual listens to music. Speed of response and related muscle activity are also topics of study, as well as eye movement patterns when a person searches for a specific target among other visual stimuli, and changes in electrical activity of the skin surface with emotion-provoking conditions.

An underlying premise in the conduct of these studies is that the information obtained will enable us to better understand the relations and interactions between physiology and behavior. Perhaps we will some day come closer to solving the mind–body problem. As Kutas and Federmeier (1998) point out, modern science recognizes the brain as the most direct substrate for the behaviors that psychophysiologists study. However, measures of heart, muscle, and other activities also aid in our understanding and development of conceptualizations regarding physiology–behavior relationships, an endeavor examined in chapter 18 of this book. At this point, it would be instructive to take a brief look at the historical development of psychophysiology.

HISTORICAL DEVELOPMENT OF PSYCHOPHYSIOLOGY

The rationale for the psychophysiological approach stems from a desire to know more about physiological processes occurring in the organism engaged in a variety of psychological activities; and, this is possible only through very careful observation or the use of specialized instruments. Just as a blood sample tells a physician something about the physical condition of an apparently healthy patient, a sampling of heart rate tells the psychophysiologist something about the emotional state of an outwardly calm individual. It is the point of view here that behavior is the result of ongoing mental processes. Thus, observed behavior is not the equivalent of mental activities, because these activities are not always translated into motor acts. However, these mental activities themselves, although not directly observable, are behaviors.

How did a desire to know more about physiological correlates of behavior develop? Records of when humans first asked about psychophysiological relationships do not exist. It is reasonable to assume that very early humans wondered about the source of our thoughts and other mental activities. There is evidence that Stone Age cavepeople may have associated headaches, distressing thoughts, or evil spirits with the inside of the head, because skulls containing holes (trephined) have been found among the remains of cave dwellers (Carson, Butcher, & Coleman, 1988). One might imagine the following scene, taking place some 250,000 years ago inside a cave illuminated by a fire: Some unfortunate caveperson, probably one who had continuous head pains or heard strange voices, is being held down by several others while an early "neurosurgeon" carefully chips away bits of skin and bone with stone tools to form an opening at the top of the skull. Scientists surmise that this trephining took place because hundreds of skulls of Stone Age cave dwellers have holes that were neatly formed and obviously made with care. In addition, the areas of healed bone around the edges of the opening (called *callus tissue*) suggest that the individual survived the procedure for some time after it was performed. Evidence of healing is more the rule than the exception. Hundreds of skulls with signs of trephination have been found all over Europe, including Denmark, Sweden, Poland, France, Spain, and the British Isles (Haeger, 1988). In one study of skulls found in Peru, there was evidence of healing in 250 out of 400 skulls examined. Special metal saws for the procedure were used as early as 300 B.C. by Celtic warrior–surgeons in Germany and Hungary (Haeger, 1988). Written records indicate that trephining was performed in medieval times presumably to allow evil spirits to escape from inside the heads of tormented or deranged individuals.

One of the earliest recorded expressions of a relationship between a body organ (brain) and mental events is found in Egyptian papyri dating from the 16th century B.C. (Edwin Smith Papyrus). These written records clearly indicate the belief that the brain was recognized as the locus of mental activity, and are all the more remarkable because they are believed to be copies of earlier writings from about 3000 B.C. (Carson, Butcher, & Coleman, 1988). In fact, the papyri reveal that at least one Egyptian physician saw the relation between head injury and difficulty in speech and movement. Smith's papyri were not translated until the early 20th century (Changeaux, 1985). Other Egyptian writings dating from about 1550 B.C. (Eber's Papyri) claim that the heart has a central role in controlling mental activities—including thought, memory, and conciousness. Later Egyptian physicians knew that brain injury could cause aphasia (disturbance in understanding language) and paralysis (Haeger, 1988).

The Greek physician Hippocrates, who was born about 460 B.C., is often referred to as the father of medicine because he systematized much of the medical knowledge of the time. He emphasized the centrality of the brain's role in human behavior by writing that the brain is the organ by which we experience sights, sounds, thoughts, joy, laughter, sorrow, and pain (Penfield & Roberts, 1959). He wrote further that the brain is our interpreter of conscious experience. Hippocrates also advanced the idea that different body fluids ("humors") could affect behavior. This emphasized the physiology–behavior interface in another way. The fluids were identified as black bile, blood, yellow bile, and phlegm. Hippocrates erroneously believed that mental problems could occur when these humors were excessive or out of balance. For example, an excess of phlegm could cause depression, whereas an excess of bile would cause excited and mischievous behavior.

Herophilus, a fourth century B.C. physician, considered to be the father of anatomy, contributed much information about the anatomy of the nervous system (Garrison, 1929). Herophilus distinguished the cerebrum from the cerebellum and wrote that the brain is the center of mental activity. He was also the first on record to distinguish between nerves that received sensations (sensory nerves) and those responsible for movement (motor nerves; Haeger, 1988).

Plato, the philosopher born in 427 B.C., believed that mental activities, and the soul, were localized in the brain. He and other philosophers of his time were concerned with the body–mind problem, or the relationship between physiological activities and spiritual (mental) events. He taught that the body and soul are separate substances (a position called *dualism*), and that the soul lives in the brain.

Aristotle, born in 384 B.C., was a pupil of Plato. He differed from his mentor in his belief that the main function of the brain was to act as a cooling system for the body, lowering the temperature of blood containing food and bringing on sleep (Changeaux, 1985). Aristotle attributed important behavioral functions to the heart because he wrote that it was the seat of mental functions such as sensations, passions, and intellect (perhaps showing the influence of the earlier Egyptians). In addition, Artistotle taught that the heart was the source of nervous control and the location of the soul. Despite his false assignment of such a menial role to the brain, Aristotle is considered to be one of the greatest biologists who ever lived. He initiated the sciences of embryology, zoology, and comparative anatomy (Garrison, 1929). Aristotle was an early contributor to psychology through his classification and accurate descriptions of the five classical senses (vision, hearing, taste, touch, and smell). He also introduced the concept of *association*, which emphasizes the connection of ideas as being critical in allowing their later retrieval from memory. Aristotle believed, contrary to Plato's view, that the body and soul comprised a single entity, a position called *monism*.

The Greek physician Galen, who lived in Rome in the second century A.D., supported the idea of many earlier scientists that the mind is located in the brain. Galen did experiments with animals and concluded that the brain played a critical role in controlling bodily and mental activity. He was convinced that the brain was an organ where mental images and intelligence arise. Galen was the first experimental neurologist; he described the cranial nerves and the sympathetic nervous system and was the first to partially sever the spinal cord of animals to produce hemiplegia (paralysis on one side of the body). However, many of Galen's ideas about function were inaccurate; for example, he claimed that animal spirits passing from the lens of the eye through hollow tubes (optic nerves) transported visual impressions to the brain (Polyak, 1957). He also believed that the most important parts of the brain were the cavities (ventricles) that supposedly contained the animal spirits that were critical for sensory and mental activity.

The important function given to the brain cavities influenced later thinkers and was even represented in anatomical sketches of the visual system by Leonardo DaVinci (Polyak, 1957). Galen also developed Hippocrates' ideas of bodily humors into a more systematic concept of physical factors that influence a person's temperament. According to Galen, the four humors had special functions: phlegm caused sluggishness; black bile induced melancholy; yellow bile caused bad temper; and blood carried vital spirits and produced a cheerful, optimistic temperament. Galen's ideas about body humors were widely accepted through the Middle Ages without much refinement. He set the stage for later theories about differences in physical features of the body as causal factors in personality differences. Most of these later theories had as little scientific verification as those proposed by Galen.

One of the first models localizing specific mental functions to discrete brain areas was advanced by a fourth century A.D. philosopher named Nemesius. He attributed mental functions to specific compartments in the brain. The compartments, or cells, were actually ventricles of the brain, the hollow areas through which cerebrospinal fluid circulates. He placed perception (cellula phantastica) in the ventricle toward the front, thinking and reasoning in the middle ventricle (cellula logistica), and memory in the rear ventricle (cellula memorialis). Centuries later, the brilliant anatomist Andreas Vesalius reformed and improved on the brain anatomy of Galen with his very accurate descriptions and drawings of the brain. His anatomical investigations showed, for example, that the optic nerves were not hollow tubes as Galen had claimed. They also showed that the ventricles were not arranged in a row from front to back as indicated in earlier drawings of the brain. Many of his drawings were so well executed that they served as standards of medical illustration into the 20th century, all the more remarkable considering Vesalius produced them in the 16th century. The work of people such as Vesalius helped to release the stranglehold of Galen's teachings on the development of anatomy and physiology.

In the latter part of the 18th century and early 19th century, a well-known physician and anatomist named Franz Gall did much to promote interest in, and research on, the relationship between brain and behavior. He originated the concept of localization of mental traits in discrete parts of the cortex. Essentially, he claimed that the surface of the brain was organized into distinct compartments, each of which controlled certain traits such as ambition, courage, and vanity. There were also areas for mathematical talent, color sense, intellect, and memory (Polyak, 1957). Furthermore, these specific traits could be determined by the raised areas on a person's skull. If a "bump" appeared in a certain area, then it would mean that a particular trait, and the underlying brain tissue, was well-developed in that individual. The bump was caused by the overgrown brain area that exerted upward pressure on the skull; the larger the bump, the more prominent the trait. Gall's ideas had a positive effect in that they stimulated research into localization of brain functions. However, under the influence of Spurzheim, his concepts degenerated into the pseudoscience of *phrenology*. The false practice and teachings of phrenology spread all over the world and functioned as a kind of personality testing, most likely providing income for its practitioners. At the same time, it stimulated scientists such as Flourens to study brain localization experimentally, partly in order to refute phrenology.

Flourens, who worked in the 1820s, removed brain areas of cats and pigeons and, indeed, did find that certain locations controlled certain behaviors. Yet, these basic activities—such as vision, hearing, and balance—were found by careful and successive removals of brain tissue and observing the behavior of the recovered animal. Flourens established that sensory and motor functions were distinctly localized in the brain. However, Flourens emphasized that the brain functioned as a whole, with all of its parts intimately connected, and with the potential for functional areas to substitute for others.

Later in the 19th century, Broca localized human motor speech in the left frontal lobe. One of his patients had lost the ability to speak; examination at autopsy revealed a lesion in the third convolution of the left frontal lobe. Broca correctly concluded that this area was responsible for motor speech, or speech production (Broca's area). The inability to speak, caused by damage to this area, is termed *motor aphasia*. Another scientist, Wernicke, discovered another brain area important for language. In the 1870s, he located a site in the left temporal lobe that was critical to the understanding of verbal language. Damage to this area led to a disorder now known as *receptive aphasia* (Wernicke's area). The physiologists Fritsch and Hitzig, in the 1870s, used electrical stimulation to specify motor centers in the outer layers of the brain (cortex) of dogs. These scientists found that direct stimulation of the motor cortex with electricity would lead to specific movements of body parts such as the forelimb or hindlimb. Stimulation of different areas produced different movements, which could be repeated each time the electricity was applied. After the work by Hitzig and Fritsch, later stimulation studies were conducted in man and other vertebrates. Visual, auditory, somatosensory, and motor areas were specified for man. In addition, other functions—such as memory for language, music, and instrument playing—were localized to cortical areas (Penfield & Roberts, 1959). Localization of function in the brain is a topic of research that continues today as scientists learn increasingly detailed information about the relationship between brain and behavior.

In this brief historical account, we see that early physicians, philosophers, anatomists, and physiologists devoted thought and experimentation to understanding the physiological correlates of behavior. French physiologists of the 19th century held that the brain is the center for perception, intelligence, and judgment, but that emotions are generated by the internal organs (Boring, 1950). In the late 19th century, this idea influenced what is now known as the James-Lange concept of emotional behavior. This concept holds that an emotional state is experienced because of the internal events, such as increased heart rate and muscle activity, produced by a provocative stimulus. According to James-Lange, if we encounter a frightening event, we feel afraid because we run; we do not run because we are afraid! The perception of danger occurs first, then escape behavior, and finally the feeling of fear. Thus, the act of escaping produces internal physiological changes that are interpreted by the brain as fear. This concept was opposed by the Cannon–Bard theory of the 1930s, which proposed that an emotional state resulted from the influence of lower brain centers (hypothalamus and thalamus) on higher ones (cortex), rather than from impulses produced by internal organs. Thus, danger is perceived first by the brain, fear is experienced, and we flee the threatening situation.

Up to this point, our brief historical excursion has emphasized the relationship between the brain and behavior. Early observers and investigators were also interested in the relationship between other physiological changes and psychological processes. In an interesting account of early psychophysiological approaches, Mesulam and Perry (1972) described observations in the practices of Erasistratos, Galen, and Ibn Sina (Avicenna), physicians who lived from the third century B.C. to the 11th century A.D. Erasistratos noticed in the third century B.C. that a teenage prince named Antiochas took ill with unexplained symptoms, including sweating, pounding heart, and palid skin coloring. The young man was confined to bed and Erasistratos determined to see whether any of the boy's visitors would bring on the symptoms. Erasistratos concluded correctly that the boy was secretly in love with his stepmother, because he showed all the of the symptoms only when she visited his sickroom. The diagnosis made by Erasistratos depended on three important assumptions: there was an interaction between psychological and physiological events; there was a type of conditioning in which a particular stimulus brought forth a variety of autonomic responses; and Antiochas might be able to conceal his love for the woman in terms of overt motor behavior, but could not hide his covert physiological responses. This is probably the first recorded instance of a "psychosomatic" disorder, in which physical symptoms were caused by psychological factors.

Four centuries later, at the beginning of the second century A.D., the physician Galen related a case history from his clinical experience. The patient was a woman suffering from insomnia, who was very restless and hesitant to answer questions about her condition. The following quote is from Galen's observation (Mesulam & Perry, 1972):

> While I was convinced the woman was afflicted not by a bodily disease, but rather that some emotional trouble grieved her, it happened that at the vey moment I was examining her this was confirmed. Someone returning from the theater mentioned he had seen Pylades dancing. Indeed, at that instant, her expression and color of her face were greatly altered. Attentive, my hand laid on the woman's wrist and I observed her pulse was irregular, suddenly, violently agitated, which points to a troubled mind. The same thing occurred to people engaged in an argument over a given subject. (p. 549)

Galen later surmised that the woman was in love with Pylades and was able to confirm this conclusion a few days later. Galen criticized the other physicians who had attended the woman for not noticing the ways in which the body could be influenced by the state of mind.

In his *Canon Medicinae*, the physician Avicenna (10th century A.D.) included a chapter on "Love Sickness." Avicenna observed that the pulse of a patient suffering love sickness "is a fluctuating pulse without any regularity whatever, as in the pulse of the fatigued. Moreover, the patient's pulse and disposition are altered when mention is made of the person he loves, and especially when this occurs suddenly. It is possible in this way to ascertain whom he loves, when he will not reveal it himself" (Mesulam & Perry, 1972, p. 550). The observations and writings of these early physicians show that they clearly understood the relationship between a psychological stimulus and physiological effects. Their interests were similar to those of contemporary psychophysiologists in that they differentiated between psychological processes through physiological changes. They were able to observe outward changes in skin color or to determine the pulse rate by feeling the patients' wrists without instruments. The modern development of psychophysiological research has depended greatly on the development of sophisticated instrumentation for measuring electrical changes that take place in body tissues, and that reflect a variety of physiological responses. These developments in instrumentation took place for the most part in the latter part of the 19th century and the early part of the 20th century.

Concepts that have implications for understanding the physiological correlates of emotional behavior and for integrating data in the field of psychophysiology are presented in chapter 18. It is clear that throughout recorded history, the brain and heart have been focal points in attempts by physicians, philosophers, physiologists, and psychologists to understand behavior. These focal points have taken a new twist since contemporary psychophysiologists have discovered interactions between heart and brain activity that have behavioral implications (see chap. 18).

CONTEMPORARY PSYCHOPHYSIOLOGY

Since the mid-1960s, there has been a tremendous growth in the number of research studies in which physiological measures, as well as behavioral ones, have been taken in the course of studying human activities and performance. That this particular field has been growing rapidly is evidenced by the increasing number of publications in the area, as well as by the increasing number of universities that offer courses and training in psychophysiology.

Applications of Psychophysiology

There is a growing trend toward applying psychophysiological techniques and information to clinical and other practical problems. One area that illustrates this interest in applications of psychophysiology is *biofeedback*. In recent years, biofeedback training has been applied to a wide variety of human ailments ranging from tension headaches to asthma and high blood pressure. There is, in fact, suggestive evidence that the provision of feedback (information) about muscle activity in the throat and facial areas may help in treating the common speech disorder known as stuttering. Because of the widespread application of biofeedback, as well as the potential importance of this field, a separate chapter is devoted to this area (see chap. 17).

Chapters 15 and 16 present examples of applied psychophysiology ranging from the controversial procedure of lie detection to the study of behavioral disorders. An important psychophysiological application involves the use of event-related brain potentials to study sensory capacities. For example, chapter 16 describes vision and hearing tests of young infants accomplished with measures of brain response.

Importance of Brain Measures

In this text, psychophysiological studies that relate brain activity (the electroencephalogram, event-related brain potentials, magnetoencephalography) to behavior play a prominent role in the overall presentation. This is partly because, as modern science recognizes, the brain is the central organ of behavior. Without it we would not be able to think, move, sense, perceive, create, or perform any of the complex functions that we associate with human endeavors. However, other physiological measures (such as heart activity, muscle activity, electrodermal responses, eye movements, pupil size, blood pressure, and blood volume changes) provide important insights into behavior that are not available through the study of brain activity. For example, regular increments in muscle activity have been associated with increased rewards for efficient performance in a motor task. Feedback from muscle to brain and back to the motor units that are responsible for muscle activity is a crucial aspect of this observed relationship.

Another reason for the prominent position given to brain measures in this text is the continued surge in cerebral psychophysiological studies since the 1960s. Much of this has been the result of applications of computer technology to the study of brain processes, enabling scientists to obtain a number of new measures, particularly event-related brain potentials (ERPs), computer analyses of the electroencephalogram (EEG), and magneto-evoked potentials. These techniques enable the noninvasive study of cortical and subcortical brain responses to specific stimuli. Various brain measures and related research are presented in chapters 3 through 7.

Physiological Measures in Relation to the Nervous System

The measures taken by psychophysiologists may include one or more of the following: the electroencephalogram (EEG), the event-related brain potential (ERP), the electromyogram (EMG, a measure of muscle activity), pupillometry (measure in changes of pupil size), electrooculography (EOG, a measure of eye movement), electrodermal activity (EDA, changes in electrical activity at the skin surface), heart responses, blood volume, and blood pressure. Some other measures obtained by psychophysiologists include respiration, oxygen consumption, salivation, skin temperature, immune function, endocrine function, and gastric motility.

The average scientist in this field normally focuses on one or several of these physiological measures, but usually not all of them, at any one time. An example of multiple physiological measurements and how some people may view the scientist in this field is illustrated in Fig. 1.1.

The physiological measures just outlined are all under the control of the nervous system. The nervous system is highly integrated, but for the sake of convenience, we can list the various measures as being primarily controlled by one or another subdivision of this system. First, a brief diagrammatic summary of the nervous system is in order. As can be seen in Fig. 1.2, it may be divided into two main branches: the central nervous system (CNS) and the peripheral nervous system. The CNS includes the brain and spinal cord. The peripheral nervous system refers to nervous tissue outside the brain and spinal cord, including the cranial and spinal nerves. The peripheral nervous system is further divided into the somatic system, concerned with muscular activities, and the autonomic nervous system (ANS), which controls visceral structures (glands and organs of the body). Finally, the ANS is subdivided into the parasympathetic nervous system (PNS), the innervation mechanisms that are dominant when the individual is at rest, and the sympathetic nervous system (SNS), which is dominant in situations requiring mobilization of energy. The PNS can be thought of as a system of rest and repair, whereas the SNS is a system of energy mobilization and work. The schematic drawing in Fig. 1.2 is imperfect, because there are parts of the ANS that are in and under the control of the CNS; for example, the hypothalamus and medulla of the brain are important in the control of ANS functions.

The assignment of physiological measures to the nervous system and its subdivisions from the point of view of general control of function would lead to the organization shown in Table 1.1.

FIG. 1.1. How some people view the psychophysiologist at work.

Nervous System

Central Nervous System
(brain and spinal cord)

Peripheral Nervous System

Somatic Nervous System
muscular activities

Autonomic Nervous System
glands + organs

Parasympathetic Nervous System
rest + repair

Sympathetic Nervous System
energy mobilization + work

TABLE 1.1
Nervous System Mechanisms in the Control
of Physiological Responses

Central Nervous System	Somatic System	Autonomic Nervous System
EEG (ongoing activity)	EMG	Heart rate (PNS, SNS)
Event-related potentials	EOG	Blood pressure (PNS, SNS)
		Electrodermal activity (SNS only)
		Pupil response (PNS, SNS)
		Blood volume (PNS, SNS)

Many of the physiological responses of interest are controlled by the ANS, and, accordingly, this is a very important system for the field of psychophysiology. The student interested in obtaining more detailed information about the anatomy and physiology of the ANS can consult such texts as those of Pick (1970) and Gardner (1975). A brief treatment of the autonomic and somatic nervous systems is presented in chapter 2.

AIMS AND ORGANIZATION OF THIS BOOK

One important aim of this text is to illustrate the kinds of questions being asked by psychophysiological researchers, the studies they are conducting, the conclusions being drawn, and the concepts that they are developing to explain their empirical findings. Conclusions are provided at the end of each major section. In some cases, specific conclusions are reached, but, in others, no definite resolutions are achieved, indicating that either more work is required to clear up an issue or that there is a stalemate. The existence of a stalemate may mean that satisfactory conclusions may never be reached with the approaches currently being used.

Other aims of this book are to provide elementary information regarding the anatomy and physiology of various body systems under discussion and examples of how the activity is measured. The purpose of this coverage is to provide basic information about how to obtain physiological measures. The student who requires more detailed information about anatomy and physiology and recording techniques can refer to specialized texts on these subjects: for example, *Gray's Anatomy* (Gray, 1977), *Basic Human Physiology* (Guyton, 1977), *Techniques in Psychophysiology* (Martin & Venables, 1980), *Psychophysiological Recording* (Stern, Ray, & Davis, 1980), and *Principles of Psychophysiology* (Cacioppo & Tassinary, 1990). Chapters 2 through 7 of this book focus mainly on the central nervous system and the relations between measures of its activity and psychological processes. Chapters 8 through 14 treat the psychophysiology of the body systems peripheral to the brain. They include, in order, the muscles, sweat glands, eyes, heart, and blood vessels. Chapters 15, 16, and 17 are concerned with applications of psychophysiology, and chapter 18 covers concepts in the field. Material in chapter 19 concerns the effects of environmental variables on physiological responses. These variables include external (e.g., temperature) and internal (e.g., hormonal and drug) influences.

Although some of the environmental studies may not be strictly psychophysiological in that they fail to manipulate psychological variables, environmental factors must be considered because of their possible interaction with both behavioral and physiological measures. The organization of this book emphasizes the brain as the central organ of behavior, with activity in the peripheral system reflecting the outflow of brain influence. This is not to minimize the role played by these peripheral systems in psychophysiology, because it is known that feedback of their activity can influence brain activity, and peripheral measures often contribute information about body–behavior relationships that measures of brain activity do not.

Once students have obtained some knowledge of the body systems, measuring techniques, and representative studies in the field, they will be ready to appreciate the theoretical issues that characterize the field of psychophysiology. Although the organization of this text reflects the view that concepts should follow empirical data, individual instructors may prefer to cover the conceptual material at some earlier point. This could have the advantage of alerting the student to issues in the field and how one or another study either supports or refutes a particular view. Other instructors may prefer to present the material dealing with the peripheral body systems prior to the material on brain activity. A feature of this text is that the coverage of the various body systems is such that each is self-contained. Hence, instructors may choose any particular chapter sequence they wish without losing the flavor of the field.

It should be noted that this book emphasizes research with humans. Animal research has been, and continues to be, crucial to the development of psychophysiology. However, a comprehensive treatment of animal studies requires a separate book.

REFERENCES

Boring, E. G. (1950). *A history of experimental psychology* (2nd ed.). New York: Appleton-Century-Crofts.
Cacioppo, J. T., & Tassinary, L. G. (Eds.). (1990). *Principles of psychophysiology: Physical, social, and inferential elements.* Cambridge, MA: Cambridge University Press.
Carson, R. C., Butcher, J. N., & Coleman, J. C. (1988). *Abnormal psychology and modern life.* Dallas: Scott, Foresman.
Changeaux, J. P. (1985). *Neuronal man.* New York: Penguin.
Furedy, J. J. (1983). Operational, analogical and genuine definitions of psychophysiology. *International Journal of Psychophysiology, 1*, 13–19.
Gardner, E. (1975). *Fundamentals of neurology* (6th ed.). Philadelphia: Saunders.
Garrison, F. H. (1929). *History of medicine* (3rd ed.). Philadelphia: Saunders.
Gray, H. (1977). *Anatomy—Descriptive and surgical.* In T. P. Pick & R. Howden (Eds.), *Gray's anatomy* (pp. 199–360). New York: Bounty Books.
Guyton, A. C. (1977). *Basic human physiology: Normal function and mechanisms of disease.* Philadelphia: Saunders.
Haeger, K. (1988). *History of surgery.* New York: Bell Publishing.
Kutas, M., & Federmeier, K. D. (1998). Minding the body. *Psychophysiology, 35*, 135–150.
Lykken, D. T. (1984). Psychophysiology. In R. J. Corsini (Ed.), *Encyclopedia of psychology* (pp. 934–937). New York: Wiley.
Mangina, C. A. (1983). Towards an international consensus in defining psychophysiology. *International Journal of Psychophysiology, 1*, 21–23.
Martin, I., & Venables, P. H. (1980). *Techniques in psychophysiology.* New York: Wiley.
Mesulam, M., & Perry, J. (1972). The diagnosis of love-sickness: Experimental psychology without the polygraph. *Psychophysiology, 9*, 13–19.
Penfield, W., & Roberts, L. (1959). *Speech and brain mechanisms.* Princeton: Princeton University Press.
Pick, J. (1970). *The autonomic nervous system.* Philadelphia: Lippincott.
Polyak, S. (1957). *The vertebrate visual system.* Chicago: University of Chicago Press.
Stern, J. A. (1964). Towards a definition of psychophysiology. *Psychophysiology, 1*, 90–91.
Stern, R. M., Ray, W. J., & Davis, C. M. (1980). *Psychophysiological recording.* New York: Oxford University Press.

2

The Nervous System
and Measurement of Its Activity

This chapter focuses primarily on the source and nature of the electrical activity of the nervous system and how it is measured. Included is a brief presentation of some neuroanatomy and neurophysiology necessary to understand the activity being measured. The material presented here forms the background for understanding some of the physiological bases of the EEG and the event-related brain potentials discussed in subsequent chapters. As outlined in chapter 1, for the sake of convenience, the nervous system may be divided into central (brain and spinal cord) and peripheral systems (nerves outside central nervous systems). These two systems are discussed briefly in separate sections of this chapter.

SOURCE OF THE BRAIN'S ELECTRICAL ACTIVITY

Electrical activity of the brain is produced by billions of brain cells called *neurons*. Activity is never absent in the living brain. Neurons are always active—when we are asleep or awake, active or passive, during meditation or hypnosis. The entire nervous system is dependent on neurons for its activity. These cells are the functional units of the brain, spinal cord, and all of the peripheral nervous system.

Although there is general agreement among scientists that neurons are the source of brain electrical activity, the exact nature of their contribution is an area of contention. For example, Noback and Demarest (1975) proposed that the EEG is produced by electrical activity at synapses (where brain cells transmit information) and by electrical activity within brain cells. They suggested further that recordings made from the scalp reflect the algebraic summation of excitatory and inhibitory activities that occur in underlying brain tissue. That is, some brain cells produce excitation and some reduce the level of activity; the resultant is the record called the EEG.

Elul (1972) made a strong argument for the position that the EEG is a resultant of activity within nerve cells in the cerebral cortex. He indicated that analyses of correlations between gross EEGs (recorded from many cells) and the activity of individual nerve cells suggest that the activity observed, at a given instant, is due to the synchronized firing of a relatively small number of cerebral neurons. Thus, according to Elul, the EEG is produced through the intermittent synchronization of cortical neurons, with different neurons becoming synchronized in successive instants. This implies that the EEG represents a series of bursts of aggregate neuronal activity, with each burst being the synchronized activity of different groups of cortical neurons. According to Elul, these bursts of activity are what we see in the EEG recording. He also pointed out that subcortical areas, such as the thalamus, have an influence over the EEG, because it is known that the thalamus plays a role in the production of at least one type of spontaneous brain activity called *sleep spindles*. He suggested, however, that other subcortical centers may also contribute to EEG rhythms.

A summary of information relating to the physiological basis of the EEG was presented by Barlow (1993). The dominant current view is that the EEG represents the summation of excitatory and inhibitory postsynaptic potentials in the pyramidal cells of the cerebral cortex. The terms *inhibitory* and *excitatory postsynaptic potentials* refer to the neuronal activity that can either reduce or increase activity of other neurons once it has traveled to other cells over an existing gap (synapse). (See Fig. 2.3 for a schematic of inhibitory and excitatory postsynaptic potentials.) Barlow explains that the EEG at the brain's cortical surface, and at the scalp surface, reflects the current flow associated with summated postsynaptic potentials in synchronously activated, vertically oriented, pyramidal cells. Rapid changes in EEG pattern from larger slower alpha waves to smaller, faster beta waves is believed to be a result of direct projections from intralaminar nuclei of the thalamus to cortical areas where they influence the "activation" of pyramidal cells. (For a description of various EEG wave patterns see Fig. 2.6.)

Barlow indicated that researchers have concluded that the theta rhythm originates in the subcortical septohippocampal system of the brain. In addition, the spindle activity of the sleeping EEG stems from the reticular nucleus of the thalamus. This reticular nucleus is crossed by almost all fibers connecting the subcortical thalamus with the cerebral cortex. Aside from the studies leading to conclusions regarding origins of theta and sleep spindles, there have been no others at a cellular level to indicate the sites of origin of other EEG waves, such as alpha and rhythms slower than theta. Let us now briefly examine the structures that produce the brain's electrical activity.

The Neuron

Neurons consist of a cell body, dendrites, and a single axon. There are an estimated 50 to 100 billion neurons in the nervous system (some estimates are much higher). The *cell body* contains the nucleus, which controls cellular activity. The *dendrites* are extensions that come off the cell body and transmit impulses to the cell. As many as 75 to 80 dendrites may be present on a motor cell, whereas sensory neurons may only have a single dendrite. Dendrites are short relative to axons. The single *axon* comes off the cell body and transmits information away from the cell body to other neurons. Axons sometimes reach a length of several feet. Diagrams of a neuron within the CNS and a motor neuron located in both the CNS and peripheral nervous system are shown in Fig. 2.1. In addition to neurons, there are billions of support cells in the nervous system, called *glia*. The most common type of glial cell is the *astrocyte*, named for its star-shaped configuration. Astrocytes are glial cells that provide support and nourishment to neurons of the CNS and play a role in forming the "blood–brain" barrier that protects neurons from effects of potentially toxic substances. The astrocytes also regulate the chemical composition of the fluid outside the neurons and provide nourishment to neurons in the form of glucose and lactate (Carlson, 1998). The fact that blood vessels of the CNS cannot transport large molecules across their walls and have astrocytes attached to their outer surfaces severely limits materials that can enter the brain. Thus, only oxygen, carbon dioxide, glucose, and certain amino acids required by the brain can pass the blood–brain barrier.

Neurons can be multipolar, bipolar, or unipolar. *Multipolar* neurons have many dendrites coming off the cell body. The motor neuron in Fig. 2.1 is an example of a multipolar neuron. Note that the break in the illustration of neuron B represents the border between the CNS above and the peripheral nervous system below. In the CNS, the oligodendrocytes, another type of glial cell in addition to astrocytes, support axons and produce a covering called the

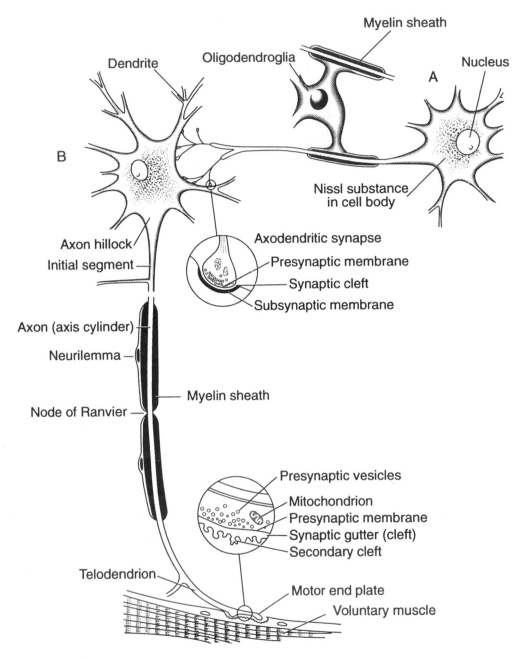

FIG. 2.1. (A) A neuron located within the central nervous system. (B) A lower motor neuron located in both the central and peripheral nervous systems. This synapses with a voluntary muscle cell to form a motor end plate. The hiatus in the nerve at X represents the border between the central nervous system above and the peripheral nervous system below.

myelin sheath. In the peripheral nervous system, Schwann cells perform the same function and also permit the regeneration of neurons. The regeneration occurs because portions of the Schwann cells, in the form of cylinders, can survive the damage and arrange themselves to provide a pathway and protection for the regenerating axon. Unfortunately, once neurons inside the CNS are destroyed through accident or disease, they do not regenerate functionally; that is, they may show some anatomical signs of regeneration, such as sprouts on the severed axon, but their function does not return. This is because they do not have the Schwann cells to help the axons find their way back to their original location.

Bipolar neurons consist of a single dendrite conducting impulses to the cell body and a single axon conducting information away from it. Schwann cells never wrap themselves around bipolar neurons, as they do with other peripheral nervous system neurons. The function of the bipolar neurons is sensory. They are found, for example, in the visual system (retina of the eye) and the auditory system (cochlea of the inner ear).

The *unipolar* neuron is composed of a single process coming off the cell body and splitting into a dendrite and an axon. Therefore, the dendrite and axon are anatomically the same. Schwann cells appear only on unipolar neurons located outside the CNS. The functions of unipolar neurons are sensory only, and they are found in the dorsal roots of spinal nerves and sensory portions of the cranial nerves.

Excitation of Neurons

Neurons are effectively excited by natural stimuli from receptor organs (e.g., in the eyes or ears) or by neural impulses coming from other nerves. They may also respond to appropriate chemical, electrical, thermal, or mechanical stimuli. Their responsiveness to artificial stimuli has enabled investigators to study electrical activity of single neurons or small groups of neurons through tiny recording microelectrodes. Because neurons are rather small, their size ranging from 4 to 100 μm (microns, or millionths of a meter), the electrodes for recording from single cells must be only a few microns in diameter to enable insertion into these cells. In experimental work, electric current has often been used to stimulate the cell because of its convenience, accuracy of quantification, and the fact that it does not damage the neuron at appropriate levels of stimulation. To produce an impulse from a neuron, a stimulus must be of a certain strength and duration. The stimulus strength just capable of producing a neuron response is termed *threshold intensity* and is usually given in terms of voltage. A stimulus must be applied for a certain period of time before it will produce a neuronal impulse. Thus, a strong stimulus will not have to be applied as long as a weak one to elicit a neuronal response. The strength of this minimal level stimulus required to produce a response is called the *threshold* or *rheobase*. The excitability of neurons can be determined by ascertaining the chronaxy or the minimum length of time it takes an electric current two times the rheobase value to create an impulse (Gardner, 1975).

A neuron must receive a certain minimal level of stimulation, or it will not fire at all. Upon adequate stimulation, it will fire with its maximum strength. This has been termed the "all-or-none principal" of neuronal firing. Once the stimulus triggers the firing of a neuron, the electrical impulse continues along the entire length of the axon and possibly to the dendrites of another neuron. Transmission to another neuron takes place across a small juncture called a *synapse*. The terminal portion of an axon branches into telodendria. At the ends of the telodendria are small structures called *terminal buttons*. These terminal buttons are responsible for the release of transmitter substances that are detected by receptors of another neuron close by. The two adjacent neurons do not touch; instead, transmission across the synapse is accomplished by chemical transmitter substances called *neurotransmitters*. Figure 2.2 shows a schematic drawing of several types of synapses, and Fig. 2.3 illustrates both excitatory and inhibitory activity at the synapse.

Neurotransmitters

The neurotransmitters act at the synapses to enable the neuron to perform its primary function of communication with other neurons. The message communicated may either cause re-

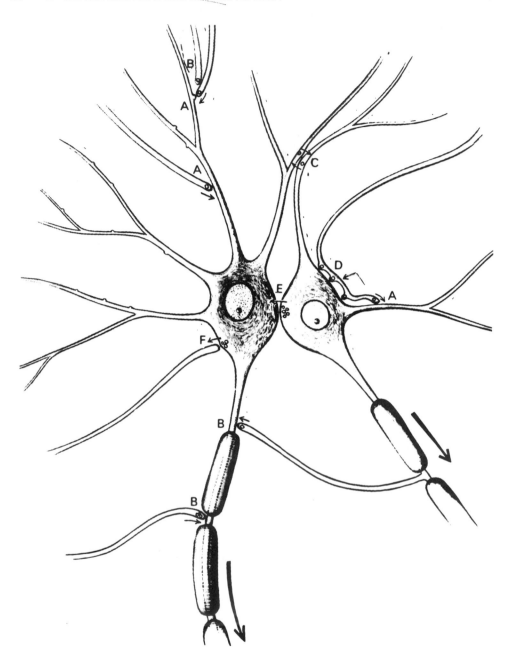

FIG. 2.2. Several types of synapses: (A) axodendritic synapses; (B) axonaxonic synapse; (C) reciprocal dendrodendritic synapses; (D) enpassant axosomatic synapses; (E) somatosomatic synapse; (F) somatoaxonic synapse.

ceiving cells to respond or it might prevent them from responding. The major neurotransmitters are amino acids, biogenic amines (acetylcholine, dopamine, norepinephrine, epinephrine, and serotonin), and peptides. The actions of each of these substances is described briefly.

Amino Acids.   The main amino acid neurotransmitters are glutamate, aspartate, glycine, and gamma-aminobutyric acid (GABA). Glutamate and aspartate are excitatory, with gluta-

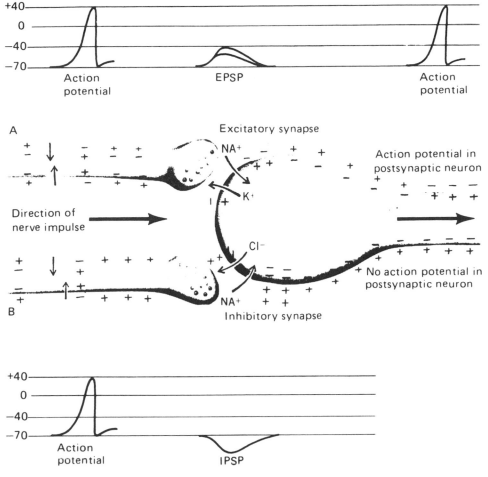

FIG. 2.3. Sequences in (A) excitatory and (B) inhibitory transmission from presynaptic neurons (left) and across synapses to postsynaptic neuron (right). (A) The action potential conducted along the presynaptic axon to an excitatory synapse produces an excitatory postsynaptic potential (EPSP), which in turn can contribute to the generation of an action potential in the postsynaptic neuron. (B) The action potential conducted along the presynaptic axon to an inhibitory synapse produces an inhibitory postsynaptic potential (IPSP), which in turn suppresses the generation of an action potential in the postsynaptic neuron.

mate acting in the brain and spinal sensory neurons and aspartate mostly in the spinal cord. When a transmitter has an excitatory effect on a postsynaptic membrane, it is referred to as an Excitatory Post Synaptic Potential (EPSP). An inhibitory effect, on the other hand, is termed an Inhibitory Post Synaptic Potential (IPSP). Glycine is an inhibitory neurotransmitter acting in spinal cord interneurons and in the lower brain stem. Bacteria that cause tetanus release a chemical that blocks glycine. The effect of this blockage inactivates glycine's inhibitory effect and causes muscles to contract continuously, resulting in spasms and the condition known as lockjaw.

GABA is also inhibitory and exerts its widespread effects in both the cerebral and cerebellar cortex. Without the inhibiting effects of transmitter substances such as GABA, the neurons in the brain would be "firing" uncontrollably. This happens in the brain event called "seizure" or convulsion, components of the disorder known as epilepsy. Some scientists believe that abnormal GABA activity may be responsible for some cases of epilepsy (Carlson,

1998). Drugs such as the benzodiazepines (e.g., valium) and barbiturates (e.g., phenobarbitol) produce their anxiety reducing, or sleep inducing, effects by enhancing the activty of GABA. Both the benzodiazepines and barbiturates have been used to control epileptic seizures.

The drug picrotoxin has the effect of inhibiting GABA and can cause convulsions (seizures) at certain dose levels. Most neuronal activity involves interactions between the excitatory and inhibitory effects of glutamate and GABA. Thus, glutamate and GABA are responsible for most of the information transmitted to and from various regions of the brain (Carlson, 1998).

Biogenic Amines and Monoamines.   Acetylcholine is primarily an excitatory biogenic amine and is the first neurotransmitter to have been identified. It is responsible for movement of both smooth (involuntary) and striated (voluntary) muscles. A sample involuntary muscle is the type that lines the inside of blood vessels, and an example of a striated muscle is the bicep of the upper arm. The drug known as curare paralyzes muscles by preventing acetylcholine from acting at the synapse between nerve and muscle. Acetylcholine is excitatory in the brain, spinal cord, and in ganglia of the autonomic nervous system. In the target organs innervated by the parasympathetic nervous system, acetylcholine can be either excitatory or inhibitory. (See Fig. 2.11 for target organs of the parasympathetic nervous system that are influenced by acetylcholine.) Neurons influenced by acetylcholine (acetylcholinergic) include those in the basal forebrain, which influence the cerebral cortex to facilitate learning, especially perceptual learning (Carlson, 1998). Others have an influence on the hippocampus, a subcortical brain area, and facilitate its role in the establishment of certain types of memories. Acetylcholinergic neurons located in the pons of the brain stem are responsible for rapid eye movement (REM) sleep, or the sleep stage associated with dreaming (see chapter 4 for a discussion of REM sleep).

The neurotransmitters dopamine, norepinephrine, epinephrine, and serotonin are classified as monoamines. Dopamine can have both inhibitory or excitatory effects, depending on the postsynaptic receptor that it influences. Dopamine plays a crucial role in controlling complex movements through the influence of dopaminergic neurons on structures in the basal ganglia of the brain (caudate nucleus and putamen). The cell bodies of these dopaminergic neurons are located in the midbrain, and if their influence on basal ganglia areas is interrupted by degeneration, then symptoms of Parkinson's disease develop. Parkinsonism is characterized by progressive difficulty in initiating and stopping movements, tremors, and rigid muscles. Symptoms can be relieved by administration of a drug called L-Dopa. Dopamine also influences parts of the limbic system of the brain, structures of which are involved in emotional and motivated behavior. In addition, dopaminergic axons excite frontal cortex regions, thus playing a role in short-term memories and planning.

Norepinephrine (also known as noradrenalin) is a neurotransmitter found in the brain and in the sympathetic nervous system. In general, the release of norepinephrine at the synapse has an excitatory effect. Synapses that are influenced by norepinephrin are referred to as noradrenergic. Stimulation of an important noradrenergic system (locus coeruleus of the pons) has a general activating effect on the brain resulting in increased attention to environmental stimuli. Noradrenergic neurons are also involved in sexual behavior and in the control of appetite. Epinephrine, also called adrenaline, is a hormone that also functions as a neurotransmitter in the brain. It has excitatory effects and can be found in the medulla and in the neurons of the sympathetic nervous system. Recent findings of Andreassi and colleagues (Andreassi, Eggleston, Fu, & Stewart, 1998) suggest that epinephrine is synthesized in the hypothalamus. The evidence for this was the detection of phenylethanolamine N-methyl-transferase (PNMT) mNRA in hypothalamic tissue of the rat brain. PNMT is the enzyme that converts norepinephrine to epinephrine. Therefore, its presence suggests that epinephrine may act as a neurotransmitter in the hypothalamus.

The monoamine neurotransmitter serotonin is also referred to as 5-HT (5-hydroxytrypta-mine). It is synthesized from the amino acid called tryptophan. Serotonin has complex effects and influences a variety of behaviors including eating, sleeping, and arousal. It also has a role in the regulation of mood. Antidepressant drugs such as amitryptyline and desipramine block the re-uptake of serotonin by the presynaptic neuron and relieve depression. The newer psychoactive drugs, or drugs that influence behavior, such as Prozac and Zoloft also act to block the re-uptake of serotonin in relieving symptoms of depression. This class of drugs are called SSRIs or Selective Serotonin Re-uptake Inhibitors, and produce their effects by making more serotonin available at the synapses. Serotonergic neurons are found in the medulla, pons, and midbrain. These neurons project their influence widely throughout the brain, including the cortex, basal ganglia, and hippocampus.

Peptides.   The peptides are chains of amino acids that occur in low concentrations in the nervous system and also have functions outside the nervous system. The endorphins (or endogenous morphines) are peptides that produce some of the effects of morphine, such as pain relief. Another peptide named substance P is a transmitter substance that brings information related to pain into the central nervous system. Angiotensin is another peptide that, when used by neurons in the CNS, copes with the loss of body fluids, for example, by producing thirst.

Neuron Conduction Velocity.   The speed of electrical impulse conduction along a neuron depends on axon diameter. Large-diameter axons transmit impulses at higher speeds. A rough estimate of transmission speed can be made from mammalian neurons that contain myelin. The diameter is multiplied by a constant of 6 to give approximate conduction speed in meters per second: $V = KD$; where V = velocity, $K = 6$, and D = diameter. Thus, for an axon 20 μm in diameter, conduction velocity is about 120 m/sec (Gardner, 1975). Myelin is a whitish material composed of protein and fat that appears on some axons in the nervous system. It is the myelin that causes masses of axons to appear as the "white matter" of the brain, as compared to the masses of cell bodies that comprise the "grey matter."

Neuron Potentials

Although the neuronal impulse can be measured in terms of changes in electrical activity, it is actually produced by physiochemical activity that occurs when the neuron is stimulated. To understand how this physiochemical activity occurs, a brief explanation of the chemicals existing inside and outside the neuron and their relation to various potential states of the neuron is given.

There is usually what is termed a *resting potential difference* on the two sides of the cell membrane, so that the inside of the cell is negative relative to the outside. This occurs because the inside of the cell has a higher concentration of potassium ions and the outside of the cell has more sodium ions. The sodium has a natural tendency to push inside the cell because its positive ions are attracted to a negatively charged area, and are also attracted to a region where there is a lesser concentration of sodium. Thus, both electrostatic and diffusion forces cause this natural push inward, but channels in the membrane are usually closed, that is, the membrane is impermeable.

When a stimulus of specific strength and duration comes along, be it electrical, chemical, or mechanical, it causes physiochemical changes to take place in which the cell membrane becomes permeable (channels open), allowing sodium to enter at a high rate and potassium to move outside the cell, thus causing a reversal of the resting potential along the entire length of the axon. This reversal of resting potential is called a *wave of depolarization*. The membrane becomes more permeable with stimulation because sodium channels along the membrane open. These channels, or gates, are located in specialized proteins embedded in the cell membrane. The channels are specialized for sodium, potassium, or chloride (Kalat, 1995). When the channel opens, sodium rushes in and increases the positivity inside the neuron. This sudden change in the membrane potential is referred to as depolarization and is responsible for the action potential. At the same time sodium enters the cell, channels open to allow potassium ions to move to the outside of the membrane. When depolarization occurs, the inside of the membrane registers a potential of about +30 mV (millivolts), a change of 100 mV from the resting potential of approximately −70 mV. Once the neuron has fired via the action potential, the cell almost returns to its original state of polarization.

At this point the resting potential is approximately restored except that now there are slightly more sodium ions and slightly fewer potassium ions inside the cell than previous to depolarization. How is the original distribution of ions restored? The answer is that a mechanism called the sodium–potassium pump operates to gradually restore the original resting potential. During this time, the molecules of the sodium–potassium pump (called sodium–potassium transporters) bring two potassium ions into the cell for each three sodium ions they pump out, the result being a net movement of positive ions out of the cell until the original state of internal negativity is restored. The advantage of the resting potential is that it prepares the neuron to respond rapidly to stimuli. Kalat (1995) likened the resting potential to the archer who pulls the bow in advance and is ready to fire his/her arrow as soon as the appropriate moment comes.

The Action Potential of the Neuron

The action potential of the neuron is made up of three components: the spike potential, the negative afterpotential, and the positive afterpotential. The *spike potential* is the large, sharply rising part of the action potential represented in Fig. 2.3. Note that the action potential may excite or inhibit activity in the postsynaptic neuron. The spike potential represents the period during which depolarization takes place. The spike potential lasts only .5 to 1 msec (thousandths of a second). The excitability of the neuron, in terms of its ability to respond to another stimulus, is greatly reduced during the spike period. In fact, during the absolute refractory period, lasting about .5 msec, no stimulus will produce another neuron response. The relative refractory period of the spike is the period during which only a stimulus of a much greater intensity than normal will produce another firing of the neuron. The relative refractory period lasts about .5 msec. An absolute refractory period of .5 to 1 msec would limit the response of an individual neuron to about 1,000 or 2,000 times a second.

The next phase of the action potential is the *negative afterpotential*, which lasts for about 5 to 15 msec and is lower in magnitude than the spike potential. The excitability of the neuron is supernormal during the negative afterpotential. This means that a stimulus of lower intensity than normal will be sufficient to cause another neuron response. Some scientists have hypothesized that this occurs because more than the usual number of sodium ions are still inside the neuron, causing it to be more excitable than normal.

The last portion of the action potential is the *positive afterpotential*, which lasts for about 50 to 80 msec. However, the neuron is in a subnormal phase during the positive afterpotential, meaning that it will take a stronger than normal stimulus to produce another spike potential during this period. One notion is that the sodium pump has pushed too much sodium outside, resulting in a lower than usual number of sodium ions inside the cell, and, therefore, a lower excitability. After about 80 to 100 msec, the normal excitability of the neuron returns.

The action potential is an example of neuronal activity that occurs in response to specific adequate stimulation. Another, more common neural activity is the graded potential, which occurs primarily in the cell bodies and dendrites of the neurons. These are continuous potentials, and they also occur in neurons in situations when stimuli are subthreshold or not intense enough to produce a spike potential.

Now that we have reviewed some aspects of electrical activity changes in neurons, it would be instructive to examine the organization of large masses of neurons in the human brain. This description of brain areas will prove useful in understanding the measures of brain activity discussed in chapters 3 through 7. For example, when the patterning of EEG responses occurs during the performance of a task, a proper interpretation requires knowledge about the brain areas contributing to this patterning.

GROSS BRAIN ANATOMY

The average weight of the adult human brain is about 1,400 g (3 lb) and the thickness of the outermost region (the cortex) is about 3 mm. The brain may be divided into three main portions for convenience of description: the cerebrum, the cerebellum, and the brain stem. The *cerebrum*, or cerebral hemispheres, occupies much of the external surface of the brain. The two hemispheres, right and left, contain virtually identical structures. The *cerebellum* overlies the posterior aspect of the brain stem. The *brain stem* is the portion that remains after the removal of the cerebral hemispheres and the cerebellum and is the structure on which the cerebellum rests. The surface of the cerebrum has many convolutions. The raised portions of these convolutions are called *gyri* (gyrus, singular) and the grooved portions are termed *sulci* (sulcus, singular) or fissures. The cerebellum is also convoluted, and the raised portions are called *folia*. There are slight differences in the shape and location of the gyri and sulci in the cerebrum of individual brains, but they are still useful in localizing various brain areas. For example, the fissure of Rolando (also called the central sulcus) travels down from the top of the brain toward the sides in both hemispheres to the lateral sulcus. It conveniently serves as a dividing line between what is termed the precentral cortex (motor functions) and the postcentral cortex (body sensory functions, such as touch), as shown in the lateral view of the cortex in Fig. 2.4. The numbers in Fig. 2.4 are from the system of functional localization of Brodman. The other drawing in Fig. 2.4 illustrates the division of the cerebral cortex into four lobes: the frontal, parietal, occipital, and temporal. Note that the fissure of Sylvius (also called the lateral sulcus) separates the temporal lobe from the frontal and parietal lobes. Neuroscientists have discovered that the cortical surface controls basic sensory and motor functions.

The primary motor area is a strip of cortex, located just in front of the sulcus of Rolando, called the *precentral gyrus* (see Fig. 2.4). Motor functions are organized such that the upper areas of this motor strip control movements in lower portions of the body (e.g., feet and legs), and areas towards the bottom control upper body muscles (e.g., head and neck). Just back of the Rolandic fissure is somatosensory cortex that, as the name infers, receives input from body sensations such as touch, temperature, and pressure. Projections from body areas mimic the motor area in that upper portions of this somatosensory strip are concerned with input from lower body locations.

The primary visual cortex is located in the occipital lobe. An area concerned with the processing of written language, called the angular gyrus, appears at the juncture of parietal, occipital, and temporal lobes. The primary auditory area for processing sounds is located in the superior temporal gyrus of the temporal lobe. An area concerned with the understanding of spoken language (Wernicke's area) is located just to the rear (posterior) of primary auditory cortex. Broca's area refers to areas 44 and 45 of the left frontal lobe and, as mentioned in chapter 1, this area controls speaking. Other areas of the frontal lobe are considered to be involved with "biological intelligence" or the ability to plan, make decisions, and solve prob-

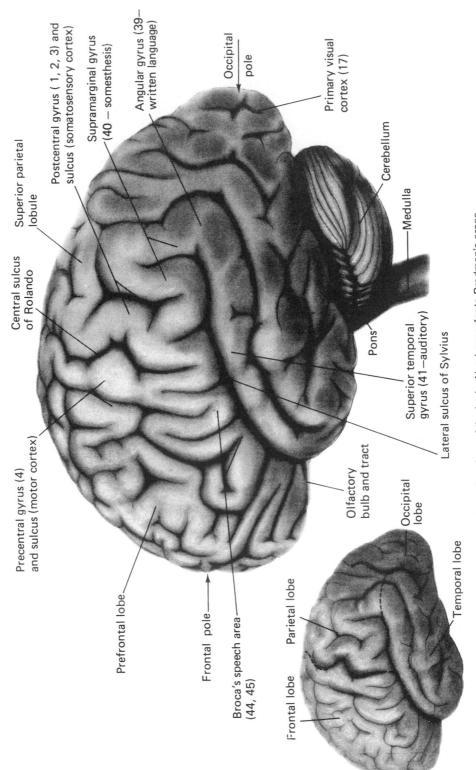

Precental gyrus (4)
and sulcus (motor cortex)

Central sulcus
of Rolando

Superior parietal
lobule

Postcentral gyrus (1 , 2 , 3) and
sulcus (somatosensory cortex)

Supramarginal gyrus
(40 — somesthesis)

Angular gyrus (39—
written language)

Occipital
pole

Primary visual
cortex (17)

Cerebellum

Medulla

Superior temporal
gyrus (41—auditory)

Lateral sulcus of Sylvius

Pons

Olfactory
bulb and tract

Prefrontal lobe

Frontal pole

Broca's speech area
(44, 45)

Frontal lobe

Parietal lobe

Occipital
lobe

Temporal lobe

FIG. 2.4. Lateral surface of the brain. Numbers refer to Brodman's areas.

22

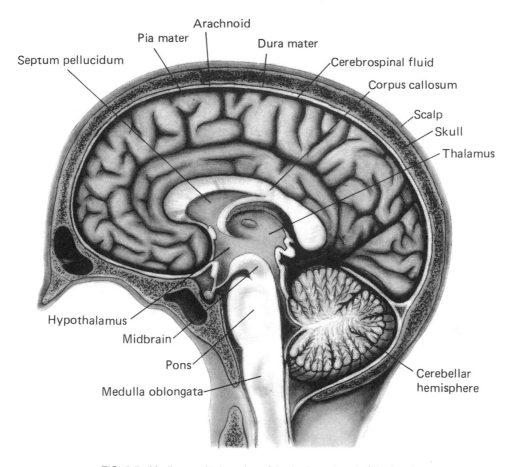

FIG. 2.5. Median sagittal section of the brain and part of the head.

lems. Areas of cortex not known to subserve specific sensory or motor functions are called *association cortex*. This cortical tissue comprises about 80% to 85% of the cortex in humans. Association cortex is believed to serve the functions of learning, planning, perceiving, and remembering.

The medial aspect is what would be seen if the brain were cut in half, from front to back (called the midsagittal section). The medial aspect is presented in Fig. 2.5. Note that if we examine the head area from outside to inside, we first see the scalp and then the skull bone. Immediately below the skull is the dura mater, which is a tough, elastic membrane covering the brain. Below the dura is the arachnoid tissue. The pia mater is a very thin, soft membrane below the arachnoid that covers the cortical surface and follows the gyri and sulci very closely. The three membranes: dura mater, arachnoid tissue, and pia mater are collectively referred to as *meninges*. The subarachnoid space contains the cerebrospinal fluid that is believed to supply nourishment to the brain as well as provide a protective envelope of liquid for the brain and spinal cord. Also in the subarachnoid space is the arachnoid trabeculae, or spider web-like filaments of tissue that criss-cross in the region between the arachnoid membrane and the pia mater. The subarachnoid space communicates with the ventricular system of the brain.

There are four ventricles in the brain: two lateral ventricles (one in each cerebral hemisphere), a third ventricle located between each thalamus, and a fourth ventricle connected to the third by a narrow channel (cerebral aqueduct of Sylvius) that runs between the brain stem and cerebellum. The ventricles are spaces through which the cerebrospinal fluid circulates in and around the brain. The subcortical brain contains many important structures that are of interest.

The thalamus (brain stem; see Fig. 2.5) has important functions as a relay station for sensory and motor input to the cortex. The thalamus contains many important nuclei, including the ventral nuclei, posteroventral nucleus, lateroventral nucleus, medial and lateral geniculate bodies, pulvinar, and reticular nucleus. The medial geniculate body is important in processing sound stimuli, receiving input from the hearing mechanisms in the cochlea of the inner ear and transmitting information to primary auditory cortex located in the temporal lobe. Another important thalamic nucleus is the lateral geniculate body, which receives information from the eyes and projects fibers to primary visual cortex located in the occipital lobe.

The reticular nucleus has a role in both general and specific cortical activity and functions. This reticular formation, running through the core of the brain stem from medulla to thalamus, has been referred to as the ascending reticular activating system (ARAS) and has important implications for behavior, especially in maintaining alertness of organisms. The hypothalamus is a relatively small, but extremely important, subcortical brain area. It has many nuclei that are variously concerned with control of eating and drinking, sexual behavior, and aggression. It also controls the autonomic nervous system and regulates the endocrine system (the hormone producing areas of the body such as the thyroid, adrenal glands, and sex glands) through its control over the pituitary gland, which is referred to as the *master gland.*

A collection of subcortical forebrain nuclei called the *basal ganglia* are concerned with the regulation of some semiautomatic movements and gross bodily adjustments. An example of semiautomatic activity is swinging of the arms while walking, and a gross adjustment would be maintenance of body posture or the initiation of sitting or standing. Major nuclei of the basal ganglia are the putamen, caudate, and globus pallidus. The putamen and caudate depend on dopaminergic neurons for their functioning, as mentioned previously in the discussion of neurotransmitters.

The midbrain contains important structures involved in visual reflexes (superior colliculi) and auditory reflexes (inferior colliculi). The midbrain reticular formation is located here as well as the substantia nigra and red nucleus. The reticular formation has a role in attention, arousal, and sleep, the substantia nigra produces dopamine and the axons of its neurons communicate with the putamen and caudate nucleus of the basal ganglia, and the red nucleus is part of the motor system that brings information from precentral cortex and cerebellum to the spinal cord.

Located between midbrain and medulla is an area of brainstem called the *pons*. The locus coeruleus of the dorsal Pons is a center for acetylcholinergic neurons that make connections with many brain areas. The Pons communicates with the cerebellum and motor cortex in coordinating movements and contains a nucleus of the auditory system (superior olivary nucleus). Traveling through the core of the Pons is the ARAS, the system concerned with sleep and arousal. The medulla is just below the Pons. It is an important center for the regulation of cardiovascular activity and respiration. It also part of the auditory pathway (inferior olivary nucleus) and the location where pyramidal decussation takes place. The decussation is a crossing over of fibers from the motor cortex of the right hemisphere to the left side of the body and from left hemisphere to the right side of the body. This organization of the voluntary motor system (pyramidal system) is responsible for contralateral motor control.

The area of brain referred to as the *limbic system* is involved in motivated and emotional behavior. Its structures include portions of the hypothalamus, thalamus, the hippocampus, hippocampal gyrus, amygdala, mammillary bodies, fornix, and the so-called *limbic cortex* (located just above the corpus callosum). The amygdala has been implicated in aggressive behavior and the hypothalamus in appetitive behavior (such as eating, drinking, sex) and in the rage response. The hippocampus plays an important role in memory since damage to this area is the primary cause of anterograde amnesia. This type of forgetting involves the inability to remember things that happen after the damage occurs, even though short-term memory (such as that involved in conversing) functions well. Another structure of special interest is the *corpus callosum*, a thick band of fibers that connects the left and right hemispheres of the brain. The corpus callosum allows the transfer of sensory and other information between the two cerebral hemispheres. This basic information about neuron and brain structures is preparatory to the material that follows in chapters on the EEG and event-related brain potential.

THE ELECTROENCEPHALOGRAM (EEG)

The electroencephalogram (EEG) or "brain wave" was first described in rabbits and monkeys by Richard Caton in 1875. Caton was interested in studying localization of sensory function in the brain. He presented visual stimuli while recording from electrodes placed directly on the exposed brains of rabbits and monkeys (Brazier, 1957). He showed that when a flash of light was presented to the animal's eyes, a change in electrical activity occurred in the occipital area. This response was probably the first sensory-evoked potential recorded from cortical tissue. Caton also noticed that when his electrodes were resting on the surface of the rabbit's cortex, with no sensory stimulation being presented, feeble oscillations occurred in his recording. He concluded that his recordings represented the electrical activity of the resting brain, and presented his findings to the British Medical Society in 1875. The work caught little attention, even though Caton later presented his findings in both the United States and Russia.

In 1902, Hans Berger began his work on brain waves with dogs, and in 1920, he started to study human EEGs. His goal from the beginning was to detect, from the scalp surface in humans, the same waves that could be obtained from the brain surface of animals. Finally, in 1929, after a great deal of work in which EEGs were recorded from many individuals, including himself and his teenage son, Berger published his findings. His paper, "On the Electroencephalogram of Man" (see Porges & Coles, 1976), identified two basic brain wave patterns: one, a relatively large, regular wave, that occurred 10 to 11 times per second, and a smaller, irregular one, at a frequency of 20 to 30 cycles per second. Berger termed the larger and slower waves *alpha* and the smaller, faster ones *beta*. Later, investigators identified other types of brain waves and continued using the Greek alphabet labels, calling them gamma, delta, theta, kappa, lambda, and mu waves. The most reliable of these later-identified waves, in terms of consistency of occurrence, have been delta and theta. The *delta* wave is characterized by very low frequency and high amplitude and was given its name by Walter (1937). The term *theta* was first used by Walter (1953) to describe a wave with a frequency between 3 and 7 cycles per second. The characteristics of some of these waves are described here and are depicted in Fig. 2.6.

The characteristic EEG patterns, frequencies, and amplitudes are rather consistent within the same individual. For example, a high degree of correlation between alpha wave recordings that were made 3 weeks apart was reported by Tomarken, Davidson, Wheeler, and Kinney (1992). The role of inheritance in development of individual EEG patterns was indicated in a study by Stassen, Lykken, and Bomben (1988). They found that the EEG patterns of identical twins were very similar, even though the twins had been reared apart. Further, they also reported that the EEG patterns of fraternal twins were significantly more similar than EEGs obtained from unrelated persons.

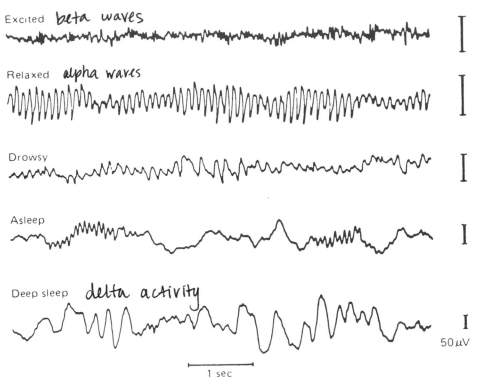

Excited *beta waves*

Relaxed *alpha waves*

Drowsy

Asleep

Deep sleep *delta activity*

50 μV

1 sec

FIG. 2.6. Electroencephalographic records during excitement, relaxation, and varying degrees of sleep. In the fourth strip runs of 14/sec rhythm, superimposed on slow waves, are termed "sleep spindles." Notice that excitement is characterized by a rapid frequency and small amplitude and that varying degrees of sleep are marked by increasing irregularity and by the appearance of slow waves.

In addition to the waves discussed so far, there are the "K complexes" and "sleep spindles" of the sleeping EEG (see Fig. 4.2 and Table 4.2). The sleep EEG is discussed in chapter 4.

Alpha Waves

The alpha wave is a rhythmic oscillation that occurs at a rate of 8 to 13 times a second (cycles per second, cps, or Hertz, Hz,) at a magnitude of about 20 to 60 μV (millionths of a volt). These waves can be produced by almost anyone sitting quietly in a relaxed position, with eyes closed. (There is a small percentage of persons who have difficulty in producing alpha waves.) As soon as the individual becomes involved in any mental or physical activity, the alpha waves generally become reduced in amplitude or disappear. For example, a person may be sitting in a chair, relaxed or not thinking of anything in particular, and at least some alpha waves will be in evidence. If the person is asked to spell a word, beta activity will usually dominate the recording. Alpha is illustrated by the second wave from the top in Fig. 2.6, labeled "relaxed." The classical view of alpha has been that it represents a relaxed state and will be disrupted with any kind of mental work. However, Shaw (1996) pointed out that there have been exceptions reported in which tasks such as mental arithmetic result in no change or even an enhancement of alpha amplitude in up to one third of the individuals tested (e.g., see Mulholland, 1969). Furthermore, there is evidence that alpha enhancement occurs before skilled actions involving aiming (shooting, archery) and golf putting (Shaw, 1996).

Beta Waves

Beta is an irregular wave that occurs at a frequency of 14 to 30 cps at an amplitude of approximately 2 to 20 μV. Beta waves are common when a person is involved in mental or physical activity as illustrated by the topmost tracing in Fig. 2.6 (labeled "excited").

Delta Waves

The delta wave is a large amplitude, low-frequency wave. It is typically between .5 and 3.5 cps in frequency, in the range of 20 to 200 μV. The delta wave appears only during deep sleep in normal individuals. If it occurs in a waking person, it could indicate some kind of brain abnormality, such as a tumor. See the bottom tracing in Fig. 2.6 for an example of delta activity.

Theta Waves

The theta wave is a relativly less common type of brain rhythm that occurs at about 4 to 7 Hz, at an amplitude ranging anywhere from 20 to 100 μV. It has been reported to occur more frequently in the spontaneous EEG recordings of children than in adults. Walter (1953) found it to occur during states of displeasure, pleasure, and drowsiness in young adults, and Maulsby (1971) reported amplitudes of 100 μV in babies experiencing pleasurable events (e.g., drinking from a bottle or being fondled by their mother).

Kappa Waves

Kennedy, Gottsdanker, Armington, and Gray (1948) discovered waves of about 10 Hz that appear to be associated with thinking. They reported that it occurred in about 30% of their subjects.

Lambda Waves

Lambda waves were discovered in humans by Evans (1952) and Gastaut (1951). They have been recorded from over the visual cortex and are considered to be a type of visual response resulting from a shifting image of some object in a person's visual field. They are triangular in shape, range from 20 to 50 μV, and last about 250 to 250 msec in response to stimulation.

Mu Waves

The mu rhythm (described by Gastaut, 1952) has sharp peaks and rounded negative portions. It appears in the normal EEG of about 7% of the population and can be recorded from over the fissure of Rolando (vertex of the scalp). The frequency is usually 8 to 13 Hz, within the alpha band, but it is independent of alpha, blocking not with eye opening but with movement or intended movement (Niedermeyer, 1987). A study by Koshino and Niedermeyer (1976) found that it was enhanced by scanning a patterned stimulus and not suppressed, as has usually been reported. These latter researchers found that 182 of 2,284 persons sampled (8.1%) showed evidence of the mu rhythm.

Gamma Waves

Gamma waves were reported on in humans by Galambos, Makeig, and Talmachoff (1981). The gamma wave can be described as a rhythmic activity that occurs to sensory stimuli such as auditory clicks or flashes of light. It has a resting frequency of 40 Hz and an amplitude of about 3 to 5 Hz. A recent paper by DePascalis and Ray (1998) described a "gamma band" of 36 to 44 Hz. Examination of Figure 1 from their paper indicates a change from a prestimulus level of 5 μV to approximately 10 μV after stimulation. DePascalis and Ray noted that 40-Hz activity is enhanced by stimulation over a wide area of cortex, but that the increase is greatest at frontal and central locations.

MEASUREMENT OF THE EEG

The various kinds of brain waves can be measured by means of electrodes attached to the scalp. This is the most common technique used by researchers studying brain activity. It must be pointed out that the amplitude of the EEG as measured from the scalp is much lower than if it were measured from the surface of the cortex (the electrocorticogram), because the electrical activity must pass through the dura mater, the cerebrospinal fluid, the skull bone, and the skin of the scalp before it reaches the scalp electrode. This greatly reduces its amplitude. The electrocorticogram is measured in millivolts, whereas the EEG is in microvolt units, showing the great disparity in magnitudes. Because of the difficulty and the hazards of penetrating the skull the electrocorticogram is rarely recorded, even in clinical cases. The EEG signal is so small at the scalp that electronic circuitry for measuring it must be very sensitive.

Electrode Location (Monopolar)

To measure EEG, one may use either a monopolar or bipolar recording technique. The monopolar method is described here, and the bipolar is discussed later. A monopolar technique involves placing one so-called active electrode in good contact with the skin over an area of interest, for example, the occipital (visual) cortex. Another electrode, termed the *reference* is placed on a relatively inactive area, such as the earlobe or tip of the nose. Because any reference electrode on the head is not completely inactive, some investigators prefer to place them on other parts of the body, for example, the back or chest. These may be difficult to use, because they could pick up muscle activity if the subject is not completely still.

A caution about the use of electrodes is in order. Because of concern over the spread of disease, such as acquired immune deficiency syndrome (AIDS) and hepatitis B virus, the Society for Psychophysiological Research set up a committee to recommend procedures to minimize such risk (Putnam, Johnson, & Roth, 1992). The recommendations include suggestions about the use of electrodes, proper sterilization techniques, and provide guidelines to protect subjects, experimenters, and laboratory technicians. The reader is encouraged to read the report published in the journal *Psychophysiology*. The diagram shown in Fig. 2.7 illustrates some commonly used scalp locations in EEG research. The locations are based on a portion of the International EEG nomenclature (Jasper, 1958). It is called the "10–20 System" because the various locations are either 10% or 20% of the distance between standard points used for measurement. For example, in obtaining the location designated O_z, a centimeter measurement is taken between the *nasion* (bridge of nose) and *inion* (a projection of bone at the back of the head found over the occipital area, also known as the occipital protuberance). Then 10% of this distance is measured (toward the nasion), and the electrode is placed at this spot. The tape measure must pass straight along the midline between nasion and inion, through those points labeled with a "z" (indicating midline). This area is designated O_z and is over the occipital cortex. Those labeled P, F, and T are over parietal, frontal, and temporal areas, respectively. The C locations are central areas, with C_z as the center of both the anterior–posterior (front–back) and coronal (side-to-side) planes. The location labeled F_p is the frontal pole and is 10% of the

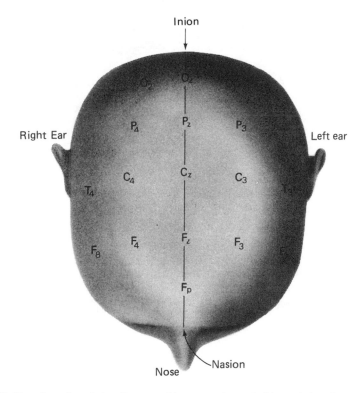

FIG. 2.7. Top view of scalp locations used by researchers studying relations between brain activity and performance. The locations are the active, or EEG-producing, areas. The reference area may be the earlobes, singly or in combination as "linked ears," or the tip of the nose. The numbering system is a portion of that used in the International EEG 10–20 system. The nasion refers to the bridge of the nose, and the inion is the occipital protuberance.

nasion–inion distance. The F_z, C_z, and P_z locations are each 20% of the nasion–inion distance back, starting from F_p. The locations along the coronal plane are based on the distance between the midpoints of the two ears taken through C_z. The other locations along this anterior–posterior line are 20% of the distance apart from each other, except for the nasion–F_2 distance of 30%. This side view is illustrated in Fig. 2.8. Note that the locations on the left side of the head are indicated by odd numbers. This system of electrode location has enabled different investigators to communicate the sites used in their EEG studies in a standard way. The method also has the advantage of being based on each subject's own head size. Anatomical studies carried out when the numbering system was first presented (Jasper, 1958) indicated that the locations do approximate the areas that they are claimed to be over, for example, occipital, parietal, frontal, or temporal lobes. There is an increasing tendency for investigators to use more scalp locations in a multiple recording array for EEG. To accommodate additional locations, the American EEG Society (1991) recommended additional sites and nomenclature for electrodes that expands on the original 10–20 system.

Electrode Attachment

The electronics of the recording equipment enable a comparison of the activity measured over the cortical area of interest with that at the reference electrode, and the difference is the written EEG record. The electrodes should be small (6–8 mm in diameter) and easy to attach. The

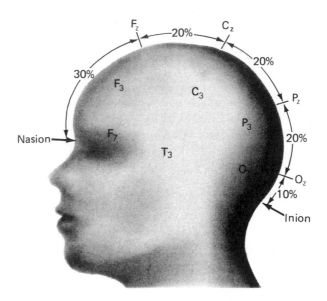

FIG. 2.8. In this diagram the 10–20 system locations are shown for the left side of the scalp. Note that left side locations have odd-numbered designations, while the right side locations are indicated by even numbers. (F, frontal; C, central; P, parietal; O, occipital; T, temporal.)

scalp area should be prepared by rubbing it with a cleansing material (alcohol on a cotton ball works well) until the skin shows a slight pink tinge. Then a standard electrode paste (a conducting agent) is carefully rubbed into the skin of the scalp until it permeates the pores. The electrode can be held firmly in place with an elastic headband with Velcro attachments, or a wide variety of other devices available commercially. Many researchers now use "electrode caps" which have prepositioned electrodes embedded at locations consistent with the 10–20 system for measurement. Simultaneous recordings from 32, 64, and even 128 electrode locations are now accomplished by some investigators with appropriate prearranged electrode arrays sold by equipment manufacturers.

The reference lead can be a convenient clip electrode, which merely is attached to the earlobe or tip of the nose after the area has been cleansed of any oils or dead skin by rubbing with alcohol. Many researchers use "linked ears" as a reference; that is, electrodes are attached to both earlobes and then connected together to serve as a common reference for scalp leads. This bilateral reference technique is especially important if one wishes to investigate hemispheric asymmetries. Electrode paste is also used when attaching the reference electrode. The resistance between the active and reference leads can be measured by impedance meters either conveniently built into the recording device or used as a separate instrument. It should read less than 5,000 ohms (units of impedance). If it does, then your electrodes are making good contact with the scalp tissue. A ground electrode may be placed on the other earlobe, on the mastoid area behind the ear, or on the tip of the nose. If activity over the two hemispheres is being compared, the investigator will want to use a reference that links both sides of the head, such as the two earlobes or two mastoid areas. Even with a good contact through careful electrode attachments, artifacts can be seen in the EEG record if subjects move about excessively or tense up the muscles of their forehead or jaw or blink their eyes. Subjects must be cautioned against producing this type of EEG artifact. Other unwanted signals, such as heart activity or skin potential responses, would be considered artifacts if they appeared in the EEG. When a fitted cap with multiple electrodes is used, it should be carefully checked periodically because slippage may occur.

Silver cup electrodes are commonly used for active leads, whereas flat silver electrodes held in a clip are convenient reference electrodes. Some investigators use gold or tin electrodes or a cellulose sponge permeated with the conducting material and held in place by an elastic headband.

Electrode Placement (Bipolar)

When using a bipolar recording technique, two active electrodes are placed over cortical areas of interest. Bipolar leads record the difference or algebraic sum of the electrical potentials beneath the two regions at every instant. Some researchers prefer bipolar recording because it avoids some of the problems of selecting an inactive reference area inherent in monopolar recording. However, bipolar recordings have the disadvantage of producing a record of combined activity at two locations. For clinical purposes (i.e., the recording of EEG to detect brain abnormalities), the interpretation of EEG records usually requires the comparison of data obtained from symmetrically placed electrodes (e.g., from two electrodes on the right frontal area compared with two on the left frontal area). The presence or absence of symmetry in the two tracings may be of clinical significance. Bipolar leads may also be used in research applications other than clinical. The monopolar technique is convenient in situations where activity produced at a specific area is monitored, for example, the left occipital area, or in recording event-related potentials (see chapter 5).

NEUROIMAGING TECHNIQUES

The EEG and a derivative measure, the event-related potential, can both be observed to change with changes in behavior. Thus, they are said to have a high degree of temporal resolution with regard to ongoing behavior. The EEG has been described briefly and is discussed further in chapters 3 and 4. The event-related potential (ERP) is described in chapters 5, 6, and 7. Another measure that has a high degree of temporal resolution with regard to behavior in progress is the magnetoencephalogram, or MEG, a measure described later in this section. However, psychophysiologists are increasingly utilizing other brain imaging techniques that, although not having the same temporal resolution as the EEG, ERP, or MEG because they develop more slowly, nevertheless offer other advantages in the study of brain structures involved in various behaviors.

In a special issue of the journal *Psychophysiology* (March, 1998), several of these imaging techniques were discussed and illustrated. What follows is a brief summary of some of the main points regarding the use of these other techniques in psychophysiological investigations. Another useful source of information is an article written by Aine (1995) that gives an overview of neuroimaging techniques in humans. Thus, we briefly discuss positron emission tomography (PET), functional magnetic resonance imaging (fMRI), and the magnetoencephalogram (MEG). These measures have enabled neuroscientists to study different aspects of brain function during attention, memory, language, motor, and sensory activities.

Positron Emission Tomography (PET)

The PET imaging technique has enabled clinicians and scientists to examine normal and abnormal brain function. The so-called PET scan allows the viewing of various brain functions through a technique that combines computed tomography (CT) and a tracer kinetic assay method (Aine, 1995). The PET technique can provide information about glucose and oxygen metabolism in brain structures, blood flow in brain tissue (cerebral blood flow), and blood volume in brain areas (cerebral blood volume). The method allows researchers to view cross sections of different brain areas that are color-coded to indicate differing amounts of activity. For example, red indicates high levels of activity whereas blue areas depict low levels of the function being measured. The PET technique requires that radioactive substances be administered to subjects. Because brain activity is greatly dependent on both glucose and oxygen the measurement of these metabolic functions offers a glimpse into which brain structures are actively using them while the individual is involved in various cognitive activities. The assumption is that more active brain areas use more glucose and more oxygenated blood, and they require a greater amount of blood. Hence, if certain brain areas are more active while the person is involved in a given behavior, then those areas have at least some part in the accomplishment of that function. One caution that must be noted here: The activation evidenced could involve inhibitory neurons, thus the overall effect would be a lessening of activity. This was discussed previously in the context of effects of inhibitory and excitatory neurotransmitters.

An example of a study that utilized PET techniques is that of Kosslyn and colleagues in which right-handed men participated in two mental rotation tasks as regional cerebral blood flow (rCBF) was measured by PET (Kosslyn, Digirolamo, Thompson, & Alpert, 1998). In one task, subjects mentally rotated and mentally compared drawings of cubes, and in another they did the same for drawings of human hands. Mental rotation of these two different kinds of objects produced activation in different brain areas: Mental rotation of cubes produced activation in parietal and occipital lobes, whereas mental rotation of hands led to activation in precentral gyrus, parietal lobe, primary visual cortex, and frontal areas. The different distribution of activity for the two tasks led the researchers to conclude that at least two different mechanisms are used in mental rotation.

In another study, PET was used to measure glucose metabolism in the thalamus and the activity was correlated with EEG measured over a 30-minute period (Larson et al., 1998). The researchers reported that greater thalamic glucose metabolism is correlated with decreased alpha, a clear demonstration of a relation between alpha EEG power and thalamic activity in humans.

Functional Magnetic Resonance Imaging (fMRI)

Magnetic Resonance Imaging (MRI) uses nonionizing radio frequency energy to provide high-resolution images of anatomical structures (Aine, 1995). To perform MRI, subjects are placed in a strong magnetic field. The resultant high resolution images are used to create a detailed photograph-like representation of the structure. Advances in data aquisition have enabled the measurement of hemodynamic changes (fMRI) such as blood oxygen concentration, blood flow, and blood volume. Thus, the fMRI allows researchers to see ongoing changes in brain activities as a person engages in cognitive tasks. Among the advantages of fMRI are better temporal and spatial resolution than PET, because it takes much more time to acquire PET displays of brain structures. However, temporal resolution of EEG- and MEG-based techniques is superior to fMRI, which can take between 500 and 1,000 msec. Spatial resolution can be defined in terms of resolving two separate sources of simultaneous activity. The PET scanners can resolve sources that are 5 to 6 mm distant, whereas fMRI can provide a resolution of about 2 mm (Aine, 1995). Other advantages over PET include briefer periods of data collection, and no requirement for the administration of radioactive materials into the body. An interesting paper—using fMRI techniques to determine activation of the visual cortex during the viewing of emotional and neutral stimuli—was published by Lang et al. (1998). Participants viewed a series of pleasant, neutral, or unpleasant pictures while images at four different locations in occipital cortex were obtained during the 12-sec picture presentation period or a 12-sec interpicture interval. Functional activation was measured as an increase in blood oxygen concentration and was shown to be greater for emotional stimuli (pleasant and unpleasant) compared to neutral stimuli. Further, there was a gender difference in that women had significantly more activity for unpleasant than pleasant stimuli in the more active right hemisphere. Men responded in the opposite direction, with greater right hemisphere activity for pleasant than unpleasant stimuli. Activity for men and women was about the same for neutral stimuli.

Biomagnetism and the Magnetoencephalogram (MEG)

Biomagnetism refers to the study of magnetic fields whose origin is in specific biological systems (Williamson & Kaufman, 1981). The weak magnetic fields of many body organs could not be practically studied until the application of the superconducting quantum interfering device (SQUID) to this type of measurement. The SQUID has been used to measure magnetic fields produced by the heart, lungs, and brain. The magnetic brain fields, called *neuromagnetism*, are among the weakest produced by biological systems. Thus, spontaneous brain activity is of extremely low magnitude when measured in terms of magnetic variations, and brain changes that occur in response to specific events, called *evoked fields*, are smaller still.

The strength of a magnetic field is indicated by the value of its magnetic induction for which the tesla (T) is the unit of measurement. Spontaneous brain activity produces such low levels of magnetic activity that it is measured in picoteslas (10^{-12} tesla). Brain activity changes produced in response to specific stimuli (evoked fields) have strengths as low as 1^{-15} tesla (femoteslas). Hence, in making biomagnetic measurements, the scientist must be able to measure extremely weak signals and must screen out possible interference from the much stronger magnetic field fluctuations in the surrounding environment (approximately 10^{-4} tesla). This requires rather elaborate procedures and instrumentation. Figure 2.9 illustrates the placement of the SQUID apparatus over temporal and occipital areas of the brain to measure magnetic brain fields in response to sound stimuli.

Neuromagnetism: The MEG and Magneto Evoked Field (MEF)

Similar to the EEG, the observed MEG represents the combined activity of millions of neurons. The advantages of being able to measure neuromagnetic fields of the brain are the following: (a) use of the SQUID eliminates the use of reference electrodes, thus allowing the MEG to compare activity in two different brains more directly; (b) the MEG measured outside the head may be better in determining subcortical sources of neural activity, because the magnetic signals are less influenced by tissue lying between the source and the sensing device—for example, asymmetries in bone density overlying two brain areas would not influence the MEG; (c) the MEG is very good for localizing sources of neuronal activity at cortical areas; (d) some currents may be detected magnetically and cannot be observed through recordings of electrical changes; and (e) the magnetic detector can conveniently scan field patterns of the brain, because the detector is not attached to the scalp surface, as in the case of fixed electrodes used to measure the EEG. The MEG may be obtained simultaneously with the EEG. Simultaneous alpha and beta activity will be observed with both kinds of records in the awake person. However, the MEG recording will not be as clear, because the very tiny signal is more susceptible to noise than EEG.

Investigators are increasingly using the MEG in studies of brain function. The MEF is a measure derived from changes in MEG activity to specific stimuli. In that respect, it is analogous to the event-related potential that is derived from averaging EEG responses that occur to discrete stimuli. Several representative studies of MEG and MEF are included in chapters on the EEG and ERP. However, a sample investigation using MEG to study brain responses in the processing of novel sounds and frequency changes is described here. The investigation

FIG. 2.9. Arrangement of magnetic sensors within a magnetically shielded room at the Neuromagnetism Laboratory at the Departments of Physics and Psychology at New York University. A 5-sensor array is supported within the dewar held over the subject's head, and two single-person units are directed inward from the sides. The latter are cooled by refrigerators and need no liquid helium to keep the sensors superconducting. (Photo by courtesy of Drs. Williamson and Kaufman of New York University.)

was carried out by Ahlo and associates (1998). It had previously been determined through event-related potential (ERP) techniques that deviant sounds, occurring in a sequence of standard sounds, produced a negative wave at about 100 msec after the deviant stimulus. This negativity was termed a mismatch negativity (MMN) and has been related to the difference between the neuronal activity caused by the deviant stimulus and a sensory memory trace of the standard sound. Ahlo and colleagues used the MMN paradigm and MEG technique to localize brain structures involved in the response. The MEG was recorded in a magnetically shielded room with a 122-channel magnetometer, termed a whole-head magnetometer and consisting of 61 dual sensor units. The standard tones were at 600 cycles per second (Hz) at 75 dB (decibels–a measure of sound intensity) and the deviants were 660 Hz at 75 dB. In one condition (ignore), the subjects were instructed to ignore the tones while they watched a silent film. In the other condition (attend), subjects counted silently the number of deviant tones presented. Subjects were also presented with infrequent novel sounds (only once in a sequence) such as a telephone ring or an electric drill. Both deviant tones and novel sounds produced a MMN in the magnetoencephalogram whether they were attended or ignored. The generators of this MEG response were located in superior planes of both temporal lobes.

Summary.   Brain imaging techniques can provide useful supplementary information for psychophysiologists seeking to discover brain areas involved in various psychological functions. Techniques such as PET and fMRI do not have the exquisite temporal resolution of EEG or MEG approaches, but have the potential to illustrate pictorially both cortical and subcortical structures involved in cognitive, perceptual, and motor activities.

THE PERIPHERAL NERVOUS SYSTEM

The peripheral nervous system allows communication between the brain and spinal cord. The communication link is made possible by 31 pairs of spinal nerves, which branch off from the spinal cord (see Fig. 2.10), and 12 pairs of cranial nerves that emerge directly from the ventral surface of the cerebrum and brain stem. The spinal and cranial nerves make possible the activities of the somatic and autonomic nervous systems. Most of the peripheral nerves (with the exception of a few cranial nerves) have both sensory and motor functions.

The Somatic System

This system consists of motor nerves that control voluntary muscle. The nerves, along with their dendrites and cell bodies, are found at different levels of the spinal cord, and form the motor portion of the spinal nerve (ventral root) at the point where spinal nerve and spinal cord meet. The ventral (motor) roots and dorsal (sensory) roots merge to form the complete spinal nerve. The spinal nerves connect to sympathetic ganglia by way of *rami communicantes*. More is said about these sympathetic ganglia when the autonomic nervous system is discussed.

The Autonomic Nervous System (ANS)

Many of the responses of interest to psychophysiologists are controlled by the ANS, thus making this a very important system for our field. The ANS is the regulator and coordinator of important bodily activities, including digestion, body temperature, blood pressure, and many aspects of emotional behavior. Its activities have traditionally been regarded to be automatic or taking place without conscious control. However, research in the area of self-regulation of physiological responses through operant conditioning techniques suggests that it might be possible to alter one's own level of ANS activity, for example, heart rate (see chapters 12 and 17).

   The main function of the ANS is to keep a constant internal body environment in the face of internal or external changes that could upset the balance. The term *homeostasis* was coined by the physiologist Claude Bernard to describe this maintenance of a stable internal environment. The ANS involves innervation of three types of cell: smooth muscle, cardiac muscle, and glandular (secretory) cells. The main neurotransmitters of the ANS are acetylcholine and norepinephrine. *Acetylcholine* is the neurotransmitter of the parasympathetic nervous system (cholinergic system) because the postganglionic axons of this system release it. *Norepinephrine* is released at most postganglionic synapses of the sympathetic nervous system (SNS). An exception is the sweat glands. These are innervated by the SNS only and postganglionic synapses use acetylcholine in this control. Other exceptions are the adrenal glands, the muscles that constrict blood vessels, and the muscles that cause the hairs of the skin to become

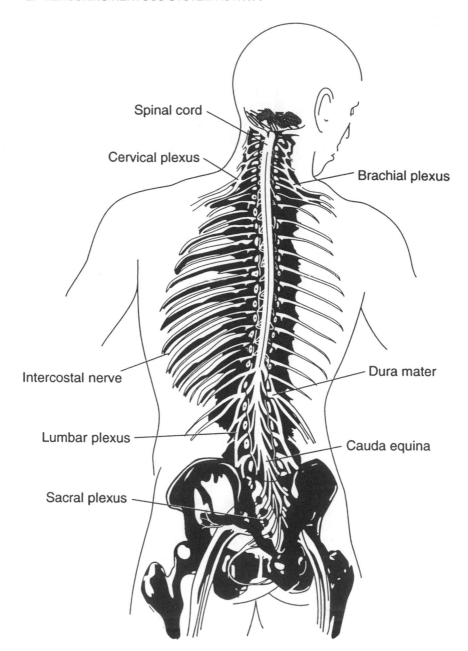

FIG. 2.10. A dorsal view of the human body, showing the routes traveled by the principal spinal nerves.

erect since they are controlled only by the SNS. Other body organs, such as the heart, pupils of the eyes, stomach, and lungs have both parasympathetic (PNS) and sympathetic input. In general, the SNS controls those activities that are mobilized during emergency and stress situations, the well-known "fight-or-flight" response, first described by Walter B. Cannon in 1915. The sympathetic reactions include expenditure of energy, the acceleration of heart rate, dilation of the pupil, increased blood pressure, increased blood sugar, enhanced blood flow to the voluntary muscles, decreased blood flow to the internal organs and extremities, and increased sweating. The rapid heartbeat, and extra glucose brings extra nutrition and oxygen to muscles, while the increased muscle tension prepares for running or physical defense. Shortness of breath induces rapid breathing, hyperoxygenating the blood. Sweating cools the body in anticipation of flight, and may also protect the skin against injury. The enlarged pupil may enable vision to be more efficient as more light enters the eye with pupillary dilation. Secretion of adrenaline into the blood makes it clot faster, if injury occurs. Thus, the sympathetic response to threat is very adaptive because it enhances survival.

The activities under parasympathetic control are also adaptive to its basic functions of rest, repair, and relaxation of the body and restoration of energy stores. The reactions under control of this system include decreases in heart rate and blood pressure, stimulation of the digestive system (including increased salivary flow and peristalsis), pupillary constriction, sexual arousal, resting, and sleep.

Although the sympathetic and parasympathetic have contrasting functions, the activities are integrated and not antagonistic. The systems tend to act in a complementary fashion with a great deal of reciprocity that usually enables a smooth flow of bodily activities and behavior.

The Sympathetic Nervous System (SNS)

The SNS is also called the thoracico-lumbar system, because all of the motor neurons of this system emerge from the spinal cord via the spinal nerves of the thoracic and lumbar regions. After emerging from the spinal cord, they make linkages to a series of 22 ganglia in the so-called "sympathetic chain." The diagram in Fig. 2.11 shows a schematic of the brain and spinal cord, the chain of SNS ganglia, the PNS ganglia, and the organs that are innervated by both systems. The organization of the chain of sympathetic ganglia enables the SNS to act as an integrated whole. This is why sympathetic reactions occur simultaneously. For example, during an emergency situation, possibly caused by fear, anger, pain, or asphyxia, the SNS activities that occur together might include increased heart rate, blood pressure, sweating, cardiac output, and respiration changes that enhance a "flight-or-fight" reaction. Note in Fig. 2.11 that the fibers from the spinal cord to the sympathetic chain are short, whereas fibers from the chain to a target organ are long. This is opposite from parasympathetic organization in which ganglia are located near the organ to be innervated, thus resulting in long preganglionic fibers and short postganglionic connections.

The Parasympathetic Nervous System (PNS)

This system is termed the *cranio-sacral* division of the ANS because its activities are controlled by motor cells whose nuclei are found in certain cranial nerves and in the sacral part of the spinal cord (Fig. 2.11). PNS activity is more specific than that of the SNS because the PNS ganglia are located near the target organ. For example, the oculomotor (third cranial nerve) regulates the iris of the eye, thus producing pupillary constriction without producing other reactions.

The PNS is the system of rest, repair, and enjoyment. It is dominant during eating, sleeping, and sexual activity. Some of its activities would include the stimulation of salivary secretions, digestive secretions in the stomach, peristalsis in the intestines, decreases in heart rate, pupillary constriction, and increased blood flow to the genitalia (erection) during sexual excitement. An example of how the PNS and SNS complement each other is in the cycle of sexual arousal, orgasm, and postorgasm. During foreplay and sexual arousal, the PNS is dominant. This dominance shifts to the SNS during orgasm and back to PNS dominance during the postorgasmic state.

The PNS influence from the sacral portion of the spinal cord is directed at the genitalia, sphincters (anal, urethral), bladder, and colon. The cranial nerves (c.n.) serving PNS functions

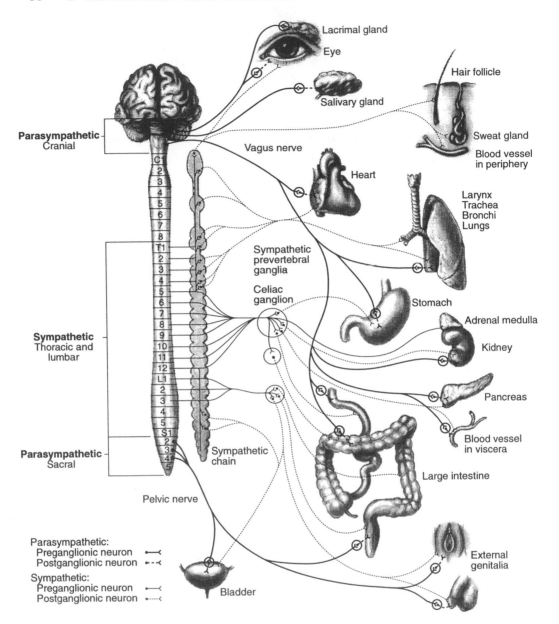

FIG. 2.11. A schematic representation of the autonomic nervous system and the target organs it serves.

are the oculomotor (third c.n.), facial (seventh c.n.), glossopharyngeal (ninth c.n.), and vagus (10th c.n.). The 12 cranial nerves and a sample of their functions are as follows:

1. Olfactory nerve or olfactory bulb (sensory)—receives impulses from olfactory cells of the upper nasal passages and transmits them to the rest of the brain through the olfactory tracts (smell).
2. Optic nerve (sensory)—a CNS tract from the retina of the eye to visual structures in the brain. Actually, the optic nerve is an extension of brain tissue (vision).
3. Oculomotor nerve (motor and PNS)—controls turning of the eyes and pupillary opening.

4. Trochlear nerve (motor)—controls oblique eye movements.
5. Trigeminal (sensory and motor)—carries sensations of touch from face, scalp, and teeth, and sends motor fibers to chewing muscles.
6. Abducens nerve (motor)—controls horizontal eye movements.
7. Facial nerve (sensory motor and PNS)—conveys taste from front two thirds of the tongue. This nerve also controls face and scalp muscles and salivary glands.
8. Auditory–vestibular nerve (sensory)—transmits stimuli from organ of hearing (cochlea) and balance (semicircular canals, utricle, and saccule) to the brain.
9. Glossopharyngeal nerve (sensory, motor and PNS)—conveys taste from back one third of tongue. It also provides motor control to vocal organs and salivary glands (parotid).
10. Vagus nerve (sensory, motor and PNS)—sensory stimuli are transmitted from thoracic and abdominal viscera (heart, stomach); sends motor fibers to tongue, heart, smooth muscle of lungs, and most abdominal organs.
11. Spinal-accessory nerve (motor)—innervates vocal organs, head, and back muscles.
12. Hypoglossal nerve (motor)—controls muscles of the tongue and neck.

Thus, we conclude a brief presentation of the peripheral nervous system, including the somatic and ANS branches and the peripheral nerves, both spinal and cranial. Now that we have considered briefly the anatomy and physiology of the nervous system, and ways of recording brain function, we are ready for a description of research on this brain activity. Chapter 3 introduces studies of EEG and behavior.

REFERENCES

Aine, C. (1995). A conceptual overview and critique of functional neuroimaging techniques in humans: I. MRI/fMRI and PET. *Critical Reviews in Neurobiology, 9,* 229–309.
Ahlo, K., Winkler, I., Escera, C., Huotilainen, M., Virtanen, J., Jaaskelainen, I. P., Pekkonen, E., & Ilmoniemi, R. J. (1998). Processing of novel sounds and frequency changes in the human auditory cortex: Magnetoencephalographic recordings. *Psychophysiology, 35,* 211–224.
American Electroencephalographic Society. (1991). Guidelines for standard electrode position nomenclature. *Journal of Clinical Neurophysiology, 8,* 200–202.
Andreassi, J. L., II., Eggleston, W. B., Fu, G., & Stewart, J. K. (1998). Phenylethanolamine N-methyltransferase mRNA in rat hypothalamus and cerebellum. *Brain Research, 779,* 289–291.
Barlow, J. S. (1993). *The electroencephalogram: Its patterns and origins.* Cambridge: MIT Press.
Brazier, M. A. B. (1957). Rise of neurophysiology in the 19th century. *Journal of Neurophysiology, 20,* 212–226.
Callaway, E. (1975). *Brain electrical potentials and individual psychological differences.* New York: Grune & Stratton.
Carlson, N. R. (1980). *Physiology of behavior* (2nd ed.). Boston: Allyn & Bacon.
Carlson, N. R. (1998). *Physiology of behavior* (6th ed.). Boston: Allyn & Bacon.
DePascalis, V., & Ray, W. J. (1998). Effects of memory load on event-related patterns of 40-Hz EEG during cognitive and motor tasks. *International Journal of Psychophysiology, 28,* 301–315.
Elul, R. (1972). Randomness and synchrony in the generation of the electroencephalogram. In H. Petsche & M. A. B. Brazier (Eds.), *Synchronization of EEG activity in epilepsies* (pp. 59–77). New York: Springer-Verlag.
Evans, C. C. (1952). Comments on: "Occipital sharp waves responsive to visual stimuli." *Electroencephalography and Clinical Neurophysiology, 4,* 111.
Galambos, R., Makeig, S., & Talmachoff, P. (1981). A 40 Hz auditory potential recorded from the human scalp. *Proc. Natl. Acad. Sci. USA, 78,* 2643–2647.
Gardner, E. (1975). *Fundamentals of neurology.* Philadelphia: Saunders.
Gastaut, H. (1952). Etude electrocorticographique de la reactivite des rhthmes rolandiques. *Revue Neurologique, 87,* 176–182.
Gastaut, Y. (1951). Un signe elelctroencephalographique peu conne: Les pointes occipitales survenant pendant 1 ouverture des yeux. *Review Neurologique, 84,* 640–643.

Jasper, H. H. (1958). Report of the committee on methods of clinical examination in electroencephalography. *Electroencephalography and Clinical Neurophysiology, 10*, 370–375.

Kalat, J. W. (1995). *Biological psychology* (5th ed.). Pacific Grove, CA: Brooks/Cole.

Kennedy, J. L., Gottsdanker, R. M., Armington, J. C., & Gray, F. E. (1948). A new electroencephalogram associated with thinkng. *Science, 108*, 527–529.

Koshino, Y., & Niedermeyer, E. (1976). Enhancement of rolandic mu rhythm by pattern vision. *Electroencephalography and Clinical Neurophysiology, 38*, 535–538.

Kosslyn, S. M., Digirolamo, G. J., Thompson, W. L., & Alpert, N. M. (1998). Mental rotation of objects versus hands: Neural mechanisms revealed by positron emission tomography. *Psychophysiology, 35*, 151–161.

Lang, P. J., Bradley, M. M., Fitzsimmons, J. R., Cuthbert, B. N., Scott, J. D., Moulder, B., & Nangia, V. (1998). Emotional arousal and activation of the visual cortex: An fMRI analysis. *Psychophysiology, 35*, 199–210.

Larson, C. L., Davidson, R. J., Abercrombie, H. C., Ward, R. T., Schaefer, S. M., Jackson, D. C., Holden, J. E., & Perlman, S. B. (1998). Relations between PET-derived measures of thalamic glucose metabolism and EEG alpha power. *Psychophysiology, 35*, 162–169.

Maulsby, R. L. (1971). An illustration of emotionally evoked theta rhythm in infance: Hedonic hypersynchrony. *Electroencephalography and Clinical Neurophysiology, 31*, 157–165.

Mulholland, T. B. (1969). The concept of attention and the electroencephalographic alpha rhythm. In C. R. Evans & T. B. Mulholland (Eds.), *Attention in neurophysiology* (pp. 100–127). London: Butterworths.

Niedermeyer, E. (1987). The normal EEG of the waking adult. In E. Niedermeyer & F. Lopes da Silva (Eds.), *Electroencephalography* (2nd ed., pp. 17–34). Munich: Urban & Schwarzenberg.

Noback, D. R., & Demarest, R. J. (1975). *The human nervous system*. New York: McGraw-Hill.

Porges, S. W., & Coles, M. G. H. (1976). *Psychophysiology*. Stroudsberg, PA: Dowden, Hutchinson & Ross.

Putnam, L. E., Johnson, R., Jr., & Roth, W. T. (1992). Guidelines for reducing the risk of disease transmission in the psychophysiology laboratory. *Psychophysiology, 29*, 127–141.

Shaw, J. C. (1996). Intention as a component of the alpha-rhythm response to mental activity. *International Journal of Psychophysiology, 24*, 7–24.

Stassen, H. H., Lykken, D. T., & Bomben, G. (1988). The within-pair EEG similarity of twins reared apart. *European Archives of Psychiatry and Neurological Sciences, 237*, 244–252.

Tomarken, A., Davidson, R. J., Wheeler, R. E., & Kinney, L. (1992). Psychometric properties of resting anterior EEG asymmetry: Temporal stability and internal consistency. *Psychophysiology, 29*, 576–592.

Walter, W. G. (1937). Electroencephalogram in cases of cerebral tumour. *Proceedings of the Royal Society of Medicine, 30*, 579–598.

Walter, W. G. (1953). *The living brain*. New York: Norton.

Williamson, S. J., & Kaufman, L. (1981). Biomagnetism. *Journal of Magnetism & Magnetic Materials, 22*, 129–202.

3

The EEG and Behavior:
Motor and Mental Activities

Many long-time EEG researchers still experience a degree of fascination and awe as they watch the pens of their physiological recorders trace out the patterns of electrical activity occurring at that instant of time in the human brain. It is very difficult to convey to an audience or a reader the sense of wonderment as the pens vibrate and quiver to the changing frequencies and amplitudes of the various brain waves. From the very beginning, the fascinating nature of EEG activity, and the fact that it was brain-generated, encouraged scientists to study relationships between brain waves and behavior. Some kinds of relationships, which seemed very logical at first, have proved very elusive to establish. One example is the effort expended in attempts to relate intelligence to EEG activity. No doubt this has been due, at least in part, to the tremendous complexity of the brain itself, and to difficulties in the interpretation of large masses of EEG data. Nevertheless, researchers have pursued questions of brain wave–behavior relationships, and a great deal of effort has been expended on this topic.

This chapter explores the effect that cognitive and physical activities have on EEG waveforms. Variations in EEG that occur with the movements involved in reaction time and other motor activities are discussed first, and then the question of whether EEG patterns can serve as an objective indicator of intelligence is considered. Right and left hemispheric asymmetries, or differences in EEG pattern as a function of type of task, remains a topic of interest to psychophysiologists. One issue among the asymmetry studies concerns the nature of differential EEG in the two hemispheres as subjects experience various emotional states. Other topics include EEG during states of hypnosis, imagery, and meditation. A consideration of environmental factors affecting EEG activity is presented in chapter 19.

MOTOR PERFORMANCE AND THE EEG

This section first examines the relationship between EEG recordings and simple motor reaction time. Then, under the subheading of visuomotor performance, we consider EEGs measured simultaneously with more complex motor performance, the kind that requires continuous eye and hand coordination.

Reaction Time and EEG

In their classic book titled *Experimental Psychology*, Woodworth and Schlosberg (1954) noted that reaction time (RT) includes the time it takes for a sense organ to react to some stimulus, brain processing time (to carry impulses to and from the brain), and muscle time (the time for muscles to contract and move some external object). One of the most common RT experiments involves one stimulus and one response (simple RT). For example, a light comes on and a subject is asked to press a response key as soon as the light is seen. The interval between the onset of the light and the response is timed to the nearest thousandth of a second and constitutes the RT in milliseconds (msec).

EEG Activation and RT.   One question that has been investigated is the relation between RT and "EEG activation" (Lansing, Schwartz, & Lindsley, 1959). Because alpha activity is often associated with relaxed wakefulness, typically with eyes closed, the desynchronization, or blocking, of alpha with stimulation is called EEG activation. When this activation occurs, alpha is replaced by low-amplitude, high-frequency beta activity. Lansing and his colleagues recorded RTs to a visual stimulus and found that RTs were significantly faster when alpha block occurred before the visual stimulus was presented. The alpha block was produced by warning signals presented shortly before the stimulus. They interpreted both the faster RT and the alpha block in terms of an alerted state produced through action of the ascending reticular activation system (ARAS). Other studies have indicated that the alpha blocking and faster RTs may not be related to each other; instead, they may be independently related to the warning signal that produces a preparatory set to react (Leavitt, 1968; Thompson & Botwinick, 1966). Leavitt (1968) rejected the concept that faster reactions were caused by a unitary arousal system such as the ARAS and suggested instead that several neural processes underlie the relation between the point in time at which the warning signal occurs and the speed of reaction. He found that when a warning signal appeared 500 msec before the stimulus, the quickest RTs occurred, along with maximal desynchronization of the EEG. At different foreperiods of 200, 1,500, and 4,000 msec, however, the degree of alpha desynchronization was not related to speed of reaction. There were times, in fact, when RT was similar whether the percentage of alpha desynchronization was 0% or 56%. This type of result would argue that RT does not differ for alpha and beta states.

Thompson and Botwinick (1968) measured the RTs and EEGs of people between the age of 19 and 35 and compared them to a group of individuals between 62 and 87 years old. They found that the younger group responded more quickly than the older group, but the groups did not differ in EEG activation.

EEG Period.   In a series of developmental studies, Surwillo (1968, 1971a, 1971b, 1974) found relationships between speed of response and period of the EEG. Period of the EEG is defined by the total number of waves recorded in the interval of time between the stimulus and the response. The average duration (period) of these waves is obtained by dividing the number of waves into the length of the interval. Thus, if the stimulus–response interval is 1.0 sec and EEG frequency is 10 cps, the EEG period is 0.1. Therefore, EEG period becomes smaller as EEG frequency increases. Surwillo (1968) reasoned that, because behavior and CNS activity occur at the same time, they should be examined at identical moments. He reported that RTs became slower and more variable in old age, and he interpreted this as being due to slower brain processes that can be measured by period of EEG. Slowing of EEG as a function of old age was reported by Hubbard, Sunde, and Goldensohn (1976). Surwillo (1971a) measured EEG period and correlated this with RT of 110 boys ranging in age from 4 to 17 years. One task used was disjunctive RT, in which the subject had to decide whether or not respond to two auditory stimuli, according to a predetermined criterion. The other task used was simple RT to an auditory stimulus. Increases in the EEG period were associated with slower RTs.

The time it took to make a movement to a sound, as well as simple auditory RT, was measured along with EEG period by Surwillo (1974). The movement time (MT) was the time it took the subject to leave a contact and touch a target 28 cm away. The subjects were boys between the age of 9 and 17. Both RT and MT decreased with age. The RT was found to be faster when EEG period was shorter, thus confirming the results of Surwillo's earlier studies. MT was not related to EEG period, however, suggesting that frequency of the EEG could not account for gross motor response time. In addition, there was no relation between MT and RT, a finding that also indicates different types of motor processes for a few small muscles as compared to a larger group of bigger muscles. Another laboratory (Sersen, Clausen, & Lidsky, 1982) has reported a significant relationship between EEG frequency and RT in the interval between stimulus and response, in agreement with Surwillo's findings. Surwillo (1975) hypothesized that speed of information processing is a function of a "cortical gating signal" that can be measured by EEG period. It is assumed that the frequency of the EEG determines frequency of the gating signal. This concept would predict a strong relationship between speed of RT and EEG frequency at the moment of stimulation, which is a very testable hypothesis.

Summary.   The positive relationship between RT and EEG observed by Surwillo has been obtained when the EEG period was used as the measure of CNS activity. Studies reporting no relation between EEG and RT (Leavitt, 1968; Thompson & Botwinick, 1966, 1968) used degree of alpha desynchronization; for example, a 50% decrease in the amplitude of the alpha rhythm for more than 200 msec (Leavitt, 1968). In fact, when Surwillo (1972) used a measure similar to alpha desynchronization, namely, blocking latency of the EEG (the time it took EEG to drop in amplitude when stimulation occurred), he found no relationship between the EEG and RT. Thus, whereas degree of alpha desynchronization may not be related to RT, other measures such as EEG period, EEG half waves (Surwillo, 1975), and average alpha frequency (Creutzfeldt et al., 1976) are related.

The following illustrates EEG Period:

$$\frac{Stimulus\text{–}Response\ Interval}{\#\ of\ EEG\ waves} = \frac{.4\ sec}{4\ waves} = .10$$

$$\text{or} = \frac{.4\ sec}{8\ waves} = .05$$

shorter period = faster RT

Visuomotor Performance

The study of RT concerns a simple abrupt type of motion. Most movements involve more complex and continuous kinds of motor adjustments also involving the visual system. A study of EEG during motor activity was conducted by Khrizman (1973), in 2- and 3-year-olds. The tasks involved continuous finger tapping and arranging checkers in rows according to color. The EEG was recorded from frontal, motor, parietal, temporal, and occipital placements. In the tapping task, the motor cortex showed the highest frequency and amplitude correlations with the lower parietal regions, whereas the checker arrangement task produced the highest correlations between the motor and frontal areas. The high motor–frontal correlations might be interpreted in terms of coordination of motor and cognitive (checker arrangement) activities believed to be a frontal lobe function. The high parietal-motor correlation (tapping task) suggests cooperation between two brain areas for a task involving simple eye-hand coordination.

EEG Coherence and Brain Function.   The use of computer analyses has enabled investigators to derive a measure of relationship between two areas of EEG recording. One such derivation is the coherence function (COH). Thus, when measuring EEG from a number of sites, a high COH from two of the locations suggests they are functionally and/or structurally connected. In one study using COH, Busk and Galbraith (1975) analyzed EEGs from over four areas of the brain while male subjects performed three motor tasks (eye tracking, hand tracking, and eye-hand tracking). The EEG was recorded from over the visual cortex (O_z), left and right motor areas (C_3 and C_4), and premotor cortex (F_z). Sites that showed the highest COH scores corresponded to areas with greatest anatomical connections.

In addition, the more difficult the task, the greater the increase in COH measures. This is an interesting finding, because it indicates an increase in required cooperation between two cortical motor areas when the task is more complicated.

In a follow-up study to further investigate COH as a measure of functional connectivity and to examine reference and artifact effects, Ford, Goethe, and Dekker (1986) measured COH during a continuous movement task. These investigators reasoned that if a person moves the right hand, for example, increased COH should be observed over the contralateral motor areas (left hemisphere) compared to the motor areas not controlling the movement (right hemisphere). This is what they found at motor and premotor sites, especially for the 9 to 12 Hz EEG band. Increased COH values were most apparent for the cortical areas known to be involved (frontal, premotor, and motor). The use of a right earlobe reference for right hemisphere sites and left earlobe for left hemisphere placements did not seem to affect the results. However, it would have been more convincing if Ford et al. had used linked ears as an additional reference. The purposeful production of eye and muscle artifact by subjects led to lowered COH values. Thus, if anything, the earlier cited Busk and Galbraith (1975) results would have been stronger if eye and muscle activity had been more carefully controlled.

EEG Patterning

The EEG patterns from bilateral temporal and occipital placements were obtained for skilled rifle marksmen in the period just before the trigger was pulled (Hatfield, Landers, & Ray, 1984). The task consisted of firing 40 shots at a target 50 ft away using the standing position. Analyses of three consecutive 2.5 sec EEG samples just prior to pulling the trigger revealed a significant shift toward right hemisphere activity as the time to fire approached. The authors suggested that the shift to right hemisphere dominance may be indicative of the subject's ability to suppress left hemisphere processes. They pointed out that many coaches and sports theorists believe that covert verbal self-instruction (left hemisphere process) can disrupt athletic performance at higher levels of skilled performance. Further, they stressed, a visual image of the desired performance is preferable to verbal instruction.

Shaw (1996) has pointed out that alpha is enhanced in the few seconds before performance of various skilled aiming tasks. For example, Salazar, Landers, Petruzzello, and Han (1990) recorded EEG during archery and found that at one second prior to arrow release alpha activity in the left hemisphere increased especially in the 10 and 12 Hz frequencies. In another study, Crews and Landers (1993) examined EEG of skilled golfers over a 3 second period before the putt. During this period left hemisphere alpha increased significantly at a motor cortex electrode. What these studies have in common is that alpha activity increased just before the action, suggesting that left hemisphere processes were suppressed. An interpretation by Shaw (1996) is that just before the relevant motor action, attention is focused on the internal action to be executed. This makes it an intentional rather than an attentional task. A distinction made by Shaw is that intention refers to the selection of an output (action) while attention concerns the selection of input (stimuli). Shaw suggests that alpha amplitude increases just before a skilled movement that is associated with some internal action plan, where attention is replaced by intention.

In a study of brain activity in continuous skilled motor performance, Sterman (1984) measured EEGs during a flight simulation task. The experiment was carried out in a mock-up of an F-16 fighter cockpit in which subjects used a joystick to achieve a series of flight paths in a video-simulated flight. The subjects were tested over a 6-hr period with six 45-min "flights" being alternated with six 15-min rest periods. Sterman found that task engagement was associated with greater activity in central cortical (motor) areas, with a decrease in pari-etal–occipital activity. Increased central activity in the 8 to 11 Hz range was associated with better performance. The author thinks that such EEG information could be used to track both alertness and competency of pilots during flight.

The finding that suppression of 7 to 13 Hz EEG occurs with motor performance and increased attentional demand was noted by Sterman and colleagues (Sterman, Mann, Kaiser, & Suyenobu, 1994). This suppression of EEG activity in mostly the alpha range has been called "event related desynchronization" (ERD) by Pfurtscheller and colleagues (Pfurtscheller & Aranibar, 1977; Pfurtscheller & Klimesch, 1991) and was first quantified by Pfurtscheller and Aranibar (1977). The ERD is a specific form of EEG alpha desynchronization, i.e., it is cir-cumscribed, phasic, and focused over specific cortical areas (Pfurtscheller, Neuper, Andrew, & Edlinger, 1997). Its topographical display allows observation of brain activation patterns in situations such as sensory discrimination, memory, and self-paced movements. Sterman et al. (1994) measured EEG from over frontal, parietal, temporal and occipital areas while adult males performed a simulated flight task. They found that visuo-motor activity produced se-lective effects on EEG frequency patterns. Four conditions included eyes closed, a stationary visual attention task involving gazing at a simulator display, instructed manipulations of a joy stick, and a simulated landing using display information and making joy stick movements (vi-sual and motor control). Five frequency bands were chosen for study (5–7, 7–9, 9–11, 11–13, and 13–15 Hz). The visual control condition resulted in posterior (occipital) suppression of all frequencies. Suppression during the motor control condition was limited to 11 to 13 Hz activity at frontal and central sites. The flight task (visuomotor) resulted in suppression at central parietal areas in the 9 to 13 Hz range. Thus, the suppression of 11 to 13 Hz activity during undirected movements was extended to the 13 to 15 Hz band during goal directed movements. The authors suggest that the parietal EEG suppression was specific to the cog-nitive processing involved in completing the task. In a follow-up study (Mann, Sterman, & Kaiser, 1996) both male and female subjects had EEG measured while engaged in a simulat-ed automobile driving task. Ten frequency bands between 6 and 17 Hz were analyzed during three different visual scanning tasks and one motor control task, in which the visual display was not activated, but subjects heard engine sounds related to acceleration and braking. The researchers reported that 11 to 15 Hz activity in lateral–central cortex was suppressed during task-directed movements. The same frequency was suppressed in temporo-parietal cortex during visual scanning movements. Hence there is additional evidence for selective suppres-sion of EEG frequencies in different cortical areas depending on the task.

Summary.   EEG coherence measures offer another way of examining possible functional and anatomical relationships between different brain areas. Increases in COH scores are great-est from cortical areas most likely to be involved in a given task. Measures of EEG during skilled visuomotor performance have yielded interesting results that have possible implications for training in those skills or in monitoring proficiency. Evidence for selective suppression ef-fects on topographic EEG frequency patterns was derived from studies using flight and auto driving simulators. The introduction of event-related desynchronization (ERD) patterns has added an important dimension to EEG research. The enhancement of alpha activity just before performance of skilled aiming tasks had led to the hypothesis that such alpha changes are relat-ed to an internal action plan. This interesting proposal requires additional empirical study.

EEG AND MENTAL ACTIVITY

This section considers research bearing on the controversial question regarding the relationship between EEG and intelligence; the intriguing findings with respect to EEG correlates of verbal and spatial performance; and some reports of EEG, hypnosis, and imagery.

EEG and Intelligence (The Search for a Culture-Free Test)

The Binet–Simon intelligence scale appeared in 1905 as an instrument to classify mentally retarded children for the purpose of educating them in the school system of Paris. This test included items related to judgment, comprehension, and reasoning, because Binet considered these as essential components of intelligence. The test also included some sensory and perceptual items, but was heavily weighted with verbal content. The Binet–Simon test and its two revisions served as a model for many tests that followed, including the well-known American version, the Stanford–Binet. One criticism that has been leveled at tests of the Binet–Simon mold is that they are not "culture-free." Living in some subcultures rather than others affects scores on these traditional intelligence tests because of at least some dependence on information learned in educational or urban settings that might be unavailable to less educated or rural populations.

Attempts to develop culture-free tests have included using items that not only make very little use of language, but that are not dependent on symbols and information of a given culture. However, psychologists have found it difficult to construct tests that are completely culture-free. At first blush, the EEG might appear to be a completely culture-free technique for assessing intelligence in a manner that would not discriminate against culturally deprived persons. The reasoning might go something like this: The brain is the seat of biological intelligence, the EEG represents brain activity, therefore one should be able to predict intelligence from EEG patterns, including amplitude and frequency. Regardless of how logical (or illogical) this argument might seem, the correlation of EEG and intelligence has proven to be a very elusive endeavor, to say the least.

After many years of research, the question of the relationship between EEG and intelligence (usually measured by intelligence test scores) is still controversial. The literature on this question was reviewed by Lindsley (1944), and it covered studies conducted in the 1930s and early 1940s. At the time of his review, Lindsley concluded that most of the studies indicated no relationship between EEG and intelligence. A review of the literature by Ellingson (1956) covered the years between 1944 and 1956. He also concluded that the available evidence did not establish a relation between EEG and intellectual performance. Later on, Vogel and Broverman (1964) argued that although no significant relationship had been found between EEG and intelligence for normal adults, such a relationship had been shown for children, mentally retarded persons, geriatric patients, and brain-damaged patients.

Ellingson (1966) reviewed the Vogel and Broverman conclusions and reported that the evidence for children and mentally retarded individuals was contradictory and inconclusive; in addition, with regard to geriatric and brain-injured patients, he noted that EEG abnormality and decreased intellectual capacity are both effects of organic brain disorder. That is, the EEG does not reflect intelligence but instead indicates decreased CNS functioning in brain-damaged and geriatric patients. Vogel and Broverman (1966) made an effective reply to Ellingson's critique and accused him of inhibiting EEG research in this area. They pointed out that there are competent and well-designed replications that support an EEG–intelligence relationship, and they accused Ellingson of minimizing the positive results.

Thus, it appears that the bulk of evidence amassed up to the late 1960s indicated a stalemate regarding the relation between EEG and intelligence. Let us examine a few of the relatively recent research efforts to see whether there have been any changes in this situation.

EEG Period.   Surwillo (1971a) criticized some of the positive findings with respect to EEG and intelligence on the basis that studies either did not control for age of the subjects or that the EEG was, in most instances, recorded when the subject was "resting" and not engaged in the task that was the measure of intelligence. One such task is the digit span of the Wechsler Intelligence Scale for Children (WISC), which tests ability to hold information in short-term memory. In digit-span, lists of digits are presented, and the subject is asked to repeat them exactly or in a reverse order. Seventy-nine normal boys ranging in age from $4^{1}/_{2}$ years to 17 years were the subjects in Surwillo's (1971a) study. The EEG period was based on recordings from occipital and parietal leads during the interval when digits were presented. Correlations between digit-span length and EEG period were in the expected direction. The greater the digit span, or capacity for short-term storage of information, the higher the EEG frequencies. When age was held constant, through a technique known as partial correlation, the relationship disappeared. Surwillo concluded that there was no evidence that digit span and EEG frequency were related in normal children.

In a well-conceived study, Giannitrapani (1969) reported that a frequency asymmetry score correlated significantly with verbal, performance, and total IQ scores in the Wechsler Adult Intelligence Scale (WAIS). He measured average EEG frequencies from frontal, parietal, occipital, and temporal sites during mental multiplication and correlated these with intelligence test performance (WAIS). A relationship was found between EEG frequency and full-scale scores, because higher frequencies went with higher IQ. This was especially true for EEG frequency from left hemisphere (parietal) derivations. Griesel (1973) investigated the relationship between EEG frequency and period and several tests of intellectual ability. The tests measured mental alertness (numerical, verbal, and reasoning ability), information processing, and ability to think analytically (Gottschaldt Figures Test). The results indicated no relationship between the intelligence test scores and the EEG frequency or period measures.

EEG Spectral Analysis.   Maxwell, Fenwick, Fenton, and Dollimore (1974) evaluated the EEG spectra (analysis based on amplitudes of the EEG at various frequencies) of 150 children (mean age of 7 years) from whom they had intelligence test scores. The children were divided into two groups, below average and above average in reading. The EEG analysis resulted in the conclusion that the poor readers used larger portions of their brain than the good readers; that is, they exerted more physiological effort to less effect. To test the hypothesis that EEG spectrum analysis would differ for poor and good readers, two new groups of subjects were tested. The subjects were 52 good readers and 52 poor readers, all of whom were 14 years of age. EEG spectrum analysis for the two groups confirmed that power generated by the poor readers was greater for all EEG frequencies measured than that of the good readers. They suggested that more neurons are used by the less proficient individual in a cognitive task, resulting in the larger EEG amplitudes observed. One might ask whether this finding can be related to that of Busk and Galbraith (1975), namely that greater amounts of EEG synchrony occurred between cortical areas in the performance of a difficult tracking task as compared to an easy one (reading could be regarded as a difficult task for the poor readers). Also, Surwillo (1971b) noted more EEG synchrony between the two hemispheres when subjects were processing longer, more difficult lists of numbers.

EEG Coherence.   In another approach, Surwillo (1971b) recorded EEGs from over the parietal and occipital cortex while subjects performed the digit-span (backward) test. The EEG period was examined from O_1–P_3 (left hemisphere) and O_2–P_4 (right hemisphere) and compared. When longer lists were processed, the EEG periods from right and left hemisphere were more alike than when shorter lists were processed. In addition, subjects who were capable of processing longer lists of digits showed more synchrony between EEG of the two hemispheres than subjects who did not do as well. Thus, Surwillo seemed to have support for the hypothesis that when increased EEG synchrony (coherence) between the hemispheres occurs, a greater amount of information is being processed.

EEG Complexity.   Positive correlations between EEG parameters and intelligence test scores were reported for separate groups of 25 mildly retarded (IQ 50–70) and 31 normal children by Gasser, Von Lucadou-Muller, Verleger, and Bacher (1983). The EEG was recorded via 8 unipolar leads overlying frontal, central, parietal, and occipital areas. The tests used were the Columbia Mental Maturity scale and the Wechsler Intelligence Scale for Children (WISC-verbal subscale). One of their findings was that children with more mature EEG (e.g., less delta and more theta) had higher test scores. Further, the correlations were higher for the mildly retarded than for normal subjects. They suggested that a certain portion of mildly retarded children have deviant brain function that is causally related to intellectual subnormality.

In a different study, the relationship between EEG complexity and intelligence was examined in adult males (Lutzenberger, Birbaumer, Flor, Rockstroh, & Elbert, 1992). Subjects were divided into two intellectual levels according to scores on the culture fair intelligence test of Cattell. The high intelligence group had an average IQ of 118, whereas the low group averaged 84 in IQ. The EEG was recorded from 15 scalp locations in frontal, central, temporal, and parietal areas while subjects rested and while engaged in both positive (erotic) and negative (loss) imagery. The authors found that the higher IQ subjects had greater EEG complexity at a greater number of EEG sites than the less intelligent persons under resting conditions, but not during the imagery task. As the authors themselves pointed out, further research with a variety of tasks and large numbers of subjects is required to assess the relationship between EEG complexity and IQ.

EEG Alpha Power.   Another interesting approach to relating EEG to intellectual level was taken by Alexander, O'Boyle, and Benbow (1996). They compared the alpha power from left and right hemispheres in three groups of subjects: gifted 13-year-olds, average-ability 13-year-olds, and college students (20-year-olds). There were an equal number of males and females in each group. The gifted group was selected on the basis of having achieved scholastic aptitude test (SAT) scores averaging 1100. This placed them in the top 0.5 percent of test scores, adjusted for age. The average group was judged so by teachers and administrative staff of their junior high schools. For all groups EEG was recorded while they focused their attention on a fixation point in the center of a screen located in a sound- and light-attenuated chamber. The investigators reported that the gifted adolescents had significantly less alpha power, from both hemispheres, than the average group, but their alpha power was similar to that of the college age students. Lower alpha power means greater brain activation, or enhanced involvement.

The EEG pattern for the gifted students suggests that they may have a developmentally advanced level of alpha activity that resembles adult levels of alpha power. The authors pointed out that the most notable change in power of specific EEG bandwidths is evidenced as a decrease in alpha power as the child grows older. Further, two critical periods in which alpha decreases occur as a function of age are from 3 to 4 years and from 10 to 11 years (Hudspeth & Pribram, 1992). Furthermore, adult levels of brain activity across the cortex are not seen until 18 to 21 years of age. Alexander and colleagues propose that gifted adolescents may be more physiologically advanced than average ability adolescents in either brain development, organization, or use of brain resources. They suggest further work to determine whether the adult-like levels of alpha power in gifted groups is maintained during the remaining years of development, and whether they change to an even higher degree as they become adults.

Summary.   Studies conducted since the 1960s do not resolve the impasse regarding the relationship between EEG and intelligence, but they do offer some hope for refining future approaches. One promising approach may involve the comparison of EEG activity from both right and left hemispheres and noting the relationship of the two hemispheres to intellectual performance. This approach resulted in two of the positive findings reported (Giannitrapani, 1969; Surwillo, 1971b). Perhaps new or more complete methods of analysis will lead to more positive results in the future. The positive results obtained by Gasser et al. (1983) were partly attributed to computer analyses of multiple scalp sites that enabled detailed examination of EEG in frequency bands ranging from delta to beta. Gale and Edwards (1983a) made a number of suggestions for improving methodology of brain activity–intelligence studies. They recommended the use of more than one IQ test, multiple EEG recording sites, heterogeneous subject populations representing the full ability range, controlling for age and gender as variables, and blind scoring techniques so that experimenters are not aware of the IQ scores of those whose brain records are under examination until completion of data analyses. They suggested these and several other procedures to avoid errors in method and interpretation. These are the kinds of steps that would be necessary to give the EEG-intelligence work a solid basis for either acceptance or rejection. Some of the newer work relating alpha power to intellectual function (e.g., Alexander et al., 1996) appears to be promising. There is a renewed interest in relating EEG parameters to aspects of intelligence. A great deal of this is due to methods of EEG power analyses and improved computerized techniques in collecting and analyzing data. Correlates of intellectual activity have also been examined with the event-related brain potential (ERP) as a dependent variable. Attempts to relate ERPs to intelligence are discussed in chapter 6.

A note of caution was advanced by Satterfield, Cantwell, Saul, and Usin (1974) that EEG abnormalities may not be a good criterion for the placement of children in special education programs. When they compared the WISC scores of 22 hyperactive young boys considered to have abnormal EEGs, with those of 63 hyperactive boys with normal EEGs, they found that those with abnormal patterns scored significantly higher (WISC full-scale scores of 106 compared to a mean of 98). This finding would seem to justify their cautionary statement.

EEG in Memory and Recall

Gamma Wave Activity.   The effects of memory load on EEG gamma wave response was examined by DePascalis and Ray (1998). In the low-memory load condition the initial stimulus (S1) was a single regular geometric figure (e.g., a triangle) and a second stimulus, appearing 3 sec later, was also a single figure. The task was to indicate whether the second stimulus was the same or different from the first. In the high memory load condition the S1 was a set of three different and irregular figures and the task was to indicate if a figure in S2 was present in the S1 stimulus memory set. A go–no go response scheme was used in which a first response condition required a key press if S1 and S2 were the same and a second condition required a key press if S1 and S2 were different. The results reported were that viewing a visual stimulus requiring a decision enhanced 40 Hz (gamma) EEG activity over a wide region of cortex. The amplitude of this 40 Hz activity increased with short-term memory load and with go–no go conditions at prefrontal, frontal, parietal, and occipital locations. In the high load condition 40 Hz activity was highest at frontal and occipital regions. This was consistent with longer RT scores obtained in the high load condition compared to the low load condition.

Event-Related Desynchronization.   An experiment by Klimesch and colleagues asked whether event-related desynchronization (ERD) in lower and upper alpha bands during encoding of words would predict later memory for these verbal materials (Klimesch et al., 1996). High ERD relates to alpha desynchronization or suppression and low ERD indicates enhancement of alpha. The low alpha band, based on average values for the individuals sampled, was 8.2 to 10.7 Hz, and the high band was set at 10.7 to 13.2 Hz. In the first part of the experiment subjects were shown 96 words and asked to categorize them as "living" or "nonliving." Later, without warning, subjects were given 5 min to recall as many of the 96 words as possible. The subjects were ranked 1 through 10 on the basis of recall performance and the top 5 were considered to be good performers whereas the bottom 5 were poor performers. Examination of EEG records indicated that good performers had significantly greater ERD in the lower alpha band for recalled as compared to nonrecalled words. In contrast, the poor performers had significantly greater ERD in the upper band for recalled words. Based on previous studies suggesting that the ERD in the lower alpha band reflects attention and that the upper band ERD relates to stimulus encoding, Klimesch and colleagues suggest that poor performers are less attentive or alert during encoding, and that good performers need less effort to encode a stimulus, as shown by the weak ERD in the upper alpha band.

These intriguing findings will require further confirmation, especially because there were only 5 individuals in the good and poor performing groups, respectively. Interestingly, Klimesch (1996) reports on a study in which Alzheimer patients with relatively good memory showed an alpha frequency which was 1.12 Hz higher than an age-related group of patients with poor memory scores on the Wechsler Memory Scale (8.14 Hz compared to 7.02 Hz). This study was presented in the context of a provocative paper in which Klimesch (1996) related results in memory research to changes in EEG activity. The interested reader is urged to examine this interesting theoretical approach proposed by Klimesch.

Summary.   One study reviewed in this section intimates that EEG gamma band activity increases with higher memory loads. The work of Klimesch and associates suggests that ERD in lower alpha bands is greater for those who do well in a recall task, but is higher in the upper alpha band for poor performers. Further, Klimesch (1997) concluded that alpha frequency of those with good memory performance is about 1 Hz higher than that of those with poor memory scores. He suggests that alpha frequency may be a factor in determining speed with which information is retrieved from memory. Moreover, he proposes that the upper alpha band is sensitive to semantic memory demands, whereas the lower alpha band reflects attentional processes. These and other provocative ideas of Klimesch require further investigation.

Hemispheric Asymmetries in the EEG

Behavioral Studies Showing Asymmetries.   The past two decades have witnessed increased interest in possible functional differences between the left and right hemispheres of the brain. This interest, among both the general population and scientists alike, was stimulated in the late 1960s by studies of Sperry and his associates. They worked with patients who had their two hemispheres disconnected by surgery to alleviate epileptic seizures (e.g., see Sperry, 1982). The result of "splitting the brain" was only noticeable when special tests were carried out because intellect and personality were unaffected by the surgery. The tests dramatically showed that the left hemisphere was specialized for language functions, whereas the right hemisphere processed spatial information more efficiently. Noninvasive techniques were required to extend these findings to normal populations, and so measures such as EEG and event-related potentials were increasingly used to determine whether various stimuli and tasks would result in differential hemisphere activity and performance differences.

The abundance of research on EEG hemispheric asymmetries reflects the fascination of scientists with this topic. Some reliable findings have emerged while others have been fleeting. This EEG section reviews representative studies in the area and presents conclusions that seem to be warranted at this time. However, before beginning the discussion of EEG studies, it is important to note that purely behavioral studies have paralleled those using brain activity. These studies have emphasized performance differences based on type of stimuli presented to the left or right hemisphere. For example, it has been reported that people can better identify words presented to the left hemisphere as compared to the right hemisphere.

The method of selective stimulation of either hemisphere makes use of the fact that the visual system is organized in a "crossed" manner, such that stimuli presented to the right of a central fixation point (right visual field) project initially to the left (contralateral) hemisphere. This type of stimulation of left or right visual field has led to an advantage in that the contralateral hemisphere responds earlier than the ipsilateral (see Andreassi, Stern, & Okamura, 1975). Similarly, auditory verbal stimuli have been found to be more effectively processed when presented to the right ear, a finding related to the fact that each ear has dominant projections to the contralateral hemisphere. Thus, words presented to the right ear stimuli reach the left (language processing) hemisphere more efficiently than left ear stimulation. This finding has arisen in studies of "dichotic listening" in which two different messages are presented simultaneously to the two ears (Kimura, 1967). Therefore, behavioral studies in normal individuals have indicated hemispheric specialization. Studies that can show both EEG and performance differences make even a stronger argument for lateralization of function.

EEG Studies Showing Asymmetries.   It has long been known that EEG activity becomes desynchronized, that is, higher in frequency and lower in amplitude, with the onset of mental activity (Ellingson, 1956). This activation of the EEG has been used as an indicant of cerebral involvement in processing information (refer also to the event related desynchronization discussed earlier in this chapter). In a study by Robbins and McAdam (1974), asymmetry was studied for identical stimuli presented in ways expected to activate one or the other hemisphere. Subjects were asked to respond to identical pictures in three different ways: to generate visual images of scenes shown, to compose a letter about the pictures, and to generate images and write a letter about the pictures. It was reported that when visual images alone were generated, the right hemisphere showed more activity. This reversed for letter composition, with the left hemisphere registering greater involvement.

The combination of the imagery and verbal tasks produced similar activity in the two hemispheres. Hemispheric asymmetry of EEG patterns was studied while subjects performed either verbal or spatial tasks (Galin & Ornstein, 1972). The results showed that right hemispheric involvement was greater in the spatial task, and left hemispheric participation was dominant during verbal activities. This finding of Galin and Ornstein was confirmed and extended by McKee, Humphrey, and McAdam (1973). They found that lower amplitude EEG activity was present (more involvement) in recordings from the right hemisphere when persons performed a musical task (detecting a theme in an unfamiliar Bach concerto). When a linguistic task was used, lower amplitude EEGs were observed from left hemisphere recordings.

Research findings have indicated that musical activities are a function of the right hemisphere. However, it has been suggested that musically trained individuals process music more analytically (left hemisphere) than nontrained persons. To examine this possibility further, Davidson and Schwartz (1977) measured EEGs of musically trained persons and those who had never received music instruction in an experiment that required all subjects to whistle, sing, and talk each of three songs. They found that nonmusically trained subjects showed a significantly greater activation of the right hemisphere while whistling the melody of a song versus speaking the lyrics of the song, as compared to musically trained persons. The musicians had similar patterns of hemispheric activation for the whistle and talk conditions. They showed EEG in the form of a ratio: R–L/R+L, in which R and L refer to amounts of alpha activity produced in right and left hemispheres. Higher numbers in this score indicate greater relative left hemisphere activity. The results indicate that individuals show different patterns of brain activity, to an identical task, depending on their training. Musically trained subjects listened to the melody analytically, thus making it a left hemisphere task rather than a right hemisphere function. The authors suggested that long-term training in a cognitive skill, such as reading and playing music, may be accompanied by permanent changes in brain activity. This also implies that structural changes have taken place in the brain.

Instead of assuming in advance that a particular task would produce verbal or visuospatial processes in subjects, Ehrlichman and Wiener (1980) had their subjects make ratings of mental processes actually used while doing a variety of tasks. They found that EEG asymmetry was related to verbal processes, but not to visual imagery. Because recordings were from over temporal and parietal areas, the researchers suggested that verbal processes may be a more important influence on EEG asymmetry at these brain areas than are visual imagery processes. They also made the point that the asymmetry was observed in the absence of external stimuli or motor responses. This was in response to a criticism of Gevins et al. (1979) that the major factor in task-dependent changes in EEG asymmetry are uncontrolled perceptual and motor differences between the tasks employed to engage the two hemispheres. Thus, Gevins and colleagues argued that EEG asymmetries were artifacts of motor and performance differences between the tasks used.

In support of the contention by Gevins and colleagues, Rugg and Dickins (1982) observed no asymmetries in alpha activity for visuospatial or verbal tasks in the absence of motor responses. However, theta activity was greater in the right hemisphere during the visuospatial as opposed to the verbal task. Further, this difference between tasks in right hemisphere theta correlated significantly with level of visuospatial performance. Another study in support of functional asymmetry carefully matched verbal and spatial tasks on performance, and EEG was recorded when no motor response was required (Davidson, Chapman, Chapman, & Henriques, 1990). The tasks were word finding and dot localization. The EEG was derived from frontal, central, and parietal areas, and power in alpha, beta, theta, and delta bands was computed. They found reliable differences in EEG asymmetry in the expected direction. The asymmetry measure most highly correlated with performance was parietal alpha. Task-dependent shifts in asymmetry in all EEG bands were such that less power (greater EEG activation) was found in the task-engaged hemisphere.

Localization of memory for faces and words to the two hemispheres, using EEG analyses, was studied by Burgess and Gruzelier (1997). Recordings were made from multiple locations over left and right hemispheres while subjects watched faces or words flashed on a screen before them and rated them for pleasantness/unpleasantness (acquisition phase). In a recognition segment subjects were asked to indicate whether the faces and words had been presented during the acquisition phase. Comparison of the acquisition and recognition phases showed significant attenuation of alpha, beta1 (13–16 Hz), and beta2 (17–30 Hz) activity in the right temporoparietal region for the faces. This is where facial information would be expected to be processed as known from other techniques used to localize cerebral activity. However, left temporoparietal changes for the word task were only seen in the women subjects. Thus it appears that EEG is validated for localizing function for facial recognition for both men and women, but only in women for word recognition.

Summary. The evidence strongly supports the contention that the type of mental activity differentially affects the two hemispheres of the brain, as indicated by EEG measures. The consensus is that the right hemisphere is involved to a greater extent than the left in the performance of spatial and musical tasks, whereas semantic, verbal, and mathematical tasks primarily involve the left hemisphere. Exceptions may arise, as in the case of musically trained individuals in whom an analytic approach to music may transform music related activities into a left hemisphere function.

In an interesting approach, Gevins et al. (1983) reported the use of multiple scalp locations, single trial analyses, and extensive intercorrelation techniques in experiments that show rapid changes in the side and site of localized brain processes during task performance. Their subjects performed a visuospatial task that required making a movement for its completion. The results showed that during the early part of the response (100 to 200 msec after initiation), brain activity is similar in both hemispheres; shortly after (around 300 msec), a right hemisphere focus occurs as subjects perform the spatial task. Finally, at approximately 400 to 600 msec, there is a left hemisphere focus as the right-handed subjects make the required motor response. Gevins and associates concluded that lateralization occurs, but that it is sometimes fleeting, shifting between hemispheres according to the activity engaged in at that instant. Furthermore, extremely rapid sampling and sophisticated analytic techniques may be required to observe these quick shifts between hemispheres and the alterations in brain activity that reflect task changes. Essentially the same conclusion was reached by Pfurtscheller and Klimesch, (1990) who studied the time course and topographical pattern of cortical activation during a visual–verbal task. They used measures of event-related desynchronization (ERD) and concluded that speech areas in the left hemisphere were maximally activated 375 to 500 msec before the verbal response, whereas activation of motor areas started about 250 msec before the verbal response.

Thus, it is safe to conclude that hemispheric specialization does exist. This is shown in differential brain activity and performance when specific materials are processed by the appropriate hemisphere. The relationship is not always as predicted, due to individual differences in skill, degree of laterality, and interpretation of the task by subjects. In the final analysis, even though each hemisphere has its special functions, the entire brain must work as a unit in the processing of stimuli and the preparation of an optimal response.

EEG Asymmetries in Emotional Expression of Infants.   Davidson and Fox (1982) reported EEG asymmetries in 10-month-old infants watching a videotape of an actress portraying sad and happy facial expressions. The positive emotion (happy) resulted in greater left hemisphere activity from over frontal lobes, there were no differences observed at left and right parietal areas. Fox and Davidson (1986) produced differing facial expressions in 2-day-old infants by placing solutions of distilled water, sugar water, or citric acid on their tongues. The EEG was recorded just after stimulation, and facial expressions were videotaped. The analyses of EEG showed greater relative left hemisphere activity with sugar water than to the citric acid. In another study, Fox and Davidson (1987) measured EEGs of 10-month-olds during approach of their mothers and compared them to when a stranger approached the babies. As expected, the infants showed positive emotional responses with the mother's approach (e.g., facial expressions of joy, positive vocalizations), and this was associated with greater relative left frontal hemisphere activity. When behavior indicating aversion or withdrawal occurred, as with the stranger, there was greater relative right frontal activation.

Fox and Davidson (1988) claimed to have identified periods of sadness, disgust, joy, and anger in 10-month-old infants. The EEGs during these periods of facial expression indicated greater right hemisphere activation during sadness and disgust, whereas the left hemisphere was more involved when joy and anger were expressed. The common elements in sadness and disgust are that they are a form of behavioral withdrawal, whereas joy and anger result in behavioral approach (Fox, 1991). For example, anger is under the approach category because it prepares the individual for a confrontation. In the same study, Fox and Davidson (1988) studied emotion produced in the infants when approached by their mothers or by a stranger. They were also interested in EEG activity that accompanied two types of smiles. They noted that the 19th-century anatomist Duchenne du Boulogne distinguished between a false smile and one that indicated genuine enjoyment. According to Duchenne, the genuine smile involved activity of muscles of the cheek (zygomatic) and around the eyes (orbicularis orbi), whereas the fake smile only involved the zygomatic muscles. According to these criteria their study found that 78% of the infants displayed genuine smiles to the mother and 75% displayed fake smiles to the stranger. Further, the real smiles were associated with greater EEG activation at the left frontal lobes and the false smiles were accompanied by right frontal activity. These are interesting findings that require further investigation.

EEG Asymmetries in Emotional Expression of Adults.   There is evidence in adults that the two hemispheres show asymmetries to stimuli associated with emotional reactions. In one study, subjects rated degree of positive or negative feelings produced by a film as EEG was measured from frontal and parietal areas of both hemispheres (Davidson, Schwartz, Saron, Bennett, & Goleman, 1979). Stimuli rated as creating positive feelings produced more left hemisphere activity from the frontal lobes. Asymmetries over parietal lobes did not discriminate between positive and negative feelings. The authors attributed their findings to the extensive anatomical connections that exist between frontal lobes and subcortical limbic system structures important in emotional expression. Tucker and Dawson (1984) designed an experiment to examine differential hemispheric involvement in two emotional states: sexual arousal and depression. The EEG was obtained from left and right frontal, central, occipital, and parietal locations as "method" actors recalled personal experiences to create states of depression or sexual arousal. The results showed greater right hemisphere activity for sexual arousal than for depression. In addition, COH measures showed higher theta coherence in right central and posterior regions during sexual arousal. This increased theta COH during sexual arousal seems consistent with a reported increase in right hemisphere theta activity during orgasm (Cohen, Rosen, & Goldstein, 1976).

Facial expression, EEG, and self-report of emotional experience were recorded while subjects were exposed to film clips that were designed to induce happiness and disgust (Ekman, Davidson, & Friesen, 1990). Brain activity was recorded from over both hemispheres in frontal, central, temporal, and parietal regions. As predicted, disgust produced higher degrees of activation from right frontal recordings, and happiness elicited greater activity from the left frontal area. In another study, large differences in frontal brain asymmetry surfaced during reward (approach) and punishment (withdrawal) related emotions (Sobotka, Davidson, & Senulis, 1992). Subjects were prewarned that a trial could either lead to a reward (winning money based on quick RTs) or punishment (losing money based on slow RTs). Once again, greater right frontal activity was recorded during punishment than reward trials, whereas reward resulted in greater left frontal activity.

Other studies by Davidson and his colleagues have indicated similar findings. In addition, they reported individual differences in frontal asymmetry to negative and positive emotional stimuli (Wheeler, Davidson, & Tomarken, 1993). They also found greater left frontal activation with more intense experiences of positive affect to positive films, and greater right frontal activation with more intense reports of negative affect in response to negative film clips. In a synopsis of work by himself and colleagues, Davidson (1992) proposed that the right anterior hemisphere is specialized for withdrawal behavior and the left anterior region for approach processes. In addition, there are individual differences in patterns of anterior asymmetry that are stable over time. The individual differences appear early since behaviorally inhibited children (31 months of age) were found to show less frontal activation than more extroverted children.

Summary.   The work of Davidson has led to interesting findings and conceptualizations regarding the physiological substrates of positive and negative affective responses. The increased right hemisphere theta activity in the recall of sexual arousal by actors (Tucker & Dawson, 1984) poses a problem for Davidson's concept since sexual arousal would not be considered a negative emotion. Davidson's work has focused on changes in activity in the alpha band of the EEG. Continued research in this area is required and should provide interesting findings.

EEG, Hypnosis, Imagery, and Meditation

Hypnosis. The phenomenon of hypnosis holds a strange fascination for most people. Mention of the word "hypnosis" might conjure up images of the stage hypnotist who causes a subject to go into a trance and do strange things, such as regression to an early stage of childhood or supporting someone's weight while lying stretched across two chairs! For many years it had been thought that hypnosis was some type of sleep during which a person could carry out various suggestions made by the hypnotist. Most contemporary evidence, however, favors the view that hypnosis is actually a modification of the waking state, with all the EEG characteristics that are indicative of such a state.

The question of the relationship between EEG and hypnotic susceptibility has been investigated by a number of researchers. For example, London, Hart, and Leibovitz (1968) reported greater amounts of alpha activity among subjects who scored high on a test of hypnotic susceptibility. Galbraith and colleagues (1970) examined this question further in a study of 59 volunteer subjects. Scores on the Harvard Group Hypnotic Susceptibility Scale (HGS) and EEG from frontal, parietal, occipital, and temporal leads were recorded. The findings supported the previous ones regarding a relationship between EEG and hypnotic susceptibility, because subjects with high HGS scores produced more alpha activity than those with low scores, especially under an "eyes-open" condition. Galbraith and his collaborators suggested that the common factor between hypnotic susceptibility and the high alpha amplitude with eyes open is "attention." Subjects with high HGS scores may be better able to attend to hypnotic suggestions among competing stimuli, thereby shutting out distracting stimuli of various kinds. Although the two studies just mentioned (and others) support a relationship between alpha and hypnotizability, they have been questioned in a paper that carefully reviews the techniques and findings of a variety of studies that explored this relationship (Perlini & Spanos, 1991). The failure to replicate the original results and errors in design are among the criticisms made by Perlini and Spanos of studies in this area, thus making conclusions regarding the alpha/hypnotizability relationship highly suspect.

Macleod-Morgan (1982) measured EEGs of persons scoring high and low on hypnotizability while resting, under hypnosis, and when given a right hemisphere "dream task" during hypnosis. The 41 highly hypnotizable persons shifted from greater left hemisphere activity during rest to a right hemisphere bias during hypnosis, a change that was even stronger with the dream task. The low hypnotizables did not show this significant shift from left to right hemisphere activity. Thus the suggestion is that hypnosis involves the right hemisphere more than the left. In another study, Macleod-Morgan and Lack (1982) claimed to have found evidence that highly hypnotizable persons also show greater shifts in EEG when performing verbal or spatial tasks; and this is especially true for tasks that are continuous rather than discontinuous. The authors suggested that low and high hypnotizables show different EEGs in focused attention and tasks involving hemispheric specialties. In these tasks, high hypnotizables seem to show greater degrees of focused cortical activation. These findings and interpretations will require replication by other investigators.

The effects of hypnotic analgesia suggestion, versus no suggestion, on EEG and pain ratings of high and low hypnotizable individuals was examined by DePascalis and Perrone (1996). Painful electrical stimulation was delivered before hypnotic induction and again, under hypnosis without suggestions of analgesia, and, finally, under a hypnosis condition with analgesia suggestions. There was a significant reduction in pain ratings for the high hypnotizable group with suggested analgesia. This group also showed significant decreases in EEG amplitude (across an entire spectrum of .5 Hz–31.75 Hz activity) at right-hemisphere locations, under the hypnotic analgesia condition only. The authors suggest that the inhibition of right hemisphere activity for this group may have played an important role in the relief of pain. The low hypnotizable subjects showed no difference in EEG activity or pain ratings under any of the conditions. Thus, there is additional evidence here for the notion that hypnosis involves the right hemisphere more than the left.

Imagery.   The word "imagery" is often used in reference to visual scenes pictured in "the mind's eye." However, imagery can also refer to other sensory experiences such as sounds, tastes, touches, and smells. In an EEG study involving imagery, a "vividness" scale was given to 71 undergraduates to assess degree of visual, auditory, and kinesthetic imagery (Gale, Morris, Lucas, & Richardson, 1972). Then, while EEG was recorded from the occipital area, subjects responded to instructions designed to produce minimal imagery, passive elicited imagery, voluntary elicited imagery, and autonomous voluntary imagery. The minimal imagery condition involved relaxing with eyes open or closed. In the passive elicited imagery task, 10 high-imagery words (e.g., acrobat) and 10 low-imagery words (e.g., answer) were presented and subjects were instructed to "see if the words suggest mental pictures." The elicited imagery task required subjects to move a circle and a triangle around in their minds. Imagining the activities of a family (father, mother, and two small children) on a beach over a 2-min period constituted the autonomous imagery task. The most clear-cut result was the decrease in alpha activity during all of the imagery tasks except the minimal imagery one. The EEG of weak and vivid imagers was differentiated by alpha frequency under the eyes-open condition; that is, it was significantly higher for the vivid imagers as compared to weak imagers.

Williamson and Kaufman (1989) used magnetoencephalography (MEG) to study suppression of alpha activity in the visual cortex during mental imagery. The task involved the matching of memories of visual images. The suppression of alpha was greatest in central regions of occipital cortex, from above the inion, and extending anteriorly toward the vertex. Functionally, the alpha suppression is correlated with both visual attention and the task of visual memory search. In a follow-up study, MEG in the alpha and beta band was measured during mental imagery (Kaufman, Schwartz, Salustri, & Williamson, 1990). Several polygon shapes were presented for subjects to remember and to mentally compare with a later "probe." One instruction required pressing a button as soon as the probe was presented, regardless of whether it was a member of the original set of shapes (simple RT). The second instruction required pressing one button if the probe was a member and another button if it was not part of the original set (choice RT). Alpha power was sharply suppressed after presentations of the probe, but it was more prolonged for the choice RT compared to the simple RT trials. The result shows that the visual cortex is involved in mental imagery, and the duration of the involvement corresponds with the duration of the task. Another interesting finding was that alpha activity was not replaced by beta during suppression, but that power in the beta band was also decreased during memory search.

Experimental studies of imagery and EEG have been relatively few in number. One problem is that it is difficult to quantify the type of imagery generated in different people by the same instructions. Other problems have included an insufficient number of EEG recording sites and the lack of a systematic research approach (Gale & Edwards, 1983b). However, an encouraging development is the use of MEG recordings during imagery tasks. The advantages of MEG have been outlined in chapter 2 and include the more accurate determination of cortical and subcortical activity during the performance of different functions.

Meditation.   In a study of physiological changes during meditation, Elson, Hauri, and Cunis (1977) matched a group of regular meditators with nonmeditating control subjects. The

EEGs of both groups were measured over a 40-min period, during which the controls were instructed to remain "wakefully relaxed" for 40 min, while the others meditated for the same amount of time. The meditators remained in a relaxed stable state of alpha and theta EEG activity, and none fell asleep. However, six of the controls fell asleep during the experiment as indicated by K-complexes and sleep spindles in their EEG records. The results indicate that meditation produces a physiological effect different from that produced in nonmeditating controls who try to relax with eyes closed for the same length of time. On the other hand, no difference in EEG responses to tone stimuli were found for a group of 17 meditators and a group of 17 control subjects (Heide, 1986). In Heide's study, experimental subjects were asked to meditate for 20 min while controls were asked to sit quietly for 20 min without falling asleep. The 1000-Hz tones were at a sound level of 80 dB and were presented on the average of once a minute. The two groups did not differ in duration of alpha desynchronization to stimuli or in time to habituate to the tones. Clearly, the lack of differences between the two groups in the Heide study was due to the auditory stimulation, which obviously intruded to an equal degree for meditators and nonmeditators.

Summary.   The recording of EEG during hypnosis, meditation, and imagery is a potentially rich source of information because it can give us data that will enable us to differentiate among these states. One interesting finding concerns the greater amount of alpha activity produced by highly hypnotizable persons compared to low hypnotizables under a variety of conditions. The greater shift to right hemisphere activity for highly hypnotizable persons suggests a degree of hemispheric specialization for hypnosis. A careful review of studies in this area has raised some doubts that can only be removed by carefully designed replications. However, findings regarding EEG changes during hypnotic suggestins of analgesia are extremely interesting and should be explored further. The use of MEG techniques also is a welcome addition to research in this area.

The evidence reviewed with respect to imagery suggests that EEG does change according to type of mental activity, regardless of whether these are produced by imposed or naturally occurring mental events. Gale and Edwards (1983b) pointed out that EEG imagery studies have not gone much beyond observing effects that occur with different kinds of imagery. There have been few attempts to predict and theorize. They also observed that most studies of EEG and imagery have not used multiple recording sites on the head, nor have they studied a wide range of variables in a systematic fashion. On the positive side, EEG evidence seems to establish meditation as a state that is different from hypnosis, autosuggestion, or sleep.

The next chapter covers EEG measures taken under different conditions of sensory stimulation, attention, and perception. Conditioning of the EEG and patterns of EEG in a variety of sleep studies are also presented in chapter 4.

REFERENCES

Alexander, J. E., O'Boyle, M. W., & Benbow, C. P. (1996). Developmentally advanced EEG alpha power in gifted male and female adolescents. *International Journal of Psychophysiology, 23*, 25–31.

Andreassi, J. L., Stern, M. S., & Okamura, H. (1975). Hemispheric asymmetries in the visual evoked cortical potential as a function of stimulus location. *Psychophysiology, 12*, 541–546.

Burgess, A. P., & Gruzelier, J. H. (1997). Localization of word and face recognition memory using topographical EEG. *Psychophysiology, 34*, 7–16.

Busk, J., & Galbraith, G. C. (1975). Electroencephalography of visual–motor practice in man. *Electroencephalography and Clinical Neurophysiology, 38*, 415–422.

Cohen, H. C., Rosen, R. C., & Goldstein, I. (1976). Electroencephalographic laterality changes during human sexual orgasm. *Archives of Sexual Behavior, 5*, 189.

Creutzfeldt, O. D., Arnold, P. M., Becker, D., Langenstein, S., Tirsch, W., Wilhelm, H., & Wuttke, W. (1976). EEG changes during spontaneous and controlled menstrual cycles and their correlations with psychological performance. *Electroencephalography and Clinical Neurophysiology, 40*, 113–131.

Crews, D. J., & Landers, D. M. (1993). Electroencephalographic measures of attentional patterns prior to the golf putt. *Med. Sci. Sports Exerc., 25*, 116–126.

Davidson, R. J. (1992). Anterior cerebral asymmetry and the nature of emotion. *Brain and Cognition, 20*, 125–151.

Davidson, R. J., Chapman, J. P., Chapman, L. J., & Henriques, J. P. (1990). Asymmetrical brain electrical activity discriminates between psychometrically-matched verbal and spatial cognitive tasks. *Psychophysiology, 27*, 528–543.

Davidson, R. J., & Fox, N. A. (1982). Asymmetrical brain activity discriminates between positive and negative stimuli in human infants. *Science, 218*, 1235–1237.

Davidson, R. J., & Schwartz, G. E. (1977). The influence of musical training on patterns of EEG asymmetry during musical and non-musical self-regeneration tasks. *Psychophysiology, 14*, 58–63.

Davidson, R. J., Schwartz, G. E., Saron, C., Bennett, J., & Goleman, D. J. (1979). Frontal versus parietal EEG asymmetry during positive and negative affect. (abstract). *Psychophysiology, 16*, 202–203.

DePascalis, V., & Perrone, M. (1996). EEG asymmetry and heart rate during experience of Hypnotic analgesia in-high and low hypnotizables. *International Journal of Psychophysiology, 21*, 163–174.

DePascalis, V., & Ray, W. J. (1998). Effects of memory load on event-related patterns of 40-Hz EEG during cognitive and motor tasks. *International Journal of Psychophysiology, 28*, 301–316.

Ellingson, R. J. (1956). Brain waves and problems of psychology. *Psychological Bulletin, 53*, 1–34.

Ellingson, R. J. (1966). Relationship between EEG and test intelligence: A commentary. *Psychological Bulletin, 65*, 91–98.

Ehrlichman, H., & Wiener, M. S. (1980). EEG asymmetry during covert mental activity. *Psychophysiology, 17*, 228–235.

Ekman, P., Davidson, R. J., & Friesen, W. V. (1990). The Duchenne smile: Emotional expression and brain physiology II. *Journal of Personality and Social Psychology, 58*, 342–353.

Elson, B. D., Hauri, P., & Cunis, D. (1977). Physiological changes in yoga meditation. *Psychophysiology, 14*, 52–57.

Ford, M. R., Goethe, J. W., & Dekker, D. K. (1986). EEG coherence and power changes during a continuous movement task. *International Journal of Psychophysiology, 4*, 99–110.

Fox, N. A. (1991). If it's not left, it's right. Electroencephalograph asymmetry and the development of emotion. *American Psychologist, 46*, 863–872.

Fox, N. A., & Davidson, R. J. (1986). Taste-elicited changes in facial signs of emotion and the asymmetry of brain electrical activity in human newborns. *Neuropsychologia, 24*, 417–422.

Fox, N. A., & Davidson, R. J. (1987). Electroencephalogram asymmetry in response to the approach of a stranger and maternal separation in 10-month old infants. *Developmental Psychology, 23*, 233–240.

Fox, N. A., & Davidson, R. J. (1988). Patterns of brain electrical activity during facial signs of emotion in 10-month old infants. *Developmental Psychology, 24*, 230–236.

Galbraith, G. C., London, P., Leibovitz, M. P., Cooper, L. M., & Hart, J. T. (1970). Electroencephalography and hypnotic susceptibility. *Journal of Comparative and Physiological Psychology, 72*, 125–131.

Gale, A., & Edwards, J. (1983a). The EEG and Human Behavior. In A. Gale & J. Edwards (Eds.), *Physiological correlates of human behavior: Vol. 2: Attention and performance* (pp. 99–127). New York: Academic Press.

Gale, A., & Edwards, J. (1983b). Cortical correlates of intelligence. In A. Gale & J. Edwards (Eds.), *Physiological correlates of behavior: Vol 3: Individual differences and psychopathology* (pp. 79–97).

Gale, A., Morris, P., Lucas, B., & Richardson, A. (1972). Types of imagery and imagery types: An EEG study. *British Journal of Psychology, 63*, 523–531.

Galin, K., & Ornstein, R. (1972). Lateral specialization of cognitive mode: An EEG study. *Psychophysiology, 9*, 412–418.

Gasser, Th., Von Lucadou-Muller, I., Verleger, R., & Bacher, P. (1983). Correlating EEG and IQ: A new look at an old problem using computerized EEG parameters. *Electroencephalography and Clinical Neurophysiology, 55*, 493–504.

Gevins, A. S., Schaffer, R. E., Doyle, J. C., Cutillo, B. A., Tannehil, R. S., & Bressler, S. L. (1983). Shadows of thought: Shifting lateralization of human brain electrical patterns during a brief visuomotor task. *Science, 220*, 97–99.

Gevins, A. S., Zeitlin, G. M., Doyle, J. C., Yingling, C. D., Schaffer, R. E., Callaway, E., & Yeager, C. L. (1979). Electroencephalogram correlates of higher cortical functions. *Science, 203*, 665–668.

Giannitrapani, D. (1969). EEG averagae frequency and intelligence. *Electroencephalography and Clinical Neurophysiology, 27*, 480–486.

Griesel, R. D. (1973). A study of cognitive test performance in relation to measures of speed in the electroencephalogram. *Psychologia Africana, 15*, 41–52.

Hatfield, B. D., Landers, D. M., & Ray, W. J. (1984). Cognitive processes during self-paced motor performance: An electroencephalographic profile of skilled marksmen. *Journal of Sport Psychology, 6*, 42–59.

Heide, F. J. (1986). Psychophysiological responsiveness to auditory stimulation during transcendental meditation. *Psychophysiology, 23*, 71–75.

Hubbard, O., Sunde, D., & Goldensohn, E. S. (1976). The EEG in Centenarians. *Electroencephalography and Clinical Neurophysiology, 40*, 407–417.

Hudspeth, W. J., & Pribram, K. H. (1992). Psychophysiological indices of cerebral maturation. *International Journal of Psychophysiology, 12*, 19–29.

Kaufman, L., Schwartz, B., Salustri, C., & Williamson, S. J. (1990). Modulation of spontaneous brain activity during mental imagery. *Journal of Cognitive Neuroscience, 2*, 124–132.

Khrizman, T. P. (1973). Characteristics of interventral relationships in electrical processes of the brain in 2 to 3 year old children during voluntary motor acts. *Voprosy Psikhologii, 19*, 107–117.

Kimura, D. (1967). Functional asymmetry of the brain in dichotic listening. *Cortex, 3*, 163–178.

Klimesch, W. (1996). Memory processes, brain oscillations and EEG synchronization. *International Journal of Psychophysiology, 24*, 61–100.

Klimesch, W. (1997). EEG-alpha rhythms and memory processes. *International Journal of Psychophysiology, 26*, 319–340.

Klimesch, W., Schimke, M., Doppelmayr, B., Ripper, J., Schwaiger, J., & Pfurtscheller, G. (1996). Event-related desynchronization (ERD) and the Dm effect: Does alpha desynchronization during encoding predict later recall performance? *International Journal of Psychophysiology, 24*, 47–60.

Lansing, R. W., Schwartz, E., & Lindsley, D. B. (1959). Reaction time and EEG activation under alerted and nonalerted conditions. *Journal of Experimental Psychology, 58*, 1–7.

Leavitt, F. (1968). EEG activation and reaction time. *Journal of Experimental Psychology, 77*, 194–199.

Lindsley, D. B. (1944). Elecstroencephalography. In J. McVHunt (Ed.), *Personality and the behavior disorders* (pp. 1033–1106). New York: Ronald Press.

London, P., Hart, J. T., & Leibovitz, M. P. (1968). EEG alpha rhythms and susceptibility to hypnosis. *Nature, 219*, 71–72.

Lutzenberger, W., Birbaumer, N., Flor, H., Rockstroh, B., & Elbert, T. (1992). Dimensional analysis of the human EEG and intelligence. *Neuroscience Letters, 143*, 10–14.

Macleod-Morgan, C. (1982). EEG lateralization in hypnosis: A preliminary report. *Australian Journal of Clinical and Experimental Hypnosis, 10*, 99–102.

Macleod-Morgan, C., & Lack, L. (1982). Hemisphere specifity: A physiological concomitant of hypnotizability. *Psychophysiology, 23*, 71–75.

Mann, C. A., Sterman, M. B., & Kaiser, D. A. (1996). Suppression of EEG rhythmic frequencies during somatomotor and visuo-motor behavior. *International Journal of Psychophysiology, 23*, 1–7.

Maxwell, A. E., Fenwick, P. B., Fenton, G. W., & Dollimore, J. (1974). Reading ability and brain function: A simple statistical model. *Psychological medicine, 4*, 274–280.

McKee, G., Humphrey, B., & McAdam, D. W. (1973). Scaled lateralization of alpha activity during linguist and musical tasks. *Psychophysiology, 10*, 441–443.

Perlini, A. H., & Spanos, N. P. (1991). EEG alpha methodologies and hypnotizability: A critical review. *Psychophysiology, 28*, 511–530.

Pfurtscheller, G., & Aranibar, A. (1977). Event-related cortical desynchronization detected by power measurements of scalp EEG. *Electroencephalography and Clinical Neurophysiology, 42*, 817–826.

Pfurtscheller, G., & Klimesch, W. (1990). Topographical display and interpretation of event-related desynchronization during a visual-verbal task. *Brain Topography, 3*, 85–93.

Pfurtscheller, G., & Klimesch, W. (1991). Event-related desynchronization during motor behavior and visual information processing. In C. H. M. Brunia, G. Mulder, & M. N. Verbaten (Eds.), *Event-Related Brain Research (EEG Suppl. 42)*, pp. 58–65.

Pfurtscheller, G., Neuper, Ch., Andrew, C., & Edlinger, G. (1997). *International Journal of Psychophysiology, 26*, 121–135.

Robbins, K. I., & McAdam, D. (1974). Interhemisphere alpha asymmetry and imagery mode. *Brain and Language, 1*, 189–193.

Rugg, M. D., & Dickins, A. M. J. (1982). Dissociation of alpha and theta activity as a function of verbal and visuospatial tasks. *Electroencephalography and Clinical Neurophysiology, 53*, 201–207.

Salazar, W., Landers, D. M., Petruzzello, S. J., & Han, M. (1990). The hemispheric asymmetry, cardiac response, and performance in elite archers. *Res. Q. Exerc. Sport, 61*, 351–359.

Satterfield, J. H., Cantwell, D. P., Saul, R. E., & Usin, A. (1974). Intelligence, academic achievement and electroencephalography abnormalities in hyperactive children. *American Journal of Psychiatry, 131*, 391–395.

Sersen, E. A., Clausen, J., & Lidsky, A. (1982). Reaction time and psychophysiological activity. *Perceptual and Motor Skills, 54*, 379–390.

Shaw, J. C. (1996). Intention as a component of the alpha-rhythm response to mental activity. *International Journal of Psychophysiology, 24*, 7–23.

Sobotka, S. S., Davidson, R. J., & Senulis, J. A. (1992). Anterior brain electrical asymmetries in response to reward and punishment. *Electroencephalography and Clinical Neurophysiology, 83*, 236–247.

Sperry, R. W. (1982). Some effects of disconnecting the cerebral hemisheres. *Science, 217*, 1223–1226.

Sterman, M. B. (1984). *Measurement and modificant of sensory system EEG characteristcs during visual-motor performance* (AFOSR Report No. 82-0335). Washington, DC: Air Force Office of Scientific Research.

Sterman, M. B., Mann, C. A., Kaiser, D. A., & Suyenobu, B. Y. (1994). Multiband topographic EEG analysis of a simulated visuomotor aviation task. *International Journal of Psychophysiology, 16*, 49–56.

Surwillo, W. W. (1968). Timing of behavior in senescence and the role of the central nervous system. In G. A. Talland (Ed.), *Human aging and behavior* (pp. 117–130). New York: Academic Press.

Surwillo, W. W. (1971a). Human reaction time and period of the EEG in relation to development. *Psychophysiology, 8*, 468–482.

Surwillo, W. W. (1971b). Interhemispheric EEG differences in relation to short-term memory. *Cortex, 7*, 246–253.

Surwillo, W. W. (1972). Latency of EEG attenuation ("blocking") in relation to age and reaction time in normal children. *Developmental Psychobiology, 5*, 223–230.

Surwillo, W. W. (1974). Speed of movement in relation to period of the EEG in normal children. *Psychophysiology, 11*, 491–496.

Surwillo, W. W. (1975). The EEG in the prediction of human reaction time during growth and development. *Biological Psychology, 3*, 79–90.

Thompson, L., & Botwinick, J. (1966). The role of the preparatory interval in the relationship between EEG, alpha-bloking and reaction time. *Psychophysiology, 3*, 131–142.

Thompson, L., & Botwinick, J. (1968). Age differences in the relationship between EEG arousal and reaction time. *Psychophysiology, 5*, 90–100.

Tucker, D. M., & Dawson, S. L. (1984). Asymetric EEG changes as method actors generated emotions. *Biological Psychology, 19*, 63–75.

Vogel, W., & Broverman, D. M. (1964). Relationship between EEG and test intelligence: A critical review. *Psychological Bulletin, 62*, 132–144.

Vogel, W., & Broverman, D. M. (1966). A reply to "Relationship between EEG and test intelligence: a commentary." *Psychological Bulletin, 65*, 99–109.

Wheeler, R. E., Davidson, R. J., & Tomarken, A. J. (1993). Frontal brain asymmetry and emotional reactivity: A biological substrate of affective style. *Psychophysiology, 30*, 82–89.

Williamson, S. J., & Kaufman, L. (1989). Advances in neuromagnetic instrumentation and studies of spontaneous brain activity. *Brain Topography, 2*, 129–139.

Woodworth, R. S., & Schlosberg, H. (1954). *Experimental psychology*. New York: Holt.

4

The EEG and Behavior: Sensation, Attention, Perception, Conditioning, and Sleep

In an influential chapter, Lindsley (1960) described patterns of EEG activity produced across behavioral states ranging from deep sleep to high alertness. Table 4.1 is adapted from Lindsley and shows his conception of a behavioral continuum, its characteristic EEG waves, associated states of awareness, and corresponding behavioral efficiency. Lindsley attributed an important role to the ascending reticular activating system (ARAS) in regulating states of attention, consciousness, sleep, and wakefulness. The functions of the ARAS also play a part in activation theory that describes the relation between levels of physiological activity and performance (see chapter 18). In 1960, Lindsley wrote:

> Attention is closely allied to arousal and wakefulness and, like wakefulness and consciousness, appears to be a graded phenomenon extending from general alerting, as in the orienting reflex, to specific alerting, as when attention is focused upon a given sense mode and dominates sensory input to the point of exclusion of other sense modes. Still higher or more finely focused attention may be restricted to a limited aspect of a given sense mode. (p. 1589)

This description of attention in general and specific form can serve as a model for contemporary psychophysiologists.

This chapter discusses various human processes and their relation to EEG activity. The sections concerned with sensory, attentional, and perceptual mechanisms are followed by a brief treatment of EEG during classical and instrumental conditioning (can a person learn to self-regulate brainwave activity?). A sample question dealt with under the heading of "attention" concerns brain activity related to efficient signal detection during a "vigil." Other issues considered in this chapter include the nature of EEG patterns during different stages of sleep, depth of sleep and capacity to respond, ability to learn during sleep, and dreaming and the EEG. Additional issues that are examined include the effects of presleep activity on sleeping EEG, and EEG changes that occur after sleep deprivation.

SENSATION, ATTENTION, PERCEPTION, AND THE EEG

In the context of this chapter, perception is considered to involve the active processing (making meaning) of sensory data. Thus, it is proposed that the registration of a stimulus (sensation) and attention to it precede perceptual integration by the individual. In this interpretation, the processes of sensation, attention, and perception are viewed as being functionally linked. The purpose of this integration is to allow the perceived material to be used in some cogni-

TABLE 4.1
Psychological States and Their EEG,
Conscious and Behavioral Correlates

Behavioral Continuum	Electroencephalogram Characteristics	State of Awareness	Efficiency
Strong, excited emotion; fear, rage, anxiety	Desynchronized: low to moderate amplitude; fast mixed frequencies	Restricted awareness; divided attention; diffuse, hazy; 'confusion'	Poor: lack of control, freezing up, disorganized
Alert attentiveness	Partially synchronized: mainly fast low-amplitude waves	Selective attention, but may vary of shift; 'concentration' anticipation; 'set'	Good: efficient, selective, quick reactions; organized for serial responses
Relaxed wakefulness	Synchronized: optimal alpha rhythm	Attention wanders—not forced; favors free association	Good: routine reactions and creative thought
Drowsiness	Reduced alpha and occasional low-amplitude slow waves	Borderline partial awareness; imagery and reverie; 'dreamlike' states	Poor: uncoordinated, sporadic, lacking sequential timing
Light sleep	Spindle bursts and slow waves (larger); loss of alphas	Markedly reduced consciousness (loss of consciousness); dream state	Absent
Deep sleep	Large and very slow waves (synchrony but on slow time bases); random irregular patterns	Complete loss of awareness (no memory for stimulation or for dreams)	Absent
Coma	Isoelectric to irregular large slow waves	Complete loss of consciousness; little or no response to stimulation; amnesia	Absent
Death	Isoelectric: gradual and permanent disappearance of all electrical activity	Complete loss of awareness as death ensues	Absent

Note. From Lindsley, D. B. (1960). Attention, consciousness, sleep & wakefulness. In J. Field, H. W. Magoun, & V. E. Hall (Eds.), *Handbook of physiology, Section I, Neurophysiology* (Vol. III, pp. 1553–1593). Washington, DC: American Physiological Society. (p. 1554)

tive activity (e.g., decision making, problem solving, or thinking). In this section, the assignment of EEG research into one of these categories is based on whether a given study is primarily concerned with stimuli, attentional processes, or perceptual–integrative functions. The separation is artificial, and the close interactive influence among sensation, attention, and perception that occurs continually in the waking person must be emphasized.

Sensation and the EEG

Stimulus Complexity.   The effects of stimulus complexity on desynchronization of the EEG alpha wave was the topic of an investigation by Berlyne and McDonnell (1965). They hypothesized that more complex and incongruous visual stimulus patterns would produce longer lasting desynchronization of alpha activity; for example, they contended that more complex stimuli, presented while subjects were in alpha, would result in a longer-lasting change to beta activity than less complex stimuli. Based on EEG recordings of 88 male subjects, their hypothesis was confirmed. The more complex or incongruous patterns produced, on the average, 500 msec longer desynchronizations than the simple patterns. An incongruous stimulus is one that is unusual, or unexpected—for example, a picture of a young woman with shaving cream on her face holding an electric razor! The result was consistent with those indicating that aspects of the external environment, such as novelty and surprise, can induce heightened levels of arousal.

This intriguing notion that stimulus complexity can affect arousal level of an observer (as measured by duration of EEG desynchronization) was examined by Christie and colleagues (1972). They criticized the Berlyne and McDonnell experiment on the basis that no measure of the subject's reaction to the stimuli was taken; that is, the experimenters themselves judged whether a stimulus was complex or simple. Another criticism was that EEG desynchronization was a relatively crude measure. Christie et al. (1972) set out to correct these shortcomings by obtaining subjective ratings of complexity and by measuring EEG amplitude in detail over a frequency range of 2 to 20 Hz. Displays presented to the subjects had differing numbers of items (2, 4, 8, 16, or 32) that corresponded to subjective complexity. The alpha activity decreased as the number of items increased. Thus, the level of complexity (as judged by subjects) did affect the amount of EEG alpha, confirming the earlier results of Berlyne and McDonnell.

Stimulus Thresholds.   The relationship between EEG alpha and detection of auditory stimuli was studied in a novel paradigm by Bohdanecky, Bozkov, and Radil (1984). Their experimental set-up enabled EEG criteria (alpha or nonalpha) to determine the automatic presentation of different intensity auditory stimuli at unexpected times for subjects. They found that the threshold for detection was higher during alpha periods than nonalpha ones. This means that the auditory system was less sensitive during periods of alpha as compared to desynchronization, as would be expected because alpha is associated with lower attention levels than desynchronization.

Odor Stimulation and EEG Pattern.   Occasionally, one reads reports in magazines or newspapers regarding claims that certain odors affect moods, alertness, and even productivity of workers. The effects of different odors on EEG and mood was studied by Lorig and Schwartz (1988). In a first experiment, spiced apple, eucalyptus, and lavender odors were presented along with a neutral odor and were found to decrease the amount of theta wave activity at the left and right posterior brain areas (T5 and T6), especially for spiced apple and eucalyptus. Self-reports indicated less anxiety and tension with the spiced apple and eucalyptus odors. In the second part, subjects smelled five similar odorous chemicals (floral) and an unscented base. The EEG alpha and theta activity in left and right hemispheres differed with the odor presented, but there was little effect on subject's mood. The shifting EEG patterns as a function of time in the experiment make the results difficult to interpret. However, the results are provocative and should lead to interesting future work because odors apparently exert effects on the human nervous system.

Martin (1998) reviewed a number of studies examining EEG changes with odorous stimulation and noted that various effects had been reported. For example, some studies have reported reductions in EEG theta and some increases in beta following exposure to olfactory stimuli. Martin believed that the various results are due to differences in EEG recording, in odor delivery technique and in the type and quality of odor presented. In a pair of carefully controlled experiments, Martin (1998) studied the effects of synthetic odors and real food odors on EEG. In the first experiment, EEG response to synthetic odors of chocolate, spearmint, almond, strawberry, vegetable, garlic, cumin, and no odor was recorded from 19 electrodes in all EEG frequencies (delta, theta, alpha, beta1, 13–22 Hz, and beta2, 23–30 Hz). Participants were instructed to breathe in through the nose and out through the mouth when odors were presented. The presentation of chocolate resulted in significant reductions in theta activity as compared to almond and cumin. Spearmint produced significant theta reduction when compared to the no-odor control. Martin noted that spearmint was rated as the most relaxing and pleasant odor and chocolate was the second-rated odor in these categories.

In the second experiment, EEG response to odors of real foods (chocolate, baked beans, rotting pork) and two controls (no odor and hot water) was recorded as in the first experiment. The odor of chocolate was associated with significantly less theta at central locations than any other odor. Thus, both experiments indicate the ability of odors to alter EEG activity. It will be interesting to follow research in this area as investigators probe to clarify the reasons for theta reduction and possible psychological properties of olfactory stimuli (e.g., ability to relax). Martin (1998) hypothesized that changes in theta activity could reflect shifts in attention, but that emotional reactions to the odor stimuli may also be necessary for the changes to occur. Another possible hypothesis is that the reduction of theta activity is related to improved detection of odors. This proposition is suggested by results from vigilance studies indicating that reductions in theta are related to superior signal detection (see next section on attention).

Summary.   Stimulus complexity and incongruity have a desynchronizing effect on the EEG. An interesting finding is that sensitivity to sound stimuli was less during periods of alpha than nonalpha. Studies of odorant stimulus effects on EEG show that some have the ability to affect the amount of theta activity. The reasons for this kind of EEG effect have yet to be discovered, but testable hypotheses have been proposed.

Attention and the EEG

A good working definition of attention is one offered by Tecce (1972). He defined it as a hypothetical process of an organism that facilitates the selection of relevant stimuli from the environment (internal or external) to the exclusion of other stimuli and results in a response to the relevant stimuli. Tecce emphasized that the process of attention has steering functions, a point previously made in definitions proposed by Berlyne (1970) and Hebb (1958). Thus, attention is seen as an active, directional process that continues up until, and perhaps after, a response to the stimulus is made.

Attention was a lively topic of psychology in the early 1900s, but research and interest in the area declined with the increased influence of behaviorism in the 1920s. Behaviorism, as a school of thought in psychology, rejected the study of attention on the grounds that it was "mentalistic" and that means for investigating it were not sufficiently objective. It was not until the 1960s and 1970s that interest in problems of attention has been revived among academic psychologists, because of developments in cognitive psychology and attempts to find neurophysiological bases of attention and related phenomena, such as the orienting response.

Attention. Psychologists have differentiated between tasks that require attention to stimuli so they can be processed (intake) and contrast them to tasks that require the exclusion of environmental stimuli (rejection) for their effective completion. The EEG pattern for intake and rejection tasks was compared by Ray and Cole (1985). An example of an intake task was to count verbs in a reading passage, whereas a rejection task required creation of sentences beginning with certain letters (exclusion of environment from focus of attention). They found that during rejection tasks alpha power was greater in the right than the left hemisphere, suggesting that different brain mechanisms underlie intake and rejection of environmental stimuli. However, different results were obtained by Valentino and Dufresne (1991) for intake and rejection tasks. This study differed from Ray and Cole's in that auditory stimuli were used instead of visual and a resting condition was added. The intake task involved detecting double letters in a chain of single letters, whereas rejection tasks included an alphabet-backward condition. They reported that both alpha and beta during intake was greater than alpha during rejection with no hemisphere differences. These results are preliminary and the conflicting findings could be due to the tasks used and differences in auditory and visual presentations.

Vigilance and Signal Detection. A bridge between early studies of attention and modern investigations was constructed by studies of vigilance in the 1940s and 1950s. The term *vigilance* was used by Mackworth (1950) and others to describe the situation in which an individual had to respond to randomly occurring and infrequent signals over an extended period of time. The original reason for studying vigilance performance was a very practical one. It was noted that detection of enemy planes by World War II radar operators dropped off drastically in a short period of time. In fact, the Mackworth studies indicated a serious drop within the first 15 to 30 min of watching the radar screen. The study of vigilance decrement has implications for other practical situations. For example, monitoring of relatively monotonous stimuli for long durations occurs in assembly-line inspection, as well as in the long-term vehicular control of truck drivers, airline pilots, and train operators. Some of the more recent studies relating brain activity to signal detection and fluctuations of attention with monotonous stimulation are presented in this chapter and in chapter 6 on event-related brain responses.

Are certain brain waves associated with better vigilance or detection of infrequent stimuli? Beatty, Greenberg, Deibler, and O'Hanlon (1974) hypothesized that learned regulation of theta activity (3–7 Hz) would affect detection performance in a prolonged monitoring task. They proposed that suppression of the occipital theta rhythm would maintain efficient detection, whereas increased theta activity would lead to greater decrements than normal in a monitoring task. The EEGs of college students were recorded from over the left occipital and parietal cortex. Twelve of the individuals were trained to suppress theta and seven to increase the amount of EEG activity in the theta band. The poorest detection performance was that of the group that produced theta during monitoring of a radar simulator. Vigilance performance for this group dropped continuously over the 2-hr period. Conversely, better monitoring performance was shown by the group that was taught to suppress theta activity. In fact, an improvement in detection was observed for the theta-suppressed group in the last segment of the experiment, a period during which the theta-augmented group showed its worst performance. This result has implications for improving the performance of persons who are involved in long-term monitoring activities, such as the inspectors, drivers, and radar operators mentioned previously. If one could teach these kinds of operators to suppress theta, then monitoring performance might be improved for certain monotonous, but critical, tasks.

In a paper submitted to a NATO symposium on vigilance, Gale (1977) made a strong argument for the use of EEG in the study and prediction of signal-detection performance. One of his own findings was that greater amounts of theta activity occurred in persons performing more poorly. Beatty and O'Hanlon (1980) reported on an experiment in which they repeated and expanded their 1974 study. They showed that the relationship between regulated theta activity and performance was stable over repeated sessions with three groups of subjects: a theta-suppress group, a theta-enhance group, and a control group (not given training in enhancement or suppression of theta). In addition, the two trained groups were able to transfer control of EEG activity from the condition where they were given feedback about EEG to one where no feedback was given. The results on EEG theta obtained under the various conditions of their experiment are shown in Fig. 4.1. Note that in the beginning there was no difference among the groups in amount of theta produced (pretest).

As training progressed, theta became differentiated and so did performance; that is, the theta-suppress group did best, followed by the control subjects, and then the augment group.

The findings regarding theta activity and vigilance were supported by Valentino, Arruda, and Gold (1993). In a comparison of a high-vigilance performance group with low-vigilance subjects, one finding was that the high group had less posterior theta and alpha than the low group. In addition, the high-performance group had greater amounts of anterior beta than the low performers. Interesting changes from the resting to task conditions included increased beta power in anterior regions, and decreased alpha and theta in posterior areas. The authors

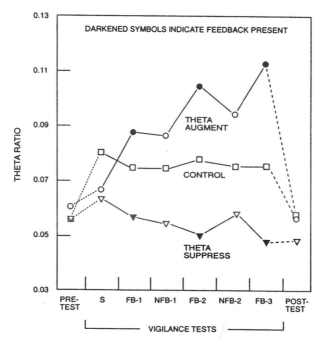

FIG. 4.1. Mean values of the theta ratio for subjects in the theta-augment, theta suppress, and control groups in the pretest, posttest, and six 1-hour vigilance tests. Darkened symbols indicate the presence of EEG-contingent feedback. The six vigilance tests are designed as follows: S = spontaneous or unregulated EEG; FB = EEG contingent feedback present for the experimental groups; NFB = EEG contingent feedback absent for the experimental but regulation attempted.

concluded that good performers could be distinguished from poor performers by their greater EEG arousal levels, as defined by higher levels of beta activity and lower levels of alpha and posterior theta. The findings regarding EEG and attention are not numerous, but those that exist are interesting. The question of how and why theta production influences signal detection requires more study.

Summary. A simplified definition is that *attention* is a process that allows an organism to select relevant stimuli from the environment. An interesting question regarding EEG during tasks that involve stimulus intake compared to those involving rejection has not yet been answered. Vigilance studies involve attention to randomly occurring stimuli that are infrequent. These kinds of studies have implications for understanding attentional mechanisms during the performance of monotonous tasks. Studies show that suppression of theta activity leads to improved signal detection, whereas increasing the amount of theta worsens vigilance performance.

Perception and the EEG

Perceptual Structuring. In an interesting approach to studying the role of perceptual processes as reflected in the EEG, Giannitrapani (1971) measured EEGs of males, aged 11 to 13, under eight conditions. Measurements were made from 16 areas over frontal, parietal, occipital, and temporal locations during (a) awake resting, (b) listening to white noise, (c) listening to a portion of Tchaikovsky's "Marche Miniature," (d) listening to a segment of Mark Twain's *Tom Sawyer*, (e) silently performing mental arithmetic, (f) looking at a poster, (g) looking through diffusing goggles, and (h) awake resting. The amount of high beta activity (21–33 Hz) increased when subjects were required to structure the stimuli. For example, listening to a portion of *Tom Sawyer* required structuring in that the verbal material is perceived by organizing sounds into words and words into a context; therefore, high beta activity increased under this condition. Conversely, the music condition showed a minimal beta effect, because it was structured for the subjects. Beta activity disappeared when the stimulus acquired the necessary structure.

Analyses of EEG coherence patterns were obtained while different groups of subjects engaged in verbal, visual, and musical creativity (Petsche, 1996). Verbal creativity involved constructing a short story using at least 10 previously chosen words; the visual task was to memorize four pictures and then mentally create a new picture; and finally, a group of professional male musicians was asked to mentally compose a short piece of their own while EEG was measured from 19 scalp locations of the 10–20 system. One striking observation was that coherence measures indicated the cooperation of distant cortical areas in all three types of tasks. For example, in the visual task, coherence increased between occipital and frontal areas in several frequency bands of the EEG. Musical composition showed enhanced contralateral cooperation between left frontal, parietal, and occipital areas and the corresponding areas of the right hemisphere. In general, the results suggest an exceptional degree of connectivity between and among cortical neurons during creative activities, even in brain areas relatively distant from one another.

Ambiguous Figures. A perceptual phenomenon that has long fascinated laymen and psychologists alike is the *ambiguous figure*. As one inspects such a figure, its perspective suddenly shifts so that the top of the figure becomes the side, or the bottom may become the top. One may need only stare a while longer and the figure surprisingly shifts back to the original form. An example of a figure that shifts into three dimensions like this is the Necker cube. In a study of EEG activity during perceptual reversals a dynamic reversible figure was used by

Basar-Eroglu and colleagues while EEG was measured from a number of scalp sites (Basar-Eroglu, Struber, Kruse, Basar, & Stadler, 1996). The figure, known as stroboscopic alternative motion (SAM), was perceived as an alternating pattern of horizontal and vertical motion. The researchers reported an increase in gamma-band activity (40 Hz) during perceptual reversals. The greatest increase in gamma activity occurred at frontal cortex suggesting that frontal lobe activity is involved in perceiving these kinds of reversals.

Summary.   Some evidence was presented for an increase in EEG beta2 activity during structuring of stimuli. This section includes a study that provides evidence for cooperation of relatively distant cortical areas in completing a creative task. The other research reviewed here indicates that enhancement of gamma band (40 Hz) EEG activity occurs during the experience of perceptual reversals, and especially implicates the frontal lobe in this type of perception.

CONDITIONING OF THE EEG

Classical Conditioning of the EEG

Shagass (1972) reviewed a number of studies that demonstrated classical conditioning of the EEG, that is, after pairing of conditioned and unconditioned stimuli, changes in EEG patterns were observed at various recording sites on the scalp with presentations of the conditioned stimulus (CS) alone. A common EEG change that occurs with conditioning is alpha blocking to the CS (the formerly neutral stimulus). In a typical experiment, the CS might be a tone and the unconditioned stimulus (US) a light. The unconditioned response (UR) is the natural alpha blocking that occurs with light stimulation, to be replaced by the conditioned response (CR) after sufficient pairings of CS and US produce alpha blocking to CS alone.

   Braggio and Putney (1980) examined the influence of US intensity, perceived US intensity, UR magnitude, and awareness of the CS–US relationship on conditioned alpha blocking. They found that UR magnitude (amount of alpha blocking to the US) was a better predictor of conditioning than either US intensity or perceived US intensity. Also, conditioned alpha blocking was apparently unrelated to a subject's awareness of the conditioning process. Shagass believes that conditioning may play an important role in determining an individual's EEG pattern, and might indicate that certain EEG characteristics, for example, amount of alpha, may be affected by conditioning.

Operant Conditioning of the EEG

There does not appear to be many recent reports in the area of classical conditioning of the EEG with awake humans. On the other hand, there are many reports of attempts to operantly condition EEG, where the presentation of some reward or reinforcement is contingent on the production of a particular EEG pattern by the subject. The operant conditioning of certain physiological activities is considered to be helpful in alleviating a variety of symptoms. For instance, beneficial effects with epileptics have been observed when specific EEG frequencies were conditioned. A more detailed discussion of studies aimed at alleviating certain symptoms through operant conditioning (commonly called biofeedback) is presented in chapter 17. Some EEG operant conditioning studies, not expressly done in a clinical context, are reviewed in this section. Thus, this section deals with the question of whether EEG can be conditioned through operant techniques. A second, more general, question is whether the operant conditioning of any physiological activity has beneficial effects in alleviating certain symptoms, for example, migraine headache. This second question is addressed in chapter 17.

Kamiya (1969) has been one of the pioneers in attempts to demonstrate that human subjects can exert operant control over their EEG activity. The control of EEG alpha activity and the mental state associated with such production was investigated by Nowlis and Kamiya (1970). A tone was presented whenever the individual produced rhythmic activity in the 8- to 13-Hz range that measured at least 20 μV. The subjects were given some trials in which they were asked to produce as much alpha as possible and others in which they tried to suppress alpha. The results showed that they were able to exert differential control over alpha production. Postsession questioning regarding how they exerted the control led to such responses as "relaxation," "letting go," and "floating" being associated with alpha production. The alpha-suppressed condition was associated with "being alert and vigilant." Brown (1970) was able to demonstrate similar effects in a situation where subjects enhanced the amount of alpha activity signaled by a blue light. They were also asked to describe the feeling states associated with keeping the blue light on. Persons who "lost all awareness" or "drifted" or "floated" tended to have greater amounts of alpha activity. The techniques used included "relaxation" or concentration on mental imagery.

A question arises as to whether the achievement of the feeling states alone can be sufficient to produce alpha activity without the use of some external signaling device (sounds or lights). Beatty (1972) showed that it was possible for individuals to control alpha activity equally well if they were given feedback when it occurred (a tone) or if they were instructed about the nature of alpha and beta activity and the feeling states associated with them, thus indicating that feedback was not critical. If given neither type of information, alpha regulation did not occur. In another study, training of theta activity was demonstrated by the ability of subjects to suppress the 3- to 7-Hz band of EEG activity when being given reinforcement to do so, and by the ability of others to increase the amount of such activity (Beatty, Greenberg, Deibler, & O'Hanlon, 1974).

The ability of subjects to recognize alpha and nonalpha states was questioned by Cott, Pavloski, and Black (1980). They reported that subjects acquired control of alpha activity during feedback through the use of specific strategies and were then able to use those strategies to control alpha when feedback was not provided, again indicating that feedback is not crucial to obtaining increased alpha. In another study, Cott, Pavloski, and Goldman (1980) determined that increases or decreases in alpha could alter mood. The factor of major influence was the instruction designed to set subjects for positive or negative alterations in feelings as a result of alpha changes. Is operant conditioning of EEG possible? A qualified "yes" must be given because, although some control has been demonstrated, there are also results to indicate that the feedback itself may not be crucial to the EEG changes observed. In addition, there are other factors in the conduct of operant EEG conditioning procedures, as indicated in the next section.

Expectancies and Noncontingent Stimuli

At least two studies show that researchers must be careful in their experimental design to eliminate or reduce the possibility of expectancy effects in the operant control of EEG (Clarke, Michie, Andreassen, Viney, & Rosenthal, 1976; Valle & Levine, 1975). In the Valle and Levine study, subjects who were led to believe that they enhanced alpha were actually able to control alpha better than those who believed they suppressed alpha. In the Clarke et al. study, both experimenters and subjects were naive, and the biasing effects of the experimenters' expectations were found to influence EEG alpha measures in the direction of the expectation.

A study by Fath, Wallace, and Worsham (1976) showed the importance of using proper controls before claiming that operant conditioning has been demonstrated. They monitored alpha EEG activity of participants divided into three groups: feedback (auditory clicks) contingent on production of alpha, noncontingent clicks, and no clicks. The noncontingent control groups produced the greatest amount of alpha, with the contingent group second and the control group third with respect to amount of alpha activity. Noncontingent control groups should be used in operant conditioning of alpha because alpha increases could otherwise be attributed to randomly occurring or noncontingent stimuli.

Eberlin and Mulholland (1976) performed an interesting experiment in which they controlled for intermittent, noncontingent stimulation in a novel way. They recorded EEG from left and right parietal–occipital locations. Presentation of a visual stimulus was contingent on the production of alpha in one hemisphere only; if the other hemisphere produced alpha, no control over the stimulus occurred. Thus, in this second hemisphere, when stimulation occurred, it would be noncontingent; that is, it had nothing to do with the type of brain activity being produced. The results showed that EEG changes were due to the contingency between EEG and stimulation, not to the effects of noncontingent stimulation.

Summary.   There is no question that EEG conditioning occurs in a classical conditioning paradigm. It also appears from the studies reviewed here that operant control of EEG alpha activity can occur. However, Johnson (1977) argued that unmediated operant control of alpha activity has not been demonstrated. In other words, the person may not be learning to produce alpha per se, but may be influencing the amount of alpha through learning something else, such as the ability to ignore distracting stimuli, or controlling moods or feelings. The study of Eberlin and Mulholland (1976) strengthened the possibility of operant control, because it is difficult to explain why mediators would affect one brain hemisphere and not the other.

SLEEP AND THE EEG

There has been a substantial amount of effort devoted to the study of EEG patterns during sleep, despite the fact that sleep studies are not at all easy to carry out. They may require that subjects sleep in a laboratory at least several nights while EEG is recorded, and they demand a considerable amount of effort and patience on the part of experimenters. The justification for this continued effort is that sleep is such an important biological activity and has implications for human performance, behavior, and well-being.

The Nature of Sleep EEG

Why should researchers be interested in a state that appears to result in such a low behavioral level? The answer is that there is actually much "behavior" going on during sleep, and investigators have been tackling such problems as levels of mental activity during sleep, depth of sleep and capacity to respond, dreaming behavior, sleep learning, effects of work schedule and exercise on sleep EEG, and effects of sleep deprivation on EEG and performance.

Behavioral studies on the depth of sleep were carried out in the 1800s and often involved the question of how loud or strong a stimulus had to be in order to wake a person from sleep. It was not until the 1930s, however, when EEG-measuring devices became widely available, that researchers were able to examine brain activity during sleep.

Contemporary sleep laboratories are equipped with physiological recorders that measure a variety of responses such as EEG, electromyogram (EMG), electrooculogram (EOG), respiration, and rectal temperature. Sleep researchers call these recordings *polysomnograms* to refer to the many physiological measures obtained during sleep. Figure 4.2 presents EEG

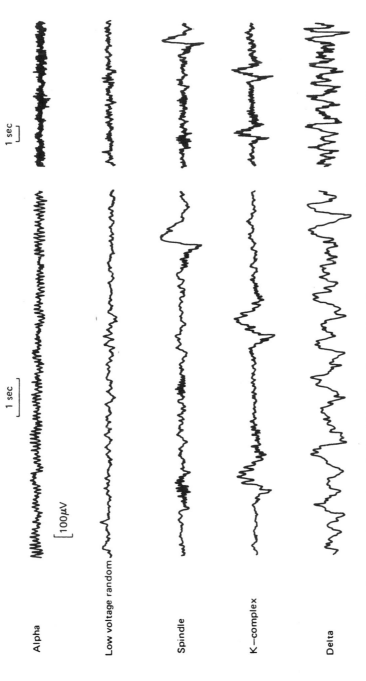

Alpha

100μV

1 sec

Low voltage random

Spindle

K–complex

Delta

1 sec

FIG. 4.2. EEG wave forms distinguishing sleep from waking. The same patterns are shown at two recording speeds: on the left, a conventional rate of 25 mm/sec; and on the right, a rate of 10 mm/sec, widely used in sleep research.

waveforms that distinguish sleep from waking. Sleep has been classified into four stages by Dement and Kleitman (1957a). The top tracing in Fig. 4.2 illustrates the regular, cyclical alpha activity of the waking state. The second line from the top illustrates Stage 1 sleep, characterized by low voltage random EEG activity. Stage 2 is shown in the third tracing and indicates an irregular EEG pattern with 12- to 14-Hz "sleep spindles" and the "K-complex," a 75-μV burst of EEG activity. Some people have sleep spindles every few seconds, whereas others have them only infrequently. Stage 3 sleep is depicted in the fourth line, and is characterized by alternate fast activity, low-voltage waves, and large, slow waves (delta). The large wave with faster frequencies superimposed on it (line 4) was first described by Loomis, Harvey, and Hobart (1938) as the *K-complex*. The K-complex is not associated with Stage 3 sleep per se but instead appears to occur spontaneously during Stages 2 and 3 of sleep. It is considered to indicate a response to some significant stimulus, similar to the orienting response of the waking state (Snyder & Scott, 1972). The term *orienting response* was introduced by Pavlov (1927) to describe reactions of animals to novel stimuli. One component of the orienting response is a change in EEG activity toward increased arousal, that is, faster and lower amplitude activity (Sokolov, 1963). The orienting response, as a concept, is discussed more fully in chapter 18.

Dement and Kleitman characterized Stage 3 sleep as containing 10% to 50% delta activity (delta being defined as those waves of at least 100 μV amplitude, with a frequency of less than 2 Hz). The last line of Fig. 4.2 shows Stage 4 sleep, defined as containing more than 50% delta waves. The method of sleep classification used today is that developed by Rechtschaffen and Kales in 1968 (cited in Rechtschaffen, 1973), shown in Table 4.2.

Differences in the amount of Stages 3 and 4 sleep in normal, healthy, young adult males was investigated by Bliwise and Bergman (1987). The percent of delta time occurring in consecutive 30-second periods (0.5–2.0 Hz, at 75 μV) was scored to determine the 20% (Stage 3) and 50% (Stage 4) criteria. Interestingly, the authors reported large ranges in amounts of Stage 3 (9.0% to 34%) and Stage 4 (7.9% to 50%) during the first 3 hrs of sleep, where slow waves are most likely to occur. Persons high in one of these stages had relatively little of the other. The reasons for these wide individual differences in slow-wave sleep are unknown, but the result supports the combining of Stages 3 and 4 sleep activity, if differences regarding the relative amounts of each is not of interest.

TABLE 4.2
Classification of Sleep EEG

Stage W (waking)	Alpha activity and/or low-voltage, mixed frequency EEG
Stage 1	Low-voltage, mixed-frequency EEG with much 2–7 Hz activity (no rapid eye movements, REM)
Stage 2	Presence of sleep spindles (12–14 Hz) and/or K-complexes (high-voltage, negative-positive spikes) on background of low-voltage, mixed-frequency EEG
Stage 3	20% to 50% of epoch with high-amplitude delta waves (2 Hz or less)
Stage 4	Delta waves in more than 50% of epoch[a]
Stage REM	Low-voltage, mixed-frequency EEG activity and episodic rapid eye movements
Stage NREM	Stages 1, 2, 3, and 4 combined, i.e., those stages with no rapid eye movements

Note. From *A Manual of Standardized Terminology, Techniques and Scoring Systems for Sleep Stages of Human Subjects* by A. Rechtschaffen and A. Kales (Eds.). Washington, D.C.: U.S. Public Health Service, U.S. Government Printing Office, 1968.
[a]Measurement epochs are 20–30 seconds.

EEG and Dreaming

The discovery that rapid eye movements (REM) were associated with dreaming was made by Aserinsky and Kleitman (1953). The eye movements they noticed varied in direction and amplitude and were 1 sec or less in duration. They reported that persons awakened during REM periods could remember their dreams 75% of the time, whereas they could remember dreams in only 7% of the non-REM (NREM) awakenings. Later estimates of the percentage of times that dreams could be vividly recalled after awakening from REM sleep vary from about 60% to 90% (Snyder & Scott, 1972). Dreaming occurs fairly commonly in NREM sleep, but the contents are not as vivid or detailed as those associated with REM awakenings (Rechtschaffen, 1973). Foulkes (1962) reported that 74% of NREM awakenings produced recall of mental activity, and 54% resulted in accounts that could be classified as dreams. Thus, dreams cannot be said to occur exclusively in REM sleep, although there are qualitative and quantitative differences between REM and NREM dreams.

The study by Aserinsky and Kleitman was classic in that it initiated the scientific study of dreaming. Researchers interested in the psychophysiology of dreaming now knew fairly precisely when dreaming occurred and could obtain reports of dreams and correlate these with various experimental manipulations and physiological responses. Some areas explored with the REM technique include: (a) changes in dream content over the night, (b) dream content among patients with differential psychiatric diagnoses, (c) effects of drugs on dream content, and (d) effects of presleep stimulation on dreaming.

Since 1953, many investigators have tried to find physiological correlates of dream content. One aspect of dream content is lucidity, or the realization that one is dreaming in the midst of the dream without awakening. It has been found that lucidity occurs most frequently within the REM stage and is not related to awakening from sleep. Tyson, Ogilvie, and Hunt (1984) tested the suggestion of an association between lucid dreams and high amplitude EEG alpha during REM sleep. They reported that lucid dreams had high alpha early in the REM period followed by a distinct lowering of REM alpha. In contrast, consistently high REM alpha was associated with prelucid dreams having bizarre, emotional dream content. They hypothesized that lucid content sometimes emerges from prelucid experiences, a suggestion that calls for further investigation of the REM alpha and lucidity relationship.

Depth of Sleep and Capacity to Respond

Cyclical variations in EEG patterns occurring throughout the night were noted by Dement and Kleitman (1957a) and indicated a progression from light (Stage 1) to deep (Stage 4) sleep and back to light sleep again. The cycle from Stage 1 back to Stage 1 takes approximately 90 to 100 min. After the first and second cycles, the deeper stages of sleep (3 and 4) rarely occur, that is, sleep becomes progressively lighter as the end of the sleep period approaches. This cyclical pattern of EEG activity throughout a night's sleep has been observed in many subjects. Figure 4.3 shows the relationship between different EEG patterns and stages of sleep. Also shown is the relative depth of sleep at various hours after a typical person has gone to sleep.

Studies have shown that the capacity of a sleeping individual to respond to stimuli depends on a number of factors, including the stage of EEG sleep, stimulus intensity, and significance of stimuli (Snyder & Scott, 1972). For example, Dement and Kleitman (1957a) found that louder sounds were required to wake subjects when they were in REM sleep as compared to onset of Stage 1 sleep. One suggestion was that this might stem from the person's involvement in the content of some dream being experienced during REM sleep (Williams, Hammack, Daly, Dement, & Lubin, 1964). Current findings indicate that wakenings by sounds is similar for REM and Stage 2 sleep.

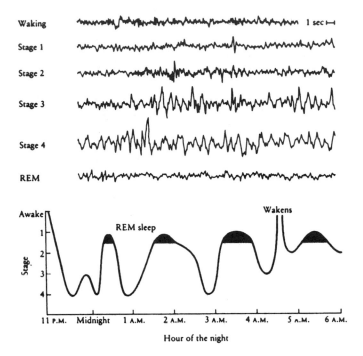

FIG. 4.3. EEG patterns during REM sleep resemble those of waking EEGs (top). Sleep increases and decreases in depth, and periods of REM sleep get longer as the night progresses. From *Brain, Mind, and Behavior* (2nd ed.), by Bloom, Lazerson, and Hofstader. Copyright 1985, 1988 Educational Broadcasting Corporation. Reprinted with the permission of W.H. Freeman and Company.

The effect of meaningfulness of stimuli on arousal from sleep has been demonstrated by a number of researchers. For example, Oswald, Taylor, and Treisman (1960) reported that a subject's name produced more EEG and behavioral responses during sleep than did the name presented backward, that is, keeping the stimuli the same but the meaning different. The EEG response was the K-complex. Williams, Morlock, and Morlock (1966) reported that the probability of responding during sleep to an auditory stimulus was increased when failure to respond resulted in punishment. The required response was closing a switch within 4 sec, and the aversive stimulus was a fire alarm about 100 dB above threshold. They suggested that these findings indicate the operation of higher nervous functions during some stages of sleep. It should be noted that 100 dB is very loud sound. Correct responses were greatest in Stage 1, and decreased progressively to Stage 4 sleep. Meaningful stimuli produced quicker awakening from sleep than nonmeaningful stimuli in an investigation by Langford, Meddis, and Pearson (1974). Criteria for awakening were both behavioral (sleeper's acknowledgement of waking) and physiological (onset of alpha rhythm).

Dreaming and REM Sleep

In general, findings suggest that in REM periods, as well as in other stages of sleep, the individual is psychologically active. Apparently, the sleeper is occupied with inner mental events, and responses to external events may depend on whether they are significant compared to ongoing events (Snyder & Scott, 1972). This theory was reinforced by the findings of Levere, Davis, Mills, and Berger (1976) regarding the hypothesized intrusion into sleep of stimuli related to reward consistency. Variations in REM duration have been related to estimates of dream duration by Dement and Kleitman (1957b). Subjects were awakened after 5 or 15 min of REM sleep and were able to estimate dream duration in 92 of 111 cases.

Figure 4.3 reveals that REM sleep is more like a waking state than a sleeping one. Other physiological measures also indicate waking characteristics during REM sleep. Some of these measures include an increase in heart rate, respiration, blood pressure, and blood volume of the genitals (erection). However, muscle activity decreases, and most body muscles become very limp. No one can really say why this divergence between the muscles and other body systems occurs. As far as the frequency and duration of REM sleep is concerned, the bottom portion of Fig. 4.3 indicates that the first REM period is the shortest (about 10 min) with later periods becoming longer. One hypothesis about the utility of REM sleep, or dreaming, is that of Crick and Mitchison (1983). They said that unsynchronized, almost random brain activity during REM sleep might represent the elimination of some connections by sets of brain neurons. The purpose of this elimination, or loosening of connections, would be to allow the brain to unlearn certain unnecessary information. Bloom, Lazerson, and Hofstader (1985) suggested that such a hypothesis might explain why infants spend so much time in REM sleep (50% versus about 20% in adults). Because babies' brains have much to learn, perhaps their long periods of REM sleep promote the establishment of new neural connections as well as eliminating some no-longer-needed connections.

Neurophysiological studies into the nature of REM sleep indicate that neurons of the visual system fire intensely, most likely because dreams involve visual scenes (Hobson, 1988). In addition, dreams are characterized by a sense of continuous movement, and brain neurons concerned with movement are very active during REM sleep. Hence, "as far as neurons are concerned, the brain is both seeing and moving in REM sleep" (Hobson, 1988, p. 171). Motor neurons, whether inhibitory or excitatory, fire intensely during REM sleep. One scientist has demonstrated that the most likely source of influence on cortical activity during REM sleep is the brainstem reticular formation, also referred to as the brainstem arousal system.

Another hypothesis about the function of REM sleep or dreaming stems from the writings of Sigmund Freud, who suggested that one function of dreams is to allow the release of anxieties and pent-up emotions that build during everyday life. This hypothesis would seem to gain some support, at least for adults, from Dement (1972). Dement's study noted that a decided increase in hostility, irritability, and unwillingness to continue in a sleep experiment occurred in subjects whose REM sleep was disturbed through awakenings. A control group consisted of subjects who were awakened an equal number of times, but during NREM periods, over the several-night laboratory sessions. This latter group did not show the same symptoms as the REM-disturbed group. When the procedure was reversed for the two groups, the symptoms emerged in the first group and disappeared in the second group.

Summary.   The discovery that rapid eye movements mean that a person is dreaming initiated the scientific study of sleep and dreaming utilizing recordings of brain activity. The capacity of an individual to respond to stimuli during sleep depends on many factors, including sleep stage, stimulus intensity, and significance of stimuli. Hypotheses regarding the function of REM sleep (dreaming) include the unlearning of unnecessary information and allowing the release of pent-up emotions or anxieties that develop during waking hours.

Learning During Sleep

The practical implications of being able to learn during sleep are considerable; but the question of whether sleep learning really occurs is a controversial one, as indicated in a review of sleep-learning research by Aarons (1976). A very basic question is whether people are really asleep when materials are being presented. In a study that used EEG criteria for sleep, Simon and Emmons (1956) tested subjects before and after sleep with 96 information items. The answers were given during sleep. Sleep was defined as the absence of alpha activity for at least 30 sec before and for 10 sec after answers were given in order to ensure that the act of giving the answer did not awaken the individual. The number of correct answers before and after sleep was the same, showing no evidence of learning.

More recent studies, however, suggest that the EEG criteria set up by Simon and Emmons may have been too restrictive. Experiments by Williams et al. (1966), Langford et al. (1974), and Levere et al. (1976) indicated that an operant response can be performed during sleep, and that meaningful materials were successful in arousing persons from sleep. These findings indicated that at least some rudimentary information processing occurs during sleep.

A study by Firth (1973) suggests that habituation of the EEG response, a very simple form of learning, can take place during sleep. Firth used auditory stimuli presented at either three regular intervals (10 to 30 sec) or three irregular intervals (8 to 36 sec). The number of K-complexes (sleeping analog of the orienting response) decreased with the number of repetitive, irrelevant stimuli. The greatest habituation occurred for the 10-sec, regular interstimulus interval. Firth suggested that earlier attempts to find habituation in sleep may have failed because stimulus intervals were too long. However, in a carefully conducted study by Johnson, Townsend, and Wilson (1975), which, in one part, duplicated the 10-sec, regular interstimulus interval used by Firth, no evidence of the EEG K-complex was found. They analyzed the K-complex during Stage 2 sleep and found that, in fact, the percentage of subjects giving K-complexes increased over trials, probably reflecting arousal within Stage 2 sleep with repeated tone presentations. On the other hand, more encouraging results were presented for the EEG K-complex by McDonald, Schicht, Frazier, Shallenberger, and Edwards (1975). They reported that a conditioned discrimination, learned during a waking condition, was carried over into Stage 2 sleep, as indicated by K-complex responses to the conditioned stimulus (tones of either 200 or 2000 Hz). The authors proposed that these results may indicate that information stored in long-term memory (processed during waking) remains available for processing during sleep, and that information from long-term memory is most available in Stage 2 and less so in Stage 4 sleep. This is somewhat similar to results showing EEG responses to meaningful stimuli, because in the McDonald et al. study, the conditioned stimuli attained meaning during the waking state. The studies reviewed thus far indicate that a response to a simple, meaningful stimulus may take place during sleep, but none show learning of complex verbal materials.

In a detailed review of sleep-learning studies, Aarons (1976) analyzed studies that monitored EEG in procedures designed to estimate learning of verbal materials during sleep. Aarons concluded that some learning was evident in all but one study. Learning of small amounts of material was shown more often for the less rigorous recognition tests than for recall tests. The consistently small amount of learning led Aarons to agree with the conclusion that sleep learning of verbal materials is possible but not practical. An examination of Aaron's data indicates that in 7 of the 10 studies showing some learning, the learning was associated with fast-wave sleep or alpha activity. It seems that the minimal amount of sleep-learning observed occurred in lighter stages of sleep (Stages 1 and 2). Another possibility is that the act of presenting the verbal materials may have served to keep subjects in lighter stages of sleep. For example, Lehmann and Koukkou (1974) found that presentations of verbal materials during sleep caused EEG activation of varying duration. Successful learning was related to higher and longer EEG activations after the presentation of the material.

Summary.   Some simple learning can take place during the lightest stages of sleep (1 and 2), especially with respect to meaningful materials. The information processed appears to extend to verbal materials. Whether the amount of verbal material retained would ever justify the extensive use of sleep-learning procedures and devices would have to be decided on the basis of practicality and possible detrimental effects stemming from the loss of restful sleep over long periods of time. It is difficult to imagine that complex conceptual materials such as calculus or physics could be processed and retained by the sleeping individual.

Effects of Work Schedule and Exercise on Sleep EEG

Work Schedule.   The daytime sleep EEGs of hospital employees, working a night shift (11:00 p.m. to 7:00 a.m.), were recorded by Kripke, Cook, and Lewis (1976). The daytime EEG sleep patterns were similar to those previously reported for young adults: Waking (W) = 2%, Stage 1 = 7%, Stage 2 = 46%, Stage 3 = 12%, Stage 4 = 13%, and REM sleep = 20%. However, REM sleep tended to occur early and was frequently interrupted, and Stages 1 and 3 occurred later than usually recorded in nighttime sleep. The authors interpreted these changes in terms of biological effects produced by inversion of the sleep–wakefulness cycle.

The day and night sleep of nursing students was found to differ with respect to both duration and pattern (Bryden & Holdstock, 1973). They fell asleep sooner during day sleep periods, but slept shorter amounts of time (6.6 hrs vs. 7.2 hrs). In addition, they showed an increased amount of Stage 1 sleep and a decrease in slow-wave sleep during daytime as compared to nighttime sleep. As in Kripke's study, REM sleep of the student nurses occurred sooner during the day sleep periods. A reduction in daytime REM sleep was also found in permanent night-shift workers and those on a weekly rotating day–night shift (Dahlgren, 1981).

Dahlgren also reported that, compared to rotating shift workers, the permanent night workers showed better adjustment of body temperature rhythm to night work and day sleep and also had fewer disturbances in sleep functions during the day sleep. The results indicate that sleep adjustment to night work is facilitated by permanent night work schedules. This is underscored by results showing that workers rotating among three shifts have periods during a 10 p.m. to 6 a.m. stretch in which they actually fall asleep (Torsvall, Akerstedt, Gillander, & Knutsson, 1989). These findings were obtained during ambulatory monitoring of EEG in 25 male papermill workers. The results also showed that sleep after night work was 2 hrs shorter than when it followed afternoon work. Because sleepiness during the night sometimes reached a level where wakefulness could not be maintained, then rotating shifts would be contraindicated when work is potentially dangerous or entails responsibility for the lives of others. In general, studies indicate that sleep onset is slower in daytime, and that total sleep is shorter. Some reduction of REM sleep occurs, with an increase in Stage 1 sleep.

Exercise.   The effects of exercise on sleep EEGs of healthy males were examined by Horne and Porter (1975). Afternoon exercise (85 minutes on a bicycle ergometer with a 15-min break at the halfway mark) resulted in increased slow-wave sleep during the first half of the night. The same amounts of morning exercise produced no changes in sleep EEGs. The authors interpreted the results as reflecting the role of slow-wave sleep in recovery from work done later in the day. Recovery from work done earlier presumably takes place during the rest of the day.

Brownman and Tepas (1976) had young males engage in progressive relaxation, light exercise, or a monotonous task (vigilance) on three separate nights, immediately prior to measurement of sleep EEGs. The three different presleep activities (approximately 45 min each) did not differentially affect sleep EEG patterns during the 7.5-hr sleep period. The subjects fell asleep fastest after the relaxation condition, whereas the exercise condition kept them awake the longest period of time. It has been suggested that slow-wave sleep (SWS or Stages 3 and 4) is a time when the body repairs and restores itself. If this is the case, then it might be expected that SWS would increase after exercise because of a depletion of bodily energy reserves. This expectation has not been confirmed, because of conflicting findings.

Bunnell, Bevier, and Horvath (1983) wondered whether having subjects exercise to a point of exhaustion during the afternoon, and quantifying the exhaustion with measures of oxygen consumption, would clarify the relationship between exercise and SWS. They recorded physiological variables on four consecutive nights: adaptation, baseline, exercise, and recovery. On the exercise day, subjects walked on a treadmill until they could go no longer, an average time of 138 min for men and 160 min for women. On the night after exercise, there was a significant increase in SWS (Stages 3 and 4), and a decrease in REM. Thus, daytime exercise can affect sleep brain activity if it is sufficient in duration and intensity.

Summary.   The studies reviewed in this section indicate that daytime sleep differs from nighttime sleep, and that the effects of exercise and presleep activities may depend on the time of day and amount of work involved. Adjustment to night work, in terms of EEG and sleep quality, is facilitated by permanent night work schedules. Daytime exercise affects sleep EEG when it is of sufficient intensity and duration.

Sleep Deprivation and Sleep Onset

Sleep Deprivation.   Naitoh (1975) distinguished among three types of sleep deprivation studies using human subjects: (a) total sleep deprivation, in which the person is kept awake throughout one or more entire sleep periods; (b) partial sleep deprivation, which involves loss of a portion of the regular sleep period; and (c) differential sleep stage deprivation, where certain sleep stages are selectively prevented from occurring, usually by arousing the person when the EEG records show signs of the particular stage to be disturbed.

A systematic review of sleep loss effects on performance was conducted by Woodward and Nelson (1974). They noted that the types of activities most likely to suffer impairment were those that involved quick reactions, short-term memory, reasoning, decision making, and attention. The amount of total sleep deprivation required to produce deficits in performance ranged from 24 hrs for monotonous, routine tasks, to 48 hrs for cognitive tasks, such as decision making. Williams and Williams (1966) studied the recovery period sleep EEGs of army men after total sleep deprivation. The sleep loss took place over a period of 64 hrs (loss of two complete sleep periods). The EEGs during recovery from sleep loss showed an increase in slow-wave sleep during the first night. The subjects showed impaired short-term memory as a result of sleep deprivation. Lubin, Moses, Johnson, and Naitoh (1974) also found impaired short-term memory during total sleep deprivation. Other sleep deprivation effects are slowing of RT, decrease in vigilance performance, increased irritability, and microsleeps (short lapses in attention). Engle-Friedman (personal communication, 1988) was of the opinion that observed deficits in short-term memory result from lapses in attention and motivational decrements caused by sleep deprivation.

A long-term study of partial sleep deprivation was conducted by Webb and Agnew (1974). The subjects had sleep EEGs measured one night a week, over a 60-day period, while on a schedule of $5\frac{1}{2}$ hrs of sleep per night. Performance on a variety of tests (vigilance, addition, word memory, grip strength, and psychological mood) was also measured once a week. Initially, the amount of Stage 4 sleep increased, but this returned to normal levels by the fifth week. The amount of REM stage sleep decreased by 25% during the course of the experiment. Performance on only one test (vigilance) decreased with continued sleep restriction. The authors concluded that a chronic loss of sleep of about $2\frac{1}{2}$ hours a night is not likely to result in major behavioral consequences. Similar results were obtained by Horne and Wilkinson (1985), although their approach was different. They paired two groups of 8-hr sleepers, and one of the groups had sleep time systematically reduced to 6 hrs per night over a 6-week period. The EEG records showed that sleep deprivation resulted in decreased REM and Stage 2 sleep. Sleep onset time was much quicker for the deprived group. Overall daytime sleepiness did not increase for the deprived group and vigilance performance was maintained. The fact that subjects in the Webb and Agnew study showed a vigilance decrement with 5^1/$_2$ hrs sleep may mean that 6 hrs of sleep is the minimum necessary to maintain successful vigilance performance in young adults.

Moses, Johnson, Naitoh, and Lubin (1975) selectively deprived subjects of either Stage 4 or REM sleep in two separate experiments. In the first experiment, they examined effects of REM deprivation or Stage 4 sleep deprivation after two nights of total sleep loss, whereas in the second experiment, effects of total sleep loss were examined after three nights of REM or Stage 4 deprivation. The number of arousals required to keep subjects from entering Stage 4 was significantly greater after sleep loss (Experiment 1) than it was in Experiment 2. The number and patterns of arousals indicate that the two nights of wakefulness increased the tendency to obtain Stage 4 sleep but not REM sleep. They interpreted the results as supporting the hypothesis from previous studies that Stage 4 has priority over REM sleep in terms of recovery from sleep loss.

The effects of graded amounts of sleep deprivation, without regard to stage, were studied by Akerstedt and Gillberg (1986). Subjects had 0, 2, 4, or 8 hrs total sleep on four experimental nights separated by 1 week, and then were allowed to sleep as long as they wanted, starting at 11 a.m. the next day. They found that during day sleep, SWS showed dramatic increases that were dependent on the amount of sleep loss. One fascinating finding was that subjects did not awaken until at least the baseline amount of SWS was obtained. This tendency of SWS to reach some quota before sleep ends, as well as its sensitivity to loss, suggests that it plays an important role in sleep regulation. Total sleep time, Stage 2, and REM showed only limited amounts of recovery compared to the loss.

Sleep, vigilance performance, and mood in response to one night of total sleep deprivation were compared for elderly and young subjects (Brendel et al., 1990). The elderly were in their 80s and the young in their 20s. The experiment consisted of three nights of baseline sleep, one night of total deprivation, and two recovery nights. Vigilance performance and mood were measured twice on each experimental day. As expected, 80-year-olds had less slow-wave sleep and more sleep awakenings than 20-year-olds. However, delta sleep and sleep continuity improved for both groups on the first recovery night. Young subjects fell asleep more easily during the day than the elderly, suggesting a greater sleep need in the younger age group. Interestingly, mood and vigilance performance were less affected in the elderly than the young. On balance, the overall results suggest that total sleep loss is more disruptive for the young than the old, and that the old need less sleep than young adults for maintenance of mood and performance.

Sleep Onset.   Although the consensus among researchers has been that reduction of alpha indicates the transition from wakefulness to sleep, some have argued for using onset of Stage 2 sleep for this purpose (Ogilvie & Wilkinson, 1988). One reason for the difficulty in locating Stage 1 sleep consistently is the variation in amount of alpha activity seen from person to person. Sleep researchers agree that people producing K-complexes and sleep spindles are asleep. Psychophysiologists doing sleep research have proposed that it would be helpful to have a behavioral measure, in addition to EEG, as an objective indicator of sleep onset. A candidate for the behavioral measure is depression of a finger switch that occurs as a result of loss of muscle tension with sleep (Perry & Goldwater, 1987).

Another is the pressing of a palm-mounted switch to turn off faint tones (5 to 10 dB). This latter procedure was used by Ogilvie and Wilkinson (1988) to study EEG and behavioral responsiveness throughout the night. They found decreasing probability of response to tones as a function of sleep stage as follows: Stage 1 = 24%, Stage 2 = 2%, Stage 3 = 0%, Stage 4 =

0%, REM = 0%. Thus, there is a very low or zero probability of response to a faint tone from Stage 2 on. The combination of Stage 2 EEG along with lack of behavioral response would seem to clearly indicate sleep onset. A problematic aspect of this study is that the 25- to 45-year-old subjects all reported having normal hearing. Hearing tests should be done routinely in situations where auditory stimuli are so faint. A general problem in sleep research is the small number of subjects used and the lack of control groups. This is due in part to the difficulties in carrying out this type of research.

Insomnia is a problem for both elderly women and men. However, it seems that although elderly women have superior patterns in terms of amount of SWS and sleep maintenance, they also complain more about poor sleep than elderly men. A possible reason for the greater complaining emerges from an investigation by Hoch et al. (1987), in which EEG patterns and self-reports about sleep were more closely related for the women, suggesting that they report sleep loss more accurately than men. With regard to insomnia in general, it has been suggested that it may represent a chronic SWS deficiency. Sewitch (1987) argued that a rapid drop in rectal temperature upon sleep onset is a necessary prerequisite for sustained SWS, defined as Stage 4 sleep. She presented a well-reasoned theory suggesting that chronic insomnia results from a failure of the thermoregulatory system to show a rapid decrease in body temperature at sleep onset, which persists for at least 1 to 2 hrs into the sleep period. This theory is certainly testable and calls for studies that examine EEG and thermoregulatory patterns in both insomniacs and normal sleepers.

A problem in treating individuals who complain of poor sleep is dealing with those who misperceive their sleep state. Often these patients say they have inadequate quantity or quality of sleep, but polygraphic measures of their sleep indicate only a mild disturbance. One consistent past finding is that poor sleepers who are awakened by sound early in their sleep period (Stage 2) are more likely to report having been awake as compared to good sleepers who perceive their sleep state more accurately (Mendelson, 1998). To determine whether this pattern for poor sleepers also holds for awakenings at later nighttime sleep periods, Mendelson (1998) awakened self-reported insomniacs (mean age 33 years) at five time points during the night with auditory tones. He found that 75% of the subjects awakened in early Stage 2 sleep reported that they had been awake, whereas later in the night, during the third NREM–REM cycle, only 25% reported having been awake. Thus, the misperception of being awake was less in the later night sleep periods. Mendelson suggests that greater durations of previous sleep may have influenced these perceptions. The early night awakening occurred after an average of 15 min of sleep, whereas the later awakenings occurred after an average of 109 min of sleep. Mendelson also noted that the tone intensity required to awaken these people was similar for Stage 2 and REM sleep (65 decibels), but was much higher for Stage 4 sleep (79 decibels).

In an interesting study entitled "An Extreme Case of Healthy Insomnia," Meddis, Pearson, and Langford (1973) described the case of a 70-year-old woman (Miss M) who slept less than 1 hr each night. She rarely experienced fatigue, and this had been her sleep schedule since childhood days. In one experiment, she remained awake for 56 consecutive hrs and then only slept for 99 min while her EEG was recorded. This sleep period was divided into the following stages: 37 min of REM sleep, 13 min of Stage 2, 31 min of Stage 3, and 18 min of Stage 4 sleep. In a second investigation, she slept in the laboratory on five consecutive nights, during which she averaged 67 min of sleep per night, without any behavioral signs of sleep deprivation. During the five nights, she spent 51% of the time in Stage 2 sleep, 23% in Stage 3, 9% in Stage 4, and 17% in REM sleep. With the exception of the absence of Stage 1 sleep, this pattern is not much different from that reported for healthy young adults (Kripke et al., 1976). This unusual woman spent much of her waking time engaged in activities that she enjoyed, such as writing and painting. She could not understand why other people slept for such long periods and wasted so much time!

Summary.   It has been shown that sleep loss can affect short-term memory in normal persons. Slower RT, poor vigilance performance, and irritability also result from sleep deprivation. The amount of slow-wave sleep increases immediately after sleep deprivation. Results from studies of long-term partial sleep deprivation do not indicate serious consequences for performance, even though the amount of REM sleep is reduced. Selective deprivation of various sleep stages indicates the apparently greater importance of Stage 4 versus REM sleep. In fact, after sleep deprivation, SWS is the stage most compensated for in the recovery period. It has been suggested that insomnia may be associated with chronic SWS deficiency. One theory says that SWS deficiency may be due to a failure of the body to show a rapid decrease in core temperature with sleep onset. Rare individuals show no detrimental effects of very little sleep on either performance or sleeping EEG pattern. Perhaps in healthy insomnia, the restorative functions attributed to sleep occur more quickly. Individuals such as Miss M may be at some extreme point of a normal distribution of sleep time requirements. Individuals at the other extreme may require 10 or 12 hrs of sleep for normal functioning, suggesting a possibly very wide range of individual differences in the amount of sleep needed.

Research in the area of brain psychophysiology has been given impetus by advances in electronics and computers and programs that enable the measurement and analysis of evoked brain potentials. These EEG-derived responses are most commonly measured from the scalp, but are also being measured directly from brain tissue. As a consequence of these developments, cerebral psychophysiology has blossomed over the past 35 years. We discuss a representative sample of these studies, and interesting concepts and hypotheses that have been proposed by researchers, in the next three chapters.

REFERENCES

Aarons, L. (1976). Sleep-assisted instruction. *Psychological Bulletin, 83*, 1–40.

Akerstedt, T., & Gillberg, M. (1986). A dose–response study of sleep loss and spontaneous sleep termination. *Psychophysiology, 23*, 293–297.

Aserinsky, E., & Kleitman, N. (1953). Regularly occurring periods of eye motility, and concomitant phenomena, during sleep. *Science, 188*, 273–274.

Basar-Eroglu, C., Struber, D., Kruse, P., Basar, E., & Stadler, M. (1996). Frontal gamma-band enhancement during multistable visual perception. *International Journal of Psychophysiology, 24*, 113–125.

Beatty, J. (1972). Similar effects of feedback signals and instructional information on EEG activity. *Physiology and Behavior, 9*, 151–154.

Beatty, J., Greenberg, A., Deibler, W. P., & O'Hanlon, J. F. (1974). Operant control of occipital theta rhythm affects performance in a radar monitoring task. *Science, 183*, 871–873.

Beatty, J., & O'Hanlon, J. (1980). Operant control of posterior theta rhythm and vigilance performance: Repeated treatments and transfer of training. In N. Birbaumer & H. Kimmel (Eds.), *Biofeedback and self-regulation* (pp. 247–258). Hillsdale, NJ: Lawrence Erlbaum Associates.

Berlyne, D. E. (1970). Attention as a problem in behavior therapy. In D. I. Mostofsky (Ed.), *Attention: Contemporary theory and analysis* (pp. 25–29). New York: Appleton-Century-Crofts.

Berlyne, D. E., & McDonnell, P. (1965). Effects of stimulus complexity and incongruity on duration of EEG desynchronization. *Electroencephalography and Clinical Neurophysiology, 18*, 156–161.

Bliwise, D., & Bergman, B. M. (1987). Individual differences in Stages 3 and 4 sleep. *Psychophysiology, 24*, 35–40.

Bloom, F. E., Lazerson, A., & Hofstader, L. (1985). *Brain, mind, and behavior*. New York: Freeman.

Bohdanecky, Z., Bozkov, V., & Radil, T. (1984). Acoustic stimulus threshold related to EEG alpha and non-alpha epochs. *International Journal of Psychophysiology, 2*, 63–66.

Braggio, J. T., & Putney, R. T. (1980). UR magnitude as predictor of conditioned alpha blocking. *Psychophysiology, 18*, 417–420.

Brendel, D. H., Reynolds, C. F., III., Jennings, J. R., Hoch, C. C., Monk, T. H., Berman, S. R., Hall, F. T., Buyse, D. J., & Kupper, D. J. (1990). Sleep stage physiology, mood, and vigilance responses to total sleep deprivation in healthy 80-year-olds and 20-year-olds. *Psychophysiology, 27*, 677–686.

Brown, B. (1970). Recognition of aspects of consciousness through association with EEG alpha activity represented by a light signal. *Psychophysiology, 6*, 442–452.

Brownman, C. P., & Tepas, D. I. (1976). The effects of pre-sleep activity on all-night sleep. *Psychophysiology, 13*, 536–540.

Bryden, G., & Holdstock, T. L. (1973). Effects of night duty on sleep patterns of nurses. *Psychophysiology, 10*, 36–42.

Bunnell, D. E., Bevier, W., & Horvath, S. M. (1983). Effects of exhaustive exercises on the sleep of men and women. *Psychophysiology, 20*, 50–58.

Christie, B., Delafield, G., Lucas, B., Winwood, M., & Gale, A. (1972). Stimulus complexity and the electroencephalogram: Differential effects of the number and the variety of display elements. *Canadian Journal of Psychology, 26*, 155–170.

Clarke, A. M., Michie, P. T., Andreassen, A. G., Viney, L. L., & Rosenthal, R. (1976). Expectancy effects in a psychophysical experiment. *Physiological Psychology, 4*, 137–144.

Cott, A., Pavloski, R. P., & Black, A. H. (1980). Operant conditioning and discrimination of alpha: Some methodological limitations inherent in response-discrimination experiments. *Journal of Experimental Psychology: General, 110*, 398–414.

Cott, A., Pavloski, R. P., & Goldman, J. A. (1980). Cortical alpha rhythm, biofeedback, and the determinants of subjective state. *Journal of Experimental Psychology: General, 110*, 381–397.

Crick, F., & Mitchison, G. (1983). The function of dream sleep. *Nature, 304*, 111–114.

Dahlgren, D. (1981). Adjustment of circadian rhythms and EEG sleep functions to day and night sleep among permanent night-workers and rotation shiftworkers. *Psychophysiology, 18*, 381–391.

Dement, W. C. (1972). *Some must watch while some must sleep.* New York: Freeman.

Dement, W. C., & Kleitman, N. (1957a). Cyclic variations in EEG during sleep and their relation to eye movements, body motility, and dreaming. *Electroencephalography and Clinical Neurophysiology, 9*, 673–690.

Dement, W. C., & Kleitman, N. (1957b). The relation of eye movements during sleep to dream activity: An objective method for the study of dreaming. *Journal of Experimental Psychology, 53*, 339–346.

Eberlin, P., & Mulholland, T. (1976). Bilateral differences in parietal–occipital EEG induced by contingent visual feedback. *Psychobiology, 13*, 212–218.

Fath, S. J., Wallace, L. A., & Worsham, R. W. (1976). The effect of intermittent auditory stimulation on the occipital alpha rhythm. *Physiological Psychology, 4*, 185–188.

Firth, H. (1973). Habituation during sleep. *Psychophysiology, 10*, 43–51.

Foulkes, W. D. (1962). Dream reports from different stages of sleep. *Journal of Abnormal and Social Psychology, 65*, 14–25.

Gale, A. (1977). Some EEG correlates of sustained attention. In R. R. Mackie (Ed.), *Vigilance* (pp. 263–283). New York: Plenum.

Giannitrapani, D. (1971). Scanning mechanisms and the EEG. *Electroencephalography and Clinical Neurophysiology, 30*, 139–146.

Hebb, D. O. (1958). *A textbook of psychology.* Philadelphia: Saunders.

Hobson, J. A. (1988). *The dreaming brain.* New York: Basic Books.

Hoch, C. C., Reynolds, C. F. III., Kupper, D. J., Berman, S., Houck, P. R., & Stack, J. (1987). Empirical note: Self-report versus recorded sleep in healthy seniors. *Psychophysiology, 22*, 69–78.

Horne, J. A., & Porter, J. M. (1975). Exercise and human sleep. *Nature, 256*, 573–575.

Horne, J. A., & Wilkinson, S. (1985). Chronic sleep reduction: Daytime vigilance performance and EEG measures of sleepiness, with particular reference to "practice" effects. *Psychophysiology, 22*, 69–78.

Johnson, S. C. (1977). Learned control of brain wave activity. In J. Beatty & H. Legewie (Eds.), *Biofeedback and behavior* (pp. 73–93). New York: Plenum.

Johnson, L. C., Townsend, R. E., & Wilson, M. R. (1975). Habituation during sleeping and waking. *Psychophysiology, 12*, 574–584.

Kamiya, J. (1969). Operant control of the EEG alpha rhythm and some of its reported effects on consciousness. In C. T. Tart (Ed.), *Altered states of consciousness* (pp. 507–515). New York: Wiley.

Kripke, D. F., Cook, B., & Lewis, O. F. (1976). Sleep of night workers: Electroencephalography recordings. *Psychophysiology, 7*, 377–384.

Langford, G. W., Meddis, R., & Pearson, A. J. D. (1974). Awakening latency from sleep for meaningful and nonmeaningful stimuli. *Psychophysiology, 11*, 1–5.

Lehmann, D., & Koukkou, M. (1974). Computer analysis of EEG wakefulness–sleep patterns during of novel and familiar sentences. *Electroencephalography and Clinical Neurophysiology, 37*, 73–84.

Levere, T. E., Davis, N., Mills, J., & Berger, E. H. (1976). Arousal from sleep: The effects of cognitive value of auditory stimuli. *Physiological Psychology, 4*, 376–382.

Lindsley, D. B. (1960). Attention, consciousness, sleep and wakefulness. In J. Field, H. W. Magoun, & V. E. Hall (Eds.), *Handbook of physiology, vol. 3* (pp. 1553–1593). Washington, DC: American Physiological Society.

Loomis, A. L., Harvey, E. N., & Hobart, G. (1938). Distribution of disturbance patterns in the human electroencephalogram, with special reference to sleep. *Journal of Neurophysiology, 1*, 413–430.

Lorig, T. S., & Schwartz, G. E. (1988). Brain and odor: I. Alteration of human EEG by odor administration. *Psychobiology, 16*, 281–284.

Lubin, A., Moses, J. M., Johnson, L. D., & Naitoh, P. (1974). The recuperative effects of REM sleep and Stage 4 sleep on human performance after complete sleep loss: Experiment 1. *Psychophysiology, 11*, 133–146.

Mackworth, N. H. (1950). Researches on the measurement of human performance (Medical Research Council Special Report No. 268). London: H. M. Stationary Office.

Martin, G. N. (1998). Human electroencephalographic (EEG) response to olfactory stimulation: Two experiments using the aroma of food. *International Journal of Psychophysiology, 30*, 287–302.

McDonald, D. G., Schicht, W. W., Frazier, R. E., Shallenberger, H. D., & Edwards, J. J. (1975). Studies of information processing in sleep. *Psychophysiology, 12*, 624–629.

Meddis, R., Pearson, A. J., & Langford, G. (1973). An extreme case of healthy insomnia. *Electroencephalography and Clinical Neurophysiology, 3*, 181–186.

Mendelson, W. B. (1998). Effects of time of night and sleep stage on perception of sleep in subjects with sleep state misperception. *Psychobiology, 26*, 73–78.

Moses, J. M., Johnson, L. C., Naitoh, P., & Lubin, A. (1975). Sleep stage deprivation and total sleep loss: Effects on sleep behavior. *Psychophysiology, 12*, 141–146.

Naitoh, P. (1975). Sleep deprivation in humans. In P. H. Venables & M. I. Christie (Eds.), *Research in psychophysiology* (pp. 153–180). New York: Wiley.

Nowlis, D. P., & Kamiya, J. (1970). The control of electroencephalographic alpha rhythms through auditory feedback and the associated mental activity. *Psychophysiology, 6*, 476–484.

Ogilvie, R. D., & Wilkinson, R. T. (1988). Behavioral versus EEG-based monitoring of all-night sleep/wake patterns, *Sleep, 11*, 139–155.

Oswald, I., Taylor, A. M., & Treisman, M. (1960). Discriminative responses to stimulation during human sleep. *Brain, 83*, 440–453.

Pavlov, I. P. (1927). *Conditioned reflexes*. Oxford: Clarendon Press.

Perry, T. J., & Goldwater, B. C. (1987). A passive behavioral measure of sleep onset in high-alpha and low-alpha subjects. *Psychophysiology, 24*, 657–666.

Petsche, H. (1996). Approaches to verbal, visual and musical creativity by EEG coherence analysis. *International Journal of Psychophysiology, 24*, 145–159.

Ray, W. J., & Cole, H. W. (1985). EEG alpha activity reflects attentional demands, and beta activity activity reflects emotional and cognitive processes. *Science, 228*, 750–752.

Rechtschaffen, A. (1973). The psychophysiology of mental activity during sleep. In F. J. McGuigan & R. A. Schoonover (Eds.), *The psychophysiology of thinking* (pp. 153–205). New York: Academic Press.

Sewitch, D. E. (1987). Slow wave sleep deficiency insomnia: A problem in thermo-downregulation at sleep onset. *Psychophysiology, 24*, 200–215.

Shagass, C. (1972). Electrical activity of the brain. In N. S. Greenfield & R. A. Sternbach (Eds.), *Handbook of psychophysiology* (pp. 263–328). New York: Holt, Rinehart & Winston.

Simon, C. W., & Emmons, W. H. (1956). Responses to material presented during various levels of sleep. *Journal of Experimental Psychology, 51*, 89–97.

Snyder, F., & Scott, J. (1972). The psychophysiology of sleep. In N. S. Greenfield & R. A. Sternbach (Eds.), *Handbook of psychophysiology* (pp. 645–708). New York: Holt, Rinehart & Winston.

Sokolov, E. N. (1963). *Perception and the conditioned reflex*. Oxford: Pergamon Press.

Tecce, J. J. (1972). Contingent negative variation (CNV) and psychological processes in man. *Psychological Bulletin, 77*, 73–108.

Torsvall, L., Akerstedt, T., Gillander, K., & Knutsson, A. (1989). Sleep on the night shift: 24-hour EEG monitoring os spontaneous sleep/wake behavior. *Psychophysiology, 26*, 352–358.

Tyson, P. D., Ogilvie, R. D., & Hunt, H. T. (1984). Lucid, prelucid, and nonlucid dreams related to the amount of EEG alpha activity during REM sleep. *Psychophysiology, 21*, 442–451.

Valentino, D. A., Arruda, J. E., & Gold, S. M. (1993). Comparison of QEEG and response accuracy in good vs. poorer performers during a vigilance task. *International Journal of Psychophysiology, 15*, 123–134.

Valentino, D. A., & Dufresne, R. L. (1991). Attention tasks and EEG power spectra. *International Journal of Psychophysiology, 11*, 299–302.

Valle, R. S., & Levine, J. M. (1975). Expectation effects in alpha wave control. *Psychophysiology, 12*, 306–309.

Webb, W. B., & Agnew, H. W. (1974). The effects of a chronic limitation of sleep length. *Psychophysiology, 11*, 265–274.

Williams, H. L., Hammack, J. T., Daly, R. L., Dement, W. C., & Lubin, A. (1964). Responses to auditory stimulation, sleep loss and the EEG stages of sleep. *Electroencephalography and Clinical Neurophysiology, 16*, 269–279.

Williams, H. L., Morlock, H. C., & Morlock, J. V. (1966). Instrumental behavior during sleep. *Psychophysiology, 2*, 208–216.

Williams, H. L., & Williams, C. L. (1966). Nocturnal EEG profiles and performance. *Psychophysiology, 3*, 164–175.

Woodward, D. P., & Nelson, P. D. (1974). *A user oriented review of the literature on the effects of sleep loss, work–rest schedules, and recovery on performance* (Tech. Rep. No. ARC-206). Arlington, VA: Office of Naval Research.

5

Event-Related Brain Potentials and Behavior I: Measurement, Motor Activity, Hemispheric Asymmetries, and Sleep

Another measure of brain activity, derived from EEG recordings, is the event-related brain potential (ERP). Unlike the EEG, which represents spontaneous brain activity, the ERP is generated as a response to specific stimuli, and is an average of a number of samples. These ERPs are time-locked to stimulus events and have proven valuable to the psychophysiologist interested in a record of brain responses to stimuli, even when no other noticeable response occurs. A great deal of research effort has been devoted to studying the relationship between ERPs and human psychological activities. Most of the work has been conducted over the past 35 years and is continuing at a high rate. What makes the ERP so appealing is the possibility of relating specific brain responses to discrete psychological states and events. The extensive research on ERPs indicates that it rivals heart activity as the most popular physiological variable studied by psychophysiologists.

The ERP has been found to be dependent on both physical and psychological characteristics of stimuli, although in some instances, ERPs are independent of specific stimuli. For example, brain responses have been found to occur at the precise time that stimuli were expected but not actually presented (Sutton, Teuting, Zubin, & John, 1967). When ERPs occur independently of external stimuli, they are called *endogenous*, indicating that they are produced by internal events. Those ERPs produced as a reaction to specific external events are called *exogenous* potentials.

Vaughan (1969) proposed the term *event-related potentials* to refer to a variety of brain responses that show stable time relationships to actual or anticipated stimuli. Those ERPs were classified by Vaughan as (a) sensory ERPs, (b) motor potentials, (c) long-latency potentials, and (d) steady potential shifts (SPS).

The sensory ERPs include those produced by visual, auditory, somatosensory (e.g., touch), and olfactory stimuli. Examples of sensory ERPs are shown in Fig. 5.1. They are based on the composite averaged potentials of eight individuals. The various negative and positive waves (components) of these ERPs can be seen in the illustration. Motor potentials (MP) refer to potentials that precede and accompany voluntary movement. Vaughan observed that the amplitude of the MP varies with the strength and speed of muscle contraction.

The long-latency potentials refer to those positive or negative components of the ERP that occur at 250 to 750 msec after some event. They reflect subjective responses to expected or unexpected stimuli, including the orienting response (see Ritter, Vaughan, & Costa, 1968). This is especially true for a positive component occurring at about 300 msec after stimulus onset, termed P300, and also referred to as P3 (discovered by Sutton, Braren, & Zubin, 1965).

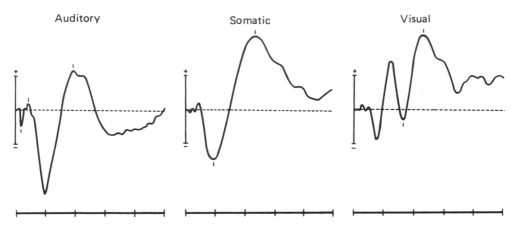

FIG. 5.1. Averaged evoked responses obtained from eight adult subjects. Each tracing is the computer average of 4,800 individual responses. Calibration 10 μV, 100 msec/division (negative down).

Another important long-latency potential is the N400, first described by Kutas and Hillyard (1980). This negative wave occurs in response to unexpected endings of sentences and is related to semantic deviations.

One example of a steady potential shift is the contingent negative variation (CNV) first described by Walter, Cooper, Aldridge, McCallum, and Winter (1964). The CNV may be observed when subjects are told that they must respond to an event some time after a warning signal is given. For example, a warning light (S1) may be given, and about 1.5 sec later a tone (S2) beeps, at which time the subject must press a button. The CNV occurs between S1 and S2. Another steady potential shift is the readiness potential (RP) of Kornhuber and Deecke (1965), which builds up just before the onset of voluntary movement. The RP was originally called *Bereitschaftspotential* by Kornhuber and Deecke, a term still used by many European scientists. Examples of the CNV, motor potential, and readiness potential are given in Fig. 5.2. The long-latency potentials and steady potential shifts are discussed further in chapter 7.

At the other extreme of long-latency potentials are the very early *far field* potentials. These were originally discovered in humans by Jewett, Romano, and Williston (1970), who demonstrated that several auditory ERPs of very short latencies (about 1 to 10 msec) could be recorded from the vertex after presentations of stimuli. These low-amplitude responses (0.5 to 1.5 μV) were attributed to electrical activity in various brain stem structures. Their existence has subsequently been confirmed by many other investigators. They are termed far field because they can be recorded from scalp electrodes (e.g., C_z or vertex) that are some distance from the source of the activity (brain stem). These brain stem potentials are discussed again in chapter 16.

ORIGIN OF EVENT-RELATED POTENTIALS (ERPs)

The specific brain areas involved in the generation of various kinds and components of ERPs are currently being sought by a number of researchers. Knowledge of these sources is important to the understanding of how brain areas participate in certain mental processes and in the application of ERP findings to practical clinical situations (Arezzo, Vaughan, Kraut, Steinschneider, & Legatt, 1986; Beck, 1975). The methods by which these sources are determined involve recording activity from subcortical and cortical brain areas that generate ERPs in

C N V   A N D   M O T O R   P O T E N T I A L

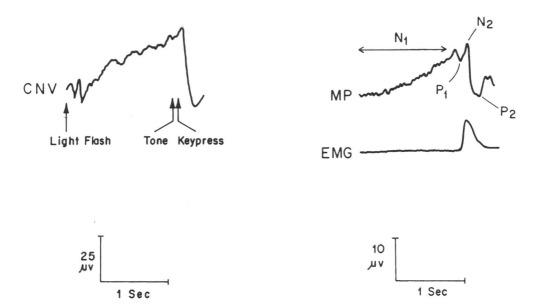

FIG. 5.2. Examples of CNV, motor potential, and Bereitschaftspotential (readiness potential). On the left is CNV (n = 6 trials) recorded from vertex (C$_z$) to right mastoid. Relative negativity at the vertex is upward. On the right (upper trace) is a motor potential (n = 400 responses) associated with dorsiflexion of the right wrist and recorded from the left Rolandic area 4 cm from midline to a linked ear reference. The lower trace on the right is the summation of the rectified EMG resulting from muscle contraction. The slow negative component "N1" is the readiness potential. (Photos courtesy of Drs. J. J. Tecce and H. G. Vaughan, Jr.)

humans and animals. Information about these areas is very fragmentary and will require much more time and effort before a more complete picture is obtained (Vaughan & Arezzo, 1988).

Other techniques involve the use of multiple electrode placements on the scalp surface to provide information about possible cortical sources for various ERPs and the use of event-related magnetic fields to suggest possible subcortical and cortical generators, and positron emission tomography (PET) scans. The use of multiple scalp locations involves the mapping out of widely distributed ERPs under various stimulus conditions, and is termed *topographical analysis*. Despite problems, which include possible summation at a particular scalp area of activity from more than one underlying brain structure, investigators have been able to suggest the sources of a number of ERP components. More recently, PET scans have helped to identify brain areas involved in certain activities through measures of increased glucose metabolism that occurs when different brain areas are actively involved in processing stimuli. The PET scan is slow responding compared to ERPs, but localization of brain areas is accurate, because the increased synaptic activity shows up in a colored X-ray-like picture. The combined techniques complement each other very well.

Brain-Stem or Far Field Potentials

There is evidence that early auditory-evoked potential components (0 to 10 msec) recorded from the scalp in humans are produced at various brain-stem locations (Jewett & Williston,

1971). Further, components of this response appear to be generated by specific structures in the auditory system. For example, a positive component occurring at about 2 msec after stimulation has been related to activity at the auditory nerve (Vaughan & Arezzo, 1988; also see Wave I of Fig. 16.1). Wave II of this brain-stem response reflects activity in the trapezoid body and neurons ascending toward the superior olive. Wave III in man has been localized to a structure called the pons, and Waves IV and V have generators near the inferior colliculus, an area in the midbrain concerned with auditory system reflexes. Waves VI and VII reflect activity of neurons that transmit auditory impulses from the thalamus to auditory cortex, the so-called thalamocortical radiations.

Sensory ERPs

The largest amplitude auditory ERP components to a brief click or tone are a negative peak occurring at 80 to 90 msec, and a positive one at around 170 msec. This negative–positive sequence is referred to as the "N1–P2 complex," and it appears to be generated at the auditory cortex in the temporal lobe (Vaughan & Arezzo, 1988).

Components of the somatosensory ERP have been related to specific brain areas. For example, a negative wave occurring at 55 msec appears to be generated in the postcentral gyrus (Goff, Allison, & Vaughan, 1978). A later somatosensory ERP, peaking around 200 msec, has been localized in primary somatosensory cortex through electrical and magnetic field recordings. With regard to visual stimulation, transient visual ERPs to low intensity flashes are largest at the occipital pole (Area 17 or striate cortex) and fall off rapidly with distance from this area. This is consistent with the idea of a principal generator located in primary visual cortex (Vaughan & Arezzo, 1988). In accord with scalp-recorded data, recordings made from the cortical surface of humans indicate that most sensory ERP components (auditory, visual, and somatosensory) seem to originate in or near the primary cortical sensory areas (Goff et al., 1978).

A component termed *N1* has also been related to attention (Hillyard, Hink, Schwent, & Picton, 1973). This N1 component, occurring about 100 msec poststimulus, was increased in size for stimuli presented in an "attended" ear. The recording was made from the vertex and there was a noticeable difference in response to stimuli from the "unattended" ear. The brain substrates for this component appear to be primary auditory cortex near the lateral sulcus (Diesch & Luce, 1997). Other studies show that the latency of this N1 component is delayed in 4- to 8-year-old children (Bruneau, Roux, Guerin, Barthelmy, & Lelord, 1997). Auditory stimulation in 4- to 8-year-olds produces a negative component peaking at about 170 msec at midtemporal locations (T_3 and T_4) and at 140 msec at the vertex. These results suggest that neural generators of surface ERPs differ depending on stage of development, and delayed latencies may reflect incomplete neuronal myelination in this age group.

Motor Potentials

Motor potentials recorded in humans with the onset of voluntary movements indicate origins in the precentral (motor) cortex at the hemisphere opposite to the moving limb (Vaughan, Costa, & Ritter, 1968). The MP has been found maximal from the precentral cortex of monkeys trained to make wrist extension movements (Arezzo & Vaughan, 1975). The relative contribution of premotor and supplementary motor cortex to scalp-recorded MPs remains to be more fully explored. Some light is shed on this by Tarkka (1994) who recorded MPs from multiple electrode sites while subjects performed finger movements. Midline sites were most active during a preparatory period just prior to voluntary movement, whereas two contralateral areas were most active during and immediately after the motor act. The pattern of MPs suggest the involvement of the supplementary motor area in preparation for the movement, the contralateral primary motor cortex during the execution of the movement, and the contralateral somatosensory cortex following the movement.

Long-Latency Potentials

As implied earlier, the long-latency potentials are strongly influenced by subjective factors (e.g., task-relevant information). Scalp recordings of late potentials indicate maximal response from over frontal cortical areas, with a secondary focus at parietal areas (Courchesne, Hillyard, & Galambos, 1975; Squires, Squires, & Hillyard, 1975). Studies of scalp distributions of the late positive components (LPCs) by Simson, Vaughan, and Ritter (1977) also suggest generators within frontal and parietal association cortex. Subcortical recordings have obtained LPCs at widespread areas of the cerebral hemispheres (Yingling & Hosobuchi, 1984). Recordings from implanted electrodes in human patients have suggested the hippocampus (a subcortical region) as a possible generator of the LPC (Halgren et al., 1980). However, there is lack of agreement about this hippocampal generator. For example, Johnson and Fedio (1986) and Johnson (1988) were still able to record the LPC (P300) in patients whose hippocampus had been removed on the same side as the recording. Even more convincing was the finding of Polich and Squire (in press). They reported that several amnesic patients with hippocampal damage on both sides of the brain had P300s that were similar to normal controls. It is likely that LPCs are derived from activity in a number of areas, including parietal and frontal association cortex and structures within the limbic region, such as hippocampus and amygdala.

The relative contributions of these areas has yet to be determined. Further, Johnson (1989) reported evidence for separate generators of P300 elicited by visual stimuli and those elicited by auditory stimuli. These findings argue against the notion of a single, modality independent generator for P300 in the brain. To identify brain structures involved in a memory workload task in neurological patients, depth electrodes were implanted in both left- and right-sided amydala and hippocampus (Beuzeron-Mangina, 1996). Increases in latency of a negative component peaking at 400 msec (N4) were noted as workload increased in both hippocampal and amygdala structures. Thus, these subcortical areas appeared to be involved in the cognitive task used, and the latency increase was attributed to greater stimulus evaluation time required as workload increased. Long-latency potentials identified as N400 and P600 have been related to memory processes. When stimuli are repeated over intervals less than a few minutes, the N400 is attenuated by repetition, whereas the P600 is enhanced. The timing of the N400 is consistent with a role in the establishment and retrieval of memories (Guillem, N'kaoua, Rogier, & Claverie, 1996). Recordings from brain regions have confirmed that frontal lobe structures contribute to the scalp-recorded N400 and P600 and, therefore, the role of prefrontal structures in memory is supported.

Steady Potential Shifts (Contingent Negative Variation and Readiness Potential)

One type of SPS, the CNV, has been found maximal over the central cortex and less pronounced at frontal and parietal areas (Cohen, 1969). This finding has been confirmed by Simson et al. (1977), who found that the later segment of the CNV is localized primarily over the central cortex. McCallum, Papakostopoulos, and Griffith (1966) recorded CNVs from areas of the human brain stem and midbrain. Delineation of CNV generators, however, is a complicated business, because, as pointed out by Vaughan and Arezzo (1988), these slow negative potentials have contributions from sensory, motor, and association cortex that vary in relative magnitude according to the nature of the stimuli, the task, and motor response requirements. According to Elbert (1993), large slow potentials (greater than $10\mu V$) have electrical sources mainly in extended cortical regions. Subcortical neurons may contribute to activity measured at the scalp, but they account for only a small part of the response. However, generators that are capable of triggering widespread cortical activity may be located in subcortical areas (e.g., thalamus or other brain-stem areas). Elbert argued that a large surface-negative potential, such as CNV, indicates activity in vast networks of cortical neurons, and an *increase* in excitability of this cortical tissue. He interpreted this as signifying that stimuli presented when cortical regions are easily excitable (as during enhanced CNV development) will be processed efficiently. Evidence presented later offers some support for this view.

Another type of SPS, the readiness potential (RP), has been recorded from areas of brain stem and midbrain in human patients by McCallum et al. (1976). These investigators reported that the RPs had distributions throughout the brain stem and midbrain. Deecke (1976) observed that the scalp-recorded RP is pronounced over parietal areas and nonexistent at frontal sites.

Summary.   There are data that link certain sensory ERPs and motor potentials to activity in or near subcortical and cortical sensory and motor areas. Results from human and animal studies have implicated contralateral precentral cortical areas in the production of MPs associated with voluntary movements. Scalp recordings of late positive components, CNVs, and RPs reveal maximal response at frontal, central, and parietal areas, respectively. The continued use of topographical approaches and the development of appropriate research using animal models and data from human clinical patients are essential to further progress in identifying the brain areas responsible for generating various ERPs. The use of MEG and PET techniques will also help in this difficult endeavor. Coles, Gratton, and Fabiani (1990) pointed out that neural structures having appropriate spatial orientations with respect to the scalp will contribute more to ERPs than other structures. Therefore, brain areas organized in layers, such as the cortex and thalamus, are more likely to contribute to scalp-recorded ERPs than those that are randomly organized such as some midbrain nuclei. Elbert (1993) indicates extended cortical areas as the main sources of the activity observed in the large slow brain potentials.

METHOD FOR OBTAINING ERPs

As pointed out previously, ERPs are derived from the EEG. Therefore, before one can obtain these potentials, the EEG must be recorded, as discussed in chapter 2. That is, the system of placing electrodes is the same, as well as the location designations, according to the "10–20 International System." If a researcher is interested in obtaining visual ERPs, he or she might place recording electrodes at O_1 and O_2 corresponding to locations over the left- and right-occipital areas. Researchers may also wish to place electrodes over other brain areas (such as parietal, temporal, and frontal) to determine how responses from these areas vary with the kind of visual stimulus (its shape or color or its meaning, e.g., pure sounds or words).

Normally, when the EEG is recorded in a relaxed person and a visual stimulus is presented, some gross activity change, such as alpha desynchronization, may be seen. The ERP will not easily be discernible in the EEG recording, because it is usually smaller than background EEG activity. Therefore, the evoked potential must be extracted from the EEG by using an averaging technique in which EEG samples are taken at the instant each successive visual stimulus is presented. The EEG samples are fed into a digital computer, which sums the individual evoked potentials to successive flashes of light, for example. Thus, the system is set up so that the presentation of a stimulus will produce sampling by a computer over a preset period of time, and depending on the ERP of interest, the sample time could vary between 20 msec (brain-stem potentials) to 2000 msec or more (CNV). It should be emphasized, therefore, that ERPs are usually averages of a number of brain responses. There are instances where an ERP may be produced by one or a few presentations of a stimulus. For example, in a study by Cooper et al. (1977), ERPs were obtained to a single stimulus; and it is common to obtain the CNV with as few as 6 to 12 stimuli. Figure 5.3 shows single ERPs recorded from occipital and parietal scalp locations in response to a visual stimulus. This single trial illustrates the beginnings of a definable brain response, with a noticeable negative peak at 200 msec and a slow wave developing between 300 and 400 msec after stimulus presentation. Note that the signal averaging begins about 200 msec before the presentation of the stimulus and includes a 10-μV calibration signal for the ERP channels and a 25-μV signal for the EOG (electrooculogram or eye movement channels). The lines labeled *lateral* and *vertical EOG* refer to the recordings of lateral and vertical eye movements. It is important to record EOG along with brain activity since the EOG signal is rather large and can easily contaminate EEG recorings. Figure 5.4 shows a trial that was excluded from the ERP average because it was contaminated by an eye blink that shows up most clearly in the channel labeled vertical EOG, but also influenced horizontal EOG, and completely distorted the brain responses that occurred at 200 msec and between 300 and 400 msec after stimulus presentation (as illustrated in Fig. 5.3).

A basic premise in obtaining averaged ERPs is that the changes in brain activity are time-locked to some event, whereas the background EEG activity stays approximately the same during stimulus presentation periods. For example, suppose a single ERP is 10 μV and the background EEG activity is 20 μV. It is assumed that the ERP will increase as a function of N samples (e.g., $N = 100$), but the background EEG will increase as function of the square root of N. This can be expressed mathematically as:

$$\frac{\text{Evoked potential amplitude }(N)}{\text{EEG amplitude }(\sqrt{N})} = \frac{10\ \mu\text{V }(100)}{20\ \mu\text{V }(10)} = \frac{1,000}{200} = 5.00$$

Thus, the value 5.00 represents an ERP that will be larger than the background activity. Usually, an averaged ERP that is twice the background EEG amplitude will be easily recognized. This ratio may be increased by increasing the number of samples.

Figure 5.5 shows a schematic drawing of the basic elements required to obtain a visual ERP. Depicted are a light source, a subject with appropriate electrode attachments, a physiological recorder, a computer to sum and store responses, and an X–Y plotter. If the light intensity is high, the visual ERP may be obtained with the eyes closed. Note that the left ear is shown as the location of a reference electrode. In actual practice, researchers prefer to place electrodes in a "linked ear" configuration, in which leads from the two earlobes are joined to form a single reference. Another popular reference is "linked mastoids," where leads from behind the lower portions of both ears are connected to form a common reference representing both sides of the head. Some prefer to use a nose reference to equate for possible spatial effects of locating a reference on one side of the head only.

Equipment manufacturers have simplified the task of the ERP researcher by developing convenient equipment packages with a number of excellent features to allow much greater flexibility than the earlier computer of average transients. These devices allow for easy acquisition of ERP data by providing programmable parameters through an interactive keyboard. For example, the researcher may enter the number of trials to be taken, the amplification for the signal, required time constants, and appropriate filtering. There can be an automatic reject feature that allows omission of eye movement or muscle artifact from the ERP by excluding any values beyond a preset criterion from the average. Sampling can continue until the programmed number of uncontaminated responses is obtained. In most systems of data acquisition, the resulting ERPs are stored onto disk for later analysis, including evaluation of amplitudes and latencies of the various ERP components through the use of a cursor-operated internal program. ERPs are typically printed out for a hard copy record, which

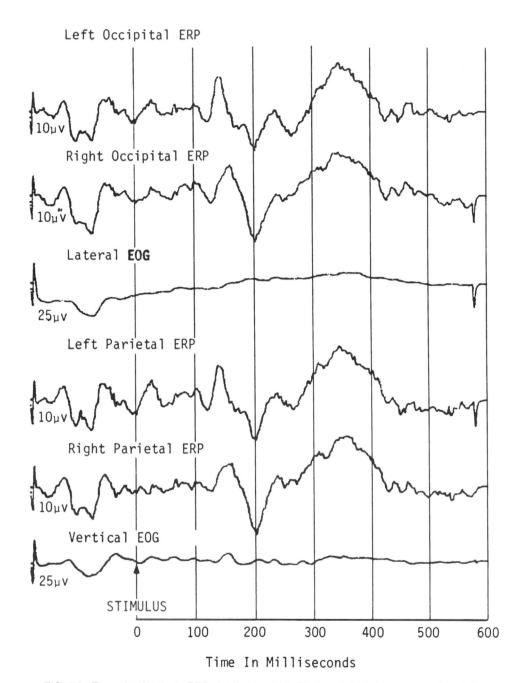

FIG. 5.3. Example of a single ERP trial (acceptable). Starting at the top, responses from left and right occipital and left and right parietal areas are shown. Also shown are lateral (horizontal) and vertical EOG (eye movements). Note that the calibration signal differs for ERP and EOG (10 and 25 μV). Note also that positivity is upward, and that a positive-going wave appears in this single trial, between 300 and 400 msec poststimulus (P300). (From author's unpublished data.)

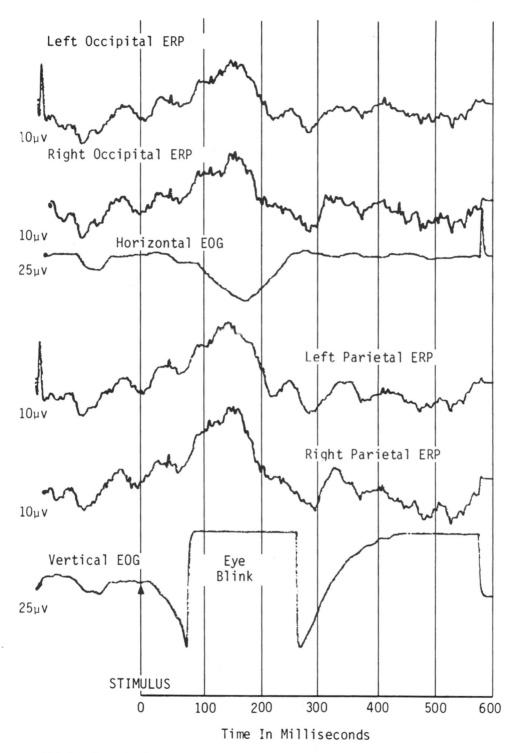

FIG. 5.4. Example of a single trial excluded because of eye movement contamination (an eyeblink). (From author's unpublished data.)

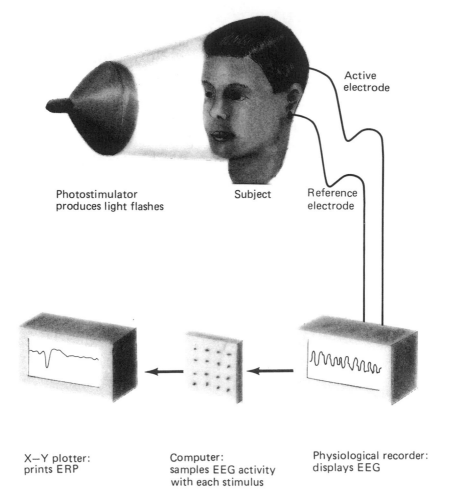

Photostimulator
produces light flashes

Active
electrode

Subject

Reference
electrode

X—Y plotter:
prints ERP

Computer:
samples EEG activity
with each stimulus

Physiological recorder:
displays EEG

FIG. 5.5. Schematic drawing of recording situation to obtain a visual ERP. A stimulus source (light flashes), electrodes, physiological recorder, digital computer, and X-Y plotter are shown in the sequence from initiation of the stimulus to the printout of the ERP. Additional equipment might be a tape system to store brain activity and an oscilloscope for additional on-line monitoring of the EEG.

includes latency and amplitude measurements for selected components. There is usually enough flexibility to obtain a variety of ERPs, from the very short latency brain-stem responses to the slowly developing CNVs. Prepackaged systems are convenient, but expensive. As a result, many different computer systems are used to obtain ERPs in the various research laboratories in the United States and abroad. Researchers with appropriate engineering support often design their own systems, making use of commercially available equipment components from different manufacturers in meeting their own needs.

QUANTIFICATION OF ERPs

There are a number of ways to designate and measure amplitude and latencies of the various positive and negative waves of the ERP. The two visual ERPs shown in Fig. 5.6 were each produced by 100 flashes of light presented to the same person. Negative components are labeled

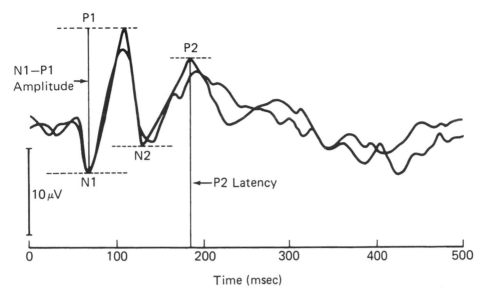

FIG. 5.6. Method for measuring amplitudes and latencies of ERP components. The amplitude of the N1-P1 component (larger of the two traces) is 17.2 μV, based on the calibrated 10 μV signal. The P2 latency is 190 msec. Each of these two ERPs was based on averaged responses to 100 light flashes, on two different occasions. Negativity is downward. (From author's unpublished data.)

as N and positive components, as P. (It should be noted that some investigators designate the downward-going component as positive, or P, and the upward one as negative, or N. This usage was originated in European laboratories.) There are two positive and two negative waves, or components, clearly visible in Fig. 5.6. The N1 component illustrated here was considered to be the first negative dip in the tracing that occurred 50 msec after presentation of the stimulus. The amplitude of the N1 component was measured as the vertical distance from "baseline" (initial horizontal portion of the X–Y plot) to the trough of this first depression. The P1 component was measured as the vertical distance from N1 to the peak of the first positive component, whereas N2 was measured as the vertical distance from the peak of P1 to the trough of the second major depression, and so on for P2. The latencies (or time after stimulus presentation) were measured to the midpoints of each positive and negative peak. If the peak is flat and appears more as a plateau, then the midpoint of the plateau is taken as the latency measurement. The amplitudes (in μV) and latencies (in msec) of the larger of the two visual ERPs in Fig. 5.6 (Condition A) were obtained according to these criteria. The amplitude of P1 will depend on the degree of negativity of N1, and so on. Therefore, it is more accurate to refer to N1–P1 amplitude when giving magnitudes of response. More detailed techniques for measuring ERP components and analyzing them are contained in Coles et al. (1990).

Vaughan (1969) suggested a flexible system for indicating polarity and latency of various ERP components. For example, a negative component at 150 msec would be labeled N150, and a positive wave at 200 msec would be designated P200. This suggestion has been adopted by most ERP workers and is used today.

The equipment for obtaining a P300 is identical to that used for sensory ERPs. However, the sample time after stimulus presentation is extended to about 1,000 to 1,500 msec. To demonstrate P300, a subject might be requested to detect an occasional different stimulus (e.g., a soft tone) interspersed in a series of loud tones. This task is called an "odd-ball" paradigm. When ERPs to soft and loud tones are summed, odd stimuli will produce a larger positive wave in the ERP than will frequent stimuli, and this will occur at approximately 300 msec after presentation.

The typical method for obtaining CNV involves the presentation of a warning stimulus (S1), followed within a fixed time period by a second stimulus (S2) to which the subject responds. The S1 may be a light, S2 may be a tone, and the response might be a key press. The interval between S1–S2 might be 1.5 sec (see Fig. 5.2). The CNV is maximally recorded with a scalp lead at C_z (vertex) with an appropriate reference site. An important consideration in the measurement of CNV is the time constant (TC) used. (The TC is the time for the amplitude of a wave to fall from 100% to 37% of its input value; Geddes, 1967.) The TC should be long with respect to the physiological event being recorded. Cooper (1976) recommended, as a rule of thumb, that the TC should be at least three times the S1–S2 interval. Cooper has mentioned that use of an insufficiently short time constant results in a CNV that falls below baseline after resolution of CNV. Tecce (personal communication, 1979) recommended a TC of 8 sec for S1–S2 intervals varying from 1 to 2 sec. The consensus among investigators is that time constants between 1 and 10 sec be used with all endogenous components, including P300. The CNV may be obtained by averaging responses to between 6 and 12 combinations (trials) of S1 and S2 (Tecce, 1972). Electrical potentials produced by eye movements and blinks are possible sources of contamination in ERPs, especially the CNV. The measurement of these eye potentials and exclusion of contaminated trials produces satisfactory results.

The readiness potential (RP) can be produced in situations that require subjects to make voluntary movements at regular intervals. The recording electrode may be placed at C_z, and brain activity is sampled for several seconds prior to the movement until shortly after the motion is completed. A typical RP between 10 and 15 μV in amplitude may be obtained by taking 32 to 64 samples of brain activity with a time constant of 5 sec (e.g., see Becker, Iwase, Jurgens, & Kornhuber, 1976). Now that a variety of ERPs have been described, we shall see how they are related to human behavior.

ERPs AND BEHAVIOR

As mentioned previously, studies using the ERP have multiplied at an increasing rate over the years. The review presented here necessarily must be restricted because of space limitations. However, an attempt is made to convey to the beginning student a sampling of past and present work in this area. The advanced student is referred to Rebert, Tecce, Marczynski, Pirch, and Thompson (1986) for an interesting account of underlying ERP physiology and theory that uses both animal and human models.

The discussion concerning ERPs and behavior has been divided among three chapters 5, 6, and 7. This chapter covers ERP correlates of motor performance, hemispheric asymmetries, and ERPs during sleep. The questions examined here include changes that occur in ERPs with more efficient RT, the effects of bisensory stimulation on RT and ERPs, motor potentials under conditions of passive and active movements, and interactions between motor and visual ERPs. Under the topic of asymmetries in the visual system, the question of how long it takes for a stimulus to travel from one hemisphere to the other is examined. This interhemispheric transfer time (IHTT) has been estimated by RT in the past, but it seems that visual ERPs may provide more accurate estimates. Does stimulation in one ear affect the contralateral auditory ERP to a greater extent than the ipsilateral response? Do speech sounds result in differential ERPs from the two hemispheres? Do probe stimuli produce hemispheric asymmetries in response depending on the cognitive task? What is the nature of the ERP to stimuli presented to sleeping persons? These are among the issues and questions covered in chapter 5. Chapters 6 and 7 consider the relationship between ERPs and other psychological functions.

ERPs and Motor Performance

Reaction Time. The time it takes to respond to an external stimulus is a function of many factors, including stimulus intensity. Studies have shown that response time of the visual system decreases as stimulus intensity increases, whether the measure of time is purely physiological or behavioral. For example, Vaughan, Costa, and Gilden (1966) reported that RT, as well as visual ERP component latencies, decreased as a function of increasing stimulus intensity. Thus, quick reactions were related to shorter ERP latencies.

Donchin and Lindsley (1966) measured RT to a flash of light, using a warning click and a variable foreperiod (from 1.0 to 2.5 sec). They found that visual ERP amplitude and RT were definitely related, with faster RTs associated with larger ERP amplitudes. Telling the subjects how quickly they responded tended to shorten RT and increase ERP amplitude. Morrell and Morrell (1966) also measured RT and visual ERP, the latter being recorded at occipital and central locations. Their results agree with those of Donchin and Lindsley in that increased amplitudes of both positive and negative ERP components were associated with faster RTs. They suggested that factors such as selective attention and fluctuations in alertness are possible determinants of the relationship between RT and VEP amplitude.

Karlin, Martz, Brauth, and Mordkoff (1971) extended the relationship found between ERP amplitude and RT to auditory stimuli. They measured ERPs during simple and choice RT tasks and found larger auditory ERP amplitudes to be associated with faster RTs. In one choice RT condition, stimuli that did not require a motor response resulted in a higher later positive component (P300) than stimuli that did require a response. Thus, it could not be said that the enhancement of late positive components was due to motor potentials. The studies reviewed thus far indicate that there is a relationship between the CNS response to a stimulus and speed of reaction. The relationship has been explained differently in terms of increased reactivity of the nervous system, arousal, or attentiveness. Karlin et al. (1971) suggested that the enhancement of the P300 component found in their study might be related to "effort, or the degree of a subject's self mobilization" (p. 135), and they proposed that holding back a response, in a context where responses are required to be made quickly, may require effort.

Auditory ERPs were measured while subjects engaged in simple RT and an auditory discrimination task involving responses to changes in pitch (Ritter, Simson, & Vaughan, 1972). They found that the P200 component did not vary much in latency under the different conditions. However, P300 latencies were longer (100 to 200 msec) when subjects were required to make auditory (pitch) discriminations. Reaction times were also longer when discriminations were required. Furthermore, P300 latencies and RTs were longer with more difficult discriminations than with relatively easy ones. The P300 component was largest at P_z, smaller at C_z, and smallest at O_z. Thus, the P300 component was related to both discrimination difficulty and response speed.

Bisensory Stimulation. The effects of bisensory stimulation on RT and the ERP were investigated by Andreassi and Greco (1975). Bisensory stimulation refers to the simultaneous, or near simultaneous, stimulation of two sensory systems (e.g., visual and auditory). Because it has long been known that RT to auditory stimuli is faster than to visual presentations, these investigators presented the visual stimuli prior to auditory to achieve simultaneity. The time difference was determined in two ways: The first, called $\Delta(RT)$, used a temporal offset equal to the difference between each subject's RT to light and sound; the second, called $\Delta(N2)$, adjusted the offset to equal the average latency difference of the N2 component to light and sound. It had already been found that N2 occurs earlier to a sound than a light stimulus.

The ERPs were measured from O_z and C_z under conditions of light alone, sound alone, light–sound offset by $\Delta(RT)$, and light–sound offset by $\Delta(N2)$. All conditions of bisensory stimulation resulted in faster RTs than did unisensory stimulation. In addition, bisensory stimulation produced larger amplitude ERPs than did auditory or visual stimulation alone. Andreassi and Greco (1975) proposed that the results indicated the occurrence of facilitative sensory interaction in the nervous system, because bisensory stimulation resulted in faster RTs. They hypothesized that a possible site for this sensory interaction is the ascending reticular formation, because it is known that this subcortical structure has a role in coordinating sensory input and attentional mechanisms (Samuels, 1959; Scheibel & Scheibel, 1967) and has diffuse projections to the cortex.

Summary.   Some studies suggest that faster RTs are associated with higher amplitude ERPs. Others indicated the relation between latencies of certain ERP components and response speed. The ERP amplitude–RT relationship could be a reflection of greater attention and CNS arousal when RTs are fast. In addition, the P300 response latencies and RT were longer when auditory discriminations were more difficult.

Motor Activity and the ERP

Movement-related brain potentials (MPs) have been detected both before and after the onset of voluntary hand movements. Kornhuber and Deecke (1965) first recorded a potential prior to voluntary movement. They found a slow negative wave beginning about 1 sec before the movement, and a large positive complex following movement. The slow negative wave is now termed the *readiness potential* and is discussed further in chapter 7. Vaughan, Costa, Gilden, and Schimmel (1965) recorded a brain potential related to voluntary movement in an RT experiment. In addition, Vaughan and colleagues (1968) found that the MP accompanying voluntary movements was maximal over the Rolandic cortex (see Fig. 5.7). Figure 5.7 shows data from Vaughan et al. (1968) in which MPs recorded from different scalp locations of one subject are illustrated for movements of the right foot. The points of maximal MP amplitude for foot, hand, and tongue movements are related to those brain areas known to produce these movements.

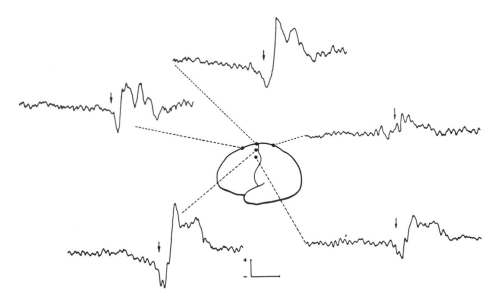

FIG. 5.7. Motor potentials (MPs) associated with dorsiflexion of the right foot. Sum of 400 contractions. Calibration 500 msec, 2.5 μV.

A unique method for examining changes in brain activity that take place during a perceptual–motor task has been developed by Gevins and colleagues (Gevins, Bressler, et al., 1989; Gevins, Cutillo, et al., 1989). The technique makes use of at least 24 recording sites on the scalp and uses a measure called event-related covariance (ERC). The ERCs compute similarity of waveform and timing between brain activity measured at the different electrode sites. This procedure has enabled Gevins and associates to examine coordinated brain activity during perceptual motor tasks. For example, Gevins et al. (1989a) used a visual cue to signal hand of response and precise amount of force to use in making a finger response (0.1 to 0.9 kg) and provided feedback about accuracy 1 sec after completion of the response. On 20% of the trials, the subjects, all right-handed, had to inhibit the response. In the early poststimulus intervals (first 250 msec), ERC patterns varied with the slant of the stimulus. In later intervals, ERCs differed with subjective interpretation of the stimulus. The ERC analyses suggest four cortical generators for the fine motor control demanded by the task: motor cortex, somesthetic cortex, premotor cortex, and prefrontal cortex (the premotor cortex is between motor cortex and prefrontal cortex as shown in Fig. 2.5). The authors also concluded that the ERC pattern for the P300 component in the inhibit response condition suggests more than one neural generator, in agreement with Johnson (1989).

Active and Passive Motor Potentials.   In a careful study of pre- and postmovement brain potentials, Shibasaki, Barrett, Halliday, and Halliday (1980a) identified eight separate components: four premotion and four postmotion. The experiment utilized brisk finger flexions and extensions while MPs were recorded from multiple locations over both hemispheres. The premotion potentials were the readiness potential, beginning 500 msec prior to movement, a negative component 90 msec before, a positive wave 50 msec before, and a negative component 10 msec prior to motion. The postmotion components included a sharp negative component at 50 msec, over the contralateral frontal region, a positive wave at 90 msec, a negative component at 160 msec, and positive component at 300 msec. This last component was maximal over the precentral brain, larger on the side opposite to the movement, and widely distributed. These same scientists then compared the MPs accompanying both passive and voluntary movements in a follow-up study (Shibasaki, Barrett, Halliday, & Halliday, 1980b).

To produce passive movement, the middle finger was tied with a string and pulled up by one of the experimenters. The voluntary movement was an extension of the same finger. There were no premotion components with passive movement, confirming that these components are related to preparation for voluntary movement. The postmovement MPs also differed, and Shibasaki and coworkers suggested that the MPs from passive movements represent kinesthetic feedback from muscle activity.

Finger Versus Foot Motor Potentials.   The MPs preceding flexion of the index fingers and feet were compared for recording sites over frontal, central, and parietal areas of both hemispheres by Brunia and Van Den Bosch (1984). These researchers proposed that, prior to finger movements, amplitudes of MPs would be larger on the same side (ipsilaterally). Their hypothesis was confirmed by the results, which, they said, point to different sources of MPs for finger and foot movements. They suggested that the ipsilateral MP prior to foot movement is due to a motor cortex source in the depths of the longitudinal fissure (the deep furrow that separates the hemispheres) at the contralateral side. Because the preparation for foot movement results in activity so close to the midline, the neuronal response is projected to the opposite hemisphere, producing what appears to be an ipsilateral response.

MP–Visual ERP Interactions.   The effects of muscular activity on the visual ERP have been studied by several investigators. Eason, Aiken, White, and Lichtenstein (1964) measured visual ERPs to flashes of light while subjects maintained a 25-lb force on a hand grip. The muscular work increased the amplitude of visual ERPs to light flashes. Andreassi, Mayzner, Beyda, and Davidovics (1970) measured visual ERPs and MPs from occipital and central areas, respectively, while subjects maintained a right-hand dynamometer grip equivalent to one eighth of their maximal squeeze. The major findings were that visual ERP was greater in magnitude with muscle tension than with a visual stimulus alone, and that the MP was also enhanced under conditions of dual stimulation as compared to squeezing only. Landau and Buchsbaum (1973) used four light intensities and two tasks (relaxation and mental arithmetic) over several days to test effects of holding 10 lbs of weight on visual ERPs. Their recordings were made from the vertex (C_z). They noted two effects: (a) an overall decrease in ERP across days when subjects held the weights, and (b) an increase in ERP amplitude under the weight condition, as compared to relaxation, on the third day of testing. They concluded that both arousal and attentional factors interact with muscle activity to influence the visual ERP.

Summary.   Investigations examining movement-related potentials indicate that brain responses occur both before and after voluntary movements. The lack of MPs with passively produced movements supports the conclusion that premotion MPs represent preparation for voluntary movements. Topographical analyses have provided insights regarding the cortical sources of MPs. The muscle tension studies, in general, indicate that impulses from two senses can interact to influence ERPs recorded at the cortex. For example, input from visual and proprioceptive (muscle) impulses summate in the nervous system and lead to enlargement of ERPs under conditions of dual stimulation. Attentional and arousal factors may also be involved, as suggested by several investigators.

HEMISPHERIC ASYMMETRIES IN ERPs

In the context of ERP research, hemispheric asymmetry refers to the observation of a difference in the ERP recorded from left and right hemispheres as a function of different stimulus or task conditions. In chapter 3, it was concluded that there was evidence for EEG asymmetry with different tasks. For example, the left hemisphere EEG was activated with numerical and verbal tasks, whereas the right hemisphere EEG showed engagement with spatial and musical activities. In this section, we consider evidence regarding ERP asymmetries under a variety of tasks and stimulus conditions.

Asymmetries With Visual Stimulation

If the eyes are fixated straight ahead, the locus of retinal stimulation varies with the position of a stimulus in the visual field. For example, if you look straight ahead while driving a car, the object you focus on will stimulate receptors in the fovea of the retina, whereas objects off to the side will produce "extra foveal" stimulation. A number of studies by Eason and his colleagues indicated a relationship between locus of retinal stimulation and visual ERPs. For example, Eason, Oden, and White (1967) recorded from over left and right hemispheres and found that the occipital area receiving primary projections from the retinal area stimulated produced larger amplitude ERPs than did the other lobe. The right lobe is primary when stimuli appear in the left visual field (LVF), and left is primary for stimuli in the right visual field (RVF). This is because the temporal retina (outside half) of the right eye and nasal retina (toward the nose) of the left eye are primarily stimulated by objects in the LVF. Both of these retinal areas project visual impulses to the right hemisphere. The opposite occurs for stimuli in the RVF.

ERPs and Interhemispheric Transfer Time (IHTT).   Common strategies in neuropsychological and psychophysiological research involve the presentation of stimuli in left and right visual fields in order to study possible processing asymmetries of the left and right hemispheres of the brain. This strategy makes use of the visual system's organization, in which primary projection of information is to the contralateral hemisphere, for example, RVF stimulation results in primary excitation of neurons in the left hemisphere. The effects of stimulus location on the visual ERP were examined by Andreassi, Okamura, and Stern (1975). They found that stimuli presented in the LVF resulted in shorter ERP latencies at the right occipital area than at the left, whereas the opposite occurred for stimuli presented in the RVF. The same size (.67 degree) stimulus was presented in seven different locations, ranging from center to 4 degrees of visual angle in the left and right fields. In addition, amplitudes of these early VEP components (N2 peaking at about 170 msec and P2 at about 200 msec) were larger with contralateral stimulation. This field effect on visual ERP latency differentials from the two hemispheres has also been reported by Andreassi, Rebert, and Larsen (1980); Ledlow, Swanson, and Kinsbourne (1978); and Rugg, Lines, and Milner (1985).

A likely explanation for the delay in visual ERP from the secondary hemisphere is that it represents the time it takes for the visual impulse to crossover from the primary projection area to the secondary one via the corpus callosum. (Recall that the corpus is a thick band of fibers that connects the two hemipheres of the brain.) The callosal transfer of neuronal response from contralateral to ipsilateral hemispheres is supported by results obtained with two individuals born without a corpus callosum (Rugg, Milner, & Lines, 1985). In both patients, visual ERPs were obtained at hemispheres contralateral to the stimulus, but the N160 component was not observable ipsilaterally. Thus, the integrity of the corpus callosum is necessary for the interhemispheric transmission of the N160 component of the visual ERP. Transmission of other component activity to the ipsilateral hemisphere was possibly due to less prominent connections between the two hemispheres, such as the anterior commissure.

Some controversy has arisen over whether estimates of the time it takes to transfer impulses from one side of the brain to the other (IHTT) are more accurate with ERPs or RT. The model of RT as a measure of IHTT says that if a stimulus is projected to the contralateral hemisphere, then the RT will be shorter if that hemisphere also controls the hand that makes the response. Thus, a stimulus in the RVF results in quicker RT if the right hand is used, because the left hemisphere controls motor activity on the right side. The difference between a right-hand and left-hand response with RVF stimulation would be the estimate of IHTT (e.g., see Berlucchi, Crea, DiStefano, & Tassinari, 1977). Estimates of IHTT using RT have reached a consensus of 2.5 msec in a number of studies (Rugg et al., 1985). Ledlow et al. (1978) used both RT and ERP measures of IHTT and concluded that RT was not as good an estimate because slight changes in hand position could result in different measures. Kinsbourne, Swanson, and Ledlow (1977) suggested that RT measures are confounded by attentional variables that produce RT variations greater than the IHTT being measured. Estimates of IHTT using ERPs range from 10 msec (Andreassi & Juszczak, 1983) to 20 msec (Ledlow et al., 1978).

The Importance of Central Fixation in Visual ERP Asymmetry Research.   The finding of contralateral ERP latency advantages has been very consistent (Andreassi & Juszczak, 1983). An exception to this contralateral advantage has been observed in strabismic subjects (Andreassi & Juszczak, 1984). Strabismus is a condition of unequal muscle balance of the two eyes. Persons with this problem have difficulty in focusing the two eyes on an object. When compared to those with normal eye balance, strabismic individuals do not show the expected latency advantage at the hemisphere contralateral to stimulation. Therefore, in using the strategy of differential visual field stimulation to study hemisphere asymmetries in function, subjects should be screened for strabismus because stimuli displaced from the central visual field (CVF) do not arrive at the contralateral hemisphere in the expected manner for these persons.

Facial and Emotional Stimuli.   The logic behind examining ERP hemispheric differences is that varied amplitudes or latencies to various kinds of stimuli suggest differential processing of these stimuli. Small (1983) conducted a study to see if visual ERPs would show hemispheric asymmetry to slides of familiar and unfamiliar faces. An early component (P100) was of similar amplitude from both hemispheres, whereas the later P300 was larger over the right hemisphere for familiar faces. This interesting finding suggests greater right hemisphere participation in the perception of faces. Evidence for a greater involvement of the right hemisphere for processing of face-like stimuli was obtained in a study by Kayser et al. (1997). In that study pictures of patients with dermatological diseases before (negative) and after (neutral) cosmetic surgery were selectively presented to left or right hemispheres through a central visual fixation technique. Asymmetries in emotional processing occurred for N2 and early P3 responses, with maximal effect over the right parietal area. The N2–P3 amplitude was increased for negative and reduced for neutral stimuli over the right hemisphere, thus pointing to right hemisphere locations in processing of affective stimuli. In addition, there is evidence from clinical studies that patients with right hemisphere damage show greater loss in facial recognition than those with left hemisphere lesions.

Asymmetries With Auditory Stimulation

Sounds.   Right and left hemisphere ERPs were recorded during conditions of monaural (one ear) and binaural (two ear) stimulation (Andreassi, DeSimone, Friend, & Grota, 1975). The stimulus used was white noise at a level of 80 dB. Andreassi and colleagues found that auditory stimulation produced larger amplitude ERPs in the contralateral hemispheres as compared to the ipsilateral. This agrees with a finding in a previous study (Butler, Keidel, & Spreng, 1969). Andreassi et al. found no difference in ERP latencies from contralateral and ipsilateral hemispheres. The amplitude results were interpreted as providing further evidence for the predominance of the contralateral pathways of the auditory system. It is known that each ear has more neuronal connections leading to the hemisphere on the opposite side than to the auditory cortex on the same side as the ear that is stimulated.

The reliability of auditory ERP measures of contralateral dominance was demonstrated in a careful experiment by Connolly (1985). He tested people on six different occasions, using recordings from T_3 and T_4, and reported consistently larger responses in the hemisphere contralateral to the ear of stimulation. Thus, the stability of the contralateral effect is strongly supported, and Connolly suggested its potential importance in assessing effects of drugs or psychopathology on brain activity.

Words.   One might expect that simultaneous stimulation of left and right ears with verbal stimuli would lead to superior detection performance by the right ear, because dominant pathways from the right ear lead to the left hemisphere, which controls language function in most people. This has been found to be the case in a number of studies in which the two ears were presented with different word stimuli at the same time (Kimura, 1961, 1967). The superiority of contralateral presentations has been consistently reported by Kimura and her colleagues in this so-called *dichotic listening paradigm.*

The effects of more complex stimuli on the ERP, such as speech stimuli and word meaning, are discussed in chapter 6. With regard to asymmetry, however, it may be noted that Morrell and Salamy (1971) found ERP amplitudes recorded from over the left hemisphere to be larger than those from the right in response to speech stimuli. Asymmetries have also been reported for linguistic information (Wood, Goff, & Day, 1971), speech versus mechanical sound-effect stimuli (Matsumiya, Tagliasco, & Lombroso, 1972), contextual meaning of words (Brown, Marsh, & Smith, 1973), and verb and noun meanings of ambiguous words (Teyler, Roemer, & Harrison, 1973). However, Grabow and Elliott (1974), who required their subjects to make either simple speech sounds (e.g., ba) or words (e.g., kangaroo), found no evidence for hemispheric asymmetries during verbalization. A similar negative finding has been reported by Galambos, Benson, Smith, Schulman-Galambos, and Osier (1975). Other attempts to find greater activity in the left hemisphere with speech stimuli have not met with success. For example, Grabow, Aronson, Offord, Rose, and Greene (1980) and Grabow, Aronson, Rose, and Greene (1980) failed to repeat the findings of L. K. Morrell and Salamy (1971) and Wood et al. (1971). Further, Woods and Elmasian (1986) found that the hemispheres had similar responses to speech or tone stimuli. Thus, functional asymmetries of the hemispheres to word or speech stimuli have yet to be demonstrated consistently through the use of ERPs.

Asymmetries and Cognitive Functions

Intelligence. Rhodes, Dustman, and Beck (1969) reported that bright children produced right hemisphere visual ERPs that were larger than their left-sided ERPs. This contrasted with dull children, who had no hemispheric amplitude asymmetries. A similar finding was obtained by Richlin, Weisinger, Weinstein, Giannini, and Morganstern (1971), who found larger right hemisphere visual ERPs in children of normal intelligence but the reverse effect with retarded children.

Verbal and Spatial Tasks. Galin and Ellis (1975) recorded visual ERPs to probe stimuli from over left and right hemispheres while subjects performed verbal and spatial tasks. It was concluded that the ERP asymmetry obtained reflected hemispheric specialization for these tasks. However, Mayes and Beaumont (1977) failed to repeat these results. They suggested that the original study of Galin and Ellis was flawed because of differences in hand–arm use and direction of gaze required in the two tasks.

Papanicolaou, Schmidt, Moore, and Eisenberg (1983) avoided the difficulties of the Galin and Ellis study by using a procedure involving the recording of ERPs to a probe stimulus while different cognitive operations were performed on the same materials. Auditory ERPs to a probe tone stimulus were recorded while subjects engaged in either an arithmetic or a visuospatial task using the same irregular geometric shapes. The probe ERP was smaller at left hemisphere sites during arithmetic computations and at right hemisphere areas with the spatial task. The researchers interpreted the decreases in ERP amplitudes as indicants of greater hemispheric engagement in a given task.

In another study, Papanicolaou, Levin, Eisenberg, and Moore (1983) recorded ERPs to a probe click stimulus while subjects listened only to the click (control), detected a given syllable (phonetic processing), or judged the emotions communicated by different speakers (affective processing). The two experimental conditions involved listening to the same taped conversation. The probe ERPs were much larger in both hemispheres under the control condition than with either phonetic (left hemisphere) or emotional (right hemisphere) processing. The results indicated dominance of the left hemisphere during phonetic processing and greater right hemisphere involvement in reacting to verbal emotional content.

The slow potential shifts (SPSs) of good and poor spatial test performers were measured during spatial and verbal processing by Vitouch, Bauer, Gittler, Leodolter, and Leodolter (1997). Those poor in spatial performance showed higher amplitude shifts and asymmetric activity in right parietal–temporal areas, whereas more efficient spatial performers showed symmetrical activity in occipito-parietal regions. The findings emphasize the importance of the right posterior cortex for spatial processing. Greater left hemisphere activity was shown for both groups during the verbal task. The fact that cortical activity was greater and more widespread in poor spatializers, especially in the right hemisphere, suggests that their brains were working harder than those with good spatial ability. This idea receives support from a PET study in which glucose metabolism was greater for those scoring more poorly in abstract reasoning, suggesting greater effort being expended by less efficient persons (Vitouch et al., 1997).

Evaluative Categorizations.   Individuals were asked to make evaluative judgments about food items (positive or negative) or nonevaluative categorizations (vegetable or non-vegetable) while P300 responses were measured from over right and left hemispheres (Crites and Cacioppo, 1996). Asymmetrical response was observed during the evaluative categorizations such that right hemisphere P300s were significantly larger. The authors proposed that this result might be due to activation of right hemisphere structures that assess the emotional importance of stimuli. In a series of follow-up experiments, Cacioppo, Crites, and Gardner (1996) confirmed the greater contribution of right hemisphere-based P300 as a function of evaluative categorizations. The result was extended to situations in which subjects judged personality traits, expressed attitudes, or judged emotionally provocative photographs. The finding that P300 amplitude is significantly larger over the right hemisphere during stimulus evaluations is consistent with the the processing of emotionally and motivationally significant information by this hemisphere, and also points to the role of P300 as an endogenous component whose form is determined by the meaning of stimuli to the individual.

Summary.   A number of studies have indicated a relationship between location of stimuli in the visual field and hemispheric asymmetries in the visual ERP. The observed latency and amplitude differences have been explained in terms of the primary projection of stimuli to the contralateral hemisphere. That a response occurs at the ipsilateral cortex at all is due to crossing of neural impulses via the corpus callosum and other commissures that connect the left and right hemispheres. Visual ERP asymmetries have also been reported for familiar faces, suggesting greater right hemisphere participation in the perception of faces.

Hemispheric asymmetries occur with auditory stimulation as a function of the ear stimulated. The higher amplitude responses from the contralateral hemispheres have been interpreted as consistent with the known contralateral predominance in the pathways of the auditory system—that is, the contralateral pathways contain a larger number of neurons than the ipsilateral. Auditory ERP asymmetries for speech and language materials have been reported by some investigators and not by others. This area is still unsettled, and perhaps we will not see any firm conclusions until techniques for testing differences have been standardized. The use of probe stimuli during hemispheric engagement with different types of materials (e.g., phonetic or emotional) seems promising in this respect.

There is some evidence to indicate that ERP asymmetries may be related to intelligence and cognitive functioning. The evidence concerning intelligence is rather tenuous, whereas that regarding cognitive functioning seems to be gaining, for example, findings regarding differential hemispheric engagement in phonetic and affective processing. Slow potential shifts have been found to occur in greater amplitude at right hemisphere sites during performance of spatial tasks. Greater and more widespread SPSs have been reported for those poor in spatial abilitity compared to those who are more efficient spatially. Categorizations of stimuli with regard to positive and negative attributes has been found to engage the P300 system of the right hemisphere, pointing to the importance of this brain area in processing emotional materials.

THE ERP AND SLEEP

The classification of sleep into distinct stages on the basis of EEG and REM was discussed in chapter 4 (see Table 4.2). These distinctions have enabled investigators to present sensory stimuli to persons in different sleep stages in order to study ERPs as a function of these stages. Shagass (1972) summarized findings regarding the somatosensory ERP (SERP) obtained during sleep as follows: (a) latencies of SERPs become longer as sleep progresses from Stage 1 to 4; (b) the SERP during REM sleep is similar to that obtained during light sleep stages; (c) amplitude changes are not as consistent as those observed for latency, but early components are generally enlarged during slow-wave sleep; and (d) the SERP gradually (taking as long as 30 min) returns to the presleep level after awakening.

Shagass and Trusty (1966) found a systematic relationship between visual ERP latencies and sleep stages, that is, progressive lengthening of latencies from Stage 1 to Stage 4. Weitzman and Kremen (1965) reported similar relationships between auditory ERP latencies and sleep stage.

Very early auditory ERPs, occurring between 1 and 10 msec after stimulation, have been found by Jewett and Williston (1971) and related to activity evoked from brain stem auditory structures. These early responses have been termed *brain stem auditory evoked responses* (BAERs). Amadeo and Shagass (1973) experimented to determine whether the BAER would differ in awake and sleeping individuals. Their results showed little difference in amplitude and latency of these brain stem potentials either between waking and sleep or between sleep stages. However, this finding is questioned by findings of Marshall and Donchin (1981), who observed delays in several components of the BAER with decreases in body temperature, and the temperature decreases occurred when the subjects slept. In another study, significant delays in Wave V latency and Wave I to IV latency in the BAER occurred during Stages 2, 3, and 4 sleep (Bastuji, Larrea, Bertrand, & Mauguiere, 1988). The delays in BAER components were clearly related to decreases in body temperature during those stages of sleep. Thus, the assumption that BAERs do not change from the waking state to sleep has been brought into question from the results of these last mentioned sleep studies.

Early components (latencies less than 40 msec) of the auditory ERP were studied during REM and Stages 2, 3, and 4 sleep by Mendel and Kupperman (1974). These early components, obtained during REM sleep, had the same latency, amplitude, and waveform as auditory ERPs elicited during other sleep stages. ERP waveforms with latencies of about 150 to 170 msec have been shown to decrease in amplitude with sleep (Naatanen & Picton, 1987). These latter researchers reported on work that confirms decreases in the 150 to 170 msec latency wave, but shows an additional later wave to auditory stimuli during NREM sleep, especially early in the night (see Naatanen & Picton, 1987, p. 407).

Buchsbaum, Ginnin, and Pfefferbaum (1975) studied the effects of sleep stage and stimulus intensity on auditory ERPs. Clicks ranging from 50 to 80 dB were used as stimuli. They found that auditory ERP amplitudes increased more with increasing stimulus intensity during Stages 2, 3, and 4 sleep than during REM sleep or when subjects were awake. Townsend, House, and Johnson (1976) exposed subjects to tone pulses 24 hrs a day for 30 days. The intensity levels were at 70, 80, and 90 dB for 10 days each, in that order. The auditory ERPs were examined in Stage 2 and REM sleep on every fifth night of the 30-day period. One finding was that the auditory ERP in Stage 2 sleep was consistently larger than in REM sleep. The main finding was that during sleep there was little habituation of the auditory ERP, even with long-term, daily exposure to the same stimulus. Thus, they concluded that the auditory ERP during sleep is similar to the K-complex (see chapter 4) in terms of resistance to habituation. (Recall that the K-complex is considered to be the sleeping EEG analog of the orienting response.) Thus, the authors pointed out that during sleep, the auditory ERP behaves as though each succeeding stimulus is a first presentation. Brain responses were compared during waking and two sleep stages (REM and NREM) to tones differing in pitch and probability (Nordby, Hugdahl, Stickgold, Bronnick, & Hobson, 1996). The N1 component occurred later and P2 was larger during sleep than when awake. The N1 to infrequent tones was larger during both sleep stages. A late negative wave was significantly larger to infrequent tones during REM sleep. The authors concluded that auditory discriminations can be made during both REM and NREM sleep. However, the longer latency of ERPs during sleep indicates that processing of external stimuli is slowed down and perhaps less accurate during sleep.

Summary.   The overall findings regarding ERPs during sleep indicate that they definitely occur, and that the later components differ from waking ERPs in latency and amplitude. Sleep is an example, therefore, of a situation where a brain response occurs to a stimulus that is probably not consciously perceived. In addition, delays in component waves of the BAER occur during sleep and seem to be related to body temperature rather than sleep stage.

Event-related brain potentials and various mental functions—including intelligence, meaning of stimuli, linguistic processing, learning, and hypnosis—are covered in the next chapter. Sensory, attentional, and perceptual processes and their relations to ERPs are also presented in chapter 6.

REFERENCES

Amadeo, M., & Shagass, C. (1973). Brief latency click-evoked potentials during waking and sleep in man. *Psychophysiology, 10*, 224–250.

Andreassi, J. L., DeSimone, J. J., Friend, M. A., & Grota, P. A. (1975), Hemispheric amplitude asymmetries in the auditory evoked potential with monaural and binaural stimulation. *Physiological Psychology, 3*, 169–171.

Andreassi, J. L., & Greco, J. R. (1975). Effects of bisensory stimulation on reaction time and the evoked cortical potential. *Physiological Psychology, 3*, 189–194.

Andreassi, J. L., & Juszczak, N. M. (1983). *Brain responses and information processing IV: Investigations of hemispheric asymmetry in event-related potentials and performance during discrimination of line orientation, color, shape, and under visual masking.* Fourth Annual Report, Baruch College, CUNY, AFOSR Contract F49620-80-C-0013.

Andreassi, J. L., & Juszczak, N. M. (1984). To fixate or not to fixate: The problem of undetected strabismic subjects in visual evoked potential research. In R. Karrer, J. Cohen, & P. Teuting (Eds.), *Brain & information: Event-related potentials* (pp. 157–161). New York: Annals of the N.Y. Academy of Sciences.

Andreassi, J. L., Mayzner, M. S., Beyda, D. R., & Davidovics, S. (1970). Effects of induced muscle tension upon the visual evoked potential and motor potential. *Psychonomic Science, 20*, 245–247.

Andreassi, J. L., Okamura, H., & Stern, M. S. (1975). Hemispheric asymmetries in the visual evoked cortical potential as a function of stimulus location. *Psychophysiology, 12*, 541–546.

Andreassi, J. L., Rebert, C. S., & Larsen, F. F. (1980). *Brain responses and information processing I: Hemispheric asymmetries in event-related potentials during signal detection.* First Annual Report, Baruch College, CUNY, AFOSR Contract F49620-80-C-0013.

Arezzo, J. C., & Vaughan, H. G., Jr. (1975). Cortical potentials associated with voluntary movements in the monkey. *Brain Research, 88*, 99–104.

Arezzo, J. C., Vaughan, H. G., Jr., Kraut, M. A., Steinschneider, M., & Legatt, A. D. (1986). Intracranial generators of event-related potentials in the monkey. In R. Q. Cracco & I. BodisWollner (Eds.), *Evoked potentials* (pp. 174–189). New York: Liss.

Bastuji, H., Larrea, L. G., Bertrand, O., & Mauguiere, F. (1988). BAEP latency changes during nocturnal sleep are not correlated with sleep stages but with body temperature variations. *Electroencephalography and Clinical Neurophysiology, 70*, 9–15.

Beck, E. C. (1975). Electrophysiology and behavior. *Annual Review of Psychology, 26*, 233–262.

Becker, W., Iwase, R., Jurgens, R., & Kornhuber, H. H. (1976). Bereitschaftspotential preceding voluntary slow and rapid hand movements. In W. C. McCallum & J. R. Knott (Eds.), *The responsive brain* (pp. 99–102). Bristol: John Wright & Sons.

Berlucchi, G., Crea, T., DiStefano, M., & Tassinari, G. (1977). Influence of spatial stimulus–response compatibility on reaction time of ipsilateral and contralateral hand to lateralized light stimuli. *Journal of Experimental Psychology: Human Perception and Performance, 3*, 505–517.

Beuzeron-Mangina, J. H. (1996). Intracerebral event-related potentials during memory workload. *International Journal of Psychophysiology, 22,* 9–23.

Brown, W. S., Marsh, J. T., & Smith, J. C. (1973). Contextual meaning effects in speech-evoked potentials. *Behavioral Biology, 9,* 755–761.

Bruneau, N., Roux, S., Guerin, P., Barthelemy, C., & Lelord, G. (1997). Temporal prominence of auditory evoked potentials (N1 wave) in 4 to 8 year olds. *Psychophysiology, 34,* 32–38.

Brunia, C. H. M., & Van Den Bosch, W. E. J. (1984). Movement-related slow potentials. I. a contrast between finger and foot movements in right-handed subjects. *Electroencephalography and Clinical Neurophysiology, 57,* 515–527.

Buchsbaum, M., Ginnin, J. C., & Pfefferbaum, A. (1975). Effect of sleep stage and stimulus intensity in auditory average evoked responses. *Psychophysiology, 12,* 707–712.

Butler, R. A., Keidel, W. D., & Spreng, M. (1969). An investigation of the human cortical evoked potential under conditions of monaural and binaural stimulation. *Acta Otolaryngologica, 68,* 317–326.

Cacioppo, J. T., Crites, S. L., & Gardner, W. L. (1996). Attitudes to the right: Evaluative processing is associated with lateralized late positive event-related brain potentials. *Journal of Personality and Social Psychology, 22,* 1205–1219.

Cohen, J. (1969). Very slow brain potentials relating to expectancy: The CNV. In E. Donchin & D. B. Linsley (Eds.), *Average evoked potentials: Methods, results, evaluations.* NASA, Washington, DC: U.S. Government Printing Office.

Coles, M. G. H., Gratton, G., & Fabiani, M. (1990). Event-related brain potentials. In J. T. Cacioppo & L. G. Tassinary (Eds.), *Principles of psychophysiology: Physical, social, and inferential elements* (pp. 413–455). Hillsdale, NJ: Lawrence Erlbaum Associates.

Connolly, J. F. (1985). Stability of pathway–hemisphere differences in the auditory event-related potential (ERP) to monaural stimulation. *Psychophysiology, 22,* 87–95.

Cooper, R. (1976). Methodology of slow potential changes. In W. C. McCallum & J. R. Knott (Eds.), *The responsive brain* (pp. 1–4). Bristol: John Wright & Sons.

Cooper, R., McCallum, W. C., Newton, P., Papakostopoulos, D., Pocock, P. V., & Warren, W. J. (1977). Cortical potentials associated with the detection of visual events. *Science, 196,* 74–77.

Courchesne, E., Hillyard, S. A., & Galambos, R. (1975). Stimulus novelty, task relevance and the visual evoked potential in man. *Electroencephalography and Clinical Neurophysiology, 39,* 131–143.

Crites, S. L., & Cacioppo, J. T. (1996). Electrocortical differentiation of evaluative and nonevaluative categorizations. *Psychological Science, 7,* 318–321.

Deecke, L. (1976). Potential changes associated with motor action, reflex responses and readiness (Chairman's opening remarks). In W. C. McCallum & J. R. Knott (Eds.), *The responsive brain* (pp. 91–93). Bristol: John Wright & Sons.

Diesch, E., & Luce, T. (1997). Magnetic fields elicited by tones and vowel formants reveal tonotopy and nonlinear summation of cortical activation. *Psychophysiology, 34,* 501–510.

Donchin, E., & Lindsley, D. B. (1966). Average evoked potentials and reaction times to visual stimuli. *Electroencephalography and Clinical Neurophysiology, 20,* 217–223.

Eason, R. G., Aiken, L. R., White, C. T., & Lichtenstein, M. (1964). Activation and behavior: II. Visually evoked cortival potentials in man as indicants of activation level. *Perceptual and Motor Skills, 19,* 875–895.

Eason, R. G., Oden, D., & White, C. T. (1967). Visually evoked cortical potentials and reaction time in relation to site of retinal stimulation. *Electroencephalography and Clinical Neurophysiology, 22,* 313–324.

Elbert, T. (1993). Slow cortical potentials reflect the regulation of cortical excitability: In W. C. McCallum & S. H. Curry (Eds.), *Slow potentials of the human brain* (pp. 1–23). New York: Plenum.

Galambos, R., Benson, O., Smith, T. S., Schulman-Galambos, C., & Osier, H. (1975). On hemispheric differences in evoked potentials to speech stimuli. *Electroencephalography and Clinical Neurophysiology, 39,* 279–283.

Galin, D., & Ellis, R. (1975). Asymmetry in evoked potentials as an index of lateralized cognitive processes: Relation to EEG alpha asymmetry. *Neuropsychologia, 13,* 45–50.

Geddes, L. A. (1967). The measurement of physiological phenomena. In C. C. Brown (Ed.), *Methods in psychophysiology* (pp. 369–452). Baltimore: Williams & Wilkens.

Gevins, A. S., Bressler, N. H., Morgan, N. H., Cutillo, B. A., White, R. M., Greer, D. S., & Illes, J. (1989). Event-related covariances during a bimanual visuomotor task. I. Methods and analysis of stimulus- and response-locked data. *Electroencephalography and Clinical Neurophysiology, 74,* 58–75.

Gevins, A. S., Cutillo, B. A., Bressler, S. L., Morgan, N. H., White, R. M., Illes, J., & Greer, D. S. (1989). Event-related covariances during a bimanual visuomotor task. II. Preparation and feedback. *Electroencephalography and Clinical Neurophysiology, 74,* 147–160.

Goff, W. R., Allison, T., & Vaughan, H. G., Jr. (1978). The functional neuroanatomy of event-related potentials. In E. Callaway, P. Teuting, & S. H. Koslow (Eds.), *Event-related potentials in man* (pp. 1–80). New York: Academic Press.

Grabow, J. D., Aronson, A. E., Offord, K. P., Rose, D. E., & Greene, K. L. (1980). Summated potentials evoked by speech sounds for determining cerebral dominance for language. *Electroencephalography and Clinical Neurophysiology, 49,* 48–58.

Grabow, J., Aronson, A. E., Rose, D. E., & Greene, K. L. (1980). Hemispheric potentials evoked by speech sounds during discrimination tasks. *Electroencephalography and Clinical Neurophysiology, 49*, 38–47.

Grabow, J., & Elliot, F. W. (1974). The electrophysiologic assessment of hemispheric asymmetries during speech. *Journal of Speech and Hearing Research, 17*, 64–72.

Guillem, F., N'kaoua, B., Rogier, A., & Claverie, B. (1996). Functional heterogeneity of the frontal lobe: evidence from intracranial memory ERPs. *International Journal of Psychophysiology, 21*, 107–120.

Halgren, E., Squires, N. K., Wilson, C. S., Rohrbaugh, J. W., Babb, T. L., & Crandall, P. H. (1980). Endogenous potentials generated in the human hippocampal formation and the amygdala by infrequent events. *Science, 210*, 803–805.

Hillyard, S. A., Hink, R. F., Schwent, V. L., & Picton, T. W. (1973). Electrical signs of selective attention in the human brain. *Science, 182*, 177–180.

Jewett, D. L., Romano, M. N., & Williston, J. S. (1970). Human auditory evoked potentials: Possible brain stem components detected on the scalp. *Science, 167*, 1517–1518.

Jewett, D. L., & Williston, J. S. (1971). Auditory evoked far fields averaged from the scalp of humans. *Brain, 94*, 681–696.

Johnson, R., Jr. (1988). Scalp-recorded P300 activity in patients following unilateral temporal lobectomy. *Brain, 111*, 1517–1529.

Johnson, R., Jr. (1989). Auditory and visual P300s in temporal lobectomy patients: Evidence for modality-dependent generators. *Psychophysiology, 26*, 633–650.

Johnson, R., Jr., & Fedio, P. (1986). P300 activity in patients following unilateral temporal lobectomy: A preliminary report. In W. C. McCallum, R. Zappoli, & F. Denoth (Eds.), *Cerebral psychophysiology: Studies in event-related potentials* (pp. 552–554). Amsterdam: Elsevier.

Karlin, L., Martz, M. J., Brauth, S. E., & Mordkoff, A. M. (1971). Auditory evoked potentials, motor potentials and reaction time. *Electroencephalography and Clinical Neurophysiology, 31*, 129–136.

Kayser, J., Tenke, C., Nordby, H., Hammerborg, D., Hugdahl, K., & Erdmann, G. (1997). Event-related potential (ERP) asymmetries to emotional stimuli in a visual half-field paradigm. *Psychophysiology, 34*, 414–426.

Kimura, D. (1961). cerebral dominance and the perception of verbal stimuli. *Canadian Journal of Psychology, 15*, 166–171.

Kimura, D. (1967). Functional asymmetry of the brain in dichotic listening. *Cortex, 3*, 163–178.

Kinsbourne, M., Swanson, J. M., & Ledlow, A. (1977). Measuring interhemispheric transfer time in man. *Transactions of the American Neurological association, 102*, 1–4.

Kornhuber, H. H., & Deecke, L. (1965). Cerebral potential changes in voluntary and passive movements inman: Readiness potential and reafferent potential. *Pflugers Archives gesamte Physiologi, 284*, 1–17.

Kutas, M., & Hillyard, S. A. (1980). Reading senseless sentences: Brain potentials reflect semantic incongruity. *Science, 207*, 203–205.

Landau, S. G., & Buchsbaum, M. (1973). Average evoked response and muscle tension. *Phsyiological Psychology, 1*, 56–60.

Ledlow, A., Swanson, J. M., & Kinsbourne, M. (1978). Reaction times and evoked potentials as indicators of hemisheric differences for laterally presented name and physical matches. *Journal of Experimental Psychology: Human Perception and Performance, 4*, 440–454.

Marshall, N., & Donchin, E. (1981). Circadian variation in the latency of brainstem responses and its relation to body temperature. *Science, 212*, 356–358.

Matsumiya, Y., Tagliasco, V., & Lombroso, C. T. (1972). Auditory evoked response: Meaningfulness of stimuli and hemispheric asymmetry. *Science, 175*, 790–792.

Mayes, A., & Beaumont, G. (1977). Does visual evoked potential asymmetry index cognitive activity? *Neuropsychologia, 15*, 249–256.

McCallum, W. C., Papakostopoulos, D., & Griffith, H. B. (1976). Distribution of CNV and other slow potential changes in human brainstem structures. In W. C. McCallum & J. R. Knott (Eds.), *The responsive brain* (pp. 205–210). Bristol: John Wright & Sons.

Mendel, M. I., & Kupperman, G. L. (1974). Early component of the averaged electroencephalic response to constant level clicks during rapid eye movement sleep. *Audiology, 13*, 23–32.

Morrell, L. K., & Morell, F. (1966). Evoked potentials and reaction times: A study of intraindividual variability. *Electroencephalography and Clinical Neurophysiology, 20*, 567–575.

Morrell, L. K., & Salamy, J. G. (1971). Hemispheric asymmetry of electrocortical responses to speech stimuli. *Science, 23*, 193–195.

Naatanen, R., & Picton, T. W. (1987). The N1 wave of the human electric and magnetic response to sound: A review and an analysis of the component structure. *Psychophysiology, 24*, 375–425.

Nordby, H., Hugdahl, K., Stickgold, R., Bronnick, K. S., & Hobson, J. A. (1996). Event-related potentials (ERPs) to deviant auditory stimuli duirng sleep and waking. *NeuroReport, 7*, 1082–1086.

Papanicolaou, A. C., Levin, H. S., Eisenberg, H. M., & Moore, B. D. (1983). Evoked potential indices of selective hemispheric engagement in affective and phonetic tasks. *Neuropsychologia, 21*, 401–405.

Papanicolaou, A. C., Schmidt, A. L., Moore, B. D., & Eisenberg, H. M. (1983). Cerebral activation patterns in an arithmetic and a visuospatial processing task. *International Journal of Neuroscience, 20*, 283–288.

Polich, J., & Squire, L. R. (1993). P300 from amnesic patients with bilateral hippocampal lesions. *Electroencephalography and Clinical Neurophysiology, 86*, 408–417.

Rebert, C. S., Tecce, J. J., Marczynski, T. J., Pirch, J. H., & Thompson, J. W. (1986). Neural anatomy, chemistry, and event-related brain potentials: an approach to understanding the substrates of mind. In W. C. McCallum, R. Zappoli, & F. Denoth (Eds.), *Cerebral psychophysiology: Studies in event-related potentials* (pp. 343–393). Amsterdam: Elsevier.

Rhodes, L. E., Dustman, R. E., & Beck, E. C. (1969). The visual evoked response: A comparison of bright and dull children. *Electroencephalography and Clinical Neurophysiology, 27*, 364–372.

Richlin, M., Weisinger, M., Weinstein, S., Giannini, M., & Morganstern, M. (1971). Interhemispheric asymmetries of evoked cortical responses in retarded and normal children. *Cortex, 7*, 98–105.

Ritter, W., Simson, R., & Vaughan, H. G. (1972). Association cortex potentials and reaction time in auditory discrimination. *Electroencephalography and Clinical Neurophysiology, 33*, 547–55.

Ritter, W., Vaughan, H. G., Jr., & Costa, L. D. (1968). Orienting and habituation to auditory stimuli: A study of short term changes in average evoked responses. *Electroencephalography and Clinical Neurophysiology, 25*, 550–556.

Rugg, M. D., Lines, C. R., & Milner, A. D. (1985). Further investigation of visual evoked potentials elicited by lateralized stimuli: Effects of stimulus eccentricity and reference site. *Electroencephalography and Clinical Neurophysiology, 62*, 81–87.

Rugg, M. D., Milner, A. D., & Lines C. R. (1985). Visual evoked potentials to lateralized stimuli in two cases of callosal agensis. *Journal of Neurology, Neurosurgery & Psychiatry, 48*, 367–373.

Samuels, I. (1959). Reticular mechanisms and behavior. *Psychological Bulletin, 56*, 1–25.

Scheibel, M. E., & Scheibel, A. B. (1967). Anatomical basis of attention mechanisms in vertebrate brains. In G. L. Quarton, T. Melnechuk, & F. O. Schmitt (Eds.), *The neurosciences: A study program* (pp. 420–437). New York: The Rockefeller University Press.

Shagass, C. (1972). *Evoked brain potentials in psychiatry.* New York: Plenum.

Shagass, C., & Trusty, D. (1966). Somatosensory and visual cerebral evoked response changes during sleep. In J. Wortis (Ed.), *Recent advances in biological psychiatry*, (vol. VIII, pp. 213–334). New York: Plenum.

Shibasaki, H., Barrett, G., Halliday, E., & Halliday, A. M. (1980a). Components of the movement-related cortical potential and their scalp topography. *Electroencephalography and Clinical Neurophysiology, 49*, 213–226.

Shibasaki, H., Barrett, G., Halliday, E., & Halliday, A. M. (1980b). Cortical potentials following voluntary and passive finger movements. *Electroencephalography and Clinical Neurophysiology, 43*, 201–213.

Simson, R. C., Vaughan, H. G., Jr., & Ritter, W. (1977). The scalp topography of potentials in auditory and visual go–no-go tasks. *Electroencephalography and Clinical Neurophysiology, 43*, 864–875.

Small, M. (1983). Asymmetrical evoked potentials in response to face stimuli. *Cortex, 19*, 441–450.

Squires, N. K., Squires, K. C., & Hillyard, S. A. (1975). Two varieties of long-latency positive waves evoked by unpredictable auditory stimuli in man. *Electroencephalography and Clinical Neurophysiology, 38*, 387–401.

Sutton, S., Braren, M., & Zubin, J. (1965). Evoked-potential correlates of stimulus uncertainty, *Science, 150*, 1187–1188.

Sutton, S., Teuting, P., Zubin, J, & John, E. R. (1967). Information delivery and the sensory evoked potential. *Science, 155*, 1436–1439.

Tarkka, I. M. (1994). Electrical source localization of human movement-related cortical potentials. *International Journal of Psychophysiology, 16*, 81–88.

Tecce, J. J. (1972). Contingent negative variation (CNV) and psychological processes in man. *Psychological Bulletin, 77*, 73–108.

Teyler, T. J., Roemer, R. A., & Harrison, T. F. (1973). Human scalp-recorded evoked potential correlates of linguistic stimuli. *Bulletin of the Psychonomic Society, 1*, 333–334.

Townsend, R. E., House, J. F., & Johnson, L. C. (1976). Auditory evoked potential in Stage 2 and REM sleep during a 30-day exposure to tone pulses. *Psychophysiology, 13*, 54–57.

Vaughan, H. G., Jr. (1969). The relationship of brain activity to scalp recordings of event-related potentials. In E. Donchin & D. B. Lindsley (Eds.), *Average evoked potentials* (pp. 45–94). Washington, DC: NASA.

Vaughan, H. G., Jr., & Arezzo, J. C. (1988). The neural basis of event-related potentials. In T. W. Picton (Ed.), *Human event related potentials: Handbook of electroencephalography and clinical neurophysiology, Vol. III* (pp. 45–96). Amsterdam: Elsevier.

Vaughan, H. G., Costa, L. D., & Gilden, L. (1966). The functional relation of visual evoked response and reaction time to stimulus intensity. *Vision Research, 6*, 645–656.

Vaughan, H. G., Jr., Costa, L. D., Gilden, L., & Schimmel, H. (1965). Identification of sensory and motor components of cerebral activity in simple reaction time tasks. *Proceedings of the 73rd Annual Convention of the American Psychological Association, 1*, 179–180.

Vaughan, H. G., Costa, L. D., & Ritter, W. (1968). Topography of the human motor potential. *Electroencephalography and Clinical Neurophysiology, 25*, 1–10.

Vitouch, O., Bauer, H., Gittler, G., Leodolter, M., & Leodolter, U. (1997). Cortical activity of good and poor spatial test performers during spatial and verbal processing studied with slow potential topography. *International Journal of Psychophysiology, 27*, 183–199.

Walter, W. G., Cooper, R., Aldridge, V. J., McCallum, W. C., & Winter, A. L. (1964). Contingent negative variation: An electrical sign of sensory motor association and expectancy in the human brain. *Nature, 203*, 380–384.

Weitzman, E. D., & Kremen, H. (1965). Auditory evoked responses during different stages of sleep in man. *Electroencephalography and Clinical Neurophysiology, 18*, 65–70.

Wood, C., Goff, W. R., & Day, R. S. (1971). Auditory evoked potentials during speech perception. *Science, 173*, 1248–1251.

Woods, D. L., & Elmasian, R. (1986). The habituation of event-related potentials to speech sounds and tones. *Electroencephalography and Clinical Neurophysiology, 65*, 447–459.

Yingling, C. D., & Hosobuchi, Y. A. (1984). Subcortical correlate of P300 in man. *Electroencephalography and Clinical Neurophysiology, 59*, 72–76.

6

Event-Related Brain Potentials and Behavior II:
Mental, Sensory, Attentional,
and Perceptual Activities

An interesting picture of brain function begins to emerge as we consider data obtained from event-related brain potential (ERP) studies. The brain can be considered as a highly integrated organ in which the many cortical and subcortical areas cooperate in carrying out its functions. We see this in the ERPs that develop over many areas of the brain simultaneously in response to a given stimulus. Thus, for example, topographical studies show that although occipital cortex may respond maximally to a word flashed on a screen, there is sufficient response from parietal and frontal areas to suggest that they are also involved in processing the stimulus. This chapter considers ERPs related to relatively more complex behaviors than those covered in chapter 5. Therefore, we consider some of the findings concerning the ERP and mental activities, including performance on intelligence tests, meaningfulness of material, linguistic processes, conditioning, resource allocation, and selectivity in attention. We also examine the ERP in the context of sensory, attentional, and perceptual functioning, including perception of shape, color, and motion. The long-latency ERPs and steady potential shifts (e.g., P300 and CNV) are discussed in chapter 7 with regard to their observed relationships to higher cognitive activities such as preparation for events, information processing, memory, selective attention, and decision making.

EVENT-RELATED POTENTIALS AND MENTAL ACTIVITY

This section considers a number of human mental processes as they have been related to ERPs. Among the issues discussed are whether the ERP can serve as a culture-free measure of intelligence, the effects of subjective factors on the generation of ERP components, and effects of stimulus meaning and emotional content on the ERP. Other topics covered include linguistic processes and ERPs, classical and instrumental conditioning of ERPs, and mechanisms of selective attention that are suggested by ERP activity. A host of questions on perception are considered. including the nature of visual ERPs with visual masking, the influence of pattern on ERP, color effects, and how the ERP is influenced by the perception of motion.

ERPs and Intelligence

The ERP as a Culture-free Measure of Intelligence? Similar to EEG, the ERP has been viewed by some as a possible culture-free technique to assess intelligence. At first glance, one might think that the ERP, with its specific form, and definable latencies and amplitudes, would offer a greater likelihood of being related to aspects of intelligence than the amorphous, general background EEG record. However, like the EEG, attempts to relate ERPs to intelligence have met with mixed results. The approach in this area has been to attempt to relate some characteristic of ERPs (e.g., latency, amplitude, waveform) to some measure of intellect, most commonly performance on some test of intelligence.

The Neural Efficiency Hypothesis.   An early experiment was performed by Chalke and Ertl (1965), who postulated that latencies of ERP components may be an index of information-processing efficiency; that is, biologically efficient organisms process data more quickly than less efficient ones, and thus their ERP latencies should be shorter. This proposal is known as the *neural efficiency hypothesis.* In their study, Chalke and Ertl obtained ERPs to light flashes using bipolar electrodes. The measure of IQ was performance on a paper-and-pencil intelligence test (Otis Higher Form A). The subjects were 33 graduate students with high Otis scores, 11 army cadets with average scores, and 4 mentally retarded individuals with very low scores. The results indicated that latencies of later ERP components (those occurring after 100 msec), were related to intelligence test scores—that is, the higher the score, the shorter the latency. Methodologically, this study is flawed because it used such a lopsided sample with scores that clustered at the high end (33 graduate students at one extreme and only 4 mentally retarded at the other). The use of a group paper-and-pencil test of intelligence is poor procedure with the mentally retarded who need the one-on-one support of individual testing procedures because they typically have difficulty following instructions. Well-established tests that require individual testing are the Stanford–Binet or the Wechsler tests (WISC for children and WAIS for adults). However, a large follow-up study by Ertl and Schafer (1969), based on a sample of 566 school children, indicated significant correlations between test scores and ERP latencies.

Investigators subsequent to Ertl have reported both negative and positive findings. On the negative side, Davis (1971) reported no relation in a large-scale study in which visual ERP latencies were measured in more than 1,000 school children and compared to test scores and school performance. This 1971 study by Davis was carried out in association with Ertl. In another study with negative findings, the auditory ERP was measured using 84 persons in a first experiment and 212 subjects in a second one (Rust, 1975). The measure of intelligence was the Mill Hill Vocabulary scale in the first experiment and the Ravens Progressive Matrices in the second experiment. Neither study found a relation between intelligence and latency measures.

Rust noted that more evidence has been produced for the visual ERP than the auditory in the intelligence context, but saw no reason for a restriction of neural efficiency to any particular sensory modality, a comment similar to that made by Callaway (1975). Callaway described studies of his own in which he found that auditory ERPs correlated positively with IQ but negatively with age. This represents a serious difficulty for the neural efficiency hypothesis of Ertl, because it is hard to explain why neural efficiency would be higher for brighter children, but not for older ones.

Some investigators who have reported positive findings are Blinkhorn and Hendrickson (1982), Hendrickson and Hendrickson (1980), Perry, McCoy, Cunningham, Falgout, and Street (1976); and Shucard and Horn (1972). Shucard and Horn (1972) measured visual ERPs and intelligence scores of 108 persons under conditions of high, medium, and low arousal. They found the greatest degree of correspondence between fast latency and high scores under the low-arousal condition. One suggested possibility was that the brighter subjects were better able to maintain alertness in the boring low-arousal condition in which subjects merely watched light flashes. Shucard and Horn argued that arousal levels of subjects must be low in order to successfully use ERP latencies to predict intelligence.

A number of visual ERP and intelligence measures were studied by Perry et al. (1976). They administered a battery of ability tests to 98 individual 5-year-old children. Visual ERPs were recorded from left and right hemispheres and occipital midline under three stimulus conditions. The measures used were amplitude, latency, and complexity (number of peaks) of ERPs. They reported significant multiple correlations between these ERP measures and Wechsler Preschool and Primary Scale of Intelligence (WPPSI). An interesting aspect of this study is that the subjects were not selected on the basis of extreme IQ scores; in fact, the mean WPPSI was 119, with a range from 94 to 141. Thus, Perry and his colleagues apparently found a relationship between intelligence test scores and a complex of ERP measures, not amplitude alone.

The String Hypothesis.   A testable hypothesis relating IQ to ERP was developed by Hendrickson and Hendrickson (1980). According to their model, IQ is positively related to complexity of the ERP trace, and complexity decreases with higher error rates in the brain. If the ERP trace is stretched out into a straight line (what the Hendricksons called a *string* measure), they predicted that longer strings will be related to higher IQs. (It should be noted that higher amplitude and more complex waveforms produce longer strings.) This hypothesis was confirmed in two studies. In the first study (Hendrickson & Hendrickson, 1980), full-scale Wechsler scores correlated highly with string length for 254 children ages 14 to 16. In the second study, by Blinkhorn and Hendrickson (1982), high correlations between string length and Raven's Progressive Matrices scores were obtained for 33 subjects. In both studies, the auditory ERP was obtained to simple tones.

P300 and Intelligence.   During the 1990s researchers began to examine the P300 response as a correlate of intelligence (O'Donnell, Friedman, Swearer, & Drachman, 1992; Polich & Martin, 1992). Polich and Martin (1992) cited suggestive evidence for linking higher P300 amplitudes and shorter latencies with superior intellectual performance. They correlated the Raven's Matrices scores and grade point average (GPA) of college students with P300 amplitudes and latencies. The only significant relationship found was a negative correlation between GPA and P300 latencies; that is, shorter latencies were related to higher GPAs. They suggested that the timing, rather than amplitude, of the P300 component may be related to cognitive ability. In another P300 study, the relationship of P300 latency to a variety of intelligence measures was recorded in subjects ranging from 20 to 88 years (O'Donnell, Friedman, Swearer, & Drachman, 1992). The measures were verbal learning, four subscales of the WAIS–R, verbal fluency, and recent and remote memory. O'Donnell et al. found that although P300 latencies slowed with age, there was also a relationship between intellectual performance and P300 latencies that was unrelated to age. The relationship was such that slower latencies were related to poorer performance, similar to the GPA portion of the Polich and Martin study. A novel approach using the P300 along with vocabulary subtests from standard intelligence measuring instruments was investigated by Connolly and colleagues (Connolly, Major, Allen, & D'Arcy, in press). They used a multiple choice version of items from the WISC III and WAIS–R in which the P300 to correct and incorrect responses could be assessed. The P300 occurred to correct answers, but not to answers the individual knew to be incorrect, or to very difficult items with which the person was not familiar. Thus, the P300 reflected knowledge of word definitions. The authors suggest that such an approach may allow one to determine intellectual functioning in patients who have suffered brain damage and cannot speak or move effectively.

Summary.   The available evidence appears to indicate some relation between the ERP and intellectual functioning. Ertl and his colleagues were the first to stimulate research in this area, but their neural efficiency hypothesis has been criticized. For example, Callaway (1975) argued that it is unlikely that a single neurophysiological factor, such as shorter ERP latencies to sensory stimuli, can be identified as the biological substrate of intelligence. Callaway rejected the Ertl hypothesis on other grounds, all of which suggest that the approach is oversimplified. The Hendrickson's theory is also appealingly simple, and, like Ertl's theory, it is testable.

A major difficulty with the Hendrickson's construct is that it relies too heavily on ERP amplitude in determining string length. Studies suggest the possibility that skull thickness can affect amplitude of response—that is, a thicker skull leads to greater attenuation of brain response than a thinner skull, and this would result in a lower ERP amplitude and would not be related to intelligence. Vetterli and Furedy (1985) also criticized two versions of the string measure. They tested one of the string measures as a predictor of IQ, and compared it to one using latency. The pure latency measure was superior, because the string measure gave inconsistent results with some in an opposite direction to the predicted relationship. Burns, Nettelbeck, and Cooper (1997) point out that only 2 of 13 studies using the string measure have reported correlations with IQ that were high enough to support the Hendrickson's theory. In a careful analysis Burns et al. found that the string measure was nonspecific because it indexes both low and high frequency event-related activity. They also affirm its dependence on ERP amplitude and concluded that the string measure is not a valid measure of ERP and should be abandoned as a possible physiological measure of intelligence, a conclusion that is warranted in view of the evidence.

Some valuable suggestions for future research in the ERP/inteligence area were made by Gale and Edwards (1983). Their strategies for future studies include repeated measurements of both EEG and ERPs in a group of subjects, obtaining both auditory and visual ERPs, multichannel topographical recordings, and tasks ranging from listening to simple tones to solving complex problems. Gale and Edwards also made a reasonable appeal for the development of a general model of brain function to help interpret present and future findings in this area. The preliminary results relating shorter P300 latencies to higher GPAs and to intelligence measures seem promising. The P300 is a measure of cognitive activity, not simply a response to sensory stimuli. Thus, there is need for additional exploration of P300 parameters and intelligence in normal persons, and its possible use to assess intellectual functioning of disabled individuals.

ERPs and Stimulus Meaning

A number of studies have been conducted to determine whether significance or meaning of a stimulus, either natural or experimentally contrived, would affect the ERP. Begleiter and Platz (1969) used taboo words (e.g., fuck) and neutral words (e.g., tile), which were printed in capital letters and equal in area, to obtain visual ERPs. Blank flashes of light were also used. They reported that ERP components appearing shortly after 100 msec were larger in amplitude for taboo words than for neutral words or flashes. A later component was larger for both types of words than the blank flash. Thus, meaning seemed to alter the late ERP components. Perhaps the taboo words produced more of a response in subjects than previously used stimuli because of the stronger inherent affective value of these stimuli as compared to those that attain such meaning through association.

An interesting demonstration of how internal factors such as expectancy might affect ERP amplitude was performed by Begleiter, Porjesz, Yerre, and Kissin (1973). In their experiment, moderate intensity light flashes elicited either large or small amplitude ERPs, depending on whether a warning tone signaled that a bright or dim flash would follow. Thus, the importance of subjective factors, independent of objective stimulus characteristics, in generating the ERP was again shown. Further, there have been reports of changes in the ERP that appeared at about the time that an expected, but absent, stimulus should have been presented.

For example, Sutton, Teuting, Zubin, and John (1967) found that an ERP would occur in the absence of an expected click. Weinberg, Walter, and Crow (1970) referred to this as an "emitted" potential, in contrast to potentials that are "evoked" by a specific stimulus. Ruchkin and Sutton (1973) reported the same result for visual stimuli, that is, a P300 response appeared with a peak latency of 400 msec at C_z and 480 msec at O_z, following the time of the missing flash. The lower amplitude and longer duration of the emitted P300 (compared to the evoked P300) was hypothesized to be due to the lack of a precisely timed external stimulus. In other words, the P300 associated with an expected, but missing, stimulus is an internally produced potential difference influenced by the variability inherent in subjective time estimates. The fact that a P300 can emerge in the absence of an external stimulus emphasizes the endogenous nature of this component.

Auditory ERPs were recorded from scalp locations over left and right hemispheres in response to words and nonsense syllables (groupings of letters that do not make words) by Molfese (1979). Brain responses that occurred between 240 and 280 msec after stimulation distinguished between meaningful and nonsense words. Both hemispheres showed differentiation between the words and nonwords, thus failing to show a processing distinction for the two hemispheres. In a study by Vanderploeg, Brown, and Marsh (1987), later ERP components (240 to 616 msec) were found to differ for positive, neutral, and negative facial expressions. They noted that processing of facial expression appeared in two stages: (a) discrimination of neutral faces involved the left hemisphere earlier (240–448 msec), and (b) continued processing of the emotional faces (positive or negative expressions) was indexed by a later right hemisphere response (448–616 msec). The results suggest a complex interhemispheric processing of emotional facial expressions, with lateralization shifting as indexed by latency of ERP components.

The influence of pleasant, unpleasant, and neutral photographs on ERPs, heart rate, and recall was studied by Palomba, Angrilli, and Mini (1997). The researchers used slides from the International Affective Picture System (IAPS). Sample slides were pleasant (smiling baby), neutral (a fork), or unpleasant (mutilated body). The earliest emotional effect was shown about 280 msec poststimulus (N2–P3) and later components (at 400–600 msec and 600–900 msec). In all cases, emotional slides (both pleasant and unpleasant) produced larger positivity in the ERP compared to neutral slides. Larger heart rate deceleration was observed with unpleasant slides compared to pleasant or neutral slides. Recall measures revealed that emotional slides (pleasant or unpleasant) were better remembered than neutral materials. Thus, in this study greater positivity in the ERP was related to perceptual intake of emotional relative to neutral stimuli.

Summary.   The studies reviewed in this section indicate that meaningfulness of stimuli alters the ERP. Factors such as stimulus content, affective value, and expectancies exert an influence on the recorded brain response. The two hemispheres appear to cooperate in a complicated way in processing emotional facial expressions. Findings regarding the greater ERP positivity observed with emotion provoking stimuli requires additional corroborating research.

ERPs and Linguistic Processes

This section is concerned primarily with ERPs to language stimuli. The recording of ERPs from the scalp makes it possible to study linguistic processes and hemispheric specialization with greater precision than can be accomplished with performance measures alone. A number of investigators have reported differences in ERPs recorded over right and left hemi-spheres, depending on whether or not stimuli were language-related. For example, Wood, Goff, and Day (1971) recorded ERPs during two auditory identification tasks: One task provided linguistic information, and the other did not. Auditory ERPs from the left hemisphere differed for the two tasks, but were identical over the right hemisphere. The authors concluded that different neural events occur in the left hemisphere during analysis of language versus nonlanguage stimuli.

Another approach was taken by Brown, Marsh, and Smith (1973), who observed that waveforms of ERPs differed acccording to the meaning of a word. For example, ERPs to the word *fire* differed when it was presented in the phrase "sit by the fire," as compared to "ready, aim, fire." The waveform differences were significantly greater from over the left hemisphere than for right hemispheric locations. In another part of the study, no hemispheric differences occurred when the meaning of the word fire was ambiguous. This was accomplished by using phrases such as "fire is hot" and "fire the gun."

Noun and Verb.   To dispel possible criticisms that the words accompanying the critical stimuli were different and therefore could have produced the asymmetries found, Brown, Marsh, and Smith (1976) conducted another experiment. They tested young adults in a situation where meaning was assigned immediately before the critical stimulus was delivered along with other words. That is, meaning was established for the ambiguous phrase "it was led" by telling subjects that the last word would be a noun, as in "the metal was lead," or a verb, as "the horse was led." The ERPs were recorded from two leads each over the left and right hemispheres. The leads were F_7 (approximately Broca's area related to speech articulation); F_8, 3 cm from T_3 (Wernicke's area related to understanding speech); and 3 cm from T_4. Again, as in the 1973 study, Brown et al. reported that ERPs from over Broca's area were dissimilar for the two meanings, whereas they were similar at the other locations.

Words and Sounds.   Auditory ERPs were produced by both spoken words and human sounds in an experiment by Friedman, Simson, Ritter, and Rapin (1975a). A sample word was "kick" and a sample sound was "pssst," both uttered by the same person. The ERPs were measured under conditions in which the sounds and words were merely listened to and where one of them served as a signal for a finger movement. They found the P300 component amplitude to be largest to signal stimuli and smallest under passive listening. Sounds produced larger P300s than words at all electrode locations (left and right hemispheres, midline). The authors suggested that this might be due to the novelty of the sounds, because they occur less frequently in everyday speech. Analyses of left–right hemispheric differences yielded only two greater left than right differences. The authors concluded that earlier studies of ERP correlates of differential hemispheric processing had design and statistical flaws and reflection of hemispheric functioning by ERPs may not be as strong as indicated by those studies.

The P300 System.   In still another experiment, Friedman, Simson, Ritter, and Rapin (1975b) recorded visual ERPs from over right and left hemispheres and vertex. The stimuli consisted of sequentially presented words that comprised a sentence. In one condition, an ingenious technique prevented the subject from knowing the meaning of the second word in the sequence until the last was shown. For example, subjects were told the form of the three sentences that were used throughout the experiment: The _eel is on the axle; The _eel is on the shoe; The _eel is on the orange. Thus, by omitting the wh, h, or p, the subject could not know the meaning of the second word until the last word in the sequence was presented. In other conditions, the meaning of the second word was known immediately. The latency of P300 to words that delivered information (last word or second) was consistently longer than to other words in the sentence. No hemispheric differences were noted. The authors interpreted the finding that all words produced P300 components as indicating that the "P300 system" is engaged whenever task-related language stimuli are used.

N400 and Semantic Mismatch.   The ERPs occurring when an inappropriate word appeared unexpectedly at the end of a sentence were studied by Kutas and Hillyard (1980). In 25% of sentences read by their subjects, the ending was moderately or strongly inappropriate. An example of moderate was "He took a sip from a waterfall" and a strong example was "He took a sip from the transmitter." They found that the inappropriate words were followed by a negative component (N400) beginning at about 250 msec and peaking at 400 msec after stimulus onset. This N400 was much larger after a strong semantic mismatch compared to a moderate one. The authors proposed that the N400 might be an ERP sign of the interruption of sentence processing by inappropriate words and an attempt to reinterpret the information (Hillyard & Kutas, 1983). This discovery of the N400 stands as one of the most significant developments in ERP studies of language processes. Many subsequent studies have related the N400 to word recognition and semantic processing. Kutas, Lindamood, and Hillyard (1984) found that words resulting in semantically appropriate endings for sentences also produced smaller N400s than words that were not good completions. For example, three endings were given for the sentence stem: "The pizza was too hot to—" "eat," "drink," or "cry." The size of the N400 grew with the inappropriateness of the completion. In that same report, they observed that expectancy of the words at the ends of sentences also affects N400 such that the least expected results in the largest response. Words that have a high degree of expectancy are said to have a high "cloze probability." This measure of expectancy is based on the probability that a particular word will be chosen to complete a given sentence context.

The N400 response has also been obtained in children (Byrne, Dywan, & Connolly, 1995). These researchers presented 10-year-old children with 90 pictures paired once with a semantically congruent word and once with an incongruent word. The N400 response was significantly larger to incongruent pairings, but only when the child understood the meaning of the words used.

Open- and Closed-Class Words.   There is suggestive evidence that ERPs to "open-class" or content words differ from those to "closed-class" or function words. Examples of open-class words are verbs and nouns, whereas prepositions and articles are in the closed-class category. The ERPs associated with open-class words resulted in larger positive ERP components between 200 and 700 msec poststimulus, and by a greater left–right asymmetry in the 400 to 700 period than ERPs to closed-class words (Hillyard & Kutas, 1983).

Summary.   Although early studies of hemispheric ERP differences to language and non-language stimuli produced promising results, recent investigations, using stringent criteria for differences, have resulted in more conservative statements regarding ERP laterality. However, studies that have related hemispheric differences to linguistic meaning have yielded more positive results. Neville (1980) suggested that when subjects perform demanding tasks designed to produce behavioral asymmetries (e.g., dichotic listening), the concurrently recorded ERPs show hemispheric asymmetries. Studies of semantically inappropriate words (N400), different cloze probabilities, and different word categories indicated that ERPs can add important information not observable with strictly behavioral approaches. The discovery of the N400 response has led to many fruitful studies of linguistic processes and related brain function.

Conditioning and ERPs

Classical Conditioning.   In relation to the number of ERP investigations in general, only a few have used the ERP in studies of human learning or conditioning. Lelord, Laffont, and Jusseaume (1976) classically conditioned ERPs in children of three intelligence levels. The three groups were normal, mildly retarded (IQ between 50 and 60) and severely retarded (IQ between 20 and 50). Sound was used as the conditioned stimulus (CS) and light as the unconditioned stimulus (UCS). After pairing of CS and UCS, the normal children showed increased amplitude of ERPs to the sound (CS), but the two retarded groups did not. Therefore, classical conditioning of ERPs occurred in normals but not in retarded subjects. In another study, the ERPs of normal and autistic children were compared in a classical conditioning situation (Martineau, Garreau, Barthelemy, & Lelord, 1984). The autistic child is characterized by extreme social withdrawal and impairment of verbal and nonverbal communication, among other symptoms. These investigators found marked ERP differences in normal and autistic children during conditioning trials. Namely, the autistic subjects showed smaller responses to stimulus pairs (sound–light) than they did to the CS (sound) alone, a finding attributed to attentional deficits usually found in autistic children.

Operant Conditioning.   There have been some reports of operant conditioning of ERPs. For example, Rosenfeld, Dowman, Silvia, and Heinricher (1984) found evidence of operant control over a P200 component at a vertex location in four of eight subjects. Correct modification of P200 was reinforced by a tone signal. Operant conditioning of slow brain potential shifts was described by Rockstroh, Birbaumer, Elbert, and Lutzenberger (1984). In their paradigm, feedback was provided by the outline of a rocket ship that moved across a TV screen. Subjects directed the ship into one of two goals, depending on instructions. One of the goals required a shift towards SP negativity, whereas reaching the other goal required a positive shift. Subjects received a monetary reward for reaching the correct goal. These investigators reported that human subjects demonstrate operant control over their own slow brain potentials within 100 to 160 trials (usually two experimental sessions). Lutzenberger, Roberts, and Birbaumer (1993) reinforced subjects for increasing or decreasing SP negativity alternatively at frontal, parietal, and central locations. Subjects engaged in a memory task (Sternberg) simultaneously with the conditioning trials. The SP was regulated differently on the negativity and positivity trials, but this was mainly at the frontal area. The lack of area-specific regulation was attributed to the attention diverted by the memory task. Such area-specific operant regulation of slow potentials was previously reported by Birbaumer, Roberts, Lutzenberger, Rockstroh, and Elbert (1992).

Summary.   The studies reviewed here indicate that changes in ERPs occur under different conditioning paradigms. Namely, ERPs were larger in amplitude to a positively conditioned stimulus. The ERPs also indicated differences in acquisition of the conditioned response of retarded and autistic children, most likely reflecting impaired intellectual and attentional functioning characteristics of these groups. There is also evidence that operant control of sensory ERPs and slow potential shifts is possible, which is a fascinating development.

SENSATION, ATTENTION, PERCEPTION, AND ERPs

As in chapter 4, the studies in this section are categorized as to whether the research is primarily concerned with stimulus variations, attentional aspects, or integrative perceptual functions.

Sensation and ERPs

Smell. Although auditory, visual, and somatosensory stimuli have been the most frequently investigated in ERP studies, it is possible to examine other forms of sensory stimulation, such as olfactory, gustatory, pain, and vestibular. For example, Smith, Allison, Goff, and Principato (1971) studied smell-generated ERPs of three patients with surgically produced smell deficits and of three normal persons. Streams of compressed air containing odorous and nonodorous substances were directed into the nostrils for 200 msec at 5-sec intervals to produce the ERP. The results indicated that the ERP (recorded from C_z) was elicited by stimulation of olfactory receptors. No ERP was obtained when jets of air, passed over distilled water flasks, were directed into the nostrils. Substantial ERPs—that is, components of 10 μV or more—could be obtained by averaging 30 responses to the olfactory stimuli.

The stimuli used apparently stimulated both smell and trigeminal nerve systems, a possibility that poses problems for studying responses to smell alone. However, a technique for successfully delivering olfactory stimuli to the nasal mucosa has been reported by Kobal and Hummel (1988). In a more recent study, olfactory ERP was observed to increase in amplitude as a function of odor concentration (Lorig, Sapp, Campbell, & Cain, 1993). Chemosensory ERPs were obtained under odorant stimulation conditions in which subjects were either inhaling (active) or not (passive) (Lorig, Matia, Peszka, & Bryant, 1996). Administration technique was affected by both odor concentration and site of ERP recording. Amplitude of P2 was greater in the passive condition suggesting that this technique may be better to determine integrity of the olfactory tract.

Olfactory ERPs were reported lower in amplitude and longer in latency for elderly subjects (mean age of 66) as compared to young adults (mean age of 26; Murphy, Nordin, de Wijk, Cain, & Polich, 1994). In an attempt to separate out possible exogenous and endogenous olfactory ERP components Pause and colleagues used an olfactory "odd-ball" paradigm (Pause, Sojka, Krauel, & Ferstl, 1996). The subject's task was to respond to a high concentration of citral by lifting an index finger, but not to the standard stimulus (low concentration of citral). The researchers report that the early components of the olfactory ERP (N1 and P2) are affected by odorant concentration, but later components (P3) vary with stimulus significance and probability. Thus, endogenous processes can contribute to the olfactory ERP.

Taste. The gustatory (taste) ERPs of humans were analyzed in detail by Funakoshi and Kawamura (1971). Demineralized water, sucrose, sodium chloride, tartaric acid, and quinine hydrochloride provided control, sweet, salty, sour, and bitter solutions, respectively. The subjects rinsed their mouths between each application of a solution to the tongue. The researchers reported the onset of an early wave at 150 msec after the stimulus was applied (10 μV in amplitude) and a late wave at about 500 msec, which was approximately 20 μV in amplitude. The early wave occurred with all solutions and with tactile stimulation of the tongue; but the later wave only appeared with the salt and tartaric acid (sour) applications. Therefore, the early component was due to the mechanical stimulation of pouring the solution on the tongue surface, and the late wave was the taste ERP. The authors suggested that the lack of ERPs to sweet and bitter may be related to the relatively small tongue areas sensitive to sweet and bitter substances. This, in turn, could result in smaller cortical responses to sweet and bitter, perhaps not visible within the limitations imposed by 40 samples.

Touch and Pain. The somatosensory ERP to stimulation of the skin was studied by Soinen and Jarvilehto (1983). The left hand was stimulated by a tactile probe that delivered stimuli ranging from those that could not be detected (below threshold) to those that were clearly felt. Tactile stimuli just above detection threshold were capable of producing a distinct somatosensory ERP. This shows that a minimal peripheral sensation (at the hand) is sufficient to activate a large number of neural elements in the brain, as indicated by the sizable ERP from over the central cortex. On the other hand, no ERP was produced to the subthreshold touch stimuli.

Pain has been produced in experimental subjects by electrically stimulating the very sensitive pulp of individual teeth (Chatrian, Canfield, Knauss, & Lettich, 1975). All subjects described the electrical stimulus to the tooth pulp as producing sharp pain of a very brief duration. The pain ERP was recorded from many scalp areas, including that over the postcentral cortex. The ERP was prominent over the somatosensory cortex, a finding that suggested the existence of a tooth pulp sensation in the somatosensory area of the postcentral gyrus. Buchsbaum, Davis, Coppola, and Naber (1981) found that both aspirin and morphine led to a reduction in somatosensory ERP to painful electrical shock stimulation. The ERP was derived from over central and somatosensory cortex.

Acceleration.   The vestibular sense provides information about body position. The receptors for linear and angular acceleration lie in the semicircular canals and utricles of the inner ear. The study of vestibular ERPs is more difficult than the study of visual or auditory ERPs, because it is difficult to produce a suitable means of stimulating the vestibular receptors. Salamy, Potvin, Jones, and Landreth (1975) studied ERPs to semicircular canal stimulation by using whole-body rotation (angular acceleration) as the stimulus. The ERP was summed for a 2-sec period simultaneous with about 84 degrees of body rotation in a swing chair. The ERP was recorded from over both hemispheres (central, parietal, temporal, and frontal leads). The investigators obtained a consistent negative–positive ERP with peaks at about 193 and 345 msec, respectively. The negative peak seemed to be the most prominent feature related to angular acceleration. Salamy et al. observed that somatosensory ERPs have negative–positive latencies peaking at about 135 and 220 msec, much earlier than ERPs obtained with acceleration, thus distinguishing them from vestibular components.

Summary.   It is possible, though more difficult, to generate ERPs to smell, taste, pain, and body acceleration. The difficulty lies in appropriate stimulation of the receptor mechanisms involved in producing these sensations. Despite the obstacles, increasing information is being obtained regarding the olfactory ERP, including the contribution of endogenous events to the brain response. Somatosensory ERPs to touch and pain stimuli have not been observed with subthreshold stimulation. A decrease in ERP amplitude to painful electric shock has been reported after analgesics have been administered. Elaborate stimulation techniques have allowed measurement of vestibular ERPs.

Attention and ERPs

The effects of attended and unattended stimuli were summarized by Hillyard and Hansen (1986) in their review of ERP correlates of attention. They pointed out that attended stimuli have more control over motor responses, are detected more accurately, and are better remembered than unattended stimuli. Attempts to find neurophysiological bases of this complex mental phenomenon in humans have used ERPs to a greater extent than raw EEG activity. A number of studies conducted in the 1960s indicated increased ERP amplitude to attended stimuli, whereas ignored stimuli produced low amplitude responses. For example, Haider, Spong, and Lindsley (1964) measured visual ERPs to signal and nonsignal stimuli during a prolonged vigilance task. They noted that lower amplitude ERPs were associated with lapses of attention, as indicated by failure to detect signals.

Although a number of other investigators reported similar results, Naatanen (1967) argued that the increased ERP amplitude did not reflect attention or cognitive activity per se, but rather the nonspecific arousal effects produced in response to expected, task-relevant stimuli. Because stimuli were presented in a regular manner, subjects could anticipate, and be prepared for, the critical stimulus, and therefore, ERP amplitude increases could be due to general cortical activation, not selective attention. In his own research, Naatanen (1967) randomly mixed relevant and irrelevant stimuli so that their occurrence could not be predicted. He found no ERP differences to relevant and irrelevant stimuli, suggesting that when differential preparation for these stimuli was precluded, ERP changes did not occur. Karlin (1970) supported Naatanen's view regarding the importance of differential preparation in producing ERP changes in the attention experiment paradigm. Karlin and Naatanen pointed out possible uncontrolled variables in selective attention experiments, including stimulus intensity, duration, sensory-modality stimulated, and peripheral orienting responses (e.g., pupil dilation).

However, a number of studies, which appear to avoid the criticisms of Naatanen and Karlin, demonstrated the role of selective attention in enhancing ERP amplitude. For example, Eason, Harter, and White (1969) presented unpredictable relevant stimuli to one visual field and irrelevant stimuli to the other field. The ERP component occurring between 120 and 220 msec increased in amplitude with presentations of relevant stimuli, those to which subjects paid more attention. Harter and Salmon (1972) presented equal numbers of relevant and irrelevant stimuli in an unpredictable manner and found enhancement of an ERP component peaking between 220 and 250 msec and a positive component at 290 to 340 msec when the stimuli were attended, as compared to when they were not attended. As later discussed for CNV, attention–arousal differences can also be demonstrated within a divided attention paradigm (Tecce, 1972).

Selectivity in Attention.   Examinations of ERP latencies have provided information regarding the point at which brain responses indicate differences to attended and unattended stimuli. A review by Hillyard and Kutas (1983) suggests that there is little evidence to support the notion that early ERP components (20 to 40 msec) are sensitive to attention shifts for different stimuli. However, under high load conditions where auditory stimuli were delivered rapidly over at least two different channels (e.g., left and right ears), a negative component 60 to 80 msec in onset was increased in size.

At first, it was thought that this ERP to attended tones was an enhancement of a peak called *N1*. Yet, because the wave also outlasted N1, the term *negative difference* (Nd) is now used to describe this attentional effect.

Hillyard and Hansen (1986) pointed out that the later portions of Nd appear to be endogenous (stimulus-independent), whereas the earlier portions overlap N1. An example of the contrast between the N1 and Nd waves is shown in Fig. 6.1. The result illustrated in the figure represents auditory ERPs to tones alternately attended to by left and right ears. Naatanen and his colleagues (e.g., Naatanen, Gaillard, & Mantysalo, 1978) referred to the Nd wave as "processing negativity," and Naatanen (1982) emphasized that this component is not just a simple increase in the exogenous (stimulus dependent) N1. Because of its short onset time, Nd was initially interpreted by Hillyard, Hink, Schwent, and Picton (1973) as indicating a tonic "stimulus set" by which relevant stimuli from the attended ear were automatically processed. Naatanen criticized this idea on the grounds that even discriminating the ear of entry required active processing that could take place as early as 60 to 70 msec. Naatanen suggested that Nd reflects decisions about whether or not a stimulus in the attended channel is a target. There is general agreement that Nd is a neural sign of stimulus processing that follows stimulus set selection (Hillyard & Kutas, 1983).

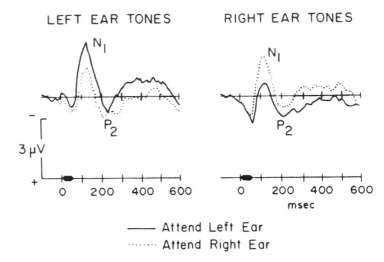

LEFT EAR TONES   RIGHT EAR TONES

—— Attend Left Ear
········ Attend Right Ear

FIG. 6.1. Auditory ERPs to standard tones in a selective listening task, in which attention was switched between tones in the two ears. Left-ear tones were 1800 Hz and right-ear tones were 2800 Hz, all at 45 dB SL and 75 msec durations. Shaded differences between attended and unattended ERPs for each ear represent the Nd component. (Grand average data over 10 subjects.)

Mismatch Negativity.   If a series of auditory stimuli suddenly changes, a negative wave at about 200 msec will occur. This N200 component is said to indicate mismatch negativity, and has been clearly described by Loveless (1983). Loveless explained that the N200 may occur with a change in physical characteristics of a repetitive stimulus, or even its omission when it is expected. This processing negativity has been conceptualized as a mismatch between the current stimulus and a neuronal model established by previous stimuli. Further, the N200 most likely reflects an automatic discrimination of stimulus change and might play a role in the initiation of the orienting response (Naatanen & Michie, 1979).

A theory of selective attention based on processing negativity has been proposed by Naatanen (1982). He suggested that selective attention involves the rehearsal of certain stimulus traces. This produces an automatic bias in the sensory system toward processing certain stimuli. The result of this selective processing is an attentional trace that lasts only as long as it is rehearsed and the sensory input is recent. The attentional trace allows rapid identification of stimulus differences when they are large enough. The Nd represents the comparison of the incoming stimulus with an internal representation and is larger and longer with increasing similarity. However, the N200 is related to a mismatch between the expected stimulus and its internal representation. Naatanen (1990) argued that mismatch negativity shows that features of auditory stimuli are processed whether or not they are fully attended. Also, precise neural representations of recent auditory stimuli are hypothesized, and these traces may underlie acoustic memory (echoic memory). The term *echoic memory* refers to the storage of auditory sensory information. According to Naatanen and colleagues, mismatch negativity (MMN) reflects the operation of automatic sensory (echoic) memory, the memory system that builds traces of the acoustic environment against which new stimuli are compared (Tiltinen, May, Reinikainen, & Naatanen, 1994).

Magnetoencephalography (MEG) was used to localize the source of MMN at the supratemporal auditory cortex (Ahlo et al., 1996). The authors also note that, although auditory memory traces are involved in MMN, it does not rule out the possibility that generators of other ERPs also participate in sensory memory for sounds. Intracranial recordings of MMN confirm that the response is localized to temporal cortex and automatically reacts to changes in a repetitive sound (Kropotov et al., 1995). The MMNs reported by Kropotov and colleagues were recorded from electrodes implanted directly in brain structures of some patients with Parkinson's disease and others with obsessive compulsive disorder. This must be taken into account since MMN in patients might be different than in healthy individuals. It is encouraging that the intracranial results were similar to those using MEG with normals. Alain and Woods (1997) have presented evidence that MMN can be modulated by selective attention and, therefore, is not completely automatic. In their experiment, MMN amplitude was higher in response to deviant stimuli presented in an attended ear than to the same stimuli presented in the unattended ear.

Theorists disagree over whether storage capacity is for only a single trace or can accommodate many traces. A study by Naatanen and colleagues (Winkler, Paavilainen, & Naatanen, 1992) indicates that at least two traces can be stored and participate in the mismatch process. Another study reported that MMN was larger over the right hemisphere regardless of the ear stimulated (Paavilainen, Alho, Reinkainen, Sams, & Naatanen, 1991). However, the N1 component was larger over the hemisphere contralateral to the stimulated ear. This result indicates that the N1 is a sensory component (exogenous), whereas MMN represents internal processes (endogenous).

Intermodal and Intramodal Selective Attention.   Visual ERPs with selective attention are more complex than for other attentional functions. The earliest changes take place when subjects attend to flashing lights in one visual field while ignoring lights in the other field (Eason & Ritchie, 1976). Hillyard and Kutas (1983) noted that in this situation, attended-field ERPs are enlarged in parietal–occipital areas and involve multiple components: P1 (80–110 msec), N1 (160–180 msec), and P2 (200–250 msec). Studies of intermodal selective attention compare ERPs during auditory and visual attention. When subjects selectively attend to auditory or visual stimuli where both are presented in mixed sequences, the ERPs to the attended modality are enhanced (Alho, Woods, Algazi, & Naatanen, 1992). Alho (1992) contended that processing negativity indicates a mechanism of intramodal selective attention in the auditory cortex, which is controlled by the frontal cortex. The mechanism is said to select auditory stimuli for further processing when they differ from unattended stimuli. Moreover, Alho asserts that the processing negativity generated during intramodal selective attention differs in scalp distribution from that obtained during intermodal selective attention. Thus, different brain mechanisms may be involved in selecting auditory stimuli from other auditory stimuli (intramodal) as opposed to selecting auditory stimuli from among visual stimuli (intermodal).

Resource Allocation.   In a concept advanced by Kahneman (1973) and Norman and Bobrow (1975), attention is limited in certain situations because we have only a certain amount of mental resources to spend on a task. If several tasks demand part of the same limited resources, then attention must be divided among the competing tasks. Allocation of resources among competing stimuli can be demonstrated by changes in ERP amplitudes. In one study, the Nd component of the ERP was found to be decreased during divided attention as compared to when attention was focused (Hink, Van Voorhis, Hillyard, & Smith, 1977). In a study by Wickens, Kramer, Vanasse, and Donchin (1983), subjects performed manual tracking while responding to probe stimuli of a secondary task. As the primary tracking task became more difficult, the ERPs elicited by the secondary task became smaller. Thus, as more resources were required for the main task, fewer were available for secondary tasks, and this was reflected in diminished ERPs.

Summary.   The ERP has contributed to understanding attentional processes in a number of ways. The preceding section has briefly discussed ERP contributions to the study of early and later processes in selective attention, processing negativity, mismatch negativity, and resource allocation. The ERP studies have also enabled psychophysiologists to make contributions to attentional theories. A discussion of attention as related to longer latency potentials is presented in the next chapter.

Perception and ERPs

In this section, we examine the existing evidence to determine whether reliable relationships have been shown between the ERP and such perceptual activities as form and pattern perception, perceptual masking, color perception, and perception of motion.

Shape.   The basic question here is whether changes in stimulus shape and pattern will influence ERPs as well as perception. An early study found that different geometric shapes (e.g., square, diamond) produced different visual ERP waveforms (John, Harrington, & Sutton, 1967). Little change in waveform of the ERP occurred with variation in the size of the figure (i.e., a small or large square evoked similar ERPs). These investigators also reported that ERPs for a blank flash were different from those produced by geometric shapes.

Pattern Size.   White (1969), using four stimulus patterns (a checkerboard, a horizontal grating, a set of concentric circles, and a set of radial lines), found striking differences in visual ERP waveforms with the different stimulus patterns. He described an additional experiment in which ERPs were recorded to the checkerboard patterns composed of different check-sizes. It was observed that larger checks produced smaller amplitude ERPs (e.g., a check-size that subtended 10 min of visual angle produced a response approximately twice the amplitude of that produced by a check that was four times larger). Visual angle depends on the size of an object and its distance from the eye. At a given distance, smaller size objects produce smaller visual angles at the eye. Visual angle is measured in seconds, minutes, and degrees of arc (60 sec of visual angle equal 1 min, and 60 min equal 1 degree).

Harter (1970) and Siegfried (1975) confirmed White's result with respect to the inverse relationship between visual ERP amplitude and check-size. Harter (1970) also reported that this relationship depends on the portion of the retina stimulated. When the foveal area (central 2 to 2.5 degrees of vision) was stimulated, relatively small checks (15 to 30 min of visual angle) evoked the greatest amplitude responses. However, when progressively more peripheral areas of the retina were stimulated (7.5 degrees out from the fovea), larger check-sizes (up to 60 min of visual angle) produced the greatest amplitude ERPs. Check-size had little effect on ERP when the retina was stimulated 12.5 to 27.5 degrees from the fovea.

Blurring and Pattern Perception.   When a checkerboard pattern was defocused (blurred), the result was a decrease in visual ERP amplitude (Harter & White, 1968). Conversely, with sharper checkerboard images, the ERP was larger. This result has led to suggestions by White (1969) that ERP amplitude differences may be used as a basis for testing vision, especially refractive errors, such as nearsightnedess (myopia). The logic behind this is that myopia results in a defocusing or blurring of images; thus smaller visual ERPs indicate that the object is not clearly seen. The technique especially lends itself to testing vision in persons who cannot verbalize well enough for testing by usual methods (e.g., the mentally retarded or young children). White's work actually led to the testing of nonverbal individuals, an application discussed further in chapter 16.

Upper and Lower Visual Fields.   Stimulation of upper and lower halves of the visual field has resulted in reports of differential visual ERP amplitudes (Eason, White, & Bartlett,

1970). Checkerboard sizes that subtended 10 min of angle produced larger ERPs in the upper field, whereas checks subtending 40 min (four times as large) were optimal for lower field stimulation. The overall ERP amplitudes suggested to Eason and his colleagues that the cortical visual system is more responsive to patterned stimuli appearing in the lower visual field than in the upper. However, the system was relatively more sensitive to smaller objects in the upper field. Why should this be the case? The investigators speculated that the differential sensitivity of the upper and lower visual fields may have survival value for humans as ground-dwelling animals. The upper field may be more attuned to "specks in the sky" that move rapidly and must be detected at a distance if the organism is to respond appropriately. However, ground objects that are close enough to pose a threat produce a larger visual angle. Therefore, the part of the visual system responding to them (lower field) may have greater sensitivity to larger objects (those that subtend angles of 30 min or more).

Perceptual Discrimination and P300.   Discriminations of line length were studied by Andreassi and Juszczak (1984). A single vertical 1.0 cm line (standard) was displayed for 40 msec and was followed randomly, 2 sec later, by 0.9 cm, 1.0 cm, or 1.1 cm (comparison) lines. Subjects were asked to judge whether the second of the lines (comparison) was "shorter" or "longer" than the first. Latencies of a P300 component (occurring between 300 and 400 msec) were longer with the 1.0 cm line compared to the other lengths. It was proposed that the difficulty experienced by subjects in judging whether the same length line was longer or shorter required more time, and this was reflected in the longer P300 latencies. Earlier papers also suggested that P300 latency is sensitive to stimulus evaluation time (Donchin, Ritter, & McCallum, 1978; McCarthy & Donchin, 1981).

In another experiment, Juszczak and Andreassi (1985) examined areal size and semantic discriminations in an ERP study of hemispheric asymmetries. In this study, subjects were required to discriminate between three sizes of rectangle whose widths were 14, 15, and 16 min of arc, respectively, and the meanings of three words. The size discrimination was much more difficult (58% correct) than word meanings (70% correct). Latencies of the P300 component were again longer with the more difficult task. This is further evidence indicating that stimulus evaluation must be completed before P300 occurs. This is useful information, because it suggests that P300 latency is an objective indicator of stimulus discriminability or task difficulty.

Pattern Recognition and NA.   A negative component of the visual ERP (designated NA) has been associated with pattern recognition by Ritter, Simson, Vaughan, and Macht (1982). This component occurs about 200 msec poststimulus, or about 100 msec prior to an N2 component thought to reflect classification of stimuli. Ritter and colleagues found support for the interpretation that NA and N2 indicate two sequential stages of information processing because the timing of NA was affected by the difficulty of a perceptual task, whereas N2 was influenced by the nature of the classification task. It should be noted that the NA component is derived via a subtraction procedure to delineate it from other, possibly overlapping, components.

Corners.   Patterns that include corners have been found to produce larger amplitude visual ERPs than those containing stripes (MacKay, 1969). Moskowitz, Armington, and Timberlake (1974) measured ERPs to rounded and sharply cornered stimuli, which varied in angularity, in 45-degree steps, from 45 to 180 degrees. The visual ERP was greatest in amplitude for the 90-degree, sharply cornered pattern. This can be seen in Fig. 6.2. Cornered and rounded-corner patterns produced larger ERPs than straight lines (180 degrees). The peak latency of responses to cornered patterns was shorter than that of responses to rounded and

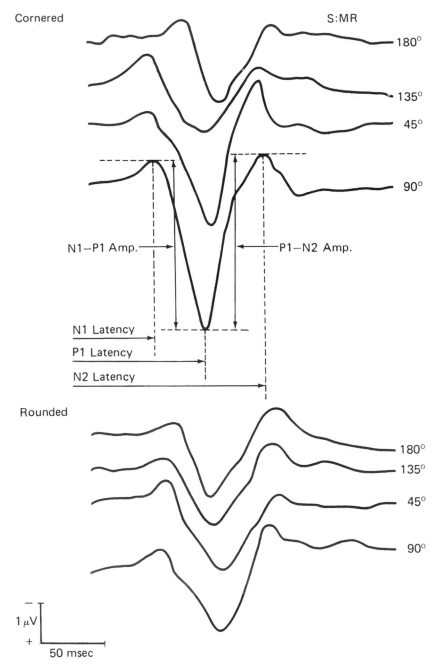

FIG. 6.2. Typical summated wave forms for one subject for each of eight experimental stimulus patterns. Positivity at the occipital electrode produced downward deflections in the recordings. Also shown is the method of amplitude and latency measurement. Note that in this figure positivity is downward.

straight patterns. Moskowitz et al. conjectured a "center-surrounded receptive field" model of the visual cortex to explain the major portion of their findings. The argument presented was that interactions between excitatory and inhibitory areas of the visual cortex allowed maximal neuronal response to occur with 90-degree cornered stimuli.

Orientation of Figures.   Maffei and Campbell (1970) presented vertical, horizontal, and oblique sets of lines (moving gratings) to subjects while visual ERPs were measured. They found ERPs to vertical and horizontal arrays to be similar, but the amplitude in response to the oblique lines was considerably smaller than to the others. They concluded that the resolving power of the visual system is greater in the vertical and horizontal orientation than in the oblique. This hypothesis was extended by Yoshida, Iwahara, and Nagamura (1975), who postulated that human visual cortical cells may be more responsive to horizontally and vertically oriented stimuli because our visual world is oriented mostly in horizontal or vertical planes. Leaning towers, such as the one in Pisa, are relatively rare in our visual environment!

Summary.   Perceptions of different forms, patterns, and orientations are paralleled by changes in visual ERPs. The various experiments with checkerboard patterns indicate that effects such as check-size, sharpness of image, and location in the visual field can influence the ERP. Visual ERPs are larger with small check-sizes, sharp images, and with stimuli in the lower visual field. Results in size discrimination studies indicate that more difficult judgments are accompanied by delayed P300 latencies. It has been suggested that stimulus evaluation must be completed before the P300 occurs. Other findings implicate a pair of negative components, NA and N2, in pattern recognition and classification, respectively. Patterns containing sharply angled corners result in larger ERPs than those with corners that are rounded or not angled as sharply. A possible conclusion is that the greater responsivity of the visual cortical system to stimuli oriented vertically and horizontally may be due to experiential factors that determine sensitivity of visual cortical cells.

Visual Masking.   There are instances where visual stimuli are presented to individuals and yet they are not perceived. For example, backward visual masking refers to a situation where presentation of a later stimulus (mask) interferes with the perception of an earlier displayed stimulus (target). The question that concerns us here is the nature of the visual ERP to the stimulus that is not perceived.

Schiller (1969) worked with a variety of visual masking known as *metacontrast.* This type of masking involves adjacent contours and is distinguished from a situation where the second stimulus completely overlaps the first. An example of this is when a large, intense patch of light follows a small, relatively dim light flash. Studies of this latter type were carried out by Donchin, Wicke, and Lindsley (1963), who measured the visual ERP under conditions in which a second (brighter) flash masked perception of the initial flash. At a 20-msec intersignal interval (ISI), when visual masking occurred, the ERPs were similar to those elicited by the second flash presented alone—the ERP to the first stimulus was completely suppressed. A similar result obtained by Donchin and Lindsley (1965) led them to conclude that the interference with the first flash by the second took place at or preceding the point at which ERPs were recorded (occipital cortex). They expressed the opinion that the same processes that are involved in perceptual suppression are involved in the ERP change. Note that in these two studies, the second flash was many times more intense than the first one (from 100 to 10,000 times), and this is probably the reason why the brain response to the first stimulus was completely obliterated.

To answer questions regarding changes in amount of contour interaction between sequential sets of stimuli, Andreassi, DeSimone, and Mellers (1976) conducted three experiments.

In the first, sequential sets of like stimuli (i.e., two grids, followed by three grids, followed by six grids) were presented, while ERPs were measured occipitally. The time between grid sets was 40 msec, and total light energy was equated for each. A schematic of the spatial and temporal arrangement of stimuli as they appeared on a CRT screen in the first experiment is shown in Fig. 6.3. In Condition A, all subjects reported two grids; in Condition B they reported seeing only the second set of three grids; while in Condition C they saw only the last set of six grids. The ERP component, which occurred at about 200 msec (P2), was significantly reduced in amplitude in Conditions B and C (masking) as compared to A (no masking). In Experiment 2, sets of the letter B were used to determine the reliability of the findings in the first experiment for a new stimulus configuration. The same results were obtained: Backward masking was accompanied by decreased P2 amplitudes. In Experiment 3, however, unlike sets of stimuli (two Bs, two Bs followed by three grids, and two Bs followed by three grids, followed by six grids) backward masking of the first set of two Bs did not occur, and neither did changes in ERP amplitude. Thus, when the amount of contour interaction between target and mask stimuli was increased to 50%, ERP amplitudes decreased with backward masking. When sets of unlike stimuli were used, the change in configuration reduced the amount of contour interaction between target and mask stimuli, thus eliminating backward masking along with ERP changes.

The effects of increasing amounts of target–mask contour interaction on perception of the target and the visual ERP was investigated by Andreassi, DeSimone, Gallichio, and Young (1976). An experiment was designed in which a single grid stimulus (target) was followed by either one, two, three, or four grid stimuli. A final condition was presentation of the target alone. In all instances, the stimulus energy of target and mask was equated. Thus, the amount of target–mask contour interaction was 0%, 25%, 50%, 75%, and 100%. Greater amounts of backward masking occurred with increases in contour interaction, and this was accompanied by increased attenuation of the P2 component of the ERP. Samples of ERP recordings from one subject under the conditions of this experiment are presented in Fig. 6.4.

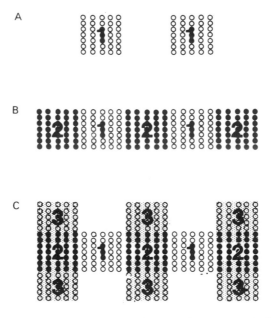

FIG. 6.3. Schematic drawing of spatial and temporal arrangement of stimuli as they appeared in the Andreassi et al. (1976a) study. Numbers merely indicate order of presentation and were not part of the actual display.

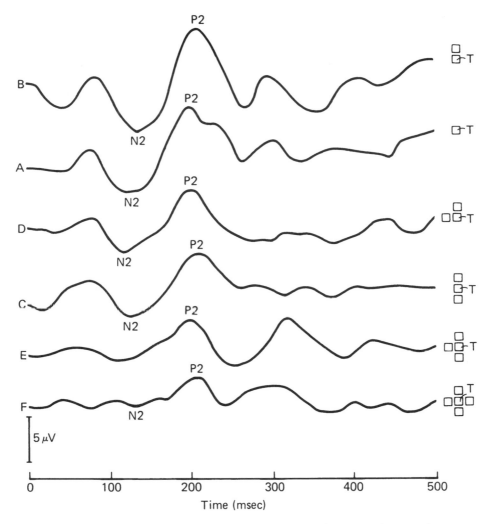

FIG. 6.4. Visual ERPs obtained under the following amount of target-mask contour interaction: Condition A = 0%, B = 25%, D = 50%, C = 50%, E = 75%, and F = 100%. In the inset, the labeled squares (T) represent the earlier presented targets, while the unlabeled elements represent masking stimuli. The ERP traces show, in general, a decrease in N2-P2 amplitude with increased amounts of contour interaction. All subjects experienced apparent motion under Condition B in which the target appeared to jump upward to a new location. This could be the reason for a lack of amplitude difference between condition B and A; i.e., contour interaction effects may be lost in apparent motion. Each trace is based on 100 responses to a target square (grid). Negativity is downward.

The effects of varying the time interval between target and mask was studied by Andreassi (1984). The target grid was followed by four masking grids at intervals of 10 msec, 40 msec, and 100 msec. The 40-msec interval produced visual masking and attenuation of the P2 component. However, the 10- and 100-msec intervals produced neither masking nor ERP reductions. This result shows that the timing and the spatial relationships are critical. If the mask is presented too close in time, the effect is lost because target and mask are perceived as one unit. If the interval is too long, target and mask are perceived sequentially. Another result observed in this study was that the ERP reduction was specific to the occipital site, because recordings from C_z differed little whether or not masking occurred. This supports the idea that topographic organization of the visual cortex, combined with excitatory–inhibitory interactions, underlie the backward visual masking phenomenon.

Summary.   A number of studies have indicated that backward visual masking was accompanied by changes in ERP amplitude or latency. An excitatory–inhibitory model has been proposed to explain the visual ERP reductions observed with visual masking: When a stimulus is presented to the visual system, it results in excitation being produced at a given location in the visual cortex. When similar stimuli follow the initial one closely in time and space, approximately adjacent areas of the visual cortex are stimulated, resulting in a reduction in response to the first stimulus. This inhibitory activity may not be sufficient to eliminate the ERP entirely, but it is enough to reduce it significantly, and the degree of reduction is related to the degree of spatial bounding of the first stimulus by later ones. The inhibition of earlier stimuli by later ones is made possible by the topographical organization of the visual system in which there is a one-to-one projection of retinal points to corresponding adjacent locations in the visual cortex.

The excitatory–inhibitory model draws support from studies that tested the feasibility of visual cortical prostheses with blind patients (e.g., Dobelle & Mladejovsky, 1974). In work of this type, direct electrical stimulation of discrete portions of visual cortex has been used to produce "electrical phosphenes" or sensations of light, in patients with peripherally caused blindness (eye damage). These electrically produced phosphenes interacted when two adjacent areas of visual cortex were stimulated (Dobelle, Mladejovsky, & Girvin, 1974). Simultaneous or sequential stimulation of two adjacent areas resulted in reports by patients of "seeing" one phosphene instead of two. The possibility that inhibitory effects can take place at the level of the visual cortex is directly suggested by these observations.

Color.   Pulses of electromagnetic energy (light) produce perceptions of color if they are within the visible spectrum for humans. The visible wavelength spectrum ranges from about 380 to 700 nanometers (nm), or billionths of a meter. The question that concerns us here is whether changes in wavelength (color) will be reflected in visual ERPs.

A number of investigators have reported that the wave form of the ERP was changed with different colors. For example, White and Eason (1966) found that components of the visual ERP varied as a function of stimulus color. Differences in ERP pattern were observed with stimulation by red, green, and blue and by the three colors simultaneously. Shipley, Jones, and Fry (1966) reported a change in ERP waveform as wavelength changed over a range of 380 to 680 nm. For instance, in the red range (640 to 680 nm), a larger positive component appeared at about 200 msec, whereas smaller, biphasic responses appeared with wavelengths in the violet range (380 to 420 nm). Regan (1972) criticized the use of large stimulus fields because they resulted in stimulation of receptors in the fovea (cones) and receptors outside the fovea (rods and cones), which have different wavelength sensitivities. Another problem pointed out by Regan is that of equating the light intensity of different wavelengths, thus making it difficult to separate color and brightness effects.

Significantly different ERPs to patterned red, green, and blue stimuli in persons with normal color vision were reported by Kinney, McKay, Mensch, and Luria (1972). Their results for one color-blind subject, who confused reds and greens but could distinguish them from blue (deuteranopia), showed ERPs that differed from normals. The ERPs for this deuteranope showed no differences in response to red and green but did show a different response to blue. Using six normals and one deuteranope, Regan and Spekreijse (1974) compared their ERPs to two-colored visual patterns. They found that the appearance of a pattern of equal intensity red and green checks produced normal ERPs in persons with normal vision, but smaller ERPs in the color-blind individual. When the brightness of the red and green checks were made equal, the amplitude of the color-blind subject's ERPs dropped sharply. Based on studies of normal color vision, these researchers concluded that the human visual system processes color information differently when the color is presented as patterned rather than as spatially unpatterned stimulation.

The experiments of Kinney et al. (1972) and Regan and Spekreijse (1974) suggest possible methods for the objective detection of color blindness. This possibility was emphasized in a study by Kinney and McKay (1974) in which ERPs of persons with normal color vision and of others with different types of color defects were measured. The color defects were deuteranopia (red–green confusion), protanopia (insensitivity to red), and tritanopia (red–blue–green confusion). Patterned stimuli varying in luminance and color were used. The normals gave pattern responses (large positive wave at about 100 msec) for both color and luminance, whereas color defectives produced ERPs only to luminance and not to any of the colors to which they were insensitive.

Summary.   Studies that have used appropriate methodological controls result in findings indicating that different ERPs occur to stimuli varying in color. Some results suggest the use of visual ERPs as objective indicators of color vision, which may be especially useful in cases where verbal responses are not possible.

Motion.   Mackay and Rietveld (1968) reported that a visual ERP occurred in response to movement of a single horizontal line, 7 cm in length. The line moved from rest at a velocity of 2 cm/sec. The presence of a reference line enhanced the ERP related to motion. This finding is associated with the fact that perceived velocity of a moving figure is increased in the vicinity of a stationary reference point.

The ERPs produced by two conditions of apparent motion and one of no motion were studied by Andreassi, Mayzner, Stern, and Okamura (1973). In all conditions, 20 Xs of identical stimulus energy and constant on and off times of 5 msec were presented sequentially on a CRT screen. Three different display orders resulted in three very different subjective perceptual experiences as follows: (a) an impression that "Xs converged toward the center from right and left," (b) "Xs diverged from the center with a small gap in the middle," and (c) the perception of "about 10 Xs with spaces in between." The ERPs, measured from O_1 and O_2, did not differ under the three conditions, indicating that, at least in this case, the brain mechanisms that produced the ERP were similar, even though the subject's perceptual experiences were very different.

Reversals in the horizontal motion of a visual noise pattern (random dots) were used to produce ERPs in an experiment by Clarke (1974). The velocity of motion was 10 degrees of visual angle per second, and motion reversal took 5 msec to occur. Clarke obtained suggestive evidence that motion-reversal ERPs were produced largely by direction-sensitive mechanisms within the human brain. He proposed tentatively that the mechanisms might be similar to the directionally sensitive neurons reported to exist in the visual cortex of the monkey. Cooper et al. (1977) measured visual ERPs when stimuli such as cars, vans, and trucks moved at unpredictable and infrequent times in a televised landscape. Measurements were made from frontal, central, parietal, and occipital areas. The main cortical sign of detecting the moving target was the occurrence of a large (30 μV) positive potential at the vertex and parietal locations shortly after the eyes fixated in the area of the vehicle (300 msec).

If you present the same object at two different points in space at the right time intervals, a person will see the object as moving from the first to the second position. This experience of motion is called the *Phi phenomenon* and often cannot be distinguished from real motion. Gallichio and Andreassi (1982) examined this type of apparent motion (calling it *discrete*) and another type in which a vertical line appeared to move smoothly from left to right, rather than making a discrete jump (*continuous motion*). The visual ERPs were recorded from O_z and C_z for the two apparent motion conditions under three different velocities (8.00 deg/sec, 13.08 deg/sec, and 19.18 deg/sec). A seventh condition was a stationary presentation of two vertical lines at the beginning and endpoints.

The main finding was that at the O_z site, the two higher velocity continuous motion conditions resulted in longer latency P200 components than the discrete motion condition. In addition, the highest velocity discrete motion condition resulted in longer P200 latencies compared to other discrete conditions. The results indicate a greater duration of brain processing time for high velocity continuous motion in the human visual system, suggesting differential processing for the two types of motion and for higher velocity movement. Because these differences were not observed at the central site (C_z), the role of the occipital area as the primary processor of differential motion and velocity is also indicated.

Another approach to studying visual ERPs to apparent motion has been to use the *breakdown effect*. The breakdown describes an effect in apparent motion in which the perception of smooth motion of a continuous stimulus alternates with the percept of two discrete stimuli (Selmes, Fulham, Finlay, Chorlton, & Manning, 1997). This breakdown has been explained in terms of adaptation to apparent motion that occurs during prolonged viewing. Selmes and colleagues recorded VERPs during periods of perceived motion and breakdown (nonmotion). They found that motion VERPs were greater in amplitude than nonmotion responses, suggesting a reduction of cortical activity during periods of breakdown.

Summary.   Investigations into the various visual ERPs produced by differerent types of perceived movement have yielded interesting results. The ERP findings provide suggestive evidence for direction-sensitive mechanisms in the human brain and larger amplitude responses accompanying the detection of a moving target. In addition, there is evidence that different types of apparent motion and velocity of motion may be processed differently in the visual system as indicated by differences in cortical responses to discrete and continuous apparent motion.

The next chapter discusses long-latency ERPs and steady potential shifts in recorded brain activity. These ERPs have been associated with the performance of various cognitive and information-processing activities and have intriguing implications with respect to understanding brain–behavior relationships.

REFERENCES

Alain, C., & Woods, D. L. (1997). Attention modulates auditory pattern memory as indexed by event-related brain potentials. *Psychophysiology, 34*, 534–546.

Alho, K. (1992). Selective attention in auditory processing as reflected by event-related brain potentials. *Psychophysiology, 29*, 247–263.

Alho, K., Tervaniemi, M., Huotilainen, M., Lavikainen, J., Tiitinen, H., Ilmoniemi, R. J., Knuutila, J., & Naatanen, R. (1996). Processing of complex sounds in the human auditory cortex as revealed by magnetic brain responses. *Psychophysiology, 33*, 369–375.

Alho, K., Woods, D. L., Algazi, A., & Naatanen, R. (1992). Intermodal selective attention. II. Effects of attentional load on processing of auditory and visual stimuli in central space. *Electroencephalography and Clinical Neurophysiology, 82*, 356–368.

Andreassi, J. L. (1984). Interactions between target and masking stimuli: Perceptual and event-related potential effects. *International Journal of Psychophysiology, 1*, 153–162.

Andreassi, J. L., DeSimone, J. J., Gallichio, J. A., & Young, N. E. (1976, December). *Evoked cortical potentials and information processing.* Fourth Annual Report, contract N00014-72-A-0406-0006. Office of Naval Research. Washington, DC.

Andreassi, J. L., Desimone, J. J., & Mellers, B. W. (1976). Amplitude changes in the visual evoked cortical potential with backward masking. *Electroencephalography and Clinical Neurophysiology, 41*, 387–398.

Andreassi, J. L., & Juszczak, N. M. (1984). An investigation of hemispheric specialization and visual event-related potentials in discriminations of line length. *International Journal of Psychophysiology, 2*, 87–95.

Andreassi, J. L., Mayzner, M. S., Beyda, D. R., & Davidovics, S. (1971). Visual cortical evoked potentials under conditions of sequential blanking. *Perception & Psychophysics, 10*, 164–168.

Andreassi, J. L., Mayzner, M. S., Stern, M., & Okamura, H. (1973). Visual cortical evoked potentials under conditions of apparent motion. *Physiological Psychology, 1*, 118–120.

Andreassi, J. L., Stern, M., & Okamura, H. (1974). Visual cortical evoked potentials as a function of intensity variations in sequential blanking. *Psychophysiology, 11*, 336–345.

Begleiter, H., & Platz, A. (1969). Cortical evoked potentials to semantic stimuli. *Psychophysiology, 6*, 91–100.

Begleiter, H., Porjesz, B., Yerre, C., & Kissin, B. (1973). Evoked potential correlates of expected stimulus intensity. *Science, 179*, 814–816.

Birbaumer, N., Roberts, L. E., Lutzenbrger, W., Rockstroh, B., & Elbert, T. (1992). Area-specific self-regulation of slow cortical potentials on the sagittal midline and its effects on behavior. *Electroencephalography and Clinical Neurophysiology, 84*, 353–361.

Blinkhorn, S. F., & Hendrickson, E. E. (1982). Averaged evoked responses and psychometric intelligence. *Nature, 295*, 596–597.

Brown, W. S., Marsh, J. T., & Smith, J. C. (1973). Contextual meaning effects on speech-evoked potentials, *Behavioral Biology, 9*, 755–761.

Brown, W. S., Marsh, J. T., & Smith, J. C. (1976). Evoked potential waveform differences produced by the perception of different meanings of an ambiguous phrase. *Electroencephalography and Clinical Neurophysiology, 41*, 113–123.

Buchsbaum, M. S., Davis, G. C., Coppola, R., & Naber, D. (1981). Opiate pharmacology and individual differences: II somatosensory evoked potentials. *Pain, 61*, 121–130.

Burns, N. R., Nettelbeck, T., & Cooper, C. J. (1997). The string measure of the ERP: What does it measure? *International Journal of Psychophysiology, 27*, 43–54.

Byrne, J. M., Dywan, C. A., & Connolly, J. F. (1995). Assessment of children's receptive vocabulary using event-related brain potentials: Development of a clinically valid test. *Child Neuropsychology, 1*, 211–223.

Callaway, E. (1975). *Brain electrical potentials and individual psychological differences*. New York: Grune & Stratton.

Chalke, F. C. R., & Ertl, J. (1965). Evoked potentials and intelligence. *Life Sciences, 4*, 1319–1322.

Chatrian, G. E., Canfield, R. C., Knauss, T. A., & Lettich, E. (1975). Cerebral responses to electrical tooth pulp stimulation in man: An objective correlate of acute experimental pain. *Neurology, 25*, 745–757.

Clarke, P. G. (1974). Are visual evoked potentials to motion-reversal produced by direction-sensitive brain mechanisms? *Vision Research, 14*, 1281–1284.

Connolly, J. F., Major, A., Allen, S., & D'Arcy, R. C. (in press). Performance on WISC-III and WAIS–R NI vocabulary subtests assessed with event-related brain potentials: An innovative method of assessment. *Journal of Clinical & Experimental Neuropsychology*.

Cooper, R., McCallum, W. C., Newton, P., Papakostopoulos, D., Pocock, P. V., & Warren, W. J. (1977). Cortical potentials associated with the detection of visual events. *Science, 196*, 74–77.

Davis, F. B. (1971). *The measurement of mental capability through evoked potential recordings*. (Education Records Research Bulletin No. 1), Greenwich, CT: Educational Records Bureau.

Dobelle, W., & Mladejovsky, M. G. (1974). Phosphenes produced by electrical stimulation of human occipital cortex and their applicaation to the development of a prosthesis for the blind. *Journal of Physiology, 243*, 553–576.

Dobelle, W., Mladejovsky, M. G., & Girvin, J. P. (1974). Artificial vision for the blind: Electrical stimulation of visual cortex offers hope for a functional prosthesis. *Science, 183*, 440–443.

Donchin, E., & Lindsley, D. B. (1965). Visually evoked respponse correlates of perceptual masking and enhancement. *Electroencephalography and Clinical Neurophysiology, 19*, 325–335.

Donchin, E., Ritter, W., & McCallum, C. (1978). Cognitive psychophysiology: The endogenous components of the ERP. In E. Callaway, P. Teuting, & S. Koslow (Eds.), *Event-related potentials in man* (pp. 349–411). New York: Academic Press.

Donchin, E., Wicke, J., & Lindsley, D. B. (1963). Cortical evoked potentials and perception of paired flashes. *Science, 141*, 1285–1286.

Eason, R. G., Harter, M. R., & White, C. T. (1969). Effects of attention and arousal on visually evoked cortical potentials and reaction time in man. *Physiology and Behavior, 4*, 283–289.

Eason, R. G., & Ritchie, G. (1976, May). *Effects of stimulus set on early and late components of visually evoked potentials*. Paper presented at the meeting of the Psychonomic Society, St. Louis, MO.

Eason, R. G., White, C. T., & Bartlett, N. (1970). Effects of checkerboard pattern stimulation on evoked cortical responses in relation to check size and visual field. *Psychonomic Science, 21*, 113–115.

Ertl, J. P., & Schafer, W. W. P. (1969). Brain response correlates of psychometric intelligence. *Nature, 223*, 421–422.

Friedman, D., Simson, R., Ritter, W., & Rapin, I. (1975a). Cortical evoked potentials elicited by real speech words and human sounds. *Electroencephalography and Clinical Neurophysiology, 38*, 13–19.

Friedman, D., Simson, R., Ritter, W., & Rapin, I. (1975b). The late positive component (P300) and information processing in sentences. *Electroencephalography and Clinical Neurophysiology, 38*, 255–262.

Funakoshi, M., & Kawamura, Y. (1971). Summated cerebral evoked responses to taste stimuli in man. *Electroencephalography and Clinical Neurophysiology, 30*, 205–209.

Gale, A., & Edwards, J. (1983). Cortical correlates of intelligence. In A. Gale & J. Edwards (Eds.), *Physiological correlates of human behavior* (Vol. 3, pp. 79–97). New York: Academic Press.

Gallichio, J. A., & Andreassi, J. L. (1982). Visual evoked potentials under varied velocities of continuous and discrete apparent motion. *International Journal of Neuroscience, 17*, 169–177.

Haider, M., Spong, P., & Lindsley, D. B. (1964). Attention, vigilance, and cortical evoked potentials in humans. *Science, 145*, 180–182.

Harter, M. R. (1970). Evoked cortical responses to checkerboard patterns: Effect of check-size as a function of retinal eccentricity. *Vision Research, 10*, 1365–1376.

Harter, M. R., & Salmon, L. E. (1972). Intra-modality selective attention and evoked cortical potentials to randomly presented patterns. *Electroencephalography and Clinical Neurophysiology, 32*, 605–613.

Harter, M. R., & White, C. T. (1968). Effects of contour sharpness and checksize on visually evoked cortical potentials. *Vision Research, 8*, 701–711.

Hendrickson, E. E., & Hendrickson, A. E. (1980). The biological basis of individual differences in intelligence. *Personality & Individual Differences, 1*, 3–33.

Hillyard, S. A., & Hansen, J. C. (1986). Attention: Electrophysiological approaches. In M. G. H. Coles, E. Donchin, & S. W. Porges (Eds.), *Psychophysiology: Systems, processes & applications* (pp. 227–267). New York: Guilford.

Hillyard, S. A., Hink, R. G., Schwent, V. L., & Picton, T. W. (1973). Electrical signs of selective attention in the human brain. *Science, 182*, 177–180.

Hillyard, S. A., & Kutas, M. (1983). Electrophysiology of cognitive processing. *Annual Review of Psychology, 34*, 33–61.

Hink, R. F., Van Voorhis, S. T., Hillyard, S. A., & Smith, T. (1977). The division of attention and the human auditory evoked potentials. *Neuropsychologia, 15*, 597–605.

John, E. R., Harrington, R. N., & Sutton, S. (1967). Effects of visual form on the evoked response. *Science, 155*, 1439–1442.

Juszczak, N. M., & Andreassi, J. L. (1985). An investigation of hemispheric asymmetry in size and semantic discriminations and related visual ERPs. *International Journal of Neuroscience, 27*, 283–297.

Kahneman, D. (1973). *Attention and effort.* Englewood Cliffs, NJ: Prentice-Hall.

Karlin, L. (1970). Cognition, preparation and sensory-evoked potentials. *Psychological Bulletin, 73*, 122–136.

Kinney, J. A. S., & McKay, C. L. (1974). Test of color-defective vision using the visual evoked response. *Journal of the Optical Society of America, 64*, 1244–1250.

Kinney, J. A. S., McKay, C. L., Mensch, A. J., & Luria, S. M. (1972). Techniques for analysing differences in VERs: Colored and patterned stimuli. *Vision Research, 12*, 1733–1747.

Kobal, G., & Hummel, C. (1988). Cerebral chemosensory evoked potentials elicited by chemical stimulation of the human olfactory respiratory nasal mucosa. *Electroencephalography and Clinical Neurophysiology, 71*, 241–250.

Kropotov, J. D., Naatanen, R., Sevostianov, A. V., Alho, K., Reinikainen, K., & Kropotova, O. V. (1995). *Psychophysiology, 32*, 418–422.

Kutas, M., & Hillyard, S. A. (1980). Reading senseless sentences: Brain potentials reflect semantic incongruity. *Science, 207*, 203–205.

Kutas, M., Lindamood, T. E., & Hillyard, S. A. (1984). Word expectancy and event-related brain potentials during sentence processing. In S. Kornblum & J. Requin (Eds.), *Preparatory states and processes* (pp. 217–237). Hillsdale, NJ: Lawrence Erlbaum Associates.

Lelord, G., Laffont, F., & Jusseaume, P. H. (1976). Conditioning of evoked potentials in children of differing intelligence. *Psychophysiology, 13*, 81–85.

Lorig, T. S., Matia, D. C., Peszka, J. J., & Bryant, D. N. (1996). The effects of active and passive stimulation on chemosensory event-related potentials. *International Journal of Psychophysiology, 23*, 199–205.

Lorig, T. S., Sapp, A. C., Campbell, J., & Cain, W. S. (1993). Event-related potentials to odor stimuli. *Bulletin of the Psychonomic Society, 31*, 131–134.

Loveless, N. E. (1983). Event-related brain potentials and human performance. In A. Gale & J. Edwards (Eds.), *Physiological correlates of human behavior* (Vol. 2, pp. 79–97). New York: Academic Press.

Lutzenberger, W., Roberts, L. E., & Birbaumer, N. (1993). Memory performance and area-specific self-regulation of slow cortical potentials: Dual-task interference. *International Journal of Psychophysiology, 15*, 217–226.

Mackay, D. M. (1969). Evoked brain potentials as indicators of sensory information processing. *Neurosciences Research Program Bulletin, 7*, 3.

Mackay, D. M., & Rietveld, W. J. (1968). Electroencephalogram potentials evoked by accelerated visual motion. *Nature, 217*, 677–678.

Maffei, L., & Campbell, F. W. (1970). Neurophysiological localization of the vertical and horizontal visual coordinates in man. *Science, 167*, 386–387.

Martineau, J., Garreau, B., Barthelemy, C., & Lelord, G. (1984). Evoked potentials and P300 during sensory conditioning in autistic children. In R. Karrer, J. Cohen, & P. Teuting (Eds.), *Brain & information* (Vol. 425, pp. 362–369). New York: Annals of the New York Academy of Sciences.

McCarthy, G., & Donchin, E. (1981). A metric for thought: A comparison of P300 latency and reaction time. *Science, 211,* 77–79.

Molfese, D. L. (1979). Cortical involvement in the semantic processing of coarticulated speech cues. *Brain & Language, 7,* 86–100.

Moskowitz, A. F., Armington, J. C., & Timberlake, G. (1974). Corners, receptive fields, and visually evoked potentials. *Perception and Psychophysics, 15,* 325–330.

Murphy, C., Nordin, S., de Wijk, R. A., Cain, W. S., & Polich, J. (1994). Olfactory-evoked potentials: Assessment of young and elderly, and comparison to psychophysical threshold. *Chemical Senses, 19,* 47–56.

Naatanen, R. (1967). Selective attention and evoked potentials. *Annales Academic Scientiarum Fennica, 151,* 1–226.

Naatanen, R. (1982). Processing negativity: An evoked-potential reflection of selective attention. *Psychological Bulletin, 92,* 605–640.

Naatanen, R. (1990). The role of attention in auditory information processing as revealed by event-related potentials and other brain measures of cognitive function. *Behavioral and Brain Sciences, 13,* 201–288.

Naatanen, R., Gaillard, A. W. K., & Mantysalo, S. (1978). The N1 effect of selective attention reinterpreted. *Acta Psychologica, 42,* 313–329.

Naatanen, R., & Michie, P. T. (1979). Early selective-attention effects on the evoked potential: A critical review and reinterpretation. *Biological Psychology, 8,* 81–136.

Neville, H. J. (1980). Event-related potentials in neuropsychological studies of language. *Brain & Language, 11,* 300–318.

Norman, D. A., & Bobrow, D. G. (1975). On data-limited and resource-limited processes. *Cognitive Psychology, 7,* 44–64.

O'Donnell, B. F., Friedman, S., Swearer, J. M., & Drachman, D. A. (1992). Active and passive P3 latency and psychometric performance: Influence of age and individual differences. *International Journal of Psychophysiology, 12,* 187–195.

Paavilainen, P., Alho, K., Reinikainen, K., Sams, M., & Naatanen, R. (1991). Right hemisphere dominance of different mismatch negativities. *Electroencephalography and Clinical Neurophysiology, 78,* 466–479.

Palomba, D., Angrilli, A., & Mini, A. (1997). Visual evoked potentials, heart rate responses and memory to emotional pictorial stimuli. *International Journal of Psychophysiology, 27,* 55–68.

Pause, B. M., Sojka, B., Krauel, K., & Ferstl, R. (1996). The nature of the late positive complex within the olfactory event-related potential (OERP). *Psychophysiology, 33,* 376–384.

Perry, N. W., Childers, D. G., & Falgout, J. C. (1972). Chromatic specificity of the visual evoked response. *Science, 177,* 813–815.

Perry, N. W., McCoy, J. G., Cunningham, W. R., Falgout, J. C., & Street, W. J. (1976). Multivariate visual evoked response correlates of intelligence. *Psychophysiology, 13,* 323–329.

Polich, J., & Martin, S. (1992). P300, cognitive capability, and personality: A correlational study of university undergraduates. *Personality and Individual Differences, 13,* 533–543.

Porjesz, B., & Begleiter, H. (1975). The effects of stimulus expectancy on evoked brain potentials. *Psychophysiology, 12,* 152–157.

Regan, D. (1972). *Evoked potentials in psychology, sensory physiology and clinical medicine.* New York: Wiley.

Regan, D., & Spekreijse, H. (1974). Evoked potentials indications of color blindness. *Vision Research, 14,* 89–95.

Rietveld, W. J., Tordoir, W. E. M., Hagenouw, J. R. B., Lubbers, J. A., & Spoor, Th. (1967). Visual evoked responses to blank and to checkerboard patterned flashes. *Acta Physiologica Pharmacologia Neerkandia, 14,* 259–285.

Ritter, W., Simson, R., Vaughan, H. G. Jr., & Macht, M. (1982). Manipulation of event-related potential manifestations of information processing stages. *Science, 218,* 909–911.

Ritter, W., Vaughan, H. G., Jr., & Costa, L. D. (1968). Orienting and habituation to auditory stimuli: A study of short term changes in average evoked responses. *Electroencephalography and Clinical Neurophysiology, 25,* 550–556.

Rockstroh, B., Birbaumer, N., Elbert, T., & Lutzenberger, W. (1984). Operant control of EEG and event-related slow brain potentials. *Biofeedback & Self-Regulation, 9,* 139–157.

Rosenfeld, J. P., Dowman, R., Silvia, R., & Heinricher, M. (1984). Operantly controlled somatosensory brain potentials: Specific effects on pain processes. In T. Elbert, B. Rockstroh, W. Lutzenberger, & N. Birbaumer (Eds.), *Self-regulation of the brain and behavior* (pp. 139–153). Heidelberg: Springer.

Ruch, T. C., Patton, H. D., Woodbury, J. W., & Towe, D. L. (Eds.). (1965). *Neurophysiology.* Philadelphia: Saunders.

Ruchkin, D. S., & Sutton, S. (1973). Visual evoked and emmited potentials and stimulus significance. *Bulletin of the Psychosomatic Society, 2,* 144–146.

Rust, J. (1975). Cortical evoked potential, personality and intelligence. *Journal of Comparative and Physiological Psychology, 89,* 1220–1226.

Salamy, J., Potvin, A., Jones, K., & Landreth, J. (1975). Cortical evoked responses to labyrinthine stimulation in man. *Psychophysiology, 12*, 55–61.

Schiller, P. H. (1969). Behavioral and electrophysiological studies of visual masking. In K. N. Leibovic (Ed.), *Information processing in the nervous system* (pp. 141–165). New York: Springer-Verlag.

Selmes, C. M., Fulham, W. R., Finlay, D. C., Chorlton, M. C., & Manning, M. L. (1997). *Perception and Psychophysics, 39*, 489–499.

Shagass, C., & Schwartz, M. (1964). Recovery functions of somatosensory peripheral nerve and cerebral evoked responses in man. *Electroencephalography and Clinical Neurophysiology, 17*, 126–135.

Shipley, T., Jones, R. W., & Fry, A. (1966). Intensity and the evoked occipitogram in man. *Vision Research, 6*, 657–667.

Shucard, D. W., & Horn, J. L. (1972). Evoked cortical potentials and measurement of human abilities. *Journal of Comparative and Physiological Psychology, 78*, 59–68.

Siegfried, J. B. (1975). The effects of checkerboard pattern check size on the VECP. *Bulletin of the Psychonomic Society, 6*, 306–308.

Smith, D. B., Allison, T., Goff, W. R., & Principato, J. J. (1971). Human odorant evoked responses: Effects of trigeminal or olfactory deficit. *Electroencephalography and Clinical Neurophysiology, 30*, 313–317.

Soinen, K., & Jarvilehto, T. (1983). Somatosensory evoked potentials associated with tactile stimulation at detection threshold in man. *Electroencephalography and Clinical Neurophysiology, 56*, 494–500.

Sutton, S., Teuting, P., Zubin, J., & John, E. R. (1967). Information delivery and the sensory evoked potential. *Science, 155*, 1436–1439.

Tecce, J. J. (1972). Contingent negative variation (CNV) and psychological processes in man. *Psychological Bulletin, 77*, 73–108.

Tiltinen, H., May, P., Reinkainen, K., & Naatanen, R. (1994). Attentive novelty detection in humans is governed by pre-attentive sensory memory. *Nature, 372*, 90–92.

Vanderploeg, R. D., Brown, W. S., & Marsh, J. T. (1987). Judgments of emotion in words and faces: ERP correlates. *International Journal of Psychophysiology, 51*, 193–205.

Vetterli, C. F., & Furedy, J. J. (1985). Evoked potential correlates of intelligence: Some problems with Hendrickson's string measure of evoked potential complexity and error theory of intelligence. *International Journal of Psychophysiology, 3*, 1–3.

Weinberg, H., Walter, W. G., & Crow, H. J. (1970). Intra-cerebral events in humans related to real and imaginary stimuli. *Electroencephalography and Clinical Neurophysiology, 29*, 1–9.

White, C. T. (1969). Evoked cortical responses and patterned stimuli. *American Psychologist, 24*, 211–214.

White, C. T., & Eason, R. G. (1966). Evoked cortical potentials in relation to certain aspects of visual perception. *Psychological Monographs: General & Applied, 80*, 1–14.

Wickens, C., Kramer, A., Vanasse, L., & Donchin, E. (1983). Performance of concurrrent tasks: A psychophysiological analysis of reciprocity of information-processing resources. *Science, 221*, 1080–1082.

Winkler, I., Paavilainen, P., & Naatanen, R. (1992). Can echoic memory store two traces simultaneously? A study of event-related potentials. *Psychophysiology, 29*, 337–349.

Wood, C. C., Goff, W. R., & Day, R. S. (1971). Auditory evoked potentials during speech perception. *Science, 173*, 1248–1251.

Yoshida, S., Iwahara, S., & Nagamura, N. (1975). The effect of stimulus orientation on the visual evoked potential in human subjects. *Electroencephalography and Clinical Neurophysiology, 39*, 53–57.

7

Event-Related Slow Brain
Potentials and Behavior

Among the more interesting brain responses are the *slow potentials* or *slow waves*. They are slow in the sense that they take longer to develop than do the sensory-evoked potentials and motor potentials discussed earlier. Two of these slow potentials are the contingent negative variation (CNV) and the readiness potential (RP), categorized by Vaughan (1969) as steady potential shifts. A third type of slow wave includes the components of the ERP that occur between 250 to 900 msec after the stimulus commonly referred to as *P300*. Some researchers prefer to call these later positive components P3 or P3b, without imposing a particular latency on the responses. The term P300 is still commonly used because the original studies by Sutton and his associates (Sutton, Braren, & Zubin, 1965) found that the response occurred about 300 msec after some initiating stimulus. All of the slow waves mentioned thus far are endogenous in nature. This means they are produced by internal (endogenous) processes and are less dependent on external (exogenous) stimuli than are the sensory or motor potentials previously described. These internal processes are among the more fascinating ones that can be studied by psychologists and include, among other attributes, intentions to move (readiness potential), expectancies regarding the occurrence of some stimulus (CNV), and decisions (P300). Because of their relation to cognitive events, many cognitive scientists have become interested in these slow waves, especially the P300.

THE CONTINGENT NEGATIVE VARIATION (CNV)

In the now classic paper by Walter, Cooper, Aldridge, McCallum, and Winter (1964), CNV was described as a steady, relatively long-lasting, negative shift in brain activity, which developed between the time of a warning signal (S1) and a second stimulus (S2) that demanded a response. Walter and colleagues referred to this slow shift in EEG baseline, in the S1–S2 interval, as a contingent negative variation because its occurrence depends on the contingency between two events and because it shows a negative drift. It was later found that CNV can occur without motor responses to S2. For example, Cohen and Walter (1966) obtained CNV in anticipation of pictorial stimuli that were used as S2. No motor response was made by the subjects. On the basis of this kind of result, Cohen and Walter suggested that the CNV reflects a state of expectancy and have used the term *E wave* as a substitute for CNV. Other investigators proposed that CNV indicates an intention to act (Low, Borda, Frost, & Kellaway, 1966), subject motivation (Irwin, Knott, McAdam, & Rebert, 1966), or attention (McCallum, 1969; Tecce & Scheff, 1969). Whatever the terminology used, it is clear that CNV is related to psychological and performance factors, and some of these are reviewed here.

The origin of CNV has been attributed mainly to the cerebral cortex when excitatory signals from the thalamus depolarize neurons over extensive cortical regions (Elbert et al., 1991). According to Elbert and colleagues, the large slow negative wave indicates periods of *increased* cortical excitability. The contributions of subcortical generators to the response, ultimately measured at the scalp, is very small because of their distance from the cortex. The amplitude of CNV measured at the vertex (central scalp) is about 15 μV in young adults. It begins within 200 to 400 msec after S1 and reaches its peak within 400 to 900 msec if the S1–S2 interval is 1,000 msec. The CNV amplitude drops abruptly with S2. The time needed to reach peak amplitude is related to CNV shape. Two basic shapes have been identified (see Fig. 7.1) and are referred to as *Type A* (fast rise time) and *Type B* (slow rise time) by Tecce (1971). Type A CNVs have been found to occur when subjects were uncertain about when S2 would occur, and Type B occurred when they were more certain about its time of appearance (see Tecce, 1972).

This CNV typology also accounts for individual differences in response to psychoactive drugs such as amphetamines and barbiturates (Tecce, Savignano-Bowman, & Cole, 1978). The magnitude of CNV appears related to stimulus intensity. When S2 intensity is very low (e.g., a barely audible tone) or very high (loud tone or intense electric shock), CNV magnitude is increased, perhaps because of enhanced attentiveness and alertness with regard to S2. When the S1–S2 interval is 4 sec or more, the CNV recordings show early and late portions. For longer S1–S2 intervals (say, 6 sec) the early negative wave will peak during the first 1 to 3 sec after S1. The late, or terminal wave peaks in the second interval before S2 presentation (Birbaumer, Elbert, Canavan, & Rockstroh, 1990). It has been proposed by Rohrbaugh and Gaillard (1983) that the early portion of the CNV reflects orienting and activation, and the later part is associated with preparation for a motor response. Psychological issues that have attracted CNV researchers include the relation between CNV amplitude and speed of response, the effects of distraction and attention on the development of CNV, and the effects of effort and reward on CNV amplitude. Other questions of interest to psychophysiologists concern stimulus variables, including uncertainty, missing stimuli, and affective value (relating to sexual preference). For a comprehensive review of CNV–behavior relationships refer to Tecce and Cattanach (1993).

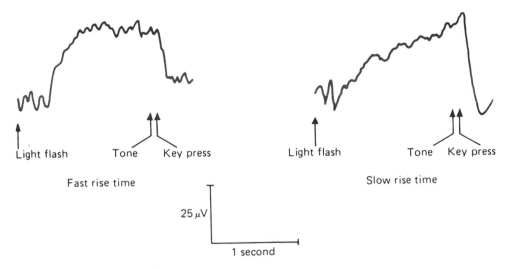

FIG. 7.1. Two types of CNV morphology based on fast (type A) and slow (type B) rise time to maximum voltage. (Photo courtesy of Dr. J. J. Tecce of Boston College.)

CNV and Reaction Time

There have been a number of reports in which an association between CNV amplitude and RT was noted, and several that indicate no relation between CNV and speed of response. For example, Cant and Bickford (1967) found that avoidable shock increased CNV amplitude and quickened RT. Therefore, when subjects were allowed to avoid shock with faster responses, the increased effort (perhaps attention) involved led to larger CNVs. Also, Tecce and Scheff (1969) observed that distraction decreased CNV amplitude and slowed RT. They found, too, that reward increased CNV and led to faster RTs. On the other hand, Naitoh, Johnson, and Lubin (1971) reported that sleep loss produced decreased CNV amplitudes but did not affect RT. Further, Rebert (1972) observed that feedback about speed of RT led to faster responses by subjects, but resulted in no CNV changes.

Rebert and Tecce (1973) performed a careful review of the literature available at the time and noted that the CNV and RT relationships that had been reported resulted from experimental manipulations and did not reflect a strong causal relationship between the two processes. They concluded that CNV and RT are relatively independent factors. Haagh and Brunia (1985) found no relation between RT and response-relevant muscle activity with its increased CNV amplitude. Muscle activity was recorded from the leg muscles as subjects waited to give a response to S2.

Summary.   CNV has been linked to speed of reaction only under experimental manipulations that are likely to affect both of them (e.g., distraction). Otherwise, CNV and RT seem to be relatively independent processes.

CNV and Distraction–Attention

An informative review of processes and concepts related to CNV was presented by Tecce and Cattanach (1987), who wrote that distraction is among the most powerful disruptors of CNV development. This is true whenever extraneous stimuli are presented in the S1–S2 interval or just prior to the interval. CNV ampitude has been found to be higher when subjects reported concentration on a task, as compared to when distracting stimuli were introduced (McCallum & Walter, 1968; Tecce & Scheff, 1969). For example, Tecce and Scheff presented four letters or numbers during the S1–S2 interval, and required subjects to recall them after their response to S2; this led to a reduction in CNV amplitude. This reduction was interpreted as being due to an interference with attention. Tecce and Hamilton (1973) introduced distraction into intertial (S1–S2) intervals by requiring subjects to do mental arithmetic (add 7s continuously). This resulted in reduced CNV amplitude and longer RTs to S2. The finding illustrates, incidentally, that slow RTs are not necessarily related to low-amplitude CNVs, but rather to the experimental manipulation that affected both processes.

The holding of a key during the S1–S2 interval has led to decreased CNV (Otto, Benignus, Ryan, & Leifer, 1977). Also, Tecce, Savignano-Bowman, and Dessonville (1984) reported that muscle tension induced in the forearm and upper torso at the time of response to S2 led to decreased CNV amplitude. It is possible that this motor activity in both studies was disruptive to the primary task of responding to S2. In addition, sleep deprivation, anxiety, and fear of failure also reduce CNV magnitude (Tecce & Cattanach, 1987). The disruptive effects of distraction (whether from external or internal sources) on CNV development is emphasized by Tecce and Cattanach (1993).

Tecce (1972) made two hypotheses: (1) CNV amplitude is monotonically related to attention; that is, as attention increases, CNV increases; and (2) the relationship between CNV amplitude and arousal can be described by an inverted-U function; that is, at low or high levels of arousal, CNV magnitude is low, and at moderate arousal levels, CNV is at its highest amplitude. Tecce, Savignano-Bowman, and Meinbresse (1976) found some evidence in support of these arousal hypotheses. Subjects were required to respond to S2, after an S1–S2 interval in which letters were presented. In one condition, they were asked to recall the letters and in another, to ignore them. The letter recall task caused a lowered CNV amplitude, lengthened RT, increased heart rate, and increased eye blinks. The reduction of CNV and RT slowing was interpreted as a distraction effect. The increased heart rate and eye blinking was attributed to increased arousal produced by distraction, an important factor in the disruption of the CNV. Thus, attention increased CNV amplitude, whereas distraction caused CNV attenuation. Other support for the arousal hypotheses are the increased CNV observed with high task interest (Fenelon, 1984) in humans, and with positive reinforcement in the monkey (Boyd, Boyd, & Brown, 1980). Reduction of CNV amplitude has been associated with lowered attention (distraction) in sleep deprivation, and in clinical populations showing impaired attention such as neurotics, depressives, and psychosurgery patients (Tecce & Cattanach, 1987).

Summary. The pattern of findings outlined here has led to formulation of a distraction–arousal model by Tecce and his associates (see Tecce & Cattanach, 1987). In this model, CNV is reduced at the highest arousal levels because of distraction, is optimal at some moderate level, and falls off again under the low attentive states of minimal arousal levels. In agreement with earlier studies, Travis and Tecce (1998) reported that CNV amplitude was decreased when a short term letter–memory task was interpolated in the S1–S2 interval. However, they also observed that when the interpolated stimuli were unexpectedly withheld, CNV increased in amplitude (a rebound effect). Although CNV amplitudes were enhanced during rebound, reaction times to S2 were slower than the control condition. If CNV amplitude reflected enhanced motor preparation for S2, then the CNV rebound would be predicted to result in faster reactions. Obviously, this did not happen and poses difficulties for those who say that late CNV merely represents a preparation for response to S2.

CNV and Effort

The amplitude of CNV increases when greater amounts of energy expenditure are anticipated to allow performance of a task (Low & McSherry, 1968). These investigators found that the anticipation of greater energy expenditure was related to higher CNV amplitudes. Further, Low, Coats, Rettig, and McSherry (1967) reported that CNV amplitude increased as S2 intensity decreased to a barely audible level. The interpretation was that greater effort was required to detect the low intensity S2 and led to enhanced CNV. However, motor activity during the S1–S2 interval does not enhance CNV. In fact, Otto et al. (1977) found that key-holding during the interval decreased CNV. Other studies indicate that increased muscular activity (fist clench) during S1–S2 reduces CNV (Tecce, Cattanach, Boehner-Davis, & Clifford, 1984).

Summary. CNV tends to be associated with anticipated or actual degree of psychological effort, and some investigators have related it to degree of motivation. Imposed muscular activity during the S1–S2 interval decreases CNV, perhaps because the muscle activity was distracting. Empirical findings argue against the position that CNV is purely due to motor activity. In fact, there are a number of studies indicating that late CNV occurs in the absence of a motor response (Tecce & Cattanach, 1993).

Stimulus Modality and the CNV

Although early studies indicated that modality of the stimulus did not appear to influence the CNV, there is some evidence that it may. Gaillard (1976) investigated the differential effects of auditory and visual warning signals on the CNV. Two S1–S2 intervals were used, 1 and 3 sec. The CNV was composed of two waves, one following S1 at about 650 msec and a second that peaked at the end of the interstimulus interval (ISI). The first wave was called an *orientation* (O) wave and the second an *expectancy* (E) wave. A modality effect was shown, because the O-wave was enhanced after an auditory S1, as compared to a visual S1. The finding that the CNV may not be a unitary potential had been previously reported in experiments by Borda (1970) based on his work with monkeys. Further, Loveless and Sanford (1974) and Weerts and Lang (1973) interpreted the O-wave as a cortical component of the orienting response to S1, and the E wave as the traditional CNV. A brief discussion of the relationship between the CNV and P300 is presented later in this chapter.

The effect of using odors or shapes as S1 was examined by Lorig, Turner, Matia, & Warrenburg (1995). Odors were presented as S1 and followed 3 sec later by S2 (a label) that was correct in 75% of the trials. The subject's task was to indicate after each S2 whether the label did or did not match the odorant. They also gave the certainty of their decision on 9-point scale. The CNV was correlated with olfactory performance in that persons with the largest odor-related CNVs had the best olfactory performance.

Other CNV Phenomena

In the course of studying the effects of stimulus presentations during the S1–S2 interval, Tecce and colleagues discovered a rebound effect in the CNV (e.g., see Tecce, Yrchik, Meinbresse, Dessonville, & Cole, 1980). When short-term memory items were presented within the S1–S2 interval, distraction effects were indicated by reduced CNV. However, when the items were then unpredictably omitted, CNV rebounded to higher than normal amplitudes. They viewed CNV rebound as a brain correlate of attention switching, that is, a shift from divided attention in the letters trials (processsing letters and responding to S2) to undivided attention when the letters were not presented in the S1–S2 interval. The absence of CNV rebound in Alzheimer's and psychosurgery patients suggests that it is a useful technique in assessing abnormal brain functioning associated with pathophysiology (Tecce & Cattanach, 1987). CNV rebound is re-established in patients with dementia of the Alzheimer's type when they are given a substance called Hydergine (Tecce, 1987).

Postimperative Negative Variation (PINV).   The term refers to a delay in CNV resolution that occurs in normals with sustained distraction (Tecce & Cattanach, 1987). What happens is that return to baseline levels is delayed long after the occurrence of S2. The PINV has also been observed in schizophrenic, depressive, and dementia patients. PINV and increased heart rate were observed in normals during mental arithmetic and were interpreted as reflecting both distraction and arousal (Tecce & Hamilton, 1973). In healthy persons, PINV occurs when there is preparation for further stimulus evaluation or when there is uncertainty about whether a preceding response was appropriate (Rockstroh, Cohen, Berg, & Klein, 1997). The PINV is reliably observed in schizophrenic patients, especially when tasks used depend on working memory functions. In their own study comparing schizophrenics and normals in a PINV paradigm, Rockstroh and colleagues found that ambiguity, whether it involved auditory or visual stimuli, affectd PINV amplitudes for both groups. The authors noted that the schizophrenic patients had larger PINVs than normals, but could not rule out the possible effects of psychotropic medication on the PINV.

S1 Frequency.   Bauer, Rebert, Korunka, and Leodolter (1992) varied the frequency of the warning signal (S1) to determine effects of different proportions of S1 on the CNV. The S1 occurred at proportions of the total number of trials equal to .10, .30, or .50 of the presentations. The CNVs were larger at frontal and central recording sites when the warning cue was the rare event, but there was no effect at the parietal site. P300s were larger when elicited by rare tones only in the .10 condition with maximum P300 amplitude at the parietal location. It is interesting that CNV can be influenced by S1 probability because it indicates that cognitive elements play a role in CNV development even at the outset of the S1–S2 interval. The fact that CNV and P300 had different scalp distributions under the various conditions is evidence that they are separate in origin, a point that will be discussed again later in this chapter.

Sexual Preference.   The CNV was found useful as an index of sexual preference in groups of 12 male and 12 female college students (Costell, Lunde, Kopell, & Wittner, 1972). The subjects were shown paired visual exposures of male nudes, female nudes, and sexually neutral silhouettes. The first presentation, serving as S1, lasted 500 msec. The second presentation (S2) was the same slide appearing after a delay of 1,500 msec and remaining on for 2,000 msec. Both male and females responded with larger CNVs to stimuli of the opposite sex than to either the same sex or neutral stimuli. In a follow-up study, designed to control for attention variations in the Costell et al. study, it was found that CNV amplitudes in anticipation of opposite sex nudes was significantly greater than for same sex nudes (Howard, Longmore, & Mason, 1992). A longer S1–S2 interval (3,500 msec) was used to distinguish early and late CNV components and a constant level of attention was assured by a match–mismatch task. The authors suggest using CNV to assess sexual object preference in sex offenders.

Missing Stimuli.   Weinberg, Walter, Cooper, and Aldridge (1974) set up an experimental situation in which possible CNVs and ERPs would be produced to an expected, but absent, stimulus. Previous research had shown that a brain potential could occur to an absent stimulus (Sutton, Teuting, Zubin, & John, 1967; Weinberg, Walter, & Crow, 1970). They also wanted to determine whether an emitted potential would be preceded by a CNV and whether the CNV would occur before or after feedback about correctness of the response. They found that emitted potentials occurred on occasions when the imperative stimulus (S2) was absent. A CNV was found to precede the emitted potential, which suggested that the expectancy of occurrence of a stimulus is important for the appearance of an emitted potential. This showed that CNV reflects the expectation to receive information.

CNV and Working Memory.   Working memory is also referred to as *short-term memory*. An example of a task used to examine working memory would be when a stimulus (S1) is held in memory for comparison with a stimulus that follows afterwards (S2). For example, in a task devised by Ruchkin and associates, the S1 was a pattern of 3 to 5 asterisks and S2 was either a match or mismatch for S1 (Ruchkin, Canoune, Johnson, & Ritter, 1995). The S1 and S2 were presented for 500 msec and the time interval between them was 3,300 msec. There was then a 1,300 msec waiting period which was terminated by a 500 msec display of a third pattern (S3). During the S1–S3 interval, a late CNV wave increased in negativity with greater memory load for the memorize task. Similar results were reported by Rohrbaugh et al. (1997) for CNVs recorded in a visual–spatial short term memory task. This time the investigators used geometric patterns presented for 100 msec, with S1 and S2 separated by 3,250 msec. The patterns randomly matched on 50% of the trials and subjects indicated same or different with a button press. The CNV was biphasic with an early wave at posterior temporal sites and a wave later in the retention interval at a midparietal site (P_z). The early wave appeared at 750 to 1250 msec post-S1 and the late wave was between 2750 and 3250 msec post-S1. It was proposed that the early wave (occipito-temporal) was related to memory encoding in the visual–spatial task, whereas the late wave (parietal) reflected ongoing rehearsal processes.

Summary.   The CNV is a fascinating phenomenon, from both a psychological and a physiological point of view. As Tecce (1972) indicated, the main hypotheses regarding the psychological performance correlates of the CNV have been expectancy, motivation, conation (intention to act), and attention. An arousal–distraction hypothesis of CNV production advanced by Tecce, Savignano-Bowman, and Meinbresse (1976) is related to attention concepts. Demonstrations that distraction disrupts CNV illustrates its relation to arousal and attentional mechanisms. Changes in CNV observed in schizophrenic, depressive, and Alzheimer's patients, and its sensitivity to drug effects, suggest possible applications for CNV research (a point taken up again in chapter 16). The PINV is a variation of the CNV that involves a delayed return to baseline long after the occurrence of S2, as, for example, when there is uncertainty about whether a just made response was appropriate. The CNV paradigms, and the resultant slow waves, offer interesting possibilities for studying sexual preference, effects of missing stimuli, and working memory.

THE READINESS POTENTIAL (RP), OR BEREITSCHAFTSPOTENTIAL

Readiness potential, or *Bereitschaftspotential*, was the term used by Kornhuber and Deecke (1965) to describe a slow-rising negative wave with amplitudes between 10 to 15 μV. It begins about 500 to 1,000 msec before a voluntary movement and peaks at the time of response (see Fig. 7.2). It has been pointed out that this potential has a slow rise time and resembles a Type B CNV (see Tecce, 1972, and Fig. 7.1). Tecce (1972) observed that when a motor response (e.g., a key

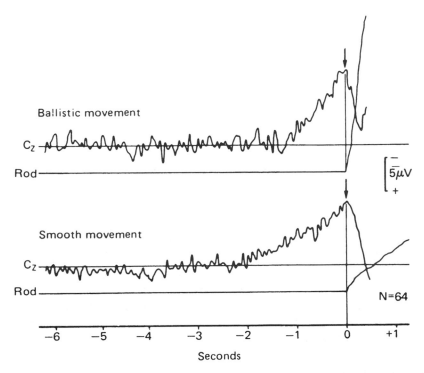

FIG. 7.2. Brain potentials preceding rapid ballistic movements (upper plot) and slow smooth movements (lower plot) in the same subject. Upper trace of pair shows average potentials at the vertex (TC = 5 sec, 64 sweeps), lower shows rod positions. In both cases, there is a clear Bereitschaftspotential.

press) is required to S2 in a CNV paradigm, both CNV and RP occur, resulting in a hybrid wave, or "CNV complex." However, when only attention to S2 is required, without an immediate motor response, only CNV occurs. Several issues that have concerned ERP researchers include the questions of how different are the CNV and RP, the role of psychological factors in production of the RP (is it purely movement-generated?), the nature of the RP in simple and complex movements, spontaneous and planned movements, contralateral representations and the development of the RP with age. These topics are discussed in the following sections.

Distinctions Between CNV and RP.   McCallum, Papakostopoulos, and Griffith (1976) recorded CNVs and RPs from areas of the human brain stem and midbrain. They reported that these slow potentials appeared to have similar, but not identical, distributions throughout the brain stem. They cautioned that the results should be interpreted conservatively, because recording electrode placement was not confirmed. Deecke (1976) observed that CNV and RP have different scalp distributions. For example, CNV can be recorded from frontal areas, but RP cannot. Whereas RP shows a distinct lateral asymmetry, CNV has only slight laterality, except where the two hemispheres are differentially activated by verbal and nonverbal stimulation (Rebert & Low, 1978). Thus, evidence derived from different experimental paradigms and as a result of recording over different brain areas indicates that the CNV and RP are separate phenomena.

Psychological Influences on the RP.   McAdam and Seales (1969) reported that the amplitude of the RP was influenced by monetary reward. They recorded the RP under reward and no-reward conditions and found that the amplitude of the RP could be approximately doubled in size with monetary reinforcement. Thus RP, like CNV, may be influenced by subject motivational level. In another study, the RP was measured as subjects prepared to solve arithmetic tasks under three degrees of time pressure (Freude, Ullsperger, Kruger, & Pietschmann, 1988). The RP was observed to be significantly greater in amplitude (in negativity) when time pressure was greater. The authors concluded that greater nervous system activation preceded mental tasks with a higher workload, and this caused increased negativity of the RP. Performance in another type of task (pattern recognition time) was also related to increased RP negativity (Freude, Ullsperger, Kruger, & Pietschmann, 1989). Single trial analyses revealed that RP was more pronounced with correct and faster pattern recognition than with incorrect and slow performance. This finding was obtained for frontal, central, and parietal scalp locations. The authors concluded that increased negativity facilitates information processing. This interesting line of work should lead to additional information regarding how the RP varies as a function of psychological manipulations.

The RP in Simple and Complex Movements

The RP has a wider scalp distribution for complex as compared to simple movements. For simple movements, it may be absent at frontal areas (Deecke, 1976), whereas for complex movements an early frontal RP may indicate the planning of a skilled motor act (Kristeva, 1984). The RP was measured from subjects instructed to vary the speed at which they pushed a 10-cm rod into a 10-cm tube (Becker, Iwase, Jurgens, & Kornhuber, 1976). They were asked to produce fast as well as slow movements. The investigators reported that the RP started 800 msec prior to fast movements and 1,300 msec before the slow, smooth movements (see Fig. 7.2). These results led them to conclude that it takes more time to prepare for voluntary, slow, smooth, movements than for quick movements. The latency results, plus the finding that the RP was greater in amplitude for smooth movements, also led them to suggest that different neural organization is involved in the production of quick movements versus slow, smooth ones. The RP was maximal at the vertex, as typically found for simple hand and finger movements.

The previous result differs from findings obtained by Deecke, Bernd, Kornhuber, Lang, and Lang (1984) in which RP was recorded during a complex visual and tactile tracking task. In this task, the subjects had to duplicate the movements of either a visually or tactually presented target. The RP preceding this task had a much wider scalp distribution than seen with simple movements. It was task-dependent, because the RP was observed in occipital sites during visual tracking, but not at parietal areas. Conversely, tactual tracking produced the RP at parietal but not at occipital sites. Kristeva (1984) examined the RP during the well-learned complex movements of skilled pianists. All the pianists had more than 20 years of experience, and RPs were recorded when playing a single note and playing a melody. Kristeva found that the RP was earlier in onset and higher in amplitude before playing a melody. In addition, both tasks produced earlier onset RPs in frontal as compared to central areas. These results "suggest that the motor plan and readiness for a complex motor sequence begin in the frontal cortex prior to its initiation in motor cortex" (Kristeva, 1984, p. 482).

Spontaneous and Planned Movements

The RP was recorded under three different instructional conditions in which subjects were required to squeeze a hand grip as follows: (a) under self-paced conditions; (b) in response to tones; and (c) to the second of two tones, separated by 1,000 msec (Kutas & Donchin, 1980). The self-paced and warned conditions (a and b) produced clear RPs at the central recording site, whereas unwarned movements did not. A difference in RPs under spontaneous and planned movement conditions was also observed by Libet, Wright, and Gleason (1982). Subjects performed finger flexions at a time of their own choosing or according to a preset signal. The spontaneous RPs were of two types: Type I had an early onset (about 1,050 msec before the movement), and a Type II RP had an onset, beginning about 575 msec prior to movement. On the basis of these results, Libet and associates proposed that voluntary acts involve more than one process. Process I is associated with an intention to act at some time in the near future, and Process II is associated with a more specific intention to act and immediately precedes the act. The Processes I and II outlined here reflect the Type I and II RPs described in the study. They also concluded that all RPs, whether self-initiated or preplanned, are specifically related to preparation for motor activity.

RP and Site of Body Response

The part of the body involved in a movement influences the scalp-recorded RP. For example, it has been found that, prior to finger movements, RP amplitudes were larger over the contralateral hemisphere (Brunia & Van Den Bosch, 1984). In contrast, prior to plantar flexion of the foot (toes pointed away from the face), RP amplitudes were larger at the same-sided hemisphere. This ipsilateral advantage prior to foot movements is due to the fact that, although the neurons controlling this movement are actually located at the contralateral side of the fissure that separates the left and right hemispheres, the source is so close that the electrical activity is projected across to the ipsilateral hemisphere. The same ipsilateral distribution for RPs was found for dorsiflexion (toes pointed toward the face) and plantar flexion of the right and left feet (Brunia & Dautzenberg, 1986).

Maturational Influences on the RP

The RPs of children age 8 to 13 were studied during skilled performance by Chiarenza, Papakostopoulos, Giordana, and Guareschi-Cazzullo (1983). The skilled performance consisted of initiating a target sweep on a screen by a button held in one hand, and stopping the sweep in a defined central area of the screen by pressing a button in the other hand. Consistent RPs were recorded in children 10 years of age and older and had a scalp distribution similar to adults, with a maximum at the vertex. From the age of 11, RP preceded muscle activity by 600 to 800 msec. Karrer and associates (Chisholm, Karrer, & Cone, 1984) found positive components preceding movement in children and preadolescents. This positively has been attributed to inhibitory processes that are needed to increase the accuracy of the motor act, and might be related to development of motor control. In the Chisholm et al. (1984) study, the RPs of children from 8 to 19 years were measured during self-paced hand squeezes. They found that RP positivity decreased with age, consistent with their own earlier results and those of Chiarenza et al. (1983).

Summary.   The RP is a brain potential that precedes both voluntary and spontaneous movements. Experimental evidence indicates that it is related to psychological and performance variables such as motivation, time pressure, perceptual accuracy, speed of movement, task complexity, site of body response, and maturational factors.

THE P300, OR P3, POTENTIAL

Sutton and colleagues (Sutton, Braren, & Zubin, 1965; Sutton, Teuting, Zubin, & John, 1967) discovered that a late positive ERP wave occurred to task-relevant stimuli that delivered significant information. Because this component had a latency of about 300 msec after stimulus presentation, and it was positive, it was referred to as *P300*. Donchin, McCarthy, Kutas, and Ritter (1983) pointed out that the term P300 is now a misnomer, because many reports since the original work by Sutton and colleagues have found the "classical P300" at anywhere from 250 to 900 msec. These positive peaks share the classical features in that they are largest at parietal scalp areas and occur in cognitive situations known to produce P300. Further, an economy in usage is achieved by referring to all of them by a common term.

The P300 response has been associated with a variety of cognitive activities, including decision making, signal probability, attention, discrimination, uncertainty resolution, stimulus relevance, and information delivery. In fact, so many cognitive events have been related to P300 and other late waves that Beck (1975) wryly commented, "One would not be greatly surprised to encounter a slow-rising late wave of 'brotherly love' " (p. 243). The proliferation of terms is due not to ambiguity of P300 as a physical occurrence, but to the variety of interpretations by different investigators who prefer to use their own labels to describe relationships found in a wide variety of experimental situations. If one were to look for a common factor to which the various cognitive activities associated with P300 were related, it would be "information processing." Donchin et al. (1983) emphasized that when researchers consider carefully the circumstances under which they observe P300, the data fall into a coherent pattern. It should be emphasized that differences in the observed P300 brain response are due to the variety of psychological circumstances orchestrated by researchers.

In this section, we examine issues of how P300 varies with decision making, decision confidence, and probability. Then, questions regarding the varieties of "P300" that occur with selective attention and the orienting response are considered. What kind of P300 occurs with the detection and discrimination of stimuli? How does the P300 vary with memory tasks such as the Sternberg paradigm and digit span? What is the relationship between P300 and CNV? Finally, some theories about P300 generation are discussed.

Number of Trials for P300.   The question of how many trials are needed to obtain a valid P300 response was answered by Cohen and Polich (1997), who used both auditory and visual stimuli with target probabilities of .20 and .80. Averaging of successive single trials revealed that P300 amplitude decreases and latency increases slightly until about Trial 20, after which both stabilize. Therefore, 20 trials appear optimal to obtain a reliable P300. Results are similar for both auditory and visual stimuli at both target probabilities used. The usual effects of stimulus modality were observed, with shorter P300 latencies for auditory stimuli than visual stimuli. This reflects the fact that auditory stimuli are registered in the brain earlier than visual because of the extra retinal photochemical activity required in processing visual stimuli (see Andreassi and Greco, 1975).

Decision Making, Decision Confidence, and P300

Some investigators have related P300 to decision making (e.g., Rohrbaugh, Donchin, & Ericksen, 1974; Smith, Donchin, Cohen, & Starr, 1970). Rohrbaugh and associates devised an experimental situation in which only the second of two rapidly successive and relevant visual stimuli permitted subjects to make a decision. Analyses of the ERPs indicated that only this second stimulus produced a prominent and enhanced P300. Rohrbaugh et al. emphasized that the subject's activity as an information processor determined the amplitude of P300, and they believed that the term "decision" is appropriate to describe its psychological correlate.

In an experiment by Woods, Hillyard, Courchesne, and Galambos (1980), young adults were required to detect auditory stimuli at split-second intervals. They found that the P300 component was fully recovered in less than 1.0 sec, but earlier N1–P2 components (latencies 100 to 180 msec) were reduced in amplitude with stimulus repetition. They proposed that the rapid recovery of P300 suggests that it is generated at the same high rates as the decision processes with which it is associated. Also, the differences in habituation to stimuli of P300 (endogenous) and earlier (exogenous) components suggest that they are generated in different brain areas, and that the P300 is not easily habituated.

Confidence in a decision regarding detection has been related to P300 amplitude such that higher amplitudes were associated with greater degrees of confidence (Hillyard, Squires, Bauer, & Lindsay, 1971). Further, Squires, Hillyard, and Lindsay (1973) used a signal detection task in which subjects had to decide whether or not a very low-level auditory signal was heard during a specified time interval. Based on their results, they made the suggestion that an early negative component of the ERP (N1, peaking between 140 and 190 msec) and P300 (354 and 450 msec) represented aspects of decision making. They also reported a relationship between P300 amplitude and decision confidence. When decision making is made easy, however, P300 varies with the probability of occurrence of a second stimulus such that higher amplitude P300 is associated with lower probability signals.

Summary.   About 20 trials are for obtaining a stable P300. The general result is that P300 amplitude is enhanced when persons are required to make decisions about stimuli. Furthermore, greater amplitude increases appear to be related to increased confidence in the decision. There is also some evidence that P300 is generated at the same rate as the decision processes with which it is related.

The P300 and Probability of Stimulus Occurrence

The studies reviewed in this section consider the relation between P300 and relative uncertainty that a stimulus will occur. Sutton, Braren, and Zubin (1965) discovered that P300 was greater in amplitude when subjects were uncertain about whether a second stimulus would be a sound or a light. This pioneering effort underscored the importance of a subjective (endogenous) reaction in the production of late ERP components, as compared to stimulus (exogenous) factors that influenced the earlier ERP components. Figure 7.3 shows auditory ERPs to certain and uncertain stimuli. Note the large dips in the ERP at around 300 msec; this is the P300. Also note in this figure that positivity is indicated by a downward deflection.

Teuting, Sutton, and Zubin (1970) found that P300 amplitude was high when the probability of a guessed outcome was low, and small when the probability of an event occurring was high. Thus, when P300 was larger, the more unexpected the outcome of the guess.

In an interesting experiment, Ruchkin, Sutton, and Teuting (1975) provided evidence that both evoked and emitted P300s were affected by stimulus probability. They devised a situation in which either the presence or absence of an auditory click provided information. The probability of stimulus presence or absence was varied between 25% and 75%. Both the emitted and evoked P300s were larger for the less frequent event and smaller for the event that had a higher probability of occurrence. The authors concluded, therefore, that evoked and emitted P300s are manifestations of the same brain processes.

A study conducted by Squires, Donchin, Herning, and McCarthy (1977) required subjects to ignore or count loud or soft tones whose probability was either high (.90) or low (.10). These researchers reported three prominent ERP components: a large negativity occurring at about 210 msec (N210), a large positive component at about 350 msec (P350), and a slow wave (SW) that appeared over the last 200 msec of the 768-msec period. They noted that the P350 component was enhanced whenever the stimulus was rare and relevant to the task. The same was true for the SW component, except that its scalp distribution was different from P350. The N210 wave was most pronounced following rare stimuli. Hence, they concluded that the P350 and SW components are related to active processing of stimulus information, whereas N210 reflects stimulus probability, independent of the task.

Summary.   A number of studies have consistently associated P300 amplitude with stimulus probability; that is, higher P300 amplitudes were related to lower probabilities of stimu-

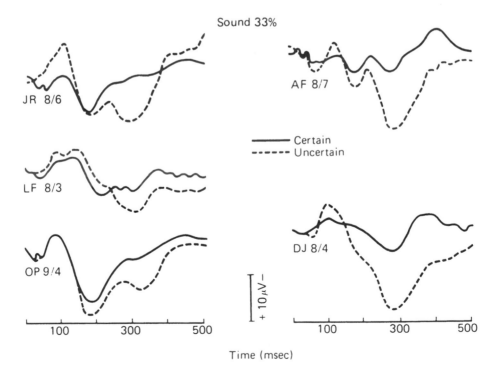

FIG. 7.3. Average wave forms for certain and uncertain (P = .33) sounds for five subjects.

lus occurrence. More detailed analyses reveal that there is more than one component of the ERP, within the latency range of the classical P300, related to stimulus probability and information processing (e.g., P3a and P3b of N. K. Squires, K. C. Squires, & Hillyard, 1975, and P350 and SW of Squires, Donchin, Herning, & McCarthy, 1977). As the research findings mount, it is becoming increasingly clear that a critical factor in the amplitude of P300 is subjective probability, or the subject's perception of the likelihood that a certain stimulus will be delivered. The importance of subjective factors in determining P300 amplitude was demonstrated by Horst, Johnson, and Donchin (1980). In that study, the largest P300s were produced when subjects were surprised that they were correct, when they thought they were wrong, and vice versa.

Selective Attention and P300

Stimulus Set and Response Set.   Auditory ERPs were recorded in persons who listened to a series of tones in one ear and ignored simultaneous tones in the other (Hillyard, Hink, Schwent, & Picton, 1973). The negative component (N1) of the ERP (peaking at 80 to 100 msec) was enlarged for the attended ear. These researchers interpreted the early ERP component as representing stimulus set and the later one as indicating response set in the selective attention situation. They proposed that stimulus set preferentially admits all sensory input to an attended channel, whereas response set facilities recognition of these specific, task-related stimuli. To illustrate this, they gave an example using the familiar cocktail party situation (with many people talking at once) in which there is a stimulus set for a particular speaker's voice and a response set to recognize the contents of speech. This helps the listener to attend to the relevant voice and ignore irrelevant background voices.

The N1 and Nd Components.   A review of the selective attention-ERP literature led Naatanen (1975) to conclude that the ERP correlates of selective attention remained to be established, especially the functional significance of the N1 component. He suggested that one reason for its apparent involvement in selective attention was that subjects were able to predict the occurrence of relevant stimuli from the pattern of stimuli in the sequence. Later, Naatanen and Michie (1979) suggested that N1 in this situation was really a part of a more complex wave that combined an endogenous negative shift with the N1 component. Hillyard and Hansen (1986) concluded that this negativity is not simply an enlargement of the exogenous N1, but represents attention effects, beginning at 60 to 80 msec, which are superimposed on N1. Because this attention-sensitive component is defined as an ERP difference between inattention and attention, Hillyard and associates referred to it as the Nd, or *negative difference* wave. Naatanen's criticisms were taken seriously by ERP researchers who utilized them to sharpen their experimental procedures in elucidating the relation between ERPs and selective attention.

The effects of tone presentation rate on selective attention was examined by Schwent, Hillyard, and Galambos (1976). The measures of attention were the auditory ERP and detection efficiency. The ISIs averaged 350 msec, 960 msec, and 1,920 msec in the fast, medium, and slow rate conditions. Interestingly, the early N1 component (latency 80 to 130 msec) was enhanced by attention only with the fast presentation rate, whereas P3 (300 to 450 msec) was larger to attended stimuli at all ISIs. Thus, the enhancement of the early component was produced by imposing a high "information load" on the subject. The authors commented that the fast stimulus presentation condition may have caused subjects to focus more intently, an observation supported by performance data because signal detection was more efficient with the faster rates. The authors interpreted their results as further evidence that the N1 and P300 components reflect different selective attention processes.

Some possible relationships between ERPs and attentional mechanisms were outlined by Callaway (1975). He suggested that early components (before 200 msec) are affected by the simpler aspects of attention, as in recognizing stimuli as being in a relevant modality. Later components (200 to 400 msec) appear most influenced by more complex processes, such as making a simple decision about stimuli. When very complex discriminations are required, the late components (400 to 500 msec) are affected. Some would disagree with the hypotheses regarding the late and early ERP components and their relation to attentional mechanisms. However, they are testable and have suggested interesting research approaches regarding patterns of ERP activity when humans are attending to stimuli.

The P3a and P3b.   Several investigations have helped to clarify some relations between attentional mechanisms and ERPs. For example, N. K. Squires, K. C. Squires, and Hillyard (1975) found evidence for two types of P300 waves. One of these they labeled P3a (latency about 240 msec), which was produced by unpredictable shifts in tone frequency and amplitude, regardless of whether instructions were to attend to or ignore the tones. The second, labeled P3b, with a latency of about 350 msec, occurred to tone changes only when subjects were actively attending to them. The P3a was apparently generated at frontal–central brain areas, whereas P3b had a parietal–central distribution (see Fig. 7.4). An experiment by Ford, Roth, and Kopell (1976) supported the notion of more than one type of P300 wave. They used a task designed to produce three levels of attention and found that P300 to the infrequent event became larger with increased attention. The P300 recorded from parietal leads was larger than that recorded from frontal areas during active attention. However, frontally recorded P300 was larger than parietal P300 during the ignore conditions.

In a review of P300 research, Pritchard (1981) pointed out that selective attention appears to be a necessary condition for producing P300. Even low probability stimuli will not produce P300 if they are not task-relevant and are ignored while a subject engages in another task.

Modality Effects.   In the past, there has been some question as to whether P300 would be influenced by the type of stimulus. More recently, Barrett, Neshige, and Shibasaki (1987) reported that auditory P300s were maximal over parietal scalp, whereas somatosensory P300s had largest amplitudes over central scalp. Johnson, Miltner, and Braun (1991) used tones and electrical stimuli to elicit auditory- and somatosensory-based P300s. The conditions required subjects to either attend or ignore the target auditory or tactile stimuli. As expected, P300s were elicited by stimuli in both modalities during the attend condition, but not when under *ignore* instructions when subjects worked on a word puzzle. Similar to Barrett et al., Johnson and colleagues found that auditory P300s were maximal at the parietal location, but somatosensory P300s had highest amplitudes over the central scalp. This indicates not only that the P300 is modality-dependent but that it is likely to have separate neural generators, depending on the eliciting stimuli.

Heredity and Age Effects.   The P300 waveform for monozygotic (identical) and dizygotic (fraternal) twin pairs was studied by Katsanis, Iacono, McGue, and Carlson (1997). The similarity in P300 amplitude and latency was much greater for identical than fraternal twins, underscoring the genetic influence on the P300 response. The authors also determined that the greater similarity of the monozygotic pairs compared to the dizygotic twins was not due to greater similarity in either head size or mental ability. Other studies have indicated heredity influences on P300 characteristics. For example, it has been reported that schizophrenic patients and their first degree relatives (e.g., siblings) have smaller amplitude and longer latency P300s than a normal sample (Blackwood, St. Clair, Muir, & Duffy, 1991). Also, children of alcoholics have smaller P300 amplitudes than children of nonalcoholics (Polich,

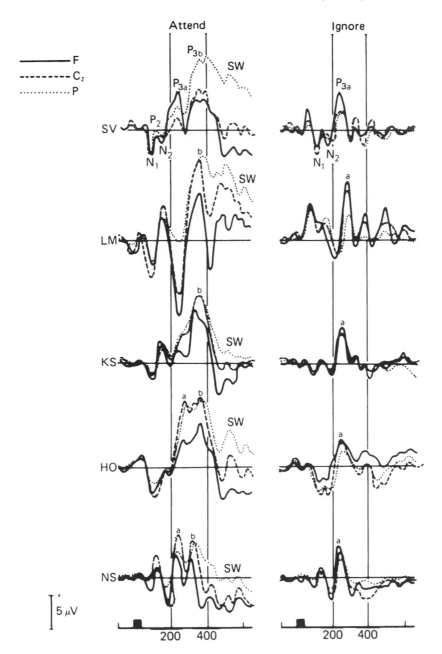

FIG. 7.4. Evoked responses to infrequent stimuli (P = .10) at three electrode locations for five subjects in the attend (left) and ignore (right) conditions. The infrequent stimulus was soft for subjects SV, LM, KS and NS, and loud for HO. For each subject the wave forms from the three electrode sites, frontal (F), vertex (Cz) and parietal (P) are superimposed.

Pollock, & Bloom, 1994). These kinds of findings suggest a possible role of the P300 as a genetic marker for identifying individuals who may be vulnerable to psychiatric disorders.

Changes in P300 amplitude and latency have been reported to occur as a function of age from preadolescence to early adulthood (Katsanis, Iacono, & McGue, 1996). The researchers studied large samples of male subjects at ages 11 to 12, 14 to 15, 17 to 18, and 20 to 21 and found that peak amplitude of P300 decreased with increasing age, whereas peak latency decreased. The authors presented evidence to argue that the reduction of amplitude and latency across the age span was not due to changes in cortical responsivity, but most likely reflects developmental changes in mental processing.

Summary.   Attentional mechanisms have been found to produce changes in both early and late components of the ERP. Most of the studies conducted after 1970 have attempted to eliminate extraneous factors such as generalized arousal or preparation as the reason for ERP enhancement in selective attention. Some investigators have postulated that enhancement of early ERP components with selective attention results from stimulus set, whereas a response set is responsible for enhancement of later components. Simply stated, this suggests that people change from reception of a stimulus to reacting to it in a very short period of time, and this is reflected by changes in brain activity.

Research reveals the complexity of the situation, because ERP components may differ according to the stimulus rate used, brain area sampled, and the level of attention required by the task. Instructions to attend or ignore have great impact on the generation of P300. Recent evidence indicates that the P300 is affected by the modality of the stimulus used to produce the response. Other evidence shows that amplitude and latency of the P300 is most similar in identical twins, indicating a strong genetic component in its generation. The age span from preadolescence to young adult is characterized by a decrease in P300 amplitude and latency.

P300 and the Orienting Response (OR)

The orienting response (OR) to novel stimuli includes a whole complex of physiological changes that occur when the organism shifts its attention to the unexpected event (see chapter 18 for a more detailed discussion of the OR). The suggestion that P300 accompanied the OR was first made by Ritter and colleagues (Ritter & Vaughan, 1969; Ritter, Vaughan, & Costa, 1968). Ritter et al. (1968) found that when the first of a series of tones was presented unexpectedly, it produced a P300 response. This also occurred when a change in pitch of the tone was unexpectedly introduced. Predictable changes in pitch did not produce a P300 response. They concluded that the P300 reflected a shift of attention associated with the OR. Ritter and Vaughan (1969) reported P300 responses when signals were detected, but not with undetected signals or nonsignal stimuli. They inferred that P300 was associated with the OR or stimulus discrimination, and that it reflected brain processes concerned with the evaluation of stimulus significance.

Habituation of P300.   One problem with relating P300 to the orienting response is that the P300 does not show substantial amplitude decrement (habituation) across large numbers of trials (Courchesne, Courchesne, & Hillyard, 1978). Because the OR usually habituates with continued presentation, one would expect the P300 to decrease in amplitude over time. Pritchard (1981) wrote that the P300 seen in orienting situations may be a different brain response than that observed with attended, task-relevant stimuli. Moreover, Donchin et al. (1983) suggested that the P300 represents neural activity that occurs whenever a neuronal model of a stimulus must be updated. This concept of a neuronal model is central to Sokolov's (1969) formulation, which says that the OR occurs whenever there is a discrepancy between a stimulus and the person's internal model of the stimulus. Donchin and colleagues further suggested that whether the model will be updated, and the extent of this revision, depends on the surprise value and relevance of the events.

Although the P300 does not habituate as easily as other physiological measures, recent evidence suggests that it will show a decrease in amplitude with repeated presentations of a target (Polich, 1989). Polich found that there was no evidence of P300 habituation with repeated auditory target presentations in the first 15 single trials analyzed. However, P300 did show a decrease in amplitude after 200 target stimuli had been presented, and this habituation of P300 showed a reversal when the pitch of the target stimulus was changed. Thus, it appears that P300 habituates and dishabituates in a way that is similar to other physiological measures of the orienting response, for example, the sensory ERP that shows amplitude decreases in relatively few trials. Polich suggested that P300 is less susceptible to habituation because subjects must continually use attention resources in order to perform the task accurately. Thus, P300 appears to be maintained to a greater degree by the attentional demands of a task, compared to other OR phenomena.

Habituation of P300 was studied under conditions of active discrimination of target and standard stimuli and under passive conditions in which subjects did not respond to either target or standard (Polich & McIsaac, 1994). The P300 was larger when subjects had to actively discriminate, but did not habituate rapidly under either condition. The authors were encouraged about the use of P300 in studying brain responses of patients who might not be able to engage in active discriminations.

P300 and the Detection and Discrimination of Stimuli

Stimulus Detection.   Psychophysiologists have designed clever experiments to determine the nature of P300 in "detection" and "guess" tasks. In the detection situation, the subject tells after a trial whether or not a stimulus was presented, but in a guess task, the subject predicts prior to the trial whether the stimulus will be presented. Hillyard et al. (1971) used a signal detection procedure in which the subject's task was to decide on each trial whether an auditory signal (at threshold) had been added to continuous background noise. They found that P300 was several times larger when signals were detected than when they were not detected. It was concluded that P300 was enlarged only when stimulus information was being actively processed and that it was associated with the occurrence of a signal and its correct detection. However, the situation is more complex than originally thought, because Ruchkin, Sutton, Kietzman, and Silver (1980) found that P300 is enlarged not only for correct detections but for correct rejections. In addition to the P300, they reported a slow wave (SW) that showed the opposite relationship, because it decreased with increasing accuracy of response. (The SW occurs at a latency of 400 to 800 msec and is positive over parietal and negative over frontal scalp areas; see Fig. 7.4). Ruchkin et al. proposed that because P300 is involved in the initial cognitive evaluation of the stimulus, it becomes larger as the amount of information provided by an event increases. On the other hand, the SW increases in amplitude as accuracy decreases, because more prolonged processing is required when the decision is more difficult.

P300 to Omitted Stimuli.   Sutton et al. (1967) and Ruchkin and Sutton (1973) found that a P300 appeared in the absence of a stimulus when the omitted signal was expected and provided information. For example, Sutton and associates asked subjects to guess, before each trial, whether the stimulus would consist of one or two clicks. The presence or absence of a second click told subjects whether their guess was correct or incorrect. In some trials, a large P300 occurred at about the same time of the second click, whether or not it had actually been presented. Sutton and colleagues interpreted the P300 as reflecting the delivery of information to the subject. Ruchkin and Sutton (1978a) noted that the emitted P300 was of lower amplitude and broader duration than the evoked P300. They suggested that this may be due to the more imprecise internal timing that occurs when a subject is estimating the time of stimulus occurrence. Ruchkin, Sutton, and Stega (1980) believed that P300s evoked by a stimulus and P300s emitted in response to the absence of a stimulus are essentially identical phenomena.

Sutton and Ruchkin (1984) examined emitted P300 and slow waves in detection and guessing tasks in which the same stimuli were used. A significant difference was found in the slow wave for the two tasks, but not for P300. For the guessing task, the slow wave was large and positive at the vertex, whereas in the detection task, it was almost zero in amplitude at the same site. The researchers suggested that the P300s reflect an intermediate stage of event evaluation that is common to more than one type of task, whereas the SW may represent a final evaluation that differs for *detect* and *guess* trials, perhaps being more complex for the guess trials. The interested reader is referred to Sutton and Ruchkin (1984), who discuss possible relationships and differences among a variety of late positive components including P300, P3b, P3a, and SW. (Most researchers in this area agree that P300 and P3b represent the classic P300 in that the latency is about 300 msec and the maximal response is recorded at P_z.) Sutton and Ruchkin presented evidence that the SW may include a tonic variety, with slow return to baseline, and a phasic type with a relatively quick return.

Discrimination of Stimuli.   The general finding has been that P300 latency increases and amplitude decreases with increased difficulty in discriminating stimuli. The latency increases have been related to the longer time for stimulus evaluation required when discriminations are difficult or ambiguous (Andreassi & Jusczcak, 1984; McCarthy & Donchin, 1981). The reduced P300 amplitude has been ascribed to "equivocation" by Ruchkin and Sutton (1978b). They used the term in reference to the reduced information resulting from the subject's uncertainty about the perceived event when discriminations are difficult. The greater variability in latency of P300 responses causes the amplitude decrease observed in equivocal situations.

The effects of varying the difficulty of target discrimination on the P300 was examined by Fitzgerald and Picton (1983) in a series of three experiments. Both easy and difficult discriminations occurred within the same condition, and RT was recorded to determine actual difficulty of the discriminations. In all experiments, the latencies of P300 were delayed and the amplitudes were smaller as a function of increasing discrimination difficulty. Also related to difficulty in discrimination of stimuli is the distance effect studied by Mecklinger, Ullsperger, Molle, and Grune (1994). This refers to greater accuracy of judgments for items that are of greater distance from each other. For example, RT is longer and accuracy lower when subjects are asked to judge whether 4 is larger than 3 compared to the judgment of whether 5 is larger than 2. Mecklinger et al. recorded ERPs along with judgments to pairs of numbers ranging from 1 to 5. Shortest RT and greatest accuracy and the largest amplitude P300 was obtained for the two numbers that were the greatest distance apart (i.e., 1 and 5). The greater P300 amplitude was attributed to higher amounts of information transmission. In a sense, the faster RTs related to higher amplitude of P300s indicate less equivocation when subjects are more sure of their judgments, as suggested by Ruchkin and Sutton (1978b).

The occurrence of P300 and a negative N400 wave in a variety of visual discrimination tasks was noted by Stuss, Picton, and Cerri (1986). In their experiment, subjects were required to name pictures presented on a screen 1 sec after a brief warning tone. A P300 occurred when a stimulus from a low-probability category was detected. The N400 (large negativity in 300–500 msec range) was observed when target stimuli came from a more extensive set of possibilities. These researchers proposed that the N400 represents a search of memory to name the object. A larger range of possibilities might result in larger amplitude N400 because of the greater effort involved in searching among stimuli stored in long-term memory.

Summary.   The P300 response becomes larger with corrrect detections. The P300 that occurs to omitted (but expected) stimuli is of lower amplitude than the usual P300. The general finding is that P300 latency increases and amplitude decreases with increased difficulty in discriminating stimuli. The latency increases have been related to increased stimulus evaluation time and the reduced amplitude to equivocation with more difficult discriminations. An interesting distance effect has been demonstrated and confirms that discrimination difficulty leads to lower amplitude P300 and slower RT. Investigators have related a late negative component (N400) to cognitive activities involving discriminations and in evaluations of appropriateness of words completing a sentence.

P300 and Memory

The Sternberg Task.   A convenient paradigm to study the P300 correlates of short-term memory is a task developed by Sternberg (1966). In a typical study, a memory set of up to six items is presented on a screen (e.g., the numbers: 9, 7, 4, 3, 1, 6). About 2 sec later, a probe stimulus (e.g., the number 3) is flashed, and the subject must decide whether it was a member of the original memory set (probability is usually set at 50%). The ERP and RT are recorded as the probe is presented. Reaction time has been found to increase linearly as a function of memory set size: The larger the set size, the more items the subject must scan in short-term memory. Sternberg's original purpose was to study the retrieval of information from short-term memory, reasoning that RT can provide clues to retrieval processes. His model proposes four stages of information processing to perform the task: stimulus encoding, serial comparison, binary decision, and response execution. Donchin and co-workers (1986) described the utility of P300 in helping to refine models of cognitive processes such as Sternberg's. For example, it has been argued that P300 latency is better than RT as an estimate of memory scanning rate, because P300 latency slope is constant when RT slope varies (e.g., for young and old subjects; Ford, Roth, Mohs, Hipkins, & Kopell, 1979).

Reaction time and P300 latency were both found to increase as memory set size increased (Gomer, Spicuzza, & O'Donnell, 1976). The delays in P300 were attributed to greater amounts of time required to do more difficult memory tasks. Further, it was reported that P300 amplitude was larger to items identified as members of the original memory set, compared to P300s to nonset members, a result observed previously for target and nontarget stimuli. In the study by Ford et al. (1979), P300 latency and RT were evaluated in a Sternberg paradigm to compare short-term memory processes in young (mean age of 23) and elderly (mean age of 81) individuals. The elderly were slower in RT to probe stimuli and evidenced a steeper increasing RT slope as a function of memory set size than did young subjects. Their P300 latencies, however, were only slightly longer than younger persons and showed similar slopes, indicating that the two age groups compared the probe with memory items at the same rate. Ford and colleagues concluded from these and other data that although older subjects encoded stimuli more slowly, they scanned memory at the same speed as younger persons.

Digit Span.   Polich, Howard, and Starr (1983) conducted a study to determine the relationship between P300 latency and the digits forward and backward tasks of Wechsler Adult Intelligence Scale. They used a total of 93 subjects, ages 5 to 87, with approximately equal numbers in each decade. Negative correlations between P300 latencies and short-term memory scores (i.e., shorter latencies were related to better scores) suggest the possibility that P300 latency is related to memory capacity. The researchers suggested that P300 latency reflects an individual's capacity to retain recently encoded information for comparison with incoming information: The greater the capacity, the shorter the latency. The authors suggested that subcortical recordings from humans, clinical observations, and animal studies point to the hippocampus and amygdala among possible subcortical contributors to the P300 response. Of particular interest is the work of Halgren et al. (1980) at UCLA, and Wood, Allison, Goff, Williamson, and Spencer (1980) and Wood, McCarthy, Squires, Vaughan,

Woods, and McCallum (1984) at Yale, in which P300 paradigms resulted in P300-like responses from hippocampus and amygdala. The subcortical recordings were made from patients undergoing treatment for epilepsy, and shared many functional characteristics of the scalp-recorded P300. Other studies have indicated, however, that P300 has multiple brain sources involved in its generation (e.g., see Johnson, 1993) and most P300 investigators agree with this position.

The von Restorff Effect.   If words in a list are made different in some respect, for example, having larger or smaller letters than others, then these items are better remembered in a later test of recall. The better recall of these "isolated" words is called the von Restorff effect. Karis, Fabiani, and Donchin (1984) predicted that such isolates would result in larger P300 amplitudes and would be better remembered. The prediction was partially correct, because there were individual differences in subjects' results. Those that showed a strong von Restorff effect also had large P300s to the isolates and remembered them better. These individuals used rote memorization (e.g., repeating the words over and over) to do the task. Those that used other memory strategies (e.g., combining the words in sentences or short stories) showed little von Restorff effect, and the P300 did not differentiate between the recalled and nonrecalled words.

In a follow-up study, Fabiani, Karis, and Donchin (1986) confirmed that P300 amplitude is related to subsequent recall. This time, subjects engaged in one task and then were asked unexpectedly to recall as many male and female names that had been previously presented. The names that were recalled had originally elicited larger P300s than names not recalled. The results supported their hypothesis that a relationship between P300 amplitude and memory emerges when elaborate rehearsal strategies are minimized. Fabiani et al. also interpreted the data as being consistent with the theory that P300 manifests processes invoked when events occur and create a need to revise representations of these events in memory.

Recognition Memory.   The exploration of P300 as a measure of recognition of recently learned words was carried out by van Hooff, Brunia, and Allen (1996). Subjects were asked to indicate recognition of recently learned words that were presented along with unlearned words. They were also presented with previously learned words (one day earlier), but were not required to overtly indicate recognition of these words. The researchers reported that recently learned words, as well as the previously learned words elicited P300, indicating a discrimination between learned and unlearned words, even after a one-day interval between learning and testing. The fact that the materials were auditory presentations and that no overt response was required to previously learned responses suggests that the P300 response would be useful in clinical situations where one wishes to evaluate the presence of information in long-term memory of patients who have difficulty verbalizing such knowledge.

A careful analysis of the scalp distribution of ERPs related to recognition of previously studied (old) versus new words was carried out by Johnson, Kreiter, Russo, and Zhu (1998). The ERPs were recorded from 32 scalp sites while subjects decided whether each presented word was old or new and pressed an appropriate button as soon as possible. The ERPs to the stimuli were elicited between 300 and 2,000 msec poststimulus. Three ERP patterns represented the old–new effect and were maximal over left frontal, left parietal–occipital, and right central–frontal areas. Three others seemed related to aspects of recognition with maxima over frontal poles, midline frontal scalp, and right frontal scalp. One other was related to decision confidence and was maximal over left central scalp. The authors take the topographical pattern as evidence that retrieval of information observed in recognition memory depends on processes that occur in a spatially and temporally distributed neural circuit.

Summary.   Rather consistent relationships have been reported by various investigators regarding P300 and decision making and P300 and stimulus probability; that is, enhancement occurs with the decision process and with less probable events. Studies of selective attention and the orienting response have indicated that the P300 is not a unitary process and may reflect variations in stimulus and response sets, in stimulus relevance, and in novelty of stimuli. Signal detection and discrimination processes have also been associated with P300 in a manner that indicates larger responses for correct detections and rejections, and decreased amplitude with increased difficulty in discriminating stimuli. Further, increased P300 latency occurs with more difficult discriminations. Experimental findings also indicate that P300 latency increases in a way showing that it reflects time to evaluate stimuli. Memory processes can also be indexed by P300 latency. For example, the greater the number of items that must be scanned in short-term memory, the longer the P300 latency. In addition, better memory scores in a digit-span task have been related to shorter P300 latencies. It has been reported that verbal materials eliciting larger P300s are recalled better by subjects (von Restorff effect). Finally, the P300 represents an efficient way to study recognition memory as it is reliably larger to previously learned materials than to new information.

We have noted in this section that the classic P300 has been separated into P3a and P3b components. Moreover, the picture of the P300 is complicated by the identification of SW and N400 components that overlap in time the appearance of the classic P300. However, now that investigators are aware of additional components, they will be able to relate them to various aspects of behavior.

Concepts and Models of P300

Is there any common psychological process to which the P300 and its related components can be attached? A number of researchers have suggested that P300 is related to active processing of stimulus information (Beck, 1975; Hillyard, Squires, Bauer, & Lindsay, 1971). In fact, many of the processes reviewed in this section—including signal detection and discrimination, selective attention and the OR, decision making and memory scanning—are aspects of active information processing and extraction. Sutton and Ruchkin (1984) proposed that P300 reflects value of a stimulus to subjects—*Value* in the sense that task-relevant events have more value than task-irrelevant events, targets have more value than nontargets, and pictures that are recognized have greater value than those that are not. The value of Sutton and Ruchkin might be equivalent to stimulus significance, and certainly both of these properties are determinants of what information is most likely to be processed by an individual.

Johnson (1986, 1988) pointed out that many constructs have been proposed to influence the occurrence of P300 and its amplitude variations, including attention, the OR, decision making, uncertainty reduction, processing demand, task relevance, and value. Johnson noted the similarities among the constructs and presented a *triarchic* model that reduces explanations of variations in P300 *amplitude* to three dimensions, thereby rejecting the notion that a single behavioral process accounts for P300. The three dimensions of his triarchic model are: (a) subjective probability, (b) stimulus meaning, and (c) information transmission. Johnson contended that the subjective probability and stimulus-meaning dimensions have independent and additive effects on P300 amplitude, and that the amplitude contributions of these two factors are dependent on the proportion of stimulus information they transmit. In a careful exposition, he presented the most systematic model to date of psychological processes, and their interactions, that affect P300 amplitude. Johnson's model is discussed further in chapter 18.

Another influential concept concerning the development of P300 is *context updating* offered by Donchin and colleagues (Donchin, 1981; Donchin & Coles, 1988). The context-updating hypothesis says that a P300 results when stimulus events require subjects to modify their currently operating set of assumptions about the environment. Further, the amplitude of the P300 response depends on the degree to which the person's model of the environment must be modified; that is, the greater the amount of change, the greater the P300. Unexpected events, for example, require greater updating of representations in working memory and, therefore, result in larger P300s. The hypothesis would predict that greater amounts of updating for a given event would lead to greater recall of that event later on. This idea is supported by the earlier presented finding that large P300s to "isolated" words were related to superior recall of these words (Karis et al., 1984).

Verleger (1988) strongly criticized the context updating hypothesis and offered his own concept to explain P300. His concept, labeled *context closure* states that P300s are elicited when expectancies are fulfilled, not when they require revision. In his view, P300s result when subjects deal with repetitive, highly structured tasks. Donchin and Coles (1988) gave a carefully reasoned rebuttal to Verleger that clarified their position and pointed out that the main focus in P300 research and theory should be on the functional significance of this component rather than the events that lead up to its occurrence. As one deficiency, they pointed out that Verleger's paper omitted mention of P300 latency, a variable that has been associated with a stimulus evaluation function.

THE RELATIONSHIP BETWEEN CNV AND P300

Some investigators have suggested that P300 and CNV are related phenomena (Karlin, 1970; Naatanen, 1970). That is, P300 is merely the return to baseline of the CNV. However, a number of studies have produced evidence that the two are separate phenomena. For example, Donald and Goff (1971) showed that P300 was enhanced by certain relevant stimuli, but that enhancement was unrelated to CNV amplitude. Friedman et al. (1973) found that P300 changed systematically with changes in stimulus probability, but CNV did not. Donchin and colleagues (1975) reported that P300 amplitude was not affected by the presence or absence of a warning stimulus, whereas CNV was elicited only for warned trials. In addition, scalp distributions of CNV and P300 differed, indicating that they are generated by different neuronal populations in the brain.

Peters, Billinger, and Knott (1977) measured CNV and P300 during verbal learning (paired-associates) and discrimination RT. They found that CNV amplitude showed an inverse relation to learning, whereas P300 increased with learning. Both waveforms were larger at central and parietal areas than at the frontal location during learning. During discrimination RT, however, the CNV was maximal at the frontal area and P300 was greatest at the parietal location. The CNV data were interpreted as reflecting early arousal and attentional processes, whereas P300 was related to the subject's decision about stimulus relevance. Peters and colleagues concluded that CNV and P300 could be regarded, on the basis of their data, as indices of learning activity taking place in the brain. The findings also indicated that they are separate processes.

The consensus at this writing is that P300 and CNV are independent phenomena. No doubt, their association with interesting psychological processes will lead to continued work on the nature of these and other slow potentials.

In the last few chapters, we have seen how brain measures are correlated with different behaviors. The next chapter, examines how changes in muscle activity are related to various human activities. This is the first of the peripheral (nonbrain) measures to be presented. Like other peripheral measures that are discussed later on, such as electrodermal and heart activity, brain and muscle activity influence each other in mutually interactive ways.

REFERENCES

Andreassi, J. L., & Greco, J. R. (1975). Effects of bisensory stimulation on reaction time and the evoked cortical potential. *Physiological Psychology, 3*, 189–194.

Andreassi, J. L., & Juszczak, N. M. (1984). An investigation of hemispheric specialization and visual event-related potentials in discriminations of line length. *International Journal of Psychophysiology, 2*, 87–95.

Barrett, G., Neshige, R., & Shibasaki, H. (1987). Human auditory and somatosensory event-related potentials. *Electroencephalography and Clinical Neurophysiology, 66*, 409–419.

Bauer, H., Rebert, C. S., Korunka, C., & Leodolter, M. (1992). Rare events and the CNV—The oddball CNV. *International Journal of Psychophysiology, 13*, 51–58.

Beck, D. C. (1975). Electrophysiology and behavior. *Annual Review of Psychology, 26*, 233–262.

Becker, W., Iwase, R., Jurgens, R., & Kornhuber, H. H. (1976). Bereitschaftspotential preceding voluntary slow and rapid hand movements. In W. C. McCallum & J. R. Knott (Eds.), *The responsive brain* (pp. 99–102). Bristol: John Wright and Sons.

Birbaumer, N., Elbert, T., Canavan, A. G. M., & Rockstroh, B. (1990). Slow potentials of the cerebral cortex and behavior. *Physiological Reviews, 70*, 1–41.

Blackwood, D. H. R., St. Clair, D. M., Muir, W. J., & Duffy, J. C. (1991). Auditory P300 and eye tracking dysfunction in schizophrenic pedigrees. *Archives of General Psychiatry, 48*, 899–909.

Borda, R. P. (1970). Drive and performance related aspects of the CNV in rhesus monkeys. *Electroencephalography and Clinical Neurophysiology, 29*, 173–180.

Boyd, E. S., Boyd, E. H., & Brown, L. E. (1980). The M-wave and CNV in the squirrel monkey: Generality of cue modality and of reward. *Electroencephalography and Clinical Neurophysiology, 49*, 66–80.

Brunia, C. H. M., & Dautzenberg, J. E. M. W. (1986). In W. C. McCallum, R. Zappoli, & F. Denoth (Eds.), *Cerebral psychophysiology: Studies in event-related potentials* (EEG Suppl. 38, pp. 238–241). Amsterdam: Elsevier.

Brunia, C. H. M., & Van Den Bosch, W. E. J. (1984). Movement-related slow potentials. I: A contrast between finger and foot movements in right-handed subjects. *Electroencephalography and Clinical Neurophysiology, 57*, 515–527.

Callaway, E. (1975). *Brain electrical potentials and individual differences*. New York: Grune & Stratton.

Cant, B. R., & Bickford, R. G. (1967). The effects of motivation on the contingent negative variation (CNV). *Electroencephalography and Clinical Neurophysiology (abstract), 23*, 594.

Chiarenza, G. A., Papakostopoulos, D., Giordana, F., & Guareschi-Cazullo, A. (1983). Movement-related brain macropotentials during skilled performances: A developmental study. *Electroencephalography and Clinical Neurophysiology, 56*, 373–383.

Chisholm, R., Karrer, R., & Cone, R. (1984). Movement-related ERPs during right vs. left hand squeeze: Effects of age, motor control, and independence of components. In R. Karrer, J. C. Cohen, & P. Teuting (Eds.), *Brain & information: Event-related potentials* (Vol. 425, pp. 445–449). New York: New York Academy of Sciences.

Cohen, J., & Polich, J. (1997). On the number of trials needed for P300. *International Journal of Psychophysiology, 25*, 249–255.

Cohen, J., & Walter, W. G. (1966). The interaction of responses in the brain to semantic stimuli. *Psychophysiology, 2*, 287–296.

Costell, R. M., Lunde, D. T., Kopell, B. S., & Wittner, W. K. (1972). Contingent negative variation as an indicator of sexual object preference. *Science, 177*, 718–720.

Courchesne, E., Courchesne, Y., & Hillyard, S. A. (1978). The effect of stimulus deviation on P3 waves to easily recognized stimuli. *Neuropsychologia, 16*, 189–199.

Deecke, L. (1976). Potential changes associated with motor action, reflex responses and readiness (Chariman's opening remarks). In W. C. McCallum & J. R. Knott (Eds.), *The responsive brain* (pp. 91–93). Bristol: John Wright & Sons.

Deecke, L., Bernd, H., Kornhuber, H. H., Lang, M., & Lang, W. (1984). Brain potentials associated with voluntary manual tracking: Bereitschaftspotential, conditioned premotion positivity, directed attention potential, and relaxation potential. In R. Karrer, J. Cohen, & P. Teuting (Eds.), *Brain & information: Event-related potentials* (Vol. 425, pp. 450–464). New York: New York Academy of Sciences.

Donald, M. W., & Goff, W. R. (1971). Attention related increases in cortical responsivity dissociated from the contingent negative variation. *Science, 172*, 1163–1166.

Donchin, E. (1981). Surprise! . . . Surprise? *Psychophysiology, 18*, 493–513.

Donchin, E., & Coles, M. G. H. (1988). Is the P300 component a manifestation of context updating? *Behavioral & Brain Sciences, 11*, 343–356.

Donchin, E., Karis, D., Bashore, T. R., Coles, M. G. H., & Gratton, G. (1986). Cognitive psychophysiology and human information processing. In M. G. H. Coles, E. Donchin, & S. W. Porges (Eds.), *Psychophysiology: Systems, processes & applications* (pp. 244–267). New York: Guilford.

Donchin, E., McCarthy, G., Kutas, M., & Ritter, W. (1983). Event-related brain potentials in the study of conciousness. In R. J. Davidson, G. E. Schwartz, & D. Shapiro (Eds.), *Conciousness and self-regulation* (Vol. 3, pp. 81–121). New York: Plenum.

Donchin, E., Teuting, P., Ritter, W., Kutas, M., & Heffley, E. (1975). On the independence of the CNV and P300 components of the human averaged evoked potential. *Electroencephalography and Clinical Neurophysiology, 38*, 449–461.

Elbert, T., Rockstroh, B., Canavan, A., Birbaumer, N., Lutzenberger, W., von Bulow, I., & Linden, A. (1991). Self-regulation of slow cortical potentials and its role in epileptogenesis: In J. G. Carlson & A. R. Seifert (Eds.), *International perspectives on self-regulation and health* (pp. 65–94). New York: Plenum.

Fabiani, M., Karis, D., & Donchin, E. (1986). P300 and recall in an incidental memory paradigm. *Psychophysiology, 23*, 298–308.

Fenelon, B. (1984). Effects of stimulus coding on the contingent negative variaton recorded in an information processing task. In R. Karrer, J. Cohen, & P. Teuting (Eds.), *Brain & information: Event-related potentials* (Vol. 425, pp. 194–198). New York: New York Academy of Sciences.

Fitzgerald, P. G., & Picton, T. W. (1983). Event-related potentials recorded during the discrimination of improbable stimuli. *Biological Psychology, 17*, 241–276.

Ford, J. M., Roth, W. T., & Kopell, B. S. (1976). Attention effects on auditory evoked potentials to infrequent events. *Biological Psychology, 4*, 65–77.

Ford, J. M., Roth, W. T., Mohs, R. C., Hipkins, W. F., III, & Kopell, B. S. (1979). Event-related potentials recorded from young and old adults during a memory retrieval task. *Electroencephalography and Clinical Neurophysiology, 47*, 450–459.

Freude, G., Ullsperger, P., Kruger, H., & Pietschmann, M. (1988). The Bereitschaftspotential in preparation to mental activities. *International Journal of Psychophysiology, 6*, 291–298.

Freude, G., Ullsperger, P., Kruger, H., & Pietschmann, M. (1989). Bereitschaftspotential and the efficiency of mental task performance. *Journal of Psychophysiology, 3*, 377–385.

Friedman, D., Hakerem, G., Sutton, S., & Fleiss, J. L. (1973). Effect of stimulus uncertainty on the pupillary dilation response and the vertex evoked potential. *Electroencephalography and Clinical Neurophysiology, 34*, 475–484.

Gaillard, A. W. (1976). Effects of warning signal modality on the contingent negative variation (CNV). *Biological Psychology, 4*, 139–154.

Gomer, F. E., Spicuzza, R. J., & O'Donnell, R. D. (1976). Evoked potential correlates of visual item recognition during memory-scanning tasks. *Physiological Psychology, 4*, 61–65.

Haagh, S. A. V. M., & Brunia, C. H. M. (1985). Anticipatory response-relevant muscle activity. CNV amplitude and simple reaction time. *Electroencephalography and Clinical Neurophysiology, 61*, 30–39.

Halgren, E., Squires, N. K., Wilson, J. W., Rohrbaugh, J. W., Babb, T. L., & Crandall, P. H. (1980). Endogenous potentials generated in the human hippocampal formation and amygdala by infrequent events. *Science, 210*, 803–805.

Hillyard, S. A., & Hansen, J. C. (1986). Attention: Electrophysiological approaches. In M. G. H. Coles, E. Donchin, & S. W. Porges (Eds.), *Psychophysiology: Systems, processes & applications* (pp. 227–243). New York: Guilford.

Hillyard, S. A., Hink, R. F., Schwent, V. L., & Picton, T. W. (1973). Electrical signs of selective attention in the human brain. *Science, 182*, 177–180.

Hillyard, S. A., Squires, K. C., Bauer, J. W., & Lindsay, P. H. (1971). Evoked potential correlates of auditory signal detection. *Science, 172*, 1357–1360.

Horst, R. L., Johnson, R., & Donchin, E. (1980). Event-related brain potentials and subjective probability in a learning task. *Memory and Cognition, 8*, 476–488.

Howard, R., Longmore, F., & Mason, P. (1992). Contingent negative variation as an indicator of sexual object preference: revisited. *International Journal of Psychophysiology, 13*, 185–188.

Irwin, D. A., Knott, J. R., McAdam, D. W., & Rebert, C. S. (1966). Motivational determinants of the "contingent negative variation." *Electroencephalography and Clinical Neurophysiology, 21*, 538–543.

Johnson, R., Jr. (1986). A triarchic model of P300 amplitude. *Psychophysiology, 23*, 367–384.

Johnson, R., Jr. (1988). The amplitude of the P300 component of the event-related potential: Review and synthesis. In P. K. Ackles, J. R. Jennings, & M. G. H. Coles (Eds.), *Advances in psychophysiology, volume 3* (pp. 69–138). Greenwich, CT: JAI Press.

Johnson, R., Jr. (1993). On the neural generators of the P300 component of the event-related potential. *Psychophysiology, 30*, 90–97.

Johnson, R., Jr., Kreiter, K., Russo, B., & Zhu, J. (1998). A spatio-temporal analysis of recognition-related event-related brain potentials. *International Journal of Psychophysiology, 29*, 83–104.

Johnson, R., Jr., Miltner, W., & Braun, C. (1991). Auditory and somatosensory event-related potentials: I. Effects of attention. *Journal of Psychophysiology, 5*, 11–25.

Karis, D., Fabiani, M., & Donchin, E. (1984). "P300" and memory: Individual differences in the von Restorff effect. *Cognitive Psychology, 16*, 177–216.

Karlin, L. (1970). Cognition, preparation, and sensory-evoked potentials. *Psychological Bulletin, 73*, 122–136.

Katsanis, J., Iacono, W. G., & McGue, M. K. (1996). The association between P300 and age from preadolescence to early adulthood. *International Journal of Psychophysiology, 24*, 213–221.

Katsanis, J., Iacono, W. G., McGue, M. K., & Carlson, S. R. (1997). P300 event-related potential heritability in monozygotic and dizygotic twins. *Psychophysiology, 34,* 47–58.

Kornhuber, H. H., & Deecke, L. (1965). Hirnpotentialanderungen bei Willkurbewegungen und passiven Berwegungen des Menschen: Bereitschaftspotential und reafferente Potentials [Cerebral potential changes in voluntary and passive movements in man: Readiness potential and reafferent potential]. *Pflugers Archives Gesamte Physiologie, 284,* 1–17.

Kristeva, R. (1984). Bereitschaftspotential of pianists. In R. Karrer, J. Cohen, & P. Teuting (Eds.), *Brain and information: Event-related potentials* (Vol. 425, pp. 477–482). New York: New York Academy of Sciences.

Kutas, M., & Donchin, E. (1980). Preparation to respond as manifested by movement-related brain potentials. *Brain Research, 202,* 95–115.

Libet, B., Wright, E. W., Jr., & Gleason, C. A. (1982). Readiness-potentials preceding unrestricted "spontaneous" vs. pre-planned voluntary acts. *Electroencephalography and Clinical Neurophysiology, 54,* 322–335.

Lorig, T. S., Turner, J. M., Matia, D. C., & Warrenburg, S. (1995). The contingent negative variation in an odor labeling paradigm. *Psychophysiology, 32,* 393–398.

Loveless, N. E., & Sanford, A. J. (1974). Slow potential correlates of preparatory set. *Biological Psychology, 1,* 308–314.

Low, M. D., Borda, R. P., Frost, J. D., Jr., & Kellaway, P. (1966). Surface negative slow potential shift associated with conditioning in man. *Neurology, 16,* 771–782.

Low, M. D., & Coats, A. C., Rettig, G. M., & McSherry, J. W. (1967). Anxiety, attentiveness–alertness: A phenomenological study of the CNV. *Neuropsychologia, 5,* 379–384.

Low, M. D., & McSherry, J. W. (1968). Further observations of psychological factors involved in CNV genesis. *Electroencephalography and Clinical Neurophysiology, 25,* 203–207.

McAdam, D. W., & Seales, D. M. (1969). Bereitschaftspotential enhancement with increased level of motivation. *Electroencephalography and Clinical Neurophysiology, 27,* 73–75.

McCallum, W. C. (1969). The contingent negative variation as a cortical sign of attention in man. In C. R. Evans & T. B. Mulholland (Eds.), *Attention in neurophysiology* (pp. 40–63). London: Butterworths.

McCallum, W. C., Papakostopoulos, D., & Griffith, H. B. (1976). distribution of CNV and other slow potentials changes in human brainstem structures. In W. C. McCallum & J. R. Knott (Eds.), *The responsive brain* (pp. 205–210). Bristol: John Wright & Sons.

McCallum, W. C., & Walter, W. G. (1968). The effects of attention and distraction on the contingent negative variation in normal and neurotic subjects. *Electroencephalography and Clinical Neurophysiology, 25,* 319–329.

McCarthy, G., & Donchin, E. (1981). A metric for thought: A comparison of P300 latency and reaction time. *Science, 211,* 77–79.

Mecklinger, A., Ullsperger, P., Molle, M., & Grune, K. (1994). Event-related potentials indicate information extraction in a comparative judgement task. *Psychophysiology, 31,* 23–28.

Naatanen, R. (1970). Evoked potential, EEG, and slow potential correlates of selective attention. *Acta Psychological supplement, 33,* 178–192.

Naatanen, R. (1975). Selective attention and evoked potentials in humans: A critical review. *Biological Psychology, 2,* 237–307.

Naatanen, R., & Michie, P. T. (1979). Early selective-attention effects on the evoked potential: A critical review and reinterpretation. *Biological Psychology, 8,* 81–136.

Naitoh, P., Johnson, L. C., & Lubin, A. (1971). Modification of surface negative slow potential (CNV) in the human brain after total sleep loss. *Electroencephalography and Clinical Neurophysiology, 36,* 191–200.

Otto, D. A., Benigus, V. A., Ryan, L. J., & Leifer, L. J. (1977). Slow potential components of stimulus, response and preparatory processes: A multiple linear regression model. In J. E. Desmedt (Ed.), *Progress in clinical neurophysiology: Vol. I. Attention, voluntary contraction and event-related potentials* (pp. 211–230). Basel: Karger.

Peters, J., Billinger, T. W., & Knott, J. R. (1977). Event-related potentials of brain (CNV and P300) in a paired associate learning paradigm. *Psychophysiology, 14,* 579–585.

Polich, J. (1989). Habituation of P300 from auditory stimuli. *Psychobiology, 17,* 19–28.

Polich, J., Howard, L., & Starr, A. (1983). P300 latency correlates with digit span. *Psychophysiology, 20,* 665–669.

Polich, J., & McIsaac, H. K. (1994). Comparison of auditory P300 habituation from active and passive conditions. *International Journal of Psychophysiology, 17,* 25–34.

Polich, J., Pollock, V. E., & Bloom, F. E. (1994). Meta-analysis of P300 amplitude from males at risk for alcoholism. *Psychological Bulletin, 115,* 55–73.

Pritchard, W. S. (1981). Psychophysiology of P300. *Psychological Bulletin, 89,* 506–540.

Rebert, C. S. (1972). The effect of reaction time feedback on reaction time and contingent negative variation. *Psychophysiology, 9,* 334–339.

Rebert, C. S., & Low, D. W. (1978). Differential hemispheric activation during complex visuomotor performance. *Electroencephalography and Clinical Neurophysiology, 44,* 724–734.

Rebert, C. S., & Tecce, J. J. (1973). A summary of CNV and reaction time. In W. C. McCallum & J. R. Knott (Eds.), *Event-related slow potentials of the brain: Their relations to behavior* (pp. 173–178). Amsterdam: Elsevier.

Ritter, W., & Vaughan, H. G., Jr. (1969). Average evoked responses in vigilance and discrimination: A reassessment. *Science, 164*, 326–328.

Ritter, W., Vaughan, H. G., Jr., & Costa, L. D. (1968). Orienting and habituation to auditory stimuli: A study of short term changes in average evoked responses. *Electroencephalography and Clinical Neurophysiology, 25*, 550–556.

Rockstroh, B., Cohen, R., Berg, P., & Klein, C. (1997). The postimperative negative variation following ambiguous matching of auditory stimuli. *International Journal of Psychophysiology, 25*, 155–167.

Rohrbaugh, J. W., Donchin, E., & Ericksen, C. W. (1974). Decision making and the P300 compnent of the cortical evoked response. *Perception and Psychophysics, 15*, 368–374.

Rohrbaugh, J. W., Dunham, D. N., Stewart, P. A., Bauer, L. O., Kuperman, S., O'Connor, S. J., Porjesz, B., & Begleiter, H. (1997). Slow brain potentials in a visual–spatial memory task: Topographic distribution and inter-laboratory consistency. *International Journal of Psychophysiology, 25*, 111–122.

Rohrbaugh, J. W., & Gaillard, A. W. K. (1983). Sensory and motor aspects of the contingent negative variation. In A. W. K. Gaillard & W. Ritter (Eds.), *Tutorials in event-related potential research: Endogenous components* (pp. 269–310). Amsterdam: North-Holland.

Ruchkin, D. S., Canoune, H. L., Johnson, R., Jr., & Ritter, W. (1995). Working memory and preparation elicit different patterns of slow wave event-related brain potentials. *Psychophysiology, 32*, 399–410.

Ruchkin, D. S., & Sutton, S. (1973). Visual evoked and emitted potentials and stimulus significance. *Bulletin of the Psychonomic Society, 2*, 144–146.

Ruchkin, D. S., & Sutton, S. (1978a). Emitted P300 potentials and temporal uncertainty. *Electroencephalography and Clinical Neurophysiology, 45*, 268–277.

Ruchkin, D. S., & Sutton, S. (1978b). Equivocation and P300 amplitude. In D. Otto (Ed.), *Multidisciplinary perspectives in event-related potential research* (pp. 175–177). Washington, DC: EPA-600/9-97-043 (Environmental Protection Agency).

Ruchkin, D. S., & Sutton, S. (1986). Latency characteristics and trial by trial variation of emitted potentials. In J. E. Desmedt (Ed.), *Cerebral evoked potentials in man*. Amsterdam: Elsevier.

Ruchkin, D. S., Sutton, S., Kietzman, M., & Silver, K. (1980). Slow wave and P300 in signal detection. *Electroencephalography and Clinical Neurophysiology, 50*, 35–47.

Ruchkin, D. S., Sutton, S., & Stega, M. (1980). Emitted P300 and slow wave event-related potentials in guessing and detection tasks. *Electroencephalography and Clinical Neurophysiology, 49*, 1–14.

Ruchkin, D. S., Sutton, S., & Teuting, P. (1975). Emitted and evoked P300 potentials and variation in stimulus probability. *Psychophysiology, 12*, 591–595.

Schwent, V. L., Hillyard, S. A., & Galambos, R. (1976). Selective attention and the auditory vertex potential: I. Effects of stimulus delivery rate. *Electroencephalography and Clinical Neurophysiology, 40*, 604–614.

Smith, D., Donchin, E., Cohen, L., & Starr, A. (1970). Auditory evoked potentials in man during selective binaural listening. *Electroencephalography and Clinical Neurophysiology, 78*, 146–152.

Sokolov, E. N. (1969). The modeling properties of the nervous system. In M. Cole & I. Maltzman (Eds.), *Handbook of Soviet psychology* (pp. 671–704). New-York: Basic Books.

Squires, K. C., Donchin, E., Herning, R. I., & McCarthy, G. (1977). On the influence of task relevance and stimulus probability on the event related potential components. *Electroencephalography and Clinical Neurophysiology, 42*, 1–14.

Squires, K. C., Hillyard, S., & Lindsay, P. (1973). Vertex potentials evoked during auditory signal detection: Relation to decision criteria. *Perception & Psychophysics, 14*, 265–272.

Squires, K. C., Squires, N. K., & Hillyard, S. A. (1975). Decision related cortical potentials during and auditory signal detection task with cued observation intervals. *Journal of Experimental Psychology: Human Perception & Performance, 104*, 268–279.

Squires, N. K., Squires, K. C., & Hillyard, S. A. (1975). Two varieties of long-latency positive waves evoked by unpredictable auditory stimuli in man. *Electroencephalography and Clinical Neurophysiology, 38*, 387–401.

Sternberg, S. (1966). High-speed scanning in human memory. *Science, 153*, 652–654.

Stuss, D. T., Picton, T. W., & Cerri, A. M. (1986). Searching for the names of pictures: An event-related study. *Psychophysiology, 23*, 215–223.

Sutton, S., Braren, M., & Zubin, J. (1965). Evoked potential correlates of stimulus uncertainty. *Science, 150*, 1187–1188.

Sutton, S., & Ruchkin, D. S. (1984). The late positive complex: Advances and new problems. In R. Karrer, J. Cohen, & P. Teuting (Eds.), *Brain & information: Event-related potentials* (pp. 1–23). *New York Academy of Sciences*, Vol. 425. New York: New York Academy of Sciences.

Sutton, S., Teuting, P., Zubin, J., & John, E. R. (1967). Evoked potential correlates of stimulus uncertainty. *Science, 155*, 1436–1439.

Tecce, J. J. (1971). Contingent negative variation and individual differences. *Archives of General Psychiatry, 24*, 1–16.

Tecce, J. J. (1972). Contingent negative variation (CNV). In E. Niedermeyer & F. Lopes da Silva (Eds.), *Electroencephalography: Basic principles, clinical application and related fields* (2nd ed., pp. 657–679). Baltimore: Urban & Schwarzenberg.

Tecce, J. J. (1987). Alzheimer's disease and CNV: Diagnosis and treatment. In R. A. Griffiths & S. T. McCarthy (Eds.), *Degenerative neurological disease in the elderly*, (pp. 188–199). Bristol: Wright.

Tecce, J. J., & Cattanach, L. (1987). Contingent negative variation. In E. Niedermeyer & F. Lopes da Silva (Eds.), *Electroencephalography: Basic principles, clinical applications, and related fields* (2nd ed., pp. 543–562). Baltimore: Urban & Schwarzenberg.

Tecce, J. J., & Cattanach, L. (1993). Contingent negative variation. In E. Niedermeyer & F. Lopes da Silva (Eds.), *Electroencephalography: Basic principles, clinical applications, and related fields* (3rd ed., pp. 887–910). Baltimore: Urban & Schwarzenberg.

Tecce, J. J., Cattanach, L., Boehner-Davis, M. B., & Clifford, T. S. (1984). CNV and myogenic functions: II. Divided attention produces a double dissociation of CNV and EMG. In R. Karrer, J. Cohen, & P. Teuting (Eds.), *Brain & information: Event-related potentials* (Vol. 425, pp. 289–294). New York: New York Academy of Sciences.

Tecce, J. J., & Hamilton, B. T. (1973). CNV reduction by sustained cognitive activity (distraction). In W. C. McCallum & J. R. Knott (Eds.), *Event-related slow potentials of the brain: Their relations to behavior* (Suppl. 33, pp. 229–237). Amsterdam: Elsevier.

Tecce, J. J., Savignano-Bowman, J., & Cole, J. O. (1978). Drug effects on contingent negative variation and eye-blinks: The distraction–arousal hypothesis. In M. A. Lipton, A. DiMascio, & K. F. Killam (Eds.), *Psychopharmacology: A generation of progress* (pp. 745–758). New York: Raven Press.

Tecce, J., Savignano-Bowman, J., & Dessonville, C. L. (1984). CNV and myogenic functions: I. Muscle tension produces a dissociation of CNV and EMG. In R. Karrer, J. Cohen, & P. Teuting (Eds.), *Brain & information: Event-related potentials* (Vol. 425, pp. 283–288). New York: New York Academy of Sciences.

Tecce, J. J., Savignano-Bowman, J., & Meinbresse, D. (1976). Contingent negative variation and the distraction–arousal hypothesis. *Electroencephalography and Clinical Neurophysiology, 41*, 227–286.

Tecce, J. J., & Scheff, N. M. (1969). Attention reduction and suppressed direct-current potentials in the human brain. *Science, 164*, 331–333.

Tecce, J. J., Yrchik, D. A., Meinbresse, D., Dessonville, C. L., & Cole, J. O. (1980). CNV rebound and aging. I. Attention functions. In H. H. Kornhuber & L. Deecke (Eds.), *Motor and sensory processes of the brain. Electrical potentials, behavior and clinical use. Progress in brain research* (Vol. 54, pp. 553–561). Amsterdam: Elsevier.

Teuting, P., Sutton, S., & Zubin, J. (1970). Quantitative evoked potential correlates of the probability of events. *Psychophysiology, 7*, 385–394.

Travis, F., & Tecce, J. J. (1998). Effects of distracting stimuli on CNV amplitude and reaction. *International Journal of Psychophysiology, 31*, 45–50.

van Hooff, J. C., Brunia, C. H. M., & Allen, J. J. B. (1996). Event-related potentials as indirect measures of recognition memory. *International Journal of Psychophysiology, 21*, 15–31.

Vaughan, H. G., Jr. (1969). The relationship of brain activity to scalp recordings of event-related potentials. In E. Donchin & D. B. Lindsley (Eds.), *Average evoked potentials* (pp. 45–94). Washington, DC: NASA.

Verleger, R. (1988). Event-related potentials and cognition: A critique of the context updating hypothesis and an alternative interpretation of P3. *Behavioral & Brain Sciences, 11*, 343–356.

Walter, W. G., Cooper, R., Aldridge, V. J., McCallum, W. C., & Winter, A. L. (1964). Contingent negative variation: An electrical sign of sensory–motor association and expectancy in the human brain, *Nature, 203*, 380–384.

Weerts, T. C., & Lang, P. J. (1973). The effects of eye fixation and stimulus and response location on the contigent negative variation (CNV). *Biological Psychology, 1*, 1–19.

Weinberg, H., Walter, W. G., Cooper, R., & Aldridge, V. J. (1974). Emitted cerebral events. *Electroencephalography and Clinical Neurophysiology, 36*, 449–456.

Weinberg, H., Walter, W. G., & Crow, H. J. (1970). Intracerebral events in humans related to real and imaginary stimuli. *Electroencephalography and Clinical Neurophysiology, 29*, 1–9.

Wood, C. C., Allison, T., Goff, W. R., Williamson, P. D., & Spencer, D. (1980). On the neural origin of P300 in man. In H. H. Kornhuber & L. Deecke (Eds.), *Progress in brain research. Motivation, motor and sensory processes of the brain* (Vol. 54, pp. 51–56). Amsterdam: Elsevier.

Wood, C. C., McCarthy, G., Squires, N. K., Vaughan, H. G., Jr., Woods, D. L., & McCallum, C. (1984). In R. Karrer, J. Cohen, & P. Teuting (Eds.), *Brain & information: Event-related potentials* (Vol. 425, pp. 681–721). New York: New York Academy of Sciences.

Woods, D. L., Hillyard, S. A., Courchesne, E., & Galambos, R. (1980). Electrophysiological signs of split-second decision-making. *Science, 207*, 655–657.

8

Muscle Activity and Behavior

The muscles of the body are critical to almost every form of human behavior. In fact, without muscle activity there would be no observable behavior. Albert Szent-Gyorgyi, who worked on muscle biochemistry, was fascinated by muscle activity. In his own words: "Muscular contraction is one of the most wonderful phenomena of the biological kingdom. That a soft jelly should suddenly become hard, change its shape and lift a thousand times its own weight, and that it should be able to do so several hundred times a second, is little short of miraculous" (McElroy, 1988, p. 82).

Studies of electromyograms (EMGs) and behavior have yielded interesting findings. Examples are the patterning of facial muscle action during the expression of different emotions, the differential patterning of EMG while an individual views pictures of positive and negative stimuli, and the EMG gradients that have been observed in motivated behavior. The first evidence that contraction of human muscles produces electrical activity was provided by in 1849 by Du Bois-Reymond (Caccioppo, Tassinary, & Fridlund, 1990). In an interesting account of historical antecedents to modern techniques for measuring muscle activity, Cacioppo and colleagues described the cumbersome procedure used by Du Bois-Reymond to record the first human electromyogram (EMG) with a galvanometer. He placed cloths on each forearm and immersed both in containers of saline solution. Each of these electrodes was connected to a galvanometer, and Du Bois-Reymond noted deflections on a meter whenever the muscles of the hand were flexed. Later experimenters built on and refined the techniques of Du Bois-Reymond to make the recording techniques much more practical.

The most common way by which modern psychophysiologists measure muscular activity in behavioral studies is through EMG recordings from the skin surface. These recordings are obtained through the placement of recording electrodes over a muscle group of interest and amplifying the tiny electrical signals that muscles produce when they are active or at rest. The EMGs may also be obtained by inserting tiny needle electrodes directly into the target muscle. However, this sometimes painful procedure is used mainly in clinical diagnosis and in some forms of muscle rehabilitation to measure activity of small portions of a larger muscle, known as motor units.

This chapter discusses briefly the anatomy and physiology of muscle and the measurement of muscular activity in the form of surface EMGs. Psychological studies of the relationship between the EMG and various behaviors, including speed of reaction, tracking, conditioning, cognition, speech, emotional expression, sleep, and conditions of motivation are topics of this chapter. More specifically, some of the questions dealt with in this chapter include: What is the relationship between ongoing level of muscle activity and readiness to respond, or quality of motor performance? Do small levels of muscle activity in the speech apparatus during reading affect reading speed? To what extent can muscle activity be conditioned? What patterns of EMG can be observed during cognition? Can measures of muscle activity reveal something about a person's motivational level? What patterns of EMG in various facial muscles might one observe during different emotional states?

THE CONTROL OF MOTOR BEHAVIOR

All of the outward behavior that we observe is the result of muscular activity. For example, an individual may have a notion to write a letter, but this is not possible without the fine motor coordination involved in moving a pen across a piece of paper to form the necessary words. The origin of the thoughts placed on paper is the brain, and the initiation of writing is controlled by the motor cortex. When writing starts, complex, rapid brain-to-muscle feedback circuits interact, and changes in both brain and muscle activity can be recorded at these times. One of the motor systems of the central nervous system (CNS) is termed the *pyramidal system*, and its origins are primarily in the precentral gyrus of the cortex (motor area). It descends through various subcortical structures to the medulla, where an estimated 70% to 90% of the fibers originating in each hemisphere cross to the opposite side and descend within the spinal cord (Gardner, 1975). The area of the medulla at which the fibers' crossover forms the shape of a pyramid, hence the name *pyramidal system*. This system is concerned with the initiation and control of fine muscle movements and is excitatory only; that is, it is involved only in the initiation of movements.

The *extrapyramidal motor system*, on the other hand, is a system that controls gross motor activities, such as those required to roll over in bed or to make postural adjustments, and it has both excitatory and inhibitory components. This complex system has its primary origin in the prefrontal cortex, but it also has origins in the precentral, postcentral, and temporal cortex. The descending fibers of this system also travel to the spinal cord after most of them crossover at the level of the medulla. However, the crossover of fibers originating in either the right or left hemisphere does not occur at the pyramidal area of the medulla, hence the name extrapyramidal motor system. The cerebellum is considered to be part of the extrapyramidal motor system, and it plays a role in the regulation and modification of motor activities, receiving input and having output to the rest of the brain and the spinal cord.

This brief review of CNS mechanisms is presented here to emphasize the fact that there are complex brain and muscle interactions that occur in carrying out behavior, interactions whose effects can be measured electrophysiologically at central (brain) or peripheral (muscle) locations. It should also been emphasized that brain–muscle interactions are not merely one-way, because varying levels of muscle involvement influence brain activity through feedback mechanisms from peripheral to central areas.

Anatomy and Physiology of Muscles

Muscles are named according to action (e.g., extensor and flexor), according to shape (e.g., quadratus), according to origin and insertion (sternocleidomastoid), and according to number of divisions (e.g., transversus). The origin of a muscle is a more fixed attachment that serves as a basis for action. The movable attachment is called the insertion. Most voluntary muscles are not inserted directly into bone, but are connected by strong fibrous cords called *tendons*. Tendons can vary in length from a fraction of an inch to longer than 12 in. Muscles that bend a limb at a joint are called *flexors* (also agonists). Those that straighten limbs at a joint are referred to as *extensors* (and antagonists). The flexor muscle must relax for the extensor to perform. If a limb is moved away from the midline of the body, an abductor is responsible; adductors move limbs toward the midline. *Levators* are muscles that raise parts of the body, and depressors lower them.

There are three types of muscle tissue in the body: skeletal, smooth, and cardiac. The *skeletal* muscles make up the voluntary motor system and are exemplified by such familiar structures as the biceps of the upper arm and the flexor digitorum of the forearm. Individual skeletal muscle fibers have striations and many nuclei, as shown in Fig. 8.1. *Smooth*, or un-striated, muscles are considered to be part of the involuntary motor system, because we ordinarily do not exert control over them. There is evidence that some influence over smooth muscle may be learned if appropriate feedback is provided (see chapter 15). The muscles of the blood vessels are good examples of smooth muscle. These muscle fibers travel in a circular path and can change the diameter of the blood vessel by constriction or dilation. Individual smooth muscle fibers have a single nucleus and no striations. *Cardiac* muscle is also classified as involuntary muscle. It is striated, similar to skeletal muscle, but is considered to be a separate variety. Skeletal muscles make up approximately 40% of total body weight, and smooth and cardiac muscle account for another 5% to 10%. The primary focus of this chapter is on the activity of skeletal (voluntary) muscle.

Skeletal Muscle.   Most voluntary muscles are attached to a bone through strong, nonelastic fibrous cords known as *tendons*. A muscle consists of groups of muscle fibers that form a primary bundle (fasciculus). A muscle is composed of a group of these *fasciculi* (see Fig. 8.2). The fasciculus, in turn, contains many muscle fibers, and muscle fibers are composed of even smaller diameter *myofibrils*. Each muscle fiber contains several hundred to several thousand myofibrils. Each myofibril has about 1,500 myosin filaments and 3,000 actin filaments, which are protein molecules responsible for muscle contraction. Viewed under a microscope, the myosin filaments are thick and dark in appearance, whereas the actin filaments are thin and light-colored. It is the myosin and actin filaments that cause the myofibrils to have alternate light and dark bands, imparting the striated appearance to skeletal muscle. The dark striations are also known as A-bands and the light ones as I-bands. Striated muscle fibers may vary in length from 1 to 40 mm (often extending the entire length of the muscle) and range in diameter between 10 and 80 μm. The sarcolemma is an electrically polarized membrane that surrounds each muscle cell. It is the cell membrane of the muscle fiber.

Mechanisms of Muscle Contraction.   Action potentials in muscle fibers are responsible for the initiation of muscle contractions. We briefly examine muscular contraction at the relatively gross level of the motor unit and at the molecular level, describing the interaction between actin and myosin filaments.

The Motor Unit.   The basic mechanism of muscle contraction is the motor unit, which consists of a nerve cell, its axon, and the muscle fibers supplied by it. The motor neuron–mus-

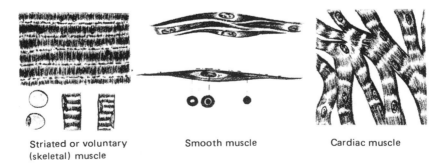

Striated or voluntary
(skeletal) muscle   Smooth muscle   Cardiac muscle

FIG. 8.1. Types of muscle cells.

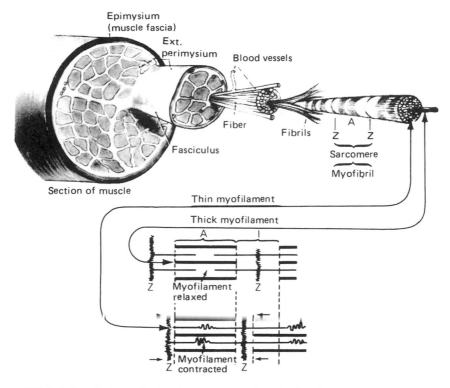

FIG. 8.2. Detail of muscle showing structure and mechanics of muscular contraction.

cle fiber link represents the last stage in the transmission of motor impulses from the cortex, down through the subcortical areas of the brain, over descending tracts of the spinal cord, and out over the motor neuron. The *final common pathway* was the name given by Sherrington to describe the motor pathway from the CNS to a muscle. The innervation ratio, or number of muscle fibers innervated by a single neuron, may range from 3:1 for those muscle fibers that control precise and rapid motor adjustments (e.g., the laryngeal and tongue muscles), to 3,000:1 for fibers involved in slow and gross postural adjustments (e.g., muscles of the lower back).

Motor units obey the all-or-none principle discussed in chapter 2. The neurons and muscle fibers that comprise the motor unit fire with their full capacity or they do not respond at all. The information regarding action potentials in neurons applies to skeletal muscle fibers, except for some quantitative differnces. For example, the resting potential is approxiamtely −85 mV in skeletal muscle fibers, slightly higher than for neurons. The duration of the muscle fiber action potential ranges from 1 to 5 msec, which is longer than for the large myelinated neuron. The biggest difference is in the velocity of conduction along a muscle fiber, because it is about 3 to 5 m/sec, or only about one eighteenth the velocity of conduction in large myelinated neurons. The skeletal muscles are normally innervated by large myelinated neurons at the neuromuscular junction (also known as the motor end plate).

The neuromuscular junction is located near the middle of the muscle fiber. Thus, the action potential spreads from the middle toward the ends, allowing all sarcomeres of the muscle to contract simultaneously. The strength of muscle contraction depends on the number of motor units contracting and the rate of contraction. The action potential of the fiber is brief, but the duration of muscle contraction may last up to 100 msec or more. Muscles are in a constant state of tonus to allow quick responses to external stimuli. The tonus is maintained by a steady flow of impulses from the spinal cord to each motor unit and varies with level of activity of the person and the nervous system. It should also be noted that feedback of activity from motor units can also affect spinal cord neurons. For example, the flow of impulses from spinal cord to muscle fibers can be reduced by purposely lowering level of muscle activity through techniques such as progressive muscle relaxation. Reduction of muscle tonus may also occur if the neuron supplying the muscle is damaged, thus preventing the constant flow of impulses. Additionally, in the case of immobilized limbs, such as those placed in a cast, the flow of impulses is reduced, and some atrophy may occur.

Muscular Contraction at the Molecular Level.   When a neuronal impulse reaches the neuromuscular junction, acetylcholine is released. The muscle fiber membrane thus becomes permeable to sodium ions, and depolarization of the membrane occurs, resulting in the action potential. The presence of acetylcholinesterase at the neuromuscular junction causes the breakdown of acetylcholine, and the muscle is ready to be stimulated again.

When an action potential travels down the muscle fiber, it causes the release of calcium ions into the sarcoplasm surrounding the myofibrils. This sets up attractive forces that cause the actin filaments to slide into spaces between the myosin fibrils. Thus, the positive calcium ions produce an energy-releasing reaction, which brings on the sliding of the myofibril filaments said to underlie muscle contraction. It is believed that the energy for this contraction is derived from the enzyme adenosine triphosphate (ATP), which is broken down into adenosine diphosphate (ADP) when the motor neuron impulse reaches the muscle fiber. The ATP is broken down to form ADP, and the hypothesis is that large amounts of energy are thereby released. A relaxing factor has been discoveared in muscle and has been postulated to react with the energizing substance of muscle to halt contraction until the next stimulus reaches the fiber (Jacob & Francone, 1970).

Muscle Fatigue.   Prolonged and strong contraction of a muscle leads to muscle fatigue. This results from the inability of the muscle fibers to maintain work output because of ATP depletion. The nerves, as well as their action potentials, continue to function properly, but contractions become weaker and weaker with time (Guyton, 1977). Continuous muscle contraction contributes to interruption of the blood supply to muscle tissue and causes fatigue in about 1 min because of nutrient loss.

Muscular Hypertrophy.   Forceful exercise, in which muscles contact to at least 75% of their maximum tension, produces an increased number of myofibrils. Thus, the diameters of the individual muscle fibers increase. In addition, the nutrients and metabolic substances, such as ATP and glycogen, are increased. Hypertrophy results from very forceful muscle activity, even though it might occur for only a few minutes each day.

THE MEASUREMENT OF MUSCLE ACTIVITY

Now that we have briefly reviewed the sources of electrical activity produced by muscles, methods for measuring this activity are presented. We then briefly review the literature to determine the kinds of changes in muscle activity that accompany the performance of various tasks.

Electromyography (EMG)

Electromyography (EMG) is the technique for measuring and recording electrical potentials that are associated with contractions of muscle fibers. The EMG is often used in the clinic to study muscular disorders. Very thin needle electrodes can be inserted into muscle tissue, and recordings can be made from limited muscle regions or even from single motor units. The EMG can also be recorded from the skin surface, because some portion of the action potentials produced in muscle fibers is transmitted to the skin. The closer the muscle tissue is to the skin surface, and the stronger the contractions, the greater will be the amount of electrical activity recorded at the surface. Most studies relating EMG to human performance deal with the activity occurring in large muscle groups.

Therefore, the information in this chapter is derived mainly from surface EMG recordings. However, subcutaneous needle electrodes can provide useful information in clinical or research settings. For example, it was reported that EMG recorded by inserting a needle electrode into the trapezius muscle directly over a trigger point indicated higher EMG levels during stress than did a nontender area of the same muscle (McNulty, Gevirtz, Hubbard, & Berkoff, 1994). (A trigger point is an area of muscle that is painful when touched. The trapezius is a large muscle located at the juncture of the upper back and neck.) The findings suggest a mechanism by which emotional factors influence muscle activity. The results have implications for studying pain associated with trigger points.

The reliability of an ambulatory EMG device was reported on by Arena and colleagues (Arena, Bruno, Brucks, Searle, Sherman, & Meador, 1994). This device enabled the recording of EMG sites on the left and right trapezius muscles for up to 18 hours per day. Twenty-six healthy individuals wore the 24-ounce instrument over a 5-day period, with application of fresh electrodes and downloading of data accomplished on each of the five mornings. The device proved to be highly reliable and offers the possibility for obtaining data away from a laboratory setting and in daily life or work situations.

General Properties of the EMG

The surface EMG records the electrical activity of many motor units, which occurs prior to contraction of a muscle (Thompson, Lindsley, & Eason, 1966). Electrodes placed on the skin over an active muscle record the algebraic sum of a large number of depolarizations that occur when a group of motor units are activated (Lippold, 1967).

Muscular Effort and the EMG.   Studies that have examined the relation between EMG level and degree of muscle tension indicate that the EMG is a fairly good indicator of tension in skeletal muscles. For example, in a sudy by Malmo (cited by J. F. Davis, 1959), EMG was recorded from the flexor muscles of the forearm while subjects varied the amount of squeeze on a hand dynamometer. (A hand dynamometer is a device used to produce and measure variations in hand grip strength.) The recordings showed regular increases in EMG amplitude (in microvolts) as grip strength increased. The data for the 9 females and 11 males indicated that, on the average, a higher EMG level was produced by females than males to maintain a given grip level. Similar results were obtained by Wilcott and Beenken (1957) for their female and male subjects. Their results are shown in Fig. 8.3. The male–female differences indicate that females must bring more motor units into action to accomplish the same amount of work as males. One could speculate about whether such striking differences would be found in contemporary times, which see regular workouts, greater participation in sports, and body building becoming more popular among women.

The EMG Waveform.   The surface EMG that accompanies muscle contraction consists of a series of spiked discharges from motor units underlying the electrode. The frequency of the components may range from 20 to 1000 Hz, with an amplitude of about 100 to 1000 μV, depending on the mass of muscle tissue beneath the recording electrodes and the degree to

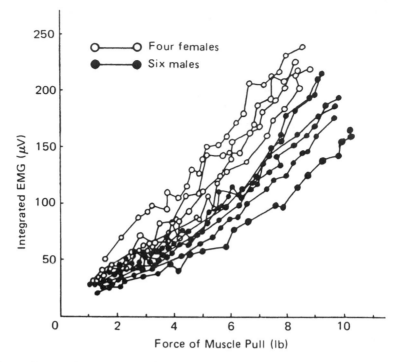

FIG. 8.3. The relation between the force of muscle pull in pounds and integrated EMG in microvolts for the bicep muscle.

which they are contracting. However, amplitudes as low as 1 to 2 μV may be recorded when a relatively small muscle is in a relaxed state. The recorded EMG waveform is not as regular as some of the other physiological measures, for example, the alpha wave of the EEG. This is why, in studies that attempt to quantify EMG and relate it to behavior, the integrated surface EMG is often derived. This is accomplished by feeding the EMG into an integrator circuit, which will show the total amount of activity over a certain period of time (e.g., 10 sec). An example of an integrated EMG record is presented in Fig. 8.4. The EMG is shown at two stages in Fig. 8.4. A first level of integration produces the EMG (first line) with no activity shown below baseline; and a second line shows the summed EMG and its calibration in microvolts, and provides a measure of total muscle activity in a given time period. The investigator in this experiment was studying the amount of forearm EMG produced during a 30-sec verbal learning trial. The other measures depicted are skin resistance and heart rate.

Electrode Placement for EMG Recording

The general principles for electrode application are the same as for other physiological measures. That is, the skin must be cleansed with alcohol or some mildly abrasive material to revove dead skin, dirt, and oils. Then, after electrode paste or gel is rubbed into the area and the excess is removed, the recording electrode containing a new supply of paste or gel is placed into the desired position. Pregelled electrodes are also commercially available for convenience purposes. The EMG is most commonly recorded with a bipolar electrode arrangement, with both electrodes located over the muscle of interest. The resistance between the electrodes should not exceed 10,000 ohms and should be lower if possible (e.g., 5,000 ohms). Too low a resistance (say, less than 1,000 ohms) should be regarded with suspicion, because it could mean there is a conducting bridge of paste between the electrodes, or that they are

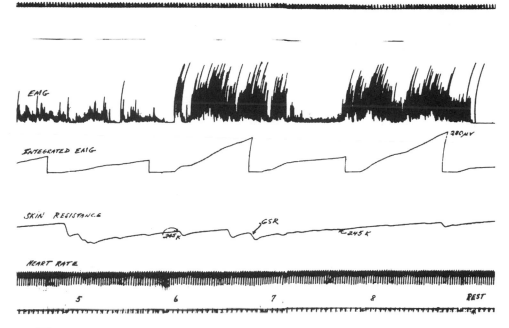

FIG. 8.4. Right forearm EMG measured during trials 5 through 8 in a verbal learning experiment. Partially integrated EMG is shown in the top trace, and integrated EMG (second line)
shows that total EMG activity over a 30-second trial (trial 8) was 280 μV. Note the sharp cessation of EMG activity at the end of trial 8 (rest). Also shown are records of skin resistance,
changes in skin resistance (GSR, or SCR when conductance is used) and heart rate. The
vertical marks in the bottom line indicate serial presentation of items to be learned in trials 5
through 8. (From author's unpublished data.)

too close. This situation could result in a short circuiting of the EMG potentials. The subject,
the EMG recorder, and the electrical equipment close to it should all be grounded to protect
the subject and to prevent 60-cycle interference in the recording. Once exposed to electrode
paste or gel, the electrodes will start to deteriorate. They must be washed in warm water and
soap after each use and then rinsed thoroughly in clear water to remove all traces of electrolyte. If a monopolar method of recording is used, then a single electrode is placed over the
muscle(s) of interest and is compared to an electrode placed at a site that is low in muscle activity. Bipolar recordings are more sensitive to variations in the gradients of muscle activity
between the two electrodes, while monopolar recordings are superior in picking up variations
in absolute levels of electrical activity. In either type of recording, the smaller the electrode
used, the greater the precision obtained in recording from a muscle group of interest.

Specific Electrode Placements

In order to place electrodes over the muscle of interest, some standardization is necessary. In
bipolar recordings, the electrode array usually consists of two active and one inactive electrode (ground). The active electrodes are placed in a bipolar pattern along the long axis of the
muscle. The amount of EMG recorded is the algebraic sum of all action potentials of the contracting fibers located between the electrodes. The exact specifications for placement of electrodes over different muscle areas have been outlined by J. F. Davis (1959) and Basmajian
and Blumenstein (1983). Examples of two common placements are given in Fig. 8.5, adapted from J. F. Davis (1959). The examples are for the frontalis muscle of the forehead and the

flexor muscles of the forearm. The placements for the frontalis muscle are obtained by measuring 2 in. to the left and right of midline (nasion as the midline reference point) and placing each electrode 1 in. above the eyebrow. One must be careful to watch for eye blink and EEG artifact with this placement.

For purposes of EMG research, there is a problem with this placement for frontalis measurement, although the specifications for other muscle groups as outlined by J. F. Davis (1959) and Lippold (1967) are satisfactory. The problem as noted by Davis, Brickett, Stern, and Kimball (1978) is: The frontales on the forehead, over each eye, are two separate muscles. Because only the potential difference between the two electrodes is amplified, activity occurring simultaneously in both muscles would not be recorded. Davis and colleagues recommend a placement in which both electrodes of a pair are placed vertically on the forehead along the longitudinal axis of a single frontalis muscle (see Fig. 8.7). The placement of an active lead over each frontalis muscle, as shown in Fig 8.5 (horizontal), is suitable for use in clinical biofeedback applications, because it provides information about within-session changes in muscle tension and allows more reliable differential EMG control than the vertical placement (Williamson, Epstein, & Lombardo, 1980).

The forearm flexor (flexor carpi radialis and flexor digitorum sublimis) electrode attachments require measurements of the distance from the medial epicondyle of the humerus to the styloid process of the radius, while subjects have their forearm on a table with palm up (see Fig. 8.5). Next, a point that is one third of the distance from epicondyle to styloid is taken. The center of Electrode A is placed over this point. Electrode B is placed 2 in. distally from the center of A. This placement should show visible movement with flexion of the middle finger of this hand. The ground may be placed at the elbow or wrist of the same arm to reduce ECG artifact. Because the EMG is susceptible to movement artifact, it is best to use relatively small electrodes and an attachment that is flexible. Placement over a pulsating artery should be avoided.

Recording the EMG

Because the EMG is a relatively small signal, a level of amplification similar to that used for EEG is required. Although the EMG produces a wide range of frequencies, some experts agree that the maximal activity occurs at the lower end of the spectrum (Goldstein, 1972). The frequencies of interest range from approximately 20 to 400 Hz. This means the filtering system must allow at least this frequency range of EMG to be recorded. Because ink-writer pen systems cannot follow the signal very well after 150 Hz, one approach has been to record the EMG on magnetic tape for later playback into a computer or to record at a slowed rate that the ink-writer can follow. Still another method utilizes a cathode-ray oscilloscope to display the EMG recording during experimental trials, because it has no difficulty in following and displaying even very high frequencies.

As mentioned previously, the technique of integration helps considerably in the analysis of EMG activity. Essentially, the integrator provides a measure of total EMG output over a given period of time. Or, alternately, it may be designed to automatically reset when a certain level of activity has occurred, for example, reset might occur after every 300 μV of accumulated EMG activity. The total integrated activity is proportional to both the positive and negative components of the EMG waveform. Goldstein (1972) pointed out a possible problem inherent in the use of integrators. Because they do not discriminate between artifacts and real muscle action potentials (MAPs), the artifacts may be integrated along with MAPs. As a precautionary measure, the researcher could monitor the raw EMG and exclude portions that have artifact. An encouraging note concerns the consistency of EMG measures in the same individual over time (Goldstein, 1972).

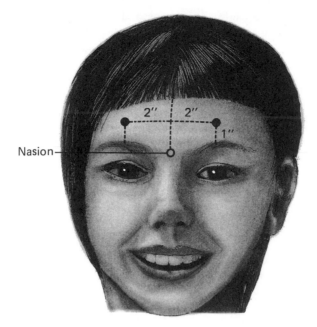

Standard Forehead Lead (frontalis muscle)

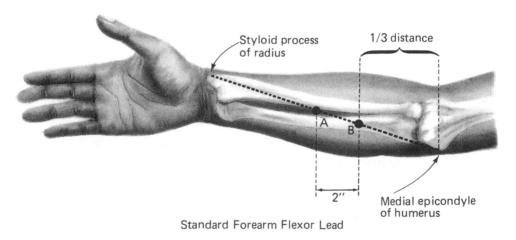

Standard Forearm Flexor Lead

FIG. 8.5. Standard forehead and forearm leads for measurement of EMG.

THE EMG AND BEHAVIOR

Many studies relating EMG to various kinds of human behavior and performance have been reviewed by Duffy (1962, 1972) and Goldstein (1972). An examination of the EMG literature from 1970 on indicates numerous EMG studies in a clinical biofeedback context. Several EMG biofeedback studies that relate to basic learning and conditioning processes are presented in this chapter, whereas representative EMG studies aimed at using biofeedback to treat some specific disorder are examined in chapter 17. Before launching into a description of EMG-behavior studies, some mention of situational and social factors that can operate in these studies should be made. Cacioppo, Tassinary, and Fridlund (1990) observed that these factors have been found to influence physiological responding. Subjects may try to figure out the purpose of the experiment and modify their behavior accordingly. The EMG is vulnerable to such distortions because it is easily influenced by voluntary actions. They may try to please the experimenter by having their responses conform to what they think the hypotheses of the study might be.

A number of tactics for minimizing social factors are suggested by Cacioppo et al. (1990) and include giving the subjects peripheral hypotheses, using cover stories to divert subject's awareness from the fact that physiological responses over which they have control are being monitored, and using dummy electrode placements over body areas other than those of primary interest. Experimenters must also keep in mind that performance on a task can be influenced just by moving the task from a nonsocial to a social context. Cacioppo et al. (1990) relate an observation of Triplett, in 1898, that subjects performed motor activities, like bicycle riding, more vigorously in a group situation than alone.

Motor Performance and the EMG

The EMG has been recorded by investigators during the performance of various kinds of motor activities, including time to react, tracking, speech production, and fatigue-producing muscular activities. Some of these studies are briefly reviewed here.

EMG and Reaction Time. In a study by R. C. Davis (1940), the EMG was recorded from the forearm extensor muscles while a subject waited to obtain a signal for his response. Muscle tension began about 200 to 400 msec after the ready signal and increased up to the moment of reaction. Two other findings were of interest: (1) the higher the muscle tension at the end of the foreperiod, the faster the RT; and (2) muscle tension was higher and RT was quicker at the end of regular foreperiods as compared to irregular ones. The finding that RT is faster with regular foreperiods is not surprising, because other investigators before and since have obtained this result. It is interesting, however, that muscle tension should be higher with regular foreperiods. Davis attributed this to a form of "set," or an increased readiness to respond on the part of subjects.

It is also of interest to relate these findings to those of other studies using different physiological measures. For example, the alpha-blocking response begins about 300 msec after the stimulus (Lansing, Schwartz, & Lindsley, 1959) or at a similar interval for the start of muscle tension buildup. Also, skin conductance has been found to be higher and RT faster during experimental conditions under which there were regular intervals between stimuli as compared to irregular intervals (Andreassi, Rapisardi, & Whalen, 1969).

The relation between EMG levels and performance of both tracking and RT was studied by Kennedy and Travis (1948). The subjects performed a pursuit tracking task over a 2-hr period while EMG was measured from the frontalis muscle. A warning light was placed off to the side of the main tracking display, and flashed on when muscle tension fell below predetermined levels. Thus, RT and tracking performance were measured at various tension levels. Kennedy and Travis reported that RTs became progressively slower with low levels of tension and faster when tension level was high. The number of failures to respond greatly increased at the low tension levels, indicating inattentiveness or drowsiness at those times. On the basis of this and other studies (Kennedy & Travis, 1947; Travis & Kennedy, 1949), they proposed that frontalis muscle tension might serve as an indicator of alertness in situations where persons are involved in monotonous tasks over prolonged periods of time.

In the R. C. Davis (1940) study, the muscle group actually involved in the response showed an increase in tension during the foreperiod, whereas in the Kennedy and Travis investigation, the frontalis muscle was not involved in the response, but the task was a visuomotor one in which subjects had to follow changes in a visual display by making hand and arm movements. Goldstein (1972) noted that with increased practice, activity in muscles not involved in the reaction tends to decrease. For example, Obrist, Webb, and Sutterer (1969) reported decreased activity in chin and neck muscles just before and during the time that subjects depressed a telegraph key with their hand. This was correlated with decreased heart rate. They interpreted this to indicate a decrease in irrelevant muscular activity that might otherwise interfere with the task that the subject was to perform.

Further study led them to suggest that EMG measured from chin muscles may be a good index of irrelevant motor activity. Obrist, Webb, Sutterer, and Howard (1970) obtained additional evidence that the decreased chin EMG was related to cardiac deceleration. Again, they found inhibition of task-irrelevant somatic activities during the foreperiod, just as the response was made in a simple RT task. It was this kind of result that led Obrist to formulate his cardiac–somatic concept in which heart rate and activity in muscles irrelevant to performance of a task covary (see chapter 18). The cardiac–somatic coupling hypothesis was investigated by Haagh and Brunia (1984), who had subjects participate in a simple auditory RT task with a constant 4-sec foreperiod. In addition to HR, the EMG of nine striate muscle groups varying in relevance to response execution were recorded. Only one muscle group was coupled to the decrease in HR noted at the end of the foreperiod, hence the results give only fragmentary support to the cardiac–somatic hypothesis (see chapter 18 for further discussion of this concept).

EMG was recorded from the masseter muscles (jaw) while a RT task was performed (Holloway & Parsons, 1972). The warning signal preceded the execution stimulus by a variable interval, and subjects were instructed to react by stepping on a foot switch. The results were similar to those of Obrist and associates, in that fast RTs were associated with less EMG during the preparatory foreperiod of the task. Notice that in this experiment, as with previous ones showing decreased EMG in the period just preceding the response, the muscle tension was measured from muscles other than those involved in the task and the response. It would have been informative if these investigators had also provided information on EMGs from responding muscle groups to enable some statement regarding the relative activity of task-involved and noninvolved muscle groups. The implication is that only activity in muscles not concerned with task execution would be reduced during the time just before and during the response.

Summary.   When a muscle group is involved in the execution of a RT task, progressively increasing activity during the foreperiod is related to faster responses. However, noninvolved muscles show a decrease in activity, presumably lessening the possibility of interference with the relevant motor response. The relationship between muscle and heart activity in these kinds of tasks forms part of the basis for Obrist's cardiac–somatic hypothesis.

EMG and Tracking.   Tracking involves the movement of some control (wheel or joystick) to keep an indicator on a moving target. Continuous motor adjustments must be made to perform the task correctly. A pilot maintaining a correct altitude and heading and a driver keeping a car in lane are performing tracking tasks. Many of the video games that occupy the time of youngsters (and some oldsters) provide good examples of tracking tasks.

Kennedy and Travis (1948) obtained results indicating a relationship between low frontalis EMG and poor tracking performance. A number of tracking studies have shown a relation between subjective effort and EMG. For example, studies by Eason and colleagues indicate, in general, that conditions requiring increased effort led to increased EMG levels and improved performance (Eason, 1963; Eason & White, 1960, 1961). Eason and White (1960) observed that EMG level increased and tracking performance improved as a function of practice trials, up to a certain point. After this point, performance dropped, even though EMG increased, suggesting that fatigue was occurring. When subjects were given 0, 10, 20, or 40 sec between trials, performance improved with intertrial interval, but the EMG was lower. This inverse relationship between EMG and performance was interpreted as evidence that muscular fatigue is partly responsible for the commonly observed superiority of distributed over massed practice in pursuit rotor tracking and in other perceptual–motor tasks. (Distributed practice refers to rests between trials, whereas massed practice requires continuous performance, trial after trial.)

Eason and White advanced a two-factor hypothesis of muscular tension. They proposed that muscular tension is positively related to both motivation and fatigue. Because motivation facilitates performance and fatigue hinders it, the tension level at any given time is a summation of the motivation and fatigue components. Results similar to those of White and Eason were reported by Mulder and Hulston (1984). They found that fatigue caused integrated EMG activity to increase, but actual muscle efficiency decreased. On the other hand, simple repetition of the task without allowing fatigue to occur led to increased efficiency. These results suggest that learning a motor skill partially involves the dropping out of irrelevant muscle activity. This idea receives support from a study by French (1980), in which a group of subjects given feedback of muscle activity while learning a pursuit tracking task had lower EMG levels and better performance than a group not receiving feedback. This kind of effect is not limited to those learning a novel motor task, as is shown in a study of skilled violin and viola players (Levine & Irvine, 1984). The musicians were provided EMG feedback as a method for removing unwanted left-hand muscle tension. Electrodes attached to the left hand during the playing of a difficult piece sounded an alarm whenever EMG exceeded a level observed during the playing of an easy scale. Irrelevant muscle activity dropped out quickly (average of 5 sessions) an effect that persisted at a 6-month follow-up check.

Summary.   Efficient tracking is related to some moderate to high EMG level. Very low muscular tension (possibly indicative of drowsiness) and very high tension (perhaps associated with over exertion or fatigue) seem to be associated with less efficient performance. The drop in efficiency with fatigue shows up in muscle output as well. A two-factor hypothesis proposes that level of muscular tension is related positively to both motivation and fatigue. Feedback from irrelevant muscles, promoting decreased EMG in those muscles, seems to benefit both skilled and unskilled performers.

EMG and Speech

The notion that thinking is nothing more than subvocal speech has commonly been attributed to behaviorists such as J. B. Watson. This position suggests that the muscles of speech operate separately from the brain. McGuigan (1981) contended that early behaviorists, including Watson, did not believe this to be the case, but thought instead in terms of many channels running between the brain and speech muscles. Goldstein (1972) reviewed a number of studies indicating that EMGs occur during thinking, but the electrical changes are not confined to the vocal mechanism (larynx), because EMG is observed in many different muscle groups. McGuigan (1981) argued that the available data justify the generalization that muscle activity accompanies all cognitive phenomena, even though EMG may be of small magnitude. There are studies that have examined subvocal speech as it occurs during reading in some individuals. Such occurrences are said to limit the rate of reading for these persons to about 150 words per minute, or approximately the maximum attainable while reading aloud.

In one study, Hardyck, Petrinovich, and Ellsworth (1966) recorded EMG activity from over the laryngeal muscle while subjects read. Subvocalization was determined by noting EMG changes that occurred when subjects were asked to read silently and then to stop reading. Of the 50 subjects tested, 17 were found to be subvocalizers. These 17 were tested further in the following manner: First, they were allowed to hear their own amplified EMG activity over headphones, then they were shown how it could be controlled, and finally they began to read under instructions to keep the EMG level at a minimum. Most subjects showed a reduction in speech muscle EMG level within 5 min. After 30 min, all 17 were able to read at an EMG level that was comparable to their resting levels.

Follow-up tests at 1 and 3 months revealed no subvocalization during reading, using the EMG as the criterion. The authors attributed this rapid, and apparently long-term, disappearance of subvocalization to the ability to make fine motor adjustments of the speech muscles on the basis of auditory feedback. This is in contrast to the situation in which attempts to reduce speech muscle activity by instructions alone were not successful. The authors cited the work of Basmajian (1963), who reported that the ability to control activity of single motor units could be learned through the aid of auditory and visual feedback.

In a later study, Hardyck and Petrinovich (1969) identified 50 college and 13 high school students who were habitual subvocalizers during silent reading. Forty-eight of the college students learned to eliminate the subvocal activity within 1 hr. The 13 high school students required from one to three sessions to abolish the subvocal speech. The immediate effect of eliminating subvocalization was that subjects reported a reduction of fatigue previously associated with reading for periods of 1 to 3 hrs. Hardyck and Petrinovich suggested that elimination of subvocal speech and reading improvement instruction should enable a high reading speed, with good comprehension, for those with sufficient ability to benefit from the techniques.

McGuigan and his associates (McGuigan & Bailey, 1969; McGuigan, Keller, & Stanton, 1964; McGuigan & Rodier, 1968) found increases in chin, lip, and tongue EMGs during silent reading as compared to resting levels. In addition, McGuigan and Rodier (1968) observed increased amplitude of chin and tongue EMG for college students during the memorization of prose materials. They also found that EMG levels were higher during silent reading when they presented auditory noise in the form of prose different from that being read. They interpreted this latter finding as indicating that subjects changed the amplitude of their covert oral behavior to facilitate the reading process.

McGuigan (1973) suggested that the higher level of oral EMG activity during silent reading in children and less proficient adults indicates that these individuals exaggerate their covert oral behavior to bring their comprehension up to a proper level. Likewise, under demanding conditions (e.g., noisy environment) the average individual enhances reading proficiency by exaggerating the amplitude of covert oral activity, sometimes reading aloud to do this, perhaps to overcome a distracting conversation in the vicinity. Contrary to the view of others who would eliminate subvocal activity related to silent reading, McGuigan believed that the covert oral response is beneficial to this and other types of linguistic tasks. McGuigan (1981) also claimed, in contrast to Hardyck, that the more rapidly a person reads, the greater the amplitude of covert speech muscle activity.

Summary.   EMG studies have detected subvocal speech during silent reading in a certain proportion of individuals tested. This type of EMG feedback may have practical applications in terms of eliminating this habit in adults who are hindered by it. However, children appear to subvocalize naturally while reading silently, and perhaps teachers should not try to eliminate this activity if it helps in comprehending the material at an early learning stage.

Muscular Fatigue and Performance

Investigations have indicated that persons can maintain maximum muscular effort (100%) for less than 1 min (McCormick, 1976). However, a level of about 25% of maximum can be maintained for 10 min or more. The implications of these findings are that muscular efficiency decreases when a high level of exertion is required for an extended period, and that this is due to muscle fatigue. With respect to performance in tracking, Eason and White (1960) contended that muscular fatigue is partly responsible for the superiority of distributed practice over massed practice. They also suggested that a fatigued subject would have to increase muscular tension in order to continue making rotary pursuit movements. Thus, additional motor units would be recruited to compensate for the reduced activity of fatigued units.

Some support for this idea is derived from a study by Wilkinson (1962). Subjects were required to perform a 20-min pencil-and-paper addition test under the following conditions: (a) after a normal night of sleep, and (b) after 32 to 56 hours of sleep deprivation. The EMG recorded from the inactive forearm indicated that persons who maintained performance best after sleep loss had the greatest increases in EMG over normal levels. Thus, the maintenance of performance level under difficult conditions is done by expending a greater amount of energy.

Localized muscle fatigue was investigated under both laboratory and factory assembly-line conditions by Ortengren, Anderson, Broman, Magnusson, and Petersen (1975). Two assembly-line stations were examined and results were comparable for both the laboratory simulation and the actual assembly line. At one station, the muscles were under heavy static load for periods of 60 secs at a time. The other station required that individuals perform much of their work above shoulder level. The EMGs were recorded from biceps, triceps, forearm, deltoid, and trapezius muscles of experienced male workers. Subjective experience of localized fatigue coincided highly with increased EMG level of various muscles. The technique enabled comparison of muscle strain for different work tasks and is useful in providing information about how jobs can be designed to make them less strenuous.

The effect of desk slant on EMG and fatigue ratings was tested by Eastman and Kamon (1976). They photographed back posture and recorded EMG from deltoid, trapezius, and spinae erector (lower back) muscles while subjects performed reading and writing tasks at flat, 12-degree tilt, and 24-degree tilt desks. The subjects worked for 2½ hrs on each of 3 days. The major finding was that EMG activity from the lower back muscles was significantly lessened with the 24-degree desk slant. Fatigue ratings were also least for the 24-degree desk.

Summary.   The several studies reviewed in this section indicate that feelings of localized fatigue are associated with increased local EMG activity. Studies of EMG activity may be useful in reducing fatigue produced by different types of work tasks and workplaces and can provide information to redesign jobs and work stations.

EMG AND MENTAL ACTIVITY

This section considers EMG in conditioning, cognitive activities, sleep, motivated performance, and emotional expression.

Conditioning of the EMG

The control of single motor units through conditioning procedures is well established, and much of the relevant work has been summarized by Basmajian (1977, 1986). The emphasis in this section is on EMG changes as revealed by surface recordings.

Operant Conditioning.   Operant conditioning of EMG was demonstrated by Cohen (1973). Two groups of subjects were reinforced for producing either 40 to 60 μV or 90 to 110

μV of chin EMG, for a minimum of .5 sec. Both experimental groups learned to emit the correct EMG level to obtain reinforcement. In another study, EMG feedback was compared with the more commonly used verbal relaxation instructions as to effectiveness in reducing frontalis muscle tension (Haynes, Mosely, & McGowan, 1975). During EMG feedback, subjects heard a tone that decreased in pitch as they became more relaxed and increased in pitch as muscular tension increased. Other subjects received instructions to relax according to either active relaxation (Jacobson) or passive relaxation (Wolpe) techniques. A control group was asked to become as relaxed as possible, but received no other assistance. A final group received noncontingent feedback in the form of a tone that was presented at random intervals and was not related to low or high EMG levels. The EMG biofeedback group achieved greater degrees of muscle relaxation than either of the other two relaxation groups and much greater than that achieved by persons in the two control groups.

Alexander (1975) questioned two basic assumptions implicit in the use of EMG feedback to achieve lowered muscular tension. These were: (a) that tension reduction in one muscle (e.g., the frontalis) is generalized to other skeletal muscles, and (b) that the subjective feeling of being relaxed is related to EMG reduction. Alexander's experimental group achieved significant decreases in frontalis EMG with feedback, but this lowering of tension did not spread to two other skeletal muscles (forearm and leg). In addition, a comparison of the ratings of relaxation made by experimental and control groups (no feedback) indicated that mild relaxation was achieved by both groups over the 5-day period of the experiment. Thus, Alexander proposed that his data do not support a claim that frontalis EMG reduction is either related to or produces general feelings of relaxation.

The generalization of muscle relaxation from frontalis to other muscles was studied by Fridlund, Fowler, and Pritchard (1980). Subjects had frontalis EMG training on 5 separate days while muscle activity was measured at 7 other sites, including the arms, legs, and neck. Frontalis EMG levels decreased significantly with feedback, but activity from the other muscles did not, thus supporting Alexander's position. A study by LeBoeuf (1980) tested the degree to which frontalis relaxation would generalize to trapezius (shoulder) and masseter (jaw) muscles. He found evidence that frontalis feedback was effective in lowering EMG in the other facial area (masseter) but not in the trapezius. This last finding indicates that generalization of relaxation from frontalis feedback may be limited to adjacent facial muscles. However, it must be emphasized that much of the research indicates that whereas biofeedback leads to reduced EMG in the targeted muscle, relaxation does not generalize to adjacent muscles (Fridlund, Cottam, & Fowler, 1982; Thompson, Haber, & Tearnan, 1981).

Summary.   Operant conditioning of surface EMG, using appropriate reinforcement, has been obtained by a number of researchers. It seems that by providing accurate information about internal processes, EMG feedback can lead to instrumental control of muscle tension level. However, the contention that lowering level of EMG in one muscle (e.g., frontalis) will generalize to other muscles has not been experimentally supported. The studies mentioned here are general in nature, because they deal primarily with the learned control of EMG. Investigations directed at the study of EMG feedback in the context of treating certain disorders, such as tension headache, are discussed in chapter 17.

Classical Conditioning.   The classical conditioning of EMG has been demonstrated in several studies. For example, Van Liere (1953) measured EMG from the masseter and forearm muscles in an experimental group, in which the CS (tone) was followed by the UCS (another tone), and in a control group, which received the CS only. As conditioning progressed, the experimental group showed a larger EMG increase to the CS than the control group, indicating conditioning of these muscles. Obrist (1968) also showed EMG activity of neck, chin, and forearm muscles during classical conditioning. Obrist et al. (1969), using a blue light as the CS and an electric shock as the UCS, found that chin EMG activity reflected a decrease in discrete movements, not in tension level.

EMG During Sleep

The question of EMG activity during sleep and dreaming was reviewed by Goldstein (1972). The consensus of several studies was that the onset of dreaming was marked by a reduction in neck and head EMG activity. This general conclusion was supported by Bliwise, Coleman, Bergmann, Wincor, Pivek, and Rechtschaffen (1974). These researchers measured chin and lip EMG during sleep on three consecutive nights. They found that EMGs decreased toward their lowest levels starting 5 min before the onset of REM sleep. The lowest EMG levels of the night occurred throughout REM sleep. The chin EMG was superior to lip recordings in identifying REM sleep. The EMG from muscles in the throat and upper air passages of persons suffering obstructive sleep apnea was studied by Guilleminault, Hill, Simmons, and Dement (1978). Sleep apnea involves a cessation of breathing during sleep. In comparison to normal controls, the apnea victims had a decrease or complete disappearance of activity in the muscles measured during parts of the sleep cycle, and this led to the obstructed airways.

EMG and Probability of Successful Performance

Forearm EMGs of subjects solving a verbal problem were measured by Clites (1936). He found that EMGs indicated greater muscle activity when subjects were successful in problem solving than when they were unsuccessful. Perhaps success led to more interest and involvement in the task and was reflected in the elevated EMG levels.

The question of probability of success and its effect on muscular effort expended in a task was investigated by Diggory, Klein, and Cohen (1964). These experimenters measured EMG from the forearms of three groups of subjects: (a) those who were led to believe that they had a high probability of success (Ps) in a task, (b) those who believed that Ps was very low, and (c) those who believed that Ps was 50–50. The investigators manipulated Ps by showing the subjects perdetermined graphs of past performance and extrapolations to future performance after each trial. The results supported the conclusion that persons who expected to succeed exerted more effort, as measured by EMG level, than those who expected to fail. Thus, there is support for the idea that the experience of success in problem solving leads to an increase in muscular activity.

This picture is complicated, however, when one considers results of studies that have varied difficulty without considering success or failure. For example, R. C. Davis (1938) measured forearm and neck EMGs while subjects solved number problems that became progressively more difficult. He reported that with increased task difficulty, EMGs at both locations increased correspondingly. The difficulty of a problem was judged by the proportion of subjects who failed it. Pishkin and Shurley (1968) measured frontalis EMGs of psychiatric patients during a concept identification task. The EMG was higher with unsolvable than with solvable problems. The investigators concluded that the EMGs represented tension associated with difficulty in processing complex information. In a later study, Pishkin (1973) reported that schizophrenics produced higher EMGs than normals as complexity of problems to be solved increased. Both groups, however, showed higher EMG activity with increased complexity.

Hence, some of the obtained results indicated heightened EMG activity when subjects were successful in their tasks. However, other findings showed increased EMG with increased task difficulty. In the latter instances, the increased EMG was related to less successful performance. The reason for this discrepancy is not clear. Perhaps the common denominator is effort, and the transfer of impulses from brain to muscle and back when a person is engaged in a difficult cognitive task. Caccioppo and Petty (1981) showed that depth of covert processing was related to oral (lip) EMG but not to nonoral (forearm) EMG or heart activity measures. The more abstract and difficult the mental coding task, the greater was the activity of the speech-related muscles. Caccioppo and Petty offered the explanation that the increased proprioceptive feedback from speech muscles to brain may help in the processing of new information. They suggested that oral EMG activity may be useful in studying central (brain) information-processing operations.

Summary.   A complex picture emerges when one considers EMG levels related to successful performance. A number of studies suggest that EMG levels increase with successful performance or with increased probability of success. On the other hand, EMG levels have also been found to increase with task difficulty and a corresponding drop in performance. Perhaps we are seeing some interaction of motivation (increased by success probability) and effort (increased in difficult tasks). It is possible that EMG may not be capable of distinguishing successful from nonsuccessful performance, or that psychophysiologists have not yet found a way to separate the effects. A possible approach would be to manipulate probability of success and task difficulty to see the effects of various combinations. For example, the effects on EMG of high and low success probability combined with high, moderate and low difficulty tasks could be studied.

EMG Gradients and Motivated Performance

Several studies have shown that EMG increased progressively from the beginning to the end of a task (e.g., Bartoshuk, 1955; Surwillo, 1956). These increases have been termed *EMG gradients* because if you plot EMG over time, you would see a line rising diagonally from left to right. There is evidence that the slope of these gradients is related to level of motivation; the steeper the slope, the higher the motivation. These findings are related to the discussion of EMG and successful performance presented in the previous section. Bartoshuk (1955) reported that EMG gradients were also related to quality of performance in mirror tracing (a difficult task in which subjects trace a pattern with vision restricted to a mirror image only). With subjects equated for practice, the gradient slope (especially for right forearm EMGs) was found to be directly related to speed and accuracy of performance. Surwillo (1956) tested the hypothesis that the slope of the EMG gradient could be increased by raising the level of incentives in a tracking task. In his first experiment, two incentive levels were produced, and the higher one resulted in steeper EMG gradients as measured from the biceps, wrist, and frontalis muscles. In a second experiment, a new group of subjects was tested at three incentive levels. Again, incentive level was found to be a factor in raising the EMG gradient.

Malmo (1975) discussed EMG gradients and their significance at some length. He hypothesized that the appearance of an EMG gradient indicates the occurrence of an organized behavior sequence. According to Malmo, the stronger the person's involvement in the task, the steeper the somatic (muscle) and autonomic (e.g., heart activity) gradients. Svebak, Dalen, and Storfjell (1981) tested the hypotheses that somatic and autonomic gradients occur jointly, and that gradients are steeper with greater involvement and effort of subjects. In two experiments, they found that a difficult continuous RT task produced steeper EMG gradients than an easier version, but that autonomic measures (heart rate, skin conductance) did not show gradients. Thus, Malmo's hypothesis was only partially supported. In another study, Svebak and Murgatroyd (1985) found that "serious-minded" subjects had steeper EMG gradients than "playful" persons while performing a video car-racing simulation. Svebak and

Kerr (1989) found a dominance of impulsive lifestyles among performers of explosive sports (sprint, jump, etc.), whereas endurance athletes had more goal-directed lifestyles. These differences led Braathen and Svebak (1990) to predict that EMG gradients in leg and "passive" forearm muscles would be greater in endurance athletes than those who participate in explosive sports. The prediction held true only for the passive forearm, as discussed in an earlier section.

Summary.   EMG gradients have been reported for both mental (e.g., listening to a story) and physical activities (e.g., tracking). These gradients have been shown to be steeper as a function of motivation and task involvement. Thus, levels of motivation, success in the task, and task difficulty can affect EMG activity, and must be taken into account in the conduct of studies relating EMG to behavior.

Facial Expression of Emotion and the EMG

The Early Work.   One of the first students of facial expressions of emotion was Charles Darwin. In his 1872 book, *Expression of the Emotions in Man and Animals*, Darwin argued that man's expressive movements are remnants of earlier ones. For example, the expression of grief in the adult is a toned down version of crying in the infant (Woodworth, 1938). The wide-open mouth of crying involves muscles of the corner of the mouth, and the slight movement of these remain as a sign of grief after vocal crying has disappeared as a response. The facial expression of disgust was described by Darwin as a combination of closing off the nose to keep out unpleasant odor and opening the mouth as if to spit out its contents.

Darwin introduced the procedure of having people judge facial expressions of emotions from photographs. The face is a logical choice, because the muscles and skin of the face are very mobile. In addition, the face is visible to others and is an important source of information in both verbal and nonverbal social communications. Another 19th century student of facial expressions in emotion was Piderit (Woodworth & Schlosberg, 1954). Piderit suggested that mental images of objects should produce the same facial response as when the object was actually viewed. Thus, with unpleasant thoughts, the mouth moves as if avoiding a bitter taste, the eye region as if avoiding an unpleasant sight, the nose as though reacting to a foul odor. Piderit mentioned also the open mouth of attention and the appraising mouth, with lips protruding. Piderit illustrated this analysis with simple line drawings: profile and front views. Later investigators such as Boring and Titchener in the 1920s used the Piderit drawings in studying judgments of emotional expressions by subjects (Woodworth & Schlosberg, 1954).

Contemporary Studies Using Facial EMG.   The procedure of using photos to study patterning in facial expressions and the question of whether they are inherited or learned has continued from the time of Darwin to the present, and has led to the interesting work of Ekman (1973), who compared cross-cultural judgments of emotion from posed facial expressions. Typically, reactions such as happiness, anger, fear, disgust, sadness, and surprise are posed in contemporary studies. In his cross-cultural work, Ekman showed that expressions such as happiness and anger are readily recognized in diverse cultures, a result that could be supportive of evolutionary origins.

The study of facial expressions of emotion entered a new phase in the 1970s with the use of EMG measures in studies by Schwartz and his associates. The 19th-century anatomist Sir Charles Bell believed that certain muscles peculiar to primates, such as the corrugators that knit the brows or the triangularis that depresses the mouth, have no other function than to express emotion (Woodworth, 1938). Schwartz and colleagues found that imagining pleasant thoughts increased muscle activity in the cheek area responsible for smiles (zygomatic muscle), whereas unpleasant imagining produced an increase in corrugator muscle activity at the eyebrows (Schwartz, Ahern, & Brown, 1979; Schwartz, Brown, & Ahern, 1980; Schwartz, Fair, Salt, Mandel, & Klerman, 1976).

Is Emotional Contagion Indicated by Facial EMG? Dimberg (1982) conducted a study to investigate whether individuals exposed to pictures of happy and angry facial expressions would be influenced by the pictured pattern through a form of social interaction. He found that facial EMG activity was differentially affected by happy and angry faces because happy faces evoked increased zygomatic activity and angry faces elicited elevated corrugator muscle response, the same pattern observed in the Schwartz studies for imagined emotional states. The patterning of response was of interest, but still to be determined was whether the pictures resulted in changed mood states or merely involved superficial mimicking on the part of subjects. This question was answered by Sirota and Schwartz (1982), who took measures of mood as well as EMG while subjects imagined scenes with elated, depressed, and neutral content. Feelings of elation and depression were elicited in approximately 70% of subjects, and among these persons, elation was accompanied by increases in zygomatic activity, whereas depression produced increases in corrugator activity. Thus, facial EMG patterning seems to be a good indicator of mood state and perhaps an index of emotional contagion.

A detailed and sophisticated computer-based analysis of facial EMG patterns during imagery and posed facial expressions was carried out by Fridlund, Schwartz, and Fowler (1984). They showed the usefulness of measuring from multiple facial sites, and confirmed the importance of corrugator activity during the experience of "negative emotions." The student interested in research methodology and possible future directions in this area should read the article by Fridlund and colleagues. Fridlund and Cacioppo (1986) presented guidelines for electrode placements in facial EMG research. Figure 8.6 shows these placements and modifications based on empirical work and anatomical review by Tassinary, Cacioppo, Geen, and Vanman (1987) and Tassinary, Cacioppo, and Geen (1989).

Facial EMG in Emotionally Charged Imagery and Visual Displays. The use of facial EMG was explored in a study of pleasant and unpleasant sexual and nonsexual arousal in a study by Sullivan and Brender (1986). Female subjects listened to four different kinds of stories—pleasant–sexual, unpleasant–sexual, pleasant–nonsexual, and unpleasant–nonsexual—while EMG was measured. Greater corrugator activity was noted for both kinds of unpleasant stimuli, but especially the one with sexual content. Zygomatic muscle activity was greater in response to sexual as compared to nonsexual stories. These interesting results argue for the use of facial EMG in studies of sexual response, but with additional recording sites to provide more information regarding differential muscle activity with different kinds of arousing or nonarousing stimuli.

Cacioppo, Bush, and Tassinary (1990) asked female subjects to view slides of social scenes (e.g., a person expressing emotion) and nature scenes (e.g., a mountain) that were pleasant, neutral, or unpleasant. In some trials, they were asked to inhibit their reaction, in others to exaggerate the reaction, and in still others no instruction was given. Facial EMG was highest in the exaggerate and lowest in the inhibit condition. Activity in the corrugator region was relatively high with unpleasant stimuli and low with pleasant ones. Facial EMG did not differ when subjects were exposed to nature versus social scenes matched for pleasantness. Results from this experiment indicated that facial EMG can vary with emotional stimuli even though the muscle activity is too small to show up as overt changes in facial expressions.

In a different approach, Cacioppo, Martzke, Petty, and Tassinary (1988) measured facial EMG and made videotapes while subjects were interviewed about themselves. Later, the individuals were asked to describe their thoughts during parts of the interview marked by in-

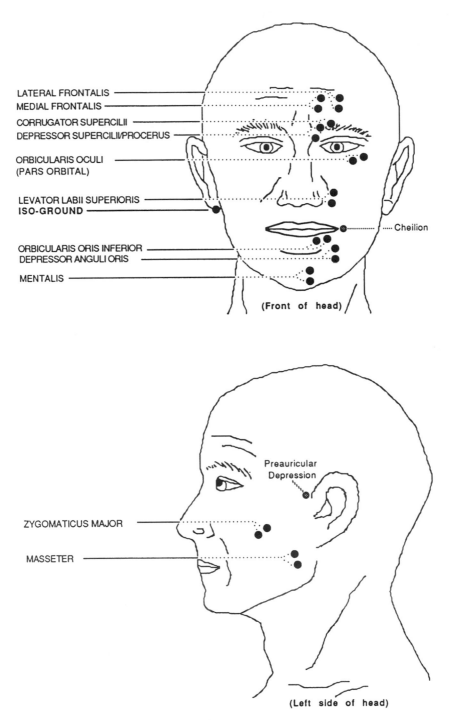

FIG. 8.6. EMG electrode placements for surface differential recording over major facial mimetic muscles. (Diagram Courtesy of Drs. Fridlund, Cacioppo and Tassinary.)

creased EMG in the brow region, but little activity elsewhere on the face. The results indicated that the EMG could detect changes in emotional processes that were too subtle or fleeting to produce observable facial expression changes during the interview.

Facial EMG was recorded as subjects imagined situations eliciting pleasure, joy, anger, and disgust (Vrana, 1993). As expected, joy and pleasure imagery produced reduced corrugator activity and increased zygomatic reactivity. Facial expression during disgust imagery was accompanied by increased activity in the levator labii (superioris and alesque nasi), which are the muscles responsible for lifting the middle of the upper lip and wrinkling the nose. The patterning of facial muscle activity in Vrana's study can be clearly seen in Fig. 8.7. Note how the levator labii activity is highest during disgust imagery and that corrugator activity is high with negative affect and dips below baseline for positive emotions (pleasure and joy).

Do People Mimic the Emotional Expressions of Others?   A systematic program of research on facial EMG patterns and emotional reactions was described by Dimberg (1990). Dimberg observed that one group of researchers has suggested that facial muscle activity serves a display function in interactions between people, communicating information about emotional state. It has also been hypothesized that the facial muscles play a role as a feedback system for the experience of emotion. In other words, the pattern of muscle activity in a person's face can provide the brain with information about emotions being experienced. Remember that the original proposal by Darwin was that facial expressions are biologically prewired and consistent between individuals. In his own research, Dimberg (1990) found that positive and negative emotional stimuli (such as happy and angry faces) produce facial EMG responses consistent with negative and emotional reactions (Dimberg, 1982; Dimberg & Thell, 1988). Dimberg and Lundquist (1990) reported gender differences.

The results indicated the expected EMG responses for angry and happy faces, but the women showed more pronounced EMG responses in both the zygomatic muscles and corrugator muscles. Dimberg interpreted this in terms of previous research showing that females are more facially expressive than males. Dimberg (1997) believes that humans are innately preprogrammed to respond with specific patterns of facial muscle activity to perceived emotions being portrayed by others. In an earlier report, Lundquist & Dimberg (1995) noted that since Adam Smith, in 1759, there have been other descriptions of people's tendency to imitate the facial expressions of others, including observations by Darwin in 1872 and Ribot in 1897. Lundquist and Dimberg (1995) measured facial EMG from zygomatic, levator labii, frontal lateralis, and corrugator supercilii muscles (see Fig. 8.6) while men and women viewed pictures of faces expressing various emotions. Emotional reactions to these pictures were also obtained. To a certain extent, subjects both mimicked and experienced emotions similar to those displayed. Although some of the results were inconsistent with the hypothesis that facial expressions are contagious, it was concluded that facial expressions are one channel through which emotional contagion can occur. Consistent with earlier research women responded with greater zygomatic muscle activity to happy faces compared to men.

One very interesting aspect of findings regarding the emotion-specific facial muscle patterns that are released when people view positive and negative stimuli is the rapidity with which they occur. Dimberg (1997) measured zygomatic and corrugator activity from a large number of individuals while they viewed a variety of negative and positive emotional stimuli. Pictures of happy faces and flowers evoked increased zygomatic activity within the first 0 to 500 msec of exposure. The corrugator muscle response was larger to angry faces than to happy ones during the initial 0 to 500 msec after stimulus onset. Pictures of snakes evoked corrugator activity almost as fast as the reaction to angry faces. Dimberg thinks that

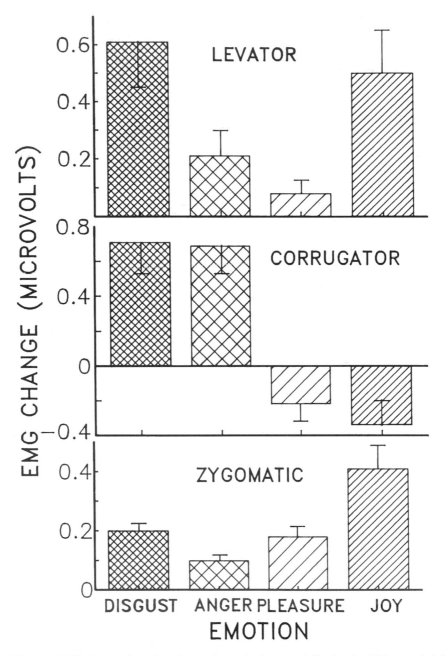

FIG. 8.7. EMG change from baseline and standard errors at the levator labii superioris/ alesque nasi, corrugator, and zygomatic muscle regions as a function of emotional content of imagery. (Figure courtesy of Dr. Scott R. Vrana of Purdue University).

the short facial EMG response time may be a general phenomenon that occurs when people are exposed to positive and negative stimuli. Further, the data suggest that emotional stimuli are rapidly processed and that facial reactions occur automatically after only a few hundred msec of exposure. This would also argue for the existence of built-in patterns of muscle activity that can be elicited by biologically relevant stimuli in a quick and automatic fashion.

Facial EMG and Anger In and Out.   Is there a difference in facial EMG patterns in persons who express anger outwardly versus those who express it inwardly? To answer this question Jancke (1996) measured frontalis, corrugator, orbicularis oculi, and zygomatic EMG from a control group and from a group of individuals who received insulting false feedback about their performance. After completing an intelligence test, the controls were given neutral feedback thanking them for their participation. The experimental group was given feedback saying their scores were unacceptable for university students, questioning their ability, and indicating that they would not receive the payment promised for participation in the study! After this feedback, all subjects were questioned about anger feelings. The experimental group was divided into those who expressed anger outwardly toward the experimenters and those who were angry about their own performance. Facial EMG patterns showed that the anger-out group had significantly higher frontalis and corrugator activity than either the anger-in or controls. Jancke concluded that the results support the notion that facial displays serve a social communication purpose rather than reflecting felt emotion. This view says that human facial displays are primarily for giving information regarding behavioral tendencies and not feelings (Fridlund, 1991).

Summary.   The use of facial EMG patterning in the study of emotional reactions is an exciting approach. The studies reviewed in this section revealed rather consistent activity in the corrugator muscles with unpleasant or negative stimuli, and increased zygomatic muscle activity with pleasant and positive stimuli. In addition, the levator labii muscle has shown increased activity to stimuli designed to produce disgust. Subjective ratings of stimuli have corresponded to reactions that could be described as positive, negative, or indicative of disgust. Gender differences have also been found, showing women to be more facially reactive than men to affect-laden stimuli. There is some evidence that facial EMG patterns are influenced by viewing pictures of emotions being expressed by others. Additional work is needed on this question of "emotional contagion." The speed of changes in muscular activity with presentation of positive or negative stimuli suggests a built-in, preprogrammed, response that is poised to be released with appropriate stimulation.

The next chapter discusses electrodermal activity (EDA) and behavior. This measure, like the EMG, is another peripheral physiological response that is very sensitive to changes in CNS activity and psychological states. The final control of EDA is via the sympathetic branch of the autonomic nervous system.

REFERENCES

Alexander, A. B. (1975). An experimental test of assumptions relating to the use of electromyographic biofeedback as a general relaxation technique. *Psychophysiology, 12,* 656–662.

Andreassi, J. L., Rapisardi, S., & Whalen, P. M. (1969). Autonomic responsivity and reaction time under fixed and variable signal schedules. *Psychophysiology, 6,* 58–69.

Arena, J. G., Bruno, G. M., Brucks, A. G., Searle, J. R., Sherman, R. A., & Meador, K. J. (1994). Reliability of an ambulatory electromyographic activity devie for musculoskeletal pain disorders. *International Journal of Psychophysiology, 17,* 153–157.

Bartoshuk, A. K. (1955). Electromyographic gradients as indicants of motivation. *Canadian Journal of Psychology, 9,* 215–230.

Basmajian, J. V. (1963). Control and training of individual motor units. *Science, 30,* 662–664.

Basmajian, J. V. (1977). Motor learning and control: A working hypothesis. *Archives of Physical Medicine and Rehabilitation, 58,* 38–41.

Basmajian, J. V. (1986). The musculature. In M. G. H. Coles, E. Donchin, & S. W. Porges (Eds.), *Psychophysiology: Systems, processes & applications* (pp. 97–106). New York: Guilford.

Basmajian, J. V., & Blumenstein, R. (1983). Electrode placement in electromyographic biofeedback. In J. V. Basmajian (Ed.), *Biofeedback: Principles & practice for clinicians* (pp. 363–378). Baltimore: Williams & Wilkins.

Bliwise, D., Coleman, R., Bergmann, B., Wincor, M. S., Pivik, R. T., & Rechtschaffen, A. (1974). Facial muscle tonus during REM and NREM sleep. *Psychophysiology, 11*, 497–508.

Braathen, E. T., & Svebak, S. (1990). Task-induced tonic and phasic EMG response patterns and psychological predictors in elite performers of endurance and explosive sports. *International Journal of Psychophysiology, 9*, 21–30.

Cacioppo, J. T., Bush, L. K., & Tassinary, L. G. (1990). Microexpressive facial actions as a function of affective stimuli: Replication and extension. *Personality & Social Psychology Bulletin, 18*, 515–526.

Cacioppo, J. T., Martzke, J. S., Petty, R. E., & Tassinary, L. G. (1988). Specific forms of facial EMG response index emotions during an interview: From Darwin to the continuous flow hypothesis of affect-laden information processing. *Journal of Personality & Social Psychology, 54*, 592–604.

Cacioppo, J. T., & Petty, R. E. (1981). Electromyographic specificity during covert information processing. *Psychophysiology, 18*, 518–523.

Cacioppo, J. T., Tassinary, L. G., & Fridlund, A. J. (1990). The skeletomotor system. In J. T. Cacioppo & L. G. Tassinary (Eds.), *Principles of psychophysiology* (pp. 325–384). New York: Cambridge University Press.

Clites, M. S. (1936). Certain somatic activities in relation to successful and unsuccessful problem solving: III. *Journal of Experimental Psychology, 19*, 172–192.

Cohen, M. J. (1973). The relation between heart rate and electromyographic activity in a discriminated escape–avoidance paradigm. *Psychophysiology, 10*, 8–20.

Darwin, C. (1872). *The expression of the emotions in man and animals.* Chicago: University of Chicago Press (1965, reprinted from the authorized edition of D. Appleton & Co. New York & London).

Davis, C. M., Brickett, P., Stern, R. M., & Kimball, W. Y. H. (1978). Tension in the frontales: Electrode placement and artifact in the recording of forehead EMG. *Psychophysiology, 15*, 591–593.

Davis, J. F. (1959). *Manual of surface electromyography* (WADC Tech. Rep. No. 59-184). Dayton, Ohio: Wright Air Development Center.

Davis, R. C. (1938). The relation of muscle action potentials to difficulty and frustration. *Journal of Experimental Psychology, 23*, 141–158.

Davis, R. C. (1940). *Set and muscular tension.* Indiana University Publications, Science Series, No. 10. Bloomington: University of Indiana Press.

Diggory, J. C., Klein, S. J., & Cohen, M. (1964). Muscle-action potentials and estimated probability of success. *Journal of Experimental Psychology, 68*, 449–455.

Dimberg, U. (1982). Facial reactions to facial expressions. *Psychophysiology, 19*, 643–647.

Dimberg, U. (1990). Facial electromyography and emotional reactions. *Psychophysiology, 27*, 481–494.

Dimberg, U. (1996). Psychophysiological reactions to facial expressions. In U. Segerstrale & P. Molnar (Eds.), *Nonverbal communication: Where nature meets culture* (pp. 32–51). Mahwah, NJ: Lawrence Erlbaum Associates.

Dimberg, U. (1997). Facial reactions: Rapidly evoked emotional responses. *Journal of Psychophysiology, 11*, 1–9.

Dimberg, U., & Lundquist, L. (1990). Gender differences in facial reactions to facial expressions. *Biological Psychology, 30*, 151–159.

Dimberg, U., & Thell, S. (1988). Facial electromyography, fear relevance and the experience of stimuli. *Journal of Psychophysiology, 2*, 213–219.

Duffy, E. (1962). *Activation and behavior.* New York: Wiley.

Duffy, E. (1972). Activation. In N. S. Greenfield & R. A. Sternbach (Eds.), *Handbook of psychophysiology* (pp. 577–622). New York: Holt, Rinehart & Winston.

Eason, R. G. (1963). Relation between effort, tension level, skill and performance efficiency in a perceptual–motor task. *Perceptual and Motor Skills, 16*, 297–317.

Eason, R. G., & White, C. T. (1960). Relationship between muscular tension and performance during rotary pursuit. *Perceptual and Motor Skills, 10*, 199–210.

Eason, R. G., & White, C. T. (1961). Muscular tension, effort and tracking difficulty: Studies of parameters which affect tension level and performance efficiency. *Perceptual and Motor Skills, 12*, 331–372.

Eastman, M. C., & Kamon, E. (1976). Posture and subjective evaluation of flat and slanted desks. *Human Factors, 18*, 15–26.

Ekman, P. (1973). Cross-cultural studies of facial expression. In P. Ekman (Ed.), *Darwin and facial expression: A century of research in review* (pp. 63–93). New York: Academic Press.

French, S. N. (1980). Electromyographic biofeedback for tension control during fine motor skill acquisition. *Biofeedback and Self-Regulation, 5*, 221–228.

Fridlund, A. J. (1991). Evolution and facial action in reflex, social motive, and paralanguage. *Biological Psychology, 32*, 3–100.

Fridlund, A. J., & Cacioppo, J. T. (1986). Guidelines for human electromyographic research. *Psychophysiology, 23*, 567–589.

Fridlund, A. J., Cottam, G. L., & Fowler, S. C. (1982). In search of the general tension factor: Tensional patterning during auditory stimulation. *Psychophysiology, 19*, 136–145.

Fridlund, A. J., Fowler, S. C., & Pritchard, D. A. (1980). Striate muscle tensional patterning in frontalis EMG biofeedback. *Psychophysiology, 17*, 47–55.

Fridlund, A. J., Schwartz, G. E., & Fowler, S. C. (1984). Pattern recognition of self-reported emotional state from multiple-site facial EMG activity during affective imagery. *Psychophysiology, 21*, 622–637.

Gardner, E. (1975). *Fundamentals of neurology*. Philadelphia: Saunders.

Goldstein, I. B. (1972). Electromyography: A measure of skeletal muscle response. In N. S. Greenfield & R. A. Sternbach (Eds.), *Handbook of psychophysiology* (pp. 329–365). New York: Holt, Rinehart & Winston.

Guilleminault, C., Hill, M. W., Simmons, F. B., & Dement, W. C. (1978). Obstructive sleep apnea: Electromyographic and fiberoptic studies. *Experimental Neurology, 62*, 48–67.

Guyton, A. C. (1977). *Basic human physiology*. Philadelphia: Saunders.

Haagh, S. S., & Brunia, C. H. (1984). Cardiac–somatic coupling during the foreperiod in a simple reaction-time task. *Psychological Research, 46*, 3–13.

Hardyck, D. C., & Petrinovich, L. F. (1969). Treatment of subvocal speech during reading. *Journal of Reading, 12*, 1–11.

Hardyck, D. C., Petrinovich, L. F., & Ellsworth, D. W. (1966). Feedback of speech muscle activity during silent reading: Rapid extinction. *Science, 154*, 1467.

Haynes, J., Mosely, D., & McGowan, W. T. (1975). Relaxation training and biofeedback in the reduction of frontalis muscle tension. *Psychophysiology, 12*, 547–552.

Holloway, F. A., & Parsons, O. A. (1972). Physiological concomitants of reaction time performance in normal and brain-damaged subjects. *Psychophysiology, 9*, 189–198.

Jacob, S. W., & Francone, C. A. (1970). *Structure and function in man*. Philadelphia: Saunders.

Jancke, L. (1996). Facial EMG in an anger-provoking situation: Individual differences in directing anger outwards or inwards. *International Journal of Psychophysiology, 23*, 207–214.

Kennedy, J. L., & Travis, R. C. (1947). Prediction of speed of performance by muscle action potentials. *Science, 105*, 410–411.

Kennedy, J. L., & Travis, R. C. (1948). Prediction and control of alertness: II. Continuous tracking. *Journal of Comparative & Physiological Psychology, 41*, 203–210.

Lansing, R. W., Schwartz, E., & Lindsley, D. B. (1959). Reaction time and EEG activation under alerted and nonrelated conditions. *Journal of Experimental Psychology, 58*, 1–7.

LeBoeuf, A. (1980). An experiment to test generalization of feedback from frontalis EMG. *Perceptual & Motor Skills, 50*, 27–31.

Levine, W. R., & Irvine J. K. (1984). In vivo EMG feedback in violin and violin pedagogy. *Biofeedback & Self Regulation, 9*, 161–168.

Lippold, O. C. J. (1967). Electromyography. In P. H. Venables & I. Martin (Eds.), *Manual of psycho-physiological methods* (pp. 245–297). Amsterdam: North-Holland.

Lundquist, L., & Dimberg, U. (1995). Facial expressions are contagious. *Journal of Psychophysiology, 9*, 203–211.

Malmo, R. B. (1975). *On emotions, needs, and our archaic brain*. New York: Holt, Rinehart & Winston.

McCormick, E. J. (1976). *Human factors in engineering and design*. New York: McGraw-Hill.

McElroy, W. D. (1988). Imaginative biochemistry (book review). *Science, 239*, 82.

McGuigan, F. J. (1973). Electrical measurement of covert processes as an explication of "higher mental events." In F. J. McGuigan & R. A. Schoonover (Eds.), *The psychophysiology of thinking* (pp. 343–385). New York: Academic Press.

McGuigan, F. J. (1981). Review of Andreassi's "Psychophysiology: Human behavior and physiological response." *American Journal of Psychology, 94*, 359–362.

McGuigan, F. J., & Bailey, S. C. (1969). Covert response patterns during the processing of language stimuli. *Interamerican Journal of Psychology, 3*, 289–299.

McGuigan, F. J., Keller, B., & Stanton, E. (1964). Covert language responses during silent reading. *Journal of Educational Psychology, 55*, 339–343.

McGuigan, F. J., & Rodier, W. I., III. (1968). Effects of auditory stimulation on covert oral behavior during silent reading. *Journal of Experimental Psychology, 76*, 649–655.

McNulty, W. H., Gevirtz, R. N., Hubbard, D. R., & Berkoff, G. M. (1994). Needle electromyographic evaluation of trigger point response to a psychological stressor. *Psychophysiology, 31*, 313–316.

Mulder, T., & Hulston, W. (1984). The effects of fatigue and task repetition on the surface electromyographic signal. *Psychophysiology, 21*, 528–534.

Obrist, P. A. (1968). Heart rate and somatic–motor coupling during classical aversive conditioning in humans. *Journal of Experimental Psychology, 77*, 180–183.

Obrist, P. A., Webb, R. A., & Sutterer, J. R. (1969). Heart rate and somatic changes during aversive conditioning and a simple reaction time task. *Psychophysiology, 5*, 696–723.

Obrist, P. A., Webb, R. A., Sutterer, J. R., & Howard, J. L. (1970). Cardiac deceleration and reaction time. An evaluation of two hypotheses. *Psychophysiology, 6*, 695–706.

Ortengren, R., Anderson, G., Browman, M., Magnusson, R., & Peterson, I. (1975). Vocational electromyography: Studies of localized muscle fatigue at the assembly line. *Ergonomics, 18*, 157–174.

Pishkin, V. (1973). Electromyography in cognitive performance by schizophrenics and normals. *Perceptual & Motor Skills, 37*, 382.

Pishkin, V., & Shurley, J. T. (1968). Electrodermal and electromyographic parameters in concept identification. *Psychophysiology, 5*, 112–118.

Schwartz, G. E., Ahern, L., & Brown, S. L. (1979). Lateralized facial muscle response to positive and negative emotional stimuli. *Psychophysiology, 16*, 561–571.

Schwartz, G. E., Brown, S. L., & Ahern, G. L. (1980). Facial muscle patterning and subjective experience during affective imagery: Sex differences. *Psychophysiology, 17*, 75–82.

Schwartz, G. E., Fair, P. L., Salt, P., Mandel, M. R., & Klerman, G. L. (1976). Facial muscle patterning to affective imagery in depressed and nondepressed subjects. *Science, 192*, 489–491.

Sirota, A. D., & Schwartz, G. E. (1982). Facial muscle patterning and lateralization during elation and depressed imagery. *Journal of Abnormal Psychology, 91*, 25–34.

Sullivan, M. J., & Brender, W. (1986). Facial electromyography: A measure of affective processes during sexual arousal. *Psychophysiology, 23*, 182–188.

Surwillo, W. W. (1956). Psychological factors in muscle-action potentials: EMG gradients. *Journal of Experimental Psychology, 52*, 263–272.

Svebak, S., Dalen, K., & Storfjell, O. (1981). The psychological significance of task-induced tonic changes in somatic and autonomic activity. *Psychophysiology, 18*, 403–409.

Svebak, S., & Kerr, J. (1989). The role of impulsivity in preference for sports. *Personality & Individual Differences, 10*, 51–58.

Svebak, S., & Murgatroyd, S. (1985). Metamotivational dominance: A multimethod validation of reversal theory constructs. *Journal of Personality & Social Psychology, 48*, 107–116.

Tassinary, L. G., Cacioppo, J. T., & Geen, T. R. (1989). A psychometric study of surface electrode placements for facial electromyographic recording: I. The brow and cheek muscle regions. *Psychophysiology, 26*, 1–16.

Tassinary, L. G., Cacioppo, J. T., Geen, T. R., & Vanman, E. (1987). Optimizing surface electrode placements for facial EMG recordings: Guidelines for recording from the perioral muscle region. *Psychophysiology, 24*, 615–616.

Thompson, J. K., Haber, J. D., & Tearnan, B. H. (1981). Generalization of frontalis electromyographic feedback to adjacent muscle groups: A critical review. *Psychosomatic Medicine, 43*, 19–24.

Thompson, R. F., Lindsley, D. B., & Eason, R. G. (1966). *Physiological psychology*. New York: McGraw-Hill.

Travis, R. C., & Kennedy, J. L. (1949). Prediction and control of alertness. III. Calibration of the alertness indicator and further results. *Journal of Comparative & Physiological Psychology, 40*, 457–461.

Van Liere, D. W. (1953). Characteristics of the muscle tension response to paired tones. *Journal of Experimental Psychology, 46*, 319–324.

Vrana, S. R. (1993). The psychophysiology of disgust: Differentiating negative emotional contexts with facial EMG. *Psychophysiology, 30*, 279–286.

Wilcott, R. C., & Beenken, M. G. (1957). Relation of integrated surface electromyography and muscle tension. *Perceptual & Motor Skills, 7*, 295–298.

Wilkinson, R. T. (1962). Muscle tension during mental work under sleep deprivation. *Journal of Experimental Psychology, 64*, 565–571.

Williamson, D. A., Epstein, L. H., & Lombardo, T. W. (1980). EMG measurement as a function of electrode placement and level of EMG. *Psychophysiology, 17*, 279–282.

Woodworth, R. S. (1938). *Experimental psychology*. New York: Holt.

Woodworth, R. S., & Schlosberg, H. (1954). *Experimental psychology*. New York: Holt.

9

Electrodermal Activity (EDA) and Behavior

The idea of studying electrical activity of the skin probably does not cause much excitement in the average person. However, as an important measure in psychophysiology, it has had a long and interesting history; and it has been a very lively topic of research. Sample issues involving electrodermal activity (EDA) are whether it can distinguish between positive and negative emotions and whether persons who show large numbers of spontaneous changes in activity are more efficient at processing information. In addition, psychophysiologists have asked questions regarding relationships between EDA and response speed, and whether it varies with learning efficiency. Researchers have investigated whether EDA can tell us anything about motivational level, and have explored it extensively in studies of the orienting response. The extent to which EDA can be classically or instrumentally conditioned has also been an important issue. Another, albeit controversial, issue regards the use of skin activity changes to indicate whether a person is lying. The topic of lie detection is discussed more fully in chapter 15 on applications of physiological measures to practical problems.

The observation that changes in electrical activity of the skin can be produced by various physical and emotional stimuli was reported by Charles Fere, a French neurologist, in 1888. Almost simultaneously, a Russian physiologist (Tarchanoff in 1890) observed similar changes in skin activity (see Woodworth & Schlosberg, 1954). The techniques of the two scientists differed. Fere's procedure involved the passing of a small current between two electrodes on the skin surface, and changes in electrodermal activity (EDA) were observed when a person was presented with various stimuli (Neumann & Blanton, 1970; Woodworth & Schlosberg, 1954). A galvanometer was used to measure the increases in skin conductance that occurred when visual, auditory, or emotion-provoking stimuli were introduced. This phenomenon was soon labeled the *psychogalvanic reflex* (PGR) and later, the *galvanic skin response* (GSR) by early investigators. Fere felt that his results with sensory and emotional stimuli showed that the responses were indicators of nervous system excitation, or arousal, to put it in more modern terms. Measures of EDA were used in the early 1900s by Carl Jung, the noted Swiss psychiatrist, to study emotional reactions of his patients to word associations.

Tarchanoff's procedure obtained similar galvanometer deflections without the use of externally applied current; that is, there were natural differences in electrical potential between two skin areas, and this potential changed when the subject was stimulated. Fere and Tarchanoff contributed what were to become two basic methods for the measurement of EDA: the recording of skin conductance (SC) and skin potential (SP). Boucsein (1992) relates that although the discovery of EDA phenomena is attributed to Fere and Tarchanoff, the history of this physiological measure dates back to 1849. The German scientist, DuBois-Reymond, noted in 1849 that electric current flowed between the two hands when they were immersed in a zinc sulphate solution. Although he observed electrodermal activity, DuBois-

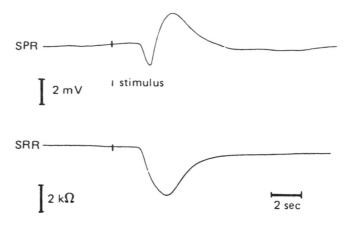

FIG. 9.1. Characteristic skin resistance and skin potential responses.

Reymond thought the current flow was due to muscle potentials. Boucsein (1992) also observed that the first person to associate psychological factors to EDA was Vigouroux in 1879. Vigouroux was an "electrotherapist" who noted that fluctuations in EDA occurred with changes in anesthesia in hysterical patients. However, he ascribed the effects to alterations in blood flow and not to local changes in the skin itself.

Figure 9.1 shows a typical change in SC and SP levels with stimulation. It must be noted that similar fluctuations can occur without any obvious physical or mental stimulation and are referred to as spontaneous EDA. The physiological bases for these responses are still not fully understood, but changes in sweat gland activity have been strongly implicated in a variety of research studies (Edelberg, 1972a). Because sweat glands are located in the skin, it is necessary to consider the anatomy and physiology of the skin in order to more fully understand the nature of the phenomena being examined in this chapter.

ANATOMY AND PHYSIOLOGY OF THE SKIN

The skin consists of two layers: an epidermis, or outer layer, which is about 1 mm or less in thickness, and a dermis, or inner layer, which ranges from about 0.5 mm over the eyelids to 6 mm over the upper back, palms of the hands, and soles of the feet. The epidermis consists of five separate cellular layers: stratum corneum (outermost layer, also known as the keratinous or "horny" layer), stratum lucidum, stratum granulosum, stratum spinosum, and stratum minativum (see Fig. 9.2). The dermis contains blood vessels, nerves, lymph vessels, hair follicles, smooth muscle, sweat glands, and sebaceous glands. Just below the dermis is the hypodermis (subcutaneous connective tissue), which contains blood and lymph vessels, the roots of hair follicles, sensory nerves, and secretory portions of the sweat glands (Woodburne, 1978).

Types and Distribution of Sweat Glands.   There are two types of sweat glands, the apocrine and the eccrine. The apocrine glands are relatively large, open into hair follicles, and begin to function after puberty (Boucsein, 1992). They are found in the genital areas and the armpits, and have not been of much interest to the psychophysiologist. The eccrine sweat glands are the ones with which we are most concerned. They have a wide distribution over the body surface and are found everywhere in the skin except on the lips, the concha (outer ear), the glans penis, the inner surface of the prepuce, the labia minora, and the clitoris. They

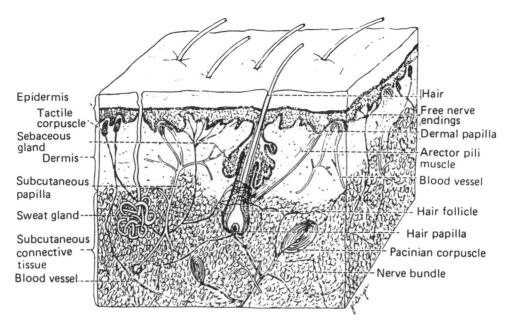

FIG. 9.2. The structure of the skin.

are most numerous in the palms of the hands and the soles of the feet; of intermediate density on the head; and least dense on the arms, legs, and trunk.

One estimate is that a square inch on the palm contains 3,000 sweat glands (Jacob & Francone, 1970). The total number of sweat glands on the body, based on studies of cadavers, ranges from 2 to 5 million (Fowles, 1986). The eccrine glands are simple, tubular structures with a rounded secretory portion and a duct that leads to the surface of the skin. The secretory portion is formed by several unequal coils rolled into a ball of about 0.3 to 0.4 mm in diameter. The secretory duct from the eccrine gland opens as a small pore at the surface of the epidermis. An example of surface epidermal sweat pores is shown in Fig. 9.3. This is a photograph of a fingertip, which was prepared in order to count the number of active sweat glands present, as indicated by chemical reactions at the pores (the dark spots).

Nervous System Control of EDA.   The secretory portion of the eccrine sweat gland has a profuse nerve supply via cholinergic fibers of the SNS. That is, although innervated by SNS fibers, the transmitting agent is acetylcholine, a chemical usually associated with PNS functions. There is evidence for a high correlation between bursts of sympathetic nerve activity and EDA (Dawson, Schell, & Filion, 1990). The controlling SNS fibers emerge from the ventral root of the spinal cord and innervate the secretory portion of the sweat gland and the muscles controlling piloerection ("goose bumps").

Discussions by Edelberg (1972a) and Venables and Christie (1973) indicate that EDA is a complex reaction with a number of control centers in the CNS. The CNS mechanisms include the premotor cortex, sensorimotor cortex, limbic and hypothalamic areas (both concerned with motivational and emotional behavior), and the reticular formation. Edelberg (1972a, 1973) proposed that the temperature regulation function of EDA is controlled by the hypothalamus, that the premotor (frontal) cortex (pyramidal system) controls changes in conductance associated with fine motor adjustments, and EDA related to gross motor adjustments (extrapyramidal) is mediated by the reticular formation. Boucsein (1992) stated that the hy-

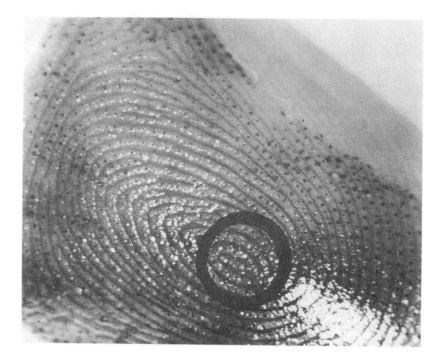

FIG. 9.3. A photograph of a fingertip prepared for a sweat gland count. The circle indicates the usual area of the ridge pattern used for counting. Active sweat glands produce black dots because of the starch-iodine reaction at the tips of the ducts.

pothalamic areas involved in thermoregulation also play a major role in the production of EDA to psychological stimulation. He further concluded that EDA results from an interaction of SNS activity and local processes in the skin. The EDA of patients with damage to various cortical areas was studied by Tranel and Damasio (1994). Damage was confirmed by neuroimaging (computed tomography and MRI). Skin conductance responses (SCRs) were elicited by both physical (noise) and psychological (photographs of nudes and mutilation) stimuli. Tranel and Damasio reported that damage to several brain locations was consistently associated with deficient SCRs: the ventromedial frontal region (right and left), the right inferior parietal area, and anterior cingulate gyrus (right and left). In a different approach, five young adults with epilepsy underwent electrical stimulation of different brain areas while SCR was measured from each hand (Mangina & Beuzeron-Mangina, 1996).

The results indicated that when right-sided limbic structures were stimulated (amygdala, anterior hippocampus, posterior hippocampus, cingulate gyrus), there was a larger SCR from the right hand than the left. This result was reversed when the same left-sided structures were stimulated. However, when cortical sites (left and right frontal and left and right midtemporal) were stimulated, SCRs were not as large and the left- and right-hand differences were not observed. The stimulation study of Mangina and Beuzeron-Mangina (1996) and lesion study of Tranel and Damasio (1994) both point to the importance of the anterior cingulate cortex in EDA. These findings were supported by Fredrikson, Furmark, Tillfors-Olsson, Fischer, Andersson, and Langstrom (1998) who confirmed the role of the cingulate cortex in EDA through the use of neural imaging (positron emission tomography). Thus, a number of brain areas contribute to EDA including cortex, reticular formation, hypothalamus (through its influence on the SNS), hippocampus, and amygdala. It appears, then, that the control of EDA entails a rather complex mechanism involving diverse areas of the nervous system. Boucsein (1992) suggested that EDA is controlled by three systems related to arousal, emotion, and locomotion. The limbic structures (hypothalamus, cingulate gyrus, hippocampus) are involved in EDA activity related to emotional responses and thermoregulation. The motor cortex and parts of the basal ganglia are involved in locomotion. And, finally, the reticular formation controls EDA related to states of arousal. Information regarding the contribution of these areas to EDA is accumulating at a faster rate with the increased use of neuroimaging techniques.

Functions of the Skin and Sweating.   Although an important function of the skin is to protect the organism it covers, for example, by keeping bacteria, parasites, and noxious chemicals out and keeping vital fluids in, it also has a role in thermoregulatory activities. The thermoregulatory contribution is produced by dilation of blood vessels in the skin and increased sweating, both of which result in decreased skin and body temperature. Blood vessel dilation increases blood flow in surface areas to enhance cooling. The increased sweat on the skin surface produces cooling through evaporation. Constriction of blood vessels in the skin (which reduces blood flow to the surface) and piloerection ("goose bumps" caused by chilling) help to maintain body warmth. Piloerection produces its effect by increasing the area of the insulating air that surrounds the skin, thus preserving heat.

An interesting aspect of sweating is that it is not merely thermoregulatory (cooling). This fact forms the basis for the behavioral studies in this chapter. Sweating, or sweat gland activity, is reflected as changes in skin potential (SP) and skin conductance (SC) in a variety of situations, including those that are emotionally arousing. For example, eccrine glands of the palms and fingers of the hand respond only weakly at certain levels of heat and strongly to psychological and sensory stimuli. You may have noticed wet or "clammy" palms in situations that were fear- or anxiety-provoking, but that were otherwise not very warm. The sweating to psychological stimuli has sometimes been termed *arousal* sweating, and some workers believe it has adaptive value (Darrow, 1933; Wilcott, 1967). Darrow suggested that the sweating of palms and soles may be an adaptive response that persisted over the course of evolution, because it aids in grasping objects. For example, the grasping of a weapon in a fight, or branches of trees during flight.

Wilcott (1967) hypothesized that arousal sweating in any part of the body toughens the skin and protects it from mechanical injury. He noted an observation by Edelberg and Wright (1962), who found that palmar skin was difficult to cut during profuse sweating. When sweating is blocked, the skin is more susceptible to mechanical injury. Hence, these interpretations of arousal sweating suggest that it has survival value for the organism, as do other SNS responses in emergency situations. In contrast to eccrine glands of the fingers and palms, those on the forehead, neck, back of the hands, and other areas respond quickly and strongly to thermal stimuli but only weakly to psychological or sensory stimuli. A suggestion by Edelberg (1972a, 1973) is that sweat gland activity helps to lower body temperature in emergency situations that require a great deal of physical effort (e.g., running or fighting). Thus, if we combine the proposals of Darrow-Wilcott and Edelberg, increased sweat gland activity can be seen as adaptive because it contributes to bodily efficiency in times of emergency.

TYPES OF ELECTRODERMAL ACTIVITY

As already noted, changes in EDA will occur with a variety of sensory and psychological stimuli. The momentary fluctuations of EDA that occur with stimulation have been termed *phasic responses*, whereas the relatively stable EDA is referred to as the *tonic level*. A classificatory scheme for the various terms relating to EDA was suggested by Venables and Martin (1967). They proposed the following designations and abbreviations:

SRR = skin resistance response
SRL = skin resistance level
SCR = skin conductance response
SCL = skin conductance level
SPR = skin potential response
SPL = skin potential level

The first four of these are related to the Fere effect because they rely on an external source of current for their observation (exosomatic), whereas the last two (Tarchanoff effect) do not require the application of current and are called *endosomatic*. Skin conductance and skin potential are considered separately, because, despite their apparent common origin, they are different phenomena. A useful distinction has been made between spontaneously occurring SCRs and those related to specific stimuli (e.g., see Dawson et al., 1990). Because spontaneous SCRs occur without apparent stimulation these are referred to as NS–SCRs (nonspecific SCRs). The SCRs that are related to known events are called ER–SCRs (event-related SCRs).

Skin Conductance

The term *skin resistance response* (SRR) refers to momentary fluctuations in SR, as did the older GSR terminology. Skin resistance level (SRL) indicates the baseline SR at any given time. Skin conductance response (SCR) and skin conductance level (SCL) are conductance unit measures of SRR and SRL, respectively. Units of conductance are preferred by many investigators instead of resistance values. One reason for this is that conductance values are more suitable for averaging and other statistical manipulations; that is, because conductance is the reciprocal of resistance, it is more likely to conform to the normal distribution of measures required for many statistical analyses. Another reason is that conductance increases with higher levels of arousal or activity of the organism and decreases at low levels, a relationship that is more logical for most persons.

The traditional unit of conductance is the mho (ohm spelled backward) to distinguish it from the ohm, which is the unit of resistance. To give an example of reciprocal transformation, a micromho (μmho) of conductance is equal to 1,000,000 ohms SRL, and 10 μmhos equals 100,000 ohms. In the last several years some EDA researchers have referred to conductance units as microsiemen, or μS, a unit that is identical to the μmho. The micromho unit will be used in this text, but the reader must keep in mind that it is interchangeable with microsiemen.

Log conductance measures go a step beyond the reciprocal of resistance and take the log of micromho values in performing averages and other statistical treatments. The log conductance measures conform to assumptions required for parametric statistical analyses of SC measures, such as analyses of variance or *t* tests. Venables and Christie (1973) proposed (because the case for the use of conductance units is strong) that the terms SCR and SCL be used to refer to exosomatic measures of EDA, and this is the usage in the remainder of this chapter.

The amplitude of the SCR depends on electrode size and this phasic change can vary approximately from 0.05 μmho to 5 μmho. Appearance of the SCR ranges from approximately 1.0 to 3.0 sec after stimulus presentation.

Skin Potential

The skin potential response (SPR) refers to changes in SP, whereas skin potential level (SPL) is the level of SP at any point in time. The recordings depicted in Fig. 9.1 show the SPR to be a biphasic (negative then positive) response measured in millivolts. However, SPR can also have a uniphasic negative wave or a uniphasic positive wave. The amplitude of the negative wave of the SPR may typically be about 2 mV, and the positive portion about 4 mV. Measures of SPR amplitudes may be difficult, because SPL is not always easy to establish. The latency of the negative SPR component is similar to that of the SCR (Venables & Christie, 1973).

ORIGIN OF EDA

In research relating performance and psychological factors to EDA, measures of SC or SP can be interpreted as mainly reflecting changes in sweating activity. For a subject during a single recording period, the amplitude of palmar SCRs and SPRs and the amplitude of sweating responses are usually found to be highly correlated (Wilcott, 1967). A model of the sweat gland and EDA was proposed by Edelberg (1972a), which relates the standing level of sweat in the ducts to tonic SCL and SCRs to increases in the level of sweat. This model is highly regarded.

THE MEASUREMENT OF EDA

Skin Conductance Level (SCL)

Fortunately, there are good commercial instruments available today that contain the appropriate amplification, filtering, and ink-writing characteristics to enable accurate recording of SCL. This includes the availability of appropriate input couplers that convert activity recorded at the skin surface into conductance units (μmhos). The circuits used to measure SCL are of two basic types: those that employ a constant voltage and those using a constant current. The constant-voltage system holds the voltage across the electrodes constant, and the current through the skin varies with conductance changes—this is what is measured on the ink-writer. If, however, the current through the skin is held constant, then the voltage, or potential difference between the two electrodes placed on the skin surface, varies with resistance. This latter system is the *constant-current technique*. Edelberg (1972a) recommended a current density of 8 μA/cm^2 (measured at either site) with the constant-current method. For the *constant-voltage technique*, he suggested a source of 0.75 to 1.0 V across the sites. Lykken and Venables (1971) endorsed the use of a constant-voltage circuit limited to 0.50 V. Most commercially available instruments for the measurement of SC use the constant-current technique, and it has proven satisfactory for many researchers. For the student or researcher interested in more detail regarding the electronic circuitry involved in SC measurements, there are several excellent sources (see, e.g., Boucsein, 1992; Edelberg, 1967, 1972a; Venables & Christie, 1973, 1980).

Skin Potential

Whereas the bipolar placement of electrodes is preferred for SCL measures, a unipolar arrangement is essential to record SPL. The active electrode may be placed on the palm of the hand and referred to a relatively inactive site on the forearm. Edelberg (1972a) mentioned the inner portion of the earlobe as an inactive area. Alternatively, an experimenter may produce an inactive area by using a dental burr to remove a portion of the epidermis or by pricking the skin under the electrode with a needle (e.g., Shackel, 1959; Wilcott, 1959). Stimulation in the form of mental multiplication, or having the individual participate in making word associations, will produce changes in SP. The SP may be measured with a sensitive DC amplifier.

Figure 9.4 illustrates the placement of electrodes to measure both SP and SC. It shows a bipolar placement on the medial phalanges of two fingers for the SCL recording. Venables and Christie (1973) recommended that the electrodes be placed on two adjacent fingers: either the second or the third or the fourth and fifth fingers. This placement allows recording from two finger areas innervated by the same spinal nerve. For the SPL measure, the active electrode is placed on the palm of the hand, and the reference electrode is located on the forearm. The inactive electrode should be placed on an abraded site (accomplished by skin pricking, rubbing with sandpaper, or skin drilling). The fingers or soles of the feet may also be used as the site of the active electrode in SP recording. The researcher must be careful to avoid skin areas that have cuts or other kinds of blemishes, because this may interfere with the response obtained. Difficulty in preparing the reference site, the possibility of skin injury, and disease transmission are factors that should be considered in the use of SP measures.

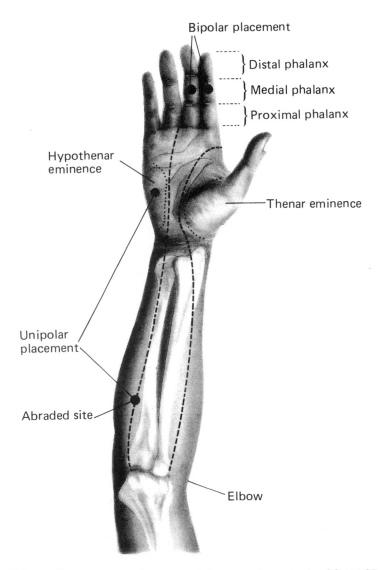

FIG. 9.4. Recommended placements of electrodes for measuring SC and SP.

Electrodes for Recording EDA

Nonpolarizing electrodes should be used for both SC and SP measurements, and these are commercially available. An appropriate technique is to use a metal coated with the salt of that metal. For example, Ag/AgCl (silver/silver chloride) or Zn/ZnSO$_4$ (zinc/zinc sulphate) electrodes. Venables and Martin (1967) recommended the use of Ag/AgCl electrodes with solutions of either KCL or NaCl as the electrolyte. Wilcott (personal communication, 1979) recommended the use of zinc electrodes, because they are easier to use than silver and are entirely adequate if kept clean and polished. Commercial electrode jellies and pastes are available.

Electrode size is significant in the recording of SCL, because resistance of the electrodes varies inversely with area. Therefore, the larger the area, the smaller the resistance. The electrolyte used should not be allowed to spread beyond the electrode site, because it increases the effective area of the electrode. A typical electrode for use in palmar or plantar (sole of foot) placements may be 1.5 to 2.0 cm in diameter. Electrodes may be held in place by strips of surgical tape, plastic adhesive, velcro strips, or elastic bands. Commercial electrodes are of appropriate size and are conveniently attached with double-sided adhesive collars.

A ground lead may not be necessary in SC or SP measurement if there is no interference present, for example, 60 Hz from room outlets. If artifact does occur, a ground electrode should be placed on an inactive site, on the same side of the body as active electrodes.

ANALYSIS OF EDA DATA

If one records directly in conductance units, several kinds of measures are possible: (a) the level of conductance (SCL) during a given period of time, (b) the number of conductance changes (SCR) during the same period, (c) the magnitude of the SCR, (d) latency of SCR (time between a stimulus and onset of SCR), (e) SCR recovery half-time (time between peak of SCR and 50% of recovery to prestimulus baseline), and SCR rise time (time between onset of SCR and peak of SCR). If SCL is at 10 μmhos, a response may be defined as any change of 0.05 μmho or greater that occurs within a specified time, say, 1.0 to 3.0 sec. The magnitude of the SCR can be treated as a percentage of SCL and thus be related to prestimulus baseline level.

When baseline changes occur, the pen of an ink-writer recorder will have to be reset and the new SCL level recorded. If many SCRs occur, this constant resetting could be cumbersome. One way to solve this problem is to use automatic resetting or, alternatively, to feed the EDA data into two channels of the polygraph: one channel for baseline SCL and another for SCR. With this latter procedure, the gain for SCL is adjusted so that it is relatively insensitive to the SCRs regarded as significantly large. Some commercial devices provide automatic recentering when SCRs occur or when SCL extends beyond certain predetermined ranges. Contemporary devices that present SCL continuously in digital form are available. Although this is sufficient if information on SCL is desired, it may be inadequate for SCR measures.

In the treatment of SP data, counts of the number of SPRs occurring in a given time period may be made. In addition, level of SP in millivolts (mV) can be recorded directly on the ink-writer paper. The SPR measure is complicated by the fact that it has negative and positive components. Investigators commonly measure the degree of negativity or positivity of the waves (in mV) and the latencies of their occurrence. Edelberg (1972a) suggested that the magnitude of the positive response should be measured from the peak of the negative component to the peak of the positive wave (in mV) without regard to whether or not the baseline is crossed. Paper speeds of 15 mm/sec are suitable for observing baseline changes in SCL or SPL and the more rapid SCRs and SPRs.

ELECTRODERMAL PHENOMENA AND BEHAVIOR

This section reviews briefly a number of areas in which EDA has been related to behavior. EDA is sensitive to a wide variety of stimuli, but psychophysiologists have been able to specifically relate it to such properties as stimulus novelty, intensity, emotional content, and significance (Dawson et al., 1990). Because EDA is sensitive to such a wide variety of stimuli, the scientist must carefully consider the situation in which the response occurred. For example, by controlling stimulus intensity, emotional content, and significance, the psychologist may infer that the EDA occurred with stimulus novelty. Therefore, the careful control of the stimulus situation and measurement of the response is critical for interpreting EDA (Dawson et al., 1990). This is true of other physiological measures as well, but especially for EDA because it is so sensitive to many stimuli.

In the remainder of this chapter we examine EDA with respect to a variety of behavioral situations. Studies relating EDA to psychological disorders are covered in chapter 16 on clinical applications of psychophysiology. It will become obvious to the reader that SC is used much more frequently than SP by investigators seeking to relate EDA to behavior. Basically, this is because SC is easier to measure and offers fewer problems of interpretation than SP.

Reaction Time

Level of Arousal.   One of the early studies of the relation between SCL and speed of reaction was conducted by Freeman (1940). He studied the RT of a single subject under various states of alertness, with the subject's condition ranging from half asleep to extremely tense. The results of 100 experimental sessions were recorded over a number of days, and Freeman found an inverted-U-shaped relation between SCL and RT, in which RTs were slower at high and low SCL levels and fastest at moderate levels. Freeman's result has often been mentioned in support of the activation or arousal concept, which describes the relation between level of physiological activity and performance as an inverted-U (e.g., Woodworth & Schlosberg, 1954). Schlosberg (1954) reported that Freeman's results had been duplicated with another subject, but a later study, using a greater number of subjects (Schlosberg & Kling, 1959), failed to replicate these findings.

In a study by Andreassi (1966b), SCL was measured continuously as subjects reacted to a fixed number of random signals occurring over a 40-min experimental period. Andreassi found evidence for the conclusion that at the highest SCL, RT is significantly faster than at moderate or low SCLs. Decreases in SCL over the course of the experimental session correlated significantly with a slowing of RT. The plotted results did not approach an inverted-U function; in fact, the relationship approached linearity, and it was suggested that this was due to a limited range of SC in a situation where level of arousal was not purposely manipulated.

Surwillo and Quilter (1965) measured RTs and SPRs of 132 healthy males, age 22 to 85 years, in an hour-long vigilance situation. The subjects were required to monitor the movements of a clock pointer and to press a key as quickly as possible when it traveled through twice the usual distance. Those above the median in SPR production were termed *labiles* (mean of 2.27 SPRs), and those below were called *stabiles* (mean of .73 SPRs) in accordance with the terminology of Lacey and Lacey (1958). The RT for labiles (488 msec) was significantly shorter than that of stabiles (540 msec). This confirmed the hypothesis that autonomic labiles (those with a large number of spontaneous autonomic responses) would have faster RTs than stabiles.

Fixed and Variable Signal Schedules.   Andreassi, Rapisardi, and Whalen (1969) measured SCL, SCRs, and heart rate while subjects detected critical signals that occurred at either fixed or variable intervals. Individuals were required to make responses, which required some effort, in order to have the opportunity to detect the signals. The results showed that SCL and SCRs were significantly higher when signals came at fixed intervals (30 sec) than when they were variable (between 11 and 66 sec, with a mean interval of 30 sec). Further, RTs were significantly faster with a fixed schedule. Records of responses made to detect signals showed typical "scalloping" patterns with fixed intervals and high steady rates with the variable signal schedules, similar to those associated with Skinnerian schedules of reinforcement. The elevated EDA observed with fixed intervals was attributed to an increased readiness to respond when subjects could anticipate the occurrence of a signal. There was evidence for "directional fractionation" in the results (see chapter 18), because HR was lower under fixed signal schedules than for variable ones, whereas SCL was higher for the fixed signals compared to the irregular pattern.

High NS–SCRs (Labiles) and Low NS–SCRs (Stabiles).   The number of spontaneous SCRs that occurred during a 40-min vigilance task was measured by Baugher (1975). Participants were divided into low-arousal and high-arousal groups on the basis of the SCL value at the time of signal occurrence. (These groups could have been termed stabiles and labiles.) The RTs to critical signals were found to be significantly faster for the high-arousal as compared to the low-arousal group. The author concluded that the direct relationship between SCRs and RT was expected (i.e., instead of an inverted-U function) because of the limited range of arousal conditions used. Andreassi (1966b) reached a similar conclusion.

Current terminology denotes individuals with a high number of nonspecific SCRs (NS–SCRs) as labiles, and those with low NS–SCRs, stabiles. Vossel (1988) found a difference in the RTs of stabiles and labiles. Not only did the labiles have significantly faster RTs, but they also had fewer errors in responding. Vossel concluded that the time required for information processing is shorter in labiles. In another study, efficiency of vigilance and perceptual speed in children (9–16 years) classified as stabiles and labiles was studied by Sakai, Baker, and Dawson (1992). They found that labiles were better able to sustain attention, and also performed faster on the assigned tasks. The authors concluded that labiles are more efficient at attending to the environment, and that their higher level of arousal enhances their performance. A relatively high frequency of NS–SCRs has also been related to cardiovascular activity. For example, persons categorized as labiles had higher heart rates than stabiles in a dichotic listening task (O'Gorman & Lloyd, 1988). In addition, labiles have been found to have greater increases in heart activity to stress than stabiles (Kelsey, 1991).

Summary.   It appears that faster RTs are associated with higher SCL. In addition, the number of spontaneous SPRs and SCRs is also related to speed of reaction, that is, a greater number of these responses are associated with faster RTs. Whether there is an inverted-U-shaped relation between SCL and RT, performance has not been established. It is likely that level of arousal (as indicated by EDA) must be actively manipulated by the experimenter to show this relationship. The high degree of nonspecific EDA in labiles may indicate elevated SNS activity in these individuals. In turn, this increased level of autonomic arousal may contribute to the faster RT and generally better performance of labiles as compared to stabiles.

MENTAL ACTIVITY AND ELECTRODERMAL PHENOMENA

Changes in electrodermal responses have been observed to occur while persons were involved in a variety of mental activities, including adding numbers, learning, and producing word associations. This section examines electrodermal activity during verbal learning, conditions of positive and negative affect (feeling), motivation, and relaxation.

Learning and Memory

Arousal.   In an early study, Brown (1937) found that quickly learned words were accompanied by larger magnitude SCRs than those not learned as readily. Andreassi (1966a) required Navy enlisted men to learn three lists of nonsense syllables on three successive days while SCL and heart rate were recorded. The lists had 100%, 53%, and 0% association values, corresponding to easy, moderately difficult, and difficult learning materials, respectively. He found that SCL and HR were significantly higher during the learning of the easy list as compared to the other two. The findings were interpreted in terms of greater subject involvement and arousal in the learning task when their performance was more successful. This conclusion was given some support from the performance of the only subject whose physiological responses did not vary with list difficulty. This subject's performance was uniformly poor, regardless of list difficulty level, and, in addition, he was the only person to fall asleep during the 2-min rest periods between lists!

Lists of eight high-arousal words (e.g., vomit) and eight low-arousal words (e.g., swim) were presented to 40 male and 40 female students (Maltzman, Kantor, & Langdon, 1966). They were asked to listen to these words while EDA was recorded, and were told that the physiological correlates of relaxation were being measured. The investigators reported that the high-arousal words produced significantly larger SCRs than the low-arousal words. Further, retention tests administered after all the items had been presented revealed that the subjects could remember more of the high-arousal words. Maltzman and his associates hypothesized that the OR facilitated the processing of high-arousal words and their retention.

The results of a number of studies have implicated SCL as a useful measure of arousal in short-term memory (STM) tasks. It is believed that EDA may reflect the registration of stimuli in central (brain) areas, just as it seems to indicate stimulus reception as part of the OR to novel stimuli. Yuille and Hare (1980) monitored SC and HR during a STM task. Subjects were required to recall words after 15 sec of interference. When the best and poorest trials were compared, they found that optimal performance was associated with the largest increases in SC and HR. The researchers interpreted these results in terms of the roles of attention and effort (as indicated by physiological response) in short-term memory.

Habituation.   A number of physiological measures, including SCL, SCRs, and heart rate (HR), were obtained during verbal learning by Andreassi and Whalen (1967). In a first experiment, after lists of materials were learned to perfection, the same material was presented for 20 overlearning trials. The overlearning phase was accompanied by significant decreases in all of the physiological measures. However, when a new list was presented subsequent to overlearning, there were increases in SCL, SCRs, and HR. In a second experiment, the initial learning phase was followed by two overlearning sessions with the same list. This time, all three measures showed progressive decreases during the first and then the second overlearning phase. The results indicated that new learning, perhaps because of the novelty of the situation and the materials to be learned, produced the highest levels of physiological activity. Overlearning, because of stimulus and situational habituation, led to significant decreases in activity.

Summary.   Studies of EDA and verbal learning indicate that more successful learning, in general, tends to be associated with greater amounts of activity. The higher levels of EDA are associated with increased alertness and effort when individuals are involved in the acquisition of novel materials. This same process is implicated in respect to SCL in short-term memory tasks. Electrodermal activity has been identified as an important component of the orienting response to novel stimuli, an area covered later in this chapter.

Positive and Negative Affect and EDA

Music and Imagery.   Affect refers to subjective feelings roughly related to like or dislike of objects, people, or events—that is, feelings that produce an emotional reaction. Music is an example of a type of stimulus that can produce an affective response. The effects of three types of music on the SCR and HR of college students were investigated by Zimny and Weidenfeller (1963). These pieces had been previously judged to be exciting, neutral, and calming by 59 other students. Selected 6-min portions of Dvorak's *New World Symphony*, Chopin's *Les Sylphides*, and Bach's *Air for the G String* were judged as exciting, neutral, and calming, respectively.

Significant SCRs occurred in response to the exciting music but not to the calming or the neutral pieces. No HR changes were observed as a function of music played. The authors interpreted the SCR results as indicating that different kinds of music produce differential EDA, and that this reflects emotional responsivity.

Skin conductance responses to a startling stimulus (unexpected 103 dB white noise) were enhanced when the stimulus came during fear imagery as opposed to its presentation while individuals were engaged in pleasant or neutral imagery (Vrana, 1995). However, it is difficult to determine whether the SCRs were enhanced because of the affective (negative) value of the stimuli, increased arousal, or a combination of the two.

Observed Violence.   The interpretation that a subject is encouraged to use with respect to observed violence appeared to influence SCRs in Geen and Rakosky (1973). The subjects were male undergraduates whose SCRs were measured while they viewed a brutal prizefight sequence from the film *Champion*. The showing of the film was preceded by narratives that described events leading to the 6-min fight scene. The narratives depicted the sequence as aggression, vengeance, or fictional vengeance. In the introductory remarks relating to fictional vengeance, subjects were reminded that the fight was not real and that the injuries were only makeup. The greatest number of SCRs were observed following the aggression narratives, whereas significantly fewer SCRs occurred after the remarks emphasizing the fictional (make-believe) aspects of the fight scene. The interpretations offered by Geen and Rakosky suggest that by emphasizing the fictional aspects of the fight scene, the subjects were able to dissociate the observed violence from their own lives.

Erotic Stimuli.   The effects of erotic and neutral stimuli on SCR, HR, and subjective ratings of females were studied by Hamrick (1974). The erotic stimuli (slides of nude males) resulted in significant increases in SCR and decreases in HR. The changes in SCR and HR to the nude males were accompanied by subjective ratings that indicated sexual arousal and positive affective reactions. The decreased HR is consistent with the work of Lacey, Kagan, Lacey, and Moss (1963), in which HR deceleration was found to accompany situations in which subjects "take in" perceptual materials.

Emotional Expression.   Lanzetta, Cartwright-Smith, and Kleck (1976) tested Darwin's assertion that freely expressing an emotion will intensify the emotional experience, whereas suppressing it will lead to a reduction of experienced intensity. In a series of experiments, subjects were asked to either conceal or exaggerate facial expressions associated with the anticipated reception of electric shocks. It was found that suppression of expressive responses led to smaller SCRs and lower pain ratings than when exaggeration of the emotional response was required. They interpreted these results as supporting hypotheses regarding the role of nonverbal displays of emotion in regulating the emotional situation itself, as well as serving a social–communicative function. Darwin's hypothesis was also supported, suggesting that a "cool" response to an emotional situation could aid in preventing reactions from spiraling out of control.

The fact that these results were contrary to the "discharge model of emotion" was explained as being due to the short-term, experimentally manipulated control of emotional expression. The discharge model predicts that active facial display of emotionality reduces physiological response to emotionally arousing situations. Support for this model was obtained by Notarius and Levenson (1979), who divided subjects into natural "expressors" or "inhibitors," based on unconstrained facial expressions to a stressful film. The more naturally expressive subjects were less physiologically reactive to an emotional stressor than nonexpressive persons, as shown by SC and HR measures. The researchers suggested that the differential physiological responding may be related to personality and cognitive style of expressive versus inhibited persons. In any event, it must be recognized that tendencies cannot be equated with experimentally manipulated emotional displays in such studies.

In a different approach, subjects were asked to generate facial expressions portraying anger, fear, sadness, and disgust as negative emotions, and happiness and surprise as postive emotions (Levenson, Ekman, & Friesen, 1990). Electrodermal activity was clearly higher during the portrayal of negative emotions.

Mother–Infant Interaction.   Interactions between mothers and babies play an important role in the formation of attachment and in determining maternal response to the infant's signals. There is research evidence that breast-feeding mothers differ from bottle-feeders in satisfaction with the experience, in acceptance of the maternal role, and emotional investment in the infant. Wiesenfeld and colleagues (1985) carried this line of investigation one step further by examining the physiological responses of breast- and bottle-feeding mothers to their infants' signals. The mothers viewed videotapes of their own infants' emotional expressions (smiling, crying, and neutral) while SC and HR were measured. Also obtained were subjective ratings of desire to pick up their infant's emotional signals. Bottle-feeders reported less desire to pick up their infants than nursing mothers. The finding that nursing mothers had lower SCL and heart rate in this situation may be related to preexisting differences in personality or attitudes. Another possibility is that maternal hormones associated with lactation may act to lower general arousal, as reflected in the lower physiological responsivity, greater relaxation during feeding, and greater satisfaction during feeding reported by nursing mothers.

Summary.   EDA can serve as an index of affective value of stimuli for a subject. This seems to be true both for nonverbal stimuli (music, film sequence) and for emotionally tinged words. Preliminary findings suggest that SCRs are enhanced when a startling stimulus is presented during negative imagery compared to negative or neutral imagery. The findings of Lanzetta et al. (1976) may have important implications for the study and control of various types of emotional behavior and should be pursued further. The work of Notarius and Levenson (1979) points up the importance of considering how the emotional expression is obtained (manipulated or naturally occurring) in predicting EDA effects. Physiological variables offer potential in differentiating responses of breast- and bottle-feeding mothers to infants' emotional signals. Finally, there is some suggestive evidence that EDA differentiates between positive and negative affective states.

Motivation and SCR Recovery Time

An additional measure of SC, called *SCR recovery rate*, was introduced by Edelberg (1970). It is used with exosomatic measures of EDA, and is based on the time it takes for SC to return to a level midway between the peak of the response and its initial level. Edelberg (1970,

1972b) related this recovery rate, also called recovery half-time, to the degree to which a subject is goal-oriented. That is, the half-time recovery is faster under conditions of goal-oriented activity than under other conditions of arousal. For example, recovery times are faster when a subject is involved in a mirror-tracing task as compared to resting with eyes open. Edelberg (1972b) concluded that the measure is stable over time, and that it is related to relative quality of performance of an individual.

Waid (1974) obtained results that supported those of Edelberg in that electrodermal recovery rate was faster during goal-oriented activity than during less directed behavior. The finding that recovery rate was slower during a timed arithmetic tasks, as compared to a verbal RT task, was interpreted as being similar to previous findings in which recovery time was slower when electric shock was threatened. However, the independence of SCR recovery time from other measures was questioned by Bundy (1974). His data showed that when an SCR was preceded by a high degree of electrodermal activity, there was a tendency for SCR recovery time to be faster than when preceded by less ongoing EDA. Edelberg and Muller (1981) obtained data that confirmed Bundy's result. They noted that although SCR recovery time may not provide unique information, it has been useful in differentiating responses to stimuli and levels of performance. However, some EDA researchers argue that it is still appropriate to treat SCR recovery time as a separate variable (e.g., see Janes, 1982; Venables & Fletcher, 1981).

Summary.   These studies of SCR recovery rate and goal orientation provide another way of analyzing EDA and correlating it with performance, as well as providing information about EDA correlates of motivation. There is some debate about the independence of SCR recovery time as a measure, but it has been found useful in a variety of investigations. The finding that this measure of EDA is related to degree of task involvement corresponds to earlier findings of Andreassi (1966a), who suggested a similar relationship for SCL and performance.

Signal Detection and EDA

In a previous section, we discussed EDA associated with RT to detected signals. This section examines some studies that have related EDA to efficiency or accuracy of signal detection in vigilance-type situations. Surwillo and Quilter (1965), found that the number of SPRs occurring within the 18-sec period before the critical signal was significantly greater for detected signals than for missed signals.

Vigilance.   Various measures were studied (i.e., SCL, HR, and neck EMG) during a vigilance task that required subjects to attend to a flashing light and to report when it stayed on longer than usual (Eason, Beardshall, & Jaffee, 1965). The most consistent finding was that during the course of a vigil, performance and SCL decreased significantly. Eason and colleagues interpreted the decreased SCL as representing a drop in SNS activity, which in turn was due to the drowsiness-producing effects of the experimental situation.

Krupski, Raskin, and Bakan (1971) measured SCL while 31 persons performed a vigilance task. The investigators were interested in the number of commission errors, that is, responding in the absence of a signal, and its relation to EDA. They found that subjects who had large amplitude SCRs when they detected a signal made fewer commission errors than those who had small detection-related SCRs. The larger SCRs were interpreted in terms of greater attention level, which resulted in superior vigilance performance. In addition, subjects who had large orienting responses (defined as the SCR amplitude to the first signal) also made fewer commission errors, a finding that would support the conclusion regarding attention level and vigilance performance.

If a signal is presented repeatedly, the SCR will decrease in amplitude, a result ascribed to habituation of response to the signal. Research has shown that persons whose SCRs habituate slowly are superior in auditory vigilance performance, because they detect more signals and show less decline in detection over time. Vossel and Rossmann (1984) extended these findings to a vigilance study that employed a complex visual monitoring task. Their slow habituators detected more signals than fast habituators. One explanation attributes the result to basic arousal differences between the groups, whereas another suggests differential sensitivity to stimuli. The question remains to be resolved through further work.

In an interesting approach, Nishimura and Nagumo (1985) used data concerning SPL and signal detection to influence vigilance performance. During their study, a bell sounded when SPLs decreased to preset levels. This procedure alerted their subjects and avoided performance decrements.

Recognition of Faces.   Electrodermal activity was used in a different type of signal detection by Tranel, Fowles, and Damasio (1985). College students observed 50 slides that included 42 unfamiliar and 8 familiar faces (famous people, e.g., Bob Hope). The SCRs to the familiar faces were reliably greater, indicating that significance of the signal had an impact on autonomic response even though no verbal report was required.

Prosopagnosia is a neurological disorder in which humans lose the ability to visually recognize familiar faces, even though they continue to recognize these persons via other senses (e.g., by voice). Tranel and Damasio (1985) used the SCR to study two patients in whom prosopagnosia had been caused by brain damage at occipital and temporal areas on both sides of the brain. These prosopagnosic subjects generated more frequent and significantly larger SCRs to faces of persons they had known, but were now unable to recognize. They did not produce such SCRs to slides of unfamiliar faces. It appears that the brain damage that blocked visual memory of the faces did not block the autonomic response (EDA), indicating different brain substrates for EDA. The fact that the EDA occurred even though there was no conscious recognition is reminiscent of findings from the "perceptual defense" literature of the 1950s. Subjects in those studies produced SCRs to words that were unidentified, but were emotionally charged. A term used to describe this effect was "autonomic discrimination without awareness" (Lazarus & McCleary, 1951), suggesting that the stimulus was processed at some level of the nervous system, but did not reach brain areas (cortical?) required for conscious recognition.

Unconscious Recognition?   Tranel and Damasio (1988) focused on the use of EDA to index "unconscious recognition" in brain-damaged patients. In a follow-up study with a larger patient sample, Tranel and Damasio tested reactions to familiar faces from a period prior to brain damage (family, friends, famous politicians, actors) and faces of persons with whom the patients had extensive contact since the damage (physicians, psychologists). The patients were also asked to rate each face for familiarity. A control set of unfamiliar faces was interspersed with familiar faces for all patients. The results clearly showed EDAs to faces that they could not recognize and for which a sense of familiarity was completely lacking. Visual acuity was normal for all subjects but brain damage was bilateral, as in the patients previously studied. It is this bilateral damage at the occipital–temporal junction or median occipital areas that seems to preclude conscious perception of faces. Tranel and associates believed that some registration of stimuli (without recognition) must take place at the visual cortex, which may then share this input with hypothalamic structures, resulting in the autonomic response to "face records." The provocative results of Tranel and colleagues will surely lead to other studies that will clarify the relationship between awareness, brain function, and EDA.

Summary.   The studies briefly reviewed in this segment indicate that higher levels of skin conductance, greater numbers of SPRs, and slower habituation of SCRs are associated with superior signal detection. Krupski et al. (1971) interpreted this type of finding in terms of higher levels of attention (reflected in EDA), which led to more efficient detection. Other possible explanations involve greater arousal and sensitivity to stimuli as indicated by EDA. There is evidence that more frequent and significantly larger SCRs occur to "familiar" faces compared to unfamiliar ones in persons whose brain damage prevents them from visually recognizing the faces of even close relatives and friends. These findings have implications for further studies of brain mechanisms mediating both autonomic responses and processing of visual information at an unconscious level.

THE ORIENTING RESPONSE AND EDA

The orienting response (OR) was first described by Pavlov in 1927 to describe a reflex that brings an immediate response to the slightest change in the environment. As the story goes, Pavlov noticed that the process of classical conditioning of dogs was briefly interrupted whenever a new person or stimulus entered the laboratory and the animal oriented its eyes and ears towards this new arrival. In his book *Attention, Arousal and the Orientation Reaction*, Lynn (1966) detailed a variety of physiological changes that occur when an organism is presented with a novel stimulus. Among these are pupil dilation, increased EMG activity, increased frequency and lower amplitude of EEG, increase in amplitude and decrease in frequency of respiration, a slowing of heart rate, and changes in EDA. Berlyne (1960) categorized stimuli that have the potential to elicit the OR as follows: novel, intense, colorful, meaningful, surprising, complex, incongrous, and conflictual.

Neuronal Model.   Sokolov (1963) presented a theory of the OR in which incoming stimuli are compared with representations of past stimuli that reside in the cortex of the brain. If a stimulus is novel—that is, if it does not match any of the existing "neuronal models"—an orienting response occurs. If the incoming stimulus is familiar, it matches a model in the cortex, and the orienting reaction does not occur. Hence, in Sokolov's theory, the match or mismatch between stimulus properties (degree of novelty) is the critical factor in producing an OR. There are a large number of studies in which EDA correlates of the OR have been studied. Many of these have dealt with issues raised by Sokolov's theory. Some researchers have confirmed and refined aspects of Sokolov's approach, whereas others have proposed modifications. Only a few of these are presented here to give a flavor of the type of research in this area and the usefulness of EDA in OR research.

Stimulus Distance and Change.   Bernstein (1969) hypothesized that increased sound intensity might signify "something approaching the organism" (p. 128), and that this could lead to a more intense OR. This hypothesis was confirmed by Bernstein, Taylor, Austen, Nathanson, and Scarpelli (1971), who measured SCRs in a situation where patterned visual stimuli were stationary or appeared to move either toward or away from the individuals tested. Frequency and amplitude of SCRs were greater under apparent motion than with the stationary perceptual condition. Further, physiological changes were more prolonged when objects appeared to approach than when they appeared to recede. These results indicated to the authors that the onset of movement in the visual field is associated with a momentary increase in perceptual receptivity. In addition, stimuli that move toward a person are more significant than those that move away, as indicated by the respective ORs.

The hypothesis that an OR to stimulus change can attenuate a subsequent OR to a second stimulus change was examined by Maltzman, Harris, Ingram, and Wolff (1971). This hypothesis was confirmed with a group of subjects who experienced the two stimulus changes at 5-, 10-, or 30-sec intervals. In addition, Maltzman and colleagues noted that the magnitude of the SCR was greater when the stimulus change was an increase in illumination as opposed to a decrease, a similar finding to that of Bernstein (1969) for auditory stimuli. Yaremko, Blair, and Leckart (1970) examined the OR (magnitude of SCR) as a function of degree of deviation from an expected stimulus. The numbers 10 through 19 were presented serially to subjects. On the next trial (when 20 should have been presented), the numbers 31, 21, 19, or 9 were delivered. Therefore, the critical number was either 1 or 11 places out of sequence in either the positive or negative direction. The SCR magnitude was related to degree of discrepancy between the expected and observed number, that is, the 11-unit discrepancy produced larger SCRs than the smaller ones, regardless of direction. The results were interpreted as supporting Sokolov's (1963) hypothesis that OR magnitude depends on the amount of stimulus change.

Habituation. The effects of repeatedly imagining a stimulus on habituation of the OR was studied by Yaremko, Glanville, and Leckart (1972). Subjects who imagined hearing a tone showed greater habituation of the SCR component of the OR to a 500-Hz tone when compared to subjects who imagined seeing a light or those in a control group. The habituation rate did not differ from that of subjects who had previously received 10 trials with a 500-Hz tone. It was suggested that the imagery process aided in the formation of a "neuronal model" (Sokolov, 1963) and facilitated habituation. According to Sokolov's theory, the repeated imagery of a tone primed the formation of a neuronal model of the stimulus, and the partially formed model functioned to inhibit the OR. Similar results were found for the sense of touch; Yaremko and Butler (1975) reported that imagining electric shocks prior to receiving actual shocks resulted in decreased SCRs.

Siddle and Heron (1978) used SCR magnitude, HR, and finger pulse volume (FPV) to test OR to a change in tonal frequency. Following habituation to a 1000-Hz tone at 70 db intensity, new tones of either 670 Hz or 380 Hz (both 70 db) were presented to subjects. Significant changes in all measures occurred to changes in auditory stimulus frequency. The results were contrary to O'Gorman's (1973) contention that the OR is only sensitive to changes in stimulus intensity or modality. In addition, SCR magnitude was greater with larger frequency differences (e.g., with 380 Hz as compared to 670 Hz). The HR and FPV measures did not vary as a function of degree of difference between training (habituated) and test (new) stimuli. Hence, EDA was the most sensitive OR component to changes in tonal frequency.

Role of Stimulus Significance. A. S. Bernstein and I. Maltzman, sought to expand the OR theory advanced by Sokolov to include cognitive activity of the individual. Recall that Sokolov stressed the match–mismatch of stimuli to neuronal models as the critical factor in producing the OR. Bernstein (1979) and Maltzman (1979) argued that stimulus significance, as well as novelty, is important in eliciting the OR. Bernstein emphasized that an interaction between stimulus uncertainty and significance triggers the OR. Maltzman believed that a "cortical set," present prior to the presentation of experimental events, influences the OR to stimuli. This set may be a relatively short-lived disposition due to task instructions, or it may be a long-standing disposition already important in determining significance and selective orienting to stimuli. As an example of a study examining the effects of preexisting set on the OR, Wingard and Maltzman (1980) found that recreational interests influenced selective orienting. Participants were selected from among members of three university clubs: surfing, chess, and fishing. Students showed significantly larger SCRs to slides depicting their recreational interest as compared to other activities and neutral slides. The findings were interpreted as support for the notion that prior experiences establish a dominant focus or cortical set for certain events and not others. Thus, in the case of recreational interests, it is familiar stimuli that lead to an OR, not unfamiliar ones as proposed by Sokolov.

In a critical article, O'Gorman (1979) questioned the need for a revision of OR theory as well as the adequacy of the changes proposed by Maltzman and Bernstein. Both Bernstein (1979) and Maltzman (1979) made thoughtful replies to O'Gorman that highlight some of the important issues in contemporary OR theory. The interested reader would do well to consult these sources. In the meantime, experimental work continues. Maltzman, Gould, Pendery, and Wolff (1982) showed that task instructions (short-term set) resulted in different rates of OR habituation as indicated by magnitude of SCRs. In an attempt to resolve the debate between Bernstein/Maltzman and O'Gorman, Ben-Shakar and colleagues have conducted a series of studies in which stimulus significance and novelty were manipulated independently while the electrodermal component of the OR was measured (e.g., Gati, Ben-Shakar, & Avni-Liberty, 1996). In this latter study the results were consistent with Bernstein's (1979) proposal because ORs to a change in stimulation (novelty) were observed only with significant test stimuli.

Information-Processing Model.   In another approach, Ohman (1979) proposed an information-processing model of the OR that combines Sokolov's ideas with constructs derived from contemporary work in attention and memory. Namely, Ohman proposed that an OR is produced when an incoming stimulus fails to find a match in short-term memory (memory function that holds items for a number of seconds). The mismatch results in a search in long-term memory (LTM), and this cognitive effort results in registration of the novel stimulus in LTM. The processing facilitates later retrieval of the stimulus, but results in inhibition of the OR, because a match between the stimulus and memory trace is made. In a study that bears on Ohman's theory, Plouffe and Stelmack (1984) examined the OR to picture stimuli during the study phase of a free-recall task. Young and elderly female subjects had larger SCRs to recalled pictures, especially uncommon ones.

In habituation trials, pictures that were not recalled produced smaller SCRs than pictures not shown in the study phase. This was taken as evidence for "stimulus priming," that is, the inhibition of the OR that occurs when a match between a stimulus and its memory trace is made. The authors concluded that the results support Ohman's proposals about the role of cognitive effort in encoding incoming stimuli, and the dependence of novel stimulus recall on production of the OR. They also suggested that the age decrement in recall may be due to a reduction of cognitive effort on the part of elderly persons.

Stimulus Omissions.   Sokolov (1963) described EDA and EEG changes at the point in time when an omitted stimulus was scheduled to appear. This is similar to the P300 brain response that occurs when an expected stimulus is omitted. If one were to use a Sokolovian explanation, it might be said that the individual does not have a neuronal model for the omitted stimulus and that is why the OR occurs when the expected stimulus does not appear. Barry (1984) hypothesized that this missing-stimulus effect was due to the emission of a voluntary OR as compared to a reflexive, involuntary OR. This led to the prediction that the EDA to missing stimluli would take longer to occur than the EDA to an actual stimulus. This hypothesis was tested by presenting a long series of visual stimuli, at regular intervals, except for a number of stimulus omissions that occurred only after habituation to the series (Barry & O'Gorman, 1987). The EDA to the missing stimulus took longer to occur, thus supporting Barry's prediction. Barry and O'Gorman concluded that the latency increase is due to the time taken for the subject's evaluation of the stimulus omission, and contrasts with the quicker process involved when the OR is involuntary or reflexive.

Alcohol Effects.   The effects of a moderate dose of alcohol on SC orienting responses were assessed by Lyvers and Maltzman (1991). The SCR evoked by novel signal, novel nonsignal, and common nonsignal stimuli was studied in subgroups of male and female "social drinkers" (no more than three periods of alcohol consumption per week, on average). Control conditions (tonic alone) were compared to alcohol conditions (vodka in tonic, sufficient to raise blood alcohol levels to .05%). It was found that alcohol-enhanced SCRs were produced by the signal tone, perhaps because of a selective depressant effect on inhibitory areas of frontal cortex. In agreement with previous findings, there was an increase in the number of spontaneous SCRs with alcohol, also suggesting a reduction of inhibitory influences. Further, alcohol led to an increase in error rate (false alarms), suggesting a disinhibiting effect on responses. Information from event-related potential studies indicate that alcohol has a depressant effect on cortical activity. It has also been reported that the SCR orienting response is absent in patients with massive lesions in the frontal cortex (Luria, 1973). Thus, the author's attribution of cortical effects seems reasonable.

Summary.   EDA has proven to be a useful physiological indicator in experimentation on the nature of the OR. Frequency and amplitude of SCRs are affected by changes in stimulus direction. Perceived approach of visual stimuli produced larger magnitude ORs. Magnitude of conceptual deviation and imagery have been related to magnitude of SCRs and tendency of the OR to habituate, respectively, in support of Sokolov. The EDA measure of OR also indicates that it can vary with changes in stimulus quality as well as intensity. The influence of both long-term and short-term dispositions (set) on the OR have been demonstrated. Effects of cognitive effort and the role of the OR in preparing for future stimulation are promising areas for exploration. It has also been demonstrated that the EDA will occur to expected, but omitted stimuli. Attempts to expand Sokolov's OR theory have resulted in some controversy, but have also stimulated new work on some of the issues. On the whole, it is obvious that Sokolov's OR theory is useful, but it requires revision to accommodate findings regarding such influences as long- and short-term set and cognitive effort.

CONDITIONING OF EDA

In the well-known Pavlovian classical conditioning paradigm, a conditioned stimulus (CS) eventually leads to a conditioned response (CR) after it has been paired with an unconditioned stimulus (UCS) a sufficient number of times. The CS is initially a neutral stimulus, for example a light, which gains importance through its association with a significant stimulus, for example food, which is termed the UCS. In the early stages of conditioning, the UCS leads to an unconditioned response (UCR) such as salivation. In the final stages of conditioning, salivation (CR) occurs to presentation of the light (CS). Pavlov was careful to measure the number of saliva drops as an indicator of the strength of conditioning. The classical conditioning of EDA and of other autonomic responses (e.g., HR) has been an extensively studied phenomenon with both animal and human subjects. Edelberg (1972a) pointed out that because of the well-defined nature of SCRs and SPRs, they serve well as the CR, because it is often possible to distinguish them from the orienting response to the CS. A wide variety of unconditioned stimuli has been used in the classical conditioning of EDA in humans. Some examples are white noise, electric shock, a puff of air, and sexually arousing stimuli (Prokasy & Kumpfer, 1973). A good UCS must produce effective ANS activation, and it should be resistant to habituation.

In the instrumental conditioning paradigm, the subject must emit some kind of response to obtain a reinforcement. The response is not defined for the subject, and in the case of EDA, the required response might be an increase in the rate of SCRs. At one time, it was believed that ANS responses could not be instrumentally conditioned. However, there is now considerable evidence that some degree of instrumental conditioning can be demonstrated with EDA (Kimmel, 1973) and other autonomic responses (e.g., heart rate). Some reinforcers that have been used in the instrumental conditioning of EDA include pleasant odors, lights presented to subjects in a dark room, lights or sounds that indicated monetary rewards, pictures of nude women presented to male subjects, and cool air for persons in a hot-and-humid chamber (Kimmel & Gurucharri, 1975).

Classical Conditioning of EDA

A discussion of a variety of independent variables that have been manipulated in studies of electrodermal conditioning has been presented by Prokasy and Kumpfer (1973). Some of these variables include the effects of interstimulus interval on the magnitude of the conditioned EDA, percentage of reinforced trials, and the modality of the CS (e.g., light or sound). Successful EDA conditioning has been observed to occur in a variety of experimental conditions. Complex variables in the classical conditioning situation were examined by Grings and Dawson (1973). These included the effects of age, sex, and intelligence on the classical conditioning of EDA. Because the classical conditioning of EDA has been presented in detail elsewhere (Grings & Dawson, 1973; Prokasy & Kumpfer, 1973) only a few sample experiments are presented here.

Prokasy, Williams, and Clark (1975) tested the hypothesis derived from Pavlov's (1927) work that if a CS is greater than or equal to the intensity of a UCS, then conditioning to that CS should not occur. The amplitude and probability of SCRs were used as the criteria of conditioning. The results indicated that conditioning was obtained even when the CS was greater in intensity than the UCS, thus refuting Pavlov's hypothesis. No difference in the amount of conditioning was associated with either CS or UCS intensity.

Verbal conditioning of EDA is an established phenomenon. For example, if subjects are informed that a UCS (electric shock) will follow a tone CS, a large SCR is observed at the first presentation of the CS, before it has been paired with the UCS. This result was long thought to be due to anxiety produced by the expected unpleasant experience. However, Pendery and Maltzman (1979) showed that similar verbal conditioning could be produced by an innocuous CS (tone) serving as a warning signal in a RT situation. These types of results can be taken as indicating the importance of cognitive factors in human conditioning.

Affective Value of the CS. In an interesting approach, Ohman and Dimberg (1978) used different facial expressions as the CS in an experiment where electric shock was the UCS. As they predicted, angry faces produced greater resistance to extinction than happy or neutral faces. Presumably, the angry faces produced a greater affective reaction in the subjects, and thereby the conditioned EDA did not extinguish as quickly. In a follow-up study, Dimberg and Ohman (1983) examined the effects of directing the angry faces toward or away from subjects. The recorded SCRs revealed that angry facial expressions gave conditioning effects that were resistant to extinction only if they were directed toward the observer. Later work by Ohman and colleagues has indicated that pictures of spiders, snakes and angry faces (CS) paired with electric shock (UCS) produced CRs (SCRs) that were very resistant to extinction (Ohman, Dimberg, & Ost, 1985). When neutral stimuli were used as the CS (e.g., pictures of flowers, geometric shapes, or happy faces), there was little resistance to extinction.

Phobias. Schell, Dawson, and Marinkovic (1991) believe that this type of research has implications for the study of phobias, because phobias involve extreme fear responses that are both irrational and highly resistant to extinction. An example would be the agoraphobia (literally, fear of open spaces) that may occur in persons with panic disorder; that is, the place where the panic attack originally occurred is avoided. The panic attack is usually accompanied by a variety of physical (racing heart, sweating, shortness of breath, dizziness) and psychological symptoms (fear of dying, fear of going crazy) that have dramatic impact. Panic victims become so fearful of an attack that they may avoid places similar to the one where the reaction first occurred (stimulus generalization), and in some severe cases the individual can become homebound for a considerable period of time.

In their own research, Schell et al. (1991) found that potentially phobic stimuli (pictures of spiders and snakes) produced SCRs that were greater during extinction than did neutral stimuli (flowers and mushrooms). Thus, we may have the beginnings of an interesting paradigm to study the nature of phobias. The initial pairing of the phobic stimulus with the fear response is accompanied by sufficient physiological response to render it very memorable. Thus, it is highly likely that both physiological and cognitive components are at work in phobic behavior, an interactive effect that makes the phobia difficult to overcome. Relevant to the question of phobias and conditioned fear reactions is research that indicates that conditioned SCRs can be generated even though subjects remain unaware of the stimulus that elicits the SCR. An example is the approach in which backwardly masked angry faces (targets) were followed by an electric shock, but happy faces were not (Esteves, Parra, Dimberg & Ohman, 1994). The face used as a mask was always neutral. Recall that in backward masking, subjects are able to report the mask but not the target (see chapter 6 for a description of backward masking as applied in visual ERP studies). Thus, even though subjects were not able to perceive the angry target face they still showed conditioned SCRs to these faces. So far, the result is limited to fear relevant conditioned stimuli (e.g., angry faces) and aversive UCSs (e.g., electric shock). The important aspect is that a conditioned fear response may be possible to a stimulus that is just below level of awareness.

Ohman and Soares (1998) used a similar backward masking paradigm in a conditioning experiment in which the fear-relevant stimuli were snakes and spiders and the fear-irrelevant conditioned stimuli were flowers and mushrooms. They also showed nonconscious conditioning to fear-relevant but not fear-irrelevant stimuli. They point up the relevance of these results in understanding the anxiety patient and suggest that nonconsciously operating fear systems alert the cognitive system (conscious), which then scans the environment *expecting* unpleasant events to occur. The topic of unconscious mechanisms in phobic fear is discussed in a very interesting and thoughtful chapter (Ohman, 1997). Ohman concludes that the data show conclusively that autonomic responses (EDA) related to fear activation can be elicited by relevant stimuli that are not consciously perceived. This could explain why many anxiety or panic disorder patients are unaware of the sources of their distress. They could very well be responding to unrecognized external or internal cues in a manner that exacerbates their condition as they are already overly sensitive to potentially threatening conscious stimuli.

Unconditioned Stimulus Probability and CS–UCS Interval.   It has been established that multiple SCRs occur in conditioning experiments where the time interval between CS and UCS is long, especially with an unpleasant UCS. The flurry of responses early in the interval has been related to the OR, whereas later ones were associated with preparation for the UCS. Backs and Grings (1985) varied UCS probability in studying EDAs during a long CS–UCS interval. The probabilities of the UCS (loud noise) occurring were .17, .50, or .83, and the interval was 8 sec. Both magnitude and frequency of early SCRs (first 4 sec after the CS) increased as a function of UCS probability. The authors suggested that preparation for a more likely aversive event resulted in greater amounts of EDA early in the CS–UCS interval. If this is true, then both orienting and preparation would be attributed to the early part of the interval.

Instrumental Conditioning of EDA

A great deal of experimental work on the instrumental conditioning of EDA was reviewed by Kimmel (1973). Basically, the review indicated that EDA, for example, the frequency or magnitude of SCRs, will be increased or decreased when the delivery of some reinforcement is contingent on this response. The reinforcement may involve either the presentation of some pleasant stimulus (e.g., monetary reward) or the avoidance of some unpleasant stimulus (e.g., electric shock). Kimmel's review will serve the student who desires more detail about this topic.

A study that explored the instrumental conditioning of EDA was conducted by Kimmel and Gurucharri (1975). Two groups of 20 subjects each were placed in a hot (115°F), humid (100% humidity) chamber while SCRs were measured. The first group of 20 experimental subjects received a burst of cool air whenever an SCR was emitted. As the experimental session progressed, the number of SCRs increased, indicating that the cool air was an effective reinforcer for producing the SCR. Twenty control subjects, who were individually matched with each experimental subject on the basis of pre-experimental level of spontaneously produced SCRs, were tested under the same conditions. Control subjects then received cool air at the same time, based on the record of when their matched experimental subject received the SCR contingent reinforcement. Thus, both groups received the same number of cool air presentations, but the control group's rewards were not contingent on producing an SCR. Nevertheless, the control group showed an increase in unelicited SCRs, although not at the same accelerating rate as the experimental subjects. Detailed examination of the SCR records of the controls indicated that they coincidentally received cool air with 38% of their SCRs, and this accounted for their increased rate of SCR production. The researchers further noted that the SCR responses of the experimental subjects resembled results from traditional instrumental conditioning studies more closely than any previously conducted SCR investigation.

Summary.   The classical conditioning of EDA has been achieved under a variety of experimental conditions. Verbal and pictorial stimuli have been effectively used as the CS. The affective value of the CS has an effect on extinction such that negative stimuli show greater resistance to extinction. Studies also suggest that EDA conditioning is of value in understanding, and possibly treating, phobias. For example, during sessions in which a therapist attempts to desensitize an individual to phobic stimuli magnitude of the SCR could be used as an indicator of improvement. It has been shown that duration of the CS–UCS interval, and probability of occurrence of the UCS affect magnitude and frequency of SCRs.

There is evidence that instrumental conditioning of EDA is possible with a variety of reinforcers. However, the effects of subjective thoughts, or cognitive meditation, have not been clearly delineated in instrumental EDA conditioning paradigms. Some investigators (e.g., Shean, 1970; Stern, 1970; Stern & Kaplan, 1967) have suggested that cognitive mediation plays a role in instrumental EDA conditioning. For example, a subject might find that a certain type of thought (e.g., a favorite activity) is related to receiving cool air, whereas, in actuality, it was the SCR produced by the arousing thought that resulted in delivery of the reinforcement. Therefore, it may be that the number of SCR-producing thoughts are increased rather than a subject's ability to influence sweat gland activity. This possibility must be investigated more closely.

The next chapter considers changes in pupillary diameter as a psychophysiological measurement. The student may be surprised to learn that a wide variety of behavioral states and activities have been associated with changes in pupil size.

REFERENCES

Andreassi, J. L. (1966a). Some physiological correlates of verbal learning task difficulty. *Psychonomic Science, 6*, 69–70.

Andreassi, J. L. (1966b). Skin-conductance and reaction-time in a continuous auditory monitoring task. *American Journal of Psychology, 79*, 470–474.

Andreassi, J. L., Rapisardi, S. C., & Whalen, P. M. (1969). Autonomic responsivity and reaction time under fixed and variable signal schedules. *Psychophysiology, 6*, 58–69.

Andreassi, J. L., & Whalen, P. M. (1967). Some physiological correlates of learning and overlearning. *Psychophysiology, 3*, 406–413.

Backs, R. W., & Grings, W. W. (1985). Effects of UCS probability on the contingent negative variation and electrodermal response during long ISI conditioning. *Psychophysiology, 22*, 269–275.

Barry, R. J. (1984). Stimulus omission and the orienting response. *Psychophysiology, 21*, 535–540.

Barry, R. J., & O'Gorman, J. G. (1987). Stimulus omission and the orienting response: Latency differences suggest different mechanisms. *Biological Psychology, 25*, 261–276.

Baugher, D. M. (1975). An examination of the nonspecific skin resistance response. *Bulletin of the Psychonomic Society, 6*, 254–256.

Berlyne, D. E. (1960). *Conflict, arousal and curiosity*. New York: McGraw-Hill.

Bernstein, A. S. (1969). The orienting response and direction of stimulus change. *Psychonomic Science, 112*, 127–128.

Bernstein, A. S. (1979). The orienting reflex as novelty and significance detector. *Psychophysiology, 16*, 263–273.

Bernstein, A. S., Taylor, K., Austen, B. G., Nathanson, M., & Scarpelli, A. (1971). Orienting response and apparent movement toward or away from the observer. *Journal of Experimental Psychology, 84*, 37–45.

Boucsein, W. (1992). *Electrodermal activity*. New York: Plenum.

Brown, C. H. (1937). The relation of magnitude of galvanic skin responses and resistance levels to the rate of learning. *Journal of Experimental Psychology, 20*, 262–278.

Bundy, R. S. (1974). The influence of previous responses on the skin conductance recovery limb. (Abstract) *Psychophysiology, 11*, 221–222.

Darrow, C. W. (1933). The functional significance of the galvanic skin reflex and perspiration on the backs and palms of the hands. *Psychological Bulletin, 30*, 712.

Dawson, M. E., Schell, A. M., & Filion, D. L. (1990). In J. T. Cacioppo & L. G. Tassinary (Eds.), *Principles of psychophysiology* (pp. 295–324). Cambridge: Cambridge University Press.

Dimberg, U., & Ohman, A. (1983). The effects of directional facial cues on electrodermal conditioning to facial stimuli. *Psychophysiology, 20*, 160–167.

Eason, R. G., Beardshall, A., & Jaffee, S. (1965). Performance and physiological indicants of activation in a vigilance situation. *Perceptual & Motor Skills, 20*, 3–13.

Edelberg, R. (1967). Electrical properties of the skin. In C. C. Brown (Ed.), *Methods in psychophysiology* (pp. 1–53). Baltimore: Williams & Wilkins.

Edelberg, R. (1970). The information content of the recovery limb of the electrodermal response. *Psychophysiology, 6*, 527–539.

Edelberg, R. (1972a). Electrical activity of the skin. In N. S. Greenfield & R. A. Sternbach (Eds.), *Handbook of psychophysiology* (pp. 367–418). New York: Holt, Rinehart & Winston.

Edelberg, R. (1972b). Electrodermal recovery rate, goal-orientation and aversion. *Psychophysiology, 9*, 512–520.

Edelberg, R. (1973). Mechanisms of electrodermal adaptations for locomotion, manipulation, or defense. *Progress in Physiological Psychology, 5*, 155–209.

Edelberg, R., & Muller, M. (1981). Prior activity as a determinant of electrodermal recovery rate. *Psychophysiology, 18*, 17–25.

Edelberg, R., & Wright, D. J. (1962). *Two GSR effector organs and their stimulus specificity*. Paper presented at the meeting of the Society for Psychophysiological Research, Denver, CO.

Esteves, F., Parra, C., Dimberg, U., & Ohman, A. (1994, October). Nonconcious associative learning: Pavlovian conditioning of skin conductance responses to masked fear-relevant facial stimuli. *Psychophysiology, 31*, 375–385.

Fowles, D. C. (1986). The eccrine system and electrodermal activity. In M. G. H. Coles, E. Donchin, & S. W. Porges (Eds.), *Psychophysiology: Systems, processes & applications* (pp. 51–96). New York: Guilford.

Fredrikson, M., Furmark, T., Tillfors-Olsson, M., Fischer, H., Andersson, J., & Langstrom, B. (1998). Functional neuroanatomical correlates of electrodermal activity: A positron emission tomographic study. *Psychophysiology, 35*, 179–185.

Freeman, G. L. (1940). The relationship between performance level and bodily activity level. *Journal of Experimental Psychology, 26*, 602–608.

Gati, I., Ben-Shakar, G., & Avni-Liberty, S. (1996). Stimulus novelty and significance in electrodermal orienting responses: The effects of adding versus deleting stimulus components. *Psychophysiology, 33*, 637–643.

Geen, R. G., & Rakosky, J. J. (1973). Interpretations of observed aggression and their effect on GSR. *Journal of Experimental Research in Personality, 6*, 280–292.

Grings, W. W., & Dawson, M. E. (1973). Complex variables in conditioning. In W. F. Prokasy & D. C. Raskin (Eds.), *Electrodermal activity in psychological research* (pp. 203–254). New York: Academic Press.

Hamrick, N. D. (1974). Physiological and verbal responses to erotic visual stimuli in a female population. *Behavioral Engineering, 2*, 9–16.

Jacob, S. W., & Francone, C. A. (1970). *Structure and function in man.* Philadelphia: Saunders.

Janes, C. L. (1982). Electrodermal recovery and stimulus significance. *Psychophysiology, 19*, 129–135.

Kelsey, R. M. (1991). Electrodermal lability and myocardial reactivity to stress. *Psychophysiology, 28*, 619–631.

Kimmel, H. D. (1973). Instrumental conditioning. In W. F. Prokasy & D. C. Raskin (Eds.), *Electrodermal activity in psychological research* (pp. 255–282). New York: Academic Press.

Kimmel, H. D., & Gurucharri, F. W. (1975). Operant GSR conditioning with cool air reinforcement. *Pavlovian Journal of Biological Science, 10*, 239–245.

Krupski, A., Raskin, D. C., & Bakan, P. (1971). Physiological and personality correlates of commission errors in an auditory vigilance task. *Psychophysiology, 8*, 304–311.

Lacey, J. I., Kagan, J., Lacey, B. C., & Moss, H. A. (1963). The visceral level: Situational determinants and behavioral correlates of autonomic response patterns. In P. H. Knapp (Ed.), *Expression of the emotions in man* (pp. 161–196). New York: International University Press.

Lacey, J. I., & Lacey, B. C. (1958). The relationship of resting autonomic activity to motor impulsivity. In J. I. Lacey & B. C. Lacey (Eds.), *The brain and human behavior* (pp. 144–209). Baltimore: Williams & Wilkins.

Lanzetta, J. T., Cartwright-Smith, J., & Kleck, R. E. (1976). Effects of non-verbal dissimulation on emotional experience and autonomic arousal. *Journal of Personality and Social Psychology, 33*, 354–370.

Lazarus, R. S., & McCleary, R. A. (1951). Autonomic discrimination without awareness: A study of subception. *Psychological Review, 58*, 113–122.

Levenson, R. W., Ekman, P., & Friesen, W. V. (1990). Voluntary facial action generataes emotion specific autonomic nervous system activity. *Psychophysiology, 27*, 363–384.

Luria, A. R. (1973). The frontal lobes and the regulation of behavior. In K. H. Pribram & A. R. Luria (Eds.), *Psychophysiology of the frontal lobes* (pp. 3–26). New York: Academic Press.

Lykken, D. T., & Venables, P. H. (1971). Direct measurement of skin conductance: A proposal for standardization. *Psychophysiology, 8*, 656–671.

Lynn, R. (1966). *Attention, arousal and the orientation reaction.* Oxford: Pergamon.

Lyvers, M., & Maltzman, I. (1991). Selective effects of alcohol on electrodermal indices of orienting reflexes to signal and nonsignal stimuli. *Psychophysiology, 28*, 559–569.

Maltzman, I. (1979). Orienting reflexes and significance: A reply to O'Gorman. *Psychophysiology, 16*, 274–282.

Maltzman, I., Gould, J., Pendery, M., & Wolff, C. (1982). Task instructions as a determiner of the GSR index of the orienting reflex. *Physiological Psychology, 10*, 235–238.

Maltzman, I., Harris, L., Ingram, E., & Wolff, C. (1971). A primacy effect in the orienting reflex to stimulus change. *Journal of Experimental Psychology, 87*, 202–206.

Maltzman, I., Kantor, W., & Langdon, B. (1966). Immediate and delayed retention, arousal, and the orienting and defensive reflexes. *Psychonomic Science, 6*, 445–446.

Mangina, C. A., & Beuzeron-Mangina, J. H. (1996). Direct electrical stimulation of specific human brain structures and bilateral electrodermal activity. *International Journal of Psychophysiology, 22*, 1–8.

Neumann, E., & Blanton, R. (1970). The early history of electrodermal research. *Psychophysiology, 6*, 453–475.

Nishimura, C., & Nagumo, J. (1985). Feedback control of the level of arousal using skin potential level as an index. *Ergonomics, 28*, 905–913.

Notarius, C. I., & Levenson, R. W. (1979). Expressive tendencies and physiological response to stress. *Journal of Personality and Social Psychology, 37*, 1204–1210.

O'Gorman, J. G. (1973). Change in stimulus conditions and the orienting response. *Psychophysiology, 10*, 465–470.

O'Gorman, J. G. (1979). The orienting reflex: Novelty or significance detector? *Psychophysiology, 16*, 253–262.

O'Gorman, J. G., & Lloyd, J. E. M. (1988). Electrodermal lability and dichotic listening. *Psychophysiology, 25*, 538–546.

Ohman, A. (1979). The orienting response, attention and learning: An information processing perspective. In H. D. Kimmel, E. H. Van Olst, & J. F. Orlebecke (Eds.), *The orienting reflex in humans* (pp. 443–471). Hillsdale, NJ: Lawrence Erlbaum Associates.

Ohman, A. (1997). Unconscious pre-attentive mechanisms in the activation of phobic fear. In G. C. L. Davey (Ed.), *Phobias: A handbook of theory, research and treatment* (pp. 95–110). New York: Wiley.

Ohman, A., & Dimberg, U. (1978). Facial expressions as conditioned stimuli for electrodermal responses: A case of preparedness? *Journal of Personality & Social Psychology, 36*, 1251–1258.

Ohman, A., Dimberg, U., & Ost, L. G. (1985). Animal and social phobias: Biological contraints on learned fear responses. In S. Reiss & R. R. Bootzin (Eds.), *Theoretical issues in behavior therapy* (pp. 123–175). New York: Academic Press.

Ohman, A., & Soares, J. J. F. (1998). Emotional conditioning to masked stimuli: Expectancies for aversive outcomes following nonrecognized fear-relevant stimuli. *Journal of Experimental Psychology: General, 127,* 69–82.

Pavlov, I. P. (1927). *Conditioned reflexes* (G. V. Anrep, Trans.). London: Oxford University Press.

Pendery, M., & Maltzman, I. (1979). Verbal conditioning and extinction of the GSR index of the orienting reflex. *Physiological Psychology, 7,* 185–192.

Plouffe, L., & Stelmack, R. M. (1984). The electrodermal orienting response and memory: An analysis of age differences in picture recall. *Psychophysiology, 21,* 191–198.

Prokasy, W. F., & Kumpfer, K. L. (1973). Classical conditioning. In W. F. Prokasy & D. C. Raskin (Eds.), *Electrodermal activity in psychological research* (pp. 157–202). New York: Academic Press.

Prokasy, W. F., Williams, W. C., & Clark, L. G. (1975). Skin conductance response conditioning with CS intensities equal to and greater than UCS intensity. *Memory & Cognition, 3,* 227–281.

Sakai, L. M., Baker, L. A., & Dawson, M. E. (1992). Electrodermal lability: Individual differences affecting perceptual speed and vigilance performance in 9 to 16 yr old children. *Psychophysiology, 29,* 207–217.

Schell, A. M., Dawson, M. E., & Marinkovic, K. (1991). Effects of potentially phobic conditioned stimuli on retention, reconditioning, and extinction of the conditioned skin conductance response. *Psychophysiology, 28,* 140–153.

Schlosberg, H. (1954). Three dimensions of emotion. *Psychological Review, 61,* 81–88.

Schlosberg, H., & Kling, J. W. (1959). The relationship between "tension" and efficiency. *Perceptual & Motor Skills, 9,* 395–397.

Shackel, B. (1959). Skin drilling: A method of diminishing galvanic skin potentials. *American Journal of Psychology, 72,* 114–121.

Shean, G. D. (1970). Instrumental modification of the galvanic skin response: Conditioning or control? *Journal of Psychosomatic Research, 1,* 155–160.

Siddle, D. A., & Heron, P. A. (1978). Effects of length of training and amount of tone frequency change on amplitude of autonomic components of the orienting response. *Psychophysiology, 13,* 281–287.

Sokolov, E. N. (1963). *Perception and the conditioned reflex.* New York: Pergamon.

Stern, R. M. (1970, October). *Operant modification of electrodermal responses and/or voluntary control of GSR.* Paper presented at the meeting of the Society for Psychophysiological Research, Washington, DC.

Stern, R. M., & Kaplan, B. E. (1967). Galvanic skin response: Voluntary control and externalization. *Journal of Psychosomatic Research, 10,* 349–353.

Surwillo, W. W., & Quilter, R. E. (1965). The relation of frequency of spontaneous skin potential responses to vigilance and age. *Psychophysiology, 1,* 272–276.

Tranel, D., & Damasio, A. R. (1985). Knowledge without awareness: An autonomic index of facial recognition by prosopagnosics. *Science, 228,* 1453–1454.

Tranel, D., & Damasio, A. R. (1988). Non-conscious face recognition in patients with face agnosia. *Behavioural Brain Research, 30,* 235–249.

Tranel, D., & Damasio, H. (1994). Neuroanatomical correlates of electrodermal skin conductance responses. *Psychophysiology, 31,* 427–438.

Tranel, D., Fowles, D. C., & Damasio, A. R. (1985). Electrodermal discrimination of familiar and unfamiliar faces: A methodology. *Psychophysiology, 22,* 403–408.

Venables, P. H., & Christie, M. J. (1973). Mechanism, instrumentation, recording techniques and quantification of responses. In W. F. Prokasy & D. C. Raskin (Eds.), *Electrodermal activity in psychological research* (pp. 1–124). New York: Academic Press.

Venables, P. H., & Christie, M. J. (1980). Electrodermal activity. In I. Martin & P. H. Venables (Eds.), *Techniques in psychophysiology* (pp. 3–67). Chichester: Wiley.

Venables, P. H., & Fletcher, R. P. (1981). The status of skin conductance recovery time: An examination of the Bundy effect. *Psychophysiology, 18,* 10–16.

Venables, P. H., & Martin, I. (1967). Skin resistance and skin potential. In P. H. Venables & I. Martin (Eds.), *Manual of psychophysiological methods* (pp. 53–102). Amsterdam: North-Holland.

Vossel, G. (1988). Electrodermal lability, errors, and reaction times: An examination of the motor impulsivity hypothesis. *International Journal of Psychophysiology, 6,* 15–24.

Vossel, G., & Rossmann, R. (1984). Electrodermal habituation speed and visual monitoring performance. *Psychophysiology, 21,* 97–100.

Vrana, S. (1995). Emotional modulation of skin. conductance and eyeblink responses to a startle probe. *Psychophysiology, 32,* 351–357.

Waid, W. M. (1974). Degree of goal orientation, level of cognitive activity and electrodermal recovery rate. *Perceptual & Motor Skills, 38,* 103–109.

Wiesenfeld, A. R., Malatesta, C. Z., Whitman, P. B., Granrose, L., & Uili, R. (1985). Psychophysiological response of breast- and bottle-feeding mothers to their infants' signals. *Psychophysiology, 22,* 79–86.

Wilcott, R. C. (1959). On the role of the epidermis in the production of skin resistance and potential. *Journal of Comparative & Physiological Psychology, 52,* 642–649.

Wilcott, R. C. (1967). Arousal sweating and electrodermal phenomena. *Psychological Bulletin, 67*, 58–72.

Wingard, J. A., & Maltzman, I. (1980). Interest as a predeterminer of the GSR index of the orienting reflex. *Acta Psychologica, 40*, 153–160.

Woodburne, R. T. (1978). *Essentials of human anatomy.* New York: Oxford University Press.

Woodworth, R. S., & Schlosberg, H. (1954). *Experimental psychology.* New York: Holt.

Yaremko, R., Blair, M. W., & Leckart, B. T. (1970). The orienting reflex to changes in a conceptual stimulus dimension. *Psychonomic Science, 2*, 115–116.

Yaremko, R. M., & Butler, M. C. (1975). Imaginal experience and attenuation of the galvanic skin response to shock. *Bulletin of the Psychomomic Society, 5*, 317–318.

Yaremko, R. M., Glanville, B. B., & Leckart, B. T. (1972). Imagery-mediated habituation of the orienting reflex. *Psychonomic Science, 27*, 204–206.

Yuille, J. C., & Hare, R. D. (1980). A psychophysiological investigation of short-term memory. *Psychophysiology, 17*, 423–430.

Zimny, G. H., & Weidenfeller, E. W. (1963). Effects of music upon GSR and heart-rate. *American Journal of Psychology, 76*, 311–314.

10

Pupillary Response and Behavior

The pupils of the eyes have been referred to as "windows to the soul." Although this romantic notion is untrue, scientists have dicovered some interesting things about pupillary size changes and behavior. Pupillometrics refers to the measurement of variations in the diameter of the pupillary aperture of the eye.

In his book on pupillometry, Janisse (1977) wrote that one of the earliest references to the pupil of the eye was made by Travisa (1495) in his translation of Bartholomaeus (Angelica Palli, 1398), in which is stated that "the blacke of theye . . . is callyd Pupilla in latyn for small, ymages ben seen therin" (Janisse, 1977, p. 1). The word *pupil* is derived from the Latin "pupilla," meaning "little girl," thus referring to the tiny reflections of persons that one can see when looking into the eyes of another. At least two different writers of the past (Joshua Sylvester, 1591, and Guillaume de Salluste) have referred to the pupillary apertures as "windows to the soul," implying that they were observation points for a person's innermost thoughts. Scientific observation of pupils is much less romantic than implied by these early writers, because we now know that dilations and constrictions of the pupil are governed by the autonomic nervous system. As we shall see in this chapter, pupillometry has provided psychophysiologists with interesting information about pupil size changes in various situations. Among the issues that have attracted researchers in this field are whether pupils dilate with positive stimuli and constrict with unpleasant ones. Changes in pupil diameter that occur during information processing, perception, short-term memory, learning, and nonverbal communication are also topics of interest. After some basic information about the pupillary response has been presented, including anatomy and physiology and how it is measured, its value in explaining psychological phenomena is discussed.

ANATOMY AND PHYSIOLOGY OF THE PUPILLARY RESPONSE

The pupil is the opening at the center of the iris of the eye through which light passes. Thus, the pupil is merely a hole surrounded by the iris muscle. A major function of the iris is to increase pupillary diameter in dim light and to decrease it in bright light. This adjusts the amount of light allowed to enter the eye according to the surrounding environment. The pupil of the human eye can constrict to 1.5 mm in diameter, it dilates to about 8 to 9 mm, and can react to stimuli in .2 sec (Guyton, 1977; Lowenstein & Loewenfeld, 1962). The constriction and dilation of the pupillary aperture is produced mainly through ANS control exerted on the muscles of the iris. More specifically, neurons of the PNS innervate circular fibers of the iris, causing pupillary constriction, whereas excitation by SNS neurons causes the radial fibers of the iris to produce dilation of the pupil.

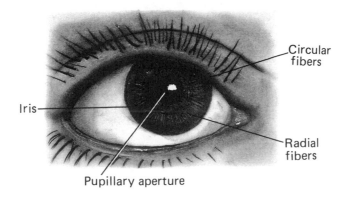

FIG. 10.1. Diagram of the eye. The diameter of the pupillary aperture is the measure used in pupillometry. Pupillary constriction occurs with contraction of circular fibers, while dilation results from contraction of radial fibers.

Both the circular and radial fibers are smooth muscle (see Fig. 10.1). The circular muscle fibers are also termed the *sphincter pupillae*, and their parasympathetic innervation begins at a group of brain cells located in the midbrain (Edinger–Westphal nucleus). The efferent parasympathetic fibers travel from this nucleus, along the oculomotor nerve (III cranial n.), to the ciliary ganglion near the eyeball, and finally to the smooth muscles surrounding the pupil. The radial fibers, also termed the *dilator pupillae*, are under control of SNS processes originating in the hypothalamus. From here, fibers project downward to the spinal cord (lower cervical and upper thoracic) and leave the cord to synapse the superior cervical ganglion. Sympathetic influence projects from this ganglion directly to the dilator pupillae of the iris. The ANS is intimately involved in emotional behavior. Janisse (1977) pointed out that the relation of pupillary response to ANS activity appears to have been accepted as early as the 1850s by investigators such as Claude Bernard. Charles Darwin, that exquisite observer of behavior, related pupil dilation to fear and other emotions in animals in his 1872 book entitled *The Expression of the Emotions in Man and Animals*. A strong emotional stimulus (e.g., an unexpected pistol firing) will cause the pupils to dilate. Thus, a dilated pupil will appear as part of a *startle reaction*, with a response occurring in as little as .2 sec and peaking in .5 to 1.0 sec. The dilation will persist even if a bright light is presented to the eye, indicating that the emotional response can override the usual pupillary constriction to intense light stimuli. Animal studies have shown that pupillary dilation occurs with stimulation of the hypothalamus, thalamus, and reticular formation. These are brain areas that have been implicated in emotional behavior and behavioral arousal.

MEASUREMENT OF PUPILLARY SIZE

Although many observations about changes in pupil size under different emotional or performance conditions have been reported, it is only within the last 30 years that the development of practical and reliable instrumentation has enabled the precise measurement of the pupillary aperture under different experimental conditions and psychological states. One problem in the measurement of pupil size is the constant fluctuation in pupil diameter that occurs during waking hours. These spontaneous changes occur simultaneously in the two eyes and are about 1 mm in amplitude. They are thought to be under control of brain mechanisms that continuously regulate pupil size according to intensity of light stimulation. Measurements obtained under normal lighting conditions must take these fluctuations into account.

Early devices in the measurement of pupil size included the use of infrared photography, which made it possible to get pictures of pupil diameter in dim light. Photoelectric methods, which measured reflected light from the iris, were also used. Both were cumbersome and not very accurate. Hakerem (1967) considered the best available device at that time to be the "Lowenstein pupillograph," which used infrared scanning of the iris to determine the amount of reflected light. This device measured the diameters of both pupils and provided information about the rate of change in pupil size. However, Janisse (1977) questioned the accuracy of the system. Hess (1972) described his device in some detail, along with procedures for its use. Essentially, it consists of a movie camera, a projector (movie or slide), a screen, and reflecting mirrors. The use of infrared film enables recordings of pupil diameter regardless of the subject's eye color. For any given visual stimulus, the averaged pupil diameter for 20 individual frames is used as the measure of pupil size for that presentation. Hess emphasized the importance of holding constant the factors of stimulus brightness and brightness contrast. Brightness contrast refers to the relative brightness of a stimulus compared to its background. The Hess technique is the most economical, but the frame-by-frame measurement of pupil size, and errors of hand measurement, make this technique time-consuming and of questionable reliability.

A widely used pupil-measuring technique in modern laboratories is the video-based pupillometer. These electronic devices use a closed-circuit TV system to observe the eye and a signal processor to measure and display pupil diameter. A low-intensity infrared light source illuminates the eye, and a low-light-level silicon matrix tube camera is used to record pupil size. Pupil diameter is presented as either a direct numerical readout or appears on a chart recorder showing continous changes in size. The system also has automatic circuitry to maintain proper measurement over a wide range of recording conditions. Pupil diameter may be measured over a 0- to 10-mm range, with provisions for expanding subintervals of this range. A more recent development uses momentary estimates of pupillary diameter, which are then continuously available for online computer analysis.

Using this approach, task-evoked pupillary responses (TEPR) can be obtained when changes in pupil size that occur with respect to certain events in a task are averaged (Beatty, 1986). With this type of averaging, changes in pupil size to significant events in the experimental trial can be specified, and background variations can be canceled out. Stern and Dunham (1990) suggested that the TEPR is an appropriate index of pupillary response. They explained that because the TEPR is measured in fractions of a millimeter, compared to background pupillary oscillations of a millimeter or more, averaging enhances the pupil response, enabling it to stand out from the background noise. This procedure requires establishing a stable baseline from which task-evoked changes in pupil diameter can be measured. The stimulus must be presented a number of times in order to obtain the averaged response.

Fatigue and Pupil Size

Lowenstein and Loewenfeld (1964) noted that pupil diameter is maximal in a well-rested individual, decreases with fatigue, and reaches a minimal diameter just before sleep. Kahneman and Peavler (1969) observed a continuous decrease in pupil size between the beginning and end of an experimental session. Hess (1972) cautioned experimenters to avoid presentation of an excessive number of stimuli in studies of pupil size, because fatigue causes the pupil to decrease in diameter.

Geacintov and Peavler (1974) measured pupil sizes of telephone operators to determine whether pupil constriction would reflect fatigue in a work environment. Each subject was measured before and after a full day's work of providing directory assistance with either the usual telephone book or an automated microfilm reader.

TABLE 10.1
Factors That May Influence Changes in Pupil Size

Factor	Effect on Pupil Size
Darkness reflex	Momentary dilation due to interruption of a constant adapting light
Consensual reflex	Stimulation of one eye affects both eyes equally
Near reflex	Constriction due to decreasing the point of focus, i.e., the pupil constricts with convergence of the eyes on a near object
Lid-closure reflex	Momentary contraction followed by redilation
Psychosensory reflex	Restoration of diminished reflexes due to external stimulation
Age	Decreased diameter and increased variability with age
Habituation	Pupil diameter decreases, speed of contraction increases, and magnitude of reflex decreases with continued stimulus presentations
Binocular summation	Constriction greater when both eyes are stimulated simultaneously

Source: Adapted from W. W. Tryon, Pupillometry: A survey of sources of variation. *Psychophysiology,* 1975, 12, 90–93.

The average pupil size for all subjects at the beginning of the day was 4.6 mm at the book position and 4.5 mm at the microfilm location. Pupil diameter decreased on the average between morning and evening measures. However, the data analyses indicated that a significant decrease (.43 mm) occurred only for the microfilm condition. Thus, a size difference between prework and postwork measurements was found with the microfilm readers but not with the book readers. Subjects reported more fatigue symptoms, such as backaches, headaches, and eyestrain, when using the microfilm device than when they used the telephone book. However, performance was superior with the microfilm reader because of the greater access speed of this automated device.

There are a number of environmental factors that can have an effect on pupil size. Some of these variables that are not otherwise mentioned in this chapter are listed in Table 10.1.

PUPILLOMETRY AND BEHAVIOR

The most influential person in the application of pupillometry to psychology was Eckhard Hess. His earliest publications in the area date back to about 1960, and stimulated a great deal of interest among psychologists. Hess's work suggested ways in which mental activities, information processing, perception, attitudes, and interests could be understood in terms of pupillary changes. He was not the first to indicate the possibility of such relationships, but his provocative work led to increased activity in this area by contemporary psychologists. It is fitting that our account of psychophysiological investigations of pupillary changes associated with different behaviors begins with a study done by Hess.

Affective Value of Stimuli and Pupil Size

Interest Value of Stimuli.   One of the most intriguing results of the original Hess study (Hess & Polt, 1960) was that pupil size appeared to be related to affect, or "feeling tone," generated by different pictures. For example, they reported that when viewing pictures of a male nude and of a baby, female subjects gave larger pupil dilation responses than males. On the other hand, males reacted with larger pupillary dilation to a picture of a nude female. The researchers concluded that the gender differences indicated greater interest in nudes of the opposite sex. As a follow-up, Hess, Seltzer, and Shlien (1965) found that homosexual males had greater pupil dilations to photographs of male nudes compared to female nudes, whereas the results for heterosexual males showed the opposite pupillary response. Others have provided support for the relation between sexual arousal and pupil size. For example, Simms (1967) reported that not only did opposite-sex pictures result in greater dilation, but that this was especially true when the photos were retouched to produce enlarged pupils. The implication of this finding is that pupil dilation in others may be subtly perceived as signifying interest on the part of that other person.

Response to Pain.   In a different approach, affective response was produced by pain stimuli and resulting changes in pupil diameter were measured (Chapman, Oka, Bradshaw, Jacobson, & Donaldson, 1999). The researchers used four intensities of electrical stimulation, applied to a fingertip, ranging from very faint to barely tolerable. Pupil diameter increased as shock intensity increased, as did subjective reports of pain intensity. The average change in pupil diameter was an 0.25 mm increase for the lowest intensity level and 0.37 mm at the highest. The average maximum intensity tolerable was 776 μA for men and 793 μA for women, a nonsignificant difference.

Summary.   The studies of Hess and colleagues have indicated reliable increases in pupil size as interest value of stimuli increases. There are also preliminary findings to suggest that pupil diameter increases with increasing subjective pain.

Sexual Arousal or Novelty?   A possible source of bias in the pupil size–sexual interest relationship was demonstrated by Chapman, Chapman, and Brelje (1969). They used "businesslike" and "carefree" experimenters to present nude male and female pinups to male subjects. Only the subjects tested by the carefree experimenter showed larger pupil dilation to the female nudes. If the two experimenters had been in different laboratories, conflicting findings would have been reported. In this same study, a large number of the male subjects showed some dilation to male nudes, leading Chapman et al. to conclude that dilation could reflect general interest and positive evaluation as well as sexual interest.

Bernick, Kling, and Borowitz (1971) measured pupil responses of heterosexual male medical students to three movies: an erotic heterosexual movie, a suspense film, and an erotic homosexual movie. The erotic heterosexual and homosexual films produced the same degree of dilation, which was greater than that to the suspense film. In addition, the degree of self-reported penile erection related closely to increases in pupil diameter during the viewing of sexual films. This finding of Bernick et al. comes closest to supporting a pupillary dilation–sexual arousal hypothesis, but, unfortunately, amount of erection was not objectively measured.

Caution is recommended for those who would use extent of pupillary dilation as an indicator of sexual preference. Not only have some studies not shown pupillary differences as a function of opposite-sex nudity (e.g., Peavler & McLaughlin, 1967), but it is also true that pupil dilation occurs to novel stimuli, and naked people are certainly more novel in our culture than clothed individuals. A study by Hamel (1974) showed pictures of females and males, in varying degrees of nudity, to female undergraduates. He found that viewing opposite-sex pictures in order of increasing nudity produced increasingly greater dilation. The greatest dilation was recorded in response to totally nude males and the smallest to fully clothed female models. Rather than sexual arousal, one could easily use the alternate explanation of novelty or interest, because total male nudity could be so categorized for these subjects, whereas female models are common pictures for them. Pupillary dilation has also been reported in response to erotic and unpleasant passages from a book presented in a tape recording (White & Maltzman, 1977). Subjects listened to 2-min passages from the same novel: one erotic, one describing mutilation, and one neutral. They found immediate dilation at the beginning of each passage, with erotic and mutilation segments maintaining this for about 60 sec. Pupil size during the neutral passage began declining within 10 sec after the reading started. These results suggest an orienting response, which was then followed by habituation to the neutral passage.

Summary.   Pupillary dilation may not merely be a reflection of sexual interest when this reaction occurs to erotic stimuli. Studies suggest that novelty initially plays a role in pupillary dilation, but that interest is required for sustaining this response. Possible experimenter effects must also be investigated more fully.

Pupil Size and Nonverbal Communication

Hess (1975) concluded that pupil size is important in nonverbal communication, because it seems to act as an unlearned mechanism in facilitating certain social behaviors such as sexual interest. In his own work, Hess manipulated pupil size in two pictures of the same attractive young woman. Male subjects described the woman with large pupils as soft, more feminine, or pretty, whereas in the smaller pupil photograph the woman was described as hard, selfish, or cold. Subjects could not distinguish between the photographs, nor could they give reasons for their preference. Other studies by Hess showed that subjects associated large pupils with happy faces and small ones with angry faces. He concluded that larger pupils are associated with attractiveness, sexual interest, and happiness, whereas small ones are related to the opposite characteristics. However, some investigators, like Janisse (1977), are still not convinced about the reliability or adequacy of pupillary communications. He pointed out that although there is information about what information the dilated pupil communicates to an observer, the validity of the communication is still questionable.

The main reason for this is that most of the data have been collected with visual stimuli where the light reflex could not be ruled out as a possible cause of pupillary change. Hess developed another research approach in which subjects are allowed to draw in pupils on line drawings of faces. Subjects consistently drew in large pupils on happy faces and small pupils on the sad faces. This result has been obtained with both adults and children as subjects. Hicks and co-workers conducted several studies to test Hess' hypotheses that females and light-eyed people are more sensitive to pupillary cues. In one study (Hicks, Williams, & Ferrante, 1979), 223 college students drew in pupils on angry and happy faces. They did find that the students drew in significantly larger pupils on the happy face, a result that supported Hess. However, male–female sensitivity did not differ. Williams and Hicks (1980) used the happy–angry faces task and reported that women and light-eyed persons were more sensitive to pupillary cues than men and dark-eyed persons.

Hess and Petrovich (1978) proposed that a relationship between eye color and sensitivity to pupillary cues is due to some evolutionary mechanism or indicates an acquired cultural effect. Possible influences of culture receive support from Tarrahian and Hicks (1979). They showed that Iranian children are sensitive to pupillary cues at an earlier age than American children. This is interesting, in view of the fact that the Iranian culture may be considered to be *pupil-intensive*, because veiled Iranian women can use only the eyes, and possibly the brows, as facial communication cues when in public. Tarrahian and Hicks noted that in the United States, where pupillary cues may be less important, the meaning of these cues might be incidentally learned when the individual begins to experience sexual situations in which increases in pupil size are likely to occur in others. Although these results seem to suggest that cultural factors may play a role in sensitivity to pupil size, there is yet no reasonable explanation as to why lighter-eyed persons or women should have greater sensitivity. In this last set of studies, it should be pointed out that pupil sizes of subjects were not measured while they drew in pupils. Pupillary size measures could be an interesting addition to these kinds of studies to indicate something about the state of the individual participant while drawing in the pupils.

Summary. Hess and his colleagues have argued for the nonverbal communication value of changes in pupillary diameter. His well-known studies in which variations in a woman's pupil size led to different judgments about her personal traits by male subjects is an example. Hess has also provided data indicating that happy faces are associated with larger pupil size than angry faces. There is some suggestive evidence that cultural factors influence sensitivity to pupillary size cues. Hypotheses regarding greater sensitivity of women and light-eyed persons have not been substantiated.

Pupil Size and Mental Activity

The amount of pupil response during mental activity has been shown to be a function of how hard an individual has to work. The first researchers to show this were Hess and Polt (1964), who asked people to do mental multiplication. Level of difficulty was gradually increased from 7 × 8 to 16 × 23, and pupil size increases reflected difficulty level. The increases ranged from 4% to 30% in diameter from prequestion to preanswer period, with pupil size decreasing immediately after the answer was given. Thus, the pupillary response appears to reflect the information-processing load placed on the nervous system by cognitive tasks. In another experiment (Polt, 1970), the threat of a mild electric shock for incorrect answers resulted in greater amounts of effort to solve problems, and this, in turn, produced greater pupil dilation. Beatty (1982) concluded that the amplitude of the task-evoked pupillary response (TEPR) is an index of a common factor related to the processing demands of memory, language processing, reasoning, and perception.

Short-Term Memory

Pupil size was observed as subjects listened to strings of three to seven digits presented at a rate of one per second (Kahneman & Beatty, 1967). After a 2-sec pause, each string was repeated by subjects at the same rate. The researchers found progressive pupillary dilation with the presentation of each digit, with maximum dilation being reached after all digits were presented. Then, as each digit was duplicated by the subject, pupillary constriction occurred and reached baseline when the last digit was repeated. Also, the amount of pupil dilation at the pause was a function of the number of items in the string, that is, it was greatest with seven digits (4.1 mm) and least with three digits (3.6 mm). The interpretation was that pupil dilation varied directly with momentary cognitive load.

In another study, Beatty and Kahneman (1966) found similar pupillary size variations when digits were retrieved from long-term memory, for example, with a familiar telephone number. Subjects were required to recall a telephone number when given a one-word cue, such as "home" or "office," and to say the numbers at a 1-sec rate. The magnitude of pupil dilation was larger with these familiar digits as compared to a string of seven unfamiliar digits presented for recall. As before, pupil diameter decreased with each digit reported, returning to baseline as the last digit was given. A number of studies by Kahneman and his associates have indicated that progressive pupil dilation occurred when lists of materials were presented for processing. Kahneman and Wright (1971) showed that pupillary response was greater when subjects were required to recall an entire series of items than when they recalled only part of the information. Stanners, Headley, and Clark (1972) reported greater pupil diameter for subjects asked to recall information from memory, as compared to a requirement to recognize items presented. They suggested that this could reflect different processing in recall and recognition, or more intense rehearsal produced by the requirement to recall information. In other words, the less the required effort, the less is pupil enlargement.

Summary.   The last two sections have presented work indicating that degree of pupillary dilation is related to workload required in performing cognitive tasks. Researchers have clearly demonstrated that in short-term memory tasks pupillary diameter increases regularly as a function of number of items to be retrieved.

Language Processing

Differential changes in pupil size occurred when persons were asked to generate visual images to abstract and concrete words (Paivio & Simpson, 1966). It was found that engagement in imagery produced increases in pupil size, with greater amounts occurring to abstract words (e.g., liberty), compared to concrete words (e.g., house). Further, time to reach maximum dilation was greater with abstract words, perhaps because it was more difficult to generate images to abstract terms. Pupillary dilation did not occur during reading or listening to passages that varied in difficulty (Carver, 1971). This led Carver to conclude that pupil size cannot be used as an objective indicator of whether or not the person is processing language. However, this conclusion is at odds with the majority of evidence. For example, Stanners et al. (1972) observed larger increases in pupillary size when more complex sentences were presented via tape recorder. In addition, task-evoked pupillary responses have been studied as subjects processed meaningful sentences differing in complexity (Ahern & Beatty, 1981). Greater degrees of grammatical complexity were reported to produce larger pupillary responses.

An interesting example of how linguistic organization of sentences affects task-evoked responses was given by Beatty (1982). Sentences composed of six words each had three levels of organization, and subjects were asked to reproduce all three types. The more disorganized sentences were harder to reproduce. As a result, a sentence reading, "Many blind roses play heavy trouble" led to larger dilations than, "Should blind people lead quiet lives?" Eliminating syntactic organization completely by using random strings of words as in "Rains children milk golden usually medals," led to the largest responses of all. Figure 10.2 depicts the task-evoked pupillary responses during the listen, pause, and report portions for the three kinds of sentences. Another experiment illustrates the finding that not only does processing of complex, meaningful, sentences take longer than processing of simpler ones, but pupil diameter is greater for the more complex materials (Just & Carpenter, 1993). The authors suggest that the pupillary response indicates the intensity of information processing. Eye fixation times increased at points in a sentence where syntax was most complex. At this point, pupil diameter increased and reached a maximum in 1.3 sec.

Summary.   A requirement to generate images of concrete versus abstract words affects pupil diameter. Sentences differing in degree of linguistic organization from organized to scrambled results in progressively enlarged pupillary diameter, suggesting that more and more effort is required in the struggle to make meaning of verbal information that is increasingly disorganized. Meaningful sentences that are more complex also result in greater amounts of pupil dilation, suggesting that intensity of processing influences dilation.

Perception

Task Difficulty.   Pupillary dilation has been related to the difficulty encountered by subjects in a pitch discrimination task (Kahneman & Beatty, 1967). The subject's task was to judge

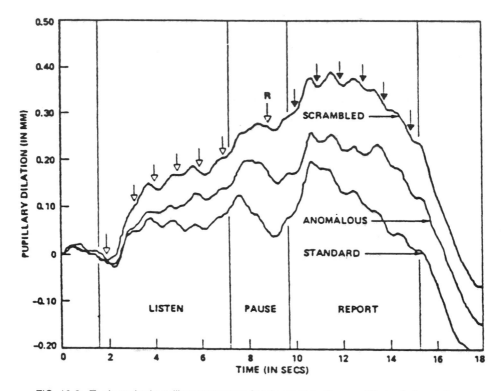

FIG. 10.2. Task-evoked pupillary responses for six-word sentences differing in linguistic organization. Standard sentences were meaningful English sentences. Anomalous sentences
used the same syntactic frames but with words interchanged between sentences to render
the strings nearly meaningless. Scrambled sentences had neither syntactic nor semantic organization. Both syntactic and semantic organization independently reduce the processing
load imposed by the sentence repetition task. Open arrows indicate presentation of words
and the response cue; filled arrows indicated timing clicks.

whether the comparison tone was higher or lower than the standard tone. When the difficulty in
distinguishing between the two became greater, subjects showed increased dilation. Hakerem
and Sutton (1966) measured pupillary response to threshold (barely perceptible) visual stimuli.
No pupillary dilation occurred to stimuli that were not detected or when the subject was not
asked to detect the weak light flashes. However, when subjects were required to detect whether
a flash was present or absent, and they correctly discriminated a flash, pupillary dilation occurred. Beatty (1975) found similar results when subjects were required to detect a weak tone
that was present during one half of the experimental trials. Pupil dilation occurred only when a
presented signal was detected by the subjects. Beatty concluded that the pupillary dilations reflected changes in nervous system activation, which accompanied perceptual processing.

Stimulus Probability.   The probability that a stimulus will be presented has been found
to affect pupil size (Friedman, Hakerem, Sutton, & Fleiss, 1973). For example, stimuli that
have a lower probability of being presented result in larger pupil responses than higher probability stimuli. Qiyuan, Richer, Wagonner, and Beatty (1985) examined the effects of probability of auditory stimuli on pupillary respones. They confirmed that probability affects pupil
response, and also reported that omitting an expected stimulus results in dilation. The finding
that stimulus omissions resulted in dilations indicates that a physical stimulus does not have
to be presented to produce a reponse, but that some mental representation of an expected

stimulus can be sufficient. In this respect, the pupillary respones is similar to the P300 component of the event-related brain potential (see chapter 6).

In a study by Beatty (1982), pupillary changes were recorded as subjects detected random target tones over a 48-min period. Signal detection perfomance deteriorated over time in the task, and this was accompanied by a decrease in the amplitude of the pupillary response over the course of the session. These results are very similar to changes reported for event-related brain potentials and visual signal detection. Beatty (1982) made the point that his pupillary results, along with the brain response data, argue for a decreased response to task-relevant stimuli as a function of time at both cortical and subcortical levels.

Affective Words.   Pupillary respones to taboo, emotional, and neutral words were measured for groups of introverts, extroverts, and ambiverts as identified by the Eysenck Personality Inventory (Stelmack & Mandelzys, 1975). Subjects were presented with 12 taboo words (e.g., whore), 12 emotional words (e.g., vomit), and 24 neutral words (e.g., field). The introverts had the largest average pupil size under all conditions. This result supported Eysenck's hypothesis that introverts have generally higher levels of physiological arousal than other personality types.

Negative Affect

Hess (1972) noted in various studies that certain types of negative stimuli produce a constriction in pupil size (e.g., pictures of crippled children). However, if the negative picture has "shock content" (e.g., a picture of a mutilated person), dilation may occur initially, followed by constriction after repeated presentations. Thus, the emotional reaction produces a sympathetic nervous system response (pupil dilation), and after it wears off, constriction occurs and reflects aversion, or "perceptual avoidance." Hess (1972) contended that "there is a continuum of pupil responses to stimuli, ranging from extreme dilation for interesting or pleasing stimuli to exteme constriction for material that is unpleasant or distasteful to the viewer" (p. 511). Other investigators have challenged this claim of bidirectionality of the pupil response.

For example, Loewenfield (1966) reviewed effects of various sensory and psychological stimuli and concluded that none, except increased light intensities, caused pupillary constriction. Woodmansee (1967) reported an opposite result, that is, pupillary dilation in 13 of 14 female college students who viewed a picture of a gruesome murder scene. Libby, Lacey, and Lacey (1973) reported that unpleasant visual stimuli produced greater dilation than pleasant stimuli. Several of their 34 subjects, however, did show consistent pupillary constriction to a few stimuli. Janisse (1974) found a positive relationship between pupil size and affect intensity, but no evidence of constriction to negative stimuli. In general, the results of other investigators cast doubt on Hess' hypothesis regarding pupillary constriction to unpleasant stimuli.

Summary.   There appears to be substantial research support for the claim that pupillary diameter increases with stimuli that produce positive affect. Pupillary constriction with negative stimuli is still controversial, and may be a response limited to a few individuals and a small range of stimulus conditions.

In previous sections, we saw that pupillary diameter enlarged with difficulty of perceptual discriminations. Lower probability stimuli result in larger diameters, possibly reflecting novelty effects. In addition, omitting expected stimuli resulted in dilations, indicating that mental representations of expected stimuli can influence pupillary response. Finally, the report of differential response of introverts and extroverts to emotional words presents some interesting possibilities for further research.

Attitudes

It has been suggested that pupil size might be a more valid index of attitude toward persons or things than more traditional methods such as interviews or questionnaires (Hess, 1972). One example is a study by Barlow (1969), who showed slides of three political leaders (Lyndon Johnson, George Wallace, and Martin Luther King) and one unknown person to White subjects classified as either liberal or conservative. The liberals showed pupillary dilation to Johnson and King, and constriction to Wallace. The conservatives showed an opposite response pattern. Thus, the pupils of subjects dilated to photographs of persons with whom they agreed, and were constricted to those of a different political persuasion. A study by Clark and Ertas (1975) questioned the use of pupil size as an index of attitude. These investigators showed pictures of 1972 presidential candidates (Richard Nixon and George McGovern) and a picture of a stranger to supporters of either of these candidates. In another condition, the candidates' last names and the name Smith were spoken. All three pictures were associated with constriction, with names producing dilation. It is obvious from these conflicting kinds of results that the question of attitude and pupil size requires a great deal of additional work.

Information Processing, Learning, and Pupil Size

Information Processing.   Poock (1973) found that pupil diameter was related to information-processing speed. He first determined maximum processing capacity (100%) by having subjects press buttons corresponding to displayed numerals as fast as possible. Then subjects alternately processed numerals at 50%, 75%, 100%, and 125% of maximum capacity. Significant increases in pupil diameter over baseline levels (viewing a blank slide) were found when subjects were required to process information at 75% and 100% of capacity. However, when the requirement was raised to 125% of capacity, pupillary constriction occurred.

Digit strings of 5, 9, and 13 were used with 14 female college students who were asked to reproduce the numbers immediately after hearing them (Peavler, 1974). There was a trend toward increased pupil size with each successive digit in the 5- and 9-digit conditions. However, the 13-digit condition revealed that dilation leveled off immediately after presentation of the 10th digit. This suggested to Peavler that information-processing effort was momentarily suspended at this instant. This point of no further dilation corresponded to the short-term memory capacity of the subjects, which was approximately 9 digits in this experiment. Thus, although the studies of Poock and Peavler agree that pupillary diameter increases with processing load, they disagree about what happens when there is an overload. Peavler reported a leveling off of increases after digit spans exceeded normal short term memory capacity (about 7 items), whereas Poock found pupillary constriction when processing load exceeded 125% of capacity.

An experiment was designed by Granholm and colleagues to clarify the nature of pupillary changes when processing demands approach or exceed available resources (Granholm, Asarnow, Sarkin, & Dykes, 1996). They recorded pupillary responses during a digit-span recall task with 5 (low load), 9 (moderate load), and 13 (excessive load) digits per string. These researchers found that memory capacity was greater than 5 digits, but less than 9 or 13 digits, a finding consistent with Miller's famous formulation which describes short-term memory capacity as the "magical number" 7, plus or minus 2 items (Miller, 1956). Granholm et al. reported that pupil dilation increased significantly when processing demands were below resource limitations (5 digits), did not change significantly during processing at or near resource limitations (9 digits), and declined significantly after demands exceeded available resources (13 digits). These results are illustrated in Figure 10.3. Thus, their findings were similar to those reported by Poock (1973) indicating that the pupil constricts when process-ing demands become excessive. Granholm and colleagues suggested that pupillary response shows an increase until resource limits are approached, then levels off and is maintained at this level as long as active processing continues, but drops when the subject ceases to allo-cate maximal resources to the task. This cessation may represent an abandonment of the task when it becomes too difficult, and the individual either refuses to perform further or is unable to do so.

Learning.   Kahneman and Peavler (1969) measured pupil diameter in a verbal learning task. The learning trials were presented under conditions of either high incentive (5-cent re-ward for each item learned) or low incentive (1-cent reward). The high incentive items were more efficiently learned than the low incentive ones (55% vs. 18%), and they produced larg-er pupillary dilations (4.04 mm vs. 3.97 mm). In another learning study, Colman and Paivio (1970) measured pupillary activity during paired-associates learning. The abstractness of the words was varied, and subjects learned the pairs under standard memorizing conditions or using imagery as an aid. Pupillary dilation was greater under the standard, more difficult learning condition. The results also showed larger pupil size with the abstract word pairs that were more difficult to learn.

The studies reviewed in this section clearly show that pupillary diameter changes occur during information processing, and that the change is related to degree of mental effort re-quired. The increases in pupillary dilation observed with heavy information-processing de-mands may be related to elevated CNS activity under higher load conditions. Beatty believed

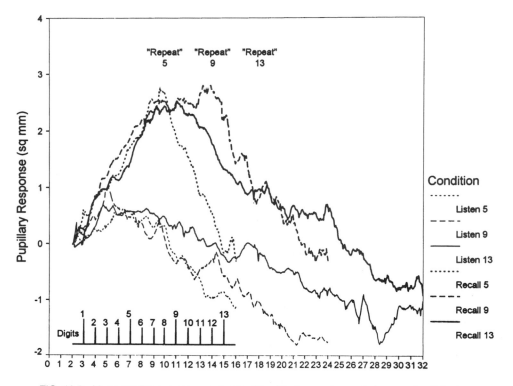

FIG. 10.3. Mean pupillary responses for the 22 subjects are shown during passive listening to and active recall of 5-, 9-, and 13-digit spans. (Figure courtesy of Dr. E. Granholm and Cambridge University Press.)

that the pupillary response provides a quantitative index of how much load is being placed on the nervous system.

Summary.   It becomes clear as one considers research in pupillometry and behavior that variables such as information-processing load and task difficulty (whether it be mental multiplication or developing images to abstract terms) will cause pupillary diameter to increase. This is true for a variety of different cognitive tasks, including short-term memory, language processing, reasoning, perceptual discrimination, and detection. However, once active processing declines, pupillary diameter decreases. Interest value and novelty of stimuli also play a role in pupillary changes. Janisse (1977) cautioned that the light reflex (constriction from increased illumination) may contaminate results when visual displays are used. However, this possibility can be reduced through the use of fixation points, constant illumination of visual displays, and auditory stimuli.

The value of pupillometry in attitude measurement and in the study of nonverbal communication has not yet been convincingly demonstrated. It is also clear that although pupillary dilations are reliably observed as responses to interesting or pleasant stimuli, the claim that constriction occurs to unpleasant or negative stimuli has not been upheld. Reliable pupillary constrictions are observed as a function of increasing fatigue. It has generally been found that pupil size decreases slowly during the day from early morning to late at night due to fatigue. One possibility is that fatigue-related decreases in pupillary diameters are primarily due to parasympathetic nervous system activity.

Pupillometry in Schizophrenia

Autonomic nervous system controlled physiological measures of schizophrenics to various stimuli, including pupillary changes, was reviewed by Zahn, Frith, and Steinhauer (1991). They noted that schizophrenics show greatly reduced pupil dilations compared to controls when performing in a guessing task. Studies suggest that, like other indices of ANS activity, pupillary response to external stimuli is less in schizophrenics compared to normals. However, one study indicated larger pupil dilations among schizophrenics when performing a digit-span task. A possible interpretation is that this represented a more difficult task for schizophrenics and they may have had to expend more effort in completing it compared to normals. This kind of finding needs repeating by other researchers.

A group of investigators hypothesized that time to reach maximal pupillary constriction could discriminate between schizophrenics who would relapse during a drug-free period and those who would not (Steinhauer, van Kammen, Colbert, Peters, & Zubin, 1992). Fifty trials of pupillary constriction to a light stimulus were averaged, and it was found that a shorter time to reach maximum pupil constriction differentiated patients who were later to relapse from those that did not relapse, thus supporting the hypothesis. The experiment was carried out in a double-blind experimental design in which patients were tested weekly over a 2-month period. Further analysis indicated that signal averaging of 15 to 20 pupillary reactions to light provided sufficient data. This type of information could be useful in deciding which patients would do well after withdrawal of medication.

It has been proposed by a number of researchers that schizophrenics have difficulty in processing sensory information and are easily overloaded by increased processing demands (Granholm et al., 1997; McReynolds, 1960). The hypothesis that pupillary response during information processing would differentiate schizophrenics from normals was tested by Granholm et al. (1997). Pupillary responses of normal controls and schizophrenic patients were observed during a working memory task (digit recall). Pupil size increased with increases in digit-span length for both groups. However, both recall performance and pupillary responses of schizophrenics were significantly lower than normals in all load conditions (low, moderate, high, and overload). These results suggest a limitation to the resources used by patients during performance of this working memory task.

Summary.   Researchers have been examining pupillary responses of schizophrenics compared to normals in various information processing situations. This approach may lead to useful information regarding the physiological bases of schizophrenia and even provide data regarding vulnerability to relapse when withdrawn from medication. The pupil response may also have promise in evaluating overload of working memory resources in schizophrenia.

The modern era of pupillometry was ushered in by the provocative work of Hess and his associates. It continues as a very interesting research area that has implications for the study of human behavior in a variety of situations. In the next chapter we consider the area of electrooculography (EOG or eye movements), and eye blinks and their relation to psychological processes.

REFERENCES

Ahern, S. K., & Beatty, J. (1981). Physiological evidence that demand for processing capacity varies with intelligence. In M. Friedman, J. P. Dos, & N. O'Connor (Eds.), *Intelligence and learning* (pp. 201–216). New York: Plenum.

Barlow, J. D. (1969). Pupillary size as a index of preference in political candidates. *Perceptual & Motor Skills, 28*, 927–932.

Beatty, J. (1975). *Prediction of detection of weak acoustic signals from patterns of pupillary activity preceding behavioral response* (Tech. Rep. No. 140). Los Angeles: University of California, Dept. of Psychology.

Beatty, J. (1982). Task-evoked pupillary responses, processing load, and the structure of processing resources. *Psychological Bulletin, 91*, 276–292.

Beatty, J. (1986). The pupillary system. In M. G. H. Coles, E. Donchin, & S. W. Porges (Eds.), *Psychophysiology: Systems, processes & applications* (pp. 43–50). New York: Guilford.

Beatty, J., & Kahneman, D. (1966). Pupillary changes in two memory tasks. *Psychonomic Science, 5*, 371–372.

Bernick, N., Kling, A., & Borowitz, G. (1971). Physiological differentiation of sexual arousal and anxiety. *Psychosomatic Medicine, 33*, 341–352.

Carver, R. P. (1971). Pupil dilation and its relationship to information processing during reading and listening. *Journal of Applied Psychology, 55*, 126–134.

Chapman, L. J., Chapman, J. P., & Brelje, T. (1969). Influence of the experimenter on pupillary dilation to sexually provocative pictures. *Journal of Abnormal Psychology, 74*, 396–400.

Chapman, C. R., Oka, S., Bradshaw, D. H., Jacobson, R. C., & Donaldson, G. W. (1999). Phasic pupil dilation response to noxious stimulation in normal volunteers: Relationship to brain evoked potentials and pain report. *Psychophysiology, 36*, 44–52.

Clark, W. R., & Ertas, M. A. (1975). A comparison of pupillary reactions to visual and auditory stimuli in a test of preferences for presidental candidates. JSAS: *Catalog of Selected Documents in Psychology*.

Colman, F., & Paivio, A. (1970). Pupillary dilation and mediation processes during paired-association learning. *Canadian Journal of Psychology, 24*, 261–270.

Darwin, C. (1872). *The expression of the emotions in man and animals*. Chicago: University of Chicago Press (1965, reprinted from the authorized edition of D. Appleton & Co., New York).

Friedman, D., Hakerem, G., Sutton, S., & Fleiss, J. L. (1973). Effect of stimulus uncertainty on the pupillary dilation response and the vertex evoked potential. *Electroencephalography and Clinical Neurophysiology, 74*, 272–283.

Geacintov, T., & Peavler, W. (1974). Pupillography in industrial fatigue assessment. *Journal of Applied Psychology, 59*, 213–216.

Granholm, E., Asarnow, R. F., Sarkin, A. J., & Dykes, K. L. (1996). Pupillary responses index cognitive resource limitations. *Psychophysiology, 33*, 457–461.

Granholm, E., Morris, S. K., Sarkin, A. J., Asarnow, R. F., & Jeste, D. V. (1997). Pupillary responses index overload of working memory resources in schizophrenia. *Journal of Abnormal Psychology, 106*, 358–367.

Guyton, A. C. (1977). *Basic human physiology: Normal function and mechanisms of disease*. Philadelphia: Saunders.

Hakerem, G. (1967). Pupillography. In P. H. Venables & I. Martin (Eds.), *Manual of psychophysiological methods* (pp. 335–349). Amsterdam: North-Holland.

Hakerem, G., & Sutton, S. (1966). Pupillary response at visual threshold. *Nature, 212*, 485–486.

Hamel, R. F. (1974). Female subjective and pupillary reaction to nude male and female figures. *Journal of Psychology, 87*, 171–175.

Hess, E. H. (1972). Pupillometrics. In N. S. Greenfield & R. A. Sternbach (Eds.), *Handbook of psychophysiology* (pp. 491–531). New York: Holt, Rinehart & Winston.

Hess, E. H. (1975). *The tell-tale eye*. New York: Van Nostrand Reinhold.

Hess, E. H., & Petrovich, S. B. (1978). Pupillary behavior in communication. In A. W. Siegman, & S. Feldstein (Eds.), *Nonverbal behavior communication* (pp. 159–179). Hillsdale, NJ: Lawrence Erlbaum Associates.

Hess, E. H., & Polt, J. M. (1960). Pupil size as related to interest value of visual stimuli. *Science, 132*, 349–350.

Hess, E. H., & Polt, J. M. (1964). Pupil size in relation to mental activity during simple problem solving. *Science, 143*, 1190–1192.

Hess, E. H., Seltzer, A. L., & Shlien, J. M. (1965). Pupil responses of hetero- and homosexual males to pictures of men and women: A pilot study. *Journal of Abnormal Psychology, 70*, 165–168.

Hicks, R. A., Williams, S. L., & Ferrante, F. (1979). Pupillary attributions of college students to happy and angry faces. *Perceptual & Motor Skills, 48*, 401–402.

Janisse, M. P. (1974). Pupil size, affect and exposure frequency. *Social Behavior & Personality, 2*, 125–146.

Janisse, M. P. (1977). *Pupillometry*. Washington, DC: Hemispheric Publishing.

Just, M. A., & Carpenter, P. A. (1993). The intensity dimension of thought: Pupillometric indices of sentence processing. *Canadian Journal of Experimental Psychology, 47*, 310–339.

Kahneman, D., & Beatty, J. (1967). Pupillary responses in a pitch-discrimination task. *Perception & Psychophysics, 2*, 101–105.

Kahneman, D., & Peavler, W. S. (1969). Incentive effects and pupillary changes in association learning. *Journal of Experimental Psychology, 79*, 312–318.

Kahneman, D., & Wright, P. (1971). Changes of pupil size and rehearsal strategies in a short-term memory task. *Quarterly Journal of Experimental Psychology, 23*, 187–196.

Libby, W. L., Lacey, B. C., & Lacey, J. I. (1973). Pupillary and cardiac activity during visual attention. *Psychophysiology, 10*, 270–294.

Loewenfield, I. E. (1966). Pupil size. *Survey of Ophthalmology, 11*, 291–294.

Lowenstein, O., & Loewenfield, I. E. (1962). The pupil. In H. Davson (Ed.), *The eye:* Vol. 3, *Muscular mechanisms* (pp. 301–340). New York: Academic Press.

Lowenstein, O., & Loewenfield, I. E. (1964). The sleep–waking cycle and pupillary activity. *Annals of the New York Academy of Sciences, 117*, 142–156.

McReynolds, P. (1960). Anxiety, perception, and schizophrenia. In D. D. Jackson (Ed.), *Etiology of schizophrenia* (pp. 248–292). New York: Basic Books.

Miller, G. A. (1956). The magical number seven, plus or minus two: Some limits of our capacity for processing information. *Psychological Review, 63*, 81–97.

Paivio, A., & Simpson, H. M. (1966). The effect of word abstractness and pleasantness on pupil size during an imaginary task. *Psychonomic Science, 5*, 55–56.

Peavler, W. S. (1974). Pupil size, information overload, and performance differences. *Psychophysiology, 11*, 559–566.

Peavler, W. S., & McLaughlin, J. P. (1967). The question of stimulus content and pupil size. *Psychonomic Science, 8*, 505–506.

Polt, J. M. (1970). Effect of threat of shock on pupillary response in a problem-solving situation. *Perception & Motor Skills, 31*, 587–593.

Poock, G. K. (1973). Information processing vs. pupil diameter. *Perceptual & Motor Skills, 37*, 1000–1002.

Qiyuan, J., Richer, F., Waggoner, B. L., & Beatty, J. (1985). The pupil and stimulus probability. *Psychophysiology, 22*, 530–534.

Simms, T. M. (1967). Pupillary response of male and female subjects to pupillary difference in male and female picture stimuli. *Perception & Psychophysics, 2*, 553–555.

Stanners, R. F., Headley, D. B., & Clark, W. R. (1972). The pupillry response to sentences: Influences of listening set and deep structure. *Journal of Verbal Learning and Verbal Behavior, 11*, 257–263.

Stelmack, R. M., & Mandelzys, N. (1975). Extraversion and pupillary response to affective and taboo words. *Psychophysiology, 12*, 536–540.

Steinhauer, S. R., van Kammen, D. P., Colbert, K., Peters, J. L., & Zubin, J. (1992). Pupillary constriction during halperidol treatment as a predictor of relapse following drug withdrawal in schizophrenic patients. *Psychiatry Research, 43*, 287–298.

Stern, J. A., & Dunham, D. N. (1990). The ocular system. In J. T. Cacioppo & L. G. Tassinary (Eds.), *Principles of psychophysiology* (pp. 193–215). Cambridge, England: Cambridge University Press.

Tarrahian, G. A., & Hicks, R. A. (1979). Attribution of pupil size as a function of facial valence and age in American and Persian children. *Journal of Cross Cultural Psychology, 10*, 243–250.

Tryon, W. W. (1975). Pupillometry: A survey of sources of variation. *Psychophysiology, 12*, 90–93.

White, G. L., & Maltzman, I. (1977). Pupillary activity while listening to verbal passages. *Journal of Research in Personality, 12*, 361–369.

Williams, S. L., & Hicks, R. A. (1980). Sex, iride pigmentation, and the pupillary attribution of college students to happy and angry faces. *Bulletin of the Psychonomic Society Society, 10*, 67–68.

Woodmansee, J. J. (1967, August). *The pupil reaction as an index of positive and negative affect*. Paper presented at the convention of the American Psychological Association, Washington, DC.

Zahn, T. P., Frith, C. D., & Steinhauer, S. R. (1991). Autonomic functioning in schizophrenia: Electrodermal activity, heart rate, pupillography. In S. R. Steinhauer, J. H. Gruzelier, & J. Zubin (Eds.), *Handbook of schizophrenia, Vol. 5: Neuropsychology, psychophysiology & information processing* (pp. 185–224). Amsterdam: Elsevier.

11

Eye Movements, Eye Blinks, and Behavior

The process of measuring eye movements in different environmental contexts is called *electroculography* (EOG). The EOG technique is concerned with measuring changes in electrical potential that occur when the eyes move. Eye movements enable the visual system to acquire information by scanning relevant aspects of the environment. Object recognition, discrimination, and other information intake by the visual system is accomplished mostly through unconscious scanning eye movements. The major part of processing the new information takes place when the eyes make brief pauses. The EOG has been useful in a wide range of applications from the rapid eye movements measured in sleep studies to the recording of visual fixations during perception, visual search, the experience of illusions and in psychopathology. Studies of reading, eye movements during real and simulated car driving, radar scanning, and reading instrument dials under vibrating conditions have been some of the practical tasks examined with eye movement recordings.

Eye blinks are easily recorded with EOG procedures and are particularly useful in studies of eyelid conditioning as a control for possible eyeblink contamination in EEG research, and as measures of fatigue, lapses in attention, and stress. There are also the periodic eye blinks that occur throughout the waking day that serve to moisten the eyeball. Still another type of eyeblink is that which occurs to a sudden loud stimulus, considered to be a component of the *startle reflex*. The startle eyeblink is largely muscular and is related to activity in the muscles that close the lids of the eye. Research on the eyeblink component of startle has revealed interesting findings that have implications for both attentional and emotional processes. The sections to follow include information about the anatomy and physiology of the system that controls movements of the eye, how these movements are measured and how psychologists have related them to behavioral phenomena.

EYE MOVEMENTS (EOG)

The Control of Eye Movements

Eye movements are controlled by cortical and subcortical systems in conjunction with cranial nerves and sets of eye muscles attached to the outside of each eyeball. The cerebral areas involved in eye fixations are the occipital and frontal cortices. Innervation of the eye muscles is by the third (oculomotor), fourth (trochlear), and sixth (abducens) cranial nerves. They influence movements of three separate pairs of eye muscles: the superior and inferior rectus, the lateral and medial rectus, and the superior and inferior obliques (see Fig. 11.1). The superior and inferior recti contract to move the eyes up or down. The lateral and medial recti allow

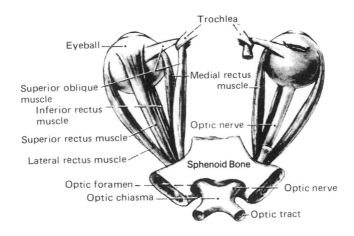

FIG. 11.1. Extrinsic muscles of the eye. (Inferior oblique muscle not shown.)

movements from side to side, and the obliques control rotation of the eyeballs. The three sets of muscles are reciprocally innervated to allow one pair to relax while another pair contracts. The purpose of eye movements is to fixate objects to allow their images to fall on the foveal region of the eye, that is, the area of sharpest vision.

Fixation movements of the eye are controlled by two different neural mechanisms (Guyton, 1977). Voluntary fixations of the eyes on some object of choice, for example, the quick movements made while reading, are controlled by a small area in the premotor cortex of the frontal lobes (Area 8). The use of positron emission tomography (PET) scans has shown increased blood flow in Area 8 while subjects looked back and forth between two fixed targets, or imagined looking at memorized targets (Wirtschafter & Weingarden, 1988). It is known that the superior colliculus of the midbrain plays an important role in successive eye fixations (saccades) in cooperation with the frontal cortical eye fields (Area 8). The maintenance of involuntary fixation and slow following movements (pursuit movements) are controlled by areas in the occipital cortex. The operation of this intricate eye movement system can be disrupted by brain damage due to disease or stroke, and by common drugs, including alcohol and barbiturates. Abnormalities of pursuit eye movements have been reported with persons suffering Korsakoff's syndrome, Parkinson's disease, Alzheimer's, and Huntington's disease, all of which involve brain damage (see chapter 16 section on "eye movements and neurological disease").

Shackel (1967) identified three common types of eye movements:

1. Saccadic—This refers to movements of the eyes from one fixation point to the next. A fixation pause lasts for about $1/4$ to 1 sec, and the saccade (movement) lasts for approximately $1/50$ to $1/10$ of 1 sec, depending on how long it takes to make the next fixation. Saccadic movements occur so quickly that they occupy only 10% of the total time spent in eye movements, whereas fixation accounts for 90% of the time (Guyton, 1977). Visual processing of information generally takes place only during fixations.

2a. Smooth Pursuit—This is the eye movement that occurs when a moving object is fixated and followed by the eyes. The rate of movement can closely approximate that of the object, up to 60 degrees per second and beyond. (In this case, perception can occur while the eye is in motion.)

2b. Smooth Compensatory—This is a movement to correct for body or head tilt to maintain an upright view of the visual field. It is an automatic or reflex activity.

3. Nystagmoid—These are oscillations of the eyes, often consisting of slow horizontal sweeps and quick returns to the original eye position. There are three causes of nystagmoid movements: (a) where eye defects or the visual field prevent adequate fixation; (b) when the vestibular, or balance, system of the inner ear is impaired; or (c) when there is impairment of visual or vestibular pathways in the CNS. It should be noted that small spontaneous saccadic drifts, and other movements, occur in the normal eye at rest. When these small movements are effectively eliminated, for example, by stabilizing an image on a certain portion of the retina through optical techniques, a fixated image gradually fades and disappears.

To these three basic varieties of eye movement, we add the rapid eye movements (REM) of sleep and lid closures known as eye blinks. The REMs of sleep occur sporadically, are variable in amplitude, and last from a few minutes to a half-hour or more. Blinking of the eyelids lasts about .2 to .4 sec and, on the average, occurs at 2- to 10-sec intervals, with wide individual variability. An exception to the .2 to .4 sec eyeblink duration is the .04 sec eyeblink that occurs when it is part of the startle response. More will be said about this eyeblink component of startle in a subsequent section.

Stern and Dunham (1990) outlined a number of saccade variables of interest to psychophysiologists who wish to relate these to behavior: *saccade latency* is the time between the presentation of a stimulus and the time it takes the eye to fixate it; *saccade amplitude* is the distance covered by the eye between initiation and termination of the saccade; *direction of movement* is a determination of vertical or horizontal movement; *velocity* is the speed of saccade; and *fixation pause time* occurs between one fixation and the next. In addition, Stern and Dunham specify several ways to analyze eye blinks. These include *blink amplitude*, *blink closure duration*, and *blink frequency*.

The Nature of Eye Blinks

An eyeblink occurs when the upper and lower lids appear to touch and the eye is temporarily hidden. Eyeblinks occur in humans and most vertebrates (Tecce, 1992). There are three types of blinks: one voluntary and two involuntary. Voluntary blinks occur with a conscious decision to momentarily close the eyes. One type of involuntary blink is considered to be protective and is produced in response to some potentially harmful stimulus such as an intense light or noise, and is referred to as a *blink reflex*. A second type of involuntary blink occurs spontaneously about 15,000 times per day (Tecce, 1992) and keeps the cornea healthy by enabling a layer of moisture to form continuously. The average blink rate for humans is about 15 to 20 times per min in a quiet, relaxed state.

The rate of blinking is closely related to psychological factors including mood state and task demands. For example, when a task requires close attention to events, then blink rate decreases. The blink rate can drop to 3 per min during reading. Blink rate increases when an individual is under time pressure or some other kind of stress. Increased blinking has also been noted when errors are made in memorizing digits, just before quitting a difficult problem-solving task, and during poor performance caused by fatigue (Tecce, 1992). A decrease in blink rate has been associated with relaxation and with successful problem solving. It has been hypothesized that increased blinking is associated with negative feelings and decreases with more pleasant psychological states.

Recording Eye Movements and Eye Blinks

Four of the basic methods commonly used to measure eye movements are the contact-lens method, the corneal reflection method, television camera scanning, and a technique termed *electrooculography* (EOG). The EOG technique is briefly outlined here and is the most commonly used by psychophysiologists in their study of eye movements. The basis for the EOG is the steady (approximately .40–1 mV) potential difference that exists between the cornea and retina of the eye. The cornea is electrically positive, whereas the back of the eye at the retina is negative. When the eyes are fixed straight ahead, recording electrodes detect a steady baseline potential. When eye movements occur, the potential across the electrodes changes and a corresponding deflection is produced in the pen of a recorder. When the eyes move, the potential at the electrode becomes more positive or negative, depending on the direction of movement. The EOG can record eye movements up to 70 degrees to the left and right of central fixation, to an accuracy of about 1.5 to 2.0 degrees. Electrode pairs placed horizontally on the skin surface, at the corners of the eyes, detect horizontal movements. Electrodes placed above and below the eyes detect vertical movements. What is really being detected is a change in DC potential that is produced when the eyes move (see Fig. 11.2).

The pen deflection in the ink-writing system will be either positive or negative, depending on the polarity of the connections, and the amplitude of the deflection is linearly related to the extent of movement, up to about 30 degrees from center. Horizontal movements may be recorded by measuring across one eye or across both eyes with electrodes placed near the external canthus (outside) of each eye (see Fig. 11.3). For monocular recording, one electrode must be at the side of the nose near the internal canthus, with the other at the external canthus. The EOG recorded from one eye is considered to reflect the position of the other eye unless stated differently. The binocular measure provides more reliable results (Shackel, 1967).

For precise recordings, the electrodes must be placed adjacent to the horizontal plane passing through the cornea of the eye. Researchers commonly use a binocular placement for horizontal eye movement, and monocular for vertical movements.

Problems in EOG Recordings.   Shackel (1967) described three problems in the recording of EOG: (a) the small magnitude of the EOG signal, (b) the existence of skin potentials in the same frequency band as EOG signals, and (c) slow drift, often caused by unclean electrodes and poor contact. The first of these problems can be overcome through the use of a suitable, sensitive recorder. Most physiological recording devices are satisfactory, provided they

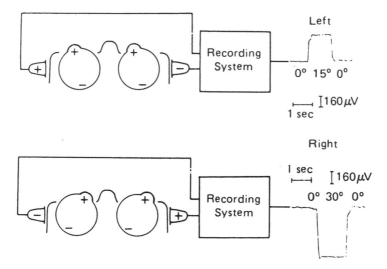

FIG. 11.2. Basis of electrooculography. The eyeball is like a small battery. As it rotates, the poles of the "battery" come nearer to the respective electrodes on the adjacent skin. The change in direct potential, and thus the angle of rotation, can be recorded.

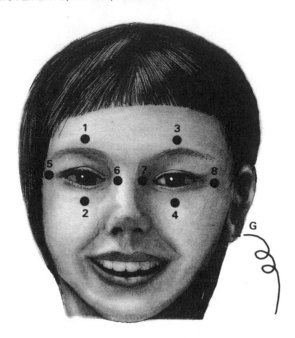

FIG. 11.3. Placement of electrodes for eye movement recordings. Electrodes 1 and 2, 3 and 4 are for vertical movement recordings. Electrodes 5 and 6, and 7 and 8 are for horizontal recordings (monocular). The most common horizontal placements are 5 and 8 (binocular). Vertical recordings are usually monocular. G, ground electrode is located at mastoid area, behind the ear.

have appropriate couplers for DC recordings. The skin potential response can be minimized by careful preparation of the skin underlying the electrode by rubbing the area with a wet cloth, a cotton ball, or with a slightly abrasive electrode paste. Another possible problem, that of slow drift, may be minimized by following the preparation routine outlined next.

Preparation of Electrodes and Subject.   The electrodes used for EOG measurement are similar to the small disc or cup electrodes used in EEG recordings. They may be made of either silver or stainless steel. The electrodes should be nonpolarizing, small, and light enough to enable attachment with surgical tape or an adhesive collar. The DC drift caused by electrode polarization can be recognized as a steady deflection of the recording pen in one direction. Electrodes should be kept in an airtight container, washed in distilled water, and then placed in a saline solution with the leads shorted together before use. Paste is then applied to the electrodes before they are placed on the skin.

When using adhesive collars, one side is attached to the electrode and paste is applied to fill the electrode through the collar opening. Then the collar is attached to the skin surface and the leads are connected to the recording device. After proper preparation, skin resistance between the electrodes should be less than 2,000 ohms. The subject's head must be kept in a fixed position with regard to the center of the visual field. Some researchers employ a chin rest to accomplish this, whereas others make an impression of the subjects' teeth in dental plastic and have them position their mouth on this "bite board" before each trial. As the head is fixed in place, the system is calibrated directly in degrees of eye movement by having subjects fixate on a series of points at known angles of eye rotation. The gain may be adjusted so that one division on the recording paper equals 1 or 2 degrees of eye movement. Typical recordings of saccadic and pursuit movements are depicted in Fig. 11.4. The records shown in Fig. 11.4 are monocular for the vertical movements and binocular for the horizontal ones.

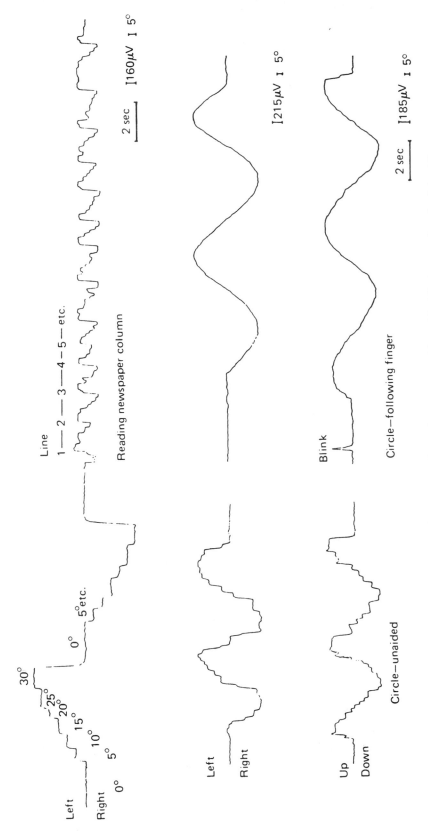

FIG. 11.4. Typical recordings of saccadic and pursuit movements. The subject fixates a series of points at 5 deg. intervals, reads a newspaper column, tries to scan smoothly around a circle by himself, and follows a fingertip drawn around the circle. Note also the typical wave form of a blink, on the vertical recording only, with sharp rise and fall and short duration.

239

The careful recording of EOG can result in a great deal of stability and repeatability of results over a period of time.

EYE MOVEMENTS AND BEHAVIOR

The next few sections discuss the measurement of eye movements during mental activities, visual search, and perception. Included under mental activities are learning, problem solving, hemispheric dominance and eye movement, reading efficiency and disabilities, and the possible utility of a particular type of EOG as a genetic marker in psychopathology.

Mental Activity and Eye Movements

The primary function of eye movements is to allow the eyes to alter their position and focus on objects of interest. Saccadic movements bring objects into foveal vision through quick adjustments, whereas pursuit motions adjust eye movements to moving objects. Psychophysiological studies of eye movement patterns have related them to mental activities, such as learning and problem solving.

Eye Movements and Learning

A series of experiments by McCormack and colleagues have used eye movements in conjunction with paired-associates learning to support a two-stage conceptualization of verbal learning. In paired-associates learning, a subject first sees two columns of words (word pairs) one at a time. After the lists have been presented, a single column (stimulus words) is presented with the request that the items in the now absent column (response words) be recalled as each stimulus word appears. It is hypothesized that subjects consolidate responses during an initial, or "response-learning," phase and then connect responses to stimuli in a second, or "hook-up" stage. These researchers have found, for example, that efficient performers spend more time fixating on the stimulus word from the outset in a learning task, as compared to inefficient learners (Haltrecht & McCormack, 1966).

In another experiment, it was found that fixation of response words decreased as learning progressed, whereas time spent viewing the stimulus words increased (McCormack, Haltrecht, & Hannah, 1967). Further, viewing time of response and stimulus words diverged more quickly when subjects learned an easy list (word pairs with high similarity) than when they performed with a difficult list (low similarity) (McCormack, Hannah, Bradley, & Moore, 1967). Thus, there is evidence here that is consistent with the idea that eye movement pattern varies with efficiency and stage of learning, and it may differ with difficulty of the learning task.

Eye Movements, Problem Solving, and Laterality

Problem Solving.   Eye movements of subjects were measured as they were presented with two horizontal arrays of pictures under three conditions: (a) when no problem solving was required, (b) when the pictures were used in the solution of a problem, and (c) after problem solving (Nakano, 1971). The average number of eye fixations was greatest when the pictures were needed to solve the problems, and lowest after problem solving was completed. Ehrlichman and Barrett (1983) studied saccadic eye movements made during two kinds of cognitive activity; verbal–linguistic and visual–imaginal, which did not require viewing of stimuli. Previous research suggested that people make more eye movements to questions calling for verbal processes than to those requiring visual imagery. A sample verbal question was

"What does this proverb mean: One today is worth two tomorrows?"; and a sample imaginal question was "What does your stove look like?" Prior work was confirmed, because resting eye movement rates were close to rates associated with imagery questions, whereas rates for verbal questions were much higher. Ehrlichman and Barrett suggested that the differences in eye movement rate reflect differences in internal sampling rate or shifts in cognitive operations. According to this view, interpreting a proverb would require more cognitive operations than generating, inspecting, and describing an image.

Hemispheric Dominance and Eye Movement.   An interesting observation by Teitlebaum (1954) concerned the movement of a person's eyes either to the left or right when reflecting on a question asked by another. This observation was investigated in more detail by Day (1964), who confirmed that the eyes move leftward or rightward in a consistent manner after persons had been asked a question requiring some thought. For example, you might ask a person to spell "Mississippi." The individual is usually unaware of the lateral movement, which can easily be seen by an observer sitting opposite to the subject. It has been hypothesized that those persons who move their eyes rightward are left hemisphere dominant, whereas those who move their eyes to the left are presumed to be right-hemisphere dominant (Bakan, 1969).

Some evidence to support this proposal was obtained by Kinsbourne (1972), who found that right-handed subjects had a tendency to move their eyes to the right for verbal problems and either up or to the left for spatial problems. Hence, the eyes moved in a direction opposite to the hemisphere involved in the solution of the problem. Kinsbourne proposed that stimulation of oculomotor areas of the left frontal lobe causes lateral eye movements to the right, whereas stimulation of frontal eye fields of the right hemisphere produces eye movements to the left.

One researcher tested right-handed males on spatial and verbal problems when sitting behind them and when facing them (Gur, 1975). The filmed eye movements showed that they moved leftward with spatial problems and rightward for verbal problems when the experimenter sat behind. This finding agreed with previous ones. However, when the experimenter faced the subjects, the eyes moved predominantly in one direction, either left or right, regardless of problem type. Thus, the influence of problem type seems to be maximized when the experimenter's presence is minimized. It has also been found that eye movements of left-handers were uncorrelated with problem type, even when the experimenter sat behind (Gur, Gur, & Harris, 1975). This result supports the view that right-handers show a higher degree of hemisphere specialization for various functions than do left-handers.

None of the studies mentioned thus far used a physiological measure of brain activation to support the concept of contralateral hemispheric activation with direction of gaze. To partially fill this empirical gap, Shevrin, Smokler, and Kooi (1980) asked whether a disposition to look either left or right to questions would be related to larger brain responses (event-related brain potentials) on the contralateral side. The subjects were right-handed, and results showed that left-looking persons had larger right hemisphere ERP amplitudes to visual stimuli. The opposite was true for right-looking subjects. Thus, the results supported the idea that the hemisphere contralateral to the direction of gaze was more responsive.

A closer link between lateral eye movements and brain activity was provided in a study that measured both simultaneously during a cognitive task (Neubauer, Schulter, & Pfurtscheller, 1988). Right-handed male subjects were used and greater EEG activation in the hemisphere contralateral to predominant direction of gaze was observed for both left-movers and right-movers. This finding was obtained under certain conditions of experimental task and recording (providing synonyms for words), EEG frequency (8–12 Hz), scalp site (temporal–anterior areas), and sampling period (EEG epoch 1 sec before the response). The findings led the authors to suggest that lateral eye movements are not the result of differential hemispheric activation, but are required for the development of a preferred hemisphere activation. This suggestion is contrary to that of Kinsbourne and further implies that lateral eye movements are required for lateralized cognitive processing. Further studies that simultaneously record EOG and hemispheric brain activity during a cognitive task will be required to clear up this issue.

Summary.   Studies of eye movements during learning show differential patterns as a function of efficiency, stage of learning, and difficulty of materials. Findings from problem-solving studies suggest that lateralization of brain function may be reflected by the direction of eye movement. The eyes move rightward for verbal analytic problems and leftward for spatial problems, indicating activation of the contralateral hemisphere. A greater degree of lateralization for right-handers is also evidenced by the experimental findings. Preliminary evidence exists for a relationship between tendency to move the eyes to the left or right during a cognitive task and brain activity in the contralateral hemisphere.

Eye Movements and Reading

Reading Efficiency.   The study of eye movements during reading has been an area of research since the early 1900s (Woodworth, 1938). Comparisons of eye movement patterns of slow and fast readers have been conducted in applied contexts to determine whether this information could be used in the development of remedial reading programs. A study by Buswell (1920), cited by Woodworth and Schlosberg (1954), examined the eye movement reading patterns of students at 13 levels from first grade to college. The results gave some insights into the development of reading skills: (a) there was a steady decrease in number of eye fixations per line of reading material with higher grade levels (18.6 in first grade and 5.9 in college); (b) the fixations became shorter in duration (660 msec in first grade and 252 msec at college level); and (c) the number of regressive movements decreased from an average of 5.1 per line for first graders to .5 for college students. Regressive movement refers to returning the eyes to earlier portions of the material being read. Studies of slow and fast readers at the same level indicated that more efficient readers made fewer and shorter duration eye fixations and had fewer regressive movements than inefficient readers.

Reading Disabilities and Eye Movements.   The study of eye movements and reading continued through the 1930s and 1940s (Venezky, 1977), but, subsequently, not much else was done in this area until researchers became interested in studying the eye movements of dyslexics and other individuals with reading difficulties. For example, Lefton (1978) studied the eye movement patterns of fifth-grade children with reading disabilities while they did a letter-matching task. For his experiment, Lefton defined reading-disabled children as those of normal intelligence and no sensory defects, whose reading scores were 1½ grades below average. The results showed that the reading-disabled children needed an unusually large number of eye fixations to do the task, more than did normal-reading third graders. Lefton argued that abnormal eye movement patterns are the result of poor reading, and that training in systematic gathering of information should help poor readers. Lefton's position has been supported by studies reporting no difference between the eye movements of dyslexics and normal controls in a tracking task (Olson, Kleigl, & Davidson, 1983; Stanley, Smith, & Howell, 1983) but abnormal eye movements for dyslexics while reading (Olson et al., 1983). However, Pavlidis (1981) reported differences between dyslexics and normal readers' eye movements in a tracking task. The chief characteristic of dyslexics was the excessive number of regressive eye movements made while fixating on sequentially illuminated rows of lights.

A number of attempts to repeat the finding of a relationship between dyslexia and faulty eye movements in nonreading tasks have not been successful (Pirozzolo & Rayner, 1988).

Pavlidis (1985) pointed out that although there is a research consensus about the erratic eye movements of dyslexics during reading, the hypotheses proposed to explain these differences vary among investigators. The three types of hypotheses are: (a) erratic eye movements reflect problems that dyslexics have with the reading material; (b) erratic eye movements cause dyslexia; (c) erratic eye movements and dyslexia are symptoms of independent but parallel brain deficits. Much of the recent research suggests that defective oculomotor control is not a causal factor in dyslexia, but that the dyslexic's abnormal eye movements in reading are due to cognitive problems such as deficits in processing information. Therefore, remedial reading programs for dyslexics should emphasize the development of thinking and information-processing strategies, not the pacing of eye movements. It has been noted that attempts to train disabled readers to make smooth, regular eye movements have been unsuccessful in remediating the problem (Pirozzolo & Rayner, 1988).

Summary.   Studies of eye movements and reading show that more experienced and more efficient readers make fewer and shorter fixations and do not regress to already fixated material as much as less experienced and inefficient readers. The majority of research findings indicate that defective eye movement control is not a causal factor in reading problems such as dyslexia. This suggests that remedial reading programs should focus on the development of information-processing strategies in assisting those with reading difficulties.

Eye Movements and Psychopathology

Schizophrenia.   A great deal of attention has been focused over the past 20 years on the link between intrusions of saccadic eye movements into smooth pursuit tracking and the presence of schizophrenia. The possibility of using deviant pursuit tracking eye movements as genetic markers in schizophrenia has been proposed by Holzman and associates (e.g., see Holzman, Proctor, & Hughes, 1973). They found that schizophrenics have difficulty following a slowly moving target that is in continuous motion. Other investigators have also reported on the inability of many schizophrenic patients to produce intact smooth eye movements (Iacono, 1988). The eye movement abnormalities have also been observed in a large proportion of relatives of schizophrenics, even though these persons are not schizophrenic themselves. This finding suggests that pursuit-tracking deficits are under genetic control and that it could possibly be used as a marker for individuals who may be predisposed to becoming schizophrenic (Iacono, 1988). Figure 11.5 shows the pursuit tracking records of three sisters (A, B, and C), all of whom were diagnosed as chronic schizophrenics. The top trace (T) shows the movement of the target and how a perfect tracking protocol would appear.

Findings that support a genetic relationship include those of Iacono and Lykken (1979), who studied eye movements of normal identical twins during tracking. The subjects were required to track a spot of light across a screen; both smooth pursuit and saccadic eye movements were analyzed. The eye movement patterns of the twins were very similar. Long-term stability was dramatized in a follow-up conducted with 52 of the original twins 2 years later (Iacono & Lykken, 1981). Smooth pursuit and saccadic eye tracking proficiency were consistent with performance measured 2 years earlier, indicating that the tasks can tap into relatively stable and inherited traits. In a large-scale study of psychotic patients, normals, and first-degree relatives, it was found that pursuit tracking dysfunction was specific to schizophrenics and their relatives and only infrequently observed in other psychotic patients and normals (Iacono, Moreau, Beiser, Fleming, & Lin, 1992). Another significant study provides evidence for a major gene, but not necessarily the only one, that affects smooth pursuit tracking dysfunction (Grove, Clementz,

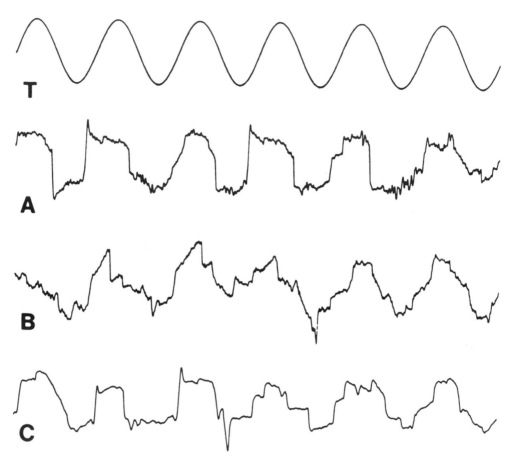

FIG. 11.5. Examples of smooth pursuit eye tracking protocols from three sisters, ages 31 (A), 27 (B), and 36 (C). All were diagnosed as having chronic schizophrenia. The uppermost tracing (T) depicts the movement of the target and indicates how a perfect tracking response should appear. In this figure the EOG was used to record the eye movement response to a target oscillating at .4Hz and traveling 20 degrees of visual arc. (Figure courtesy of Dr. William G. Iacono).

Iacono, & Katsanis, 1992). Taken together, these results suggest that eye tracking difficulties may one day serve as a genetic marker for schizophrenia risk.

One researcher contended that in schizophrenics, eye movement deficits occur because of frontal lobe dysfunction (Levin, 1984). She further suggested that the disorder in frontal eye fields manifests itself as an inability to inhibit saccades and that is why they intrude into the smooth pursuit eye tracking of schizophrenics. Other researchers have reported that male college students identified as having impaired smooth pursuit eye movements were more likely to have a "schizotypal" personality diagnosis than those who are high-accuracy trackers (Siever, Coursey, Alterman, Buchsbaum, & Murphy, 1984). They suggested that the tracking deficit might reflect a vulnerability for this type of disorder.

The significance of saccadic interruptions in smooth pursuit EOGs is still not certain, despite suggestions that it might be a biological marker of schizophrenia. Still unanswered is whether the saccades that are present during poor pursuit performance introduce error through their appearance, or whether they represent attempts to correct errors in pursuit tracking. Also requiring greater definition are the precise nature of the tracking deficit, and the pattern of familial transmission (see Iacono, 1988; Iacono & Clementz, 1993). In a recent study, Yee, Nuechterlein, and Dawson (1998) asked whether eye-tracking deficiencies found in recent-onset schizo-phrenics could be improved with strategies that enhance attentional mechanisms. One of their suggestions was that attentional functioning might deteriorate in chronic schizophrenia as a re-sult of long-term medication effects and adaptation to chronic illness. Indeed, the researchers found that attentional enhancement improved eye-tracking performance of recent-onset schizo-phrenics more than it did with normal controls over a 1-year period. The attentional manipula-tion involved introducing color changes in the pursuit tracking target, and reminders to keep fol-lowing the target. One possible explanation offered by the authors is that voluntary attention may be diminished as schizophrenia progresses and they call for additional studies of the rela-tionship between defective pursuit tracking and ability to maintain voluntary attention.

Manic Depression.   A study by Gooding, Iacono, Katsanis, Beiser, and Grove (1993) was conducted to see whether tracking performance of manic-depressive patients on lithium carbonate medication would differ from patients not receiving medication. The results indi-cated that lithium carbonate did not worsen pursuit performance, and overall patient per-formance supports the idea that smooth pursuit dysfunction is specific to schizophrenia.

Summary.   There is consensus that schizophrenics have deficits in pursuit tracking. The questions of attentional and long-term medication effects still need to be settled. Tracking performance is stable over time, and there is evidence that a major gene affects eye-tracking dysfunction. It has been suggested that the deficit has its basis in a disorder affecting the frontal eye fields (Area 8 in the frontal lobes). Others have suggested a contribution of brain stem mechanisms to the eye tracking difficulties. Workers in the field have proposed that eye-tracking dysfunction may one day serve as a genetic marker for schizophrenia.

Eye Movements and Perception

The measurement of eye movements has been utilized by several investigators interested in the problems of pattern recognition and discrimination. In a study by Gould and Schaffer (1967), subjects were alternately instructed to find patterns that either matched or did not match a standard pattern. Eye movement recordings indicated that subjects spent more time fixating patterns that exactly matched a memorized standard than on those that differed, sug-gesting that detailed comparisons of features were being made.

Scan Paths.   Noton and Stark (1971a, 1971b) analyzed eye movements of subjects while they viewed different patterns in a "learning" phase and during a "recognition phase." In the learning stage, they viewed five different patterns for 20 sec each. In the recognition phase, these five patterns were again viewed, along with five new ones. Analyses of eye movements indicat-ed that subjects followed similar paths for a given pattern, and the sequence of movements was usually the same in the recognition phase as it was in the learning stage. This led Noton and Stark to suggest that memory for features of a picture is established sequentially by the memory of eye movements required to look from one feature to the next. They termed the characteristic pattern of eye movements for a subject viewing a given stimulus a *scan path*. However, Luria and Strauss (1975) did not find consistent scanning strategies in their study. This led them to suggest that the use of a characteristic scanning technique may depend on the type of search task.

Pictoral Information.   What have eye movement studies revealed about how people look at pictures? A study by Mackworth and Morandi (1967) indicated that portions of a picture rated as highly informative by one group of people were fixated more frequently by another group of individuals who examined the pictures while their eye movements were measured.

Yarbus (1967) found different patterns of eye movements while subjects viewed the same painting of a family scene under a variety of instructions. For example, when asked to estimate the wealth of the family, fixations centered on furniture and on clothing worn by women. When asked to estimate the ages of people in the picture, eye fixations on faces became the most numerous. Thus, the information one wishes to derive from a visual scene will determine the pattern of eye movements used in examining the picture. In Fig. 11.6, eye movement patterns show the greatest number of fixations around the eyes, nose, mouth, and ear of the ancient Egyptian sculpture of queen Nefertiti during a free examination period of three minutes.

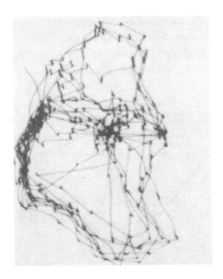

FIG. 11.6. The bottom photograph is a record of eye movements made during free examination of the top photograph with both eyes for 3 minutes.

Loftus (1972) found that durations of eye fixations did not affect recall of a picture, but the number of fixations made during a fixed period of viewing did affect later recognition. The greater the number of fixations, the more likely the person was to recognize the picture at another time. In another study, 20 subjects rated the informativeness of various regions in 10 pictures, and another 20 people viewed each of the pictures for 20 sec while their eye movements were measured (Antes, 1974). The findings were like those of Mackworth and Morandi (1967) because informative regions of pictures were fixated immediately. However, Antes also found that, whereas initial fixations were on informative areas, the less informative detail received a greater proportion of the fixations later in the viewing sequence. Data from this and previous experiments also suggest that observers use information from peripheral vision to fixate immediately on informative areas. Gould (1974) pointed out that people tend to fixate on contours more frequently than on other areas of a picture. This is because contours carry critical information as to the shape, and therefore the identification, of objects in the picture.

Summary.   Research findings on visual search indicate that significant portions of visual stimuli attract eye fixations. Characteristic scan paths appear to exist, but their role in pattern recognition has not been established. In looking at pictures, people tend to fixate on those areas that contain the most information, especially in the early stages of viewing. The purpose of viewers, in terms of the the type of information they are trying to extract, will also determine how they examine a scene. A higher number of fixations during a viewing period seems related to superior recall of that picture.

Eye Movements and Illusions

Muller–Lyer Illusion.   There has been some attention paid to the study of eye movements while persons experience various kinds of visual illusions. The familiar Muller–Lyer figure is one example. It will be recalled that the line with an attached arrowhead directed inward looks shorter than an identical line with the arrowhead directed outward. It has been found that with prolonged inspection, the magnitude of the illusion decreases, although it does not disappear completely. One explanation for this concerns feedback provided by erroneous eye movements regarding the nature of the distortion. If eye movements are restricted to one portion of the figure, less information will be fed back, and the illusion will persist to its full extent. An experiment that supports this eye movement hypothesis was conducted by Festinger, White, and Allyn (1968). They found that the Muller–Lyer illusion became less powerful when eye movements were made over the entire figure than when only one part of the figure was fixated. A similar result was found for the Oppel–Kundt figure, which also produces illusory differences in length of line (Coren & Hoenig, 1972). In the Oppel–Kundt illusion, a divided horizontal space (e.g., four equally spaced dots) is seen as having greater linear extent than a solid horizontal line of identical length (see inset of Fig. 11.7). Two groups of 15 subjects each observed this illusion. One group made saccadic eye movements over the entire length of the illusion, whereas the other group fixated on the junction between the divided and undivided space. The illusion decreased over time for the eye movement group but not for the fixation group (see Fig. 11.7).

Rebound Illusion.   Eye movements were recorded while subjects experienced a "rebound illusion" (Mack, Fendrich, & Sirigatti, 1973). The rebound illusion occurs when the eyes pursue a luminous object in the dark. Experiments by Mack and colleagues indicated that the illusion is caused by an overshoot of the target by the eye, at the point at which the

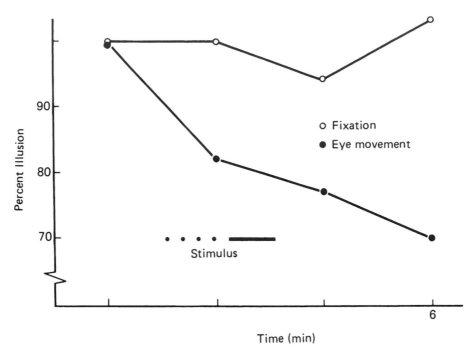

FIG. 11.7. Percentage of illusion is plotted against inspection time in minutes. The inset
shows the Oppel-Kundt stimulus configuration used in the experiment.

target stops. Thus, it appears that eye movement studies may provide valuable information regarding the bases for various kinds of visual illusion.

The Eye Blink (EB) in Cognition, Information Processing, and Stress

Tecce (1992) reviewed physical characteristics of blinks and their relation to some psychological phenomena. A typical blink, recorded via EOG, is about 380 μV in amplitude and lasts
120 msec. Spontaneous eye blinks occur throughout the day, at an average of 15 to 20 times
per minute for a relaxed person. Tecce indicates that since adults need only 2 to 4 blinks per
minute to keep the eyeball moist, most blinks are unecessary from a physiological viewpoint.

Cognitive Activity and Eye Blinks.   Activities that require thought lead to an increase
in blinking. For example, Andreassi (1973) reported a significant increase in EB frequency
when subjects were required to solve anagrams mentally, in a darkened room with eyes
closed, as compared to when they were resting with eyes closed. Tecce (1992) observed that
persons responding to interview questions or engaging in conversation show increases in
blink frequency. He also noted that blink frequency decreased when individuals gave close
attention to outside visual events, perhaps to facilitate information processing. Stern (1980)
observed that the oculomotor control system is very sensitive to fatigue, boredom, and lapses in attention.

Information Processing.   Stern and his associates found that long closure duration, the
time the eyes remain closed during blinking, is related to reduced alertness. They also noted
that during reading there is an inhibition of blinking, which becomes more pronounced as a
function of the reader's interest in the material. A flurry of blinks then occurs as the reader
turns the page. In one experiment, blink rate was found to increase from an initial average rate

of 15.7 blinks per min to 26.2 per min at the end of a 1-hr reaction time experiment (Stern, 1980). Blink closure duration followed a similar pattern, and was closely related to measures of reaction time performance.

In a study out of Stern's laboratory (Goldstein, Walrath, Stern, & Strock, 1985), it was discovered that blink rate and duration were both less in a visual task than an auditory one. Bauer, Strock, Goldstein, Stern, and Walrath (1985) argued that blink suppression is due to increased cognitive demand that directs attention to task-relevant stimuli. Their study of blinking during an auditory discrimination task led them to conclude that blinks are delayed until decisions about external stimuli have been made and responses to those stimuli completed. Thus, such variables as blink rate and duration may be related to cognitive functions such as decision making and discrimination.

An interesting association was found between saccades and blinking by Fogarty and Stern (1989). They found blinking to be time linked to saccadic eye movements in a way that would minimize the disruption of visual information processing. Another approach by Stern and his colleagues involved the recording of blink rate, duration and latency while individuals were engaged in a modified Sternberg task (Goldstein, Bauer, & Stern, 1992). A lower blink rate was found for a 6-item than a 2-item memory set. The authors suggested that the lower blink rate reflects the greater attention demanded of subjects performing the more difficult task involving 6 items.

Stress.   According to Tecce (1992), increased blink frequency generally reflects negative mood states, such as nervousness, stress, and fatigue. As an example of the blink-stress relationship Tecce cites the so-called "Nixon effect." During president Nixon's resignation speech he blinked over 50 times per minute when discussing his being forced from office. He also showed rapid bursts of blinks (3 per second), showing the overall stress and negative emotional impact of his departure from the presidency. Additionally, it was found that negative emotional states that accompany poor performance have been related to increases in blinking. On the other hand, more positive states are accompanied by decreased blink frequency. For example, Tecce observed that blink rate slows after relaxation has been hypnotically induced and during successful problem solving. Tecce (1992) concluded that observations of these kinds offer support for the hedonia-blink hypothesis, which states that decreased blinking is related to pleasant feelings, whereas increased frequency of blinks accompanies unpleasant mood states.

The Eye Blink Component of the Startle Response in Attention, Emotion, and Clinical Research

Eye Blink and the Startle Response.   The *startle response* refers to a complex of bodily reactions to a strong, rapid and unexpected stimulus. Woodworth and Schlosberg (1954) state that the most effective and convenient stimulus used to elicit a startle reflex in the 1930s was a pistol shot (a .22 caliber blank cartridge) fired closely behind someone's head! The physiological changes produced by this type of stimulus included increases in eye blink (EB), heart rate, skin conductance, and a wide variety of muscular responses. The startle pattern has been thoroughly analyzed by Landis and Hunt in work reported in 1939 as cited by Woodworth and Schlosberg (1954). These investigators found that the fastest and most stable component of the response was EB with a latency of 40 msec. The other fast components identified were: widening of the mouth (70 msec), forward head movement (80 msec), tightening of neck muscles (90 msec) and a wave of muscular response to the shoulders, abdomen, and reaching the knees in about 200 msec. The heart rate and skin conductance changes take longer to occur, but show up within 1 sec or less. The rapid eye closure that occurs during the reflexive EB reflects an abrupt increase in EMG activity of the orbicularis oculi, the muscle that surrounds the eye (Lang, 1995).

The EB Component of the Startle Response in Attention.   Graham (1975) initiated research on the startle EB as a means to study attentional mechanisms. She proposed that use of the startle paradigm could enable distinctions between intensity-dependent effects of stimuli and attentional effects. Further, the effects of processing short duration and sustained stimuli could also be separated. Studies by Graham and her students indicated that a weak tone of 70 dB, of only 20 msec in duration, effectively reduced the startle EB to an intense (104 dB) white noise presented 120 msec after the onset of a lead stimulus.

In an additional series of studies, Graham and colleagues found that if the weak lead stimulus was increased from 200 msec to 2,000 msec in duration, the EB was progressively facilitated, in both latency and amplitude, reaching a maximum at 2,000 msec. A possible explanation for this is an activating effect produced through the reticular formation, a structure that runs through the core of the brain stem (see chapter 18 describing the activation concept and the influence of the reticular activating system).

Inhibition of the EB Startle Response.   Later research has indicated that this weak lead stimulus (or prepulse, as it is referred to in contemporary research) works to inhibit the EB if it is short (about 250 msec or less) and to enhance the EB if it is longer than approximately 500 msec (Filion, Dawson, & Schell, 1993). It should also be pointed out that the time from prepulse onset to onset of the startle stimulus is referred to as *lead interval*. The prepulse can be discrete, in which case it is brief and ends some time before the startle stimulus. In a continuous prepulse, it lasts until the startle stimulus begins. Both discrete and continuous prepulses have been used. It has been reported that with long lead intervals the EB magnitude to an auditory, blink-producing, stimulus is enhanced when attention is focused on an auditory prepulse, and the increase is even greater when the auditory prepulse is of high interest value compared to one of low interest (Anthony & Graham, 1985).

One proposal has been that when attention is allocated to a stimulus from one modality (hearing, for example) then there is a facilitation in processing of other stimuli in the same modality. The EB inhibition that occurs at short lead intervals, on the other hand, occurs regardless of modalites of the prepulse or startle eliciting stimulus. One suggestion is that inhibition of the EB may reflect an attempt to protect the processing of the prepulse (Graham, 1980). A related view is that EB inhibition regulates sensory input to the brain and allows early stages of information processing to occur without disruption (Braff and Geyer, 1990). This sensorimotor view is distinguished from the protection of processing hypothesis because it holds that startle inhibition reflects an exclusion of external stimuli (auditory, visual, etc.) as well as internal ones such as thoughts (Filion, Dawson, & Schell, 1998).

Attentional Processing With Short and Long Lead Intervals.   The sensitivity of short and long lead intervals to attentional processing, using EB modification, was examined by Filion et al. (1993). Both attended and ignored tones were prepulses for an EB eliciting burst of white noise presented at intervals of 60, 120, 240, and 2,000 msec following prepulse onset. They hypothesized that if short and long lead interval modifications of the startle EB do reflect attentional processes, then the attended prepulse should produce greater startle inhibition at the short lead intervals and greater facilitation at the long intervals. The hypothesis was confirmed; that is, the attended prepulse produced significantly greater blink inhibition at the 120 msec interval and greater blink facilitation at the 2,000 msec interval. They suggest that the EB modification at the short interval may reflect not only protection of preattentive processing (Graham, 1980), but also an early evaluation of the significance of the prepulse.

Further, although the attended prepulse produced the largest amount of EB inhibition (indicating sensitivity to attentional mechanisms), the ignored tones also produced inhibition, indicating the operation of automatic processes. Thus, the authors believe that the short lead interval paradigm has potential for probing early stages of information processing. The finding that greater startle facilitation occurred with attended than ignored prepulses at the 2,000 msec interval suggests that long lead intervals are useful for studying later stages of information processing.

Allocation of Attentional Resources.   Studies indicating that greater EB startle facilitation follows attended than ignored lead stimuli have been interpreted as reflecting greater allocation of attentional resources to the attended tone (Filion et al., 1998). Other evidence that allocation of attention plays a role in modifying the EB reflex comes from a study by Zelson and Simons (1986), who reported that performance in a visual vigilance task inhibited the EB to an intense acoustic stimulus and that when the task was more difficult the inhibition was even greater.

The modification of the EB component of startle has also been used as a measure of attentional resource allocation by Jennings, Schell, Filion, and Dawson (1996). They reasoned that startle facilitation would show an increase across lead intervals since greater attention should be paid closer to the end of a prepulse tone when judgement of tone duration is required. Tones of 5- and 7-sec duration, of either high or low pitch, were presented with instructions to count the longer tones of either pitch, thereby requiring judgements of tone duration. Startle probes of 100 dB intensity were presented after the tone at four intervals varying from 120 msec to 6,000 msec. Startle EB inhibition took place at the short intervals, whereas it was facilitated at long intervals, both for the experimental (active attention) and the control (passive attention) groups. Further, it could be concluded that attention to the tone enhanced both the inhibition and the facilitation effect, with greater inhibition and facilitation, respectively, produced by the attended tone. Also noted was that the attended tone facilitation was greater at a 4,500-msec lead interval than a 2,000-msec interval. What this suggests is that startle EB modification may index changing attentional demands of a task at different stages of information processing in both active and passive attentional conditions. It also indicates that, as the authors suspected, the amount of startle facilitation at long lead intervals is a function of degree of attentional processing.

The EB Component of the Startle Response in Emotion.   The use of a high intensity noise burst (95 dB for 50 msec) to elicit a startle response while college students viewed pleasant and unpleasant slides produced interesting results (Vrana, Spence, & Lang, 1988). The investigators found that the startle response, as measured by EB magnitude, was largest when subjects viewed unpleasant stimuli and smallest for positive stimuli, as compared to neutral slides (see Fig. 11.8). Examples of pleasant stimuli were happy babies, appetizing food, and attractive nudes; unpleasant stimuli included aimed guns, poisonous snakes, and pictures of violent death; neutral stimuli were umbrellas, hair dryers, and other common household objects.

The pleasantness–unpleasantness of stimuli was confirmed by participant's ratings. The author's explanation for the results centered about the strengthening or weakening of the reflex response to an aversive stimulus (the loud noise). The stimuli's "affective valence," that is, whether it produces a positive approach response or a negative avoidance response, either adds to or subtracts from the startle response to the aversive noise. Thus, the EB response to the unpleasant stimuli is increased because avoidance or escape behavior is strengthened. Conversely, startle is inhibited when the viewed stimulus evokes a positive reaction. Vrana and Lang (1990) conducted a follow-up study in which they found that subjects asked to

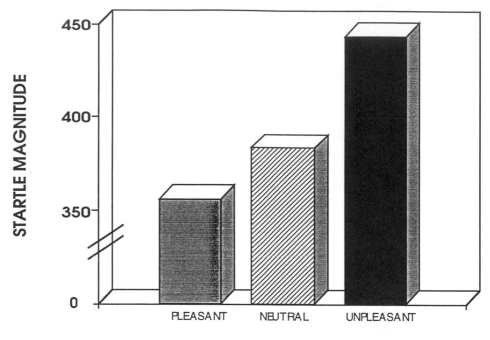

FIG. 11.8. Mean magnitude of the eyeblink response (A-D units) elicited by an acoustic startle probe during viewing of positive, neutral, and negative affective slides. (Figure courtesy
of Drs. P. Lang, E. Spence, and S. Vrana and the American Psychological Association.)

imagine fearful experiences showed augmented EB responses to the high intensity noise
bursts. The startle probes were again at a level of 95 dB and were presented at unpredictable
times when subjects engaged in fearful imagery associated with previously memorized sentences, or when they recalled neutral material. Thus, the startle response was again facilitated by a negative affective context, this time during aversive imagery. The authors suggested
that the EB component of startle be used as an objective measure in research on emotion,
emotional development, and the psychopathology of affect, since it is automatic and the individual has minimal influence on the response.

Emotional Valence and Physiological Arousal.   In order to sort out the effects of emotional valence (positive–negative) and physiological arousal (low and high), Witvliet and Vrana
(1995) compared EB startle magnitude and latency under conditions of negative and positive
imagery that included both high- and low-arousal components. For example, fear and joy are
negative and positive, respectively, and both are high-arousal events. In contrast, sadness
(negative) and pleasant relaxation (positive) can be considered low arousal. They found that
EB magnitudes were larger and latencies were faster during negative, as compared to positive, imagery. In addition, higher arousal also resulted in larger magnitude and shorter latency EBs. These results are especially interesting because the imagery represents a situation
where the EB component of startle was modified by subjectively generated stimuli as opposed to external visual or auditory stimuli. The effects of both emotional valence and arousal level of stimuli was investigated by Cuthbert, Bradley, and Lang (1996). The EBs were
elicited by startle probes of 80, 95, and 105 dB while participants viewed pictures varying in
both pleasure (pleasant, neutral, and unpleasant) and arousal (low, moderate, and high). The

EB potentiation during unpleasant content and EB attenuation during pleasant content were strongest for pictures that were rated high in arousal. This effect occurred with all three probe intensities.

Positive and Negative Sensory Experience. The EB component of the startle reflex has also been used to evaluate the emotional effects of postively and negatively rated odors (Miltner, Matjak, Braun, Diekmann, & Brody, 1994). The unpleasant odor used was hydrogen sulfide and the pleasant one was vanillin. The EB amplitude was compared for positive, negative, and neutral air stimulation. The hydrogen sulfide significantly enhanced EB amplitude in comparison with neutral air, but the reduction in EB with vanillin was not significant. Miltner and colleagues suggested that this may have occurred because the emotional valence of vanillin was only about half as positive as the valence of hydrogen sulfide was negative. This study was followed up by Ehlichman and colleagues (Ehrlichman, Kuhl, Zhu, & Warrenburg, 1997), who used a design in which participants experienced either a pleasant odor or an unpleasant one, but not both, and a no-odor control. They also used odors whose emotional valence was equal in terms of rated pleasantness or unpleasantness. The pleasant odor was a coconut fragrance, whereas the unpleasant one was limburger cheese. Their results showed that the unpleasant odor increased the magnitude of the EB, and, unlike the Miltner et al. study, the pleasant odor now attenuated the EB component of the startle reflex.

The EB Component of Startle in Clinical Research. The notion that schizophrenics have difficulty with assimilation of percepts or processing sensory stimuli has existed for quite some time (e.g., see McReynolds, 1960). More recently, inhibition of the EB component of the startle reaction has been of interest in the study of schizophrenia because it can index deficits in early information processing, and may be related to underlying vulnerability factors (Filion et al., 1998). The question is whether schizophrenics show deficits in startle inhibition, which could indicate difficulty in processing stimuli. A number of studies have indicated that schizophrenic inpatients show reduced startle inhibition at short prepulse intervals (see Grillon, Ameli, Chamey, Kryotal, & Braff, 1992). In addition, normal individuals who score as "psychosis prone" according to measures of the MMPI (Minnesota Multiphasic Personality Inventory) also show less startle inhibition compared to control individuals.

Modulation of the EB startle reflex was studied in persons with high fear (phobics) and low fear (nonphobics) of animals or mutilation (Hamm, Cuthbert, Globisch, & Vaitl, 1997). All participants viewed color slides of fear-relevant, unpleasant, neutral, and pleasant scenes. Those with the animal and mutilation phobias showed significantly larger EB facilitation when viewing slides of their specific phobic objects than when viewing other unpleasant scenes. Further, they showed greater EB magnitudes when viewing feared pictures than the nonphobics viewing the same or other unpleasant slides. The authors suggest that the EB startle reflex indexes the individual's basic motivational disposition and can provide information for the assessment of fear responses. Other studies, reviewed by Filion et al. (1998) indicate that modulation of the EB reflex, with larger responses during negative than positive affect, is sensitive to affective states in the normal and pathological range. For example, individuals with simple and social phobias, posttraumatic stress disorder, and panic disorder all show enhancement of the startle EB while imagining scenes or viewing pictures that are threatening.

Summary. A rich literature has developed in the area of startle eyeblink modulation as it relates to attentional and emotional processes. As has been indicated in the studies reviewed here, the human startle EB is modified by both cognitive and emotional factors. It appears that, at short-lead intervals, startle inhibition may reflect protection of processing, sensorimotor gating, and early stages of attentional processing (Filion et al., 1998). Modifications at long-lead intervals include those related to attentional processes and modification by emotional factors. Potentiation of the eyeblink reflex by negative emotional stimuli—whether they be pictorial, induced through imagery, or odoriferous—has implications for greater understanding of affective stimuli in emotion and even in psychopathological states. Clinical research utilizing startle EB modification has resulted in some provocative findings relating to schizophrenia, phobias, posttraumatic stress and panic disorder.

The next three chapters cover measures of cardiovascular activity and their relation to behavior. A representative summary of the voluminous research on the associations between heart activity and psychological functioning is presented in chapters 12 and 13. Discussions of blood pressure and blood volume are the topics of chapter 14.

REFERENCES

Andreassi, J. L. (1973). Alpha and problem solving: A demonstration. *Perceptual & Motor Skills, 36*, 905–906.

Antes, J. R. (1974). The time course of picture viewing. *Journal of Experimental Psychology, 103*, 62–70.

Anthony, B. J., & Graham, F. K. (1985). Blink reflex modification by selective attention: Evidence for the modulation of "automatic" processing. *Biological Psychology, 21*, 43–59.

Bakan, P. (1969). Hypnotizability, laterality of eye movement and functional brain asymmetry. *Perceptual & Motor Skills, 28*, 927–932.

Bauer, L. O., Strock, B. D., Goldstein, R., Stern, J. A., & Walrath, L. C. (1985). Auditory discrimination and the eyeblink. *Psychophysiology, 22*, 629–635.

Braff, D. L., & Geyer, M. A. (1990). Sensorimotor gating and schizophrenia: Human and animal studies. *Archives of General Psychiatry, 47*, 181–188.

Buswell, G. T. (1920). An experimental study of the eye–voice span in reading. *Supplemental Education Monograph, 17*, 505–510.

Coren, S., & Hoenig, P. (1972). Eye movements and decrement in the Oppel–Kundt illusion. *Perception & Psychophysics, 12*, 224–225.

Cuthbert, B. N., Bradley, M. M., & Lang, P. J. (1996). Probing picture perception: Activation and emotion. *Psychophysiology, 33*, 103–111.

Darwin, C. (1872). *The expression of the emotions in man and animals.* Chicago: University of Chicago Press (1965, reprinted from the authorized edition of D. Appleton & Co., New York & London).

Day, M. E. (1964). An eye-movement phenomenon relating to attention, thought and anxiety. *Perceptual & Motor Skills, 19*, 443–446.

Ehrlichmann, H., & Barrett, J. (1983). "Random" saccadic eye movements during verbal–linguistic and visual–imaginal tasks. *Acta Psychologica, 53*, 9–26.

Ehrlichmann, H., Kuhl, S. B., Zhu, J., & Warrenburg, S. (1997). Startle reflex modulation by pleasant and unpleasant odors in a between-subjects design. *Psychophysiology, 34*, 726–729.

Festinger, L., White, C. W., & Allyn, M. R. (1968). Eye movements and decrement in the Muller–Lyer illusion. *Perception & Psychophysics, 3*, 376–382.

Filion, D. L., Dawson, M. E., & Schell, A. M. (1993). Modification of the acoustic startle-reflex eyeblink: A tool for investigating early and late attentional processes. *Biological Psychology, 35*, 185–200.

Filion, D. L., Dawson, M. E., & Schell, A. M. (1998). The psychological significance of human startle eyeblink modification: A review. *Biological Psychology, 47*, 1–43.

Fogarty, C., & Stern, J. A. (1989). Eye movements and blinks: Their relationship to higher cognitive processes. *International Journal of Psychophysiology, 8*, 35–42.

Goldstein, R., Bauer, L. O., & Stern, J. A. (1992). Effect of task difficulty and interstimulus interval on blink parameters. *International Journal of Psychophysiology, 13*, 111–118.

Goldstein, R., Walrath, L. C., Stern, J. A., & Strock, B. D. (1985). Blink activity in a discrimination task as a function of stimulus modality and schedule of presentation. *Psychophysiology, 22*, 629–635.

Gooding, D. C., Iacono, W. G., Katsanis, J., Beiser, M., & Grove, W. M. (1993). The association between lithium carbonate and smooth pursuit eye tracking among first-episode patients with psychotic affective disorders. *Psychophysiology, 30*, 3–9.

Gould, J. D. (1974). *Looking at pictures* (Research Rep. No. RC 4991). Yorktown Heights, NY: IBM.

Gould, J. D., & Schaffer, A. (1967). Eye-movement parameters in pattern recognition. *Journal of Experimental Psychology, 74*, 225–229.

Graham, F. K. (1975). The more of less startling effects of weak prestimulation. *Psychophysiology, 12*, 238–248.

Graham, F. K. (1980). Control of reflex blink excitability. In R. F. Thompson, L. H. Hicks, & V. B. Shvyrkov (Eds.), *Neural mechanisms of goal-directed behavior and learning* (pp. 511–519). New York: Academic Press.

Grillon, C., Ameli, R., Chamey, D. S., Krystal, J., & Braff, D. (1992). Startle gating deficits occur across prepulse intensities in schizophrenic patients. *Biological Psychiatry, 32*, 939–943.

Grove, W. M., Clementz, B. A., Iacono, W. G., & Katsanis, J. (1992). Smooth pursuit ocular motor dysfunction in schizophrenia: Evidence for a major gene. *American Journal of Psychiatry, 149*, 1362–1368.

Gur, R. E., Gur, R. C., & Harris, L. J. (1975). Cerebral activation, as measured by subjects' lateral eye movements, is influenced by experimenter location. *Neuropsychologia, 13*, 35–44.

Guyton, A. C. (1977). *Basic human physiology: Normal function and mechanisms of disease.* Philadelphia: Saunders.

Haltrecht, E. J., & McCormack, P. D. (1966). Monitoring eye movements of slow and fast learners. *Psychonomic Science, 6*, 461–462.

Hamm, A. O., Cuthbert, B. N., Globisch, J., & Vaitl, D. (1997). Fear and the startle reflex: Blink modulation and autonomic response patterns in animal and mutilation fearful subjects. *Psychophysiology, 34*, 97–107.

Holzman, P. S., Proctor, L. R., & Hughes, D. W. (1973). Eye tracking patterns in schizophrenia. *Science, 181*, 179–181.

Iacono, W. G. (1988). Eye movement abnormalities in schizophrenic and affective disorders. In C. W. Johnston & F. J. Pirozzolo (Eds.), *Neuropsychology of eye movements* (pp. 115–146). Hillsdale, NJ: Lawrence Erlbaum Associates.

Iacono, W. G., & Clementz, B. A. (1993). A strategy for elucidating genetic influences on complex psychopathological syndromes (with special reference to ocular motor functioning and schizophrenia). In L. J. Chapman, J. P. Chapman, & D. C. Fowles (Eds.), *Progress in experimental personality & psychopathology research* (pp. 11–65). New York: Springer.

Iacono, W. G., & Lykken, D. T. (1979). Electrooculographic recording and scoring of smooth pursuit and saccadic eye tracking: A parametric study using monozygotic twins. *Psychophysiology, 16*, 94–107.

Iacono, W. G., & Lykken, D. T. (1981). Two-year retest stability of eye tracking performance and a comparison of electro-oculographic and infrared recording techniques: Evidence of EEG in the electro-oculogram. *Psychophysiology, 18*, 49–55.

Iacono, W. G., Moreau, M., Beiser, M., Fleming, J. A. E., & Lin, T.-Y. (1992). Smooth-pursuit eye tracking in first-episode psychotic patients and their relatives. *Journal of Abnormal Psychology, 101*, 104–116.

Jennings, P. D., Schell, A. M., Filion, D. L., & Dawson, M. E. (1996). Tracking early and late stages of information processing: Contributions of startle eyeblink reflex modification. *Psychophysiology, 33*, 148–155.

Kinsbourne, M. (1972). Eye and head turning indicates cerebral lateralization. *Science, 176*, 539–541.

Lang, P. J. (1995). The emotion probe: Studies of motivation and attention. *American Psychologist, 50*, 372–385.

Lefton, L. A. (1978). Eye movements in reading disabled children. In J. W. Senders, D. F. Fisher, & R. A. Monty (Eds.), *Eye movements and the higher psychological function* (pp. 225–237). Hillsdale, NJ: Lawrence Erlbaum Associates.

Levin, S. (1984). Frontal lobe dysfunction in schizophrenia: I: Eye movement impairments. *Journal of Psychiatric Research, 18*, 27–55.

Loftus, G. R. (1972). Eye fixations and recognition memory for pictures. *Cognitive Psychology, 3*, 525–551.

Luria, S. M., & Strauss, M. S. (1975). Eye movements during search for coded and uncoded targets. *Perception & Psychophysics, 17*, 303–308.

Mack, A., Fendrich, R., & Sirigatti, S. (1973). A rebound illusion in visual tracking. *American Journal of Psychology, 86*, 425–433.

Mackworth, N. H., & Morandi, A. J. (1967). The gaze selects informative details within pictures. *Perception & Psychophysics, 2*, 547–552.

McCormack, P. D., Haltrecht, E. J., & Hannah, T. E. (1967). Monitoring eye movements during the learning of successive paired-associate lists. *Journal of Verbal Learning and Verbal Behavior, 6*, 950–953.

McCormack, P. D., Hannah, T. E., Bradley, W. J., & Moore, T. E. (1967). Monitoring eye movements under conditions of high and low intralist response (meaningful) similarity. *Psychonomic Science, 8*, 517–518.

McReynolds, P. (1960). Anxiety, perception, and schizophrenia (pp. 248–292). In D. D. Jackson (Ed.), *The etiology of schizophrenia* (pp. –). New York: Basic Books.

Miltner, W., Matjak, M., Braun, C., Diekmann, H., & Brody, S. (1994). Emotional qualities of odors and their influence on the startle reflex in humans. *Psychophysiology, 31*, 107–110.

Nakano, A. (1971). Eye movements in relation to mental activity of problem solving. *Psychologia: An International Journal of Psychology in the Orient, 14*, 200–207.

Neubauer, A., Schulter, G., & Pfurtscheller, G. (1988). Lateral eye movements as an indication of hemispheric preference: an EEG validation study. *International Journal of Psychophysiology, 6*, 177–184.

Noton, D., & Stark, L. (1971a). Scanpaths in saccadic in eye movements while viewing and recognizing and recognizing patterns. *Vision Research, 11*, 929–942.

Noton, D., & Stark, L. (1971b). Eye movements and visual perception. *Scientific American, 224*, 34–43.

Olson, R. R., Kleigl, R., & Davidson, B. J. (1983). Dyslexic and normal reader's eye movements. *Journal of Experimental Psychology: Human Perception and Performance, 9*, 816–825.

Pavlidis, G. Th. (1981). Do eye movements hold the key to dyslexia? *Neuropsychologia, 19*, 57–64.

Pavlidis, G. Th. (1985). Eye movements in dyslexia: Their diagnostic significance. *Journal of Learning Disabilities, 18*, 42–50.

Pirozzolo, F. J., & Rayner, K. (1988). In C. W. Johnston & F. J. Pirozzolo (Eds.), *Neuropsychology of eye movements* (pp. 65–80). Hillsdale, NJ: Lawrence Erlbaum Associates.

Shackel, B. (1967). Eye movement recordings by electroculography. In P. H. Venables & I. Martin (Eds.), *Manual of psychophysiological methods* (pp. 299–334). Amsterdam: North-Holland.

Shevrin, H., Smokler, I., & Kooi, K. A. (1980). An empirical link between lateral eye movements and lateralized event-related brain potentials. *Biological Psychiatry, 15*, 691–697.

Siever, L. J., Coursey, R. D., Alterman, I. S., Buchsbaum, M. S., & Murphy, D. L. (1984). Impaired smooth pursuit eye movement: Vulnerability marker of schizotypal personality disorder in a normal volunteer population. *American Journal of Psychiatry, 141*, 1560–1566.

Stanley, G., Smith, G. A., & Howell, E. A. (1983). Eye-movements and sequential tracking in dyslexic and control children. *British Journal of Psychology, 74*, 181–187.

Stern, J. A. (1980). *Aspects of visual search activity related to attentional processes and skill development* (Final Report, Contract F49620-79-C0089). Washington, DC: Air Force Office of Scientific Research.

Stern, J. A., & Dunham, D. N. (1990). The ocular system. In J. T. Cacioppo & L. G. Tassinary (Eds.), *Principles of psychophysiology* (pp. 193–215). Cambridge, England: Cambridge University Press.

Tecce, J. J. (1992). Psychology, physiology and experimental psychology. In , Ed. *McGraw-Hill yearbook of science & technology* (pp. 375–377). New York: McGraw-Hill.

Teitelbaum, H. A. (1954). Spontaneous rhythmic ocular movements: Their possible relationship to mental activity. *Neurology, 4*, 350–354.

Venezky, R. L. (1977). Research on reading processes: An historical perspective. *American Psychologist, 32*, 339–345.

Vrana, S. R., & Lang, P. J. (1990). Fear imagery and the startle-probe reflex. *Journal of Abnormal Psychology, 99*, 189–197.

Vrana, S. R., Spence, E. L., & Lang, P. J. (1988). The startle probe response: A new measure of emotion? *Journal of Abnormal Psychology, 97*, 487–491.

Wirtschafter, J. D., & Weingarden, A. S. (1988). Neurophysiology and central pathways in oculomotor control: Physiology and anatomy of saccadic and pursuit eye movements. In C. W. Johnston & F. J. Pirozzolo (Eds.), *Neuropsychology of eye movements* (pp. 5–30). Hillsdale, NJ: Lawrence Erlbaum Associates.

Woodworth, R. S. (1938). *Experimental psychology*. New York: Holt.

Woodworth, R. S., & Schlosberg, H. (1954). *Experimental psychology*. New York: Holt.

Yarbus, A. L. (1967). *Eye movements and vision*. New York: Plenum.

Yee, C. M., Nuechterlein, K. H., & Dawson, M. E. (1998). A longitudinal analysis of eye tracking dysfunction and attention in recent-onset schizophrenia. *Psychophysiology, 35*, 443–451.

Zelson, M. F., & Simons, R. F. (1986). Sustained attention in Type A and Type B subjects: A blink reflex analysis. *Psychophysiology, 23*, 385–392.

12

Heart Activity and Behavior I: Developmental Factors, Motor and Mental Activities, Perception, Attention, and Orienting Responses

Why should the heart be of interest in psychophysiological research? After all, it is merely a muscular pump that pushes out blood to the rest of the body. This is true, but as we noted in chapter 1, there are written records to show that very early scientists observed that changes in cardiac activity were related to psychological phenomena and emotions such as "love sickness." In fact, it is more than likely that changes in heart activity that occurred in amorous or fear-producing situations were noticed by cavepeople thousands of years ago. The association of the heart with love, cupid's bow, and Valentine's day also reflects individual perceptions of heartbeat changes that occur with emotional reactions. Contemporary cardiovascular psychophysiologists (and *cardiovascular* is a subspecialty within psychophysiology) are not usually concerned with heart activity on Valentine's day. Rather, they are interested in more general issues; for example, whether perceptual accuracy varies with changes in heart activity, or if differential changes in heart rate occur in various emotional states, whether individuals are capable of accurate detection of changes in their own cardiac responses, or if perception of heart rate change can influence the emotion experienced by a person.

Today, we use scientific methods to study changes in heart activity not only during emotional or stressful situations but also in the performance of more subtle tasks, such as signal detection and problem solving. We find that experimental evidence indicates significant interactions of heart activity with somatic (muscle) and central (brain) activity. These findings have been elaborated in the cardiac–somatic concept of Paul Obrist and the intake–rejection formulation of the Laceys, as discussed in chapter 18. In this and the next chapter, changes in heart activity that occur in various behavioral situations are considered. The areas examined in this chapter include such issues as how heart activity varies in infants and children as a function of attentional states and emotion. Questions about relationships between heart activity and speed of response, and as a function of complex motor performance, are explored. Issues regarding cardiovascular response during various cognitive activities are probed (verbal learning, problem solving, and imagery). Also considered are cardiac changes during perception, attention, and orienting reactions.

The next chapter considers heart activity as it relates to emotions, stress, motivation, personality, and social factors. Also included is a discussion of conditioning and interactions between heart and brain. The next section of this chapter reviews the anatomy and physiology of the heart, and how its activity is measured, to enable a better appreciation of the behavioral studies covered in these chapters.

ANATOMY AND PHYSIOLOGY OF THE HEART

The heart is a muscular, four-chambered organ whose main function is to supply blood, with its nutriments and oxygen, to the tissues of the body. The heart is about the size of a man's fist. It weighs approximately 300 gm in the male and 250 gm in the female. The four chambers are the right and left atria (on top) and the right and left ventricles (on the bottom). Figure 12.1 is a cutaway drawing that shows the various heart chambers. The atria are receiving chambers for blood that has been returned to the heart by the veins. The ventricles pump blood via arteries to the lungs and the rest of the body.

Heart Structures Involved in Blood Circulation

The right atrium receives blood from all body tissues except the lungs. The veins that bring blood to the right atrium are (a) the superior vena cava (blood from the upper body), (b) the inferior vena cava (blood from the lower body), and (c) the coronary sinus blood (blood from the heart itself). The blood flows from the right atrium to the right ventricle and from there to the lungs (via the pulmonary artery). In the lungs, carbon dioxide is removed from the blood and oxygen is added. The oxygenated blood is then returned to the left atrium by four pulmonary veins. From there, it goes to the left ventricle, which then pumps the oxygenated blood through the aorta to the rest of the body.

Control of the Heartbeat (Cardiac Cycle)

The heartbeat, which we can hear through a stethoscope and record with the eletrocardiograph, represents the contraction that the heart does to pump blood to other body areas. The human heart normally contracts at a rate of about 72 beats per minute (BPM) at rest. This average rate translates to just over 100,000 times per day and between 2.5 and 3.0 billion times in a lifetime of 70 to 80 years. The control of this beating is by mechanisms both internal and external to the heart.

Internal Cardiac Control

The internal mechanism of the heartbeat consists of a system of specialized fibers, including: (a) the sinoatrial (S–A) node, (b) the atrioventricular (A–V) node, (c) the A–V bundle, and (d) the left and right bundles of conducting fibers (Guyton, 1977). The S–A node is located on the rear wall of the right atrium, and its regular electrical discharge produces the normal rhythmic contraction of the entire heart. The S–A node is also known as the *pacemaker*, with a rate of 120 BPM at normal body temperature. However, the vagus nerve (the 10th cranial nerve) inhibits the pacemaker and holds the rate down to approximately 70 to 80 BPM. The impulse for contraction is slightly delayed at the A–V node before passing into the ventricles. The A–V bundle then conducts the impulse into the ventricles, and Purkinje fibers conduct the impulse for contraction to all parts of the ventricles. The contraction phase of the heart is known as *systole*, whereas the relaxation phase is termed *diastole*.

External Cardiac Control

The normal regular rate of contraction may also be influenced by external factors, that is, by nerves from the autonomic (ANS) and central (CNS) nervous systems. The parasympathetic (PNS) system influences the S–A and A–V nodes via the vagus nerve. Its influence results in the slowing of the heartbeat (also called a negative chronotropic effect). This influence is pro-

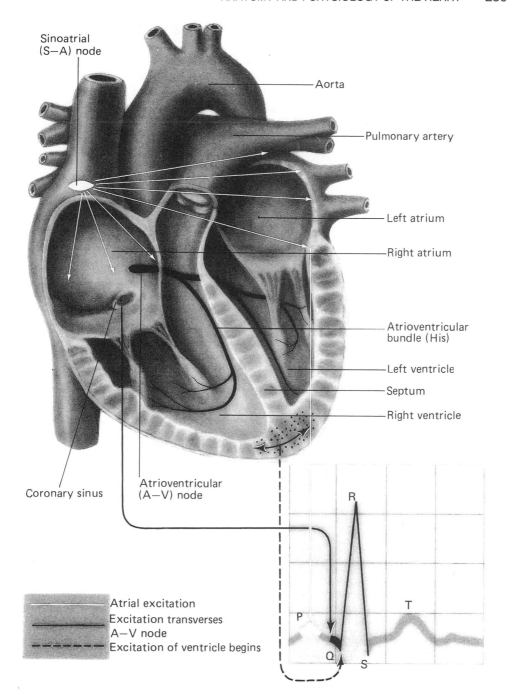

FIG. 12.1. Conducting system of the heart showing source of electrical impulses produced on electrocardiogram.

duced by the release of the neurotransmitter acetylcholine at the vagus nerve endings, which, in turn, results in the slowing of activity at the S–A node (cardiac pacemaker) and a slowing of the cardiac impulse passing into the ventricles (Guyton, 1977). The SNS has the opposite effect; that is, it produces an increase in heart rate (positive chronotropic effect). It exerts this effect through the release of norepinephrine at the sympathetic nerve endings. This results in (a) an increase in the rate of S–A node discharge, (b) increased excitability of heart tissue, and (c) an increase in force of contraction of both atrial and ventricular musculature. The heart muscle is also known as the myocardium.

The SNS acts to increase cardiac output in certain emotional situations or at extreme levels of exercise. However, it should be noted that HR increases are often due to decreased vagus verve inhibition (PNS). Thus, changes in heart rate depend on SNS and PNS activity, such that an increase in rate can occur due to a decrease in PNS activity or an increase in SNS activity. Cardiac output refers to the amount of blood pumped by the heart. At rest, this is approximately 5 to 6 liters per min, but it can increase to five times that amount with heavy exercise. Also changing during vigorous exercise is the distribution of blood in various body tissues. For example, the muscles receive 15% to 20% of the cardiac output of blood at rest, but the amount changes to 80% to 85% with strenuous exercise or work (Astrand & Rodahl, 1977).

At one time, it was thought that the medulla exerted the primary control over certain reflex actions concerned with influencing heart rate. However, it is now known that other CNS structures—including the hypothalamus, cerebellum, and amygdala—also contribute to these reflexes.

Carotid Sinus Reflex

Baroreceptors (pressure sensitive) are present in the carotid sinus, located in the neck at about the level of the chin. The carotid sinus is supplied by fibers from the glossopharyngeal (9th) cranial nerve. When pressure on the walls of the carotid sinus is low because of decreased blood pressure, this information is transmitted to a cardiac acceleration center in the medulla. At this point, sympathetic fibers are brought into action to increase heart rate and, in addition, to bring the pressure of the carotid sinus up to an acceptable level. The basic function of the baroreceptors is to ensure an adequate blood supply to the brain. Thus, we see the operation of a feedback mechanism that maintains heart rate and blood presssure within certain limits. The reader who is interested in more detail on this topic may want to consult a review of central mechanisms in the control of heart rate by Cohen and MacDonald (1974). There are other internal and external factors that can influence heart rate, including the metabolism of the heart itself, chemical factors, and hormonal influences.

MEASUREMENT OF HEART ACTIVITY
(ELECTROCARDIOGRAM OR ECG)

The study of electrical changes occurring during the heart's contractions was made possible by the work of Willem Einthoven in 1904 (Pardee, 1933). He developed an instrument sensitive and quick enough to follow the small, rapidly varying currents produced by the heart. It had been known since 1856 that the heart's contraction was accompanied by the production of an electric current. In 1887, Waller showed that the current could be recorded from the surface of the body if proper contact was made between wires from a galvanometer and two body locations on either side of the heart. Einthoven's string galvanometer made the recording of heart activity practical in the early 1900s, and it soon became widely used in European clinics. This early recording device and modern ones take advantage of the fact that a portion of the electrical impulse that passes through the heart during contraction spreads to the surface of the body. If electrodes are placed on the skin, the electrical potentials generated by the heart can be recorded. When these potentials are amplified and recorded on an ink writer, the resulting measurement is called the electrocardiogram (ECG). The normal ECG is composed of characteristic deflections referred to as P, Q, R, S, and T waves. These wave components

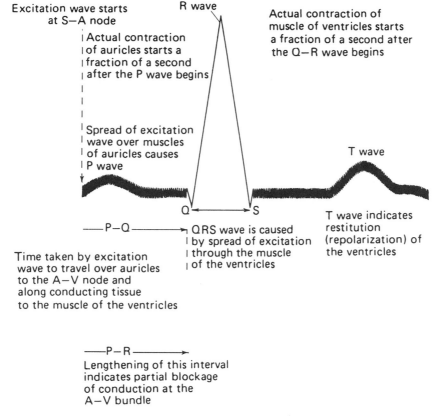

FIG. 12.2. Electrocardiogram.

of the ECG are depicted in Fig. 12.2. The relatively small P wave is produced by electrical currents generated just before contraction of the atria.

The QRS complex is caused by currents generated in the ventricles during depolarization just prior to ventricular contraction. Note that the R wave is the most prominent component of the QRS component. The T wave is caused by repolarization of the ventricles. Atrial repolarization does not result in a separate ECG wave because it is masked by the more pronounced ventricular-related changes. The depolarization and repolarization that occurs in cardiac muscle fibers is similar in principle to the depolarization and repolarization that occurs in neurons. That is, depolarization occurs as the ionic activity inside of the fiber becomes positive with respect to the outside, and repolarization is a return to internal negativity and external positivity.

Wave Component Durations

The time between the start of the P wave and the beginning of the QRS complex (or P–Q interval) is about 160 msec (Guyton, 1977). The Q–T interval, or the time from the beginning of the Q wave to the end of the T wave, is about 300 msec. Because the cardiac cycle lasts about 830 msec (based on a rate of 72 bpm), there are approximately 370 msec between the end of the T wave and the beginning of the next atrial contraction. The heart actually spends less time contracting than relaxing; for instance, with a cycle of 800 msec, it is in ventricular systole for 300 msec and in diastole for 500 msec.

Limb Leads for Recording the ECG

There are several standard limb leads for ECG recording. They are as follows:

Lead I: Electrodes are attached just above the wrists on the insides of the right and left arms. The polarity is selected so that when the left arm lead is positive, with respect to the right, there is an upward deflection of the P and R segments of the ECG.

Lead II: Electrodes are attached above the right wrist and above the left ankle. The polarity is chosen such that there is an upward deflection of the P and R waves of the ECG when the ankle lead is positive relative to the arm placement.

Lead III: Electrodes are attached above the left wrist and above the left ankle. Again, the polarity is selected so that there is an upward deflection of the P and R waves when the ankle placement is positive relative to the arm lead. Normal ECG records obtained through the use of these three lead placements are shown in Fig. 12.3.

The leads just described are adequate in situations where subjects are lying down or sitting or standing in one place. However, for active subjects, sternal or axillary leads are preferred. Sternal leads are placed over the breast bone (sternum), and are therefore relatively immune to movement artifacts (see Fig. 12.4). The placement of chest leads in Fig. 12.4 shows the upper electrode placed on the manubrium of the sternum and the lower lead on the xiphoid process of the sternum. An upward deflection on the ECG is obtained when the upper electrode is positive relative to the lower one. The axillary (underarm) leads are also depicted in Fig. 12.4 and show placements at the level of the heart. They are moderately free from movement artifacts, but because they are over muscle tissue, arm movements may produce EMG artifacts.

Amplitude and Recording Characteristics of the ECG

In the normal ECG, Lead II produces an R wave that ranges in amplitude up to about 2 mV (Brener, 1967). This 2-mV peak is much larger than that encountered in either EEG or EMG recordings. The 2-mV peak amplitude must be amplified by a factor of 2,500 to bring it to us-

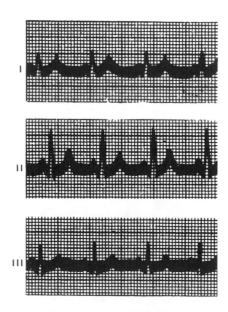

FIG. 12.3. Normal electrocardiograms recorded from three standard electrocardiographic leads.

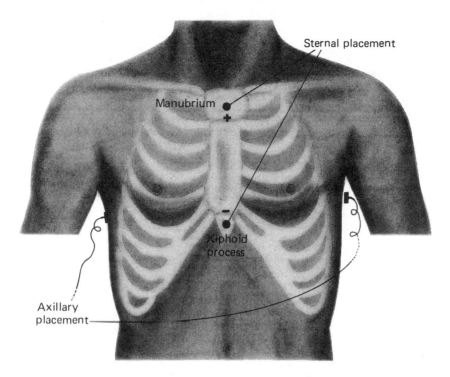

FIG. 12.4. Placement of electrodes at manubrium and xiphoid process of sternum enables recording of ECG with active subjects. The axillary placements are not as free from EMG artifact as are the sternal leads.

able level. The procedure in clinical work is to use a gain (amplification) setting that will allow a vertical deflection of 1 cm equal to 1 mV. A slightly higher gain would be used by researchers in psychophysiology. Paper speeds of 25 mm/sec enable good resolution of the various components of the ECG, and are necessary when investigators want information on interbeat intervals. When information on rate only is desired, speeds of 5 or 10 mm/sec are adequate.

Measures in Research

In studies of human performance, heart rate (HR) or heart period (HP) are commonly used as measures of heart activity. The HR is based on the number of beats per unit of time, for example, in beats per minute (BPM). It is based on the occurrence of the most prominent component of the ECG, the R wave. Thus, continuous recordings of HR may be taken and then BPM may be computed. Alternatively, 10 or 20 sec of the activity in a given minute may be sampled and taken as the HR for that period. The HR may also be continuously monitored by electronic counters, which can automatically print out the rate for given time periods.

The HP measures the time between one R wave and the next. Another way of referring to HP is the interbeat interval (IBI). The HP, or IBI, is expressed in milliseconds, and may be automatically measured by an event per unit time (EPUT) meter (Brown, 1972). This device is commercially available and can be connected to a printer to obtain a numeric readout of each heart period. Contemporary psychophysiologists more commonly use computers and appropriate software to process the signals generated by the ECG equipment. Researchers interested in changes in heart activity that can occur within a single cardiac cycle make use of the HP, or IBI, measure. Those interested in longer-term changes that occur over a period of 30 sec or more may use BPM. Still another way of looking at cardiac changes is in terms of HR variability. This is a measure of the stability of HR during baseline or during the performance of a task. For example, it has been suggested that attention-demanding tasks that require information processing result in less variation of HR from reading to reading (Walter & Porges, 1976). An important paper on heart rate variability as a psychophysiological variable was reported by a committee of experts in the use of the measure (see Berntson et al., 1997). This report covers the origins of heart rate variability, its measurement, and warnings about its interpretation.

Those interested in an alternate view of examining HR variability, other than using a variance statistic, may want to consult Heslegrave, Ogilvie, and Furedy (1979). They presented evidence to show that the combination of a successive difference mean square (SDMS) procedure as a variability statistic and IBI for the HR measure is best for assessing changes in HR variability under certain conditions. In addition, IBI may be preferable to BPM for showing average HR changes between conditions. Another measure proposed for use is T-wave amplitude. Recall that the T wave of the ECG represents repolarization of the ventricles and is positive going in the Lead II recording. It has been found to become less positive as SNS influence on the ventricles increases (Furedy & Heslegrave, 1983).

The ECG can be recorded on any physiological recorder that provides a pen deflection of 1 to 15 mm for each millivolt of signal and can process frequencies from 0.1 to 125 Hz (Brown, 1972). It is recorded with an AC amplifier. The ECG is not difficult to obtain, because it is a relatively large signal and does not require as much amplification as some other measures (e.g., EMG or EEG). With lower degrees of amplification, one is less likely to pick up unwanted electrical activity. Stern, Ray, and Davis (1980) pointed out that because HR has a frequency of about 1 Hz (1 cycle per sec), a filter can be set at 20 to 30 Hz, reducing the problem of 60-Hz noise and removing most muscle artifact. However, as with other physiological measures, the proper use and application of electrodes is critical in obtaining a good recording.

Impedance Cardiography.   The impedance cardiograph (ZCG) technique can provide valuable information about physical functions of the heart, as a supplement to electrical data provided by the ECG. The kinds of physical functions that may prove useful to psychophysiologists include cardiac output, stroke volume, ventricular ejection time, myocardial contractility, and total peripheral resistance.

The recording principle in impedance cardiography is that when a high frequency (e.g., 100 KHz), constant-current (4 mA) signal is passed across the thoracic cavity (chest), the impedance measured between two electrodes will vary with the volume of the cavity. The impedance decreases as volume increases. Double strips of electrode tape are placed around the neck and the chest at diaphragm level (see Miller & Horvath, 1978; and see especially Sherwood, Allen, Fahrenberg, Kelsey, Lovallo, & Van Doornen, 1990, who provide an important set of methodological guidelines for impedance cardiography). The top and bottom electrode strips are connected to a high frequency signal source, while the middle two record impedance changes (see Fig 12.5 for a schematic). Impedance cardiograph devices are available commercially, as are the strip chart recorders to which they are attached. The records may be hand scored from the chart paper for student exercises or, if recorded on FM tape, they may be processed offline with a computer program in research applications.

As explained earlier, cardiac output is a measure of the amount of blood, in liters, that the heart pumps per minute. Other measures that may be estimated with impedance cardiography include stroke volume (the amount of blood pumped per beat), myocardial contractility (the degree to which the heart muscle contracts in pumping blood), ventricular ejection time (the time it takes for the left ventricle to eject blood), and total peripheral resistance (resistance to

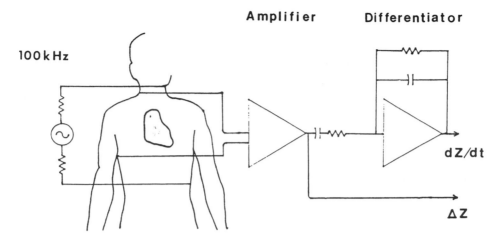

FIG. 12.5. Schematic diagram of impedance cardiograph. (Courtesy of Dr. Glenn Albright, Baruch College, C.U.N.Y.)

blood flow in the body). Figure 12.6 illustrates an impedance cardiograph record and how the various values are derived.

The Z_o value is the total impedance between Leads 2 and 3 (the two inner leads); dZ/dt is the first derivative of the change of impedance during a cardiac cycle; VET is ventricular ejection time; and R–Z is the time interval from the R wave of the ECG to maximum ejection as indicated by the peak of dZ/dt. Tursky and Jamner (1982) explained that psychophysiologists see promise for impedance cardiography as a method for measuring relative contributions of the PNS and SNS to cardiac function and as a useful technique in studies of hypertension. The technique also has clinical applications in measuring cardiac function before and after heart surgery. Miller and Horvath (1978) concluded that impedance cardiography gives a reliable within-subject estimate of relative changes in measures such as stroke volume and cardiac output, but is not as useful for comparing measures between subjects. In making impedance cardiograph recordings, subjects must be carefully instructed to hold their breath while several cardiac cycles are obtained (about 10 sec), otherwise breathing artifacts will appear in the record. Thus,

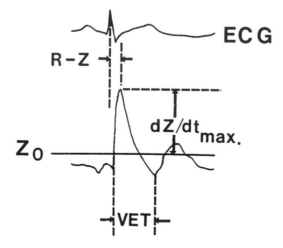

FIG. 12.6. Measurements taken from the impedance cardiograph. (Courtesy of Dr. Glenn Albright, Baruch College, C.U.N.Y.)

the researcher must take precautions in using this technique. An ambulatory monitor for impedance cardiography was described by Gonneke et al. (1996) and compared to standard impedance devices in the laboratory and during a 24-hr period during which the 26 subjects moved about and recorded their activities in a diary. The signal processor obtains input from 6 electrodes, 4 placed on the chest and 2 on the back. The values obtained with the portable device, except for stroke volume and cardiac output, correlated highly with standard laboratory impedance equipment. Thus, this device offers promise as a way to obtain information about important cardiovascular functions in real-life settings. As pointed out later in this chapter, studies of cardiovascular activity using impedance techniques are increasing in number.

Electrodes in ECG Recordings

A number of good commercially available electrodes may be used for research purposes. Electrodes can be made of stainless steel or silver. They are usually in the shape of flat discs, or cups, measuring from $1/2$ in. to 2 in. across. They are held in place by adjustable rubber straps, suction cups, surgical tape, or adhesive plastic strips. Some excellent electrodes have been developed in connection with the space program, and are especially suited for long-term recordings of 24 hr or more. One example is a silver disc embedded in a rubber suction cup with a center-mounted sponge that contains the electrolyte.

Electrodes should be applied to hairless sites, if possible. The area of application may be briskly rubbed with a gauze pad until the skin is slightly pink. Then, electrode jelly or paste is applied to the electrode before it is attached to the recording site. Electrodes should not be so tightly attached that they cause discomfort or muscle tremor, both of which can cause artifacts in the record. On the other hand, they must be prevented from moving, because this will also result in distorted recordings. As mentioned previously, the sternal lead is preferred for the moving subject. It also has the advantage of producing a large R wave. Leads II and III also produce large R waves. The large R wave is important in terms of ease of analyzing the data and providing a suitable signal for triggering automatic counters. Brown (1972) has recommended that the amplified R wave be used to activate a Schmitt trigger, a device that will enable signals to activate counters or cardiotachometers in a reliable manner. This kind of triggering is used less in psychophysiology laboratories as computer programs are now used increasingly to recognize the R wave and process the ECG.

For a freely ranging subject, telemetry or portable recorders may be used. Telemetry is far more comfortable for subjects. The subject wears electrodes and a small FM or AM transmitter (as light as 18 g), capable of sending heart signals to a recorder at another location, where the information may be recorded on FM tape. Miniature portable recorders enable ECGs to be obtained from subjects or patients as they go about their daily activities (e.g., see Gunn, Wolf, Block, & Person, 1972). Electrodes attached to the sternum and rib cage are fed into a small recorder that amplifies the signal and records it on tape. Modern recording units that can record ambulatory HR, systolic, diastolic, and mean arterial pressure weigh as little as 12.6 ounces. The measures obtained are equivalent to those obtained using the cuff/stethoscope auscultation method. Recordings can be made for up to 48 hours and the unit may be programmed to take samples at predetermined times or the patient can initiate readings. The large mass of data obtained can be downloaded onto a computer for offline analyses.

HEART ACTIVITY AND BEHAVIOR

The number of new behavioral studies using heart activity as a measure continues to be large. The heart and brain are still the favorite organs for psychophysiological research. The studies cited in this chapter are, by necessity, only representative of the large volume of research conducted in the last 30 years or so. Cardiac activity in relation to development, motor performance, cognition, perception, attention, emotional reactions, motivation, personality factors, and conditioning are covered in this chapter.

Developmental Factors

Monitoring of fetal HR in hospital maternity wards prior to delivery is a common practice. The use of ultrasonic technology makes the recording relatively noninvasive, and useful information about fetal distress during maternal contractions, and at other stages prior to delivery, can be obtained. Typically, the near-term fetal HR is about 140 bpm. During labor contractions, this rate goes up to about 160 bpm. The newborn baby has a HR of about 140 bpm and this rate drops to about 120 bpm after the first year. The 10-year-old child has an average HR of about 90 bpm, compared to the resting adult value of about 70 bpm for men and 76 bpm for women.

Attention and Heart Rate (HR).   Research on cardiac activity of infants and children in behavioral contexts has produced some interesting results. It has been found that newborns and young infants show HR decelerations ranging from 2 to 4 bpm when auditory or visual stimulation is terminated (Berg, 1974; Porges, Stamps, & Walter, 1974). This "offset response" reminds one of the HR deceleration that occurs in adults engaged in tasks requiring attention to stimuli. Richards (1988) studied the HR offset response of infants from 14 to 26 weeks of age, employing procedures in which attention to the interrupted stimuli was assured. Visual stimulation was used and the offset response was small but reliable. Richards also reported that infants with high levels of respiratory sinus arrhythmia (RSA) showed higher HR offset responses than low RSA infants. The RSA is being used increasingly as a measure of vagus nerve control (parasympathetic) of heart activity (see Berntson, Cacioppo, & Quigley, 1993). The RSA is basically a measure of HR variability due to respiratory activity, that is, HR accelerates shortly after respiration begins and decreases shortly after the start of exhalation. Psychophysiologists think that RSA may reflect capacity to pay attention to stimuli. In general, it has been found that HR slows and variability decreases during intensive attention to stimuli.

Heart rate variability during attentional phases in young infants was studied by Richards and Casey (1991). The subjects were groups of infants tested at 14-, 20-, or 26-weeks-old. Visual presentations consisted of a "Sesame Street" program, the onset of which produced HR deceleration. When HR returned to prestimulus levels, a computer-generated pattern replaced "Sesame Street," either immediately or after a delay. Heart rate variability decreased during attention and returned to prestimlulus levels 5 sec after termination of attention. Baseline RSA increased over the age range used. As in previous studies, high RSA infants showed sustained HR deceleration during attention compared to low RSA infants. Also, the HR response during sustained attention increased with age.

The auditory system of the human fetus is mature at about 6 months gestational age, and there is some evidence that the fetus may respond to sound as early as 3 months. An investigation of infants tested less than 24 hr after birth revealed that they responded with significant HR deceleration to recordings of their mother's spontaneous speech (Ockleford, Vince, Layton, & Reader, 1988). The results show discrimination between the mothers' and strangers' voices and suggest that the mother's voice is of particular significance to the newborn. These provocative results require replication.

Emotional Reactions in Children.   The relationship between HR variability and emotional reactivity of children was examined by Fox (1989). Infants were tested as newborns, and then again at 5 and 14 months of age. The data suggest that infants with high RSA (high vagal tone) were more reactive to both positive ("peek-a-boo") and negative (restraint) events at 5 months than those with low RSA (low vagal tone). Further, those with high vagal tone were more sociable and approachable, and spent less time close to their mothers at 14 months of age. Hence, the reactive infant at 5 months was the more sociable toddler at 14 months. It is suggested that the differences in behavior are a stable dimension during the first year and that they are associated with varying degrees of parasympathetic influence.

In another study, preschool children (average age of 5 years) and second graders (mean of 7 years) watched three film clips (70 sec) while HR was monitored (Eisenberg, Fabes, Bustamante, Mathy, Miller, & Lindholm, 1988). Children in both age groups showed HR acceleration during a film used to provoke anxiety, introduced by the experimenters as a "film about a little boy and girl who are scared during a thunderstorm." On the other hand, HR deceleration was found while subjects viewed a film that induced sadness, "about a girl who was sad because her pet died" and for another used to generate feelings of sympathy "about a girl who had a problem walking and had to use crutches." Observed facial expressions and self-report data confirmed that the young subjects had the expected reactions. Thus, in this study, different patterns of IIR were obtained for situations likely to induce various emotional reactions. Taken together, the two studies suggest that children evidence differential HR that may depend on vagal tone and their interpretation of an emotion-provoking situation.

Temperamental categories labeled "inhibited to the unfamiliar" and "uninhibited to the unfamiliar" have been used by Kagan and associates to classify children (Kagan, Reznick, & Snidman, 1988). Inhibited children are shy with unfamiliar people, timid in unfamiliar situations, and fearful when presented with novel situations, in contrast to the uninhibited child. Kagan and colleagues reported that inhibited children show larger HR and blood pressure increases to mental and physical stress than the uninhibited children. Studies by the same group indicated that the combination of high motor activity and frequent irritability (high reactivity) in response to unfamiliar stimuli predicted later fearfulness. The highly reactive infants were most likely to become behaviorally inhibited later on (Kagan & Snidman, 1991). The question of relationships between cardiac data and temperamental characteristics of high and low reactivity was explored by Kagan and associates (Snidman, Kagan, Riordan, & Shannon, 1995). A longitudinal study was conducted in which initial heart activity data were collected approximately 2 weeks before birth and again at intervals from 2 weeks to 21 months of age. Cardiac measures at 2 weeks and 2 months of age were better predictors of the temperamental categories than later measures of the same variables.

Summary.   Young infants show HR deceleration and decreased variability to both onset and offset of stimuli, a response similar to adults engaged in attentional tasks. High respiratory sinus arrhythmia (RSA) was correlated with greativity reactivity to both positive and negative stimuli in a sample of 5-month-old infants. Older children (5 and 7 years) have shown differential patterns of HR in situations that produced various emotional reactions. In all of these respects, the responses of infants and young children is similar to those of adults. Investigations by Kagan and colleagues suggest that cardiac function early in life may be a good predictor of temperamental behavior, such as high and low reactivity at 4 months of age and fear of the unfamiliar in the second year.

Performance and Heart Activity

It is well known that vigorous muscular activity produces a requirement for increased blood supply, and that heart activity speeds up under these conditions. There is a shift of blood flow away from the skin, gastrointestinal tract, and kidneys to the skeletal muscles. Hence, under continued strenuous motor performance, increases in HR would be expected. However, there are motor activities, for example, simple RT, that require only periodic and brief movements, involving muscles to a minimal degree. In this section, we examine two categories of motor activities: (a) the type associated with quick, unstrenuous responses, as in reaction time, and (b) those in which continuous, complex, or strenuous motor performance is required as in continuous tracking or exercise.

Reaction Time.   An interesting body of research concerns the relationship between cardiac activity and RT. A number of investigators have found that decreased HR occurs during the fixed foreperiod of simple RT experiments (e.g., Lacey, 1967; Obrist, Webb, & Sutterer, 1969; Webb & Obrist, 1970). There have been suggestions that greater magnitudes of HR slowing are related to faster RTs.

Although HR deceleration has sometimes been associated with faster RTs in situations where fixed foreperiods are used, this does not appear to hold when HR is controlled by external factors or when no warning signal is used. For example, the HR of cardiac patients with pacemakers was manipulated and no relation was found between RT and different rates of cardiac pacing (Nowlin, Eisdorfer, Whalen, & Troyer, 1970). In another study, Surwillo (1971) measured HR and RTs of 100 healthy males in three experimental sessions. Stimuli occurred at random (no warning or foreperiod), and RTs were collected as HR varied spontaneously. Cardiac deceleration to stimuli was not observed under these conditions. Thus, these last two studies indicate that HR slowing and RT were unrelated when an external cardiac pacemaker was used and when stimuli were presented without regular foreperiods.

The relationship among RT, HR, and measures of task-irrelevant somatic activity (eye movements and blinks, chin EMG, and general bodily activity) was studied in groups of children and an adult reference group (Obrist, Howard, Sutterer, Hennis, & Murrell, 1973). The children were groups of 4-, 5-, 8-, and 10-year-olds. The purpose was to study the cardiac–somatic hypothesis that HR and ongoing somatic activities vary in a similar direction. All groups showed a decrease in HR and a drop in task-irrelevant activities coincident with making the relevant response. However, there was no relation between age and degree of HR deceleration, although RT was faster in older children. Klorman (1975) measured HR and RT in groups of preadolescent (10 years of age), adolescent (14 years), and young adult (19 years) males. The task was simple RT with a relatively long (5-sec) foreperiod. His HR findings agreed with those of Obrist et al. (1973) in that there was no systematic age difference in cardiac deceleration, even though older subjects had quicker RTs.

B. C. Lacey and J. I. Lacey (1977) used a fixed-foreperiod RT paradigm and measured heart period (R–R interval) as a function of time at which an imperative stimulus was presented in the cardiac cycle. They found that magnitude of HR deceleration during the preparatory interval depended on where in the cardiac cycle the imperative signal was presented. If it occurred early (4th decile) in the cycle, deceleration was much greater than if the imperative signal came late (10th decile) in the cycle. Earlier stimuli produce HR deceleration because they have more time to exert an influence (Velden, Barry, & Wolk, 1987). The Laceys attributed the speed of this HR deceleration to the quick action of the vagus nerve.

Phasic cardiac responses were studied during choice RT by Jennings and Wood (1977). The cardiac cycle time was varied by presenting stimuli at either the R wave or 350 msec later. An interesting finding was that when responses occurred early in the cycle, anticipatory deceleration ended and shifted to acceleration within the same heartbeat. However, if responses occurred later than 300 msec after the R wave, the shift from slowing to speeding was delayed until the next heartbeat. To explain this, Jennings and Wood hypothesized that the vagal inhibitory activity responsible for slowing HR ends when a task is completed, and, therefore, the shift to speeding depends on the time course of inhibition by the vagus nerve. The RT data showed that magnitudes of both HR deceleration and accelerative recovery were larger for faster responses. However, speed of RT was not related to time of stimulation within the cardiac cycle. Coles, Pellegrini, and Wilson (1982) found that both warning stimuli and stimuli to respond produced a decelerative effect on HR. Deceleration was not found with slow HR subjects while they were breathing in, suggesting that vagus nerve influence on HR slowing was modified by level of HR and phase of the respiratory cycle. Coles and colleagues found no evidence for a cardiac cycle time effect on RT speed. Methodologically, their results suggest the importance of considering respiratory phase in evaluating cardiac cycle time effects.

Summary.   It is well established that HR deceleration occurs during the fixed foreperiod of an RT task. The relationship between magnitude of HR slowing and speed of RT is still a point of controversy. It is clear that when an RT task is performed under conditions in which HR is externally manipulated, or without fixed foreperiods or warning signals, there is no HR decrease associated with the period just prior to the response or during the response itself. The general findings suggest that unmanipulated cardiac deceleration represents a preparaton to respond when an individual expects a significant stimulus. Differential changes in HR deceleration have not been found across age groups for children, although RT is faster in adolescents and young adults than in children. Findings also indicate that magnitude of HR deceleration during the preparatory interval of an RT task depends on time of event occurrence within the cardiac cycle. In addition, it has been found that when RT responses occurred early enough in a cycle, deceleration ended and shifted to acceleration within the same heartbeat. Speed of RT has not been found to be related to time of stimulation in the cardiac cycle. Inhibitory activity of the vagus nerve has been proposed as a mechanism responsible for HR slowing observed in these situations.

Complex Motor Performance and Heart Activity.   Ohkubo and Hamley (1972) obtained measures of HR during a 5-day period while individuals learned to drive a car. The subjects were instructed in driving along an isolated course five times during each day of training. As proficiency increased, a marked decrease was observed in HR during both rest and driving periods. A more convenient way of measuring HR responses in a stressful situation was used by Lewis, Ray, Wilkinson, and Ricketts (1984), who introduced the "zipwire" slide. In this situation, a person slides down a 60-ft wire, via a pulley, from a 35-ft height. The task allows experimenters to repeat a number of trials over a relatively brief period of time. In their study, Lewis and collaborators had male and female subjects without previous risk sport experience (e.g., no skydiving) complete eight runs on the zipwire while HR and self-reports of anxiety level were obtained. Telemetered HR was obtained at seven stages, from climbing the ladder to reaching the ground. The HR peaked during the slide, and levels for males and females were similar. However, females reported more anxiety than males. An interesting sex difference emerged because females who had the greatest increases in HR also reported the highest anxiety, but males with the greatest HR increases reported the lowest anxiety levels. One might speculate that the more anxious males could hide this fact in the self-report, but not in their HR measures.

An intriguing observation is that HR often increases more during the performance of certain motor tasks than would be expected purely on the basis of increased energy expenditure. This was first reported for a reaction time-avoidance task where subjects were required to react quickly to avoid an electric shock (Obrist et al., 1973). Increases in HR occurred after the response was made, and motor activity was not very great. Turner, Caroll, and Courtney (1983) examined HR and respiration changes while subjects played the computer game "Space Invaders," and also when the game proceeded automatically, and subjects did not affect the outcome. It was clear that the HR increases during actual playing of the game were much greater than expected from the amount of energy used. Also, some subjects showed larger-than-average HR reactivity to the "Space Invader" task, a mean of 15.7 BPM compared to 1.9 BPM for low reactors. The study affirms previous findings that HR does increase beyond metabolic requirements in a challenging perceptual motor task, and that some individuals may be classified as high HR reactors.

A number of studies have indicated that a combination of exercise and psychological stress produces greater cardiovascular response than either alone. One investigation used impedance cardiography derived measures of HR, stroke volume, cardiac output, and pre-ejection period and found the same result (Rouselle, Blascovich, & Kelsey, 1995). The psychological stressor was mental arithmetic (4 min) and the physiological one was pedaling on a bicycle ergometer under a 50-watt workload, also for 4 min. These findings indicate that exercise did not mask the increased cardiovascular activity evoked by a psychological stressor.

Summary.   Habituation of heart rate was shown as subjects learned to drive a car over a 5-day period. Anxiety generated through participation in a threatening zipwire ride produced expected increases in HR, but self-reports of anxiety correlated positively with HR levels for women and negatively for men. The fact that HR increases during performance of certain motor tasks, at a level greater than would be expected from merely increased metabolic requirements, points up the emotional impact of performing such tasks as well as individual differences in cardiovascular reactivity. The emotional impact of performing psychologically stressful tasks is not masked by physical activity as shown by findings indicating that, although both physical activity and psychological stress produce increased cardiovascular activity, simultaneous exercise and stress result in even greater increases.

Heart Activity and Mental Performance

This section considers heart activity and mental performance in situations where the task or task situation was not intended to be stressful or provoke an emotional reaction. The latter type of relationship is examined in a subsequent section. This section focuses on the relationship between cardiac activity and verbal learning, problem solving, and cognitive activity (thoughts and imagery).

Verbal Learning.   In one study of verbal learning, Andreassi (1966) investigated the relationship between HR, SCL, SCRs, and difficulty of materials to be learned. (The SCL and SCR findings were discussed in chapter 9.) The mean HR was significantly higher when subjects learned the easiest list than when they performed with lists of moderate or high difficulty. Thus, superior performance was related to elevated HR. The results suggested that during superior performance, the individuals became more involved in the learning task, and this effect was reflected in the increased HR. A similar finding was reported by Malmo (1965), who found that HR was consistently higher during tracking trials where performance was better, as compared to the poor-performance trials. This could be taken as evidence that good performance is motivating.

Andreassi and Whalen (1967) reported that the HR of college students was significantly elevated during learning verbal materials compared to resting. When the same materials were presented for 20 more trials after original learning (an "overlearning" sequence), HR showed a significant decrease. Finally, the requirement to learn a new list of materials again produced a significant increase in HR. The original learning presented a sufficient cognitive challenge to subjects, and HR increased accordingly. However, habituation of HR occurred when subjects were no longer required to assimilate novel materials.

Problem Solving.   Lacey presented a theoretical framework that relates HR to a subject's interaction with the environment (see Lacey, 1967; Kagan, Lacey, & Moss, 1963). According to this theoretical orientation, decreased HR during performance of a task is associated with increased sensitivity to stimulation, and occurs when a situation requires mental intake of environmental stimuli. This theory further states that increased HR accompanies mental elaboration, as during the solution of a problem. Steele and Lewis (1968) found support for the second of these hypotheses. They measured HR of subjects in four age groups while problems involving mental arithmetic were solved. The age groups were 6 to 8, 9 to 11, 12 to 15, and 16 to 27 years. The researchers reported an immediate acceleration of HR with each problem, an effect that lasted for three cardiac cycles and then fell below resting levels. This was true for all subjects in all age groups. Thus, the results support the hypothesis that cardiac acceleration accompanies the mental elaboration, or active processing of information necessary in problem solving and other cognitive tasks. Note that the task is much more complex here compared to when a subject waits for a stimulus to occur after a warning signal. In this latter instance, as discussed previously, HR deceleration occurs during that waiting period.

In another approach, HR and SCL were monitored continuously while undergraduates solved either seven riddles (humorous) or seven problems (Goldstein, Harman, McGhee, & Karasik, 1975). One theory of humor suggests that it is basically a problem-solving process, involving both a perception and a resolution of certain features of the joke. Riddles were chosen for comparison with problems, because they have structural similarities; that is, they have a similar question (Q) and answer (A) format. Goldstein and associates tested the hypothesis that physiological arousal would occur during the Q portion of the riddle or problem, and drop to the prestimulus level shortly after the punch line or answer is provided. The riddles were unsolvable because the subjects never heard them before, and the problems were also insoluble because the 3 seconds between Q and A was not sufficient to allow solutions. A sample riddle was: Q: "How can you tell an honest politician?" A: "When he's bought, he stays bought." A sample problem used was: Q: "What is the least common multiple of 3, 8, 9, and 12?" A: "72." Heart rate increased once a riddle or problem was presented, and decelerated when the solution was given. Thus, HR did not differentiate between riddles and problems, which is not surprising given their structural similarities. However, the basic results are similar to those of other experiments because HR increases occurred when the information of the riddle was being processed and then dropped as the answer was given and the person waited for the next item.

Imagery and Meditation.   The question here concerns the effects of thoughts and images on heart activity. Although common experience might tell us that thinking about certain activities can produce a physiological response, the verification of this intuitive truth is not simple. Suppose an experimenter asks a subject to imagine being fearful while HR is being measured? If a change is observed, a problem then arises concerning whether the physiological response results from the instruction to "image" or the imagery itself. Although there has not been much research in this area, the findings obtained are suggestive. For example, Schwartz (1971) developed a procedure to obtain cardiac responses to specific internal (thought) stimuli in the absence of external stimuli. Immediately on the presentation of a tone, subjects were asked to think of a number sequence. The number sequence was followed by thoughts of letters (e.g., A, B, etc.) or of emotional words (e.g., rape, death). The subjects were asked to experience any thoughts that accompanied these letters or words. The results showed that subjects had significantly higher HRs when thinking about emotional words than when thinking about letters. The data clearly indicated that different thought sequences can produce different cardiac responses.

A promising technique that uses imagery to evoke different emotional states has been described by Roberts and Weerts (1982). Subjects were carefully selected according to their ability to imagine arousing emotional scenes during a screening interview. There were significant HR increases for the high anger and fear imagery versus the low intensity conditions. It was also suggested that subjects showing the largest physiological changes focused on their responses in the emotional imagery, rather than the stimuli.

Imagery has been used to determine whether people who have exaggerated concerns about their health ("hypervigilants") show excessive HR activity when imagining threats to their health (Brownlee, Leventhal, & Balaban, 1992). Previously, Lang and his colleagues (e.g., Lang, 1984; Lang, Levin, Miller, & Kozak, 1983) reported that persons whose memory structures include physiological components show stonger ANS responses during imagery. Brownlee et al. (1992) asked subjects to listen to descriptions of two illnesses and to imagine they were the person being described. Neutral and exercise scenes were employed as controls. Compared to control subjects, the HR of "hypervigilant" subjects increased while listening to the illness descriptions and took longer to return to baseline levels. The authors believed that the results lend support to a theory of intrusive memory (Horowitz, 1985) in which anxiety-provoking images are reflected in cardiovascular activity. Sinha, Lovallo, and Parsons (1992) employed visual imagery of situations designed to evoke fear, anger, action, sadness, or joy. Compared to baseline, HR acceleration averaged 13 bpm for anger imagery and 12 BPM for fear and imagery involving activity. Imagery involving sadness and joy produced HR increases of 8 BPM.

A number of physiological responses were recorded while subjects practiced transcendental meditation (TM) according to the method of the Maharishi Mahesh Yogi (Wallace & Benson, 1972). During meditation, HR slowed, SCL decreased, and EEG alpha activity increased. The subjects were described as being in a wakeful, but very relaxed state. In fact, the investigators observed that the physiological changes during TM, a relatively easily learned technique, were very similar to those observed in highly trained yoga experts and in Zen monks, who have had 15 to 20 years of experience in meditation. These results led the authors to suggest that the possibilities for clinical application of this relaxing technique should be investigated further.

The effects of imagining various scenes on persons classified as Type A or Type B personality was studied by Baker, Hastings, and Hart (1984). Scenes were either neutral or designed to provoke the Type A personality in accordance with the concept of Type A as being impatient, competitive, and hard-driving. A sample provocative scene was, "You are standing in a slowly moving line at the store. Although the sign says '10 items, cash only,' the person in front of you has 15 items and wants to write a check." Scenes such as these produced much higher increases in HR and neck EMG in Type A persons, but neutral scenes did not differentiate the groups.

Summary. It has been observed that elevated HR occurs during the acquisition phase of verbal learning, especially if performance is successful. Continued repetition of familiar materials will produce habituation of the HR response. Decreased HR has been reported in tasks requiring mental intake of stimuli. Conversely, cardiac acceleration accompanies mental elaboration in a problem-solving task. Imagery involving highly charged emotional words or situations led to significantly higher HR than imagery of nonemotional stimuli. Individuals described as having exaggerated health concerns show high HR when imagining illness compared to control subjects. It also took their HR longer to return to baseline levels than controls. On the other hand, practice of transcendental meditation results in HR slowing. Personality factors have also been linked to HR reactivity. There is much need for further work in this area to reveal the cardiac effects of various qualities and intensities of mental and imaginal experience.

Heart Activity and Perception

This section examines cardiac correlates of perceptual thresholds and stimulus significance.

Perceptual Thresholds. Auditory thresholds were measured under conditions designed to test J. I. Lacey et al.'s (1963) suggestion that lowered HR could lead to greater sensory sensitivity (Edwards & Alsip, 1969). According to Lacey, decreases in HR facilitates sensory intake because decreased baroreceptor pressure leads to greater cortical activity. The rest of the hypothesis is that increased HR improves mental work (not simple sensory intake) because it facilitates rejection of potentially distracting environmental stimuli. In a study by Edwards and Alsip, 25 tones (near threshold levels) were presented during high HR, and 25 during periods of low HR. Edwards and Alsip found no difference in the number of correct detections under high and low HR, indicating a lack of support for the baroreceptor hypothesis. Another approach has been to examine phases within a cardiac cycle for differences in performance since, for example, baroreceptor activity is greater during ventricular systole (QRS) than diastole (P and T wave). The idea that subjects would be most sensitive to visual stimuli during the P wave, and least sensitive during the QRS complex was tested by Elliott and Graf (1972). They presented subjects with 96 stimuli at four phases of the cardiac cycle: P, QRS, T, and T–P. No detection differences were found at any of these four phases. Velden and Juris (1975) also failed to find variations in perceptual performance when tracing signal detectability in steps of 66, 100, and 200 msec of the cardiac cycle. However, when examining steps of 33 msec, they did find a systematic variation with phases of the cardiac cycle. Their subjects were required to detect a 1000-Hz tone from a white noise background while heart activity was measured.

Although a relationship between sensory sensitivity and cardiac cycle has not been firmly established, Schell and Catania (1975) presented some evidence that a general cardiac deceleration is related to increased sensory acuity. Their subjects were tested under conditions in which a warning signal preceded the threshold stimulus by a time sufficient to allow a cardiac response. Greater HR deceleration occurred when the threshold visual stimulus was detected than when it was not. The authors concluded that degree of sensitivity to the environment may be predicted by observing cardiac activity. Carriero and Fite (1977) also found superior perceptual performance related to cardiac deceleration. In their experiment, individuals judged the relative positions of a black bar projected on a screen. They found that accurate judgments were accompanied by greater cardiac deceleration to stimulus onset than were inaccurate judgments. However, they noted that this relationship existed only during the first half of the experiment.

Stimulus Significance. The effects of a 1000-Hz tone (70 dB) on HR were studied by Keefe and Johnson (1970). They reported a complex HR response that consisted of an initial small deceleration followed by a more marked acceleration and then by another deceleration. A similar finding for a 100-Hz tone (85 dB) was reported by Graham and Slaby (1973), that is, a triphasic HR response of deceleration-acceleration-deceleration. However, for broadband white noise (50–10000 Hz at 85 dB), a diphasic cardiac response was obtained with acceleration followed by deceleration (see Fig. 12.7). The differential effects of these two types of auditory stimulation should be taken into account in studies of cardiac response to auditory stimulation.

In related work, Hatton, Berg, and Graham (1970) found that if sound intensity is high enough, rapid rise time produces HR acceleration that occurs within the first second of stimulus onset. However, if rise time is gradual, acceleration begins only after a 1- or 2-sec delay, even with high intensities.

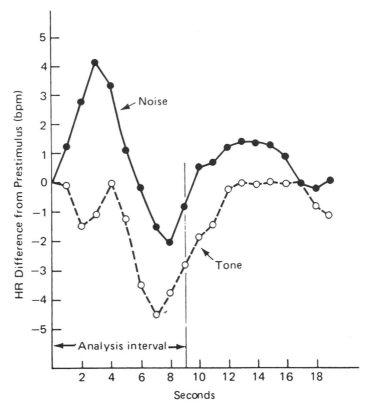

FIG. 12.7. HR change from a prestimulus period averaged over 10 presentations of 5-second 85-dB white noise and a 1000 Hz tone.

The heart responses of students to a high-speed dental drill were measured by Gang and Teft (1975). Sixteen of the subjects were dental hygiene students, and 22 were liberal arts majors. The sound level of the dental drill ranged from 90 to 95 db. Cardiac accelerations were obtained to the sound of the dental drill, but they were most pronounced in those subjects who had unpleasant experiences in the dental office as patients and who were not familiar with the high-speed drill. Those who had pleasant experiences in the dental office and were familiar with the drill had the smallest amount of HR acceleration. The authors concluded that the subjects were responding not only to the intensity of the stimulus but also to its meaning.

Summary.   The suggested relationship between perceptual sensitivity and phase of the cardiac cycle has not been confirmed by research findings. However, there is some evidence that cardiac deceleration, in general, may be related to superior perceptual performance. These results are similar to those reported for RT and cardiac activity. Auditory stimuli will result in HR changes. The responses to pure tones versus white noise are different. The response to a meaningful stimulus (dental drill) tended to be greater than to nonmeaningful stimuli. In general, the initial HR response is a decrease with moderate intensities (less than 75–80 db) and an increase with higher intensities (Turpin, 1986).

Heart Activity, Attention, and the Orienting Response

Attention refers to the act of focusing awareness on some aspect of a stimulus situation. Over the years, a great deal of evidence has accumulated to show that physiological changes accompany variations in attention. One common observation is that HR slows briefly either before an expected event or following a significant, but unexpected, occurrence. Jennings (1986) discussed some situational characteristics that influence HR deceleration. Included among these are: (a) the event must be a significant one to the person; (b) the estimate of event occurrence must be fairly precise; (c) when anticipation ends, the deceleration stops; and (d) detection difficulty enhances deceleration. Thus, a decrease in HR is an indicator of the initiation and termination of an attentional state. A widely accepted model that addresses the question of HR deceleration in RT tasks is given by Jennings' capacity hypothesis (1986, 1992). According to Jennings, HR deceleration indexes the holding of available capacity to perform mental operations on expected input. On the other hand, HR acceleration indicates that processing capacity is allocated to ongoing mental and motor activities. The notion that HR deceleration reflects preparations that facilitate the intake of stimuli rather than response preparation was empirically supported by DePascalis, Barry, and Sparita (1995). In a fixed-period RT task that also required recognition of visual stimuli, they found HR decreases in the interval immediately before the target stimulus, and even greater decreases just before the onset of a signal that gave feedback about the subject's performance. Because greater HR deceleration occurred before a feedback signal (no motor response required) than for the probe stimulus, it was concluded that HR deceleration expresses stimulus processing rather than preparation to respond.

Theorists have differing perspectives regarding the role of HR deceleration in attentional situations. In the view of Lacey and Lacey (1980), the decrease in HR enhances receptivity to new stimuli and improves response effectiveness. Graham (1979) interpreted cardiac deceleration mainly in terms of enhancing the input of stimuli. In contrast to the Laceys and to Graham, Obrist (1981) emphasized the decrease in motor activity that accompanies HR deceleration. To Obrist, the HR change is not a direct effect of attention, but an indirect one caused by a quieting of motor activity. Thus, in the case of stimulus intake, the drop in HR reflects the general somatic quieting observed in that kind of situation. These conceptual viewpoints are discussed further in chapter 18.

Graham and Clifton (1966) reviewed the hypotheses of Sokolov (1963) and J. I. Lacey et al. (1963) regarding heart activity during the orienting response (OR). They noted that Sokolov proposed cardiac acceleration as the OR to novel stimuli, whereas Lacey et al. hypothesized HR deceleration as facilitating the reception of stimuli. Graham and Clifton reviewed a number of studies in which HR changes took place in response to weak and moderate stimuli and showed habituation over trials. They concluded that the OR was accompanied by HR deceleration and that HR acceleration most likely represented a "defense reaction" to stimuli of "prepain" intensity. Pursuing this question further, Raskin, Kotses, and Bever (1969) found that an 80-dB stimulus resulted in a brief HR deceleration, whereas one of 120-dB produced HR acceleration (see Fig. 12.8). Thirty males received 30 presentations of .5 sec white noise at each level of stimulation. The brief HR deceleration to the 80-dB stimulus was interpreted as representing the OR, whereas the acceleration to the 120-dB stimulus reflected a defensive reaction (DR). Turpin and Siddle (1983) filled in the range of stimuli by using tones of 45, 60, 75, 90, and 105 dB while recording HR. Stimuli up to 75 dB produced cardiac deceleration, whereas the higher intensities elicited acceleration. These results supported the Graham–Clifton formulation of the OR and DR. Note that the HR analysis in Fig. 12.8 is based on beat-by-beat changes. The abbreviations PA and BC in Fig. 12.8 stand for forehead-skin pulse amplitude and forehead-skin blood content, respectively.

As discussed in chapter 4, REM sleep has been associated with dreaming. Periods of rapid nystagmoid eye movements, called *eye bursts*, occur during REM sleep and have been related to orientation to dream content. Taylor, Moldofsky, and Furedy (1985) hypothesized that if eye bursts represent orientation to dream content, then HR deceleration should occur, just as it occurs in the waking OR. In support of their hypothesis, they found that HR decelera-

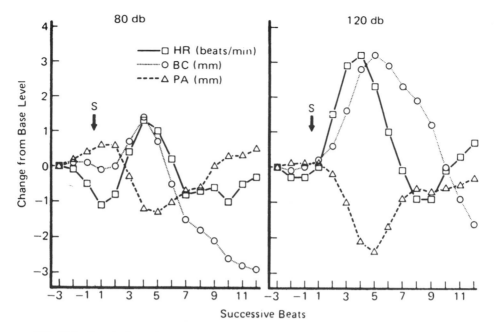

FIG. 12.8. Beat-by-beat changes in mean PA (pulse amplitude), BC (blood content) and HR from prestimulus beat 3 produced by 30 presentations of two stimulus intensities.

tions preceded eye bursts in REM sleep. There is suggestive evidence that dream intensity is high during eye burst periods, but Taylor and colleagues failed to waken their subjects for dream reports during eye burst or more quiet periods. Nevertheless, their study suggests some interesting possibilities for further work.

In another approach to studying the OR, Hare (1972) used slides of homicide victims to study HR response to unpleasant stimulation. Forty-nine college students participated in this experiment, in which a beat-by-beat analysis of HR was performed. Hare reported three different groups of responders based on the HR data. One group of 9 subjects showed acceleration, 12 gave marked deceleration, and the remaining 28 persons produced moderate deceleration. The results support the contention that the OR consists of HR deceleration and that the DR consists of HR acceleration. However, the generalizability of the finding is somewhat limited as a result of the individual differences found. The result regarding individual differences was followed up by Hare (1973).

In this study, he recorded HR of 10 subjects who feared spiders and compared them to 10 others who did not fear spiders. The 20 subjects viewed spider slides and slides of neutral objects, for example, landscapes. It was predicted that those persons who feared spiders would show a DR in the form of accelerated HR. The prediction was confirmed, as Hare observed that subjects with spider fears had HR acceleration and those without showed deceleration, especially when they found the slides interesting. The two groups showed no differences with respect to the neutral slides. Thus, the type and intensity of stimuli used and the possible role of individual differences should be considered in studies of the OR and DR. This latter point was made clear in a study by Eves and Gruzelier (1984). They found evidence for individual differences in response to very high intensity tones (112 to 127 dB). Initial HR acceleration was followed by another large increase in one group of subjects (accelerators), but this secondary increase did not occur in another group (decelerators). Subjects apparently differed in their evaluation of the aversiveness of, and response to, identical stimuli, as also noted in the study using a dental drill. There is good support for the hypothesis that HR deceleration is associated with the OR and stimulus intake, whereas HR acceleration accompanies the DR and stimulus rejection.

In a study of persons listening to continuous verbal text, Spence, Lugo, and Youdin (1972) found a decrease in HR when they directed their attention to external stimlul. The individuals listened to a taped psychoanalytic interview while HR was measured. Cardiac deceleration was associated with the main theme of the therapeutic interview, that is, references to termination of the patient's treatment. Although this experiment did not investigate the OR in terms of a reaction to a discrete stimulus, the general result is congruent with the notion that attention to external stimuli results in cardiac deceleration.

Summary.   The main theme of this section is that HR deceleration is related to stimulus intake and the orienting response, whereas HR acceleration accompanies stimulus rejection and the defensive response. This theme has been supported by a number of converging studies including those using relatively low-intensity sounds and very high-intensity auditory stimuli, reactions of phobics and nonphobics to spiders and homicide scenes, correlations of HR deceleration with eye bursts in REM sleep, and listening to a taped interview. Thus, there is a consistent body of work that confirms the relation between changes in heart activity and orienting and defensive responses.

REFERENCES

Andreassi, J. L. (1966). Some physiological correlates of verbal learning task difficulty. *Psychonomic Science, 6*, 69–70.

Andreassi, J. L., & Whalen, P. M. (1967). Some physiological correlates of learning and overlearning. *Psychophysiology, 3*, 406–413.

Astrand, P., & Rodahl, K. (1977). *Textbook of work physiology.* New York: McGraw-Hill.

Baker, L. J., Hastings, J. E., & Hart, J. D. (1984). Enhanced psycho-physiological responses of Type A coronary patients during Type A-relevant imagery. *Journal of Behavioral Medicine, 7*, 287–306.

Berg, W. K. (1974). Cardiac orienting responses of 6- and 16-week-old infants. *Journal of Experimental Child Psychology, 17*, 303–312.

Berntson, G. G., Cacioppo, J. T., & Quigley, K. S. (1993). Respiratory sinus arrhythmia: Autonomic origins, physiological mechanisms, and psychophysiological implications. *Psychophysiology, 30*, 183–196.

Berntson, G. G., Bigger, J. T., Jr., Eckberg, D. L., Grossman, P., Kaufmann, P. G., Malik, M., Nagaraja, H. N., Porges, S. W., Saul, J. P., Stone, P. H., & Van Der Molen, M. W. (1997). Heart rate variability: Origins, methods, and interpretive caveats. *Psychophysiology, 34*, 623–648.

Brener, J. (1967). Heart-rate. In P. H. Venables & I. Martin (Eds.), *Manual of psychphysiological methods* (pp. 103–131). Amsterdam: North-Holland.

Brown, C. S. (1972). Instruments in psychophysiology. In N. S. Greenfield & R. A. Sternbach (Eds.), *Handbook of psychophysiology* (pp. 159–195). New York: Holt.

Brownlee, S., Leventhal, H., & Balaban, M. (1992). Autonomic correlates of illness imagery. *Psychophysiology, 29*, 142–153.

Carriero, N. J., & Fite, J. (1977). Cardiac deceleration as an indicator of correct performance. *Perceptual & Motor Skills, 44*, 275–282.

Cohen, D. H., & MacDonald, R. L. (1974). A selective review of central pathways involved in cardiovascular control. In P. A. Obrist, A. H. Black, J. Brener, & L. V. DiCara (Eds.), *Cardiovascular psychophysiology* (pp. 33–59). Chicago: Aldine.

Coles, M. G. H., Pellegrini, A. M., & Wilson, G. V. (1982). The cardiac cycle time effect: Influence of respiration phase and information processing requirements. *Psychophysiology, 19*, 648–657.

DePascalis, V., Barry, R. J., & Sparita, A. (1995). Decelerative changes in heart rate during recognition of visual stimuli: effects of psychological stress. *International Journal of Psychophysiology, 20*, 21–31.

Edwards, D. C., & Alsip, J. E. (1969). Stimulus detection during periods of high and low heart rate. *Psychophysiology, 5*, 431–434.

Eisenberg, N., Fabes, R. A., Bustamante, D., Mathy, R. M., Miller, P. A., & Lindholm, E. (1988). Differentiation of vicariously induced emotional reactions in children. *Developmental Psychology, 24*, 237–246.

Elliott, R., & Graf, V. (1972). Visual sensitivity as a function of phase of cardiac cycle. *Psychophysiology, 9*, 357–361.

Eves, F. F., & Gruzelier, J. H. (1984). Individual differences in the cardiac response to high intensity auditory stimulation. *Psychophysiology, 21*, 342–352.

Fox, N. A. (1989). Psychophysiological correlates of emotional reactivity during the first year of life. *Developmental Psychology, 25*, 364–372.

Furedy, J. J., & Heslegrave, R. J. (1983). A consideration of recent criticisms of the T-wave amplitude index of myocardial sympathic activity. *Psychophysiology, 20*, 204–211.

Gang, M. J., & Teft, L. (1975). Individual differences in heart rate responses to affective sound. *Psychophysiology, 12*, 423–426.

Goldstein, J. H., Harman, J., McGhee, P. E., & Karasik, R. (1975). Test of an information-processing model of humor: Physiological response changes during problem and riddle-solving. *Journal of General Psychology, 92*, 59–68.

Graham, F. K. (1979). Distinguishing among orienting, defense and startle reflexes. In H. D. Kimmel, E. H. Van Olst, & J. F. Orlebeke (Eds.), *The orienting reflex in humans* (pp. 137–167). Hillsdale, NJ: Lawrence Erlbaum Associates.

Graham, F. K., & Clifton, R. K. (1966). Heart-rate change as a component of the orienting response. *Psychological Bulletin, 65*, 305–320.

Graham, F. K., & Slaby, D. A. (1973). Differential heart rate changes to equally intense white noise and tone. *Psychophysiology, 10*, 347–362.

Gunn, C. G., Wolf, S., Block, R. T., & Person, R. J. (1972). Psychophysiology of the cardiovascular system. In N. S. Greenfield & R. A. Sternbach (Eds.), *Handbook of psychophysiology* (pp. 457–489). New York: Holt.

Guyton, A. C. (1977). Basic human physiology: Normal function and mechanisms of disease. Philadelphia: Saunders.

Hare, R. D. (1972). Cardiovascular components of orienting and defensive responses. *Psychophysiology, 9*, 606–614.

Hare, R. D. (1973). Orienting and defensive responses to visual stimuli. *Psychophysiology, 10*, 453–464.

Hatton, H. M., Berg, W. K., & Graham, F. K. (1970). Effects of acoustic rise time on heart rate response. *Psychonomic Science, 19*, 101–103.

Heslegrave, R. J., Ogilvie, J. C., & Furedy, J. J. (1979). Measuring baseline-treatment differences in heart rate variability: Variance versus successive differences mean square and beats per minute versus interbeat interval. *Psychophysiology, 16*, 151–157.

Horowitz, M. (1985). Disasters and psychological responses to stress. *Psychiatric Annals, 15*, 161–167.

Jennings, J. R. (1986). Bodily changes during attending. In M. G. H. Coles, E. Donchin, & S. W. Porges (Eds.), *Psychophysiology: Systems, processes & applications* (pp. 268–289). New York: Guilford.

Jennings, J. R. (1992). Is it important that the mind is in a body? Inhibition and the heart. *Psychophysiology, 29*, 369–383.

Jennings, J. R., & Wood, C. C. (1977). Cardiac cycle time effects on performance, phasic cardiac responses and their intercorrelation in choice reaction time. *Psychophysiology, 14*, 297–307.

Kagan, J., Reznick, J. S., & Snidman, N. (1988). Biological bases of childhood shyness. *Science, 240*, 167–173.

Kagan, J., & Snidman, N. (1991). Infant predictors of inhibited and uninhibited profiles. *Psychological Science, 2*, 40–44.

Keefe, F. B., & Johnson, L. C. (1970). Cardiovascular responses to auditory stimuli. *Psychonomic Science, 19*, 335–337.

Klorman, R. (1975). Contingent negative variation and cardiac deceleration in a long preparatory interval: A developmental study. *Psychophysiology, 12*, 609–617.

Lacey, B. C., & Lacey, J. I. (1977). Change in heart period: A function of sensorimotor event timing within the cardiac cycle. *Physiological Psychology, 5*, 383–393.

Lacey, B. C., & Lacey, J. I. (1980). Cognitive modulation of time-dependent primary bradycardia. *Psychophysiology, 17*, 209–221.

Lacey, J. I. (1967). Somatic response patterning and stress: Some revisions of activation theory. In M. H. Appley & R. Trumbell (Eds.), *Psychological stress: Issues in research* (pp. 14–42). New York: Appleton-Century-Crofts.

Lacey, J. I., Kagan, J., Lacey, B. C., & Moss, H. A. (1963). The visceral level: Situational determinants and behavioral correlates of autonomic patterns. In P. H. Knapp (Ed.), *Expression of emotions in man* (pp. 161–196). New York: International Universities Press.

Lang, P. J. (1984). Cognition in emotion: Concept and action. In C. Izard, J. Kagan, & R. Zajonc (Eds.), *Emotions, cognition, and behavior* (pp. 192–226). New York: Cambridge University Press.

Lang, P. J., Levin, D. N., Miller, G. A., & Kozak, J. J. (1983). Fear behavior, fear imagery, and the psychophysiology of emotion: The problem of affective response integration. *Journal of Abnormal Psychology, 92*, 276–306.

Lewis, D., Ray, W. J., Wilkinson, M. O., & Ricketts, R. (1984). Self-report and heart rate responses to a stressful task. *International Journal of Psychophysiology, 2*, 33–37.

Malmo, R. B. (1965). Physiological gradients and behavior. *Psychological Bulletin, 664*, 225–234.

Miller, J. C., & Horvath, S. M. (1978). Impedance cardiography. *Psychophysiology, 15*, 80–91.

Nowlin, B., Eisdorfer, C., Whalen, R., & Troyer, W. G. (1970). The effect of exogenous changes in heart rate and rhythm upon reaction time performance. *Psychophysiology, 7*, 186–193.

Obrist, P. A. (1981). *Cardiovascular psychology: A perspective.* New York: Plenum.

Obrist, P. A., Howard, J. L., Sutterer, J. R., Hennis, R. S., & Murrell, D. J. (1973). Cardiac-somatic changes during a simple reaction time task: a developmental study. *Journal of Experimental Child Psychology, 16*, 346–362.

Obrist, P. A., Webb, R. A., & Sutterer, J. R. (1969). Heart rate and somatic changes during aversive conditioning and a simple reaction time task. *Psychophysiology, 5*, 696–723.

Ockleford, E. M., Vince, M. A., Layton, C., & Reader, M. R. (1988). Responses of neonates to parents' and others' voices. *Early Human Development, 18*, 27–36.

Ohkubo, T., & Hamley, E. J. (1972). Assessment of human performance in learning a skill involved in driving. *Journal of Human Ergology, 1*, 95–110.

Pardee, H. B. (1933). *Clinical aspects of the electrocardiogram* (3rd ed.). New York: Harper.

Porges, S. W., Stamps, L. E., & Walter, G. F. (1974). Heart rate variability and newborn heart rate responses to illumination changes. *Developmental Psychology, 10*, 507–513.

Raskin, D. C., Kostes, H., & Bever, J. (1969). Cephalic vasomotor and heart rate measures of orienting and defensive reflexes. *Psychophysiology, 6*, 149–159.

Richards, J. E. (1988). Heart rate offset responses to visual stimuli in infants from 14 to 26 weeks of age. *Psychophysiology, 25*, 278–291.

Richards, J. E., & Casey, B. J. (1991). Heart rate variability during attention phases in young infants. *Psychophysiology, 28*, 43–53.

Roberts, R. J., & Weerts, T. C. (1982). Cardiovascular responding during anger and fear imagery. *Psychological Reports, 50*, 219–230.

Rouselle, J. G., Blascovich, J., & Kelsey, R. M. (1995). Cardiorespiratory response under combined psychological and exercise stress. *International Journal of Psychophysiology, 20*, 49–58.

Schell, A. M., & Catania, J. (1975). The relationship between cardiac activity and sensory acuity. *Psychophysiology, 12*, 147–151.

Schwartz, G. E. (1971). Cardiac responses to self-induced thoughts. *Psychophysiology, 8*, 462–467.

Sherwood, A., Allen, M. T., Fahrenberg, J., Kelsey, R. M., Lovallo, W. R., & Van Doornen, L. J. P. (1990). Methodological guidelines for impedance cardiography. *Psychophysiology, 27*, 1–23.

Sinha, R., Lovallo, W. R., & Parsons, O. A. (1992). Cardiovascular differentiation of emotions. *Psychosomatic Medicine, 54*, 422–435.

Snidman, N., Kagan, J., Riordan, L., & Shannon, D. C. (1995). Cardiac function and behavioral reactivity during infancy. *Psychophysiology, 32*, 199–207.

Sokolov, E. (1963). *Perception and the conditioned reflex*. New York: MacMillan.

Spence, D. P., Lugo, M., & Youdin, R. (1972). Cardiac change as a function of attention to and awareness of continuous verbal text. *Science, 176*, 1344–1346.

Steele, W. G., & Lewis, M. (1968). A longitudinal study of the cardiac response during a problem solving task and its relationship to general cognitive function. *Psychonomic Science, 11*, 275–276.

Stern, R. M., Ray, W. J., & Davis, C. M. (1980). *Psychophysiological recording*. New York: Oxford.

Surwillo, W. W. (1971). Human reaction time and endogenous heart rate changes in normal subjects. *Psychophysiology, 8*, 680–682.

Taylor, W. B., Moldofsky, H., & Furedy, J. J. (1985). Heart rate deceleration in REM sleep: An orienting reaction interpretation. *Psychophysiology, 22*, 342–352.

Turner, J. R., Caroll, D., & Courtney, H. (1983). Cardiac and metabolic responses to "space invaders": An instance of metabolically exaggerated cardiac adjustment? *Psychophysiology, 20*, 544–549.

Turpin, G. (1986). Effects of stimulus intensity on autonomic responding: The problem of differenting orienting and defense reflexes. *Psychophysiology, 23*, 1–14.

Turpin, G., & Siddle, D. A. (1983). Effects of stimulus intensity on cardiovascular activity. *Psychophysiology, 20*, 611–624.

Tursky, B., & Jamner, L. D. (1982). Measurement of cardiovascular functioning. In J. T. Cacioppo & R. E. Petty (Eds.), *Perspectives in cardiovascular psychophysiology* (pp. 19–92). New York: Guilford.

Velden, M., Barry, R. J., & Wolk, C. (1987). Time dependent bradycardia: A new effect. *International Journal of Psychophysiology, 4*, 299–306.

Velden, M., & Juris, M. (1975). Perceptual performance as a function of intracycle cardiac activity. *Psychophysiology, 12*, 685–692.

Wallace, R. K., & Benson, H. (1972). The physiology of meditation. *Scientific American, 226*, 84–90.

Walter, G. F., & Porges, S. W. (1976). Heart rate and respiratory responses as a function of task difficulty: The use of discrimination analysis in the selection of psychologically sensitive physiological responses. *Psychophysiology, 13*, 563–571.

Webb, R. A., & Obrist, P. A. (1970). The physiological concomitants of reaction time performance as a function of preparatory interval and preparatory interval series. *Psychophysiology, 6*, 389–403.

Willemsen, G. H. M., De Geus, E. J. C., Klaver, C. H. A. M., Van Doornen, L. J. P., & Carroll, D. (1996). Ambulatory monitoring of the impedance cardiogram. *Psychophysiology, 33*, 184–193.

13

Heart Activity and Behavior II: Stress, Emotions, Motivation, Personality, Social Factors, Brain Interactions, and Conditioning

This chapter examines the question of whether differential heart activity occurs in various emotional situations. It also covers the effects of stress, motivational state, personality, and social factors on changes in heart rate. Cardiac reactivity, or how much of a change in HR occurs from baseline to a task situation, is another important aspect examined in this chapter. In addition, questions about interactions between heart and brain activity and the classical and instrumental conditioning of cardiac activity are also reviewed. We start with a consideration of stress, anger, frustration, and fear as *affective* processes.

HEART RATE AND AFFECTIVE PROCESSES

Affective processes, as considered here, include HR changes that have been recorded in situations likely to produce emotional reactions in people. Some situations that qualify are those that involve stressors, fear, anger, frustration, competition, and motivation.

Stress

Research on cardiovascular responses to stressors is currently an active area. The approaches are interesting and consider factors such as whether an individual copes actively or passively with a stressor, the type of task, parental history of cardiovascular disease, and personality factors, such as the Type A/B dichotomy. Many studies examine systolic and diastolic blood pressure as well as HR changes (for this reason they are discussed in chapter 14 on Blood Pressure and Behavior).

There are a number of experiments that have used electric shock as a stressor and examined heart activity in response to the shock itself or in anticipation of the shock. Elliott (1974) reviewed several studies that showed a decrease in HR just prior to the shock. However, he pointed out that the change was a phasic one; that is, it occurred in the few seconds before the stressful stimulus. Elliott observed that when one looks at the longer-term (tonic) effects, say over a period of minutes, HR increases occur under threat of an electric shock. An example of a short-term (phasic) decrease in HR is a result obtained by Obrist, Webb, and Sutterer (1969), in which deceleration took place in anticipation of a "very painful" electric shock. On the other hand, tonic acceleration was reported by Deane (1969), who told subjects that they would receive a shock at a specific point in a sequence of numbers. Interestingly, Deane's subjects showed increased HR at the beginning of the number series and a decrease just before and during the expected time of the shock.

The effects of a real-life stress on HR of 12-year-old girls was studied by Shapiro (1975). A novel aspect of Shapiro's study is that he compared the responses of girls raised in a Kibbutz with those of other Israeli girls raised in an urban setting. The measures were taken as the girls received immunization injections. In addition to HR, three behavioral measures were taken: (a) a self-rating about fear of needles, (b) a self-rating regarding expected intensity of pain, and (c) ratings of reactions by a nurse in the injection area. The measures of HR were taken 1 day before the injection, at the time of the injection, and 1 week after. The lower HR for the Kibbutz girls (72 BPM) compared to the urban subjects (79 BPM) corresponded with behavioral measures, indicating a more relaxed attitude to needle penetration. Shapiro postulated that educational policies in the Kibbutz, which emphasize the helpfulness of medical personnel, may have been responsible for the physiological and behavioral differences observed.

Another technique that has been used to produce stress involves asking participants to perform a demanding task. Frankenhaeuser and Johansson (1976) had people perform three tasks of varying difficulty while they measured HR and epinephrine excretion. They found, as have previous investigators, that performance did not deteriorate much when the task became more demanding. However, physiological arousal did increase as a function of task difficulty as indicated by both increased HR and epinephrine production. In addition, subjective ratings of distress increased with demanding tasks. The authors interpreted the results as showing evidence of the high physiological cost of adapting to stressful situations. In other words, our performance may not drop under stressful conditions, but we pay for this with increased energy expenditure.

Research on adults has indicated moderate to high consistency in HR and blood pressure responses across various psychological stressors such as mental arithmetic, mirror tracing and speech tasks (e.g., Turner, Sherwood, & Light, 1990). Examples of studies evaluating consistency of children's responses to laboratory stressors are those of Musante, Raunikar, Treiber, Davis, Dysart, Levy, and Strong, 1994, and Malpass, Treiber, Turner, Davis, Thompson, Levy, and Strong, 1997. In the first of these, Musante and colleagues (1994) evaluated responses of 341 children (mean age of 11 years) to a mix of physical and psychological stressors (e.g., cold pressor, and a video game). They reported consistent reactivity across stressors for HR, blood pressure, cardiac output (CO), and total peripheral resistance (TPR), with the highest correlations for CO and TPR. In the second study Malpass et al. (1997) studied the ability of cardiovascular responsivity to standard laboratory stressors to predict resting cardiovascular measures in young (6–7 yrs) boys and girls 1 year later. At initial testing heart rate, blood pressure, CO, and TPR were assessed at rest and during a variety of physical stressors (treadmill exercise, cold pressor, and postural change). At the follow-up, it was found that HR responses to postural change were predictive of later resting levels as were systolic and diastolic blood pressure to the cold pressor. Thus, in general, for this sample of young boys and girls, cardiovascular stress responses were predictive of future resting cardiovascular functioning. The authors call for longitudinal studies to determine whether cardiovascular stress responses can predict resting function over longer periods of time, and whether they may serve as early indicators of cardiovascular disease.

Summary.   Both phasic decreases and tonic increases in HR have been obtained in studies where the anticipation of an electric shock is a prominent component. These results are not contradictory, but merely indicate momentary HR decreases just prior to to occurrence of the shock and a generally elevated HR over the extended course of an experimental session. The momentary decrease in HR is similar to the deceleration observed in a fixed foreperiod RT situation. The experiment by Shapiro regarding a real-life stressor, and its differential effects on two social groups, is provocative and should provide a model for research in a variety of situations. Other real-life evaluations have revealed higher HR in naval pilots during takeoff and landing on airfcraft carriers than during bombing runs (Roman, Older, & Jones, 1967), and elevated HR in physicians during stressful periods of daily life (Ira, Whalen, & Bogdonoff, 1963).

Cardiovascular response shows some consistency across different stressors and over time for both adults and children. Researchers are interested in pursuing the question of whether cardiovascular response in children can be predictive of response as adults, and implications for predicting the development of cardiovascular disease.

EMOTIONAL RESPONSE

Patterns of Emotional Response

As discussed in chapter 1, changes in physiological activity that occur in different emotional states are important considerations in theories set forth by Cannon and by James-Lange. Coles (1983) pointed out that in Cannon's approach, physiological changes are only by-products of emotional states that are generated by brain processes, whereas to James-Lange, the physiological responses constitute the main part of the emotional experience with the brain processes occurring secondarily. Coles further pointed out that contemporary researchers have attempted to answer three questions that are generated by these theories: (a) Do different emotional states reveal themselves in specific patterns of physiological activity?, (b) Can individuals detect their own patterns of physiological activity?, and (c) How does perception of physiological activity influence the emotional reaction?

With regard to (a), there is little doubt that HR will rise under the threat of shock or in an anger-producing situation (Elliott, 1974). Other studies of fear and frustration also indicate HR increases related to these feeling states. One of the difficult questions over the years has been whether patterns of HR change will enable one to differentiate between emotional reactions, for example, fear and anger. In a classic experiment by Ax (1953), HR, skin conductance responses, and blood pressure were greater in fear than in anger. Ax produced fear and anger through scenarios threatening electric shock or involving verbal abuse by an experimenter, respectively. However, although this result suggested different patterns of physiological response in fear and anger, Elliott (1974) believes the finding may be related to whether the subjects were more inclined to action by a fear of electrocution than they were by anger toward an insult. Elliott believed that the accumulated research has not shown HR to be useful in differentiating emotional states. On the other hand, Ekman, Levenson, and Friesen (1983) observed differential HR with posed facial expressions of various emotions. In addition, the subjects (actors and scientists) were asked to relive emotional experiences for 30 sec. In the posed emotion task, subjects were told precisely which muscles to contract in producing expressions of fear, anger, disgust, sadness, happiness, and surprise. Heart rate changes associated with anger, fear, and sadness were all greater than for happiness, surprise, and disgust. The relived emotional task was not as effective in producing cardiac changes, but higher skin conductance was found for sadness, as compared to other negative emotions. Ekman and colleagues concluded that voluntary contractions of facial muscles into universal expressions of emotion produced differential autonomic activity that resembled physiological patterns obtained when using the relived emotions task.

In a follow-up study, Levenson, Ekman, and Friesen (1990) conducted four separate experiments and found: (a) voluntary production of facially expressed emotions produced self-reports of that emotion, and (b) there were reliable physiological differences among the negative emotions of anger, disgust, fear, and sadness, and positive emotions of happiness and surprise. Larger HR increases for anger, fear, and sadness were found compared to the negative emotion of disgust and the emotion of surprise. For skin conductance, the emotions of fear and disgust produced larger increases than happiness and surprise, noting: (c) autonomic differences among emotions found in group data were also found in data from individuals, and (d) the findings were not limited to male or female subjects or only to people experienced with emotional expressions (e.g., actors). Thus, the results of Levenson et al. come down strongly on the side of differential physiological responding in different emotional states. The fact that differences were found among negative emotions indicates that the results are not due merely to high arousal associated with negative affect versus relatively low arousal connected with positive affect. Also lending strength to the conclusion of differential responding is the finding of distinctions among negative emotions across a number of experiments.

Detection of Physiological Changes in Emotion

The second question raised by Coles, regarding sensitivity to internal physiological changes, has received some preliminary answers. Individual differences in sensitivity to HR have been found to be influenced by providing knowledge of results (Ashton, White, & Hodgson, 1979). Similar findings have been reported for the improvement of sensitivity to blood pressure changes through knowledge of results about such changes (Greenstadt, Shapiro, & Whitehead, 1986). Thus, with appropriate feedback, individuals can be trained to be sensitive to internal physiological changes. In a study by Ludwick-Rosenthal and Neufeld (1985), subjects were successful at "tracking" their own heartbeat. The tracking consisted of tapping their index finger in synchrony with their ongoing HR. They further reported that subjects who performed better had higher HR and higher levels of current anxiety than those whose "interoceptive acuity" was not as high. Information regarding HR led to improved detection performance. The tendency was for individuals to greatly underestimate their HR prior to receiving HR information.

Influence of Physiological Response on Felt Emotion

The question regarding effects of physiological changes on emotional reaction has produced some controversy. The results of a Schachter and Singer (1962) study suggest that generalized physiological activation causes the subject to explain the perceived changes in terms of some emotion appropriate to the current situation. College students were injected with adrenalin and put into situations designed to arouse either *euphoria* or *anger* through the use of "stooges" (accomplices of the experimenters). The emotion was labeled according to the situation produced. Plutchik and Ax (1967) objected to the suggestion that all emotional states are physiologically identical and differentiated only by cognitive factors. They criticized many aspects of the Schachter and Singer study, but agreed with the basic idea that emotional states are due to interactions of physiological arousal and cognitive factors.

Frustration and Fear

A number of studies have examined physiological changes in situations designed to produce frustration and fear. The effects of frustration on cardiac response were studied by Rule and Hewitt (1971). Subjects were asked to learn lists of verbal materials during sessions in which verbal reinforcement was provided by a peer. Three groups of subjects each received either an easy list with neutral comments from their peers, a difficult list with neutral comments, or a difficult list with derogatory comments. This last condition was considered to be "highly thwarting" in that it involved both frustration and insult. The other two conditions were considered as being low or moderate in amount of "thwarting," and thus merely frustrating. The persons subjected to both frustration and insult did not differ in cardiac rate during the learning period, but when made aware of an opportunity to administer electric shock to their peers, in a role reversal, this "highly-thwarted" group displayed elevated HR, compared to the low and moderate groups. Thus, the insulted subjects did not show greater HR increases than the other groups until given the opportunity to retaliate against their tormentors!

Klorman and colleagues conducted a series of studies in which HR measures were taken while subjects viewed fearful or neutral stimuli. For example, Klorman, Wiesenfeld, and Austin (1975) categorized 32 women as either high or low in fear of mutilation. The subjects viewed neutral (photographic poses), mutilation (burn and accident victims), and incongruous slides (e.g., a bald man with lemons attached to his ears) as HR was measured. The fearful subjects showed increased HR to mutilation slides, whereas the low-fear persons showed cardiac deceleration. Both groups responded to incongruous stimuli with HR deceleration. These results were interpreted as indicating defensive reactions in fearful individuals and orienting responses in the low-fear subjects.

The authors saw these results as extending Hare's (1973) results with spider-phobic persons to those with a fear of mutilation. Similar results were obtained by Klorman, Weissberg, and Wiesenfeld (1976) when mutilation slides produced cardiac acceleration in fearful persons and lowered HR in low fear subjects. Neutral (standard photographs) and incongruous (e.g., a young woman with shaving cream on her face and an electric razor in her hand) resulted in HR decreases in additonal samples of high- and low-fear persons. The results support Hare's (1972) conclusion that individual differences in reaction to a supposed fear stimulus will determine whether HR acceleration or deceleration will occur.

Summary.   There is evidence that pattern of physiological responding varies with different emotional states, that sensitivity to internal changes may be enhanced by training, and that physiological arousal interacts with cognitive factors in producing an emotional state. It has been observed that frustration plus insult will lead to an increase in HR when the victim has a chance to retaliate. A series of investigations of reactions to fearful stimuli support the notion that HR will accelerate in persons who actually fear the stimulus and will decelerate in those who do not fear the unpleasant stimulus, but instead find it morbidly interesting. These latter results produce a conceptual fit with the hypothesis that HR deceleration accompanies stimulus intake and the orienting response, whereas HR acceleration is associated with stimulus rejection and the defensive response.

MOTIVATION

Incentive and Competition Effects

Elliott (1974), on the basis of his own prior research, concluded that the effects of increasing the amount of an incentive (e.g., money) usually produced an increase in tonic HR during the performance of a relevant task (Elliott, 1969; Elliott, Bankart, & Light, 1970). Evans (1971) reported that rivalry (a desire to win) caused significant increases in tonic HR, that is, HR measured over at least a 1-min period. He interpreted this increase as indicating the incentive nature of competition. In a follow-up study, Evans (1972) measured HR of 64 men and 64 women while they placed objects of different sizes and shapes into a form board. Half of the males and half of the females completed the task under competitive and noncompetitive conditions. The introduction of competition resulted in an average increase in HR of 10 BPM, regardless of resting HR level. Evans interpreted this result as supporting Elliott's work, indicating that incentive increases are accompanied by elevations in tonic HR.

Fowles (1983) made a strong case for the view that HR is closely linked to appetitive motivational states (positive incentives). In a test of this notion, Fowles, Fisher, and Tranel (1982) used money rewards and took HR measures during the performance of a continuous motor task. They found that HR was significantly higher when subjects were paid 2 cents for each success, compared to subjects given feedback only. A follow-up study by Tranel, Fisher, and Fowles (1982) showed that the increases in HR were related to the amount of the reward; more money led to higher HR. Also, when the money reward was discontinued, HR decreased. These and similar results by Fowles and his colleagues led them to repeat pleas by other psychophysiologists (e.g., Stern, Farr, & Ray, 1975) to study physiological responses in situations that are pleasurable. Fowles et al. (1982) wrote: "To this end, we might modify the traditional view that cardiac acceleration occurs in anticipation of fight or flight to read "fight, flight, or fun . . ." (p. 512).

Summary.   Increased incentive levels are effective in producing an elevation in cardiac rate. In addition, the introduction of competition may be inferred to have incentive or motivational effects, because it results in tonic HR acceleration. However, the possible roles of fear of failure or apprehension about comparisons, or individual reactions to rivalry, have not been delineated in HR studies that have used competition as an independent variable. Greater use of HR and other physiological measures is encouraged in studies of response to pleasure.

CARDIOVASCULAR REACTIVITY (CVR), PERSONALITY, AND SOCIAL FACTORS

Cardiovascular Reactivity

The concept of cardiovascular reactivity refers to the magnitude and patterns of cardiovascular responses from baseline to task levels, including exposure to stressors. Psychophysiologists and health psychologists are interested in the hypothesis that exaggerated reactivity to psychological stressors may play a role in the development of cardiovascular disease (coronary heart disease, high blood pressure). An overview of cardiovascular reactivity research was presented by Sherwood and Turner (1992). They pointed out that HR and blood pressure have been the main measures of reactivity, but that others are increasingly being used (e.g., cardiac output, total peripheral resistance). These measures provide convenient indices of cardiovascular arousal compared to some baseline—usually a state of rest. An individual who shows an increase in HR of 30 bpm from baseline when asked to perform some task is more reactive than one who increases by 10 bpm for the same task. Sherwood and Turner emphasized that it is these individual differences in reactivity that are of interest to psychophysiologists because they have been shown to have predictive significance for health outcomes—for example, the development of high blood pressure (see Light, Dolan, Davis, & Sherwood, 1992).

In addition to individual differences shown in reactivity research, it is also evident that different tasks elicit different patterns of reactivity. For example, a study of young male college students showed widely different reactivity to two stressors (Sherwood, Davis, Dolan, & Light, 1992). They reported that a reaction time task produced HR and systolic pressure increases, but the cold pressor task (ice pack on forehead for 3 min) evoked large changes in diastolic pressure and very little HR reactivity. According to Sherwood and Turner, cardiovascular reactivity is assumed to be a behavioral trait. In keeping with the notion of such a trait, the stability of measures of reactivity are constant over time, and also in response to different stressors. For example, Kamarck, Jennings, Debski, Glickman-Weiss, Johnson, Eddy, and Manuck (1992) found five measures of reactivity to be highly reliable (HR, systolic and diastolic blood pressure, stroke volume, and pre-ejection period).

Sherwood and Turner (1992) concluded that some individuals appear to be generally more reactive than others in showing typically large magnitude cardiovascular responses to a variety of stressful stimuli. The mechanisms responsible for these responses are relatively stable, suggesting that cardiovascular reactivity has attributes of a psychophysiological trait.

Personality

The concept of a Type A behavior pattern characterized by impatience, competitiveness, and hostility and related to an increased risk for coronary heart disease (CHD) was advanced by Friedman and Rosenman (1974). The Type B pattern is relatively free of these behavioral traits and presents a picture of a generally more relaxed person who shows little aggressive drive and who is not always in a hurry. Coronary heart disease is a major cause of death and is thought to result from damage to the coronary arteries from atherosclerosis (a thickening of the arterial walls). The disease results in myocardial infarction (death of heart tissue), angina pectoris (a syndrome of chest pain caused by insufficient oxygen supply to heart muscle), and sudden death. Researchers have been attempting to relate Type A/B personality to patterns of physiological change, especially changes involving the cardiovascular system. Studies focusing on changes in diastolic and systolic blood pressure are covered in chapter 14. Investigations emphasizing HR are discussed here.

Most studies have identified individuals as Type A either through a structured interview or the Jenkins Activity Survey (a paper-and-pencil survey). The interview consists of a detailed list of questions about behavior, but also places emphasis on the individual's reactions during the interview, such as speed of speech. The Jenkins Survey is a self-report about behaviors with questions such as "Has your spouse or a friend ever told you that you eat too fast?", "When you have to 'wait in line' at a restaurant, a store, or at the post office, what do you do?", and "Do you ever set deadlines or quotas for yourself at work or at home?" In general, studies have shown that Type As have increased cardiovascular activity over baseline rates, compared to Type Bs, when engaged in a task (Krantz, Glass, Shaeffer, & Davia, 1982).

The differences between As and Bs seem to be more reliable when the structured interview or extreme Jenkins scores are used to categorize individuals as As or Bs. This has been shown in a variety of populations, including college students, working-class adults, and coronary patients. However, qualifications must be made because differences in A/B reactions seem to depend on the type of task or experimental environment. For example, Type A/B differences are observed in situations that involve challenge, competition, or harrassment. Differences in A/B HR reactivity emerged in a competitive task involving cognitive (short-term memory) activity, but not while performing an engaging video perceptual motor task (Juszczak & Andreassi, 1987). Type A/B differences did not emerge in response to the cold pressor test or balloons bursting; tasks that could be considered irrelevant to Type A characteristics (Goldband, 1980). In accord with this notion, Stern and Elder (1982) found that the effectiveness with which Type As reduced their own HR depended on the challenge produced in a biofeedback situation. For example, when told that HR reduction was rare ability, Type As reduced HR more than did Type Bs. When told that HR reduction was a common ability, Type Bs achieved greater reduction. These results suggest interesting possibilities for exploiting Type A behavior in reducing Type A symptoms.

Parental History of Hypertension as a Factor

Two risk factors for CHD, Type A behavior and parental history of hypertension, were investigated along with cardiovascular reactivity to challenging tasks (Allen, Lawler, Mitchell, Matthews, Rakaczky, & Jamison, 1987). College males were categorized as Type A or B on the basis of both the structured interview of Rosenman and Friedman and the Jenkins Activity Survey. Results showed that Type As, based on the structured interview classification, had higher HR levels than Bs on all tasks (cold pressor, reading comprehension, backward digits, handgrip exercise). In addition, those with parental history of hypertension also had higher HR on all tasks. The study results also reflect the previously mentioned finding that the structured interview seems to differentiate between Type As and Bs more consistently than other psychometric techniques, especially in those factors related to differential cardiovascular activity in As and Bs. Also suggested is the possible role of parental history in cardiovascular reactivity.

Heart rate reactivity and parental history of hypertension were examined as predictors of cardiovascular reactivity to mental tasks (Sausen, Lovallo, & Wilson, 1991). Those subjects (all males) who had high HR reactivity on a cold pressor task had higher HR on the cognitive tasks (mental arithmetic, digit span) than low reactors. Subjects with a hypertensive parent had greater systolic and diastolic blood pressures than those without such a history. Persons classified as Type A by the Jenkins Activity Survey did not differ from Type Bs on any of the physiological variables. However, it has been previously noted that Type A/B differences are most likely to show when either the structured interview or extreme Jenkins scores are used.

The cardiovascular reactivity of men who had suffered heart attacks versus healthy controls was studied by Sundin, Ohman, Palm, and Strom (1995). These groups were also classified as Type A or B by a structured interview. The patient group had suffered a myocardial infarction from 2.2 years to 6 months prior to the study. The tasks included complex mental arithmetic, isometric exercise (squeezing a hand grip), and a cold pressor (left hand immersed in ice water for 1 min). The patients showed significantly greater cardiac output and systolic blood pressure during mental arithmetic and higher total peripheral resistance and lower stroke volume and cardiac output during the physical tasks compared to the healthy controls. The Type A men, regardless of whether they were patients or nonpatients, showed higher systolic and diastolic blood pressure to both mental and physical stressors than did the Type Bs.

Not as much research was devoted to cardiovascular reactivity of women as a function of personality prior to 1990. The few reported results prior to that time rarely indicated differences. One exception was that reported by Lawler, Huck, and Smalley (1989) who identified Type A and B behavior in college women with the Jenkins Activity Survey. A real-life stressor was used (a midterm examination) while HR and blood pressure were measured. The results showed higher HR and blood pressure for Type A women. Thus, when the stressor was a real exam, Type A women showed elevated cardiovascular response compared to Bs. Lawler and colleagues reviewed the literature on Type A/B women and reactivity and concluded that small sample sizes may have accounted for many of the mixed findings (Lawler, Schmied, Armstead, & Lacy, 1990). In the 18 studies reviewed involving Type A women and reactivity, exactly half had sample sizes under 30. The cardiovascular reactivity of 32 Type A women was compared to 32 Type Bs in a study conducted by Fichera and Andreassi (1998). The HR activity did not differ for Type A/B with the two tasks used (reaction time and an oral quiz), but Type As had significantly greater blood pressure reactivity to both tasks. In a second experiment, involving a 6-minute speech in a classroom situation, women, showed significantly greater HR response than men, whereas men reacted to a greater extent with respect to blood pressure increases (Fichera, 1997). The finding of differential cardiac and blood pressure responding for women and men has been reported in a number of previous studies.

Hostility and Cardiovascular Reactivity

Hostility has been defined as "having a set of negative attitudes, beliefs and appraisals concerning others" (Smith, 1992, p. 139). High scores on a measure of hostility (Cook–Medley Hostility scale) have been shown in a longitudinal study to be associated with increased risk of coronary heart disease (CHD) and severity of atherosclerosis (Barefoot, Williams, & Dahlstrom, 1983). It has been proposed that one mechanism contributing to CHD is excessive SNS-mediated cardiovascular reactivity to environmental stressors. In a study by Suarez and Williams (1989), cardiovascular reactivity of young men with high versus low hostility scores was evaluated while they solved anagrams with or without harassment. Compared to performing the task alone, harassment resulted in increased cardiovascular activity (HR, blood pressure) that was more pronounced for the high hostility subjects compared to those scoring low on the scale. Further, harassment led to increases in self-ratings of anger and irritation, but it was only among those with high hostility scores that increased anger and irritation led to exaggerated cardiovascular reactivity.

In a follow-up study, Suarez and Williams (1990) refined items from the hostility scale into factors called *antagonistic hostility* (anger expressed outwardly) and *neurotic hostility* (suppressed anger). The results showed that those high in antagonistic hostility had elevated systolic blood pressure to harassment, whereas those high in neurotic hostility had higher forearm blood flow under harassing conditions. Suarez and Williams suggested that the use of standard laboratory tasks such as mental arithmetic or anagrams without harassment, may account for findings showing no asociation between hostility/anger measures and cardiovascular reactivity. Fichera and Andreassi (1998) found that women who scored high in hostility (Cook–Medley scale) had greater blood pressure reactivity, but no HR differences, than women who scored low.

Ambulatory HR and blood pressure were obtained in male paramedics during a 24-hr work shift to see the effects of work stress on cardiovascular response (Jamner, Shapiro, Goldstein, & Hug, 1991). Hostility was measured by the Cook and Medley scale and an additional measure called "defensiveness" was obtained by the Marlowe–Crowne Social Desirability Scale. Defensiveness may be defined as a coping style characterized by avoiding threatening information and a denial of distress and negative emotions. The real-life stressor involved interpersonal conflicts in a hospital setting and those paramedics who scored high in both hostility and defensiveness had higher HR than those high in hostility but low in defensiveness. The same pattern was observed for blood pressure.

Social Factors

Social Support and Coping.   An interesting finding is that cardiovascular response is greater when persons are capable of exerting some control over a potential stressor compared to when they are not. For example, Obrist, Gaebelein, Teller, Langer, Grignolo, Light, and McCubbin (1978) found that when subjects were able to avoid an electric shock through good performance on a reaction time task, HR and systolic pressure were higher than when they had no control over the shock. Obrist and his colleagues have referred to this ability to control the stressor as "active coping" and to the no-control situation as "passive coping."

Active coping in a social context was studied by Smith, Allred, Morrison, and Carlson (1989). They found that male subjects attempting to influence opinions of others in order to earn a reward showed higher cardiovascular reactivity (HR, blood pressure) than those not making such an attempt. A second experiment showed that both men and women had elevated responses when preparing to influence another person and when making the attempt. Thus, the cardiovascular effects of control appear to be similar in a social interaction as well as in isolation. In a follow-up study, Smith, Baldwin, and Christensen (1990) asked subjects to prepare and deliver a persuasive communication. The same communication was delivered under an incentive condition (money for sucessfully influencing others) or no incentive. Again, the preparation and delivery of the message produced elevated HR and blood pressure, but only under the incentive condition. Thus, the cardiovascular effects of being actively involved in determining the outcome appear to be similar in situations involving other persons as well as those merely using a solitary measure (e.g., reaction time). Another factor that must be considered here is the monetary reward, previously found to influence HR in studies by Fowles and his colleagues.

The effects of social support on age-related changes in cardiovascular response were examined by Uchino, Kiecolt-Glaser, and Cacioppo (1992). They began by citing evidence that between the ages of 30 and 70 the muscle mass and contractility of the heart decrease to produce a drop in stroke volume. Further, a decline in maximal HR by about 24 BPM also contributes to a reduction in cardiac output. Older persons also have been found to show less HR reactivity to an active coping task than younger subjects. In their study, Uchino et al. (1992) looked at the effects of aging, chronic stress, and social support on cardiovascular reactivity. The subjects were a group of family caregivers for Alzheimer's disease patients (average of 8 years of care) and a group of controls matched in age and gender. All performed two active coping tasks while cardiovascular activity was monitored. Those caregivers who rated high in social support (number and quality of outside support persons) had decreases in HR reactivity, typically shown for older persons. However, those low in social support showed increases in HR reactivity. Uchino and colleagues suggested that sufficient social support can moderate cardiovascular reactivity, especially in those subjected to chronic stress.

Social support as a moderating factor on cardiovascular reactivity during challenging laboratory tasks was examined by Kamarck, Manuck, and Jennings (1990). College students recruited a friend to accompany them during the experiment. Two tasks were used (mental arithmetic and concept formation) and the presence of a friend significantly lowered cardiovascular reactivity. Subjects in the *Alone* condition showed more than two times the magnitude of reactivity to mental arithmetic compared to those accompanied by a friend. The results for the concept formation task were in the same direction, but were not as striking. Studies of social affiliation effects on cardiovascular reactivity may translate to the real world in terms of the effects of social isolation on susceptibility to illness.

Social Context.   It is well known that both HR and blood pressure increase when people speak; and people usually speak in a social context. In a study designed to explain why speech produces cardiovascular reactivity, Tardy and Allen (1998) used speech tasks varying in self-disclosure and cognitive preparation and measured HR and blood pressure of Caucasian and African-American men and women subjects. They reported that an extemporaneous speech task resulted in lower systolic blood pressure than a prepared speech task, perhaps because of evaluation apprehension during the preparation period. Talking about another person produced greater diastolic blood pressure than talking about one's self. The data also revealed gender differences because men had higher diastolic blood pressure when speaking, whereas women had elevated HR. This type of study opens up the possibility for further study that varies the intimacy of self-disclosure and presentation of complex versus simple materials in a speech task.

Cognitive Dissonance.   As several of the previous studies indicate, an emerging area of research concerns the effects of social factors on physiological reactivity or "social psychophysiology" (see Cacioppo & Petty, 1983). An approach that might be taken in this promising area is to measure physiological changes in the context of various social psychological phenomena such as attitude change, cognitive dissonance, or emotional communication. An example is the use of physiological measurements to confirm the existence of tensions and their subsequent release in cognitive dissonance. The concept of cognitive dissonance was introduced by Festinger to describe the state produced when there is a difference between a person's attitude and behavior. The conflict is resolved by a change in attitude to match the behavior, but in the meantime, the individuals are said to experience a tension that they are motivated to relieve. Croyle and Cooper (1983) used HR and EDA as measures of tension or arousal in a dissonance situation in which one half of the subjects were asked to write an essay supporting a campus ban on alcohol, even though an attitude survey had shown them to be opposed to the ban. The other subjects wrote an essay in agreement with their attitudes. Those in the dissonant condition were more aroused after writing the essay than other subjects. However, the arousal was observed as increased EDA, because HR showed no dissonance effect.

In another study, a positive effect for HR was found because attitude toward a stimulus was influenced by the subject's perceived response. In this experiment, Valins (1966) asked men to examine pictures of *Playboy* centerfolds while they listened to what they believed was their own HR. False feedback was given, and HR did not vary while they viewed one half of the nude photos, and increased or decreased for the other half. The men later rated the photos that were accompanied by HR change (either up or down) as more attractive than the others. Therefore, subject's evaluations of stimuli may have been influenced by their perceived HR changes. Cross-fertilization between the fields of psychophysiology and social psychology has yielded some fascinating findings.

Summary.   Cardiovascular reactivity has been described as an individual trait that has a degree of stability over time (Sherwood & Turner, 1992). Individual differences in personality play a role in reactivity. In general, Type As show greater cardiovascular reactivity than Bs, with findings being more reliable when the structured interview or extreme Jenkins scores are used as measures of Type A/B. Extreme scores would include those scoring in the upper quartile (75th percentile and above) to denote Type A and the lower quartile (25th percentile and below) to designate Type Bs. Most studies have been based on male samples, but recent years have seen an increase in the amount of research on women. Preliminary results show that individuals with a parental history of hypertension (either one or both parents) evidence greater reactivity.

There is emerging evidence that individuals who score high in hostility show considerable cardiovascular reactivity to stressors. Real-life stressors may produce greater amounts of cardiovascular activity than laboratory tasks. Further refinements of the hostility measure suggest that measures of so-called antagonistic or neurotic hostility may offer more specific information.

Cardiovascular response has been found to be greater when the individual can exert some control over a potential stressor. This situation has been referred to as *active coping* and the no-control condition as *passive coping*. Perceived or actual social support moderates cardiovascular reactivity. The greater arousal experienced in a cognitive dissonance situation is expressed as increases in EDA, but not HR. Some preliminary evidence suggests that evaluations of stimuli may be influenced by perceived changes in HR.

INTERACTIONS BETWEEN HEART AND BRAIN ACTIVITY

One of the main aspects of the intake-rejection hypothesis of the Laceys (see chapter 18) is that changes in cardiovascular activity influence brain activity. For example, the decreased HR that occurs under instructions to detect signals leads to a decrease in the inhibitory influence of baroreceptors on cortical function, resulting in enhanced brain activity and improved performance. The limited evidence to support performance effects of HR acceleration–deceleration was discussed earlier, but there is evidence that brain activity is influenced by cardiac events. Walker and Sandman (1979) measured evoked brain potentials to light flashes when subject's HR were low, high, or moderate. The P2 component of the visual ERP from over the right hemisphere was larger at low HR than for moderate or high rates, indicating greater cortical sensitivity at the low HR. However, left hemisphere responses did not differ as a function of HR. Sandman, Walker, and Berka (1982) reported that these findings are consistent with those suggesting that tasks requiring attention to the environment are associated with low HR and ERPs recorded from the right hemisphere. They proposed that the heart may influence perceptual/attentional functions by selectively influencing right hemisphere activity.

Sensitivity to Signals

As mentioned previously, there is a lack of evidence regarding performance changes within the single cardiac cycle even though there are baroreceptor changes when the ventricles contract and relax. Wolk and Velden (1987) suggested that one reason for the lack of evidence was that investigators failed to sample enough points during the cycle. They pointed to the study of Velden and Juris (1975), which obtained suggestive evidence for cycle effects, but only because sampling was done at 33-msec intervals. Later (Wolk and Velden, 1987) performed a signal detection experiment in which signals were presented many times at 25-msec intervals up to 500 msec after the R wave (21 sample points). They found that perceptual performance oscillated about every 100 msec (10 Hz), and suggested that it was time-locked to both the cardiac cycle and the alpha rhythm of the brain (8 to 12 Hz).

They speculated that increased baroreceptor activity at these intervals indirectly exerts an inhibitory effect on performance by producing alpha activity, which interferes with the passing of sensory information at the level of the thalamus. Through this hypothesis, the authors expanded on the Lacey's assumption about the modulating effects of cardiac activity on the brain and performance. Their chain of reasoning takes a number of speculative leaps, but it is interesting, and verifiable through additional research. It would help if measures of EEG and baroreceptor activity could also be taken at frequent intervals during the cardiac cycle to confirm the relationships suggested by Wolk and Velden.

Hemispheric Differences in Brain–Heart Interactions

Further evidence for cardiovascular–brain influences was reported by Walker and Walker (1983). The EEG recorded from over left and right hemispheres was comprised of slower frequencies during ventricular systole than EEG sampled during diastole. The results were extended to the enhancement of auditory ERPs observed when tones were presented during the diastolic phases of pulse pressure, a period of lowered cardiovascular activity (Sandman, 1984). The effect appeared most reliably in responses recorded from the right hemisphere. An experiment by Hantas, Katkin, and Reed (1984) provided findings indicating that perception of cardiovascular activity may be processsed more effectively in the right hemisphere. Subjects classified as "right hemisphere preferent" were better at detecting their own heartbeat than those classified as "left hemisphere preferent." When knowledge of results was given, all subjects showed significant improvements in performance, but the right hemisphere preferent individuals maintained their superiority. Weisz, Szilagyi, Lang, and Adam (1992) presented evidence that the right hemisphere plays a greater role in regulation of HR than the left. They suggested that the two hemispheres have differential effects on sympathetic activities. They concluded that heart activity was selectively influenced by the right hemisphere through its influence on sympathetic innervation of the sinoatrial node (pacemaker) of the heart.

The CNV and Heart Activity

In chapter 5, the contingent negative variation (CNV) was described as a long duration brain response that slowly develops between a warning stimulus (S1) and a required response (S2). This is the same type of paradigm that produces HR slowing in the fixed period RT tasks previously described. Friedman, Putnam, and Hamberger (1990) were interested in studying the relationship between HR deceleration and the CNV in a situation where old, young, and middle-aged subjects performed a memory task involving RT. Their findings failed to find a relationship between magnitude of HR deceleration and performance, or between CNV and RT. Friedman and colleagues indeed found that the amount of HR slowing was attenuated significantly with age, but that the magnitude of the CNV was not related to age. The relationship between CNV development and HR slowing for each of the age groups is shown in Fig. 13.1.

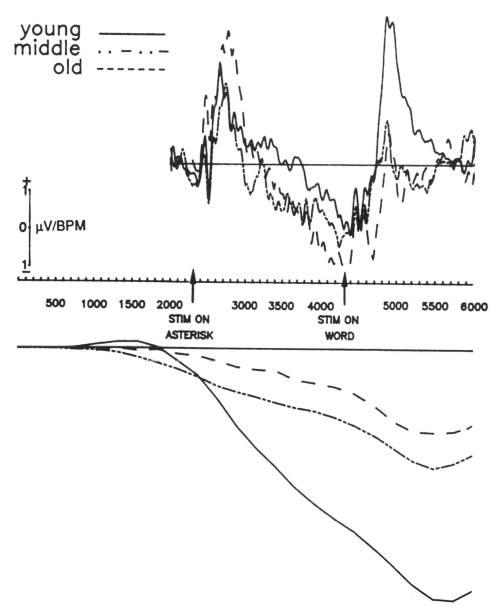

FIG. 13.1. ERPs (top) recorded at P$_z$, and cardiac decelerations (bottom) averaged across subjects within each age group elicited during the S1 (asterisk) - S2 (word) interval in the P.M. session. The data depicted were elicited by correct detections of "old" (i.e., presented in the A.M.) items. First arrow marks asterisk onset, second arrow marks word onset. Time lines every 100 msec. Calibration is 1µV for ERPs and 1 bpm for cardiac deceleration. (Figure courtesy of Dr. David Friedman.)

Note the steep negative-going wave that occurs between "stim on asterisk" (S1) and "stim on word" (S2) for all three age groups. Then, note that the slope for cardiac deceleration is greatest for the young group and least for the old group. The authors proposed that the decrease in HR slowing with age may mean that attentional capacity is reduced in older persons. This hypothesis requires further research, but Friedman and colleagues produced a clear demonstration of a relationship between cardiac deceleration and a brain response.

Summary. The studies reviewed here indicate interesting interactions between cardiovascular and brain activity, and demonstrate that the brain's influence on the heart is not a one-way street. The results thus far also suggest that cyclic physiological events, such as cardiac systole and diastole, may modulate the impact of external stimuli on the central nervous system. The questions of possible performance differences with changes in cardiac–cortical interaction, and cardiac cycle effects, and the meaning of hemispheric asymmetries require further investigation.

CONDITIONING OF HEART ACTIVITY

A brief discussion of classical and operant conditioning procedures was presented in chapter 9. This section discusses some representative investigations of classical and instrumental conditioning of cardiac activity.

Classical Conditioning

It has long been known that ANS responses can be modified by classical conditioning. For example, Kimble (1961) mentioned changes in EDA and respiration that were produced by the CS in various experiments, in addition to the well-known salivary response (e.g., Pavlov's dog). Heart rate has also been classically conditioned, that is, a CS formerly paired with a pleasant (food) or unpleasant (electric shock) stimulus can produce a change in HR. For example, Notterman, Schoenfeld, and Bersh (1952) measured HR in a classical conditioning situation and reported cardiac deceleration just before the onset of the UCS (shock). Obrist et al. (1969) also observed a conditioned HR deceleration that took place in the CS (light)–UCS (shock) interval. Although these studies indicate conditioned deceleration of HR, Van Egeren, Headrick, and Hein (1972) obtained results that revealed individual HR differences in an aversive classical conditioning experiment. These investigators used two experimental paradigms in studying the cardiac responses of two groups of subjects during classical conditioning. The HR changes indicated three kinds of response during the CS–UCS interval: initial acceleration followed by deceleration, deceleration-only, and initial deceleration followed by acceleration. The findings illustrate the importance of considering individual differences in experiments dealing with the conditioning of heart activity. Recall also that Hare and Blevings (1975) showed HR acceleration in spider-phobic individuals prior to the UCS (spider slides).

The possible effects of respiration on concurrent HR changes during conditioning were examined by Headrick and Graham (1969). Three groups of 20 persons each were given conditioning trials as follows: respiration controlled at normal rates, controlled at fast rates, or uncontrolled. Significant HR responding occurred in all three groups during the CS (tone)–UCS (electric shock) interval. There were three components to the HR response: deceleration immediately after the CS, followed by a brief acceleration, and a large deceleration just prior to the UCS. Thus, this study seems to rule out respiration effects in classical conditioning of HR.

Obrist (1976) offered explanations of anticipatory HR deceleration during the CS–UCS interval in terms of both behavioral and biological strategies. The behavioral approach explains the HR changes in terms of physiological interactions. For example, Obrist's data have indicated that HR deceleration is due to a momentary increase in vagal (parasympathetic) excitation, which overrides sympathetic acceleration effects.

Furedy and Poulos (1976) explored the possible use of body tilt as a UCS in conditioning a decrease of HR. In a first experiment, they established that tilting the body from a head-up to a head-down position produced a mean cardiac deceleration to less than 60 BPM by the 9th sec after UCS onset. (The subjects were strapped to a "tilt-table," and the duration of the tilt was 9 sec.) In a second experiment, these same investigators demonstrated that classical conditioning of HR deceleration could be accompanied by using a tone as the CS and body tilt as the UCS. This time, 32 tilts were each performed after a 1.7-sec duration tone. However, the 12 subjects produced a mean conditioned deceleration of only 4 BPM. This was a small conditioned response relative to the large unconditioned response of over 30 BPM in the first experiment. An encouraging aspect of this study is that the classically conditioned cardiac deceleration was obtained with a stimulus other than the often-used electric shock. A test of the hypothesis that relevant imagery enhances classical conditioning of HR was conducted by Arabian (1982). Using head tilt as the UCS, one group of subjects was instructed to imagine the tilt-UCS whenever the CS was presented, whereas the other group imagined a car ride (irrelevant imagery). The hypothesis was supported because the relevant imagery group showed a much larger conditioned HR deceleration.

Summary. The classical conditioning of HR has been reported in a number of experiments. The most common UCS has been electric shock, which has usually produced cardiac deceleration. The role of individual differences may explain variations in cardiac patterning sometimes observed in the CS–UCS interval. The possible influence of respiratory variations on HR changes seems to have been ruled out. Investigators have implicated vagal (parasymphatetic) excitation in producing HR deceleration in the CS–UCS interval.

Instrumental Conditioning

The term *instrumental conditioning* refers here to changes in physiological activity that occur as a result of reinforcement contingencies. For example, individuals are provided with a continuous display of their heart activity and are reinforced when HR rises above a certain level. The rise in HR is thus instrumental in obtaining the reinforcement. The reinforcement may be the achievement of a desirable event (e.g., monetary reward) or the avoidance of something unpleasant (e.g., an electric shock). The terms *instrumental* and *operant* conditioning are used interchangeably, although some workers in the field (e.g., Kimmel, 1973) prefer to use the word *operant* to refer to unique instrumental conditioning procedures in which responses are "emitted" independently of identifiable external stimuli. Recall that in the classical conditioning situation, the reinforcement (UCS) is presented whether or not the subject makes a particular response.

For quite some time (from the late 1930s to the early 1960s), most investigators agreed that the modification of ANS responses by instrumental conditioning was not possible, but that these same visceral responses were amenable to classical conditioning. Kimble (1961) reflected the thought of the time when he stated that "autonomic responses apparently cannot be instrumentally conditioned at all" (p. 108). However, some research findings have accumulated since then, indicating that subjects can learn to modify their HR and other autonomic responses in an instrumental conditioning paradigm. An important aspect is the provision of feedback, or knowledge of results, to the individuals so that they know that the desired response is being achieved (e.g., see Bergman & Johnson, 1972). Early demonstrations of instrumental conditioning of HR were provided by Shearn (1962) and Hnatiow and Lang (1965). Shearn (1962) used a conditioning paradigm in which HR increases postponed the delivery of an electric shock. The experimental subjects produced more HR accelerations over the five sessions than the control subjects. Shearn reported changes in respiration, which, he suggested, could have mediated the HR change. However, after being alerted to this possible contaminating effect of respiration, experimenters have either monitored or controlled breathing in studies conducted since then. Hnatiow and Lang (1965) reported the successful stabilization of HR when subjects were instructed to keep their heart rates as steady as possible and were provided with a visual display of HR. Control subjects, who were provided with false feedback, did not show a reduction in HR variability. Lang (1974) pointed out that the magnitude of HR control achieved in various studies has been modest, especially HR deceleration, and he attributed this partially to the difficulties in providing all the environmental controls necessary to perform instrumental conditioning studies with humans (e.g., subject isolation, powerful reinforcers). He also suggested that HR control is a type of skill learning, and some individuals are better at it than others.

The importance of individual differences in learning control of HR was underscored by McCanne and Sandman (1976) in an extensive review of operant HR conditioning. They suggested that individual differences in physiological responding occur during instrumental HR conditioning and that a study of these differences might help to understand how voluntary control is achieved over HR. They had earlier ruled out changes in respiration, muscle activity, and cardiac–somatic interaction (with the CNS as the control mechanism) as possible bases for operant control over HR. However, this is controversial, because critics have emphasized the difficulty of demonstrating HR changes without concurrent somatic changes, for example, respiration (Blanchard & Young, 1973; Katkin & Murray, 1968). Thus, this area is rather unsettled in terms of comprehending the underlying mechanisms that allow instrumental control of HR. Hatch, Borcherding, and Norris (1990) took a step in the direction of specifying a possible mechanism in the voluntary control of heart activity. A group of healthy subjects successfully raised and lowered HR from resting baseline. The experiment was conducted over five sessions and visual feedback of heart period was provided. The changes in HR were closely paralleled by changes in cardiac vagal tone; that is, when vagal influence (parasympathetic) was greater HR was slower. Respiration rate and amplitude was not related to HR slowing or speeding. Individual differences in cardiac vagal tone were unrelated to HR.

The effects of varying incentive (monetary) on the voluntary control of HR speeding and slowing were investigated by Lang and Twentyman (1976). Fifty subjects received four HR control sessions over a 3- to 4-week period. The results showed that subjects can alter HR directionally, and that performance was improved with monetary incentives. Frequent reinforcement, additional incentives, and practice with feedback produced optimal HR change performance. The researchers postulated that the findings support an interpretation of HR feedback training as being similar to the learning of a motor skill. This implication is stronger for HR speeding than for HR slowing, because only incentive altered slowing, whereas speeding was also influenced by other factors that were manipulated.

Fairly large increases in HR were instrumentally conditioned by Hatch (1980). Further, intermittent delivery of the feedback was more effective than continuous feedback in producing the result. Slowing of HR was also brought under voluntary control, but the schedule of reinforcement did not affect the degree of deceleration. Hatch used a wide range of motor tasks to test the hypothesis that voluntary HR control was related to motor skills. The results were contrary to the hypothesis that the same abilities underlie skeletal motor and visceral (HR) learning. In an interesting approach, McKinney, Gatchel, Brantley, and Harrington (1980) obtained fairly large HR reductions (9 BPM, on the average) in a training procedure that combined feedback with tangible rewards. During a generalization test (no feedback), the tangible reward group produced an average HR decrease of 13 BPM, compared to virtually no HR reduction in a continuous-feedback-only group. Thus, we see a sizable HR deceleration when subjects receive rewards in addition to information regarding changes in HR.

One possible application of instrumental control of HR might be the reduction of cardiovascular reactivity in a stressful situation. There is some experimental evidence that this may be possible. For example, McCanne (1983) found that practice at controlling HR led to reduced HR while viewing stressful scenes in a film. Self-reports of beliefs about ability to control HR were related to the reductions observed during film viewing. This suggests that expectancy effects may reduce autonomic responding during stress. Perski, Engel, and McCroskery (1982) reviewed several studies showing that humans can be taught to control HR while anticipating or experiencing a variety of aversive stimuli.

For example, Victor, Mainardi, and Shapiro (1978) demonstrated that HR acceleration produced by placing a hand in ice water can be modified by training in HR slowing. Ratings of painfulness decreased during HR slowing. Perceptions of stimuli and reactions to them may be changed by the instrumental conditioning procedure. One question that has arisen is whether baseline levels of systolic blood pressure (SBP) can affect the discrimination of one's own heartbeat. It was reported that persons with elevated SBP were more able to accurately perceive their heartbeats, both before and after feedback training, compared to those with normal levels (O'Brien, Reid, & Jones, 1998). The average baseline SBP for the elevated group was 111 mmHg, whereas it was 124 mmHg for the normal group. The authors posited that those with higher blood pressure levels had stronger stimulus cues than the normals.

Summary.   Research on the instrumental conditioning of HR indicates that cardiac activity may be brought under some degree of voluntary control. It appears that increases are more easily atttained than decreases, although the role of tangible reward has not been fully explored. The exact mechanisms underlying this voluntary control are not known, although there are findings to suggest that operant HR speeding is associated with a decrease in cardiac vagal tone, and HR slowing with an increase in cardiac vagal tone. Researchers have variously suggested that the HR changes are mediated by respiratory factors, by muscle activity, and by factors similar to those that influence the learning of a motor skill (e.g., practice with feedback, motivation, and frequent reinforcement). This area is still controversial, and, so far, the hypothesis proposing the similarity of visceral and motor learning has not been supported. It has been reported that individuals with higher levels of systolic blood pressure are better able to perceive their own heartbeats than people with lower levels. The possibility of voluntary control over HR has important clinical implications, regardless of the source of this control. The effects of baseline blood pressure on perception of HR merits further study. Some of the findings have indicated that HR control may lessen responsivity to stressful stimuli. Clinical applications of biofeedback are discussed in chapter 17.

Research on the relationship between cardiac activity and behavior continues to occupy the time of many researchers. Many empirical findings and some interesting concepts have stemmed from these studies (e.g., those of the Laceys and Obrist and colleagues, which are discussed more fully in chapter 18). Chapter 14 discusses two physiological measures, blood pressure and blood volume, and their relation to behavior.

REFERENCES

Allen, M. T., Lawler, K. A., Mitchell, V. P., Matthews, K. A., Rakaczky, C. J., & Jamison, W. (1987). Type A behavior pattern, parental history of hypertension, and cardiovascular reactivity in college males. *Health Psychology, 6,* 113–130.

Arabian, J. M. (1982). Imagery and Pavlovian heart rate decelerative conditioning. *Psychophysiology, 19,* 286–293.

Ashton, R., White, K. D., & Hodgson, G. (1979). Sensitivity to heart rate: A psychophysical study. *Psychophysiology, 16*, 403–406.

Ax, A. R. (1953). The physiological differentiation between fear and anger in humans. *Psychosomatic Medicine, 15*, 147–150.

Barefoot, J. C., Williams, R. B., Dahlstrom, W. G. (1983). Hostility, CHD incidence and total mortality: A 25-year follow-up study of 255 physicians. *Psychosomatic Medicine, 45*, 59–63.

Bergman, J. S., & Johnson, H. J. (1972). Sources of information which affect training and raising of heart rate. *Psychophysiology, 9*, 30–39.

Blanchard, E. B., & Young, L. D. (1973). Self-control and cardiac functioning: A promise yet unfulfilled. *Psychological Bulletin, 79*, 145–163.

Cacioppo, J. T., & Petty, R. E. (1983). *Social psychophysiology*. New York: Guilford.

Coles, M. G. H. (1983). Situational determinants and psychological significance of heart rate change. In A. Gale & J. A. Edwards (Eds.), *Physiological correlates of human behavior* (pp. 171–186). New York: Academic Press.

Croyle, R. T., & Cooper, J. (1983). Dissonance arousal: Physiological evidence. *Journal of Personality and Social Psychology, 45*, 782–791.

Deane, G. E. (1969). Cardiac activity during experimentally induced anxiety. *Psychophysiology, 6*, 17–30.

Ekman, P., Levenson, R. W., & Friesen, W. V. (1983). Autonomic nervous system activity distinguishes among emotions. *Science, 22*, 1208–1210.

Elliott, R. (1969). Tonic heart rate: Experiments on the effects of collative variables lead to a hypothesis about its motivational significance. *Journal of Personality and Social Psychology, 12*, 211–288.

Elliott, R. (1974). The motivational significance of heart rate. In P. A. Obrist, A. H. Black, J. Brener, & L. V. DiCara (Eds.), *Cardiovascular psychophysiology* (pp. 505–537). Chicago: Aldine.

Elliott, R., Bankart, B., & Light, T. (1970). Differences in the motivational significance of heart rate and palmar conductance: Two tests of a hypothesis. *Journal of Personality and Social Psychology, 14*, 166–172.

Evans, J. F. (1971). Social facilitation in a competitive situation. *Canadian Journal of Behavioral Science, 3*, 276–281.

Evans, J. F. (1972). Resting heart rate and the effects of an incentive. *Psychonomic Science, 26*, 99–100.

Fichera, L. V., & Andreassi, J. L. (1998). Stress and personality as factors in women's cardiovascular reactivity. *International Journal of Psychophysiology, 28*, 143–155.

Fowles, D. C. (1983). Motivational effects on heart rate and electrodermal activity: Implications for research on personality and psychopathology. *Journal of Research in Personality, 17*, 48–71.

Fowles, D. C., Fisher, A. E., & Tranel, D. T. (1982). The heart beats to reward: The effects of monetary incentives on heart rate. *Psychophysiology, 19*, 506–513.

Frankenhaeuser, M., & Johansson, G. (1976). Task demand as reflected in catecholamine excretion and heart rate. *Journal of Human Stress, 2*, 15–23.

Friedman, D., Putnam, L., & Hamberger, M. J. (1990). Cardiac deceleration and E-wave potential components in young, middle-aged and elderly adults. *International Journal of Psychophysiology, 10*, 185–190.

Friedman, M., & Rosenman, R. H. (1974). *Type A behavior and your heart*. New York: Knopf.

Furedy, J. J., & Poulos, C. X. (1976). Heart-rate decelerative Pavlovian conditioning with tilt as UCS: Towards behavioral control of cardiac dysfunction. *Biological Psychology, 4*, 93–106.

Goldband, S. (1980). Stimulus specificity of physiological response to stress and the type A coronary-prone personality. *Journal of Personality & Social Psychology, 39*, 670–679.

Greenstadt, L., Shapiro, D., & Whitehead, R. (1986). Blood pressure discrimination. *Psychophysiology, 23*, 500–509.

Hantas, M. N., Katkin, E. S., & Reed, S. D. (1984). Cerebral lateralization and heartbeat discrimination. *Psychophysiology, 21*, 274–278.

Hare, R. D. (1972). Cardiovascular components of orienting and defensive responses. *Psychophysiology, 9*, 606–614.

Hare, R. D. (1973). Orienting and defensive responses to visual stimuli. *Psychophysiology, 10*, 453–464.

Hare, R. D., & Blevings, G. (1975). Defensive responses to phobic stimuli. *Biological Psychology, 3*, 1–13.

Hatch, J. P. (1980). The effects of operant reinforcement schedules on the modification of human heart rate. *Psychophysiology, 17*, 559–567.

Hatch, J. P., Borcherding, S., & Norris, L. K. (1990). Cardiopulmonary adjustments during operant heart rate control. *Psychophysiology, 27*, 641–648.

Headrick, M. W., & Graham, F. K. (1969). Multiple component heart rate responses conditioned under paced respiration. *Journal of Experimental Psychology, 79*, 486–494.

Hnatiow, M., & Lang, P. J. (1965). Learned stabilization of cardiac rate. *Psychophysiology, 1*, 330–336.

Ira, G. H., Whalen, R. E., & Bogdonoff, M. D. (1963). Heart rate changes in physicians during daily "stressful" tasks. *Journal of Psychosomatic Research, 7*, 147–150.

Jamner, L. D., Shapiro, D., Goldstein, I. B., & Hug, R. (1991). Ambulatory blood pressure and heart rate in paramedics: Effects of cynical hostility and defensiveness. *Psychosomatic Medicine, 53*, 393–406.

Juszczak, N. M., & Andreassi, J. L. (1987). Performance and physiological responses of Type A and Type B individuals during a cognitive and perceptual motor task. *International Journal of Psychophysiology, 5*, 81–90.

Kamarck, T. W., Jennings, J. R., Debski, T. T., Glickman-Weiss, E., Johnson, P. S., Eddy, M. J., & Manuck, S. B. (1992). Reliable measures of behaviorally-evoked cardiovascular reactivity from a PC-based test battery: Results from student and community samples. *Psychophysiology, 29*, 17–28.

Kamarck, T. W., Manuck, S. B., & Jennings, J. R. (1990). Social support reduces cardiovascular reactivity to psychological challenge: A laboratory model. *Psychosomatic Medicine, 52*, 42–58.

Katkin, E. S., & Murray, E. N. (1968). Instrumental conditioning of autonomically mediated behavior: Theoretical and methodological issues. *Psychological Bulletin, 70*, 52–68.

Kimble, G. A. (1961). *Hilgard and Marquis' conditioning and learning.* New York: Appleton-Century-Crofts.

Kimmel, H. D. (1973). Instrumental conditioning. In W. F. Prokasy & D. C. Raskin (Eds.), *Electrodermal activity in psychological research* (pp. 225–282). New York: Academic Press.

Klorman, R., Weissberg, R. P., & Wiesenfeld, A. R. (1976, October). *Individual differences in fear and autonomic reactions to affective stimulation.* Paper presented at meeting of Society of Psychophysiological Research, San Diego, CA.

Klorman, R., Wiesenfeld, A. R., & Austin, M. L. (1975). Autonomic responses to affective visual stimuli. *Psychophysiology, 12*, 553–560.

Krantz, D. S., Glass, D. C., Shaeffer, M. A., & Davia, J. E. (1982). Behavior patterns and coronary disease: A critical evaluation. In J. T. Cacioppo & R. E. Petty (Eds.), *Perspectives in cardiovascular psychophysiology* (pp. 315–346). New York: Guilford.

Lang, P. J. (1974). Learned control of human heart rate in a computer directed environment. In P. A. Obrist, A. H. Black, J. Brener, & L. V. DiCara (Eds.), *Cardiovascular psychophysiology* (pp. 392–405). Chicago: Aldine.

Lang, P. J., & Twentyman, C. T. (1976). Learning to control heart rate: Effects of varying incentive and criterion of success on task performance. *Psychophysiology, 13*, 378–385.

Lawler, K. A., Huck, S. W., & Smalley, L. B. (1989). Physiological correlates of the coronary-prone behavior pattern in women during examination stress. *Physiology & Behavior, 45*, 777–779.

Levenson, R. W., Ekman, P., & Friesen, W. V. (1990). Voluntary facial action generates emotion-specific autonomic nervous system activity. *Psychophysiology, 27*, 363–384.

Light, K. C., Dolan, C. A., Davis, M. R., & Sherwood, A. (1992). Cardiovascular responses to an active coping as predictors of blood pressure patterns 10 to 15 years later. *Psychosomatic Medicine, 54*, 217–230.

Ludwick-Rosenthal, R., & Neufeld, R. W. J. (1985). Heart beat interoception: A study of individual differences. *International Journal of Psychophysiology, 3*, 57–65.

Malpass, D., Trieber, F. A., Turner, J. R., Davis, H., Thompson, W., Levy, M., & Strong, W. B. (1997). Relationships between children's cardiovascular stress responses and resting cardiovascular functioning 1 year later. *International Journal of Psychophysiology, 25*, 139–145.

McCanne, T. R. (1983). Changes in autonomic responding to stress after practice at controlling heart rate. *Biofeedback & Self-Regulation, 8*, 9–24.

McCanne, T. R., & Sandman, C. A. (1976). Human operant heart rate conditioning: The importance of individual differences. *Psychological Bulletin, 83*, 587–601.

McKinney, M., Gatchel, R., Brantley, D., & Harrington, R. (1980). The input of biofeedback manipulated physiological change on emotional state. *Basic & Applied Psychology, 1*, 15–21.

Musante, L., Raunikar, R. A., Treiber, F., Davis, H., Dysart, J., Levy, M., & Strong, W. B. (1994). Consistency of children's hemodynamic responses to laboratory stressors. *International Journal of Psychophysiology, 17*, 65–72.

Notterman, J. M., Schoenfeld, W. N., Bersh, P. J. (1952). A comparison of three extinction procedures following heart rate conditioning. *Journal of Abnormal and Social Psychology, 47*, 674–677.

O'Brien, W. H., Reid, G. J., & Jones, K. R. (1998). Differences in heartbeat awareness among males with higher and lower levels of systolic blood pressure. *International Journal of Psychophysiology, 29*, 53–63.

Obrist, P. A. (1976). The cardiovascular-behavioral interaction as it appears today. *Psychophysiology, 13*, 95–107.

Obrist, P. A., Gaebelein, C. J., Teller, S. E., Langer, A. W., Grignolo, A., Light, K. C., & McCubbin, J. A. (1978). The relationship among heart rate, carotid dP/dt and blood pressure in humans as a function of the type of stress. *Psychophysiology, 15*, 102–115.

Obrist, P. A., Lawler, J. E., Howard, J. L., Smithson, K. W., Martin, P. L., & Manning, J. (1974). Sympathetic influences on the heart in humans: Effects on contractility and heart rate of acute stress. *Psychophysiology, 11*, 405–427.

Obrist, P. A., Webb, R. A., & Sutterer, J. R. (1969). Heart rate and somatic changes during aversive conditioning and a simple reaction time task. *Psychophysiology, 5*, 696–723.

Perski, A., Engel, B. T., & McCroskery, J. H. (1982). The modification of elicited cardiovascular responses by operant conditioning of heart rate. In J. T. Cacioppo & R. E. Petty (Eds.), *Perspectives in cardiovascular psychophysiology* (pp. 296–314). New York: Guilford.

Plutchik, R., & Ax, A. F. (1967). A critique of "Determinants of emotional state by Schachter, J., & Singer, J. E. (1962)." *Psychophysiology, 4*, 79–82.

Roman, J., Older, H., & Jones, W. L. (1967). Flight research program: VII. Medical monitoring of Navy carrier pilots in combat. *Aerospace Medicine, 38*, 133–139.

Rule, B. G., & Hewitt, L. S. (1971). Effects of thwarting on cardiac response and physical agggression. *Journal of Personality and Social Psychology, 19*, 181–187.

Sandman, C. A. (1984). Augmentation of the auditory event related potentials of the brain during diastole. *International Journal of Psychophysiology, 2*, 11–19.

Sandman, C. A., Walker, B. B., & Berka, C. (1982). Influence of afferent cardiovascular feedback on behavior and the cortical evoked potential. In J. T. Cacioppo & R. E. Petty (Eds.), *Perspectives in cardiovascular psychophysiology* (pp. 189–222). New York: Guilford.

Sausen, K. P., Lovallo, W. R., & Wilson, M. F. (1991). Heart rate reactivity, behavior pattern, and parental hypertension as predictors of cardiovascular activity during cognitive challenge. *Psychophysiology, 28*, 639–647.

Schacter, S., & Singer, J. E. (1962). Cognitive, social and physiological determinants of emotional state. *Psychological Review, 69*, 379–399.

Shapiro, A. H. (1975). Behavior of Kibbutz and urban children receiving an injection. *Psychophysiology, 12*, 79–82.

Shearn, D. N. (1962). Operant conditioning of heart rate. *Science, 137*, 530–531.

Sherwood, A., Davis, M. R., Dolan, C. A., & Light, K. C. (1992). Effects of self-challenge on cardiovascular reactivity. *International Journal of Psychophysiology, 12*, 87–94.

Sherwood, A., & Turner, J. R. (1992). A conceptual and methodological overview of cardiovascular reactivity research. In J. R. Turner, A. Sherwood, & K. C. Light (Eds.), *Individual differences in cardiovascular response to stress* (pp. 3–32). New York: Plenum.

Smith, T. W. (1992). Hostility and health: Current status of a psychosomatic hypothesis. *Health Psychology, 11*, 139–150.

Smith, T. W., Allred, K. D., Morrison, C. A., & Carlson, S. D. (1989). Cardiovascular reactivity and interpersonal influence: Active coping in a social context. *Journal of Personality & Social Psychology, 56*, 209–218.

Smith, T. W., Baldwin, M., & Christensen, A. J. (1990). Interpersonal influence as active coping: Effects of task difficulty on cardiovascular reactivity. *Psychophysiology, 27*, 429–437.

Stern, G., & Elder, R. D. (1982). The role of challenging incentives in feedback-assisted heart rate reduction for coronary-prone adult males. *Biofeedback & Self Regulation, 7*, 53–69.

Stern, R. M., Farr, J. H., & Ray, W. J. (1975). Pleasure. In P. H. Venables & M. J. Christie (Eds.), *Research in psychophysiology* (pp. 208–233). New York: Wiley.

Suarez, E. C., & Williams, R. B. (1989). Situational determinants of cardiovascular and emotional reactivity in high and low hostile men. *Psychosomatic Medicine, 51*, 404–418.

Suarez, E. C., & Williams, R. B. (1990). The relationships between dimensions of hostility and cardiovascular reactivity as a function of task characteristics. *Psychosomatic Medicine, 52*, 558–570.

Sundin, O., Ohman, A., Palm, T., & Strom, G. (1995). Cardiovascular reactivity, Type A behavior, and coronary heart disease: Comparisons between myocardial infarction patients and controls during laboratory-induced stress. *Psychophysiology, 32*, 28–35.

Tardy, C. H., & Allen, M. T. (1998). Moderators of cardiovascular reactivity to speech: Discourse production and group variations in blood pressure and pulse rate. *International Journal of Psychophysiology, 29*, 247–254.

Tranel, D. T., Fisher, A. E., & Fowles, D. C. (1982). Magnitude of incentive effects on heart rate. *Psychophysiology, 19*, 514–519.

Turner, J. R., Sherwood, A., & Light, K. C. (1990). Generalization of cardiovascular response: Supportive evidence for the reactivity hypothesis. *International Journal of Psychophysiology, 11*, 207–212.

Uchino, B. N., Kiecolt-Glaser, J. K., & Cacioppo, J. T. (1992). Age-related changes in cardiovascular response as a function of a chronic stressor and social support. *Journal of Personality & Social Psychology, 63*, 839–846.

Valins, S. (1966). Cognitive effects of false heart-rate feedback. *Journal of Personality and Social Psychology, 4*, 400–408.

Van Egeren, L. F., Headrick, M. N., & Hein, P. L. (1972). Individual differences in autonomic responses: Illustration of a possible solution. *Psychophysiology, 9*, 626–633.

Velden, M., & Juris, M. (1975). Perceptual performance as a function of intracycle cardiac activity. *Psychophysiology, 12*, 685–692.

Victor, R., Mainardi, J. A., & Shapiro, D. (1978). Effects of biofeedback and voluntary control procedures on heart rate and perception of pain during the cold pressor test. *Psychosomatic Medicine*, 216–225.

Walker, B. B., & Sandman, C. A. (1979). Human visual evoked responses are related to heart rate. *Journal of Comparative & Physiological Psychology, 93*, 717–729.

Walker, B. B., & Walker, J. M. (1983). Phase relations between carotid pressure and ongoing electrocortical activity. *International Journal of Psychophysiology, 1*, 65–73.

Weisz, J., Szilagyi, N., Lang, E., & Adam, G. (1992). The influence of monocular viewing on heart period variability. *International Journal of Psychophysiology, 12*, 11–18.

Wolk, C., & Velden, M. (1987). Detection variability within the cardiac cycle: Toward a revision of the "baroreceptor hypothesis." *Journal of Psychophysiology, 1*, 61–65.

14

Blood Pressure, Blood Volume, and Behavior

Blood pressure (BP) is one of the most frequently measured physiological variables. Its measurement in the physician's office and the hospital or clinic far exceeds its use as a variable in psychological research. This is because of its importance as a general index of cardiovascular function and health. Research on the effects of psychological stimuli on blood pressure dates back to at least the 1920s, when Nissen, as one example, obtained blood pressure readings of patients in a dentist's chair. Pressures rose sharply as soon as the dentist entered the room! (Woodworth & Schlosberg, 1954).

Blood volume (BV) is much less familiar than blood pressure. It refers to the amount of blood that is present in a certain portion of body tissue at a given time. Blood volume changes occur as a function of local metabolic requirements, and an important factor affecting it is the behavior in which the individual is engaged. Early studies of blood volume include those of Shepard, who reported in 1906 that the expectation of a stimulus led to decreased hand blood volume and an increase in brain volume (Woodworth & Schlosberg, 1954). This chapter examines BP and BV as physiological variables in psychological research. Some questions of interest regarding blood pressure include the effects of cognitive load and problem solving on this measure. Important issues concerning effects of stress, frustration, hostility, and anger on changes in blood pressure are also considered, as are the relationships between Type A/B personality and this vital measure. In addition, social factors such as crowding and communications are examined with respect to their influence on blood pressure. The extent to which blood pressure can be conditioned through classical and instrumental procedures is also covered.

With regard to blood volume changes as a function of psychological processes, there is less coverage because the research in this area is not as extensive as for blood pressure. Nevertheless, there are important issues concerning the use of blood volume measurements in research on sexual response of both women and men, and blood volume changes during the orienting response and instrumental conditioning. The BP and BV responses, and their relation to behavior, are presented after a brief discussion of the anatomy and physiology of these measures.

ANATOMY AND PHYSIOLOGY OF THE BLOOD VESSELS

Blood vessels may be divided into several categories on the basis of their size, function, and microscopic characteristics. These categories include the large elastic arteries, medium-size arteries, small arteries (arterioles), capillaries, veins, and venules (Jacob & Francone, 1970). The blood vessels are composed of three layers: an inner tunica intima, a middle tunica media, and an outer tunica adventitia. (Note the direct use of the Latin word for a layer of clothing or *tunica* in each of these terms.) Table 14.1 outlines the structures of these various kinds of blood vessels. Figure 14.1 illustrates the structural layers of arteries and veins.

Basically, the arteries are tubes with thick walls, branching out from the aorta to carry blood to all parts of the body. Arteries are made up of smooth muscle fibers and elastic membrane tissue. This gives them an elastic property, enabling them to stretch when pressure is applied and then readily return to normal when pressure is relaxed.

The arterioles are the smallest arteries in the body. They enable blood to enter capillary beds (Guyton, 1977). The capillaries are tiny vessels, one cell layer thick (about 10 μ), that allow the actual exchange of carbon dioxide and oxygen in the lungs and of nutrients and wastes in body tissues. The blood leaves the capillary beds by small venules, which form into small veins and eventually into larger veins, which carry blood back to the heart. Veins are not as muscular as arteries, their walls are thin, and they have valves that prevent the backflow of blood.

Innervation of Blood Vessels

All of the blood vessels of the body, except the capillaries, are innervated by nerve fibers from the SNS alone (Guyton, 1977). The SNS produces varying degrees of constriction of the blood vessels. This is controlled via the vasomotor center, which is located in the reticular substance of the brain (lower pons and upper medulla). The hypothalamus of the brain can exert powerful inhibitory or excitatory effects on the vasomotor center. Cortical effects have not been as well defined.

The vasomotor center maintains what is called *sympathetic vasoconstrictor tone*, which is essential in keeping arterial blood pressure at an appropriate functioning level. Normal sympathetic tone keeps almost all of the blood vessels of the body constricted to about half of maximum diameter. With increased SNS activity, vessels can be further constricted. On the other hand, by inhibiting the normal tone, blood vessels can be dilated. Thus, normal sympathetic tone allows both vasoconstriction and vasodilation of blood vessels. The PNS exerts no direct influence over the peripheral blood vessels (Gardner, 1975). The sympathetic vasoconstrictor substance is norepinephrine, which acts on the smooth muscle tissue of blood vessels.

TABLE 14.1
Structure of Blood Vessels

Vessel	Outer Layer: Tunica Adventitia	Middle Layer: Tunica Media	Inner Layer: Tunica Intima
Large arteries (elastic)	Thick layer, consisting of connective tissue	Layer consists largely of elastic fibers with some muscle	Thin endothelial cells resting on connective tissue
Muscular arteries (medium)	Thick layer, consisting of connective tissue	Fewer elastic fibers, more smooth muscle	Thin endothelial cells resting on connective tissue
Small arteries (arterioles)	Thin	Consists of muscular tissue	Layer composed almost entirely of endothelium
Capillaries	Absent	Absent	Endothelial layer, one cell thick
Veins	Thin layer	Thinner, little muscle or elastic tissue	Endothelial lining with scant connective tissue

Source: Taken from S. W. Jacob and C. A. Francone, *Structure and function in man* (2nd ed.). Philadelphia: W. B. Saunders, 1970.

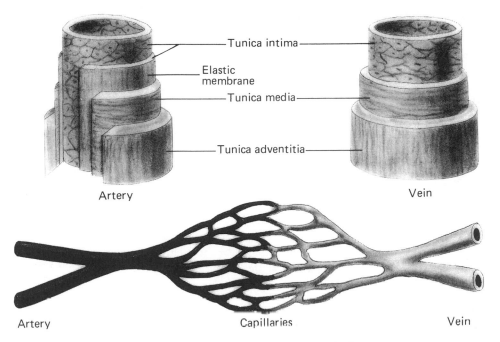

FIG. 14.1. Component parts of arteries and veins.

Regulation of Blood Pressure

Jacob and Francone (1970) listed five factors that function to maintain arterial blood pressure:

1. Cardiac factor: This refers to the volume of blood expelled each time the left ventricle contracts.

2. Peripheral resistance: This is produced primarily by the arterioles, which vary their diameter over wide range.

3. Blood volume: Blood volume refers here to the relatively constant volume of blood cells and plasma within the whole circulatory system. If blood volume is low, then blood pressure is reduced.

4. Viscosity: Increased viscosity of blood causes a greater resistance to flow and, therefore, a higher arterial pressure. If blood hematocrit increases, so does the friction between successive layers of blood, and viscosity increases drastically. (The hematocrit refers to the percentage of blood that is composed of cells. Thus, if a person has a hematoccrit reading of 42, it means that 42% of the blood volume is composed of cells and 58% is plasma). The hematocrit value of a normal man is about 42, whereas that of a normal woman is about 38 (Guyton, 1977).

5. Elasticity of arterial walls: When elasticity of the larger arteries decreases, systolic pressure rises. Systolic blood pressure refers to the pressure exerted on arterial walls during ventricular systole (contraction of the heart muscle), whereas diastolic pressure is related to ventricular diastole (resting of the heart muscle).

Stretch receptors (baroreceptors) in the carotid sinuses and in the aorta transmit signals to the vasomotor system of the brain stem according to arterial pressure. These baroreceptors are spray-type nerve endings, lying in the walls of the arteries, which are stimulated when stretched. The baroreceptors are not stimulated by pressures between 0 and 60 mm Hg, but above this level they progressively increase their firing rate until a maximum is reached at about 180 mm Hg (Guyton, 1977). Heart rate and blood pressure are inversely related through the baroreceptor reflex, so that a drop in arterial pressure quickly leads to an increase in heart rate (Steptoe, 1980). However, under certain conditions, such as exercise or unpleasant stimulation, BP and HR may increase together. Usually, if blood pressure becomes elevated, reflex signals from the vasomotor center slow the heart and dilate the blood vessels. Thus, stimulation of baroreceptors by pressure in the arteries reflexively causes arterial pressure to decrease, whereas low pressure produces the opposite effect; that is, pressure is reflexively caused to rise back toward normal. Although the baroreceptor reflex is important in regulating moment-to-moment changes in arterial pressure, it is unimportant in the long-term control of blood pressure, because the baroreceptors adapt in 1 or 2 days to a given pressure level. The more long-term control of BP is determined by the balance between fluid intake and output, in which the kidneys play an important role. Blood pressure varies within the cardiac cycle, for example, it rises sharply with ventricular systole. Blood pressure level also changes from beat to beat, posing difficulties in measurement (e.g., see Tursky, Shapiro, & Schwartz, 1972).

Systemic arterial blood pressure is important in regulating blood flow to body organs (Papillo & Shapiro, 1990). Systemic blood pressure is a resultant of cardiac output (CO) times total peripheral resistance (TPR). As pointed out in chapter 12, CO is a function of heart rate × stroke volume, and TPR is the level of resistance to blood flow caused by the state of constriction of blood vessels in the circulatory system.

Regulation of Blood Volume

The normal adult has a blood volume of approximately 5,000 ml (5 liters). This figure varies with such factors as age, sex, build, race, environment, and disease (Grollman, 1964). In this chapter, we are interested in examining changes in blood volume that occur in the performance of various mental and physical tasks. That is, shifts in the blood volume of various body parts that occur in different kinds of activities. These shifts in blood volume are dependent on the arterial blood flow into an area and the venous outflow from an area. Therefore, those factors mentioned earlier with respect to vasoconstriction or vasodilation of blood vessels (e.g., SNS activity, baroreceptor reflex) are also of importance in regulating blood volume. There is also a reflex for the control of blood volume (Guyton, 1977). For example, if blood volume of the body increases, stretch receptors in the atria and large veins transmit signals to the vasomotor center. Reflex signals involving both the vasomotor center and the hypothalamus then cause the kidneys to increase their fluid output, thus reducing total body fluid and blood volume.

MEASUREMENT OF BLOOD PRESSURE

The methods we describe for the measurement of blood pressure are known as *indirect techniques*. The true measurement of blood pressure can only be achieved by penetrating an artery to insert a sensing device. This direct measurement of intra-arterial BP would be a problem in the psychophysiology laboratory using human subjects, because of discomfort for participants and possible medical complications.

The most familiar blood pressure measuring technique involves the use of a sphygmomanometer (from the Greek word *sphygmos*, meaning "pulse"). The method involves the use of a pressure cuff, a rubber bulb, a mercury (Hg) manometer, and a stethoscope. The pressure cuff is wrapped around the upper arm and inflated to a level well above the expected systolic pressure (say, 175 mm Hg). The stethoscope, which has been placed over the brachial artery, picks up no sound at this level, because the artery has been collapsed by the cuff pressure. The cuff pressure is then very gradually reduced, until sounds are heard. Gradual reductions of about 2 mm Hg per sec on the mercury manometer allows fairly accurate measurements of BP. The sounds are produced by small amounts of blood passing through the cuff and are called Korotkoff sounds, after the man who first used this method in the early 1900s. The pressure on the manometer is noted when the first sound is heard with each pulsation. This is the systolic pressure (SBP) and, for a normal adult, ranges between 95 and 140 mm Hg, with 120 mm Hg being average (Cromwell, Arditti, Weibell, Pfeiffer, Steele, & Labbock, 1976). The pressure in the cuff is then reduced further, until the sounds are no longer heard. When the sounds disappear, the manometer reading at that point indicates diastolic pressure (DBP). Normal diastolic pressure ranges between 60 and 89 mm Hg for the adult. The Korotkoff sounds are believed to be caused by blood jetting through the partly collapsed artery. The jet causes turbulance in the open artery beyond the cuff, and this sets up the vibrations heard in the stethoscope. This technique is termed the *auscultatory method* of obtaining blood pressure, and is adequate for the physician who is mainly concerned that patients fall within a normal range. However, for psychophysiological research, it is necessary to have automated, accurate techniques that enable frequent measurements of blood pressure. It should be noted, too, that the systolic reading is obtained when the heart is contracting to push blood into the arteries, whereas the diastolic reading is obtained when the heart relaxes between beats.

Another measure of blood pressure determined by the difference between systolic and diastolic is called *pulse pressure*. *Mean arterial pressure* (MAP) refers to the average pressure during the cardiac cycle and is estimated by the following: $MAP = \frac{1}{3}(SBP - DBP) + DBP$. Some commercial BP measuring equipment provides digital readouts of MAP along with systolic and diastolic pressure. Papillo and Shapiro (1990) observed that MAP is an important measure of BP because it reflects the average effective pressure that drives the blood through the circulatory system. The MAP must be sufficient to cause the cardiac output of blood to flow through the resistance in the blood vessels.

Tursky (1974) explained that the auscultatory method leads to an underestimate of systolic blood pressure. This is because the pressure in the cuff must be lower than that in the artery in order for Korotkoff sounds to be heard. A problem also exists in measuring diastolic pressure by this means, because it, too, depends on changes in sound. Tursky et al. (1972) developed an automated constant-cuff pressure system to overcome this error of measurement. This technique determines the relationship between a fixed-cuff pressure and arterial pressure at each heartbeat. The presence and absence of the Korotkoff sound is then used to establish a median pressure. The system was tested on a patient who had arterial pressure recorded directly from the brachial artery of the left arm while systolic pressures were obtained from the right arm with the constant-cuff procedure. Measures on five sets of 32 beats showed a close correspondence in systolic pressure obtained with each method (all comparisons were less than 2 mm Hg apart).

Gunn, Wolf, Black, and Person (1972) briefly described a portable device for the automatic measurement of blood pressure. Since that time, ambulatory blood pressure monitoring devices have become increasingly miniaturized and can provide accurate measures of blood pressure over a 48-hr period. The numerous noninvasive BP measures are recorded for later downloading into a computer for detailed analyses. The instrument can be worn by a freely moving person, enabling the continous recording of blood pressure as the individual responds to physical or psychological demands that occur during the course of a day (Harshfield & Pulliam, 1992). The use of these portable devices has great potential for researchers who wish to study BP reactions to daily events, and for physicians desiring to measure effects of antihypertensive medications. Contemporary commercially available units have become lighter in weight (less than 16 ounces) and can record systolic, diastolic, and mean arterial pressure as well as HR. A hospital nursery was the site where ambulatory monitoring was used to measure BP and heart rate in newborn infants (Hall, Thomas, Friedman, & Lynch, 1982). The device detected pressure pulsations in the cuff and recorded them automatically. The lowest BP readings were obtained when the 77 infants were sleeping (78 systolic, 40 diastolic), and the highest (82 systolic, 45 diastolic) occurred while they were sucking. The HR was lowest while they slept (126 BPM), and it was highest when they cried (144 BPM).

MEASUREMENT OF BLOOD VOLUME

Brown (1967) pointed out that *plethysmography* is a term used to describe various techniques of measuring blood volume changes in a limb or segment of tissue. The term is derived from the Greek *plethysmos*, which means "an enlargement." Brown described three basic types of devices for recording blood volume changes:

1. Hydraulic or pneumatic systems, in which fluids or air detect a volume change in an observed part and transmit this to a recording device.
2. Electrical impedance, which reflects changes in impedance by tissue to the passage of high-frequency alternating current, as a function of volume change.
3. Photoelectric transducers, which measure changes in the intensity of a light passed through a tissue segment, for example, a fingertip or an earlobe. The intensity varies as a function of the amount of blood in the tissue from moment to moment. It should be noted that photoelectric techniques do not reflect absolute blood volume but only changes within a given person. Comparisons across subjects cannot be made.

Because blood volume measures are relative, most investigators examine changes within each subject from some baseline period and compare this to effects produced by the experimental conditions. Stern, Ray, and Davis (1980) observed that change between baseline and treatment conditions may be expressed as a percentage, and the magnitude of change measured as the difference between the lowest point of a pulse and its peak. Photoelectric devices to measure blood volume changes have been described by Tursky and Greenblatt (1967) and Lee, Tahmoush, and Jennings (1975). The device described by Tursky and Greenblatt involves the use of a pair of fiberoptic light guides. One guide is connected to a regulated light source that tramsmits light to the skin, and a second, attached to a photocell, records changes in reflected light corresponding to volume changes. Lee et al. (1975) used a reflective transducer that combines an infrared light-emitting diode (LED) and a silicon phototransistor. This device can be applied to almost any area of the body to measure changes in vascular activity (see also Tahmoush, Jennings, Lee, Camp, & Weber, 1976).

Cook (1974) pointed out that there are two elements of plethysmographic change that can be measured. These are the relatively slow engorgement of an area, just described as blood volume, and a rapid component referred to as *pulse volume* or *pulse amplitude*. Pulse volume represents the pumping action of the heart as represented in local blood vessels. Blood volume and pulse volume can be measured with the same photoplethysmographic device, using different coupling and gain settings, on separate channels of a recorder. Blood volume measurements obtained with a photoplethysmograph require the use of a DC amplifier with a preamplifer and appropriate transducer (e.g., photoelectric cell placed on an earlobe). Pulse volume measures require AC coupling of the amplifier because the changes that occur are more rapid. Figure 14.2 shows sample traces of blood volume, pulse amplitude, and blood flow. The tracings show that all the measures are sensitive to an environmental stimulus, in this case, a 95-db tone presented simultaneously to the two ears.

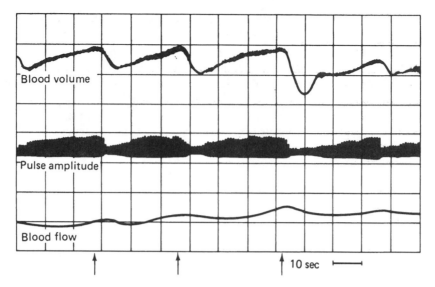

FIG. 14.2. Blood volume, pulse amplitude, and blood flow responses from the finger to a 95-dB, 1000-Hz tone. Arrows mark the onset of stimulus presentation.

A vaginal photoplethysmograph has been developed (see Geer, Morokoff, & Greenwood, 1974; Sintchak & Geer, 1975) for measuring changes in vaginal blood volume. This device, in addition to a penile strain gauge, was used by Heiman (1977) in a study on sexual arousal patterns in males and females. Briefly, the vaginal device is a hollow cylinder, $1^3/_4$ in. long and $^1/_2$ in. in diameter, and houses a small lamp and a photocell. It is inserted into the vagina, and the indirect light reflected back to the photocell from the vaginal wall is measured. The amount of reflected light varies with changes in vaginal blood volume.

The penile strain gauge fits around the shaft of the penis, near the coronal ridge, and measures changes that occur with erection or return to the flaccid state. Laws and Bow (1976) described a penile strain gauge of this type in detail. Figure 14.3 illustrates some data obtained by Laws and Bow from a single subject during the viewing of a 3-min segment of pornographic film. Depicted is the course of penile erection from zero to maximum and the return to baseline.

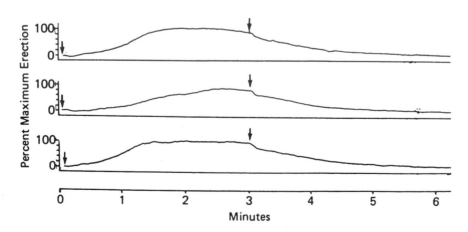

FIG. 14.3. Sample polygraph tracings showing measurement characteristics of penile transducer. Arrows indicate onset and offset of 3-minute film segments.

BLOOD PRESSURE AND BEHAVIOR

In this segment, we examine a number of studies that have employed blood pressure as one of the physiological variables in studies relating to human behavior. There is no question that BP increases with most types of mental and physical activity. Questions that investigators are interested in concern the amount of change, moderating effects of various kinds of mental activities, emotional and stress effects, environmental influences, and personality factors. Also discussed in this section are the conditioning of blood pressure and effects of motor activities and fitness on BP. Researchers have provided some answers to these questions, but they have also uncovered new questions requiring new answers.

Mental Activity and Blood Pressure

Mental Load and Problem Solving.   The relationship between a number of physiological variables and "mental load" was investigated by Ettema and Zielhuis (1971). The physiological measures included blood pressure, HR, and respiration rate. The researchers manipulated mental load by varying the amount of information processed by young adult subjects in a given period of time. High and low tones were presented over earphones in a random sequence. Each of the subjects had the physiological measures recorded during rest and during processing of 20, 30, 40, or 50 signals per minute. Systolic and diastolic blood pressure showed systematic increases as information-processing load increased. The same was true for HR and respiration rate. The authors concluded that increased cardiovascular and respiratory functions are useful indices regarding mental load and may be important in assessing this aspect of industrial work.

The effects of solving difficult problems on BP and other cardiovascular measures was studied by McCubbin, Richardson, Langer, Kizer, and Obrist (1983). The subjects were male undergraduates who were promised bonus money if they completed a series of problems rapidly and accurately. Systolic pressures increased from 127 to 138 mm Hg from pretest to test periods, and an average increase from 70 to 79 mm Hg was observed for diastolic pressures. Heart rates for the same comparisons increased from 64 to 71 BPM. Cardiovascular measures were found to covary with levels of plasma epinephrine and norepinephrine, causing the investigators to conclude that SNS-adrenal gland responsivity may be an important mechanism of individual differences in response to the mental stress involved in solving difficult problems.

Blood pressure and HR of mild hypertensives and normotensives were monitored during rest, mental arithmetic, and head-up tilt (Drummond, 1983). The BP and HR of the hypertensives were higher than the normals when both were at rest. In addition, BP levels increased more in hypertensives while doing mental arithmetic and performing head-up tilt. The greater responsivity of hypertensives in this study supports the view that excess sympathetic nervous system activity contributes to the elevated BP levels observed in hypertension.

Meditation.   There are some kinds of mental activity that can lead to a lowering of BP. For example, lower systolic pressures were observed in 112 persons practicing transcendental meditation (TM) when their values were compared to a matched control group (Wallace, Silver, Mills, Dillbeck, & Wagoner, 1983). The difference was also independent of diet and exercise. Those who had meditated for more than 5 years showed lower levels than meditators with less than 5 years' experience. In another study, the effects of TM were compared to progressive muscle relaxation (PMR) with respect to influence on BP and HR (Throll, 1982). Physiological variables were measured in a pre-experimental session and again at 5, 10, and 15 weeks after practicing each technique. The TM group had greater decreases during meditation and during activity than the PMR group. The groups had shown no pre-experimental differences. The more pronounced results for meditators were explained in terms of the greater amount of time the TM group spent on their technique, in addition to the difference between the two techniques themselves.

Summary.   Information processing load affects blood pressure as does engagement in problem-solving tasks. The relationship between cardiovascular activity and levels of epinephrine and norepinephrine emphasized the role of SNS and hormones in the response to workload. Hypertensives appear to have elevated BP levels during rest and work as compared to normotensives. The practice of transcendental meditation can result in BP decreases.

EMOTIONAL REACTIONS, STRESS, AND BLOOD PRESSURE

Frustration and Aggression.   It has been reported that both frustration and attack produced increased levels of diastolic and systolic blood pressure (Gentry, 1970). In that study, 30 males and 30 females were subjected to frustration (interrupted and not allowed to complete an intelligence test), attack (personal insults by an experimenter), or control conditions. A gender difference was found, in that males generally had greater increases in systolic pressure than did females, with no differences noted for diastolic changes. Doob and Kirshenbaum (1973) measured blood pressure and digit-symbol performance in four groups of subjects, after they were subjected to various combinations of frustration and aggression. The blood pressure and digit-symbol performance were recorded both before and after the following conditions: (a) not frustrated, viewed neutral film; (b) not frustrated, viewed aggressive film; (c) frustrated, viewed neutral film; and (d) frustrated, viewed aggressive film. Persons in Group (d) showed the greatest increase in systolic BP from the first to second reading. Those in Groups (b) and (c) showed a small increase, whereas individuals in Group (a) had slight decreases. The authors interpreted the results as contrary to the idea that movies depicting aggression are tension reducing for either frustrated or nonfrustrated persons; rather, the effects of frustration and aggression seem to be additive in terms of cardiovascular response.

Along similar lines, Geen and Stonner (1974) found that subjects who were given electric shocks, and who then viewed an aggressive film about revenge, showed higher BP levels at the conclusion of the film than did persons who were not shocked and who were told that the theme of the film was either altruism or professionalism. Geen and Stonner suggested that the meaning attached to observed violence affects aggression by lowering inhibitions against aggressiveness and by raising arousal levels. Geen (1975) followed this study with another, in which the effects of being shocked and viewing "real" violence were compared with neutral treatment and observing a film of "fictional" violence. The combination of prior shock (attack) and observation of real violence produced the highest levels of BP. This and the prior study indicated to Geen that the observation of violence facilitated the expression of aggression by raising the viewer's level of emotional arousal.

Effects of emotional expression on cardiovascular response played a role in results obtained by Harburg, Blakelock, and Roeper (1979), who analyzed coping styles in a frustrating situation. They tested the hypothesis that certain coping reactions to an angry boss would be conducive to elevated BP. The subjects were 492 males and 252 females (age 25–60) who completed a questionnaire measuring three types of coping: (a) suppressing anger by ignoring or walking away from the conflict situation; (b) venting anger; and (c) analyzing the problem and restoring a fair job situation. The individuals using the first two strategies had significantly higher BP levels than those using the third one. Thus, giving vent to anger or ignoring the situation completely seem to be maladaptive both from a behavioral and cardiovascular perspective.

Emotional Imagery.   The question of cardiovascular response differences with various emotional imagery was examined by Schwartz, Weinberger, and Singer (1981). College students were asked to produce imagined states of happiness, sadness, anger, fear, relaxation, and a control imagery state, while seated and when they exercised. Anger imagery produced the greatest overall increases in BP, and HR and was very similar under seated and exercise conditions. Similar results were obtained by Roberts and Weerts (1982), who examined cardiovascular responding during fear and anger imagery. They, too, found greater BP increases for anger than fear imagery.

Naturalistic Stress.   Matthews, Manuck, and Saab (1986) used a naturalistic stressor (giving a 5-min speech in class) to evaluate cardiovascular response in anxious and in angry high school students. Anxious students showed elevated systolic BP and HR while giving the speech, whereas adolescents who were frequently angry, and expressed their anger outwardly, had elevated diastolic BP. Adolescents who had exaggerated cardiovascular responses ("reactors") to mental subtraction and mirror-tracing in an additional laboratory test also showed elevated BP and/or HR in the field setting (class speech). This finding suggests that responses in laboratory settings may be good indicators of responding in everyday life situations. This also fits in with findings of McKinney et al. (1985), who showed that laboratory measures of BP using standard stressors (e.g., cold pressor test) were related to ambulatory measures of BP taken at home and at work. In several of the studies reviewed here, anger played a prominent role in elevated BP whether it was naturally present or derived through imagery. This basic research could have important health implications. Williams and his associates (e.g., Williams, Barefoot, & Shekelle, 1985) are involved in research investigating the roles of anger and hostility in producing cardiovascular disease.

A real-life stressor was used to evaluate the link between hostility and cardiovascular reactivity by Jamner, Shapiro, Goldstein, and Hug (1991). They obtained ambulatory HR and BP in male paramedics during a 24-hr work shift to see the effects of work stress on cardiovascular response. The real-life stressor involved interpersonal conflicts in a hospital setting, especially with emergency room physicians, and those paramedics who scored high in both hostility and a measure of defensiveness had greater HR and BP reactivity than those high in hostility, but low in defensiveness. Defensiveness was defined as a coping style characterized by avoiding threatening information and a denial of negative emotions. Studies using ambulatory measures of blood pressure in naturalistic settings were reviewed by Carels, Sherwood, and Blumenthal (1998). Some of the findings were that male medical students reported greater psychological distress and had higher SBP and DBP during pre-exam and examination periods than when the exams were over. Also reported was a study of working women, some of whom cared for someone at home after work. Both caregivers and noncaregivers showed similar ambulatory BP in the clinic and at work, but caregivers showed a significant increase in SBP when they returned home, yet the noncaregivers showed a decrease in BP after leaving work. Studies such as these suggest that perceived or actual stress in an individual's surroundings may influence BP levels.

Job Strain.   Research indicates that job strain can produce work-related stress and could have health consequences. Job strain is defined as the combination of high psychological demands along with low decision latitude (little control) on the job (Carels et al., 1998). A number of investigations into job strain and ambulatory BP were summarized by Carels and colleagues. Seven of 10 studies with men indicated that increased job strain was correlated with elevated SBP or DBP (sometimes both) at work. Two of the three studies with women (also ambulatory) found an association between BP level and job strain. On balance, then, it appears that stressful work settings can lead to elevated BP levels.

Active and Passive Coping in Cardiovascular Reactivity to Stress.   The idea that *active* coping to a stressor produced greater cardiovascular reactivity than *passive* coping was introduced by Obrist and colleagues. Active coping refers to the subject's ability to influence the outcome of a situation through mental or physical performance, whereas passive coping indicates that the person has no control over the outcome of an event. An example of a task that allows for active coping is one where the subject can avoid a shock by quick reaction times. If a shock is unavoidable, or if a hand is placed in a bucket of ice, then the subject must cope passively.

Cardiovascular responsivity to stress is currently receiving a great deal of attention. Research designs are complex and consider such factors as type of task, whether an individual is able to actively cope with a stressor, history of parental hypertension, and personality factors (e.g., hostile, angry, defensive). *Stress* can be defined as the body's response to some demanding psychological or physical stimulus. The stimulus itself is the "stressor." An example of a psychological stressor might be a mental multiplication task, whereas a physical stressor might be submerging a hand in a bucket of ice water (cold pressor).

Light and Obrist (1983) reported that persons high in cardiovascular reactivity show larger systolic BP and HR responses during tasks requiring active coping. In their study, 72 young men had measures taken while performing a reaction time task where winning money was easy, difficult, or impossible. The subjects termed "high reactors" were those who showed greater HR increases when the task started, and who maintained this higher level over lower HR reactors, regardless of task difficulty. Lovallo, Pincomb, and Wilson (1986) also studied high and low reactors in active and passive coping and obtained similar results. Both BP and HR were more highly elevated during active coping for the high HR reactors. The passive condition involved exposure to noise and electric shock.

Allen, Sherwood and Obrist (1986) compared cardiovascular and respiratory responses to a cold pressor, three levels of exercise on a bicycle ergometer, and under instructions to react quickly to avoid an electric shock to the leg. The cold pressor and reaction time stress both produced an increase in systolic BP of about 17%, but the diastolic increase was much greater for the cold pressor (25%) than for reaction time (7%). Also of interest was the finding that graded increases in the bicycle exercise resulted in steady increases in systolic BP, but no increase in diastolic BP. What might be considered as examples of physical stressors (cold pressor and bicycle pedaling) produced very different effects on diastolic BP.

It is noted that there was a considerable disparity in tasks used to produce active or passive coping situations. For example, mental arithmetic versus RT for active coping, and cold pressor versus exercise for passive coping. In order to control for the possible confounding effect of tasks, Sherwood, Dolan, and Light (1990) designed a task that was identical in all respects under active and passive coping with the exception that only the active member of a team of two subjects influenced the outcome. The results for this matched task were similar to past findings for less well-matched ones. Both active and passive members of a team showed increases in systolic and diastolic blood pressure, but the increases were greater for the active member. An interesting difference, however, was found for total peripheral resistance (TPR) because decreases occurred for the active member and increases the passive member. Another difference was that cardiac output was greater for the active member, indicating a greater increase in HR and stroke volume than for the passive member. This finding led the authors to conclude that active coping resulted in increased cardiac activity and dilation of peripheral blood vessels, whereas passive coping produced less of an increase in cardiac activity, but a constriction of peripheral blood vessels. In a refinement of the active–passive coping view, it was hypothesized that active coping leads to greater heart activity, whereas passive coping leads to greater changes in peripheral blood vessels (Sherwood et al., 1990).

An important link has been found between cardiovascular reactivity to an active coping task and later measures of blood pressure (Light, Dolan, Davis, & Sherwood, 1992). A sample of 51 men, originally tested at age 18 to 22, were assessed 10 to 15 years later. Original measurements were of systolic and diastolic pressure and HR during RT under the threat of shock. At follow-up, blood pressure and HR were measured during work, social, and leisure activities through ambulatory monitoring during waking hours. Men with higher systolic and diastolic readings during the original task showed similar results at follow-up. In addition, those with initially high HR reactivity showed higher systolic, diastolic, and HR levels at follow-up than low HR reactors, even though their BP levels had not differed at the first testing. Thus, an initial assessment of cardiovascular reactivity taken in a laboratory was useful in predicting reactivity 10 to 15 years later under real-life stress conditions that occurred during the waking day. The job of researchers now is to find out whether high reactivity is just a marker or if it contributes to the development of hypertension.

Summary. Changes in blood pressure occur in laboratory situations where subjects are frustrated or threatened with electric shock. The combination of being attacked or frustrated and viewing an aggressive film seems to result in reliable increases in BP. Anger, whether naturally occurring or induced through imagery, results in BP increases. The use of ambulatory BP monitoring devices enables recordings while individuals experience "real-life" stress. Sample findings were briefly summarized and include BP reactivity in paramedics, working women, and medical students in their daily settings.

The effects of stress on BP have been shown in a variety of studies. The mechanisms are complex, however, as indicated by results showing higher BP in tasks that allow active coping, and the differential responding by those categorized as "high reactors" emphasizes the role of individual differences in physiological response in a given situation. The interaction effect between active coping and high reactivity is dramatic. It is likely that an individual's cardiovascular reactivity to stress is influenced by a combination of factors, including physiological predisposition, personality, type of stressor and the setting. There is evidence that earlier measures of cardiovascular reactivity in a laboratory situation can predict reactivity years later with real-life stressors.

Social–Environmental Factors and Blood Pressure

Social Communication. The effects on BP of verbally communicating with other individuals have been studied and reveals interesting findings. For example, elevations in BP were observed in both normotensive and hypertensive persons while talking to others (Lynch, Long, Thomas, Malinow, & Katcher, 1981). Subjects with higher resting BP showed greater increases while talking than people with lower pressures. In some hypertensive persons, increases in BP of 25% to 40% occurred within 30 sec after the initiation of speech. In another study, increased BP was found for 40 college students when they engaged in a variety of verbal activities with either a high-status person or an equal-status person (Long, Lynch, Machiran, Thomas, & Malinow, 1982). However, the BP increases of the 20 subjects speaking to a high-status person were significantly greater than those who interacted with an equal-status individual. Thus, part of the BP increase was related to the process of verbally communicating and part to the social distance between individuals.

The cardiovascular responses of a group of 30 nurses were measured before and after they spoke to an individual or a group of nurses (Thomas, Friedman, Lottes, Gresty, Miller, & Lynch, 1984). Blood pressures and heart rates were higher when speaking than when at rest, and higher still when speaking in front of a group. It is clear that interacting socially through verbal communication will cause increases in BP. Other important factors include relative status of the two individuals, the number of people involved, and pre-experimental levels of BP.

Effects of Sociotropy.   Sociotropic cognition refers to a heightened preoccupation with being accepted by others. It was hypothesized by Ewart and colleagues that adolescent girls who scored high in a measure of sociotropic cognition would show elevated BP in reaction to interpersonal stress (Ewart, Jorgensen, & Kolodner, 1998). Sociotropy was measured by a scale that required subjects to indicate how strongly they agree with statements such as "I am nothing if a person I love doesn't love me," or "If others dislike you, you cannot be happy." A sample of adolescent girls (mean age of 14), had BP and HR measured while completing a mirror tracing task and while undergoing a social competence interview. The hypothesis was supported since both SBP and DBP were significantly elevated for those scoring high in sociotropy compared to low scorers, but only for the socially relevant social competence interview. Girls who did not place a high value on social acceptance had similar BP on the social competence and tracing tasks, but those who had a high need for social acceptance had increased cardiovascular reactivity to the task with an interpersonal focus.

Crowding.   Environmental psychologists and sociologists have been interested in the effects of crowding on human behavior and welfare. D'Atri, Fitzgerald, Kasl, and Malinow (1981) conducted a study that relates to this question. They investigated the effects of crowded housing on BP of 568 male prison inmates. The prisoners, whose average age was 25, showed significant increases in systolic BP when transferred from single-occupancy cells to multiple-occupancy dormitories. Those who remained in single cells showed no BP increase, and those who returned to cells after a short stay in dormitories had a drop in BP. Crowding is probably not the only factor in causing the increased BP noted in this study. Other important factors are the threat to life and safety and the increased vigilance that must be exercised by prisoners in a dormitory situation.

Effects on BP of city and country living were examined by Rao, Inbaraj, and Subramaniam (1984). They measured BPs of a random sample of 961 rural and 1,073 urban women in southern India. For both the systolic and diastolic BPs, the urban values were significantly higher than the rural. Crowding may be a factor in this urban–rural comparison, but other differences in lifestyle between country and city should also be considered, including type of job, socioeconomic level, and availability of housing.

Pets.   The presence of a dog has been found to lead to a lowering of BP in humans. In one study, a group of 9- to 16-year-olds had BP and HR measured while resting or reading in the presence of a friendly animal (Friedmann, Katcher, Thomas, Lynch, & Messent, 1983). Having a dog present led to lowered BP and HR under all conditions. The effect was greater when the dog was present initially than when it was introduced in the second half of the experiment. Similar results were obtained by Baun, Langston, and Thoma (1984), who measured BP and HR while subjects age 24 to 74 petted a known dog, an unfamiliar dog, or read a book. The lowest cardiovascular activity levels occurred while petting a familiar dog and when reading. In such experiments, the presence of a friendly animal may cause subjects to modify their perceptions of the experimenter and the experimental situation by making them appear more casual and less threatening.

Social Support.   The effects of social situations involving family, friends, and strangers on BP responses was evaluated by Spitzer and coworkers using ambulatory techniques (Spitzer, Llabre, Ironson, Gellman, & Schneiderman, 1992). They reported that SBP and DBP were significantly lower in the presence of family members as compared to friends and strangers. We have already discussed how job strain can lead to elevated BP. There is also evidence that the association of job strain with elevated DBP is greater in persons who have low social support (Schnall, Landsbergis, & Baker, 1994). These results were obtained through ambulatory BP measures of a large number of workers at their job site. Thus, it appears that associating with family members may have a beneficial influence on BP and the same could be said for supportive relationships with respect to effects of job strain.

The relationship between depressed mood and cardiovascular response was investigated by Light and colleagues (Light, Kothandapani, & Allen, 1998). They tested the hypothesis that women scoring in the upper 25% on a measure of depression (Beck Depression Inventory) would show higher levels of cardiovascular response, before and during behavioral stressors, than those scoring in the lower quartile of the group sampled. The mean scores on the Beck were 16.7 for the upper quartile and 2.2 for the low scoring group. None of the individuals tested met the criteria for a diagnosis of clinical depression. The stressors were a speech task where the participant was asked to talk for 3 min about a recent incident that made her angry, and a postural challenge task (rising from sitting to standing for 3 min). Women with higher Beck scores showed higher SBP and DBP during both of the stressors, and also during baseline and recovery. These results, along with findings of decreased HR variability and shortened pre-ejection period, led Light et al. to conclude that healthy young women with subclinical depression evidence an increase in tonic SNS activity and elevated sympathetic responsivity to behavioral stress. They also reported that the Beck scores correlated highly with a lack of perceived social support, suggesting a link between social isolation and depressive symptoms.

Summary.   Verbal communications with other individuals lead to elevated BP, especially if the other person is of higher status. The effects of crowding are difficult to single out because of other factors that could affect BP levels, such as socioeconomic status or safety. The company of pet dogs and family members results in a lowering of BP. Social support, in general, is related to lower BP readings at the job site. Among a sample of healthy young women, the presence of depressive symptoms was related to increased BP both at rest and during the performance of stressful tasks.

Competition, Auditory Stimulation, and Fitness

Competition.   Measurements of BP and heart rate of male college students were made while they participated in a competitive perceptual–motor task (TV tennis) (Dembroski, MacDougall, Slaats, Eliot, & Buell, 1981). In an interesting approach, the health records of participants were examined to determine frequency of minor ilnesses. Dembroski and colleagues reported that subjects who responded during the contest with extreme increases in diastolic BP and heart rate were more likely to have frequent minor illnesses than those responding with low or moderate increases.

Auditory Stimulation.   In a study by Ray, Brady, and Emurian (1984), subjects performed a synthetic work task over a period of 3 days while BP, HR, and pulse amplitude were recorded. Auditory stimulation, in the form of 93-dB noise was presented for 10 min of each 30-min task period. Performance of the task alone led to increases in BP and HR, and drops in pulse amplitude. The addition of noise produced further increases in BP and decreases in pulse amplitude, but no further changes in heart activity. This last finding is reminiscent of those that report increased BP and hypertension for workers in noisy factories as compared to workers in relatively quiet factories (e.g., Jonsson & Hansson, 1977). Similar effects were observed by Carter and Beh (1989) who presented bursts of sound at 92 dB over two loudspeakers during performance of a 55-min vigilance task. Diastolic BP and mean BP were more sensitive to noise presentations than SBP. They both increased with noise relative to pretest measures, and remained elevated throughout the task period. The authors believed that the noise affected blood pressure directly, but another possibility is that subjects exerted extra effort to overcome the distraction of having to detect signals in a noisy environment. They suggested that noise may have a deleterious effect on blood pressure, especially because there is no evidence of habituation of cardiovascular response over relatively long time periods.

Aerobic Fitness.   It is well known that regular, vigorous exercise training decreases cardiovascular response to fixed amounts of exercise. The observed pattern of lower heart rate and increased stroke volume represents more efficient functioning of the heart. However, results concerning effects of training on BP during rest and exercise have not been consistent. Some have reported lower pressures at rest in trained normotensives, whereas others have not.

Hull, Young, and Ziegler (1984) conducted a study to determine whether physical fitness is correlated with lower responsivity of BP and heart rate to various kinds of stressors. These responses were measured during four kinds of stress: (a) passive psychological stressor (film of industrial accidents); (b) Stroop word–color interference (active psychological stress); (c) cold pressor (passive physical stress); and (d) running to exhaustion on a treadmill (active physical stress). The subjects were men and women, age 21 to 64, who spent at least 30 min per day in exercise or a hobby. They were divided into four groups varying in aerobic fitness. Fitness was defined in terms of length of time spent on a treadmill before feeling exhausted. Among persons 40 years of age or older, fitness was associated with lower resting SBP and lower DBP to both types of psychological stress and to active physical stress. However, more and less fit persons under age 40 did not differ on any of the cardiovascular measures. As reported in previous studies of this type, heart rates were lower in fit persons at most times.

Similar results were obtained by Light, Obrist, James, and Strogatz (1987). The subjects were 174 men, age 18 to 22, divided into low, moderate, and high exercise groups based on self-reports about weekly aerobic exercise. Low exercise individuals showed greater cardiovascular response to both a stressful reaction time task and exercise than those in the high exercise group. This greater response was shown by group differences in SBP and heart rate. The topic area of aerobic fitness and cardiovascular response to stressors is one that certainly deserves more research attention. So far, the suggestive results argue in favor of the cardiovascular benefits of being physically fit.

Personality Factors Affecting Blood Pressure

Type A and B Personality Patterns.   In the 1970s and 1980s, research on personality factors was dominated by comparisons of Type A and Type B individuals with respect to their cardiovascular reactions, mostly in "stressful" situations. The Type A concept was developed by two cardiologists to describe individuals who are competitive, impatient, and hostile achievers (Friedman & Rosenman, 1974). Individuals relatively lacking in these characteristics are labeled Type B. Clinical studies suggest that Type A individuals are three times more likely to suffer from a variety of cardiovascular disorders, such as coronary heart disease (CHD) and atherosclerosis (Jenkins, 1976), than Type Bs. One view is that these disorders may be due in part to greater cardiovascular and neuroendocrine reactivity of Type As compared to Type Bs (Matthews, 1982). In general, studies indicate that cardiovascular response of Type A males is greater than Type Bs in a variety of situations. (The results are not as consistent for women.) For instance, Type As have shown differential responding under a variety of different experimental situations that involved the manipulation of different stressors, such as uncontrollable noise, harassment, competition, presence of a hostile individual, task difficulty, challenge, and incentives.

To illustrate, Dembroski, MacDougall, Heard, and Shields (1979) randomly assigned 80 Type A and B males to conditions of high or low challenge while they engaged in RT and cold pressor tasks. Type A subjects had greater systolic BP and heart rate increases than Type Bs. This finding of elevated systolic BP is a consistent finding in a variety of situations. Harassment by a hostile individual during a competitive task led to increases in systolic BP and heart rate of Type As, but not Type Bs (Glass et al., 1980). Higher elevations of systolic BP was found for Type As compared to Type Bs even before the start of an arithmetic task in which money rewards were given (Contrada, Wright, & Glass, 1984). Holmes, McGilley, and Houston (1984) had 30 Type A and 30 Type B subjects work on a short-term memory task that was easy, moderate, or difficult. Again, systolic BP increased more for As than Bs, but only during the difficult task.

Contemporary researchers are aware that the relationship between personality and cardiovascular reactivity is complex. In order to predict whether a personality variable is likely to influence reactivity one needs to consider other conditions or environmental variables. Carels et al. (1998) have stated that . . . "if a Type A has both a need for control as well as a need to be conforming and submissive, these conflicting needs are likely to create inner conflict and subsequently increase BP. When an angry/hostile person feels that he or she must not or cannot express his or her anger (i.e., social desirability), these conflicting needs may give rise to increased BP. Likewise, the interaction of psychological factors and environmental circumstances also appear to influence BP level. For example, the Type A who is constantly interrupted by noise, the hostile individual that feels his or her authority is challenged and the high-effort coper on exam day are all likely to manifest high BP." (Carels et al., 1998, p. 125).

Children and Teens.   Research findings support the possible utility of the Type A concept with teenage and younger children. In one study, 3- to 6-year-old boys who scored high on competitiveness, impatience/anger, and aggression (components of Type A behavior) responded to challenge with a greater increase in systolic BP than Type Bs (Lundberg, 1983). A review of studies that examined BP reactivity in children revealed that three of them found reactivity to be predictive of later BP levels (Sallis, Dimsdale, & Caine, 1988). Sallis and colleagues cited the work of Hines and associates who, in 1937, measured BP reactivity of 300 school children ages 7 to 17. After 27 years, 207 subjects had BP reassessed. Four of 40 children who were initially hyperreactive to the cold pressor test were hypertensive, whereas none of the 167 normal reactors were hypertensive at follow-up. In an unusual procedure, BP measurements were collected on 142 of the original subjects at a 45-year follow-up. In 1982, 71% of the hyperreactors were classified as hypertensive, as compared to only 19% of the normal reactors. The strong suggestion is that BP reactivity in childhood is a strong predictor of later development of high blood pressure. Sallis et al. (1988) pointed out that race, obesity, Type A, and family history of hypertension are associated with BP reactivity in children.

Systolic BP of teens (13–18 years) was also found to be related to Type A behavior (Siegel, Matthews, & Leitch, 1983). An additional finding was that high variability in systolic BP was related to high levels of hostility and the rapid speech pattern characteristic of Type A persons. The factors of Type A behavior, potential for hostility and parental history of hypertension, as influences on cardiovascular responses to stressors were investigated by McCann and Matthews (1988). The subjects were 171 adolescents (99 female) in grades 6 to 12 and the stressors were mental arithmetic, mirror star tracing, and maintaining hand grip tension for $2\frac{1}{2}$ min. Those adolescents with a hypertensive parent had larger DBP responses during all three stressors, and the effect was especially pronounced for Type As. Individuals rated as high on potential for hostility had elevated SBP and DBP, particularly during the muscle tension condition. This represents the first time that early signs of hostility as a risk factor have been related to psychophysiological responses thought to be important in the development of cardiovascular disease.

Type A and B Women.   Many of the investigations into the relationship between Type A/B behavior and cardiovascular response have used males as subjects. Research with females has thus far indicated that there are some differences as compared to findings with males. For example, MacDougall, Dembroski, and Krantz (1981) reported that, unlike males studied earlier, female Type As and Bs did not differ in their systolic or diastolic BP to a RT or cold pressor task. However, they did show elevated systolic BP during a structured interview and an oral history quiz given by another woman. Thus, under a challenging interpersonal exchange, Type A women may show more cardiovascular response than Type Bs.

In another study, Lane, White, and Williams (1984) reported that Type A and B women had similar BP and heart rate increases to a mental arithmetic task. Thus, the Type A women were not hyperresponsive compared with Type Bs. However, the authors reported that a subsample of Type A women, those with a positive family history of high blood pressure, had larger cardiovascular responses under challenging conditions. Thus, family history of hypertension and gender are additional factors to consider in studying the relations between Type A/B behavior and cardiovascular response. Lawler, Schmeid, Mitchell, and Rixse (1984) also reported no difference in cardiovascular responding of college-age Type A and B women to cognitive tasks.

In an examination of possible relationships between family history of hypertension and Type A/B behavior, Lawler and Schmied (1986) investigated cardiovascular responsiveness of a larger sample of Type A and B women subjected to interpersonal and competitive stressors (oral quiz and Stroop color–word interference). Women with positive family histories did have higher levels of systolic BP, but this was not related to Type A behavior. In other words, there were Type Bs who had family histories of hypertension. The authors concluded that Type A behavior is not related to cardiovascular responsivity in young adult women. Therefore, although fairly well established for males, the cardiovascular-A/B relationship still required further investigation in women.

There is obviously a research gap because the amount of work on cardiovascular response of Type A/B men far outweighs the number of studies on Type A/B women. Because coronary heart disease is the leading cause of death of women in the United States, it is of critical importance that researchers address the psychosocial and biological risk factors for women with regard to this disease (Lawler, Schmied, Armstead, & Lacy, 1990). The findings thus far have suggested that Type A women show more cardiovascular reactivity than Type Bs under conditions that involve an interpersonal challenge and a realistic stressor (e.g., taking an actual test for a grade). An additional factor differentiating Type A and B women called "desire for control" (Burger & Cooper, 1979) can now be added to the brief list. In a study by Lawler et al., (1990) two groups of college-age women were assessed for Type A/B behavior and desire for control in two experiments. Those who were classified as Type A by the Jenkins Survey or by another survey, and who also scored above the median on an instrument designed to measure desire for control, had larger increases in HR to a difficult reaction time task than any other group. In addition, Type A women had more reactive SBP than Type Bs in the first experiment; and in the second experiment, Type A women with a high desire to control were more reactive than Type As scoring low on desire for control. The authors proposed that desire for control may be a critical factor linking Type A behavior to cardiovascular reactivity in Type A women.

Lawler et al. (1990) reviewed a number of studies on Type A women and found that those using an older population, or working women (as opposed to college students) have observed increased reactivity for Type As, especially if the Type As feel they lack control (as among clerical workers). The suggestion by Lawler and colleagues that "desire for control" may be an important coronary-prone component of the Type A behavior pattern in women deserves additional study. In a recent study, Type A women were reported to have higher BP responses compared to

Type Bs in reaction to behavioral stressors (Fichera & Andreassi, 1998). The women were classified as Type A or B according to extreme scores on the Jenkins Activity Survey (upper and lower quartiles). The college participants came from diverse ethnic backgrounds: 31% White, 29% Hispanic, 28% Black, and 12% Asian and were at a mean age of 26, older than the usual college sample. The women competed for a $50 prize, dependent on performance during the two tasks (RT and a timed Oral IQ Quiz during which questions were asked by a woman using a demanding tone of voice). The Type A participants had greater reactivity on both tasks, but especially with the IQ Quiz, which had greater interpersonal impact than the RT task.

Cardiovascular Reactivity, Hostility, and Anger.   There is an increasing trend towards a focus on hostility and anger as the active components of the Type A personality that predisposes them to coronary heart disease (CHD). Cardiovascular reactivity refers to a change in level of physiological response (e.g., blood pressure, heart rate) from resting baseline to task performance. A prominent hypothesis in this area of research is that degree of reactivity may be predictive of later development of cardiovascular disease, including hypertension and CHD (Light et al., 1992). There is evidence that cardiovascular reactivity is an enduring individual trait (Sherwood & Turner, 1992) with a degree of stability across tasks and over time. A common measure of hostility is the Cook–Medley Hostility scale. Hostility may be defined as an enduring negative attitude toward the environment and other people and is a cognitive process. Scales from the State–Trait–Anger Expression Inventory developed by Spielberger and colleagues (1985) are frequently used as an anger measure. Anger can be defined as feelings ranging from mild irritation to rage and is an emotional reaction rather than a cognitive process.

High scores on the Cook–Medley Hostililty (Ho) scale have been shown in a longitudinal study to be associated with risk of cardiovascular disease in men (Barefoot, Dodge, Peterson, Dahlstrom, & Williams, 1989; Barefoot, Williams, & Dahlstrom, 1983). The Cook–Medley scale is a 50-item instrument derived from the Minnesota Multiphasic Personality Inventory (MMPI). The scale assesses anger proneness, resentment, suspicion, and distrust (Smith & Allred, 1989). Investigators using the scale consider it to be a measure of cynical hostility or mistrust.

Suarez and Williams (1989) studied the cardiovascular reactivity of young men with high versus low hostility scores while they solved anagrams with or without harassment. Compared to performing the task alone, harassment resulted in increased cardiovascular activity (HR, BP) that was more pronounced for the high-hostility subjects compared to those who scored low on the scale. Further, harassment led to increases in self-ratings of anger, but it was only among those with high hostility scores that increased anger led to exaggerated cardiovascular reactivity.

In a follow-up study, Suarez and Williams (1990) refined items from the hostility scale into factors called *antagonistic hostility* (anger expressed outwardly) and *neurotic hostility* (suppressed anger). The results showed that those high in anger-out had elevated blood pressure and forearm blood flow to harassment, whereas those high in suppressed anger only had higher forearm blood flow to harassing conditions. Suarez and Williams suggested that the use of standard laboratory tasks such as mental arithmetic or anagrams without harassment may account for findings showing no association between hostility/anger measures and cardiovascular reactivity. Cardiovascular responses of high- and low-hostility males were obtained during a social interaction (Smith and Allred, 1989). The subjects were given the task of presenting their position in a series of discussion topics. The high-hostility group had larger systolic and diastolic reactivity during the presentations. In another study, both men and women classified as high in hostility showed higher levels of systolic and diastolic BP when measured during a typical working day, using ambulatory monitoring, as compared to levels recorded in a laboratory (Brownley, Light, & Anderson, 1996).

What would happen if there was a mismatch between the cognitive attitude of hostility and anger-expression behavior? Findings by Bongard, al'Absi, and Lovallo (1998) indicated that High Anger-Out/Low-Hostile men displayed the greatest increases in blood pressure and HR while performing two tasks. They proposed that this occurred because of an internal conflict between having a low degree of hostility, but a propensity to express anger outwardly. In contrast, individuals with low hostility and low anger-out and those who were high hostiles and high anger-out were least reactive because of the compatibility between the cognitive and emotional components. The final grouping consisted of persons high in hostility and low in anger expression, whose reactivity was the second highest of the four groups, because of the mismatch. The task involving a social challenge (preparing for and delivering a 4-minute talk) resulted in greater reactivity than mental arithmetic for all groups.

Summary.   The interaction between personality factors and cardiovascular reactivity is complex. Besides the personality variables, there are task (e.g., social vs. nonsocial stressors), context (e.g., harassment vs. no harassment) and environmental (e.g., job vs. home) variables. Although the Type A/B dichotomy is still being studied, researchers have begun to focus on other behavioral variables such as hostility, anger, depression, defensiveness, desire for control, and sociotropy. From what has been written here, whether you are male or female, if you are a Type A, hostile, angry, defensive, controlling person, you would most likely demonstrate extremely elevated cardiovascular reactivity when given a challenging task! However, as Lawler (1998) points out we have yet to define the mechanisms by which these behavioral variables cause reactivity in the first place. Another question relates to how much is contributed by each of these behavioral variables and how they interact with each other, in different social contexts and in real-life situations. Laboratory studies of cardiovascular reactivity to different tasks are very useful in suggesting relationships and variables for study, but the increasing use of ambulatory monitoring devices is important in providing more information about reactivity in real-life settings, of normal and hypertensive persons, as a function of behavioral variables. Areas deserving more research effort include studies of reactivity of children and teens, such as those of Matthews and colleagues (for example, McCann & Matthews, 1988) along with the use of longitudinal data to trace the progress of cardiovascular reactivity and disease.

Heredity as a Factor in Cardiovascular Reactivity.   A number of studies support the conclusion that individuals with a family history of hypertension (one or both parents) show greater cardiovascular reactivity to stress than those without a positive history. However, there is evidence that differential responding may also be related to type of task. For example, Ditto (1986) compared reactivity of 24 males with positive family histories to 24 males without this hereditary factor while they performed two active-coping and one passive-coping task. As predicted, family-history subjects showed greater systolic BP increases than non-family-history persons to the two active-coping stressors. Another study designed to study the cardiovascular reactivity of males with and without parental histories of hypertension was conducted by Miller and Ditto (1991). Through the use of drug and placebo conditions, these researchers were able to compare responses of the two groups in an active-coping stress situation. They concluded that the sympathetic nervous system is responsible for the exaggerated cardiovascular response of those with a parental history of hypertension. Lamensdorf and Linden (1992) evaluated the cardiovascular reactivity of normotensives with and without family histories of hypertension. They found greater diastolic BP and HR reactivity for those with a positive history to a variety of laboratory tasks.

In another study, a large sample of men and women, with and without family histories of hypertension, were tested on a social and nonsocial stressor (Lawler et al., 1998). The social stressor was an interview during which subjects recalled a time when they were really angry at someone close to them, and the nonsocial task was mental arithmetic. One of the major findings was that persons with positive family histories, both men and women, had higher levels of BP whether measured at rest or recovery or during either stressor. The anger recall interview resulted in larger increases in systolic and diastolic BP, mean arterial pressure and total peripheral resistance, while the math produced larger increases in HR and cardiac output. Therefore, the anger recall produced a greater vascular response, whereas the math induced more of a myocardial response. Lawler and her associates also found that persons in the positive family history group who reported low anger expression had higher BP levels during stress. This fits with previous findings indicating that suppressed hostilty is associated with higher resting and task BP levels reported for positive history individuals.

The hypothesis that men with a positive family history of hypertension, who also scored high in hostility, would show elevated cardiovascular response during interpersonal conflict was tested by Miller, Dolgoy, Friese, and Sita (1998). The results indicated higher cardiac output and forearm blood flow for positive history/high hostile men under harassment. The authors suggest that their findings lend support to the notion that excessive cardiac output and peripheral blood flow may initiate hypertension because of the pressure this places on arterial walls.

Summary.   Parental history of hypertension has been linked to cardiovascular reactivity. Findings have indicated that both men and women with positive family histories have elevated BP levels at both rest and during task performance. Suppressed anger and hostility have been emerging as personality variables that may moderate cardiovascular responsivity to stressors of those with positive family histories of hypertension.

Conditioning of Blood Pressure

Much of the basic research on changing BP levels through instrumental conditioning has been motivated by the possible development of a technique for the treatment of patients who suffer from essential hypertension. This disorder is one of elevated blood pressure without a demonstrable cause and is implicated in heart disease and strokes. This segment considers attempts to instrumentally condition blood pressure level in normal subjects, whereas chapter 17 considers the use of this technique with hypertensive patients.

The pioneering work of DiCara and Miller (1968), in which instrumental conditioning of blood pressure of rats was attempted, has prompted other researchers to try a similar approach with humans. For example, Shapiro, Tursky, Gershon, and Stern (1969) provided normal male subjects with information (feedback) about their systolic pressure and reinforced half of them for decreasing it and the other half for increasing it. They developed an application of the auscultatory technique to provide automatic feedback of systolic pressure at each successive heartbeat; that is, feedback regarding upward or downward changes in pressure was given with each beat. Short duration lights and tones signaled blood pressure that was in the right direction. After every 20 signals of this type, the subjects received a reinforcement. The reinforcer was a nude centerfold from the pages of *Playboy* magazine, projected on a screen for 5 sec. The results indicated that systolic blood pressure can be modified by external feedback and operant reinforcement. This occurred in a single session consisting of 25 trials.

In a follow-up study, Shapiro, Tursky, and Schwartz (1970) found that the changes in blood pressure levels were independent of HR. Shapiro, Schwartz, and Tursky (1972) extended their findings to diastolic pressure in another study of instrumental conditioning in normal males. This time, the reinforcers consisted of slides of landscapes, slides of nude women, and money. Measures of HR and respiration were also obtained. The group reinforced for pressure increases had a mean diastolic pressure difference of 7.0 mm Hg (10% of baseline level) as compared to the decrease group (up increased 4 mm Hg, down decreased 3 mm Hg). The authors expressed optimism about the possible application of this technique to hypertensive patients, especially in view of the relatively brief (25 or 35 min) training periods used in the studies.

The work of Shapiro and colleagues has been criticized by Blanchard and Young (1973) for using different feedback modes (visual and auditory) and reinforcers (slides and monetary rewards). They also criticized the lack of a no-feedback control group. These criticisms were addressed in a study by Fey and Lindholm (1975), in which two groups of normal subjects received feedback contingent on either increases or decreases in systolic BP, and two other groups received either noncontingent feedback or no feedback. The subjects participated in three 1-hr experimental sessions over a 3-day period. Progressive and significant drops in systolic pressure were seen in the decrease group over the 3-day period. No systematic changes were observed in the other three groups. The authors pointed out that visual feedback alone seemed to be as effective as the feedback-reinforcer combination previously used in the instrumental conditioning of blood pressure. They concluded that contingent feedback is effective in lowering BP and that ability to do this is improved with practice over a few days.

In a related line of research, investigators have been studying ability to discriminate variations in one's own blood pressure. Shapiro, Redmond, McDonald, and Gaylor (1975) found that six hypertensive persons were able to detect up or down variations in BP when asked to report every 30 sec whether pressure had changed. Discriminations were better with larger BP changes. In another study, Cinciripini, Epstein, and Martin (1979) recorded BP of moderately hypertensive individuals who had daily BP variations of at least 15 mm Hg. Significant improvements in estimation were observed when subjects were given immediate knowledge of results regarding BP levels. In a larger-scale study, Greenstadt, Shapiro, and Whitehead (1986) examined the benefits of discrimination training on the ability of 72 normotensive males to detect changes in their own BP. The subject's task was to decide whether his BP was higher during the first or second of two consecutive 5-sec periods. Immediate feedback was provided regarding correctness of decisions, and accuracy was rewarded with money. The results showed that, when given feedback, subjects showed a significant improvement in ability to discriminate BP in only two sessions. There was also evidence for the relative independence of systolic and diastolic BP. Still unresolved was the mechanism by which subjects learned to make the discrimination; that is, whether cues came from internal sources or were the result of variations in the pressure cuff itself.

This brief review has shown that modest, but consistent, decreases in BP have been instrumentally conditioned in a number of studies. In addition, there is some evidence that people can learn to discriminate changes in their own BP levels when given immediate feedback. This line of research has both academic interest in terms of physiological responses that can be instrumentally conditioned and is also of potential clinical importance in the treatment of essential hypertension. Since high blood pressure is not usually associated with noticeable body sensations, techniques that produce greater awareness of this condition have the potential to alleviate what has been termed a "silent" disease.

BLOOD VOLUME AND BEHAVIOR

The studies in this section fall into three main categories: blood volume and sexual response, orienting reflexes and blood volume, and conditioning of blood volume responses.

Blood Volume and Sexual Response

Direct measures of genital changes have become increasingly important methods in the study of sexual behavior and preferences. The main genital change that occurs in sexual arousal is the vasocongestion of vaginal, clitoral, and penile tissue. The blood that flows to these areas remains and causes the tissue to become enlarged and warmer. Psychophysiologists have taken advantage of these facts in devising techniques to measure changes in genital temperature, blood volume, and blood flow in studying sexual arousal in a variety of situations. As Geer (1975) observed, nongenital measures have not proven as useful in sex research as the more direct genital ones.

Devices to monitor male erection have been in existence since 1944 (Geer & Head, 1990). The earliest instrument consisted of a ring that fit around the penis and gave information about the presence or absence of erection. A penile strain gauge described by Laws and Bow (1976) was described earlier in this chapter.

The studies of Masters and Johnson (1966) on the human sexual response indicated that increased blood volume and muscle tension throughout the pelvic area was consistently associated with sexual arousal in humans. The work of researchers such as Geer and his associates has resulted in the development of satisfactory devices for the measurement of genital blood volume in the female (Geer et al., 1974; Sintchak & Geer, 1975). Levine and Wagner (1983) developed a sophisticated device that measures blood flow in vaginal tissue. A device for measuring temperature from the labia majora of female genitalia was described by Henson and Rubin (1978), and they reported that increases in labial temperature were related to viewing an erotic film.

Two penile strain gauges for measuring changes in penis circumference with sexual arousal were described by Richards and associates (Richards, Bridger, Wood, Kalucy, & Marshall, 1985). Additionally, groin skin temperature has been proposed by Rubinsky, Hoon, Eckerman, and Amberson (1985) as a measure of psychosexual arousal for both males and females. When compared to penile circumference and vaginal blood volume and pulse amplitude measures, during erotic film viewing, similar results were obtained with groin temperature for most of the subjects (10 males and 10 females). Let us now review some representative work in this field.

According to Geer, O'Donohue, and Schorman (1986), the field of psychophysiology has contributed information on sex differences and practical problems in sexuality. For example, it had been assumed that women were not as responsive to explicitly erotic stimuli as were men. However, a study using physiological measures found that women are quite responsive to erotic stimuli even when there is no romantic context (Heiman, 1977). Geer and collaborators (1974) used a device to measure vaginal blood volume and pulse volume during the presentation of erotic and nonerotic films to female college students. Two female experimenters described the research to subjects in detail during the first session.

In the second session, the subjects inserted the vaginal probe, in privacy, and after a 3-min rest period, viewed the two films. The erotic film was 8 min in duration and showed a young man and woman engaged in foreplay, oral–genital sex, and intercourse. The 8-min nonerotic film depicted scenes of battles and court life during the time of the Crusades. Both blood volume and pulse volume were significantly higher during viewing of the erotic film than during the nonerotic film. In another study, Geer (1974) described a procedure used in his laboratory in which young men and women were asked to imagine an arousing sexual scene while they were alone in a private, comfortable room. Measures of penile volume and vaginal pulse volume were made in the room without observers and with no erotic stimuli present. After 2 to 3 min, increases in the size of the penis and elevated vaginal pulse volume were observed. A postrecording questionnaire indicated that the subjects were sexually aroused by their fantasies.

Vaginal blood volume and pulse volume were obtained as adult women (age 19 to 35) masturbated to orgasm (Geer & Quartararo, 1976). Pulse volume increased greatly during masturbation and postorgasm periods over baseline levels. Although blood volume increased during masturbation and postorgasm, it decreased dramatically at the onset of, and during, orgasm. The researchers postulated that the drop in blood volume during orgasm reflects SNS activity. This is consistent with the model of sexual activity that proposes that sexual arousal is controlled by the PNS, whereas orgasm is under SNS influence.

Heiman (1977) compared the sexual arousal of males and females, using a combination of genital and subjective measures. In Heiman's study, 59 female and 9 male undergraduates completed three sessions during which genital blood volume and pulse volume were measured. The subjects listened to various kinds of tapes: erotic, erotic–romantic, romantic, or control (contained neither erotic nor romantic materials). A 2-min, subject-generated fantasy preceded and followed each tape. The main findings were that (a) erotic and erotic–romantic contents resulted in similar increases in genital pulse amplitude and blood volume in both sexes, (b) there was high agreement between subjective ratings of sexual arousal and the genital measures, and (c) individuals became aroused during sexual fantasy.

The question of whether women show a change in sexual arousal at different stages in the menstrual cycle was investigated by Hoon, Bruce, and Kinchloe (1982). The subjects were sexually experienced women ranging in age from 20 to 28. Vaginal blood volume, pulse amplitude, and labial temperature were measured while subjects listened to erotic tapes and when they engaged in erotic fantasies. Measures were taken at the premenstrual, menstrual, follicular, ovulatory, and luteal stages of the cycle. All three physiological measures and a rating scale of self-arousal indicated increases in sexual arousal with erotic stimulation. Most importantly, the researchers reported that arousability was the same at all stages of the menstrual cycle.

Cognitive factors have been found to play a role in male sexual arousal. For example, Geer and Fuhr (1976) found that distraction produced by engagement in a cognitive task resulted in lower arousal to erotic stimuli. A similar result was found for women subjects in an experiment by Adams, Haynes, and Brayer (1985). Vaginal blood volume and pulse amplitude were recorded while women listened to descriptions of explicit sexual activity. The cognitive distractor was a visually presented addition task. There was significant physiological and subjective arousal to erotic materials. However, when the distractor was added, physiological arousal decreased dramatically. A sizable sample of women participated in a study designed to explore the relationship between genital and subjective arousal (Laan, Everaerd, Van Der Velde, & Geer, 1995). The researchers hypothesized that conditions producing large changes in genital arousal would be paralleled by changes in subjective reports of arousal. Genital arousal was measured through vaginal pulse amplitude and subjective judgements were made continuously via a lever adjusted by subjects to indicate "no genital sensations" at one extreme to "complete wetness of the vagina" at the other. The subjects viewed erotic films taken from women-made videotapes. The hypothesis was supported in that a linear relationship was found between subjectively perceived genital sensations and objective genital arousal in over 70% of the participants. According to the authors, the results suggest that women use the stimulus situation and their own sensations of genital arousal to rate subjective sexual arousal.

Summary.   A number of studies have used measures of genital blood volume or pulse amplitude to indicate genital responses to sexual stimuli, sexual activity, subjective sexual arousal, and sexual fantasy. In addition, measures of genital response have provided scientific evidence to dispel the idea that women are only sexually responsive during certain phases of the menstrual cycle. The detrimental effects of a distractor on sexual arousability has also been extended from males to females.

Blood Volume and the Orienting Response

Changes in blood volume are an important part of the orienting reflex as described by Sokolov (1963). Sokolov reported increases in forehead blood volume with novel or unexpected stimuli and decreases when stimuli were painful or threatening. According to Sokolov, increases in cephalic blood volume reflect the orienting reflex (OR), and the OR leads to improved perceptual ability. Conversely, decreases in blood volume reflect a defensive response (DR) that protects the organism by making it less sensitive to threatening or painful stimuli. The OR is said to habituate with continued stimulus presentation, and the DR is said to be immune to this effect. Although Sokolov's theory still remains to be established, it has been found that blood volume changes do occur in various parts of the body as a result of unexpected or novel stimuli.

The orienting response and its speed of habituation were investigated by Levander, Lidberg, and Schalling (1974). Young male subjects were presented with a series of 100-db tones (1-sec duration) at intervals varying between 35 and 610 sec. Decreases in finger blood volume and pulse volume were used as the physiological measures of the OR. Both responses were relatively large with the presentation of the first tone, and both habituated (i.e., decrease in response amplitude) as a function of additional tone presentations. The researchers noted that the pulse volume responses habituated faster than the blood volume responses, suggesting a degree of independence between these measures.

The effects of stimulus repetition on habituation of the OR was also studied by Ginsberg and Furedy (1974). They measured finger blood volume and pulse volume of 20 subjects who listened to a series of 80-dB tones. They found that pulse volume responses habituated to the repetitive stimulation, but blood volume did not.

The effects of stimulus intensity and rise time on the OR were tested by Oster, Stern, and Figar (1975). They used tones of 70 and 90 dB, with fast (10 μsec) and slow (100 msec) rise times. Sixty subjects had blood volume responses recorded from the head (temporal artery) and finger. As Sokolov predicted, head (cephalic) blood volume shifted from dilation to constriction with increased sound intensity. However, the constriction response habituated, thus not meeting one of Sokolov's criteria for a DR. Completely different types of stimuli and procedures were used by Hare (1973) in assessing blood volume as an indicator of the OR and DR. The subjects were young women, half of whom feared spiders (spider-phobic) and half who did not. The fearful group responded with decreased forehead blood volume to pictures of spiders, whereas the nonfearful group had the opposite response. The vasoconstriction would indicate the DR, whereas the vasodilation would suggest the OR, thus providing results in line with Sokolov's theory.

Summary.   Blood volume and pulse volume appear to change with the introduction of new or unexpected stimuli. With regard to blood volume responses, some of the research findings partially support Sokolov's theory regarding the relation between cephalic vasoconstriction and vasodilation and the DR and OR, respectively. Differences between habituation rate of the blood and pulse volume responses may indicate a partial physiological independence of these two measures.

Conditioning of Blood Volume

Conditioning of the vasomotor response has been reported with both classical and instrumental approaches. For example, Shean (1968) produced a classically conditioned finger blood volume decrease in a situation where the CS was the word "boat" and the UCS was an electric shock. Acquisition and extinction of the vasoconstriction response was observed in those subjects who later indicated they were aware of the relationship between the CS and UCS.

Blood volume changes have also been instrumentally conditioned. For example, Christie and Kotses (1973) found that cephalic (head) blood volume could be brought under stimulus control in subjects who participated in six separate sessions. A photoplethysmographic device was positioned over the temporal artery of the head to detect blood volume changes. Some subjects received feedback and reinforcement for vasodilation, whereas others were conditioned to produce vasoconstriction. The persons reinforced for vasodilation showed this response in the period during which the reinforcement was available, whereas the others reliably produced vasoconstriction. The authors suggested further investigation of this technique for possible use in the treatment of migraine headache, because this disorder has been linked to vasodilation of cephalic arteries.

Chapters 15, 16, and 17 cover practical applications of physiological measures. Chapters 15 and 16 are concerned with diverse applications, ranging from lie detection to neurological disorders. Chapter 17 considers applications of biofeedback to clinical problems.

REFERENCES

Adams, E. A., III, Haynes, S. N., & Brayer, M. A. (1985). Cognitive distraction in female sexual arousal. *Psychophysiology, 22*, 689–696.

Allen, M. T., Sherwood, A., & Obrist, P. A. (1986). Interaction of respiratory and cardiovascular adjustments to behavioral stressors. *Psychophysiology, 23*, 532–541.

Barefoot, J. C., Dodge, K. A., Peterson, B. L., Dahlstrom, W. G., & Williams, R. B. (1989). The Cook–Medley Hostility Scale: Item content and ability to predict survival. *Psychosomatic Medicine, 51*, 46–57.

Barefoot, J. C., Williams, R. B., & Dahlstrom, W. G. (1983). Hostility, CHD incidence and total mortality: A 25-year follow up study of 255 physicians. *Psychosomatic Medicine, 15*, 59 63.

Baun, M., Langston, N. F., & Thoma, L. (1984). Physiological effects of human/companion animal bonding. *Nursing Research, 33*, 126–129.

Blanchard, E. B., & Young, L. D. (1973). Self-control of cardiac functioning: A promise as yet unfulfilled. *Psychological Bulletin, 79*, 145–163.

Blumenthal, J. A., Lane, J. D., Williams, R. B., McKee, D. C., Haney, T., & White, A. (1983). Effects of task incentive on cardiovascular response in Type A and Type B individuals. *Psychophysiology, 20*, 63–70.

Bongard, S., al'Absi, M., & Lovallo, W. R. (1998). Interactive effects of trait hostility and anger expression on cardovascular reactivity in young men. *International Journal of Psychophysiology, 28*, 181–191.

Brown, C. C. (1967). The techniques of plethysmography. In C. C. Brown (Ed.), *Methods in psychophysiology* (pp. 54–74). Baltimore: Williams & Wilkins.

Burger, J. M., & Cooper, H. M. (1979). The desirability of control. *Motivation and Emotion, 3*, 381–393.

Carels, R. A., Sherwood, A., Blumenthal, J. A. (1998). Psychosocial influences on blood pressure during daily life. *International Journal of Psychophysiology, 28*, 117–130.

Carter, N. L., & Beh, H. C. (1989). The effect of intermittent noise on cardiovascular functioning during vigilance task performance. *Psychophysiology, 26*, 548–559.

Christie, D. J., & Kotses, H. (1973). Bidirectional operant conditioning of the cephalic vasomotor response. *Journal of Psychosomatic Research, 17*, 167–170.

Cinciripini, P. M., Epstein, L. H., & Martin, J. E. (1979). The effects of feedback on blood pressure discrimination. *Journal of Applied Behavioral Analysis, 12*, 345–353.

Contrada, R. J., Wright, R. A., & Glass, D. C. (1984). Task difficulty, Type A behavior pattern, and cardiovascular response. *Psychophysiology, 21*, 638–646.

Cook, M. R. (1974). Psychophysiology of peripheral vascular changes. In P. A. Obrist, A. H. Black, J. Brener, & L. V. DiCara (Eds.), *Cardiovascular psychophysiology* (pp. 60–84). Chicago: Aldine.

Cromwell, L., Arditti, M., Weibell, F. J., Pfeiffer, E. A., Steele, B., & Labbock, J. A. (1976). *Medical instrumentation for health care*. Englewood Cliffs, NJ: Prentice-Hall.

D'Atri, D. A., Fitzgerald, E. F., Kasl, S. V., & Malinow, K. L. (1981). Crowding in prison: The relationship between changes in housing mode and blood pressure. *Psychosomatic Medicine, 43*, 95–105.

Dembroski, T. M., MacDougall, J. M., Heard, J. A., & Shields, J. L. (1979). Effect of level of challenge on pressor and heart rate responses in Type A and B subjects. *Journal of Applied Social Psychology, 9*, 209–228.

Dembroski, T. M., MacDougall, J. M., Slaats, S., Eliot, R. S., & Buell, J. C. (1981). Challenge-induced cardiovascular response as a predictor of minor illnesses. *Journal of Human Stress, 7*, 2–5.

DiCara, L. V., & Miller, N. E. (1968). Instrumental learning of systolic blood pressure responses by curarized rats: Dissociation of cardiac and vascular changes. *Psychosomatic Medicine, 30*, 489–494.

Ditto, B. (1986). Parental history of hypertension, active coping, and cardiovascular reactivity. *Psychophysiology, 23*, 62–70.

Doob, A. N., & Kirshenbaum, H. M. (1973). The effects on arousal of frustration and aggressive films. *Journal of Experimental Social Psychology, 9*, 57–64.

Drummond, P. D. (1983). Cardiovascular reactivity in mild hypertension. *Journal of Psychosomatic Research, 27,* 291–297.

Ettema, J. H., & Zielhuis, R. L. (1971). Physiological parameters of mental load. *Ergonomics, 14,* 137–144.

Ewart, C. K., Jorgensen, R. S., Kolodner, K. B. (1998). Sociotropic cognition moderates blood pressure response to interpersonal stress in high-risk adolescent girls. *International Journal of Psychophysiology, 28,* 131–142.

Fey, S. B., & Lindholm, E. (1975). Systolic blood pressure and heart rate changes during three sessions involving biofeedback or no feedback. *Psychophysiology, 12,* 513–519.

Fichera, L. V., & Andreassi, J. L. (1998). Stress and personality as factors in women's cardiovascular reactivity. *International Journal of Psychophysiology, 28,* 143–155.

Friedman, E., Katcher, A. H., Thomas, S. A., Lynch, J. J., & Messent, P. R. (1983). Social interaction and blood pressure: Influence of animal companions. *Journal of Nervous & Mental Diseases, 17,* 461–465.

Friedman, M., & Rosenman, R. H. (1974). *Type A behavior and your heart.* New York: Knopf.

Gardner, E. (1975). *Fundamentals of neurology* (6th ed.). Philadelphia: Saunders.

Geen, R. G. (1975). The meaning of observed violence: Real vs. fictional violence and consequent effects on aggression and emotional arousal. *Journal of Research in Personality, 9,* 270–281.

Geen, R. G., & Stonner, D. (1974). The meaning of observed violence: Effects on arousal and aggressive behavior. *Journal of Research in Personality, 8,* 55–63.

Geer, J. H. (1974, August). *Cognitive factors in sexual arousal: Toward an amalgam of research strategies.* Paper presented at the annual convention of the American Psychological Association, New Orleans, LA.

Geer, J. H. (1975, May). *Sexual functioning—Some data and speculations on psychophysiological assessment.* Paper presented at the Behavior Assessment Conference, West Virginia University.

Geer, J. H., & Fuhr, R. (1976). Cognitive factors in sexual arousal: The role of distraction. *Journal of Consulting & Clinical Psychology, 44,* 238–243.

Geer, J. H., & Head, S. (1990). The sexual response system. In J. T. Cacioppo & L. G. Tassinary (Eds.), *Principles of psychophysiology: Physical, social, and inferential elements* (pp. 599–630). Cambridge, England: Cambridge University Press.

Geer, J. H., Morokoff, P., & Greenwood, P. (1974). Sexual arousal in women: The development of a measurement device for vaginal blood volume. *Archives of Sexual Behavior, 3,* 559–564.

Geer, J. H., O'Donohue, W. T., & Schorman, R. H. (1986). Sexuality. In M. G. H. Coles, E. Donchin, & S. W. Porges (Eds.), *Psychophysiology: Systems, processes & applications* (pp. 407–430). New York: Guilford.

Geer, J. H., & Quartararo, J. D. (1976). Vaginal blood volume responses during masturbation and resultant orgasm. *Archives of Sexual Behavior, 5,* 1–42.

Gentry, W. D. (1970). Sex differences in the effects of frustration and attack on emotion and vascular processes. *Psychological Reports, 27,* 383–390.

Ginsberg, S., & Furedy, J. J. (1974). Stimulus repetition, change, and assessments of sensitivities of and relationships among an electrodermal and two plethysmographic components of the orienting reaction. *Psychophysiology, 11,* 35–42.

Glass, D. C., Krakoff, L. R., Contrada, R., Hilton, W., Kehoe, K., Mannucci, E. G., Collins, C., Snow, B., & Elting, E. (1980). Effect of harassment and competition upon cardiovascular and plasma catecholamine responses in Type A and Type B individuals. *Psychophysiology, 17,* 453–463.

Greenstadt, L., Shapiro, D., & Whitehead, R. (1986). Blood pressure discrimination. *Psychophysiology, 23,* 500–509.

Grollman, S. (1964). *The human body.* New York: Macmillan.

Gunn, C. G., Wolf, S., Black, R. T., & Person, R. J. (1972). Psychophysiology of the cardiovascular system. N. S. Greenfield & R. A. Sternbach (Eds.), *Handbook of psychophysiology* (pp. 457–489). New York: Holt, Rinehart & Winston.

Guyton, A. C. (1977). *Basic human physiology.* Philadelphia: Saunders.

Hall, P. J., Thomas, J. A., Friedman, E., & Lynch, J. J. (1982). Measurement of neonatal blood pressure: A new method. *Psychophysiology, 19,* 231–236.

Harburg, E., Blakelock, E. H., & Roeper, P. J. (1979). Resentful and reflective coping with arbitrary authority and blood pressure. *Psychosomatic Medicine, 51,* 189–202.

Hare, R. D. (1973). Orienting and defensive responses to visual stimuli. *Psychophysiology, 10,* 453–464.

Harshfield, G. A., & Pulliam, D. A. (1992). Individual differences in ambulatory blood pressure pattern. In J. R. Turner, A. Sherwood, & K. C. Light (Eds.), *Individual differences in cardiovascular responses to stress* (pp. 51–61). New York: Plenum.

Heiman, J. R. (1977). A psychophysiological exploration of sexual arousal patterns in females and males. *Psychophysiology, 14,* 266–274.

Henson, D. E., & Rubin, H. B. (1978). A comparison of two objective measures of sexual arousal of women. *Behaviour Research & Therapy, 16,* 143–151.

Holmes, D. D., McGilley, B. M., & Houston, B. K. (1984). Task-related arousal of Type A and Type B persons: Level of challenge and response specificity. *Journal of Personality & Social Psychology, 46,* 1322–1327.

Hoon, P. W., Bruce, K., & Kinchloe, B. (1982). Does the menstrual cycle play a role in sexual arousal? *Psychophysiology, 19*, 21–27.

Hull, E., Young, S. H., & Ziegler, M. G. (1984). Aerobic fitness affects cardiovascular and catecholamine responses to stressors. *Psychophysiology, 21*, 353–360.

Jacob, S. W., & Francone, C. A. (1970). *Structure and function in man* (2nd ed.). Philadelphia: Saunders.

Jamner, L. D., Shapiro, D., Goldstein, I. R., & Hug, R. (1991). Ambulatory blood pressure and heart rate in paramedics: Effects of cynical hostility and defensiveness. *Psychosomatic Medicine, 53*, 393–406.

Jenkins, D. C. (1976). Recent evidence supporting psychologic and social risk factors for coronary disease. *New England Journal of Medicine, 294*, 1033–1038.

Jonsson, A., & Hansson, L. (1977). Prolonged study of a stressful stimulus (noise) as a cause of raised blood pressure in man. *Lancet, 1*, 86–87.

Laan, E., Everaerd, W., Van Der Velde, J., & Geer, J. (1995). Determinants of subjective experience of sexual arousal in women: Feedback from genital arousal and erotic stimulus content. *Psychophysiology, 32*, 444–451.

Lamensdorf, A. M., & Linden, W. (1992). Family history of hypertension and cardiovascular changes during high and low affect provocation. *Psychophysiology, 29*, 558–565.

Lane, J. D., White, A. D., & Williams, R. B. (1984). Cardiovascular effects of mental arithmetic in Type A and Type B females. *Psychophysiology, 21*, 39–46.

Lawler, K. A. (1998). Individual differences and cardiovascular responsivity. *International Journal of Psychophysiology, 28*, 113–116.

Lawler, K. A., Kline, K., Seabrook, E., Krishnamoorthy, J., Anderson, S. F., Wilcox, Z. C., Craig, F., Adlin, R., & Thomas, S. (1998). *International Journal of Psychophysiology, 28*, 207–222.

Lawler, K. A., & Schmied, L. A. (1986). Cardiovascular responsivity, Type A behavior and parental history of heart disease in young women. *Psychophysiology, 23*, 28–32.

Lawler, K. A., Schmied, L. A., Armstead, C. A., & Lacy, J. E. (1990). Type A behavior, desire for control, and cardiovascular reactivity in young adult women. *Journal of Social Behavior and Personality, 5*, 135–158.

Lawler, K. A., Schmied, L. A., Mitchell, V. P., & Rixse, A. (1984). Type A behavior and physiological responsivity in young women. *Journal of Psychosomatic Research, 28*, 197–204.

Laws, D. R., & Bow, R. A. (1976). An improved mechanical strain gauge for recording penile circumference change. *Psychophysiology, 13*, 596–599.

Lee, A. L., Tahmoush, A. J., & Jennings, J. R. (1975). An LED-transistor photoplethysmograph. *IEEE Transactions on Biomedical Engineering, 22*, 248–250.

Levander, S. E., Lidberg, L., & Schalling, D. (1974). Habituation of the digital vasoconstrictive orienting response. *Journal of Experimental Psychology, 102*, 700–705.

Levine, R. J., & Wagner, G. (1983). Haemodynamic changes of the human vagina during sexual arousal assessed by a heated oxygen electrode. *Journal of Physiology, 275*, 23–24.

Light, K. C., Dolan, C. A., Davis, M. R., & Sherwood, A. (1992). Cardiovascular responses to an active coping challenge as predictors of blood pressure patterns 10 to 15 years later. *Psychosomatic Medicine, 54*, 217–230.

Light, K. C., Kothandapani, R. V., & Allen, M. T. (1998). Enhanced cardiovascular and catecholamine responses in women with depressive symptoms. *International Journal of Psychophysiology, 28*, 157–166.

Light, K. C., & Obrist, P. A. (1983). Task difficulty, heart rate reactivity, and cardiovascular responses to an appetitive reaction time task. *Psychophysiology, 20*, 301–312.

Light, K. C., Obrist, P. A., James, S. A., & Strogatz, D. S. (1987). Cardiovascular responses to stress: II. Relationships to aerobic exercise patterns. *Psychophysiology, 24*, 79–86.

Long, J. M., Lynch, J. J., Machiran, N. M., Thomas, S. A., & Malinow, K. L. (1982). The effect of status on blood pressure during verbal communication. *Journal of Behavioral Medicine, 5*, 165–172.

Lovallo, W. R., Pincomb, G. A., & Wilson, M. G. (1986). Heart rate reactivity and Type A behavior as modifiers of physiological response to active and passive coping. *Psychophysiology, 23*, 105–112.

Lundberg, U. (1983). Note on Type A behavior and cardiovascular responses to challenge in 3–6 yr old children. *Journal of Psychosomatic Research, 27*, 39–42.

Lynch, J. J., Long, J. M., Thomas, S. A., Malinow, K. L., & Katcher, A. H. (1981). The effects of talking on the blood pressure of hypertensive and normotensive individuals. *Psychosomatic Medicine, 43*, 25–33.

MacDougall, J. M., Dembroski, T. M., & Krantz, D. S. (1981). Effects of types of challenge on pressor and heart rate responses in Type A and Type B women. *Psychophysiology, 18*, 1–9.

Masters, W. H., & Johnson, V. E. (1966). *Human sexual response*. Boston: Little-Brown.

Matthews, K. A. (1982). Psychological perspectives on the Type A behavior pattern. *Psychological Bulletin, 91*, 293–323.

Matthews, K. A., Manuck, S. B., & Saab, P. G. (1986). Cardiovascular responses of adolescents during a naturally occurring stressor and their behavioral and psychophysiological predictors. *Psychophysiology, 23*, 198–209.

McCann, B. S., & Matthews, K. A. (1988). Influences of potential for hostility, Type A behavior, and parental history of hypertension on adolescents' cardiovascular responses during stress. *Psychophysiology, 25*, 503–511.

McCubbin, J. A., Richardson, J. E., Langaer, A. W., Kizer, J. S., & Obrist, P. A. (1983). Sympathetic neuron function and left ventricular performance during behavioral stress in humans: The relationship between plasma catecholamines and systolic time intervals. *Psychophysiology, 20,* 102–110.

McKinney, M. E., Miner, M. H., Ruddel, H., McIlvain, H. E., Witte, H., Buell, J. C., Elliot, R. S., & Grant, L. B. (1985). The standardized mental stress test protocol: Test–retest reliability and comparison with ambulatory blood pressure monitoring. *Psychophysiology, 22,* 453–463.

Miller, S. B., & Ditto, B. (1991). Exaggerated sympathetic nervous system response to extended psychological stress in offspring of hypertensives. *Psychophysiology, 28,* 103–113.

Miller, S. B., Dolgoy, L., Friese, M., & Sita, A. (1998). Parental history of hypertension: A psychophysiological analysis. *International Journal of Psychophysiology, 28,* 193–206.

Oster, P. J., Stern, J. A., & Figar, S. (1975). Cephalic and digital vasomotor orienting responses: The effect of stimulus intensity and rise time. *Psychophysiology, 12,* 642–648.

Papillo, J. F., & Shapiro, D. (1990). The cardiovascular system. In J. T. Cacioppo & L. G. Tassinary (Eds.), *Principles of psychophysiology: Physical, social, and inferential elements* (pp. 456–512). Cambridge, England: Cambridge University Press.

Rao, P. S., Inbaraj, S. G., & Subramaniam, V. R. (1984). Blood pressure measures among women in south India. *Journal of Epidemiology & Community Health, 38,* 49–53.

Ray, R. L., Brady, J. V., & Emurian, H. H. (1984). Cardiovascular effects of noise during complex task performance. *International Journal of Psychophysiology, 1,* 335–340.

Richards, J. C., Bridger, B. A., Wood, M. M., Kalucy, R. S., & Marshall, V. R. (1985). A controlled investigation into the measurement properties of two circumferential penile strain gauges. *Psychophysiology, 22,* 568–571.

Roberts, R. J., & Weerts, T. C. (1982). Cardiovascular responding during anger and fear imagery. *Psychological Reports, 50,* 219–230.

Rubinsky, H. J., Hoon, P. W., Eckerman, D. A., & Amberson, J. I. (1985). Groin skin temperature: Testing the validity of a relatively unobtrusive physiological measure of psychosexual arousal. *Psychophysiology, 22,* 488–492.

Sallis, J. F., Dimsdale, J. E., & Caine, C. (1988). Blood pressure reactivity in children. *Journal of Psychosomatic Research, 32,* 1–12.

Schnall, P. L., Landsbergis, P. A., & Baker, D. (1994). Job strain and cardiovascular disease. *Annu. Rev. Public Health, 15,* 381–411.

Schwartz, G. E., Weinberger, D. A., & Singer, J. A. (1981). Cardiovascular differentiation of happinesss, sadness, anger, and fear following imagery and exercise. *Psychophysiology, 22,* 488–492.

Shapiro, A., Redmond, D. P., McDonald, R. H., & Gaylor, M. (1975). Relationships of perception, cognition, suggestion and operant conditioning in essential hypertension. *Progress in Brain Research, 42,* 299–312.

Shapiro, D., Schwartz, G. E., & Tursky, B. (1972). Control of diastolic blood pressure in man by feedback and reinforcement. *Psychophysiology, 9,* 296–304.

Shapiro, D., Tursky, B., Gershon, E., & Stern, M. (1969). Effects of feedback and reinforcement on the control of human systolic blood pressure. *Science, 163,* 588–590.

Shapiro, D., Tursky, B., & Schwartz, G. E. (1970). Differentiation of heart rate and systolic blood pressure in man by conditioning. *Psychosomatic Medicine, 32,* 417–423.

Shean, G. D. (1968). Vasomotor conditioning and awareness. *Psychophysiology, 5,* 22–30.

Sherwood, A., Dolan, C. A., & Light, K. C. (1990). Hemodynamics of blood pressure responses during active and passive coping. *Psychophysiology, 27,* 656–668.

Sherwood, A., & Turner, J. R. (1992). A conceptual and methodological overview of cardiovascular reactivity research. In J. R. Turner, A. Sherwood, & K. C. Light (Eds.), *Individual differences in cardiovascular response to stress* (pp. 3–32). New York: Plenum.

Siegel, J. J., Matthews, K. A., & Leitch, C. J. (1983). Blood pressure variability and the Type A behavior pattern in adolescence. *Journal of Psychosomatic Research, 27,* 265–272.

Sintchak, G., & Geer, J. H. (1975). A vaginal plethysmograph system. *Psychophysiology, 12,* 113–145.

Smith, T. W., & Allred, K. D. (1989). Blood pressure responses during social interaction in high- and low-cynically hostile males. *Journal of Behavioral Medicine, 12,* 135–143.

Sokolov, E. N. (1963). *Perception and the conditioned reflex.* New York: Macmillan.

Spielberger, C. D., Johnson, E. H., Russell, S. F., Crane, R., Jacobs, G. A., & Worden, T. J. (1985). The experience and expression of anger: Construction and validation of an anger expression scale (pp. 5–30). In M. A. Chesney & R. H. Rosenman (Eds.), *Anger and hostility in cardiovascular and behavioral disorders.* Washington, DC: Hemisphere.

Spitzer, S. B., Llabre, M. M., Ironson, G. H., Gellman, M. D., & Schneiderman, N. (1992). The influence of social situations on ambulatory blood pressure. *Psychosomatic Medicine, 54,* 79–86.

Steptoe, A. (1980). Blood pressure. In I. Martin & P. Venables (Eds.), *Techniques in psychophysiology* (pp. 247–274). New York: Wiley.

Stern, R. J., Ray, W. J., & Davis, C. M. (1980). *Psychophysiological recording.* New York: Oxford.

Suarez, E. C., & Williams, R. B., Jr. (1989). Situational determinants of cardiovascular and emotional reactivity in high and low hostile men. *Psychosomatic Medicine, 51*, 404–418.

Suarez, E. C., & Williams, R. B., Jr. (1990). The relationships between dimensions of hostility and cardiovascular reactivity as a function of task characteristics. *Psychosomatic Medicine, 52*, 558–570.

Tahmoush, A. J., Jennings, J. R., Lee, A. L., Camp, S., & Weber, F. (1976). Characteristics of a light emitting diode-transistor photo-plethysmograph. *Psychophysiology, 13*, 357–362.

Thomas, S. A., Friedman, E., Lottes, L. S., Gresty, S., Miller, C., & Lynch, J. J. (1984). Changes in nurses' blood pressure and heart rate while communicating. *Research in Nursing & Health, 7*, 119–126.

Throll, D. A. (1982). Transcendental Meditation and progressive relaxation: Their physiological effects. *Journal of Clinical Psychology, 38*, 522–530.

Tursky, B. (1974). The indirect recording of human blood pressure. In P. A. Obrist, A. H. Black, J. Brener, & L. V. DiCara (Eds.), *Cardiovascular psychophysiology* (pp. 93–105). Chicago: Aldine.

Tursky, B., & Greenblatt, D. J. (1967). Local vascular and thermal changes that accompany electric shock. *Psychophysiology, 3*, 362–371.

Tursky, B., Shapiro, D., & Schwartz, G. E. (1972). Automated constant cuff-pressure system to measure systolic and diastolic blood pressure in man. *IEEE Transactions on Biomedical Engineering, 19*, 271–276.

Wallace, R. K., Silver, J., Mills, P. J., Dillbeck, M. C., & Wagoner, D. E. (1983). Systolic blood pressure and long term practice to the Transcendental Meditation and TM–Sidhi programs. *Psychosomatic Medicine, 45*, 41–46.

Williams, R. B., Barefoot, J. C., & Shekelle, R. B. (1985). The health consequences of hostility. In M. A. Chesney & R. H. Rosenman (Eds.), *Anger and hostility in cardiovascular and behavior disorders* (pp. 173–186). Washington: Hemisphere.

Woodworth, R. S., & Schlosberg, H. (1954). *Experimental psychololgy*. New York: Holt.

15

Applied Psychophysiology I: Detection of Deception, Vigilance, Job Design, and Workload

Over the years, psychophysiologists have developed, or stimulated the development of, increasingly sensitive and sophisticated instruments to measure the physiological variables in their psychological studies. The refined instruments and techniques have led to a precision that allows the measurement of physiological responses in many practical applications. The next two chapters address the question: How might the measurement of physiological responses help in the solution of practical problems? In order to find answers, we examine a number of research studies in a variety of areas. The main difference between the studies described here and those in earlier chapters is that applied research is generally performed to provide an answer to a specific problem, the solution of which has practical value. This is not to say that basic research is valueless, because it often leads to applications of information or techniques that eventually prove to be very useful. Thus, applied and basic research often support and complement each other.

The applications that we consider in this chapter are concerned with detection of deception, vigilance, and personnel considerations including ergonomics, workload, job satisfaction, job strain, human–computer interactions, and personnel selection. In the next chapter, we examine applications to sensory system testing, mental retardation, nervous system disorders, and behavior disorders.

DETECTION OF DECEPTION

Historical Background.   The use of physiological measures to determine when an individual is lying is a controversial area with a long history. The controversy exists over the accuracy of the techniques and their use in personnel selection and in granting security clearances, as well as in criminal investigations. Woodworth and Schlosberg (1954) observed that the principle of SNS discharge (arousal) and its effects on inhibiting salivary secretion was used by the ancient Chinese in lie detection. The unfortunate suspect was given rice powder to chew on and then forced to spit it out. If the powder was still dry, the suspect was guilty! It was assumed that the guilty person would be fearful because of lies told during the interrogation process, and that this fright interfered with salivation. Obviously, a guilty person would not be able to moisten the dry rice! Furedy (1986) wrote that the earliest written account of psychophysiological observation in the detection of deception came from a Hindu medical source dating about 900 B.C. In this account, persons who lied about using poison on others showed such physiological changes as blushing, and behaviors such as rubbing their hair. Thus, vasodilation of facial blood vessels was the physiological change taken to indicate deception.

Over 90 years ago, Munsterberg (1908) suggested that measures of emotional reactions, such as changes in heart rate, blood volume, skin conductance, and respiration, should be investigated as possible aids in distinguishing between the innocent and the guilty suspect. He recommended caution in the use of this approach, because "the innocent man, especially the nervous man, may grow as much excited on the witness stand as the criminal when the victim and the means of the crime are mentioned; his fear that he may be condemned unjustly may influence his muscles, glands and blood vessels as strongly as if he were guilty" (p. 132). Munsterberg suggested instead that the measures be used in situations where a certain item of information could only be known to a witness of the crime. Later, Marston, a student of Munsterberg, attracted the interest of two police officers in using physiological measures to detect lying (Kleinmuntz & Szucko, 1984). The forerunner of the modern polygraph was developed by one of these police officers (Larson) and perfected by the other (Keeler). This equipment became the mainstay of professional polygraphers, and is known as the *Keeler polygraph*. The lay public has come to associate the word *polygraph* with an instrument that detects deception. In truth, any instrument that measures more than one physiological response simultaneously can be termed a polygraph. The Keeler device measures electrodermal activity, blood pressure, and respiration. From the foregoing account, it is apparent that the main measures used in detection of deception have been autonomic responses. More recently, the event-related potential (ERP) has been explored as a possible window to concealed information. Specifically, the P300 component of the ERP has been utilized as a technique in detection of deception (Farwell & Donchin, 1991; Johnson & Rosenfeld, 1992; Rosenfeld, Angell, Johnson, & Qian, 1991).

The approach suggested many years ago by Munsterberg has more recently been described by Lykken (1959, 1974) as the guilty knowledge test (GKT). Lykken distinguished the GKT from the lie detection (LD) approach, because in LD the interrogator asks direct relevant questions such as, "Did you rob the bank?" mixed with irrelevant ones such as, "Are you sitting down?" In contrast, the GKT involves the preparation of questions so that a multiple-response situation is created. Thus, for example, in a situation where a robber pretended that he wanted to take out a loan for paying doctor bills, before showing his gun, the interrogator would tell the suspect that the guilty person will know the supposed purpose of the loan. Then, the interrogator lists five possibilities (e.g., car, vacation, gift, doctor bills, new appliance) and the suspect repeats each of them while the various physiological measures are recorded. Lykken found only one field study of the LD technique that he thought adequate in terms of the criteria against which LD validity could be measured. Unfortunately, this real-life study by Bersh (1969) did little to establish the validity of the physiological response portions of the test. Lykken (1974) deplored the increasing use of the LD test in industry and suggested that it is worthless in both screening employees and in detecting thieves. At the time, he estimated that there were 3,000 persons giving over several million polygraph tests in industry each year.

The GKT was classified as an information test by Podlesny and Raskin (1977) because its use presumes that a person's critical information can produce differential physiological responses to various items. Information tests are distinguished from deception tests, which are based on the assumption that differential physiological response occurs to certain questions when the person is deceptive. This presumed differential physiological responding is the basis for the control question test (CQT) described by Podlesny and Raskin (1977). Furedy, Davis, and Gurevich (1988) criticized the CQT on the basis of differential significance between the relevant and control questions. As an example, they cited a case involving alleged child sexual abuse in which one relevant question was "Did you lick X's vagina?" The control question used as a comparison was "Did you ever do anything you were ashamed of?" On the basis of greater physiological response to the relevant question, the suspect, a 74-year-old crossing guard, was accused of the crime. Furedy and colleagues argued that, even for an innocent examinee, the impact of such a "relevant" question could far outweigh that of the so-called "control" question, in a test where both are presumed to have equal significance for an innocent person. This potential impact of a very provocative question on physiological response is the same point that Munsterberg made many years ago.

In comparing the two questioning techniques, the GKT is superior to the CQT. This is because the GKT can be standardized, as any psychological test should, whereas the CQT cannot. Additionally, error rates can be specified with GKT, and it is less vulnerable to faking (Furedy & Heslegrave, 1988). The widespread adoption of the GKT by professional polygraphers (most of whom are not scientists) is unlikely, because the CQT is procedurally entrenched.

Two extensive reviews of lie detection have appeared as chapters in books (Barland & Raskin, 1973; Orne, Thackray, & Paskewitz, 1972). In addition to the criminal investigation and industrial applications of LD, Orne et al. (1972) pointed out that it is commonly used for screening individuals for security purposes, especially in government agencies that have access to "secret" or "top secret" information. Orne and his colleagues detailed the procedures followed by interrogators in real-life situations. Professional polygraphers rarely vary their techniques in a systematic way, a practice that makes it difficult to establish the validity of the various aspects of the procedure. For example, Orne et al. asked whether the polygrapher makes a decision of "guilty" or "innocent" on the basis of a pretest interview, the person's dossier or file, the physiological response, a posttest interrogation, or some other subtle behaviors that an experienced criminal investigator might notice. Orne et al. (1972) concluded, as did Woodworth and Schlosberg (1954), that LD in a real-life situation is an art rather than a science, and the same comment applies today. Scientific evaluation of the contribution of physiological responses to the LD situation is, therefore, very difficult, because it is only one part of a comprehensive procedure. An important question is whether the use of physiological measures helps in detecting deception. To test this adequately, all other potential influences on a decision about truthfulness must be controlled.

The fact that most professional polygraphers are not trained psychologists has contributed to the lack of scientific validation of the techniques. Kleinmuntz and Szucko (1984) accused psychologists of having neglected the study of polygraphic lie detection. They contended that this procedure is a psychometric instrument that, thus far, has not been demonstrated to possess sufficient reliability and validity. (In psychometric terms, *reliability* refers to consistency of a test in measuring the phenomenon of interest, whereas *validity* evaluates the degree to which a test actually measures what it claims to measure.) Further, Kleinmuntz and Szucko cited studies in which as many as 37% to nearly 50% of innocent subjects were classified as guilty or lying. This represents a high rate of "false positives" (i.e., in this case, incorrectly classifying innocent persons as guilty). However, Raskin, Barland, and Podlesny (1977) assessed the reliability and validity of polygraph techniques and presented a much more promising picture. They evaluated the results of eight experiments that included field studies of criminal suspects and laboratory "mock crime" experiments. They also examined the belief that psychopathic criminals can "beat the polygraph," a contention based on the observation that psychopaths are practiced and habitual liars and have little guilt about the consequences of their actions. The main conclusions were that polygraph examinations using the CQT or GKT were approximately 90% accurate when properly conducted and evaluated. They also reported that deception in diagnosed psychopaths was as easy to detect as in nonpsychopaths. A review of GKT validity studies (Ben-Shakar & Furedy, 1990) indicates an accuracy rate of 84% for guilty subjects and 94% for innocent subjects. Unlike results for the CQT, these findings indicate that false negatives are more likely to occur than false positives in a GKT polygraph examination.

In a study of LD in psychopaths and nonpsychopaths, Raskin and Hare (1978) obtained additional results regarding the notion that psychopaths can beat the polygraph. They used a sample of 48 prisoners, half of whom were diagnosed psychopaths. Half of each group were "guilty" of taking $20 in a mock crime, and the other half were "innocent." A polygraph examination was conducted after a field-type interview. The measures were electrodermal activity, cardiovascular response, and respiration. The test results yielded 88% correct decisions, 4% wrong, and 8% inconclusive. The psychopaths were as accurately detected as nonpsychopaths. In addition, psychopaths showed evidence of stronger electrodermal responses and HR decelerations in the CQT used. Lykken (1978) criticized this conclusion about psychopaths on the basis that the mock crime situation used had nothing to do with fear or guilt, and was probably viewed as an interesting game by the subjects. He also questioned Raskin's claim of 90% accuracy of detection and, based on his own analysis of past studies, Lykken concluded that the accuracy rate is more like 64% to 71% (with 50% being a chance result). Coupled with Lykken's estimate of 49% to 55% of false positives, a serious indictment against polygraphic LD using the CQT is delivered. The finding of no difference between detection rate for psychopaths and nonpsychopaths also raises some concern. If the physiological measures do not differentiate between those who do and do not feel guilty about lying, then what is being measured?

The debate about polygraph examinations has continued. Lykken (1981) affirmed his skepticism about the lie detection industry, and at the same time attempted to stimulate interest in the psychophysiological investigation of lie detection for the purpose of criminal investigation. Kleinmuntz and Szucko (1984) pointed out that more psychophysiologists should do research in this area because of the important social and political implications of lie detection. At present, polygraph testing is not only done in criminal investigations but for preemployment screening of those applying for sensitive positions in law enforcement or national security. Therefore, psychologists have an obligation to use their scientific skills to resolve some of the issues and prevent potential abuse through the use of inadequately validated techniques.

Laboratory Studies in the Detection of Deception

Several investitgators have pointed out that there is no unique pattern of physiological response to deception (e.g., Lykken, 1981; Orne, 1975). However, laboratory studies are necessary to establish which physiological measures offer the greatest promise for detecting deception. According to Podlesny and Raskin (1977), the main advantage of laboratory studies is that the truthfulness of the response can be controlled and compared with the physiological response given. This is in contrast to real-life situations, in which the decision about truthfulness or deception may never be verified in some cases. On the other hand, the laboratory subject may not be highly motivated to evade detection and may not be representative of a typical population of criminal suspects.

In a laboratory study (Thackray & Orne, 1968), subjects were told that they would be interrogated as though they were suspected of being spies. They were given a set of code words and were questioned by an experimenter who did not know the words but who had a list of questions that were related to these words. The physiological measures obtained during interrogation were skin conductance, skin potential, systolic blood pressure, finger volume, and respiration. They found that SCRs, SPR, and finger blood volume were effective in discriminating deception in this situation. They observed that several previous studies had indicated SCR as the best single index of deception. Systolic blood pressure and respiration amplitude gave inconsistent results. Orne et al. (1972) noted that most laboratory studies agree that SCR is superior to other physiological variables in the detection of deception. Similarly, Barland

and Raskin (1973) concluded that SCR has shown the greatest success in discriminating between truthfulness and deception in the laboratory. Recent laboratory results with the P300 component of the ERP suggest that it has promise as a physiological indicator of deception (Farwell & Donchin, 1991). This development is discussed further later in this section.

The usefulness of SCR in field situations has been disputed. Most field examiners claim that blood pressure and respiration are more useful in detecting deception than EDA measures. In their opinion, the SCR is too sensitive to be useful in differentiating between relevant and irrelevant questions in a highly emotional criminal interrogation (e.g., Arthur, 1971). The issue is still not resolved, and would seem to be one that could benefit from scientific cooperation between professional polygraphers and psychophysiologists.

The use of the GKT assumes that suspects who are aware of crime-relevant information will show greater physiological responsivity to questions about the relevant items than to irrelevant ones. To test this assumption, three groups of innocent subjects were given the same crime-relevant information as members of a group that were guilty of a mock crime (Bradley & Warfield, 1984). The physiological measure was EDA. The results showed that detection scores of guilty subjects were higher than those in any of the innocent groups. Thus, only those persons who were attempting to deceive were detected with a high rate of accuracy. Thus, motivation to deceive is a factor in detection of deception. In another study, Bradley and Ainsworth (1984) examined the effects of alcohol on lie detection. The main finding was that alcohol intoxication during a mock crime reduced detectability with detection scores based on EDA.

The Use of Countermeasures in Detection of Deception.   An issue of special importance to investigations that utilize polygraph techniques is the extent to which the subject can use physical or psychological *countermeasures* to alter their physiological response and contribute to an erroneous decision regarding guilt. Examples of physical countermeasures are self-induced pain, muscular movements, or changes in breathing when critical questions are being asked. Mental countermeasures include thinking about relaxing scenes or exciting situations during interrogation. The effects of physical countermeasures (pressing toes to floor, biting tongue) on the accuracy of the CQT was tested by Honts, Hodes, and Raskin (1985). They found that guilty subjects in a mock crime experiment could produce enhanced responses to control questions and thus be classified as innocent.

An example of a mental countermeasure is the use of mental arithmetic during control questions (Raskin, 1989). This activity affected the outcome of a CQT examination to the extent of producing 35% false negatives and 30% inclusives. In a systematic study, Elaad and Ben-Shakar (1991) manipulated attention level and type of mental countermeasure to determine effects on GKT results. Attention levels were: High (motivational instructions, verbal response to questions, and monetary reward) and Low (no verbal response to questions, no reward). The mental countermeasures were: Continuous (counting sheep during the entire procedure), Item-specific (counting silently from 1 to 10 each time the relevant item was presented), and Neutral (no countermeasure instruction). The physiological measure was SCR. The High attention condition enhanced physiological response to the relevant stimuli. The continuous dissociation technique diverted attention from the relevant items and lowered detection. On the other hand, the Item-specific countermeasure increased physiological responsivity to relevant items. This happened because the subject had to identify the relevant item before using the mental dissociation. The implications of these studies on countermeasures is important because the utility of techniques subject to purposive distortion is questionable.

Measures of EDA, respiration, blood pressure, pulse amplitude, pulse volume, and heart rate have been frequently used in studies of deception. Podlesny and Raskin (1977) suggested that several other measures may have potential value as correlates of deception and should be further investigated. These include muscle activity, ocular activity (including eye blinks and eye movements), pupillary diameter, EEG, and voice analyses. Voice analyses include the study of frequency and amplitude changes in the vocal pattern during deception. Kubis (1973) evaluated two voice analysis techniques in LD and compared the results with those yielded by a polygraph test in a mock crime situation. Accuracy obtained with both voice analysis techniques gave results that were no different from chance, whereas the traditional polygraph test produced significant numbers of correct detections. Horvath (1978) obtained essentially the same results as Kubis when he compared a voice analysis technique (Psychological Stress Evaluator) with electrodermal activity. Accuracy with the stress evaluator was at chance levels, but hit rates based on EDA were significantly higher.

The P300 Component of the ERP in Detecting Deception.   Several studies have examined the P300 as a possible physiological measure in LD. The feasibility of using the ERP in a GKT paradigm was tested by Farwell and Donchin (1991). In their experiment, 20 subjects participated in one of two fictional spy scenarios, and were tested for their knowledge of both scenarios. All stimuli consisted of short phrases, some of which were called "probes" and were related to the scenarios and some which were designated as "targets" by the experimenters. The rest of the items were "irrelevants." Subjects responded by pressing one switch following targets and another to probes and irrelevants. As expected, targets elicited large P300s in all subjects, but P300s were only elicited by probes related to the scenario in which a given subject participated. The irrelevants did not produce a P300 response. There were no false positives or false negatives, that is, whenever a decision could be made based on the P300, it was accurate. However, a decision could not be reached in 12.5% of the cases (indeterminates).

In a second experiment, four college students who had minor brushes with the law (for example, being arrested for underage drinking) were examined with ERPs. Target stimuli and probes related to a given subject's offense produced large P300s. Irrelevant stimuli and probes not related to the offense produced either a very small or no P300 at all. Determinations were 100% correct in this second experiment.

Rosenfeld and colleagues also looked into the feasibility of using ERPs in LD (Rosenfeld, Angell, Johnson, & Qian, 1991). In one of their studies, a CQT procedure was used along with necessary conditions for producing P300 responses. The subjects were 32 males, randomly assigned to equal groups of 16 "guilty" and 16 "innocent." The accuracy of detection was 89%. Johnson and Rosenfeld (1992) measured ERPs while subjects were presented with a list of eight antisocial acts and one target-response phrase to which a "yes" button press was required. After the ERP was obtained, truth was established by having subjects fill out an innocent/guilty checklist of antisocial acts. On this basis, there were 17 guilty and 14 innocent subjects. The P300 response criteria yielded 87% accuracy.

The results with ERP measures of LD are promising, especially the Farwell and Donchin procedure. In this approach the P300 component of the innocent person does not occur to the probe or irrelevant stimuli, but does react to the designated targets. The guilty person responds with a P300 to probes and targets, but not irrelevants. Thus, there is a built-in control here in that responses to targets by innocent and guilty subjects show that a lack of P300 to probes is not due to the inability to produce P300s, but that the probe is an irrelevant stimulus to the innocent person. Possible advantages of using ERPs are that they are not as dependent on emotional responses to stimuli as are the traditional ANS measures used in polygraphy, and they may be less vulnerable to countermeasures compared to autonomic responses, especially because they are quicker (latency of 300–400 msec poststimulus compared to 1,000–2,000 msec for the SCR). Further study is necessary to test the effects of emotion and attempted countermeasures on the ERP.

The value of scientific controversy as to the validity of polygraphic lie detection is that it has led to open discussion of the issues and, hopefully, will lead to empirical studies to resolve some of the questions. Furedy (1986) argued that a "specific effects" approach must be used in evaluating polygraphy. This would require that improvements in detection of deception by an examiner using polygraphy be precisely defined. Another consideration is the issue of accuracy afforded by the polygraphic charts alone (i.e., scored "blind," or without direct contact between the scorer and the examinee). According to Lykken, this accuracy level is about 70%, versus a 50% chance level, compared to Raskin's extimate of 90% accuracy. Clearly, both these estimates are above chance, but the protagonists disagree about how much better than chance. Furedy also suggested that factors affecting accuracy should be subjected to scientific scrutiny, especially in field studies. Another set of relevant issues can be studied in the more controlled laboratory setting and include obtaining information about psychological factors (e.g., memory, incentives, beliefs about effectiveness of detection apparatus), as well as phyiological ones (e.g., the most reliable measures, drug effects, environmental effects) that influence detection of deception.

Furedy (1993) wrote about what he called the "CQT Polygrapher's Dilemma." He argued that an ethical dilemma exists for those polygraphers who use the CQT because (1), some innocent persons are classified as deceptive and (2), those classified as nondeceptive never receive the benefit of a debriefing concerning their feelings of unease raised by the control questions that are designed to elicit a strong emotional response. Because of this dilemma, and other problems with CQT procedures, Furedy called for an end to the use of this technique, but not for the more standardized GKT. Honts, Kircher, and Raskin (1995) responded to Furedy's critique and claimed that his arguments for banning the CQT are based on inaccurate representations, for example, that the CQT is not a standardized method. Honts et al. agreed that some field examiners may be poorly trained and may apply the technique inappropriately, but that this should not lead to dismissal of a useful psychophysiological tool in criminal investigation. They also mention new developments in LD not mentioned in Furedy's critique. These are the use of the "directed lie" technique, in which individuals are told to lie when asked a given question during the test, and the development of computer-based statistical evaluation of physiological data. Honts and colleagues believe that to abandon the CQT would be contrary to scientific evidence and not to the interests of our society.

Summary.   The message of this section is that the validity and usefulness of polygraphic lie detection is controversial. Part of the problem is to determine whether physiological responses vary with the act of lying or whether they reflect anxiety stemming from justified guilt or the possibility of being wrongly accused. It is unimportant whether the false positive (error) rate is 10% or 40% with any technique of questioning. In human terms, this means that between 10% and 40% of individuals examined may be falsely accused and their reputations destroyed, and this makes any error rate unacceptable. Another part of the problem concerns a lack of standardization of techniques and procedures of questioning. Psychophysiologists should take up the challenge of lie detection research and apply their scientific procedures to the problem instead of cringing when they hear about alleged abuses of LD in law enforcement or in governmental agency settings. They can cooperate to a greater extent with professional polygraphers to learn more about field procedures used in an attempt to identify factors that influence reliability and validity of the technique. It is clear that we still need additional information. Once this information has been generated, we may either witness detection of deception procedures based on physiological measures and sound psychometric and theoretical foundations, or we may have evidence for limiting the use of polylgraphic lie detection in our society to special situations.

Physiological Correlates of Vigilance and Workload

Vigilance.   The problem of vigilance decrement, enunciated so well by Mackworth (1950), is still with us. There has been increasing attention to the physiological changes that occur during the course of a vigil. Mackie (1977) discussed the variety of situations and the kinds of physiological measures used. For example, prolonged night automobile driving and physiological changes were studied by O'Hanlon and Kelly (1977). In three separate experiments, the performance of 41 young males was monitored while measures of EEG and HR were taken. The main performance indicator was the frequency of drifting out of lane, that is, the number of times the white line or road shoulder were touched during the drive. All driving was done on actual roads in California. The time of driving ranged from 109 to 315 min and averaged 200 min. Each driver used the same vehicle and started the run at 10:00 p.m. An observer was present in the vehicle at all times. The subjects were divided into groups of 21 "better" and 20 "poorer" drivers on the basis of the lane-drifting measure. The better drivers tended to have higher rates of heart activity and lower heart rate variability than the poorer ones.

The HRs of both groups decreased progressively over the course of the drive. In three cases, the observer took control of the vehicle when performance became very erratic, and the subject seemed more asleep than awake. The EEG records of these subjects confirmed this, revealing bursts of delta or theta activity. The drivers were unaware that the experimenter took control, suggesting that persons who were at a dangerously low level of arousal while driving did not realize it. More studies of this type are needed, especially when the tremendous losses in traffic accidents and other kinds of accidents are considered. One might visualize night drivers, radar operators, or pilots of the future wearing physiological monitors that sound an alerting bell or buzzer when the recorded activity signals a potentially dangerous low level of alertness.

The effects of achievment motivation on vigilance performance and two measures of heart activity were examined by Beh (1990). Subjects were either high or low scorers on the need for achievment scale of the Edwards Personal Preference Survey. The vigilance task involved the detection of 60 randomly presented visual signals over a 30-min period. Those persons who scored high in achievement motivation had higher HR and lower HR variability than the low scorers during performance of the task. Prior to the vigilance task, the two groups did not differ in these measures. In addition, vigilance performance, measured in terms of decision time and movement time, was significantly superior for the high scorers. The findings indicate that subjects high in achievement motivation expend greater mental effort in task performance and that this effort results in cardiovascular activation.

The combined effects of night shift work and noise on vigilance task performance and physiological response were studied by Boucsein and Ottmann (1996). Participants worked either a day shift (8 a.m. to 6 p.m.) or night shift (8 p.m. to 6 a.m.) over a 5-day period. All worked under simulated traffic noise (80 db) or no noise (50 db) conditions while skin conductance and heart rate were measured. The results indicated higher skin conductance and heart rate values during day shifts, and this was associated with faster reaction times in the vigilance task. Lower conductance values and slower heart rate were observed during the night shift conditions. A large decrease in HR was observed during the second half of the shift in the night condition, but not during the day shift. The noise partly attenuated the drop in HR during the night shift. Because the participants were students not accustomed to night work, the authors caution generalizing to shift workers in the actual labor force. Boucsein and Ottmann proposed three different arousal systems to explain day/night differences and noise effects, and they call for additional research with experienced night workers.

Psychophysiology in Ergonomics.   Historically, the term *ergonomics* refers to designing equipment, jobs, and work environments while keeping the capacities and limitations of the human operator in mind. This particular endeavor has come under a variety of names over the years including human factors engineering and human engineering. The object in the psychophysiology in ergonomics is to establish the patterns of physiological activity under different conditions of work with the aim of improving human performance and comfort.

Measurement of physiological activity can give the researcher some idea of the "physiological cost" of performing certain jobs. The field of ergonomics has been in existence for a number of years and the measurement of physiological activity in real and simulated work environments has also existed for some time. However, a recent focus on this area is evidenced in the formation of a special interest group "Psychophysiology in Ergonomics" as a new technical group of the International Ergonomics Association. The formation of this group is a welcome addition to applied psychophysiology, and several of the studies to be described in this section exemplify the work of this group.

The job of air traffic controller (ATC) is very demanding and complex and serves as a good model for the study of workload effects on physiological response. From a practical standpoint, the increase in air traffic all over the globe makes it imperative that we understand more about the psychological and physiological effects of increased workload. The effects of momentary workload on physiological responses of controllers as they performed ATC tasks was the focus of a study by Brookings, Wilson, and Swain (1996).

In their research, experienced Air Force controllers performed under three scenarios on a simulator. One scenario varied aircraft volume over the 45-min session such that 6, 12, and 18 planes were handled in succesive 15-min intervals. The second scenario held the workload constant over the 45 min, but varied complexity of the task in terms of changing arrival/departure ratios, pilot miscommunications, and variety of aircraft types. The third situation was pure overload in that controllers were presented with 15 aircraft to handle in 5 min in order to overwhelm them. The variables of volume, complexity, and overload affected performance detrimentally. The measures of EEG reflected changes in complexity and volume. For example, theta activity increased with increasing task difficulty, especially at central and parietal sites. The authors suggest that increased theta may reflect cognitive activity in the simulation used. Beta activity increased with increasing complexity, primarily over frontal and central locations. Eye blink rate decreased with higher workload, indicating that visual attention increases with greater task demands. Decreases in eye blink frequency with increased processing demands have been reported by previous investigators (e.g., Fogarty & Stern, 1989). Brookings and colleagues also reported increases in respiration rate with increased task demand. The authors suggested that eye blinks and respiration could be used as online monitors of cognitive demand during actual ATC situations as they represent measures that can be recorded continuously in an unobtrusive manner. The EEG measures were most sensitive to task variables and offer promise as differential indicators of workload factors not detected by other physiological recordings.

Mental workload is a concept often mentioned in applied research of this type. The mental workload is considered to be high when the difference between task demands and capacity of the operator is small (Veltman & Gaillard, 1996). A number of physiological variables were measured by Veltman and Gaillard as subjects performed a complex flight simulator task. Workload was manipulated by introducing a secondary task (auditory memory) and varying difficulty level of the flight. The subjects were all from a Dutch military academy. The researchers report that eye blink duration decreased during flight and landing. Blink frequency decreased only during landing, again confirming that high visual processing load leads to decreased duration and frequency of eye blinks. Increases in blood pressure and heart rate were observed during more difficult segments of the task.

The electrooculogram (EOG) data of partially sleep-deprived subjects were obtained while they performed in a flight simulation for a 4.5 hr period (Morris & Miller, 1996). The subjects were Air Force trained pilots who had an average of 12.7 years of flying experience. They reported to the laboratory at 1 a.m. and remained awake until the simulator flight which took place between 1 p.m. and 5:30 p.m. Subjects averaged only 2.4 hr. of sleep the night before the experiment. Analyses of the data indicated that performance decreased over time and subject's ratings of sleepiness increased during the experimental session. A number of EOG measures predicted performance decrement due to fatigue. These were blink amplitude, long closure rate (number of closures longer than 500 msec), blink rate, and blink duration. The authors suggest that a measure that combines blink amplitude, long closure, rate, and duration would provide the best predictor of performance decrement.

Job Strain.   There is a great deal of concern about the effects of stress on both health and job performance. An influential concept regarding this problem has been the job strain model as proposed by Karasek and Theorell (1990). They defined *Job strain* as the combination of high demands at work with little control over how the work is carried out. Several studies using ambulatory monitoring of blood pressure (BP) have indicated a relationship between job strain and BP. For example, Theorell et al. (1991), studied a large sample of borderline hypertensive men and found a significant correlation between job strain and diastolic blood pressure (DBP) at work and at night after work.

In another study, Light, Brownley, Turner, and Hinderliter (1992) examined a large sample of nonhypertensive men and women and found that men with high job strain showed higher BP on the job as compared to men with low job strain. The authors emphasized that their findings demonstrate that in a sample of young, healthy, nonhypertensive working men, high job strain is not associated with elevated blood pressure in measures taken in a clinic environment, but shows significant increases over a full workday. In that same study, job strain and BP levels were unrelated for women. In general, higher levels of job strain are associated with higher BP in men. The results are not as clear for women. Positive results were reported by Theorell, Ahlberg-Hulten, Jodko, Sigala, and de la Torre (1993) who indicated a relationship between job strain and both SBP and DBP at work for women hospital personnel.

In addition, Blumenthal, Towner Thyrum, and Siegel (1995) found that job strain was related to SBP among mildly hypertensive women. The women with high job strain had higher SBP than low job strain women and they also had higher SBP than men with either high or low job strain. It has been suggested that other factors such as job status or social support, hypertensive status, age, and ethnicity might influence the association between job strain and BP levels in women (Carels, Sherwood, & Blumenthal, 1998). Some support for this suggestion comes from a study by Light et al. (1995) in which it was shown that women who had high status jobs had higher DBP at work and in the laboratory than other women. The women scored high on a measure of "high effort coping," which was characterized by endorsement of such items as "Hard work has really helped me to get ahead in life," and "I don't let my personal feelings get in the way of doing a job." This 12-item scale was not related to measures of hostility or Type A/B behavior.

The job strain model has been criticized for inadequately specifying demand and control (Steptoe, Evans, & Fieldman, 1997). Steptoe and colleagues pointed out that the control dimension may be particularly important as a risk factor for cardiovascular disease. One study has shown that after adjustments are made for factors such as age, BP, cholesterol level, smoking, alcohol consumption, and family history that lack of control over one's work was associated with heart disease (Alterman, Shekelle, Vernon, & Burau, 1994). No relationship between job demand and disease was found. This does not mean that demand should be eliminated from the model, but only that it helps to more precisely indicate the influences on job demand characteristics. In their own laboratory research, Steptoe and colleagues have manipulated control by varying the extent to which subjects have a perception of either self-pacing or external-pacing of tasks on which they work. For example, in one experiment men aged 55 to 65 years had larger increases in SBP and DBP in externally-paced as compared to the self-paced situations (Steptoe, Fieldman, Evans, & Perry, 1993).

A follow-up study expanded on the number of subjects in addition to evaluating responses of women (Steptoe et al., 1997). Here, 132 adults (64 men and 68 women) were randomized to self-paced and externally paced conditions. The self-paced group carried out visual matrix problem solving and mirror tracing at their own pace. The work requirement for the externally-paced group was set to equal the rate of the self-paced group. This was done to equalize work demand, thus making the only difference between the groups the perception of who was actually controlling the work. Both SBP and electrodermal responsivity were significantly greater under external pacing of the mirror tracing task. No differences were found for the matrix task and for DBP and heart rate. Steptoe and associates note that the perceived lack of controllability for the matrix task was less than in their previous study, and that this may have influenced physiological responsivity. This is an important area of research that requires further study.

PERSONNEL APPLICATIONS

Job Satisfaction and Design.   The relationship among job satisfaction, perceived effort, and HR was measured in 40 female factory workers (Khaleque, 1981). The average HR of satisfied workers was significantly lower than that of dissatisfied ones. In addition, there was a significant correlation between job satisfaction and HR—that is, greater satisfaction was related to lower HR. There was no relation between perceived effort and HR. The results have possible health implications with regard to the long-term cardiovascular effects of job dissatisfaction. A number of studies have shown that repetitive industrial tasks are associated in some workers with job dissatisfaction and in others with emotional stress. Assembly-line inspection or production tasks are common examples of industrial jobs that are repetitive and, potentially, very boring. The effects of four different repetitive tasks on several physiological measures was examined by a group of researchers (Weber, Fussler, O'Hanlon, Gierer, & Grandjean, 1980). All of the repetitive tasks were associated with depressed EEG alpha, increased HR, and elevated adrenaline excretion. Two of the tasks required discrimination and were accompanied by higher neck EMG and less boredom and drowsiness. The results point up the possible stressful effects of repetition, and the importance of job design, or redesign in reducing these effects. Another consideration is that of job strain, which was defined earlier. A study of 73 men and women found increased systolic blood pressure during working hours for those reporting high strain compared to those with low job strain (Theorell, Perski, & Akerstedt, 1988). The occupations sampled included air traffic controllers, waiters, airplane mechanics, physicians, symphony orchestra musicians, and baggage handlers.

Job Workload.   Donchin, Kramer, and Wickens (1986) made a case for the potential utility of ERPs in studying job workload and the design of tasks. They cited studies indicating that P300 is sensitive to perceptual demands of a primary task, because P300 amplitude to a secondary task probe decreases with increased difficulty of a primary task. Thus, it may serve as a good index of the relative demands of primary and secondary tasks on an operator. This is an important consideration in the design of jobs in modern complex man-machines systems where multiple tasks must be performed. Because ERPs have been found useful in studying cognitive activities, Donchin and his coworkers advocated their use as analytical tools in measuring and understanding mental workload.

The effects of workload on a variety of physiological measures was the topic of study for Fournier, Wilson, and Swain (1999). These researchers compared effects of performing a single task with multiple tasks that varied in complexity. In the single task condition, participants monitored and responded to audio messages. In the multitask conditions, they were required to monitor messages, keep watch over four different gauges, detect the offset and onset of lights, and keep a green circle within a moving rectangle (tracking task). The results showed that heart rate was significantly higher in the multitask conditions compared to the single task. Respiration rate was also significantly faster during the multitask conditions as was eye blink rate. Other EOG measures showed increased eye blink amplitude and decreased blink duration in the multitasks relative to the single task. As a manipulation check, Fournier et al. (1999) obtained self-reports of workload level on a low (1) to high (10) scale covering mental, physical, performance, time, effort, and frustration demand. The reports indicated significantly higher demand ratings for the multitasks.

Human–Computer Interaction.   The control of computer functions by eye movements was successfully demonstrated for normal individuals by Tecce, Gips, Olivieri, Pok, and Consiglio (1998). In their research, protocol eye movements derived from electrooculography (EOG) were used to move a cursor on a letter grid that contained the 26 letters of the alphabet. After only 5 min of practice, subjects were able to compose a number of simple sentences such as "get the car." The task was to sequentially select the letters needed plus two spaces separating the words for a total of 11 characters. Processing time averaged 2.5 seconds per letter during the sentence construction task. The authors point out that the use of eye movements offers promise for computer control by handicapped individuals who lack manual control and have no speech capability, such as those with quadriplegic cerebral palsy.

Personnel.   Reports from the Navy Personnel Research and Development Center in San Diego, California, suggest that ERPs are more accurate in predicting on-the-job performance of Naval personnel than are traditional psychological tests (Lewis, 1983a, 1983b). Research results suggest that ERPs are related to success or failure in a remedial reading program, that ERPs distinguished between prematurely discharged recruits and those of equal aptitude who successfully completed training, and in predicting performance of antisubmarine warfare sonar operators. These are promising results that require replication with other tasks.

Summary.   Several studies were cited to indicate that physiological measures have possible applications to job situations. Physiological variables have been related to decreased alertness in nighttime driving, and vigilance performance in monotonous tasks. Psychophysiology in ergonomics, or the study of work and work environments, is gaining momentum. Research in this area has focused on the physiological responses of persons working in air traffic control simulators and flight simulators. One recent approach examined the physiological responses of sleep-deprived pilots on a flight simulator. The prime predictors of performance were EOG measures (blink rate, duration and closure time). Job strain has been defined as being due to a combination of high work demand and a low level of control over the work process. Studies of men in high- versus low-strain jobs have indicated higher levels of blood pressure for high-strain jobs. Results for women are not as clear-cut, but recent results suggest that women in high-status jobs show elevated DBP both at work and in the laboratory. There is also evidence to suggest that external pacing of work rate leads to higher levels of BP than self-paced work. Other intriguing findings concern the lower HR of satisfied workers, the use of eye movements to control computer functions, and the use of ERPs to predict job performance of Naval personnel.

REFERENCES

Alterman, T., Shekelle, R. B., Vernon, S. W., & Burau, K. D. (1994). Decision latitude, psychological demand, job strain, and coronary heart disease in the Western Electric Study. *American Journal of Epidemiology, 139*, 620–627.

Arthur, R. O. (1971). The GSR unit. *Journal of Polygraph Studies, 5*, 1–4.

Barland, G. H., & Raskin, D. C. (1973). Detection of deception. In W. F. Prokasy & D. C. Raskin (Eds.), *Electrodermal activity in psychological research* (pp. 417–477). New York: Academic Press.

Beh, H. (1990). Achievement motivation, performance and cardiovascular activity. *International Journal of Psychophysiology, 10,* 39–45.

Ben-Shakar, G., & Furedy, J. J. (1990). *Theories and applications in the detection of deception: psychophysiological and cultural perspectives.* Berlin: Springer.

Bersh, P. J. (1969). A validation of polygraph examiner judgments. *Journal of Applied Psychology, 53,* 399–403.

Blumenthal, J. A., Towner Thyrum, E., & Siegel, W. C. (1995). Contribution of job strain, job status, and marital status to laboratory and ambulatory blood pressure in patients with mild hypertension. *Journal of Psychosomatic Medicine, 39,* 133–144.

Boucsein, W., & Ottmann, W. (1996). Psychophysiological stress effects from the combination of night-shift work and noise. *Biological Psychology, 42,* 301–322.

Bradley, M. T., & Ainsworth, D. (1984). Alcohol and the physiological detection of deception. *Psychophysiology, 21,* 63–71.

Bradley, M. T., & Warfield, J. F. (1984). Innocence, information, and the Guilty Knowledge Test in the detection of deception. *Psychophysiology, 21,* 683–689.

Brookings, J. B., Wilson, G. F., & Swain, C. R. (1996). Psychophysiological responses to changes in workload during simulated air traffic control. *Biological Psychology, 42,* 361–377.

Carels, R. A., Sherwood, A., & Blumenthal, J. A. (1998). Psychosocial influences on blood pressure during daily life. *International Journal of Psychophysiology, 28,* 117–129.

Donchin, E., Kramer, A., & Wickens, C. (1986). Applications of brain event-related potentials to problems in engineering psychology. In M. G. H. Coles, E. Donchin, & S. W. Porges (Eds.), *Psychophysiology: Systems, processes & applications* (pp. 702–718). New York: Guilford.

Elaad, E., & Ben-Shakar, G. (1991). Effects of mental countermeasures on psychophysiological detection in the guilty knowledge test. *International Journal of Psychophysiology, 11,* 99–108.

Farwell, L., & Donchin, E. (1991). The truth will out: Interrogative polygraphy ("lie detection") with event-related brain potentials. *Psychophysiology, 28,* 531–547.

Fogarty, C., & Stern, J. A. (1989). Eye movements and blinks: Their relationship to higher cognitive processes. *International Journal of Psychophysiology, 8,* 35–42.

Fournier, L. R., Wilson, G. F., Swain, C. R. (1999). Electrophysiological, behavioral, and subjective indexes of workload when performing multiple tasks: Manipulations of task difficulty and training. *International Journal of Psychophysiology, 31,* 129–145.

Furedy, J. J. (1986). Lie detection as psychophysiological differentiation: Some fine lines. In M. G. H. Coles, E. Donchin, & S. W. Porges (Eds.), *Psychophysiology: Systems, processes & application* (pp. 683–701). New York: Guilford.

Furedy, J. J. (1993). The "control" question "test" (CQT) polygrapher's dilemma: Logico-ethical considerations for psychophysiological practitioners and researchers. *International Journal of Psychophysiology, 15,* 263–267.

Furedy, J. J., Davis, C., & Gurevich, M. (1988). Differentiation of deception as a psychological process: A psychophysiological approach. *Psychophysiology, 25,* 683–688.

Furedy, J. J., & Heslegrave, R. J. (1988). The forensic use of the polygraph: A psychophysiological analysis of current trends and future prospects. In J. R. Jennings, P. K. Ackles, & M. G. H. Coles (Eds.), *Advances in psychophysiology* (Vol. 4, pp. 121–142). Greenwich, CT: JAI Press.

Hare, R. D. (1968). Psychopathy, autonomic functioning and the orienting response. *Journal of Abnormal Psychology Monographs, 73,* 1–24.

Hare, R. D. (1975). Psychopathy. In P. H. Venables & M. J. Christie (Eds.), *Research in psychophysiology* (pp. 325–348). New York: Wiley.

Honts, C., Hodes, R. L., & Raskin, D. C. (1985). Effects of physical countermeasures on the physiological detection of deception. *Journal of Applied Psychology, 70,* 177–187.

Honts, C., Kircher, J. C., & Raskin, D. C. (1995). Polygrapher's dilemma of psychologist's chimaera: A reply to Furedy's logico-ethical considerations for psychophysiological practitioners and researchers. *International Journal of Psychophysiology, 20,* 199–207.

Horvath, F. (1978). An experimental comparison of the psychological stress evaluator and the galvanic skin response in detection of deception. *Journal of Applied Psychology, 63,* 338–344.

Johnson, M. M., & Rosenfeld, J. P. (1992). Oddball-evoked P300-based method of deception detection in the laboratory II: Utilization of non-selective activation of relevant knowledge. *International Journal of Psychophysiology, 12,* 289–306.

Karasek, R. A., & Theorell, T. (1990). *Healthy work.* Basic Books: New York.

Khaleque, A. (1981). Job satisfaction, perceived effort and heart rate in light industrial work. *Ergonomics, 24,* 735–742.

Kleinmuntz, B., & Szucko, J. J. (1984). Lie detection in ancient and modern times. *American Psychologist, 39,* 766–776.

Kubis, J. F. (1973). *Comparison of voice analysis and polygraph as lie detection procedures* (Contract DAADO5-72-C-O217). U.S. Army Land Warfare Laboratory, Aberdeen Proving Ground, Aberdeen, MD.

Lewis, G. W. (1983a). Event-related brain electrical and magnetic activity: Toward predicting on-job performance. *International Journal of Neuroscience, 18*, 159–182.

Lewis, G. W. (1983b). *Bioelectric predictors of personnel performance: A review of relevant research at the Navy Research and Development Center.* NPRDC TR 84-3, Navy Personnel Research and Development Center, San Diego, CA.

Light, K. C., Brownley, K. A., Turner, J. R., Hinderliter, A. L., Girdler, S. S., Sherwood, A., & Anderson, N. B. (1995). Job status and high-effort coping influence work blood pressure in women and Blacks. *Hypertension, 25*, 554–559.

Lykken, D. T. (1959). The GSR in the detection of guilty. *Journal of Applied Psychology, 43*, 385–388.

Lykken, D. T. (1974). Psychology and the lie detector industry. *American Psychologist, 29*, 725–739.

Lykken, D. T. (1978). The psychopath and the lie detector. *Psychophysiology, 15*, 137–142.

Lykken, D. T. (1981). *A tremor in the blood.* New York: McGraw-Hill.

Mackie, R. R. (1977). *Vigilance: Theory, operational performance and physiological correlates.* New York: Plenum.

Mackworth, N. H. (1950). *Researches on the measurement of human performance.* (MRC Spec. Rep. 268). London: H. M. Stationery Office.

Morris, T. L., & Miller, J. C. (1996). Electrooculographic and performance indices of fatigue during simulated flight. *Biological Psychology, 42*, 343–360.

Munsterberg, H. (1908). *On the witness stand.* New York: Doubleday, Page & Co.

O'Hanlon, J. F., & Kelly, G. R. (1977). Comparison of performance and physiological changes between drivers who perform well and poorly during prolonged vehicular operation. In R. R. Mackie (Ed.), *Vigilance: Theory, operational performance and physiological correlates* (pp. 87–109). New York: Plenum.

Orne, M. T. (1975). Implications of laboratory research for the detection of deception. In N. Ainsley (Ed.), *Legal admissibility of the polygraph* (pp. 94–119). Springfield, IL: C. C. Thomas.

Orne, M. T., Thackray, R. I., & Paskewitz, D. A. (1972). On the detection of deception. In N. S. Greenfield & R. A. Sternbach (Eds.), *Handbook of Psychophysiology* (pp. 743–785). New York: Holt, Rinehart & Winston.

Podlesny, J. A., & Raskin, D. C. (1977). Physiological measures and the detection of deception. *Psychological Bulletin, 84*, 782–799.

Raskin, D. C. (1989). *Psychological methods in criminal investigation and evidence.* New York: Springer.

Raskin, D. C., Barland, G. H., & Podlesny, J. A. (1977). Validity and reliability of detection of deception. *Polygraph, 6*, 1–39.

Raskin, D. C., & Hare, R. D. (1978). Psychopathy and detection of deception in a prison population. *Psychophysiology, 15*, 126–136.

Rosenfeld, J. P., Angell, A., Johnson, M., & Qian, J. (1991). An ERP-based, control-question lie detector analog: Algorithms for discriminating effects within individuals' average waveforms. *Psychophysiology, 38*, 319–335.

Steptoe, A., Evans, O., & Fieldman, G. (1997). Perceptions of control over work: Psychophysiological responses to self-paced and externally-paced tasks in an adult population sample. *International Journal of Psychophysiology, 25*, 211–220.

Steptoe, A., Fieldman, G., Evans, O., & Perry, L. (1993). Control over work pace, job strain and cardiovascular responses in middle-aged men. *Journal of Hypertension, 11*, 751–759.

Tecce, J. J., Gips, J., Olivieri, C. P., Pok, L. J., & Consiglio, M. R. (1998). Eye movement control of computer functions. *International Journal of Psychophysiology, 29*, 319–325.

Theorell, T., Ahlberg-Hulten, G., Jodko, M., Sigala, F., de la Torre, B. (1993). Influence of job strain and emotion on blood pressure in female hospital personnel during work hours. *Scand. J. Work Environ. Health, 19*, 313–318.

Theorell, T., Perski, A., & Akerstedt, T. (1988). Changes in job strain in relation to changes in physiological state. *Scand. J. Work Environ. Health, 14*, 189–196.

Theorell, T., de Faire, U., Johnson, J., Hall, E., Perski, A., & Stewart, W. (1991). Job strain and ambulatory blood pressure profiles. *Scand. J. Work Environ. Health, 17*, 380–385.

Thrackray, R. I., & Orne, M. T. (1968). A comparison of physiological indices in detection of deception. *Psychophysiology, 4*, 329–339.

Veltman, J. A., & Gaillard, A. W. K. (1996). Physiological indices of workload in a simulated flight task. *Biological Psychology, 42*, 323–342.

Weber, A., Fussler, C., O'Hanlon, J. F., Gierer, R., & Grandjean, E. (1980). Effects of repetitive work on physiological response. *Ergonomics, 23*, 1033–1046.

Woodworth, R. S., & Schlosberg, H. (1954). *Experimental psychology.* New York: Holt.

16

Applied Psychophysiology II: Auditory and Visual System Tests, Nervous System Disorders, and Behavior Disorders

CLINICAL APPLICATIONS OF PHYSIOLOGICAL MEASURES

Physiological measures have been applied in a variety of clinical situations by psychologists, neurologists, and psychiatrists. Some of the applications have included testing of vision, hearing, and brain responses in retarded individuals, and brain activity in neurological and behavior disorders. Examples of how physiological responses have been used in these various clinical situations, which are of importance to psychologists, audiologists, neurologists, psychiatrists, and others, are briefly described in the next sections.

Auditory System Tests

The Brain Stem Potential. In the adult, the auditory brain stem response is a complex series of waves (see Fig. 16.4). The normal newborn infant shows only Waves I, III, and V in response to the high frequency click stimuli (Stapells & Kurtzberg, 1991). Wave I is produced by neural activity in the 8th cranial nerve (auditory) and Wave III is generated by activity in the pons of the brain stem. Wave V arises from activity in the midbrain in the vicinity of the inferior colliculus. At-risk infants, that is, those of low birth weight, or those who suffered asphyxia at birth, have shown abnormal brain stem responses (Majnemer, Rosenblatt, & Ridig, 1988). The latencies between peaks of the brain stem potential were delayed in these infants compared to normal controls. Thus, the brain stem response is a potential diagnostic tool for indicating infants who may have suffered damage to the auditory system.

The use of auditory ERPs to assess hearing deficits in retarded children, infants, and children with multiple handicaps (e.g., those with cerebral palsy) has been increasing in recent years. Because traditional auditory testing requires that subjects indicate verbally or by gesture that they have heard a sound, a technique that can evaluate the integrity of the auditory system without requiring such a response would be of value for testing certain individuals. Rapin (1974) observed that the auditory ERP is a powerful physiologic test of hearing because it indicates that stimulation by sound has caused a response to occur in the auditory system and the brain. She found that early diagnosis of hearing deficits with ERPs can allow early remediation. For example, infants have been fitted with hearing aids before the age of 6 months because ERPs showed their hearing to be impaired. Rapin expressed the belief that evoked potential audiometry is too demanding a technique for routine use with cooperative patients, but that it is justified with selected cases, similar to those just mentioned.

Rapin, Graziani, and Lyttle (1969) studied behavioral responses to sound and auditory ERPs of 51 children whose mothers had German measles (rubella) during the first 3 months

344

of pregnancy. Of 38 children judged to be hearing impaired with behavioral responses, 27 had abnormal auditory ERPs.

Children who require intensive care as newborns, because of low birthweight or other medical complications, have a higher incidence of sensory deficits and speech and language disorders. In one study, 28% of infants with histories of low birth weight or neonatal asphyxia had auditory ERP abnormalities (Cone-Wesson, Kurtzberg, & Vaughan, 1983). These abnormalities represent dysfunction in the auditory system. Because auditory system integrity is essential in speech development, hearing assessment in early infancy is very important and may dictate the use of intervention strategies such as hearing aids. Kurtzberg, Hilpert, and Kreuzer (1984) found that cortical auditory ERPs to speech sounds /da/ and /ta/ and to 800-Hz tones were less mature for low birth weight (less than 3.3 lb) infants than full-term babies, even though they were tested at the same age. The differences lessened at subsequent age levels of 2 and 3 months, but Kurtzberg and Vaughan (1985) speculated about the possible detrimental impact of these early abnormalities on later language development. Kurtzberg and colleagues (1984) recorded auditory ERPs of newborn infants in response to the speech sounds /ba/, /da/, and /ta/. The different waveforms obtained with three positive components that varied in latency according to the stimulus used indicates that the newborn auditory system discriminates between speech sounds (see Fig. 16.1). These researchers suggested that the ability of the newborn brain to discriminate among speech sounds may provide a useful tool for early diagnosis of defective auditory system processing.

The auditory ERPs of newborns was obtained to determine if they would respond to a change in pitch (frequency) of an auditory stimulus (Alho, Sainio, Sajaniemi, Reinikainen, & Naatanen, 1990). In this study, a 1000-Hz tone served as a standard, and a 1200-Hz tone was the "odd-ball." The newborns detected the difference and the 1200-Hz stimulus produced an ERP wave with longer latency and a larger amplitude than the 1000-Hz tone. Kurtzberg, Stapells, and Wallace (1988) used an odd-ball paradigm to test infants in discriminating the speech sounds of /da/ and /ta/. They also reported a longer latency and larger response to the

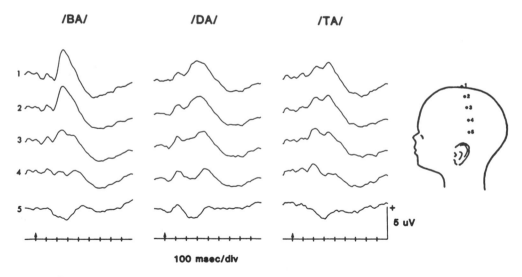

FIG. 16.1. Mean cortical auditory ERP recorded from a group of newborns to the speech sounds /ba/, /da/, and /ta/. Note the waveshape differences between responses recorded at the midline from those recorded overlying the lateral surface of the temporal lobe. These responses have a differential maturational course. The waveshape and amplitudes of the responses differ as a function of the auditory stimulus. Stimulus onset at arrow. (Photo courtesy of Dr. D. Kurtzberg.)

odd-ball stimulus in normal infants. However, at-risk infants did not show this discrimination response.

Summary.   The information presented here indicates that auditory ERPs can be especially useful in detecting auditory system deficits in cases where other testing is not feasible, for example, with infants or retarded individuals. The use of both brain stem and cortical auditory ERPs in newborns will aid in the early diagnosis of conditions that could lead to speech and language problems in later life.

Visual System Tests

Visual ERPs and Visual System Defects.   A number of studies have indicated that visual ERPs could be used to detect the presence of lesions at various levels of the visual system (Regan, 1972). In an early study, Vaughan, Katzman, and Taylor (1963) found that patients suffering from hemianopia produced visual ERPs that were 50% greater in amplitude from the unaffected part of the brain. *Hemianopia* refers to defective vision in which there is blindness in half of the visual field. The patients studied by Vaughan and colleagues had homonymous hemianopia, which affected either the right or left halves of the visual fields of both eyes; thus, damage involved either the right or left occipital areas. The hemianopic patients could be differentiated, with ERPs, from both normal persons and from brain-damaged persons who did not have visual defects. The most striking difference was the depressed amplitude of an early positive wave, peaking between 50 and 60 msec. A follow-up study by Vaughan and Katzman (1964) confirmed the usefulness of positive (latency 50–60 msec) components of the ERP in identifying patients with hemianopic defects involving the central 10 degrees of visual field. In addition, they reported that visual disorders could be localized by recording both ERPs and the electroretinogram (ERG). For example, retinal disease was found to be associated with changes in both ERP and ERG (electrical activity of the retina) with stimulation of the involved eye. Optic nerve disease was indicated by loss or suppression of the ERP with stimulation of the involved eye, accompanied by a normal ERG. Damage of areas before the optic chiasm (optic nerve) were associated with loss of the ERP. Damage in areas between the lateral geniculate bodies and visual cortex were associated with loss of the early visual ERP components and preservation of the later ones.

The results of a number of studies suggest that the visual ERP may be used as a test of visual acuity. For example, Harter and White (1968) found that when a checkerboard stimulus pattern was in sharp focus, there was a large negative visual ERP component at 100 msec and a positive wave at 180 msec. As the image was defocused (contours of the checkerboard pattern were degraded), there was a progressive decrease in amplitude of these two components. White and Bonelli (1970) found that ERP amplitude with binocular stimulation was greater with focused than with defocused images. Further, the degree of binocular summation shown by the VEPs was also related to quality of the image, because summation was maximal with sharply focused patterns. In addition, White and Hansen (1975) tested the effects of presenting images, which differed in focus, to the two eyes. This technique produces image relationships similar to clinical cases of amblyopia, in which the image seen by one eye is extremely dim or defocused. In some cases, it was observed that one eye gave a stronger contour response than the other. The studies by White and his colleagues show that the visual ERP can be used to test visual acuity and can prove useful in the prescription of corrective lenses to a population that is difficult to test—for example, the very young and other nonverbal individuals.

Visual ERPs were measured in children suffering from amblyopia by Lombroso, Duffy, and Robb (1969). The visual ERP to a patterned light was abnormally depressed when obtained with the amblyopic eye, whereas unpatterned light produced no difference for normal and amblyopic eyes. This suggested that the cortex is the major site of defect in this condition because it is here that cells responding to pattern or shape are found. A volume edited by Bodis-Wollner (1982) contains accounts of a number of studies that used visual ERPs in neurology and in diagnosing visual problems. The articles include studies of visual ERPs in glaucoma, retinal disease, and amblyopia. This volume is recommended to those interested in a more detailed account of clinical applications in this field.

An interesting application of the visual ERP has been described by Kinney and McKay (1974), who have used it to distinguish between individuals with differing types of color vision defects. They tested normals, deuteranopes (red–green confusion), protanopes (insensitivity to deep red), and one tritanope (red–blue–green confusion). The persons with normal color vision produced visual ERPs to patterns formed by color differences, whereas the color-defective individuals produced no ERPs to targets formed of colors they could not discriminate. Again, this type of approach could be used in testing color vision of persons incapable or unwilling to give accurate verbal responses.

Developmental Visual ERPs.   The visual ERP to light flashes was obtained for low birth weight infants and compared to a group of full-term infants at 40 weeks postconceptional age for both groups (Kurtzberg, 1982). Only 51% of the low birth weight infants had normal occipital visual ERPs at 40 weeks postconceptional age. Visual ERP abnormalities persisted in 75% of the low weight babies at the age of 1 year.

Another technique of stimulation to obtain visual ERPs is that of pattern stimulation, involving reversals of black-and-white checkerboards or gratings. The occipital pattern ERP from the full-term newborn consists of a small positive wave at about 175 msec, followed by a negative component at 250 msec, and a positive peak at about 350 msec after reversal (Kurtzberg & Vaughan, 1985). The pattern ERP recorded from various scalp areas at various ages from newborn to 6 months is shown in Fig. 16.2. Note the prominence of components at the occipital location and the increasing complexity of waveforms with age. The prominent occipital component indicates the importance of this area in pattern perception, and the increase in wave complexity reflects development of neurons in the infant's visual system.

By changing the size of elements within the pattern (e.g., check-sizes) it is possible to estimate visual acuity of infants. If a visual ERP is not obtained with one check-size, then larger checks are used until a response is elicited. If no ERP is obtained, even with large check-sizes, then a visual problem might exist. The visual ERPs to varying check-sizes are a function of maturation level of the infant and integrity of the visual system.

Visual ERPs in Down's Syndrome Infants.   A study was done to compare visual ERPs of Down's Syndrome infants with age (6 months) and gender-matched non-Down's Syndrome babies (Karrer, Karrer, Bloom, Chaney, & Davis, 1998). Behavioral differences have not been widely reported in Down's Syndrome infants during the first 6 months of life. In their study, Karrer found no differences in attentional behavior of their two groups of infants, but could differentiate them through ERPs. The Down's Syndrome infants had significantly larger ERPs and showed little decrease in ERPs with repetitive stimulus experience (little habituation, a simple form of learning) compared to normals. The authors concluded that their results support the hypothesis that inhibitory cerebral processes and memory processes are deficient in the brains of Down's Syndrome infants.

The N400 in Dyslexia.   It has been estimated that 4% of children have difficulty in learning to read or to write (Helenius, Salmelin, Service, & Connolly, in press). Deficits in auditory and visual processing of verbal materials appear to be involved in the disorder.

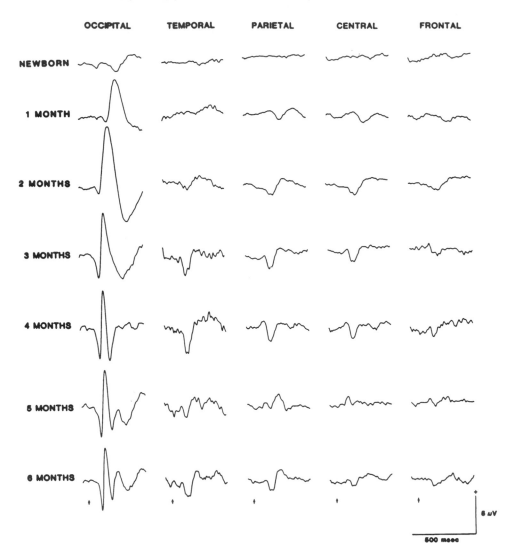

FIG. 16.2. Mean pattern visual ERP recorded from a group of normal full-term infants from birth through 6 months. The occipital response recorded in the newborn consists of a small positive-negative-positive complex with peak latencies of 175, 250 and 350 msec after pattern reversal. The latency of the major positive component progressively decreases throughout the first 6 months of life. Secondary components begin to develop at 1 month, but do not become prominent until 2 months. Pattern reversal occurs at arrow. (Photo courtesy of Dr. D. Kurtzberg.)

Helenius and colleagues noted that at least one previous study showed that the N400 response was delayed in dyslexics compared to controls. Recall that the N400 component of the ERP occurs when sentences end with inappropriate or unexpected words (see chapter 6). Helenius et al. used MEG to study ERPs of dyslexic and normal readers. The N400 responses to inappropriate endings were maximal at left superior temporal cortex for both groups. Where the dyslexics differed was in the latency and amplitude of the N400 response, because it began about 100 msec later and was weaker in the dyslexics. The N400 was judged as the most negative peak occurring between 300 and 600 msec postcritical word. The authors concluded that word recognition for the dyslexic group was not as efficient.

Summary.   The visual ERP shows development of the infant visual system and can provide estimates of visual acuity. Normative developmental data could allow the prescription of corrective lenses in infants whose acuity is deficient. Visual ERPs show differences in Down's Syndrome infants that may not show up behaviorally prior to 6 months of age. Preliminary evidence indicates that the N400 response of dyslexics to inappropriate sentence-ending words are slower in latency and smaller in amplitude than for normal readers.

EEG and ERP in the Evaluation of Nervous System Disorders

The EEG in Epilepsy and Other Abnormalities.   Soon after Berger's (1929) publication about recording brain activity from the intact human scalp, clinicians began to use the technique in diagnosing neurological problems. Among the disorders that produce abnormal EEG patterns are tumors, encephalitis, epilepsy, meningitis, and drug overdose. The most significant abnormalities in the waking adult are (a) delta waves, (b) spike activity, (c) theta waves of 4 to 7 Hz (not always abnormal), and (d) asymmetry of wave frequency in the two hemispheres. Brain lesions may suppress the alpha rhythm on the side of damage. Delta waves are commonly associated with brain damage (from hemorrhage or tumor) when they occur in an awake person, and are often observed over the injured area. Spike wave activity is often seen in convulsive disorders, such as epilepsy. In patients with petit mal epilepsy (less severe than grand mal), a 3-per-second spike wave is common. (See Fig. 16.3 for a sample of some normal and abnormal brain wave patterns.) Patients with temporal lobe or "psychomotor" epilepsy often show spike complexes that occur over the affected lobe. The EEG is a safe, noninvasive procedure that is useful in detecting abnormal brain activity. One drawback of the EEG is in the interpretation of "borderline" records, because these types of records show up in about 20% of the normal population (Simpson & Magee, 1973).

The ERP in "Brain Death."   The "isoelectric" or "flat line" EEG is considered an indicator of brain death when confirmed at two examinations within 24 hrs (Trojaborg & Jorgensen, 1973). The EEG is judged to be flat if it is less than 2 μV in amplitude. Trajaborg and Jorgensen explored the question of whether visual or somatosensory ERPs could be recorded in 50 patients who were unconscious, artificially respirated, and had an isoelectric EEG. Nineteen of the patients evidenced ERPs to visual and somatosensory stimulation, and nine of these subsequently regained spontaneous cortical activity. Three of nine patients recovered consciousness, and one was discharged from the hospital before the completion of the study. If the flat-line EEG was used as the criterion for brain death, then the three persons who subsequently regained consciousness might have been taken off their respirators.

Beck, Dustman, and Lewis (1975) also found ERPs to be more useful than EEG in determination of "brain death." They cited a case of a 41-year-old woman in a coma who produced a flat EEG. However, stimulation with flashes of light resulted in a visual ERP indicating that her brain, although severely damaged, was still alive and could respond to sensory stimulation. These results argue for the superiority of the ERP to raw EEG in the evaluation of brain death.

Brain Stem Potential Recordings in Neurological Diagnoses.   The finding by Jewett, Romano, and Williston (1970) that responses from the subcortical brain stem of humans could be elicited by auditory stimuli and recorded at the vertex on the scalp has led to the use of this technique in evaluating subcortical function. Starr and Achor (1975) reported auditory brain stem potentials to be useful in evaluating the mechanisms of coma and in localizing midbrain and brain stem tumors. They pointed out that the brain stem potential is independent of attention level, that latencies and components vary systematically, and they are abolished by damage to the auditory system. The response consists of a series of seven com-

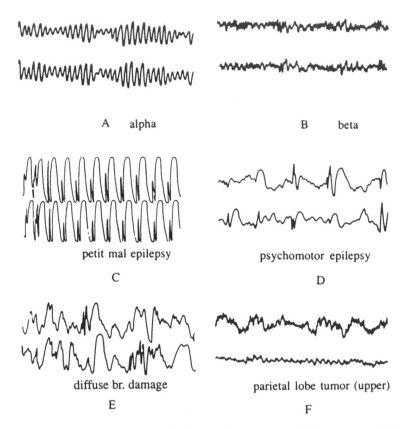

A   alpha

B   beta

petit mal epilepsy

C

psychomotor epilepsy

D

diffuse br. damage

E

parietal lobe tumor (upper)

F

FIG. 16.3. Electroencephalograms. (A) Normal alpha rhythm. (B) Beta waves. (C) Three-per-second spike waves in petit mal epilepsy. (D) Spikes and spike waves from temporal lobes in psychomotor epilepsy. (E) Numerous abnormal wave forms in a child with diffuse brain damage ("hypsarrhythmia"). (F) Delta wave focus (upper portion) in parietal lobe tumor.

ponents (labeled I through VII) that occur during the first 10 msec after stimulation and are of very low amplitude (less than 1 μV). Responses to binaural stimulation can be measured by placing an active electrode at C_z and the reference electrode on the right earlobe. Stimulation may be provided by auditory clicks at a rate of 10 per second. Figure 16.4 shows an auditory brain stem potential.

Starr and Achor (1975) compared the brain stem responses of six normal subjects with a variety of patients whose potentials were measured at bedside. They concluded that the finding of normal brain stem potentials in a comatose patient suggests that the coma is due to metabolic (e.g., uremia) or toxic (e.g., drug overdose) causes, and that the brain stem has been spared. The absence of all components after Wave III was associated with a tumor that damaged the midbrain. The absence of all waves after I was correlated in another case with damage to the cochlear nucleus (medulla). Wave I was related to activity in the auditory portions of the 8th cranial nerve.

In another set of clinical observations, Starr and Hamilton (1976) correlated abnormalities of the auditory brain stem potential with confirmed (at operation or autopsy) locations of brain damage. They reported that the midbrain must be intact for Waves IV through VII to occur. Widespread brain stem lesions were correlated with the absence of all components after Wave I. Extensive brain stem lesions followed anoxia in three patients who showed a Wave I that was normal in amplitude but delayed in latency. Wave I represents the initial com-

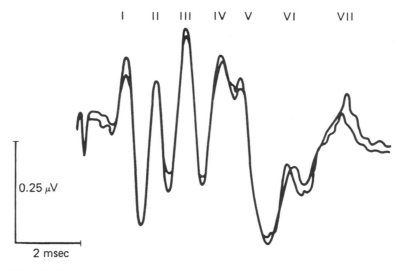

FIG. 16.4. Auditory brain stem responses from normal subject in response to monaural click signals, 65 dB SL, presented at 10 per second. Clicks were presented to right ear and recordings derived from vertex and right earlobe electrodes (C_z-A_2). Total of 2,048 click trials were used to form each of two averages presented. Roman numerals I through VII designated sequence of upward peaks comprising response. Note that amplitude calibration is in submicrovolt range and sweep duration is 10 msec. In this figure, positivity at vertex (C_z) electrode is in upward direction.

ponent of 8th cranial nerve activity. The second wave includes secondary activity in the 8th nerve plus activity in the superior olive and trapezoid body (both lower pons). Wave III has been localized to the pons, whereas IV and V appear to be generated near the inferior colliculus. Waves VI and VII reflect activity in the neurons transmitting impulses from thalamus and to auditory cortex (Vaughan & Arezzo, 1988).

ERPs in Clinical Neurology

Multiple Sclerosis.   The use of pattern-evoked visual ERPs in clinical neurology gained impetus after the report of Halliday, McDonald, and Mushin (1973), in which delays in the visual ERP were recorded in patients suffering from multiple sclerosis (MS). A combined battery of ERPs to different check-sizes, brain stem-evoked potential, and somatosensory ERP was compared to magnetic resonance imaging (MRI) in the diagnosis of MS (Geisser et al., 1987). The visual ERP was considered abnormal if the P100 was greatly delayed or if the waveform was deviant or absent. The criteria for abnormal brain stem potentials were long central transmission (latency difference between Waves I and V) and poorly defined or absent components of the waveform. The somatosensory ERP was considered abnormal if central transmission was delayed. The MRI was used to detect areas where neurons lost their myelin covering. The ERP battery had a sensitivity of 90.5%, compared with 71.4% for MRI in diagnosing 23 patients with possible MS. The authors pointed out that although ERPs may fail to show lesions well-defined by MRI, they detect degeneration too small to be detected by MRI. Thus, MRI and ERPs are complementary diagnostic techniques. A follow-up study by Novak, Wiznitzer, Kurtzberg, Geisser, and Vaughan (1989) evaluated 111 patients with suspected MS, and 16 with a definite diagnosis, with pattern ERPs. They found that the use of several check-sizes, along with half visual field stimulation, led to increased sensitivity of visual ERPs in diagnosing MS.

CNS Degenerative Disease.   Cerebral and spinal somatosensory ERPs were recorded in children with CNS degenerative disease by Cracco, Bosch, and Cracco (1980). The ERPs were obtained at various spinal cord levels, and at C_z, to peroneal nerve (back of knee) stimulation. The cerebral ERPs were absent in 14 of the 17 patients, and conduction velocity over spinal cord segments was delayed in 12 of the patients. Celesia (1982) reported that delayed or absent pattern visual ERPs have been reported in optic neuritis, optic atrophy, and compression of the optic nerve. He stated that ERPs are useful in determining early lesions of the optic nerves and in monitoring early compression of the optic nerve by tumors. Further, the ERPs can be used to quantify the effects of surgery, because they show restoration with postoperative improvement in visual function.

Huntington's Chorea.   Huntington's Chorea (HC) is a severe degenerative disease of the CNS that is inherited. It is considered to be a "subcortical dementia" because brain degeneration occurs in subcortical structures such as the midbrain. Patients with subcortical dementias, including Parkinson's disease and HIV disease, show delayed ERP for sensory components (N1 and P2) as well as for later cognitive components such as N2 and P300 (Johnson, 1992). However, persons with "cortical dementia," such as Alzheimer's, show normal sensory ERPs but delayed latencies for late components. Persons who had one parent afflicted with HC are said to be at-risk for developing this disease. At least two studies have found decreased visual ERPs in patients already suffering from HC. Lawson, Barrett, Kriss, and Halliday (1984) studied the visual ERPs of 9 HC patients, 18 at-risk individuals, and 15 control subjects. The P100 responses for HC patients were reduced in amplitude, but the at-risk and control groups did not differ.

Parkinson's Disease.   Parkinson's is a motor disorder caused by a deficiency in dopamine delivery to basal ganglia structures important in the control of movement. A study was conducted to compare the auditory ERPs of nondemented, medicated, Parkinson's patients with age- and education-matched controls (Philipova, Gatchev, Vladova, & Georgiev, 1997). The medication was to supplement dopamine levels. Participants counted tones in one condition and discriminated low and high tones, through a speeded reaction time task, in another (sensorimotor task). The investigators reported a decrease in N1 and P3 amplitudes and a prolongation of N2 latency during the sensorimotor task. Parkinson's patients also had slower RT than normals.

Alzheimer's Disease.   This is a progressive and degenerative neurological disease that is often difficult to diagnose definitively. A definitive diagnosis is possible only after histological studies of brain tissue at biopsy or autopsy. The disease is characterized by severe behavioral changes due to loss of cognitive functions, with memory loss being the most noticeable.

It has been pointed out that most studies of auditory ERPs in Alzheimer's disease have found prolonged P300 latency compared to elderly controls (Holt et al., 1995). The researchers used an auditory odd-ball paradigm to compare probable Alzheimer disease patients with controls matched for age, sex, handedness, and education. The P300 was measured at frontal, parietal, central, and occipital locations, at midline and over right and left hemispheres. The Alzheimer's group had smaller P300s compared to controls at all sites, and the difference was most pronounced at parietal and central locations. Also, in the Alzheimer's group, P300 was largest at frontal sites, whereas the controls had the largest P300s at parietal locations. It was concluded that P300 is reduced (not abolished) in Alzheimer's and is differently distributed, providing "some support for the hypothesis of multiple generators of P300 that are differentially affected by the disease process" (Holt et al., 1995, p. 264). In another approach, the N400 component was recorded in patients with probable Alzheimer's and asymptomatic elderly controls (Casteneda, Ostrosky-Solis, Perez, Bobes, & Rangel, 1997). The ERPs were recorded during a semantic categorization task in which 50% of the stimuli were congruent and 50% were incongruent. Significantly smaller N400s occurred to incongruent stimuli in patients compared to controls. The N400 to congruent stimuli did not differ. The investigators suggest that the difficulty of probable Alzheimer's patients in processing incongruent stimuli could be due to damage in cortical association areas.

Progressive Supranuclear Palsy.   A relatively rare type of subcortical dementia (progressive supranuclear palsy (PSP) was examined with ERPs (Johnson, 1992; Johnson, Litvan, & Grafman, 1991). This degenerative disorder involves a number of subcortical structures, but spares cortical connections. In Johnson et al. (1991), early and late components of the ERP were examined in PSP patients and matched controls during choice reaction time. Compared with normal controls, the PSP patients had reduced amplitudes and delayed responses for both the P2 and P300 components. Reaction times were slower and errors more numerous in patients. Nevertheless, the scalp distributions of all components were unaltered in the PSP patients as was the manner in which the ERP component amplitudes varied with the experimental variables. The pattern of results indicated that stimulus identification or categorization processes are disrupted in PSP patients. Johnson (1992) used a variety of psychological tasks, including short-term memory, sentence completion, and left–right mental rotation tasks with PSP patients and matched controls. The delayed and less prominent P2 and P300 components for patients versus controls during the performance of these tasks indicates that a slowing and degradation of information processing beginning in the sensory processing stages underlie the cognitive deficits shown in PSP. Johnson suggested that neuronal loss in the caudate nucleus of the basal ganglia is a possible physiological substrate for the deficit.

Human Immunodeficiency Virus (HIV).   Human immunodeficiency virus (HIV) infection is associated with neurological complications in many patients. Estimates of the frequency of behavioral, motor, and cognitive deficits in acquired immunodeficiency disease (AIDS) patients varies from 32% to 87% (Ollo, Johnson, & Grafman, 1991). There are specific HIV infections that can occur, such as HIV encephalitis. The appearance of dementia in late stages of HIV disease may occur with other opportunistic infections, tumors, or metabolic changes. Both the ERP and EEG have been found useful in detecting nervous system changes before behavioral changes occur. For example, Ollo et al. (1991) recorded ERPs from HIV-positive men with no physical illness or neurologic involvement. One-half of the subjects had AIDS or AIDS-related complex (ARC). This latter half showed reduced P300 amplitudes and delayed P2 and P300 responses to auditory and visual stimuli. The P300 results show alterations in stimulus evaluation and processing speed at early stages of the disease, a time when cognitive deficits are not noticeable through other measures.

In another study, P300s were recorded from 76 HIV positive subjects either two or three times over a 6-month period (Messenheimer, Robertson, Wilkins, Kalkowski, & Hall, 1992). The P300 latencies increased over time for both symptom-free and individuals infected with AIDS and ARC. The ERP changes were not associated with any clinically apparent progression of the disease. Baldeweg et al. (1993) pointed out that motor problems are among the earliest and most common signs of brain impairment produced by HIV disease. Baldeweg and colleagues used EEG to study both symptomatic and asymptomatic HIV patients. They found that motor performance did not differ for patients, but that the EEG in patients with symptoms showed consistent increases in theta, alpha, and beta wave amplitudes. The amplitude increases were observed from different scalp areas during resting compared to motor activation. These findings suggest simultaneous involvement of several motor areas perhaps due to an impairment in subcortical integration. The authors suggested that because the EEG showed changes and motor performance did not, then the EEG may be a more sensitive way to assess treatment effects before motor abnormalities appear in HIV patients.

Summary. A number of studies indicate the potential usefulness of EEG and ERPs in the detection and diagnosis of neurological disorders. Although only a few representative studies have been presented here, there are many investigations in progress at various hospitals, clinics, and laboratories, indicating that brain electrophysiology in general, and ERP in particular, is serving the clinician as an important diagnostic tool, and as a means for understanding various disorders. Some of the disorders examined include Alzheimer's disease, Parkinson's disease, multiple sclerosis, progressive supranuclear palsy, Huntington's chorea, and the neurological consequences of AIDS.

Physiological Responses and Behavioral Disorders

Brain ERPs and Psychiatric Diagnosis. Several investigators have developed approaches that result in differential ERPs with psychiatric patients and normal subjects. For example, Callaway, Jones, and Layne (1965) recorded auditory ERPs to 1000- and 600-Hz tones from schizophrenic patients and normal control subjects. The tones were presented randomly and were equated for loudness at about 65 db. In normal subjects, the two tones produced very similar ERPs, but in schizophrenics, the ERPs were different. This difference was later attributed to greater variability in the responses of schizophrenics (Callaway, Jones, & Donchin, 1970). Callaway (1975) suggested that the high degree of ERP variability in schizophrenics is partly related to the unstable and variable thought processes of these patients. However, he believed that ERP variability is of limited value in studying schizophrenia, because, among other reasons, patients differing in diagnostic category (e.g., depression) also produce highly variable ERPs.

Another approach has been that of Shagass and associates, who used the somatosensory ERP to study "recovery functions" in psychiatric and nonpsychiatric patients (Shagass, 1972). The technique involved the presentation of two electric shock stimuli, in close succession (intervals between stimuli varied from 20–200 msec), and measuring the amplitude of the second ERP relative to the first. The amplitude ratio of the second ERP to the first is the measure of recovery of cortical excitability after stimulation. The higher the ratio, the greater the recovery. Figure 16.5 from Shagass and Schwartz (1964) shows that somatosensory ERP recovery ratios during the first 20 msec were greater in nonpatients than in patients. Thus, the initial phase of recovery was delayed or reduced in patients with behavior disorders. The amount of recovery in the visual ERP was also found to be reduced in psychiatric patients in a number of studies cited by Shagass (1972).

The ERP approach of Callaway in studying psychiatric disorders tended to emphasize changes in the response that took place 100 msec or more after the stimulus, and that of Shagass focused on components that occurred within 100 msec after stimulus presentation, especially the first 20 msec. Another approach is to examine the relationship between psychiatric disorders and the CNV. For example, McCallum and Walter (1968) reported that persons suffering from severe anxiety neurosis had CNV waves that were much lower in amplitude than those of normal controls, especially when a distracting stimulus was introduced.

An interesting finding is that of increased frontal CNV in schizophrenics (Tecce & Cole, 1976). The observation that frontal CNV amplitude also increases in head injury suggests to Tecce and Cattanach (1987) that neural disinhibition (or less brain control) might be a factor in producing this effect. An international pilot study, which standardized procedures in various laboratories, studied CNV in mental illness (Timsit-Berthier et al., 1984). Depressed patients displayed disruption in CNV development, and a portion of the CNV wave (designated *M2*) was selective for schizophrenia.

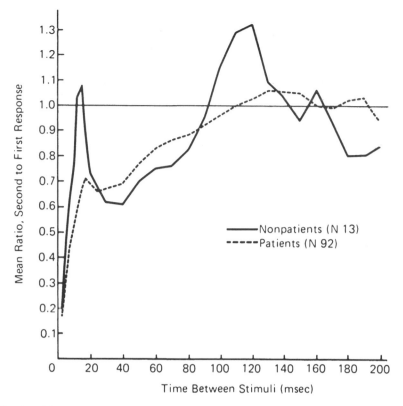

FIG. 16.5. Mean somatosensory (primary component) recovery curves for 13 nonpatients and a heterogeneous sample of 92 psychiatric patients. Note biphasic pattern of curve in nonpatients and greater recovery at 20 msec. than by patients.

Another ERP that has been studied in relation to behavior disorder is the P300. For example, Roth and Cannon (1972) compared this late positive wave in 21 schizophrenics and a group of controls matched for age and race. The late waves of the schizophrenics were significantly lower in amplitude than for nonpatients. It was also reported that schizophrenics evidenced reduced P300 amplitudes and increased RTs to low probability targets, and decreased P180 latencies to high probability nontargets (Roth, Pfefferbaum, Kelly, Berger, & Kopell, 1981). Later investigators have asked whether the reduced P300 amplitudes observed are due to behavioral differences that affect information processing or to an underlying brain abnormality. This question was partially answered in a study by Salisbury et al. (1994), who noted that reduced amplitude of P300 in schizophrenics and especially as recorded from over the left temporal lobe have been reported. In their own study, Salisbury and colleagues manipulated the difficulty of auditory stimulus discriminations (loudness and pitch) as ERPs were measured in schizophrenics and normal controls. Reduced amplitude P300s were found at left temporal areas for schizophrenics and the researchers believe that this reflects a deficit in the brain areas responsible for generating P300. This conclusion is supported by the fact that when discriminations were easy, and performance improved, they still observed reduced P300 amplitudes and these abnormal P300 asymmetries in schizophrenics.

An extensive study that included 135 patients at the onset of their first psychotic episode, 146 relatives, and 113 normal controls was undertaken by Katsanis, Iacono, and Beiser (1996). Visual ERPs were measured while all groups were presented with light flashes of four different intensities. The visual ERPs for patients diagnosed as schizophrenic, at this early stage of their illness, did not show deficits in processing of simple sensory stimuli when compared to the other groups.

Summary.   A number of studies have reported altered ERPs for psychiatric patients. It is still not clear whether these differences are due to behavioral factors that affect these patients or to some underlying brain abnormality. Recent evidence suggests that, at least for chronic schizophrenics, there may be some underlying brain pathology.

Psychopathy.   The P300 responses of psychopaths and nonpsychopaths were recorded to targets and nontargets in a visual performance task (Raine & Venables, 1988). The P300s differed for the two groups in that the psychopaths had longer P300s to targets and more sustained positivity than nonpsychopaths. The authors interpreted these results as indicating enhanced ability to attend to events of interest. In a review of ERP studies of psychopathic adults and antisocial adolescents, Raine (1989) argued that under certain circumstances, psychopaths evidence information-processing proficiencies and are clearly different from schizophrenics in terms of P300 responses. Raine contended that when a task is of interest, the psychopath shows evidence of increased attentional processes, hence the larger P300s in those instances. On the other hand, when the task is one requiring sustained attention to stimuli of little interest, then one may expect to see diminished P300s. Based on the findings of enhanced attentional processing with interesting stimuli, Raine concluded that a sensation-seeking model of psychopathy is supported. By this, he meant that the psychopath is a pathological stimulation-seeker, and as such would be expected to be especially attracted to stimulating events. Raine explained that it is important to provide hypotheses around which further research may be done, and the main weakness in ERP studies of psychopathy is that they were conducted outside a conceptual framework, resulting in different methodologies and fragmented findings that are difficult to integrate.

When studies of the relationship between ERPs and behavior disorders were first begun in the 1960s, researchers had high hopes for the use of the technique both for differential diagnosis, and as an aid to understanding the neurological bases of these disorders. These early goals have still not been completely realized, but slow progress is being made.

EEG and Schizophrenia.   In a review, Itil (1977) concluded that the most important finding in EEG research relating to schizophrenia is that patients have less well-organized alpha activity and more low voltage fast activity (beta) than normals. He postulated that available data support the position that desynchronized high frequency beta activity may be the physiological correlate of a genetic predisposition to schizophrenia. In a representative study, Itil, Hsu, Klingberg, Saletu, and Gannon (1972) found that a sample of 100 schizophrenics had significantly higher voltage beta activity (ranging from 24–33 Hz) than a sample of 100 normal subjects. Itil (1977) suggested that further work is needed to correlate quantitative EEG findings with possible biochemical factors in schizophrenia. According to one biochemical theory, schizophrenics have an excess of the neurotransmitter dopamine in their brains. This notion would be tentatively supported by the high-frequency EEG usually reported for schizophrenics.

Buchsbaum (1977) summarized some EEG research comparing schizophrenics with normals and wrote that patients generally show diminished alpha, faster and more prolonged blocking of alpha by a stimulus, and greater effect of eye opening on alpha. The pattern of high beta and low alpha occurs in normals engaged in processing information. Buchsbaum suggested that these findings indicate that the resting schizophrenic is in a constant state of cortical processing, a condition consistent with psychological models of deficient filtering of sensory input or sensory overload in schizophrenics.

Research on measures of brain activity and schizophrenia increasingly points to structural and metabolic brain abnormalities as underlying factors in the condition. Investigations using neuroimaging techniques, including positron emission tomography, magnetic resonance imaging, and computed tomography have provided evidence for degeneration of brain cortical tissue (Sponheim, Clementz, Iacono, and Beiser, 1994). The resting EEGs of schizophrenic patients have been found to contain more delta (1–3 Hz), theta (3–8 Hz), and beta (13–30 Hz), and less alpha (8–13 Hz) than controls (Sponheim et al., 1994).

In their own study, Sponheim and colleagues examined the EEGs of 102 schizophrenics and 102 normals. Their main purpose was to determine the effects of length of illness, and therefore treatment, on the EEGs of schizophrenics. Hence, the patient group was divided into 44 first-episode and 58 chronic schizophrenics. First, they report that the EEGs of patients contained more delta and theta and less alpha than normals. Second, they found no EEG differences in the acute and chronic schizophrenic patients, suggesting that EEG abnormalities are independent of duration of illness. They presented evidence that EEG abnormalities reflect brain pathology in schizophrenia and not years of treatment, eye movements, or other electrophysiological artifacts. They concluded that the EEG, complemented by neuroimaging techniques, offers promise for discovering defective brain mechanisms in schizophrenia.

Electrodermal Activity and Behavioral Disorders.   In a study by Gruzelier and Venables (1973), larger electrodermal responses were recorded from the right hand than the left in schizophrenics. These and other results supported the idea that schizophrenia is associated with dysfunction in the opposite hemisphere; in this case the left, because a lack of inhibitory influence would be indicated by the excessive right-hand EDA. Depressed patients showed an opposite asymmetry, supporting a theory that these two psychoses are associated with dysfunction of opposite hemispheres. Later work (Gruzelier, 1984), indicated differential EDA in two varieties of schizophrenia. Patients with larger right-hand responses had blunted affect, emotional withdrawal, and reduced energy level, among other symptoms. Those with larger left-hand responses showed more "florid" features, including delusions, hallucinations, and flight of ideas. These results suggest that a control mechanism disruption occurs in the left hemisphere for those with low affect and in the right hemisphere for patients with florid features.

Lader and Noble (1975) observed that patients categorized as anxiety neurotics show elevated levels of skin conductance (SCL) and greater numbers of spontaneous fluctuations (SCRs) than do normal controls. Venables (1975) reviewed a number of studies that investigated the relationship between EDA and schizophrenia. The trend of results seems to indicate that (a) higher-than-normal levels of skin conductance occur in some schizophrenics; (b) chronic schizophrenics appear to show a faster recovery to baseline SCL than normals; (c) chronic schizophrenics show higher levels of spontaneous SCRs than normals; and (d) schizophrenics who give orienting responses do not habituate to the stimulus as quickly as normals. The general trend for EDA seems to support the contention of some investigators that chronic schizophrenics are overaroused, because high levels of EDA indicate elevated SNS activity.

In an application of EDA measures to learning disability, Mangina and Beuzeron-Mangina (1988) proposed that presentation of a variety of stimuli, although maintaining subjects within an "optimal" range of physiological activity, leads to improved academic performance. The EDA measured bilaterally (both hands) is kept within a pre-established optimal range of 6.5 to 8.5 μmhos, during the processing of information. When SCL falls below 6.5 μmho an alerting tone is presented automatically to increase level of arousal. If the SCL continues to drop, light flashes and postural manipulations are used. Relaxation techniques were used when SCL rose above the optimal level. This technique is said to derive its beneficial effects through stimulation of underdeveloped synaptic connections in the brains of the learning disabled. This approach is an application of EDA and activation theory (see chapter 18).

Measures of SCRs and finger pulse volume were recorded in criminals who scored either high or low on a scale of psychopathy (Schalling, Lidberg, Levander, & Dahlin, 1973). They found that the group scoring high in psychopathy had fewer spontaneous SCRs during a tone stimulation period and a poststimulation rest period than the other group. The investigators suggested that the lower degree of responsivity to stimuli in the highly psychopathic subjects might be related to the hypothesis that states of low cortical arousal are a main correlate of psychopathy (see Hare, 1975). No differences in finger pulse volume were found. Beh and Harrod (1998) reported that persons scoring high on a scale measuring psychoticism (P-scale of Eysenck's Personality Questionnaire) showed elevated SCRs and two measures of heart activity that indicated greater sympathetic nervous system arousal than those scoring low on the scale. However, the difference was shown only in a condition where the subjects could avoid an aversive stimulus through their own action (active coping), not under a passive coping condition.

Cardiovascular Activity and Behavioral Disorders.   Venables (1975) indicated that there has been little research attempting to relate heart activity to schizophrenia. A sample study is that of Spohn, Thelford, and Cancro (1971), who reported HR deceleration to pictorial slides in both normal and schizophrenic subjects. These results agree with earlier ones indicating HR deceleration with attention to external stimuli by normal subjects.

Panic Disorder.   Patients suffering from panic disorder were monitored over a 24-hr period with ambulatory HR measurements (Taylor, Telch, & Havvik, 1983). When panic attacks occur, patients often experience a wide variety of unpleasant symptoms, including palpitations, shortness of breath, sweating, faintness, nausea, and sweating, indicating a massive sympathetic nervous system response. The HR monitoring showed significantly elevated levels during panic episodes and suggest the usefulness of this technique with individuals suffering frequent attacks with HR greater than 110 BPM. The monitoring is useful in adjusting the level of medication required to relieve the person's anxiety and bring the excessive physiological response under control. Persons experiencing a panic attack for the first time often show up in hospital emergency rooms because of fears that they are "going crazy" or having a heart attack. In many cases, patients with panic disorder become agoraphobic. Agoraphobia literally means "fear of open spaces." When a panic attack occurs in a particular place, say a theater, the patient may then start to avoid theaters. Often the avoidance generalized to other public places and may start to include supermarkets, malls, or restaurants. Thus, agoraphobia, when it accompanies panic attacks, is characterized by subjective, behavioral, and bodily symptoms. Sometimes the agoraphobic reaction becomes so severe that the patient becomes homebound. In a study by Roth, Telch, Taylor, and Agras (1988), patients suffering from agoraphobia with panic attacks, and a control group, were tested in a laboratory and on a walk in a shopping mall. The patients were tested before and after 15 weeks of treatment with a placebo and exposure therapy or a drug (imipramine) and exposure therapy. The exposure therapy consisted of intensive therapist-assisted exposure to feared situations. On the first test day, patients showed higher HR, SCL, and SCRs in the laboratory, and higher HR before and during the walk than controls. Clinical ratings improved after treatment, and this was associated with reductions in SCL in the patient groups. However, HR levels decreased in patients on the placebo and increased in patients on the drug. Imipramine is known to cause an acceleration in HR. Thus, because the placebo group showed as much improvement as the drug group, the results argue for the use of exposure therapy alone, especially because drugs like imipramine can cause undesirable side effects.

Attention Deficit Hyperactivity Disorder (ADHD).   The effects of a stimulant drug, methylphenidate (Ritalin), on autonomic responses (including HR and SCRs) of hyperactive children with attention deficit disorder was studied by Solanto and Conners (1982). Some workers in this field think that Ritalin is effective because hyperactive children are actually underaroused, and the excessive activity represents an attempt to compensate for the low arousal level. The researchers found that HR was significantly increased with Ritalin but

EDA was not. Improvements in motor performance (RT) were attributed to the reduction of extraneous motor activity produced by the medication. Obviously, much remains to be done in this area, especially on the long-term effects of Ritalin on physiological response and associated health implications.

Depression.   Electroconvulsive therapy (ECT) is still an option used in the treatment of severe depression. Pulse rate and forearm blood flow were measured in depressed patients before and after a series of electroshock treatments (Noble & Lader, 1971). Clinical improvement subsequent to shock treatments was accompanied by increased forearm blood flow. Pulse rate did not change. These investigators suggested that depressive illness is related to a decrease in blood flow, which may involve a disturbance of hypothalamic control.

Psychopathy.   In a review of physiological measures that have been studied in relation to psychopathy, Hare (1975) indicated that most of the cardiovascular research in this area is conceptually based on the orienting response and on Lacey's (1967) hypothesis that sensory intake is associated with HR deceleration, and that rejection of the sensory environment goes with HR increases. In a representative study, Hare (1968) found that the cardiovascular components of the OR (i.e., HR deceleration and finger vasoconstriction) were relatively slow to habituate in psychopaths. This suggests that psychopaths responded as though the stimuli were still novel for a longer time than normals.

Obsessive–Compulsive Disorder.   Obsessive–Compulsive Disorder (OCD) is a disabling condition in which patients experience disturbing obsessive thoughts and are compelled to perform repetitive, often ritualistic, activities to reduce the obsessional anxiety. A number of studies, using EEG and a variety of neuroimaging techniques, have led to suggestions that OCD may be due to dysfunctional activity in the frontal lobes (McCarthy, Ray, & Foa, 1995). In their own study, McCarthy et al. examined heart rate activity and EEG in OCD patients and in both high- and low-anxious control groups. The tasks used were designed to produce intake and rejection on the part of subjects. Intake tasks require concentration on external stimuli; whereas, in rejection tasks, individuals ignore external events that could interfere with performance. One of the study questions had to do with whether cardiac deceleration would occur with intake and acceleration with rejection for OCDs as with normals. One thought was that because OCD patients are so focused on internal events, they might not show the usual pattern; however, they did, as did the high- and low-anxious subjects. Where they differed was in EEG pattern such that, for OCDs, there was elevated low-frequency activity at the right frontal lobe during both intake and rejection tasks. Thus, the results were suggestive of frontal lobe dysfunction specific to OCD patients.

Summary.   The work briefly reviewed here merely scratches the surface with respect to the number of studies that have attempted to relate physiological response to various behavior disorders. However, it is hoped that a feeling for the type of work in the area has been conveyed. Much more remains to be done and established in this potentially fruitful area.

EYE MOVEMENTS AND NEUROLOGICAL DISEASE

The ability to track, or follow, objects with the eyes is impaired in a variety of neurological disorders, including Wernicke's syndrome, Parkinson's disease, Huntington's disease, Alzheimer's dementia, and other diseases that involve brain structures. To maintain a clear image of a moving target, the oculomotor system uses both saccadic and smooth-pursuit eye movements. Saccades correct for errors of position between the fovea and the target, whereas pursuit tracking moves the eye at a speed that matches that of the target. Kenyon, Becker, and Butters (1984) and Kenyon, Becker, Butters, and Hermann (1984) measured both saccadic and smooth-pursuit movements in Wernicke–Korsakoff's syndrome. Korsakoff's syndrome is due to chronic alcoholism coupled with thiamine deficiency. In the acute Wernicke state, the patient is confused and suffers visual disorders. After treatment, the patient reverts to the chronic Korsakoff state characterized by inability to learn new information and impaired ability to recall events prior to onset of illness. Among the perceptual changes are chronic deficits in ability to process visual information. Kenyon et al., (1984) found abnormal saccadic movements 2 to 7 years after the onset of Korsakoff's, a result consistent with cerebellar and frontal lobe dysfunction. Smooth-pursuit eye movements are also abnormal in these patients, indicating that eye movement disorders are a feature of Korsakoff's syndrome and reflect the diffuse damage that this condition produces in the nervous system.

Parkinson's disease causes impairments of movement and is accompanied by mild dementia in half of the patients, and can become severe in a few. The disease is caused by degeneration of pathways that bring dopamine from the substantia nigra of the midbrain to the caudate nucleus and putamen of the basal ganglia. The clinical effects include tremor at rest, rigidity of muscles, and slowness of movement. Parkinson's patients show a number of abnormal eye movements (Kuskowski, 1988). Smooth pursuit movements are interrupted by saccades. Saccadic movements tend to be slowed down so that many saccades are needed to follow a target object. Treatment with L-Dopa does not seem to help the abnormal eye movements (Kuskowski, 1988).

The existence of eye movement abnormalities in patients with Huntington's disease has been known for some time. In fact, the ability to follow a moving finger with the eyes is part of a diagnostic procedure because oculomotor abnormalities are some of the first signs of the disease. Huntington's is an inherited disorder that causes degeneration of the basal ganglia and is characterized by progressive lack of motor control, jerking, writhing movements, dementia, and death. A general absence of rapid eye movements have been noted in these patients, and saccadic movements were missing during reading and REM sleep (Kuskowski, 1988). In addition, smooth pursuit movements are impaired, saccades are slow, and there is difficulty in maintaining eye fixation.

Testing of Alzheimer's patients, depressed patients, and normal elderly control subjects on their ability to track a spot of light across a screen was done by Hutton, Nagel, and Loewenson (1984). The smooth-pursuit tracking performance of Alzheimer's patients was worse than in the other groups, and there was a correlation between tracking dysfunction and severity of the brain disease. Thus, both eye-tracking dysfunction and severity of Alzheimer's are related to the severity of brain deterioration. Diffuse atrophy of cortical neurons occurs in Alzheimer's and degeneration in frontal eye fields (frontal lobes) and parietal cortex affects eye movements (Kuskowski, 1988). A group of Alzheimer's patients was followed over a 1-year period to determine if disease progression was related to eye movement disorders and measures of mental status (Hutton, 1985). Indeed, the findings showed that mental status and quality of smooth pursuit declined over time in the patients. Kuskowski believed that smooth-pursuit tracking will be a useful measure for estimating cognitive ability in severe cases of Alzheimer's when psychological testing becomes difficult.

Summary.   Chapter 11 contained some information regarding abnormal EOG patterns in various behavior disorders. The preceding section indicates that these abnormal patterns are also observed in neurological disorders. Perhaps an underlying feature is some brain anomaly in both the behavior and neurological disorders.

Chapters 15 and 16 have indicated the diversity in applied psychophysiology. Another area of application is that of biofeedback, in which the clinical goal is the learned self-regulation of some physiological response to alleviate a disorder. Many published reports have appeared on this topic over the past 30 years. As a result, the next chapter is devoted solely to a consideration of those biofeedback applications whose expressed purpose has been to treat various ailments, ranging from tension headache to high blood pressure.

REFERENCES

Alho, K., Sainio, K., Sajaniemi, N., Reinikainen, K., & Naatanen, R. (1990). Event-related brain potential of human newborns to pitch change of an acoustic stimulus. *Electroencephalography and Clinical Neurophysiology, 77*, 151–155.

Baldeweg, T., Gruzelier, J. H., Stygall, J., Lovett, E., Pugh, K., Liddiard, D., Muller, J., Riccio, M., Hawkins, D., & Catalan, J. (1993). Detection of subclinical motor dysfunctions in early symptomatic HIV infection with topographical EEG. *International Journal of Psychophysiology, 15*, 227–238.

Beck, E. C., Dustman, R. E., & Lewis, E. G. (1975). The use of the Averaged Evoked Potential in the evaluation of central nervous system disorders. *International Journal of Neurology, 9*, 211–232.

Beh, H., & Harrod, M. E. (1998). Physiological responses in high-P subjects during active and passive coping. *International Journal of Psychophysiology, 28*, 291–300.

Berger, H. (1929). Uber das elektrenkephalogramm des menschen. Translated and reprinted in P. Gloor, Hans Berger on the electroencephalogram of man. *Electroencephalography and Clinical Neurophysiology (Supp. 28)*, 1969, Amsterdam: Elsevier.

Bodis-Wollner, I. (1982). *Evoked potentials.* Annals of the New York Academy of Sciences, Vol. 388. New York: New York Academy of Sciences.

Buchsbaum, M. S. (1977). Neurophysiological aspects of the schizophrenic syndrome. In L. Bellak (Ed.), *The schizophrenic syndrome* (pp. 152–180). New York: Grune & Stratton.

Callaway, E. (1975). *Brain electrical potentials and individual psychological differences.* New York: Grune & Stratton.

Callaway, E., Jones, R. T., & Donchin, E. (1970). Auditory evoked potential variability in schizophrenia. *Electroencephalography & Neurophysiology, 29*, 421–428.

Callaway, E. Jones, R. T., & Layne, R. S. (1965). Evoked responses and segmental set of schizophrenia. *Archives of General Psychiatry, 12*, 83–89.

Castaneda, M., Ostrosky-Solis, F., Perez, M., Bobes, M. A., & Rangel, L. E. (1997). ERP assessment of semantic memory in Alzheimer's disease. *International Journal of Psychophysiology, 27*, 201–214.

Celesia, G. (1982). Steady state and transient visual evoked potentials in clinical practice. In I. Bodis-Wollner (Ed.), *Evoked potentials* (pp. 290–305). New York: New York Academy of Sciences.

Cone-Wesson, B., Kurtzberg, D., & Vaughan, H. G., Jr. (1983, March). *Detection of auditory system dysfunction in very low birth weight infants.* Paper presented at the meeting of the Society for Ear, Nose, & Throat Advance in Children, San Diego, CA.

Cracco, J., Bosch, V. V., & Cracco, R. Q. (1980). Cerebral and spinal somatosensory evoked potentials in children with CNS degenerative disease. *Electroencephalography and Clinical Neurophysiology, 49*, 337–445.

Geisser, B. S., Kurtzberg, D., Vaughan, H. G., Jr., Arezzo, J. C., Aisen, M. L., Smith, C. R., LaRocca, N. G., & Sheinberg, L. C. (1987). Trimodal evoked potentials compared with magnetic resonance imaging in the diagnosis of multiple sclerosis. *Archives of Neurology, 44*, 281–284.

Gruzelier, J. H. (1984). Hemispheric imbalances in schizophrenia. *International Journal of Psychophysiology, 1*, 227–240.

Gruzelier, J. H., & Venables, P. H. (1973). Skin conductance responses to tones with and without attentional significance in schizophrenic and non-schizophrenic psychiatric patients. *Neuropsychologia, 11*, 221–230.

Halliday, A. M., McDonald, W. I., & Mushin, J. (1973). Visual evoked responses in the diagnosis of multiple sclerosis. *British Medical Journal, 4*, 661–664.

Hare, R. D. (1968). Psychopathy, autonomic functioning and the orienting response. *Journal of Abnormal Psychology Monographs, 73*, 1–24.

Hare, R. D. (1975). Psychopathy. In P. H. Venables & M. J. Christie (Eds.), *Research in psychophysiology* (pp. 325–348). New York: Wiley.

Harter, M. R., & White, C. T. (1968). Effects of contour sharpness and check-size on visually evoked cortical potentials. *Vision Research, 8*, 701–711.

Helenius, P., Salmelin, R., Service, E., & Connolly, J. F. (in press). Semantic cortical activation in dyslexic readers. *Journal of Cognitive Neuroscience.*

Holt, L. E., Raine, A., Pa, G., Schneider, L. S., Henderson, V. W., & Pollock, V. E. (1995). P300 topography in Alzheimer's disease. *Psychophysiology, 32*, 257–265.

Hutton, J. T. (1985). Eye movements and Alzheimer's disease: Significance and relationship to visuospatial confusion. In J. T. Hutton & A. D. Kenny (Eds.), *Senile dementia of the Alzheimer type* (pp. 3–33). New York: Liss.

Hutton, J. T., Nagel, J. A., & Loewenson, R. B. (1984). Eye tracking dysfunction in Alzheimer-type dementia. *Neurology, 34*, 99–102.

Itil, T. M. (1977). Qualitative and quantitative EEG findings in schizophrenia. In L. R. Mosher (Ed.), *Schizophrenia* (pp. 61–79). Rockville: National Institute of Mental Health.

Itil, T. M., Hsu, W., Klingberg, H., Saletu, B., & Gannon, P. (1972). Digital-computer-analyzed all-night sleep EEG patterns (sleep patterns) in schizophrenics. *Biological Psychiatry, 4*, 3–16.

Jewett, E. L., Romano, M. N., & Williston, J. S. (1970). Human auditory potentials: Possible brainstem components detected on the scalp. *Science, 167*, 1517–1518.

Jewett, D. L., & Williston, J. S. (1971). Auditory evoked far-fields averaged from the scalp of humans. *Brain, 94*, 681–696.

Johnson, R., Jr. (1992). On the relation between exogenous and endogenous ERP component activity: Evidence from patients with a subcortical dementia. *Electroencephalography and Clinical Neurophysiology*.

Johnson, R., Jr., Litvan, I., & Grafman, J. (1991). *Neurology, 41*, 1257–1262.

Karrer, J. H., Karrer, R., Bloom, D., Chaney, L., & Davis, R. (1998). Event-related brain potentials during an extended visual recognition memory task depict delayed development of cerebral inhibitory processes among 6-month-old infants with Down syndrome. *International Journal of Psychophysiology, 29*, 167–200.

Katsanis, J., Iacono, W. G., & Beiser, M. (1996). Visual event-related potentials in first-episode psychotic patients and their relatives. *Psychophysiology, 33*, 207–217.

Kenyon, R. V., Becker, J. T., & Butters, N. (1984). Oculomotor function in Wernicke–Korsakoff's syndrome: II. Smooth pursuit eye movements. *International Journal of Neuroscience, 25*, 53–65.

Kenyon, R. V., Becker, J. T., Butters, N., & Hermann, H. (1984). Oculomotor function in Wernicke–Korsakoff's syndrome: I. Saccadic eye movements. *International Journal of Neuroscience, 25*, 53–65.

Kinney, J. A. S., & McKay, C. (1974). Test of color-defective vision using the visual evoked response. *Journal of the Optical Society of America, 64*, 1244–1250.

Kurtzberg, D. (1982). Event-related potentials in the evaluation of high-risk infants. In I. Bodis-Wollner (Ed.), *Evoked potentials* (Vol. 388, pp. 557–571). New York: New York Academy of Sciences.

Kurtzberg, D., Hilpert, P., & Kreuzer, J. A. (1984). Differential maturation of cortical auditory evoked potentials to speech sounds in normal full term infants and very low birthweight infants. *Developmental Medicine & Childhood Neurology, 16*, 466–475.

Kurtzberg, D., Stapells, D. R., & Wallace, I. F. (1988). Event-related potential assessment of auditory system integrity: Implications for language development. In P. M. Vietze & H. G. Vaughan, Jr. (Eds.), *Early identification of infants with developmental disabilities* (pp. 160–180). New York: Grune & Stratton.

Kurtzberg, D., & Vaughan, H. G., Jr. (1985). Electrophysiologic assessment of auditory and visual function in the newborn. *Clinical in Perinatology, 12*, 277–299.

Kuskowski, M. A. (1988). Eye movements in progressive cerebral neurological disease. In C. W. Johnston & F. J. Pirozzolo (Eds.), *Neuropsychology of eye movements* (pp. 147–176). Hillsdale, NJ: Lawrence Erlbaum Associates.

Lacey, J. I. (1967). Somatic response patterning and stress: Some revisions of activation. In M. H. Appley & R. Trumbull (Eds.), *Psychological stress: Issues in research* (pp. 14–44). New York: Appleton-Century-Crofts.

Lader, M., & Noble, P. (1975). The affective disorders. In P. H. Venables & M. J. Christie (Eds.), *Research in psychophysiology* (pp. 259–281). New York: Wiley.

Lawson, E., Barrett, G., Kriss, A., & Halliday, A. M. (1984). P300 and VEPs in Huntington's Chorea. In R. Karrer, J. Cohen, & P. Teuting (Eds.), *Brain and information: Event-related potentials* (Vol. 425, pp. 592–597). New York: New York Academy of Sciences.

Lombroso, C. T., Duffy, F. H., & Robb, R. M. (1969). Selective suppression of cerebral evoked potentials to patterned light in amblyopia ex anopsia. *Electroencephalography and Clinical Neurophysiology, 27*, 238–247.

Majnemer, A., Rosenblatt, B., & Ridig, P. (1988). Prognostic significance of the auditory brainstem evoked response in high-risk neonates. *Developmental Medicine and Child Neurology, 30*, 43–52.

Mangina, C. A., & Beuzeron-Mangina, J. H. (1988). Learning abilities and disabilities: Effective diagnosis and treatment. *International Journal of Psychophysiology, 6*, 79–90.

McCallum, W. C., & Walter, W. G. (1968). The effects of attention and distraction on the contingent negative variation in normal and neurotic subjects. *Electroencephalography and Clinical Neurophysiology, 25*, 319–329.

McCarthy, P. R., Ray, W. J., & Foa, E. (1995). Cognitive influences on electrocortical and heart rate activity in obsessive–compulsive disorder. *International Journal of Psychophysiology, 19*, 215–222.

Messenheimer, J. A., Robertson, K. R., Wilkins, J. W., Kalkowski, J. C., & Hall, C. D. (1992). Event-related potentials in human immunodeficiency virus infection: A prospective study. *Archives of Neurology, 49*, 396–400.

Noble, P., & Lader, M. (1971). Depressive illness, pulse rate and forearm blood flow. *The British Journal of Psychiatry, 119*, 261–266.

Novak, G. P., Wiznitzer, M., Kurtzberg, D., Geisser, B. S., & Vaughan, H. G., Jr. (1989). The utility of visual evoked potentials using hemifield stimulation and several check sizes in the evaluation of suspected multiple sclerosis. *Electroencephalography and Clinical Neurophysiology, 66*, 16–30.

Ollo, C., Johnson, R., Jr., & Grafman, J. (1991). Signs of cognitive change in HIV disease: An event-related brain potential study. *Neurology, 41*, 209–215.

Philipova, D., Gatchev, G., Vladova, T., & Georgiev, D. (1997). Event-related potentials in Parkinsonian patients under auditory discrimination tasks. *International Journal of Psychophysiology, 27*, 69–78.

Raine, A. (1989). Evoked potentials and psychopathy. *International Journal of Psychophysiology, 8*, 1–16.

Raine, A., & Venables, P. H. (1988). Enhanced P3 evoked potentials and longer P3 recovery times in psychopaths. *Psychophysiology, 24*, 191–199.

Rapin, I. (1974). Testing for hearing loss with auditory evoked responses—Successes and failures. *Journal of Communication Disorders, 7*, 3–10.

Rapin, I., Graziani, L. J., & Lyttle, M. (1969). Summated auditory evoked responses for audiometry: Experience in 51 children with congenital rubella. *International Journal of Audiology, 8*, 371–376.

Regan, D. (1972). *Evoked potentials in psychology, sensory physiology, and clinical medicine*. London: Chapman & Hall.

Roth, W. T., & Cannon, E. H. (1972). Some features of the auditory evoked response in schizophrenics. *Archives of General Psychiatry, 27*, 466–471.

Roth, W. T., Pfefferbaum, A., Kelly, A. F., Berger, P. A., & Kopell, B. S. (1981). Auditory event-related potentials in schizophrenia and depression. *Psychiatry Research, 4*, 199–212.

Roth, W. T., Telch, M. J., Taylor, C. B., & Agras, W. S. (1988). Autonomic changes after treatment of agoraphobia with panic attacks. *Psychiatry Research, 24*, 95–107.

Salisbury, D. F., O'Donnell, McCarley, R. W., Nestor, P. G., Faux, S. F., & Smith, R. S. (1994). Parametric manipulations of auditory stimuli differentially affect P3 amplitude in schizophrenics and controls. *Psychophysiology, 31*, 29–36.

Schalling, D., Lidberg, L., Levander, S. E., & Dahlin, Y. (1973). Spontaneous autonomic activity as related to psychopathy. *Biological Psychiatry, 1*, 83–97.

Shagass, C. (1972). *Evoked potentials in psychiatry*. New York: Plenum.

Shagass, C., & Schwartz, M. (1964). Evoked potential studies in psychiatric patients. *Annals of New York Academy of Sciences, 112*, 526–542.

Simpson, J. F., & Magee, K. R. (1973). *Clinical evaluation of the nervous system*. Boston: Little, Brown.

Solanto, M. V., & Conners, C. K. (1982). A dose-response and time action of autonomic and behavioral effects of methylphenidate in attention deficit disorder with hyperactivity. *Psychophysiology, 19*, 658–667.

Spohn, H. E., Thetford, P. E., & Cancro, R. (1971). The effects of phenothiazine medication on skin conductance and heart rate in schizophrenic patients. *Journal of Nervous and Mental Disease, 152*, 129–139.

Sponheim, S. R., Clementz, B. A., Iacono, W. G., & Beiser, M. (1994). Resting EEG in first-episode and chronic schizophrenia. *Psychophysiology, 31*, 37–43.

Stapells, D. R., & Kurtzberg, D. (1991). Evoked potential assessment of auditory system integrity in infants. *Clinics in Perinatology, 18*, 497–518.

Starr, A., & Achor, L. J. (1975). Auditory brainstem responses in neurological disease. *Archives of Neurology, 32*, 761–768.

Starr, A., & Hamilton, A. E. (1976). Correlation between confirmed sites of neurological lesions and abnormalities of far-field brainstem responses. *Electroencephalography and Clinical Neurophysiology, 41*, 595–608.

Taylor, C. B., Telch, J. J., & Havvik, D. (1983). Ambulatory heart rate changes during panic attacks. *Journal of Psychiatric Research, 17*, 261–266.

Tecce, J. J., & Cattanach, L. (1987). Contingent negative variation. In E. Niedermeyer & F. Lopes da Silva (Eds.), *Electroencephalography: Basic principles, clinical applications and related fields* (pp. 657–679). Baltimore: Urban & Schwarzenberg.

Tecce, J. J., & Cole, J. O. (1976). The distraction–arousal hypothesis, CNV, and schizophrenia. In D. E. Mostofsky (Ed.), *Behavior control and modification of physiological activity* (pp. 162–219). Englewood Cliffs, NJ: Prentice-Hall.

Timsit-Berthier, M., Gerono, A., Rousseau, J. C., Mantanus, H., Abraham, P., Verhey, F. H. M., Lamers, T., & Emonds, P. (1984). An international pilot study of CNV in mental illness: Second report. In R. Karrer, J. Cohen, & P. Teuting (Eds.), *Brain & information: Event-related potentials* (Vol. 425, pp. 629–637). New York: New York Academy of Sciences.

Trajaborg, W., & Jorgensen, E. O. (1973). Evoked cortical potentials in patients with "isoelectric" EEGs. *Electroencephalography and Clinical Neurophysiology, 35*, 301–309.

Vaughan, H. G., Jr., & Arezzo, J. C. (1988). The neural basis of event-related potentials. In T. W. Picton (Ed.), *Human event-related potentials* (Vol. III, pp. 45–96). Amsterdam: Elsevier.

Vaughan, H. G., Jr., & Katzman, R. (1964). Evoked response in visual disorders. *Annals of the New York Academy of Sciences, 112*, 305–319.

Vaughan, H. G., Jr., Katzman, R., & Taylor, J. (1963). Alterations of visual evoked response in the presence of homonymous visual defects. *Electroencephalography and Clinical Neurophysiology, 15*, 737–746.

Venables, P. H. (1975). Psychophysiological studies of schizophrenic pathology. In P. H. Venables & M. J. Christie (Eds.), *Research in psychophysiology* (pp. 282–324). New York: Wiley.

White, C. T., & Bonelli, L. (1970). Binocular summation in the evoked potential as a function of image quality. *American Journal of Optometry and Archives of the American Academy of Optometry, 47*, 304–309.

White, C. T., & Hansen, D. (1975). Complex binocular interaction and other effects in the visual evoked response. *American Journal of Optometry and Physiological Optics, 52*, 674–678.

17

Clinical Applications of Biofeedback

Biofeedback means providing immediate information regarding physiological processes about which the individual would normally be unaware. Thus, a person might be provided with information regarding muscle potentials in the forearm, or level of blood pressure, heart rate, or perhaps the type of brain wave being produced at that moment. According to a basic premise in biofeedback applications, if an individual is given information about biological processes, and changes in their level, then the person can learn to regulate this activity. Therefore, with appropriate conditioning and training techniques, an individual can presumably learn to control body processes that were long considered to be automatic and not subject to voluntary regulation. As outlined in this chapter, there is some evidence to support the basic premise that the provision of feedback has specific effects, for instance, that information about skin temperature and muscle tension can lead to self-altered and regulated levels of each.

The basic premise regarding learned control over physiological responses has theoretical and practical implications. On the theoretical side, it means certain physiological processes controlled by the autonomic nervous system (e.g., blood pressure, heart rate, skin temperature) must be reexamined to determine the extent to which they are subject to voluntary control. On the practical side, it offers the possibility that physical maladies, such as hypertension (high blood pressure) or cardiac arrhythmias (irregular heartbeats), may be alleviated by self-regulation.

The studies reviewed in this chapter represent only a small portion of the clinically oriented biofeedback research that has been generated in the past 30 years, and, hence, they can only be considered as a representative sample of the work performed. The attempt is to describe what clinical researchers have been doing and concluding about their applications of biofeedback to specific human disorders. The potential benefits of this research are great. However, overenthusiastic or premature claims about therapeutic effectiveness could harm the field by reducing its credibility. Again, biofeedback researchers and therapists would do well to heed the advice of Miller (1974), who said that, "this is a new area in which investigators should be bold in what they try but cautious in what they claim" (p. xviii).

An additional research area covered in this chapter is "psychoneuroimmunology." As the name implies, this field examines the relationships among behavior, brain function, and the immune system. It is included in this chapter because factors that influence the immune response, either negatively or positively, have been studied in the context of stress, relaxation and self-regulation. The Association of Applied Psychophysiology and Biofeedback has been active in encouraging psychoneuroimmunology research through inclusion of presentations by keynote speakers and empirical papers at its annual meetings.

There are a number of questions regarding biofeedback training (BFT) that require answers. For example:

1. What is actually learned as a consequence of BFT? Is it an awareness of some internal response, or is it an awareness of associations between stimuli and responses?
2. What are the variables that influence learning, and how do they exert their effect? For example, what are the effects of the quality and quantity of reinforcements used to promote learning?
3. Which physiological responses are most appropriate to modify with respect to a specific disorder? For example, is lowering of blood pressure best achieved through feedback of BP, or is feedback of hand skin temperature more effective?
4. To what extent does transfer of training take place from the clinic or laboratory to real life? That is, can the individual self-regulate a physiological response at home as well as in the clinic?
5. How are the factors of motivation and expectancies to be handled in BFT? Are persons with greater motivation and expectations of success better able to learn physiological self-regulation?
6. To what degree does the BFT situation operate as a placebo effect? Are there nonspecific influences created by the equipment and related procedures because patients believe in their effectiveness?
7. How does BFT compare with other possible approaches to altering physiological response, such as relaxation, meditation, suggestion, or hypnosis?

At the conclusion of this chapter, the reader should have some information about the extent to which these questions have been answered by the representative summary of BFT research presented. Problems of a theoretical and empirical nature that confront biofeedback researchers are discussed by Black and Cott (1977). The question of whether BFT has a specific effect on a target physiological function has sparked a lively debate among psychophysiologists. Comments by Furedy (1987) regarding placebo versus specific effects hold that specific effects of biofeedback still need to be demonstrated. Schellenberger and Green (1987) countered that biofeedback has no specific effects, because it is not the treatment. They contended that studies demonstrate the value of self-regulation (the treatment) for symptom alleviation. These opposing positions require resolution through research showing that BFT leads to self-regulation and that this produces effects that are clinically beneficial. Prior to examining clinical studies, a typical biofeedback situation, aimed at training a person to increase production of alpha EEG, is described.

AN EXAMPLE OF A BIOFEEDBACK TRAINING (BFT) SITUATION

The production of alpha waves may be achieved by almost any person who can generate a relaxed state, with eyes closed, in a quiet room. We define alpha activity here as a regular EEG signal, occurring between 8 and 13 cycles per second, at an amplitude of approximately 20 to 60 μV. It is more difficult to produce alpha activity with the eyes opened (e.g., Brown, 1974).

Let us suppose that our objective is to train increases in the production of alpha activity under eyes-opened conditions and compare this with alpha training under an eyes-closed condition. The EEG may be recorded by some standard bipolar or monopolar electrode placement from over the occipital or parietal areas. Some commercially available equipment only permits the use of the bipolar technique. In this case, an O_2–P_2, or an O_1–P_1 derivation may be used. The EEG activity is filtered and amplified by equipment that is set to produce a signal whenever the activity meets the criteria set up for alpha; in this instance, waves that occur at a frequency of 8 to 13 Hz and at an amplitude between 20 and 60 μV (see Fig. 17.1). The equipment is set up to provide the subject with a tone over headphones every time activity in the alpha range is detected. The tone that occurs with alpha is the feedback indicating to in-

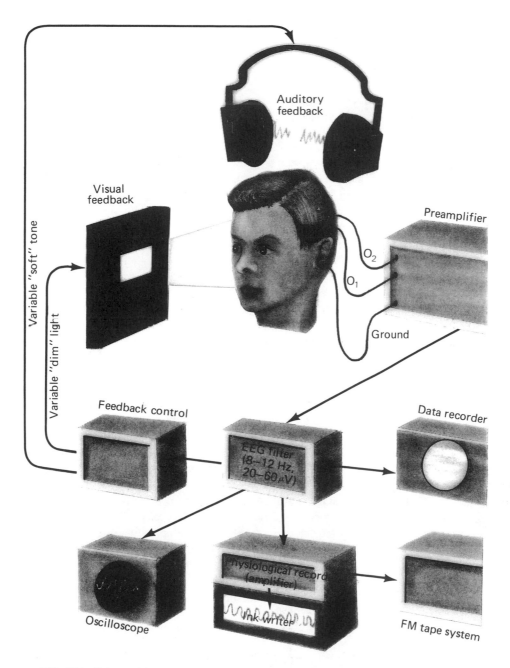

FIG. 17.1. Schematic drawing of alpha wave feedback instrumentation similar to that which might be used in a research setting. The physiological recorder and oscilloscope enable monitoring of the accuracy of EEG biofeedback. The amount of alpha activity is accumulated on the data recorder, which can provide digital readout or printout. Information about amount of alpha production is fed back to the subject via headphones (tone) or visual display (light). This basic equipment array can be used to feed back information of a variety of physiological responses, according to researcher's needs. Sophisticated computer graphics may be displayed to subjects to provide more accurate feedback than simple lights or tones.

367

dividuals that they are achieving the desired response. The output of our alpha detecting equipment will also go to another device that records the amount of alpha activity produced during a given time period, for example, during a 1-min or a 10-min interval. Hence, a tone results when a person is producing alpha waves, and no tone occurs in the absence of alpha. The subject might simply be asked to keep the tone on as long as possible. At the end of each training segment (say, 1 min), the person is informed about the actual amount of alpha produced or is simply told, "Very good, keep up the good work," and is encouraged to keep the tone on for a longer period of time during the next training interval. Monetary rewards or other incentives can also be provided for good performance. The experimenter keeps a record of the amount of alpha activity produced over a number of training trials.

The BFT may continue for a number of days or weeks and a record of performance, plotted as a "learning curve" over the period of the experiment, may be kept. The procedure should include the alteration of "alpha-on" trials with "no alpha" trials. In the latter case, the person is asked to prevent the tone from sounding. The object of this procedure is to allow the subject to clearly differentiate between the alpha and nonalpha state, and it also ensures that increased alpha production is not merely due to unlearned baseline changes. The training in alpha-on and alpha-off (or bidirectionality) helps to clarify for the person what is being done and the sensory consequences involved. It is important, too, because it demonstrates the learned control of being able to turn a physiological response on or off as desired. An eventual goal of BFT is to have the person produce the desired physiological response without the benefit of the electronic equipment providing the feedback.

Ways to achieve this include having subjects practice the production of alpha without the provision of feedback during regular training sessions, between sessions at home, and after training has been completed. Performance with and without feedback can determined—that is, in terms of the percentage of alpha activity—under the two conditions. Alternatively, the feedback signal can be gradually removed so that it is less and less frequently presented over sessions, until it is completely absent. During the gradual removal of the feedback signal, subjects are informed about their level of alpha production after each trial. Subjects may return several months after completion of training to test their retention of alpha-producing skills and for possible retraining sessions. This same basic procedure can be used in attempts to train regulation of other physiological responses such as blood pressure, heart rate, EMG, EDA, and skin temperature. A simple equipment configuration for providing EMG feedback is shown in Fig. 17.2. Many persons practicing BFT use a simpler form of instrumentation. Other practitioners, especially those working in clinic settings, employ sophisticated compter graphics to illustrate control of physiological activity and the degree to which training goals are being met.

The next section, considers physiological measures that have been used in a BFT context in attempts to alleviate specific disorders.

THE ELECTROMYOGRAM (EMG) IN BIOFEEDBACK APPLICATIONS

The EMG has been used extensively in biofeedback applications ranging from the treatment of tension headache to attempts at the alleviation of stuttering.

EMG and Tension Headache

Tension headache usually results from sustained contraction of skeletal muscles of the forehead, scalp, and neck (Friedman & Merritt, 1959). Budzynski, Stoyva, and Adler (1970) re-

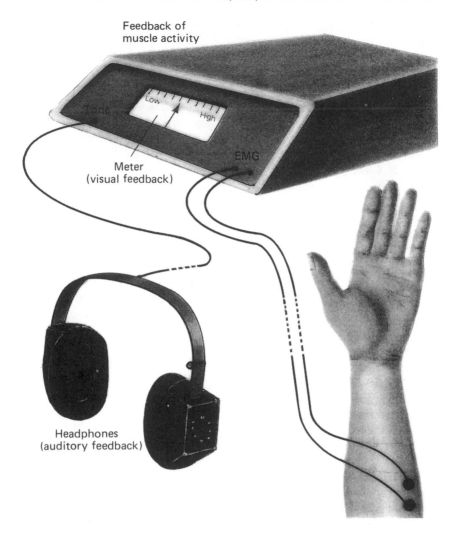

FIG. 17.2. A much simpler biofeedback system than that depicted in Figure 15.1 may be used in clinical applications. The EMG system shown above illustrates the provision of information regarding changes in forearm EMG level. Decreased or increased EMG may be indicated by changes in tone, or lights and amount of change read off a visual scale.

ported alleviation of tension headache by having patients reduce EMG levels in frontalis (forehead) and splenius (neck) muscles through BFT.

The effectiveness of frontalis EMG biofeedback and passive relaxation instructions in treating tension headache was studied by Haynes, Griffin, Mooney, and Parise (1975). The college-student subjects were assigned to a BFT group, a relaxation group, or control group (no treatment). Both of the treatment procedures were more effective than no treatment in reducing the frequency of headaches. Hutchings and Reinking (1976) compared the effectiveness of three forms of muscle relaxation training in tension headache control. The group that had EMG biofeedback-assisted relaxation showed larger gains than the relaxation alone groups. A follow-up study of these patients (Reinking & Hutchings, 1981) indicated that at 6 and 9 months after sessions ended, the most important variable in continued sucess was whether patients still practiced relaxation exercises. Thus, although EMG-assisted relaxation led to faster acquisition of lower muscle activity, other variables were important in determining whether patients continued to use what was learned. Among these were belief in the treatment process and reported changes in personality variables following treatment. The importance of continued practice of relaxation techniques and transfer of the relaxation response to everyday situations are very important for continuance of the improvement initially attained. Thus, EMG/BFT, relaxation techniques, and combinations of the two help to alleviate tension headaches. More information is needed about the duration of the beneficial effects and the relative effectiveness of the various techniques in treating tension headaches.

Reviews of the literature indicate that EMG feedback either alone or combined with relaxation training typically reduces tension headache activity by about 40% to 60% (see Bogaards and ter Kuile, 1994). Rokicki, Holroyd, France, Lipchik, France, and Kvaal (1997) used a combination of EMG feedback and relaxation with a group of young adults with chronic tension headache and compared their progress over six sessions of treatment compared to a matched control group. They also tested a hypothesis regarding the contribution of cognitive factors to improvement by using a headache self-efficacy scale to measure beliefs that headache pain could be managed, and confidence in ability to control headaches in various situations. The results revealed the treatment group to be significantly improved in headache activity and use of pain medication compared to the untreated controls. However, improved scores on the self-efficacy scale indicated that the combination of feedback and relaxation changed beliefs that headaches were beyond control and increased confidence that strategies could be used to prevent or control headaches. In fact, the authors conclude that the cognitive changes produced by the treatment were responsible for the improvements observed, and not reductions in EMG activity. Further research on cognitive changes induced by biofeedback and relaxation is needed.

Summary.   In several of the studies cited, relaxation techniques were as effective as EMG feedback in alleviating tension headache. Clinical researchers need to provide an answer to the following valid question: Why use the EMG devices if relaxation alone can benefit the patient? A number of good relaxation techniques do exist, and these include progressive muscle relaxation, autogenic phrases, breathing exercises, visual imagery techniques, meditation, and various combinations of these. Thus, the clinician has a large number of techniques that could be used alone or in combination with physiological feedback. Whenever relaxation techniques are combined with BFT, it will be difficult to separate out the effects of each in the clinical or research situation. However, most clinicians feel comfortable using BFT combined with relaxation strategies because they maintain that it is important in achieving criterion levels of physiological activity and in selecting the most effective relaxation techniques. Many argue that the biofeedback equipment provides objective indications of physiological change, and the amount of change, as treatment progresses, and it helps to convince patients that they can learn to self-regulate certain physiological responses (such as skin temperature, muscle tension, and heart rate). The relaxation techniques are seen as vehicles to lower autonomic, skeletal, and CNS activity to produce physiological levels that are then reinforced by feedback from the equipment. There is at least one study indicating that frontalis EMG biofeedback led to improvements in tension headache sufferers when relaxation techniques alone failed (Blanchard et al., 1982). The possibility still exists that the equipment produces at least some beneficial results through a placebo effect, that is, a nonspecific influence that the equipment has because the patient believes in its effectiveness.

As stated previously, this is an issue that biofeedback researchers need to address in order to separate out specific and placebo effects. With regard to equipment placebo effects, researchers could compare the effectiveness of BFT provided by equipment versus feedback provided verbally, with no equipment visible, in promoting physiological change. There is some evidence that persons who suffer chronic pain may not be as proficient at discriminating muscle tension build-up as compared to normals (Flor, Schugens, & Birbaumer, 1992). A group of chronic back pain patients and another group of patients who suffered from temporomandibular (TMJ) pain were compared to normals in ability to discriminate levels of muscle tension in the jaw and back muscles, and patients did not fare as well as the normal group. The use of appropriate EMG feedback could help to remedy this deficiency in ability to perceive muscle tension. Flor and Birbaumer (1991) reported that both TMJ pain and chronic back pain patients showed improvements in their symptoms when given EMG feedback that improved their ability to discriminate muscle tension levels.

EMG Feedback and Stuttering

It has been estimated that from 40 to 50 million children in the Western world have a bad stutter (Coleman, 1976). This speech disorder is characterized by blocking of speech or the repetition of initial sounds of words, especially in a socially stressful situation. In an application of EMG feedback to stuttering, Guitar (1975) trained three adult male stutterers to reduce facial and neck EMG prior to speaking selected sentences. Decreases in stuttering were associated with decreased lip EMG in one patient, lower EMG at a laryngeal site in another, and a combination of lip and laryngeal EMG decrease in the third. A systematic program was then instituted with a 32-year-old male stutterer, in which feedback training to reduce EMG during speech resulted in the elimination of stuttering during both telephone and face-to-face conversations. A follow-up showed that stuttering was still substantially improved 9 months after laboratory training had ended.

Lanyon, Barrington, and Newman (1976) found that feedback of masseter (jaw) muscle activity led to a reduction of muscle tension. The reduction in tension was associated with a major reduction in stuttering in the six persons studied. Lanyon (1977) taught 19 stutterers to relax their masseter muscles under conditions of EMG feedback. In a series of three studies, it was found that reduced muscle tension was followed by reduced stuttering. Lanyon also reported that relaxation was generalized to periods of no EMG feedback after explicit instructions and constant reminders to do so were given.

A hypothesis made by Craig and Cleary (1982) was that EMG of the speech musculature is higher for stuttered than for nonstuttered words. They confirmed this hypothesis in a clinical study with three young males (age 10, 13, and 14). The patients were trained to reduce speech muscle tension (levator and superior orbiculoris oris muscles) with EMG feedback. Stuttering was reduced in the clinic, and then was reduced 60% to 80% in the home environment. A 9-month follow-up showed continued improvement.

Summary.   The case studies reported here are uncontrolled; that is, there is no comparison of results for individuals who did not receive the treatment over the study period. However, the use of EMG biofeedback may offer a viable treatment for stuttering. As with any application, further clinical trials and controlled investigations are required to separate biofeedback effects from other treatment variables such as therapist attention, verbal exchanges, suggestions for managing stress, the clinical atmosphere, or simply participating in a self-help program.

EMG Feedback in Neuromuscular Disorder

The amplification and feedback of EMG signals has been found to be helpful in neuromuscular reeducation. Basmajian, Kukulka, Narayan, and Takebe (1975) used EMG feedback to assist patients in improving the strength and voluntary control of muscles that are weak, unreliable, and poorly controlled as a result of a stroke. One condition that may occur after a stroke is "foot drop." Paralytic foot drop is characterized by an inability to contract the muscles that bend the ankle to raise the foot. The patient often wears a brace to assist in walking. Basmajian and colleagues divided 20 patients with foot drop into two therapeutic groups: The first had 40 min of exercise, three times a week for 5 weeks; the second had 20 min of exercise and 20 min of EMG/BFT over the same period. The tibialis anterior muscle (lower leg) was selected for training, because it is the main muscle involved in lifting the ankle. The group receiving BFT showed an improvement in both strength of flexion and range of movement that was approximately twice as great as the other group. In addition, three patients in the BFT group were able to discard their braces.

In another clinical study, Takebe and Basmajian (1976) found that patients treated with a peroneal nerve (leg) stimulator for 5 weeks and those treated with BFT for 5 weeks showed and maintained improvement of their walking pattern as compared to patients who received physical therapy only. These investigators believe that feedback indicating residual muscle activity can play an important role in muscular re-education in stroke patients. Later, Basmajian, Regenos, and Baker (1977) reported that, of 25 patients treated for foot drop, 16 were able to discard their leg braces entirely after 3 to 25 sessions. In addition, age of the patient and duration of the foot-drop condition did not affect the treatment outcome. Failures were related to poor motivation, discontinuance of treatment, spasticity, or concurrent illnesses.

Middaugh (1977) reported on the use of EMG/BFT with patients suffering neuromuscular problems due to nervous system damage. The patients were asked to produce 30-sec contractions in a muscle that was below functional strength. The EMG feedback, in each of the two sessions, was a continuous tone that varied in pitch proportional to the amount of activity. A comparison of results for feedback versus no-feedback trials revealed that EMG activity was an average of 16% higher on feedback trials (a significant difference). Time since injury was not a factor, and all patients showed a positive effect. Thus, Middaugh concluded that EMG feedback had a substantial effect on motor unit recruitment that was independent of locus of nervous system damage or time since occurrence of the injury.

A variety of clinical studies in which EMG feedback was used in attempts to treat symptoms of a wide variety of disorders—including cerebral palsy, poliomyelitis, hemiplegia, torticollis, and rectosphincter incontinence—were discussed by Engel-Sittenfeld (1977). Fairly successful results were achieved with torticollis and rectosphincter responses. Torticollis is a movement disorder in which spasms in the neck muscles cause the head to be twisted back and disrupt normal head control. Alleviation of torticollis through the reduction of muscle tension via EMG feedback has been reported by several investigators (e.g., Cleeland, 1973). Control of the rectal sphincter muscle was achieved by six incontinent patients, age 6 to 54, with BFT (Engel, Nikoomanesh, & Schuster, 1974). Follow-ups at periods ranging from 6 months to 5 years found four patients completely continent and the other two improved.

The use of monetary incentives to enhance EMG control with feedback was studied in five stroke patients with paralysis on one side of the body (Santee, Keister, & Kleinman, 1980). Integrated EMG from tibialis and gastrocnemius muscles during flexion of the affected foot was recorded. The EMG feedback training produced greater range of motion than unassisted practice, and the addition of monetary incentives improved the effects. Biofeedback was used to treat urinary incontinence in four stroke patients by Middaugh, Whitehead, Burgio, and Engel (1989). The training sessions taught patients to attend to bladder sensations, inhibit bladder contractions, and improve voluntary sphincter muscle control. All of the patients were able to achieve and maintain urinary continence.

Summary.   The promising results obtained thus far argue for further clinical evaluation of BFT in treating neuromuscular disorders. Basmajian and Hatch (1979) concluded that

EMG biofeedback is a significant tool in the re-education of weak muscles and the relaxation of hyperactive ones.

EMG Feedback and Anxiety

It is estimated that 5% of persons in the United States suffer from chronic anxiety: "a persistent or recurrent state of dread or apprehension accompanied by signs of physiological arousal" (Raskin, Johnson, & Rondestvedt, 1973, p. 263). The effects of muscle relaxation, achieved through frontalis muscle BFT, on chronically anxious patients was investigated by Raskin et al. (1973). The patients in the Raskin study had not been helped by psychotherapy or medication for the 2-year period before the investigation. All patients reached the criterion of 2.5 μV/min of EMG activity or less, averaged over a 25-min period. The training time of the daily sessions varied from 2 to 12 weeks. Forty percent of the patients improved in self-ratings of anxiety level. The relaxation training had impressive effects on insomnia in 87% of the patients who reported sleep disturbances. In addition, patients with headaches experienced a reduction in frequency and intensity of this symptom.

The effectiveness of frontalis EMG/BFT and muscle relaxation training were compared for 28 anxiety neurotics (Canter, Kondo, & Knott, 1975). One half of them reported panic episodes (e.g., tachycardia, difficulty breathing, etc.) associated with the anxiety. The EMG/BFT resulted in lower levels of muscle activity and greater relief of anxiety than progressive muscle relaxation alone for the majority of patients. Gatchel, Korman, Weis, Smith, and Clarke (1978) showed BFT to be more effective in EMG reduction than false feedback, but there was no differential effect on anxiety reduction. A positive result was obtained by Weinman, Semchuk, Gaebe, and Mathew (1983), who hypothesized that BFT along with relaxation training would be more effective for anxious patients with high amounts of recent life stress than those with low amounts. The results supported the hypothesis, as the high-stress group showed changes on anxiety measures, depression, and EMG, whereas the low-stress individuals showed no change after 10 sessions of biofeedback-assisted relaxation. The high-stress group attributed improvement to the belief that they were in control of their minds and bodies.

Summary. The evaluation of these anxiety studies is made difficult because most of them were uncontrolled. However, the results of several clinical studies and the one controlled investigation suggest that EMG/BFT is helpful with certain types of anxiety.

EMG Feedback and Asthma

Asthma is characterized by episodes of bronchospasm, during which the person has great difficulty in breathing. The bronchospasm (bronchoconstriction) may be initiated by allergens in the environment, by emotional reactions, or both (Bates, Macklem, & Christie, 1971). The effects of frontalis muscle relaxation on peak expiratory flow rate (PEFR) scores in asthmatic children was investigated by Kotses, Glaus, Crawford, Edwards, and Scherr (1976). The PEFR is a measure of efficiency in expelling air from the lungs. The subjects were 36 asthmatic summer campers ranging in age from 8 to 16 years. They were divided into a contingent feedback group, a noncontingent feedback group, and a no-treatment group. The contingent feedback group received a tone for changes in EMG, whereas the noncontingent received tones that were not related to EMG in any systematic way. These two groups participated in nine sessions spread over 3 weeks. PEFR was obtained daily from all 36 subjects by persons who were unaware that it would be used in a study. The EMG training group showed an increase in PEFR over the pretraining level, whereas the noncontingent and no-treatment groups did not evidence a change. The researchers concluded that the reduction of frontalis EMG through BFT was associated with the alleviation of some symptoms of bronchial asthma.

Kotses and his associates repeated these results in a follow-up study (Kotses, Glaus, Bricel, Edwards, & Crawford, 1978). Other studies indicated that PEFR was influenced by changes in facial EMG and not in limb muscles, an effect seen in both asthmatics and normals (Kotses & Glaus, 1981). According to these workers, only facial muscle feedback and airways resistance feedback (information about resistance in breathing structures and lung airways) have produced short-term breathing improvements in asthmatics. Long-term effects of these procedures were examined in a study by Kotses et al. (1991). One group of asthmatic children had BFT to reduce facial tension and a control group of asthmatic children were trained to maintain facial tension at a stable level. The children were followed for a 5-month period after initial training and results led the investigators to conclude that facial relaxation improved long-term lung function in asthmatic children. The long-term improvements depended on both BFT and home practice.

Kotses and colleagues recommended the inclusion of EMG/BFT as a component of asthma self-management programs. They believe that facial relaxation may interrupt the chain of events leading to an asthmatic attack and may lessen or prevent the attack. An interesting aspect of the study was an attitude improvement regarding asthma and a reduction of anxiety measures obtained during the last follow-up session. These changes are reminiscent of those reported for persons undergoing EMG/BFT and relaxation for tension headache discussed previously. Cognitive changes induced by the treatment program may provide a sense of control over the condition for both headache and asthma patients.

A proposed mechanism to explain the underlying relationship between increases in facial muscle tension and decreased pulmonary function was offered by Kotses, Hindi-Alexander, & Creer (1989). They hypothesized that asthma symptoms are worsened by stress via a reflex through which impulses from the facial muscles influence the trigeminal nerve, which then produces increases in vagal activity, thus causing bronchoconstriction. Lehrer, Generelli, and Hochron (1997) attempted a test of this hypothesized vagal–trigeminal pathway in stress-induced asthma. Their experiment was also designed to test another hypothesis that links pulmonary function with thoracic (chest) muscle tension. In the study, asthmatics alternately tensed forehead and shoulder muscles while frontalis and trapezius EMG, EKG, and repiratory impedance were measured.

Kotses' hypothesis would predict decreased pulmonary function (increased respiratory sinus arrhythmia and impedance) during induction of frontalis tension. The thoracic breathing theory would predict decreased pulmonary function during tensing of trapezius muscles. Their findings did not support the Kotses hypothesis that facial muscle tension induced changes in vagal activity are related to changes in pulmonary function. However, Lehrer and colleagues pointed out that their results do not definitively disprove the vagal–trigeminal hypothesis. The data did offer some support for the thoracic breathing theory and an approach to treating asthma that reduces tension in thoracic muscles through training in abdominal breathing and EMG feedback (Peper & Tibbetts, 1992).

A pilot study was conducted to compare the feasibility of respiratory sinus arrhythmia (RSA) versus neck/trapezius EMG as biofeedback techniques with asthmatic patients (Lehrer, Carr, et al., 1997). The RSA refers to heart rate fluctuations during inhalation and exhalation, that is, heart rate speeds up during inhalation and slows during exhalation. Three groups of participants were given RSA biofeedback, EMG feedback, or were wait-list controls. Results supported the further investigation of RSA biofeedback to treat asthma.

In a follow-up study Lehrer and colleagues (Lehrer, Hochron, et al., 1997) re-examined data from a large sample of asthmatics to determine the relationship between EMG and RSA during relaxation training. Two indices of cardiac vagal tone were amplitude of RSA and heart interbeat interval. (Both RSA and interbeat interval are related to activity of the vagus nerve, the main parasympathetic influence on the heart and lungs.) Measures of RSA and frontalis EMG were taken for 33 participants doing progressive muscle relaxation, 31 listening to relaxing music, and 30 wait-list controls. Eight sessions were administered to the two treatment groups. Measures of lung capacity were taken before and after the first and last sessions. The investigators reported evidence of increased vagal tone during relaxation and a relation between relaxation-induced decreases in pulmonary function and increased vagal influence on the heart. There was no association between decreased facial muscle tension and decreased vagal tone or improved pulmonary function of the asthmatic patients. In an interesting conclusion, Lehrer, Hochron, et al. (1997), stated that "Our data also would suggest that it would be unwise for asthmatic individuals to relax during an acute asthma attack, because relaxation may produce a short-term autonomically-mediated further decline in pulmonary function, which may exacerbate their asthma still further" (p. 190).

The findings of Lehrer and colleagues suggest that some form of biofeedback-assisted relaxation training is good for asthmatics over the long run, but that relaxation might not be helpful in acute asthmatic attacks as bronchoconstriction (a parasympathetic response) could occur. As pointed out in Lehrer, Hochron, et al. (1997), mildly stressful active coping tasks such as mental arithmetic and reaction time tend to produce bronchodilation (sympathetic response) among asthmatics, and bronchodilation is what helps their breathing during acute episodes.

Another approach involves training asthmatics to respond to provoking stimuli with slow diaphragmatic breathing and relaxation (Peper & Tibbetts, 1992). These researchers reported on a 15-month follow-up study that used upper back muscle EMG feedback and feedback from a Voldyne inspirometer (a simple device that measures amount of inhaled air). At follow-up, all patients reported significantly reduced EMG tension and increased inhalation volumes. Reductions were shown for asthma symptoms, medication use, emergency room visits, and breathless episodes. In summary, the underlying physiological mechanisms for beneficial effects of EMG biofeedback with asthma are unclear. As stated previously, the entire treatment package and possible cognitive changes concerning attitude about control over the ailment, along with anxiety reductions, may be playing an important role in observed improvements and these possibilities need to be explored more thoroughly.

Summary. Reductions in facial EMG appears to help asthmatics. The mechanism by which this improvement is produced is unknown. Another approach suggests that RSA and EMG feedback can help asthma patients over the long run, but that relaxation may not be appropriate for the asthmatic suffering an acute attack. Training in diaphragmatic breathing has also shown preliminary promise in treating asthmatics. It is obvious that more work is needed in this area.

EMG Feedback and Hyperactivity

The term *hyperactivity* is used to describe a group of symptoms that include overactivity, short attention span, impulsivity, low frustration tolerance, and in some cases, aggressive behavior. Hyperactivity is often associated with attention deficit disorder (ADD). A drug widely used to control hyperactivity is methylphenidate (Ritalin), a stimulant that paradoxically acts as a tranquilizer on children. According to a 1987 estimate by the drug's manufacturer, it is prescribed for 500,000 patients annually. Possible side effects are nausea and stunted growth with long-term use.

The effects of frontalis EMG/BFT and progressive relaxation was examined with 15 hyperactive children between 6 and 13 years of age and 15 nonhyperactives ranging from 6 to

15 years (Braud, 1978). Both EMG and progressive relaxation exercises resulted in muscular tension reductions in all subjects over 12 sessions. In the hyperactives, improvements in behavioral ratings (especially aggression) and test scores (digit span, coding) were observed. The improvements occurred in both medicated and unmedicated hyperactives, but were more pronounced in the nonmedicated individuals. One possibility is that the nonmedicated children were more motivated to learn the self-control techniques because they could not depend on drugs.

A study using EMG-assisted relaxation training with hyperactives was reported by Denkowski, Denkowski, and Omizo (1984). Forty-eight hyperactive males, ages 11 to 14, were assigned to treatment and control groups. The treatment consisted of frontalis EMG feedback combined with imagery relaxation techniques once every 2 weeks over a period of 12 weeks. The controls attended sessions without feedback or relaxation being introduced. Pre- and postsession measures showed EMG reduction and improved reading and language scores for the treatment group, but not for controls. In addition, locus of control changed from external to internal for the biofeedback group, suggesting a greater feeling of self-control. A follow-up study by Denkowski et al. (1984) implicated locus of control as a predictor of success in EMG treatment of hyperactivity. This suggests that internally oriented individuals are better at gaining control over their own physiological processes.

Summary.   A variety of results with hyperactives indicate improved academic performance, increased self-control, and a decrease in disruptive behavior as a function of EMG-assisted relaxation. Hence, this approach certainly merits further consideration as a primary or adjunct treatment for hyperactivity.

THE ELECTROENCEPHALOGRAM (EEG) IN BIOFEEDBACK APPLICATIONS

EEG Biofeedback and Epilepsy

Three delineated forms of epilepsy—grand mal, petit mal, and psychomotor—produce seizures or attacks that are accompanied by disturbances in the EEG pattern. There are many neurological conditions that lead to epileptic seizures, and, therefore, the cause of seizures may differ from one patient to another. The Epilepsy Foundation estimates that there are 4 million epileptics in the United States. About 20% to 25% of epileptics have poorly controlled seizures, even with medication (Birbaumer et al., 1994).

Attempts to treat epilepsy have focused on influencing the EEG pattern through BFT. The use of EEG/BFT to reduce incidence of seizures stems from the work of Sterman and colleagues, who noted an increase in 12- to 16-Hz EEG in cats given reinforcement for suppressing a bar-pressing response. This 12- to 16-Hz activity was termed the *sensorimotor rhythm* (SMR), because it was most prominent over sensorimotor cortex. The findings that cats previously trained to enhance SMR activity were able to delay the onset of seizures induced by a convulsant drug led Sterman and associates to try SMR training in epileptic patients. For example, Sterman and Friar (1972) reported the suppression of seizures in an epileptic patient who had been conditioned to produce 11- to 14-Hz EEG through BFT. Sterman (1973) suggested that the SMR may be an EEG phenomenon related to brain mechanisms that mediate motor suppression. The reduction of seizures in severe epileptics using SMR training has been reported subsequently by a number of investigators.

Sterman, MacDonald, and Stone (1974) reported that four epileptics had a reduction in seizure frequency when biofeedback was used to train the production of 12- to 14-Hz EEG from over the Rolandic (central) cortex. Seifert and Lubar (1975) worked with three male and three female adolescent epiletics whose seizures were not well controlled by drugs. The patients were provided with feedback whenever they produced a half-second of 12- to 14-Hz activity of a specified magnitude. They observed a significant reduction in the number of seizures during the first 3 to 4 months of treatment in five of the six epileptics. The BFT sessions were 40-min long and scheduled three times a week.

Sensory motor rhythm training was used with eight epileptics whose seizures were frequent, severe, and not controlled by anticonvulsant drugs (Lubar & Bahler, 1976). Six of the eight patients were studied in an extension of SMR training initiated by Seifert and Lubar (1975). In addition to 12- to 14-Hz activity, patients were provided feedback of 4- to 7-Hz activity that indicated epileptiform spike activity. They were to suppresss their epileptiform activity. The patients continued to show improvements in the form of decreased seizure frequency. The addition of feedback regarding epileptiform activity enabled some patients to develop the ability to block many of their seizures. The more successful patients demonstrated an increase in the amount and amplitude of SMR during the training period.

A lack of relation between the SMR and seizure reduction was reported by Kuhlman and Allison (1977). These investigators used both contingent and noncontingent feedback to train 9- to 14-Hz Rolandic EEG activity. Although seizure reduction occurred in three of the five patients, it was associated with increases in the amount and frequency of alpha, and not with enhancement of the SMR. Kuhlman (1978) suggested that the human analog of the 12- to 16-Hz SMR in cats is an EEG of 8- to 13-Hz, and he called this rhythm *Mu*. The features of Mu that distinguish it from alpha are that it is localized to the sensorimotor area, it occurs in the absence of movement, and it is not attenuated by visual stimulation. The contention that the SMR in cats does not have a human analog in the same frequency range is controversial, and has not yet been resolved. Kuhlman (1978) trained an increase in 9- to 14-Hz EEG from sensorimotor area of five patients. He controlled for placebo effects by giving 12 initial sessions during which feedback was noncontingent to the EEG. After 50 training sessions, seizure reductions occurred in 3 to 5 patients (average of 60% decrease). The EEG changes were mixed: One successful patient showed increased alpha, one shifted to higher frequencies, and the third one had a decrease in slow-wave activity. Kuhlman suggested that a "normalization" of EEG occuured for these three patients.

A study was conducted to examine EEG/BFT with eight epileptics suffering severe symptoms (Whitsett, Lubar, Holder, Pamplin, & Shabsin, 1982). All patients experienced multiple seizures each month, and were not helped by drugs. The study was conducted double-blind so that neither patients nor technicians knew the feedback contingencies. The patients were reinforced for (a) suppression of 3- to 7-Hz activity, (b) enhancement of 12- to 15-Hz activity, or (c) simultaneous suppression of 3- to 7-Hz and enhancement of 12- to 15-Hz activity. Sleep recordings of EEG provided support for the hypothesis that EEG/BFT led to changes in epileptic EEG that were reflected in sleep recordings. Thus, they concluded that BFT can produced changes in epileptic patients that result in an alteration of both seizure pattern and the sleep EEG.

A novel approach was used by Sterman (1984), who reported on the use of a computer soccer game to provide feedback of SMR. In the game, a ball moves into the goal area when 12- to 15-Hz activity occurs, and the goal defense is eliminated when 4- to 7-Hz activity is suppressed. Training sessions were carried out for 6 weeks, with three per week. Sterman reported a reduction of seizure rates by more than 50% with contingent BFT. Comparison of pre- and post-BFT sleep EEG showed that normalization of abnormal EEG with contingent SMR enhancement and 4- to 7-Hz suppression was related to greater amounts of seizure reduction (60%). Sterman believed that the changes seen with SMR training are due to decreases in abnormal thalamocortical excitability that occur with training.

In a different approach, Birbaumer and associates (1994) trained epileptic patients to control slow cortical potentials using performance in a rocket ship game as reinforcement for producing the desired response. The patients were epileptics whose seizures were not controlled with medication. Seizure frequency varied from one per week to over 60 per week, with an average of 11.5. Median seizure frequency was calculated for an 8-week baseline period and then during a 1-year follow-up period, subsequent to 28 training sessions. Data were based on 18 persons who completed the 1-year monitoring period. Six of them became seizure-free, another seven showed decreased frequencies of seizure compared to baseline, and the remaining five showed no change. Degree of improvement was related to learned ability to control slow cortical potentials and age, with younger patients having better results.

Summary.   In summary, suggestive findings indicate a relation between EEG/BFT and seizure reduction in epilepsy. Training in a specific EEG frequency does not seem necessary for achieving "normalization" of brain wave pattern. The best approach for training seems to involve suppressing epileptiform activity and enhancing normal EEG or measures of brain electrophysiology, regardless of the particular frequency. The combined procedure of enhancing 12- to 15-Hz activity while reducing 4- to 7-Hz activity appears to have promise. The disabling nature of epileptic seizures for so many individuals and the detrimental side effects of medications used are strong arguments for continued funding of this type of research. Work on EEG/BFT with epileptics is time-consuming and costly; however, the potential benefits are great.

EEG Biofeedback and Attention Deficit Hyperactivity Disorder (ADHD)

According to the Diagnostic and Statistical Manual of the American Psychiatric Association (DSM–IV, 1994) attention deficit hyperactivity disorder (ADHD) is a persistent pattern of inattention and/or hyperactivity–impulsivity that is more frequent and severe than observed in other individuals at a comparable stage of development. Also, at least some of the inattentive, hyperactive, or impulsive symptoms must have been noticeable before the age of 7. A number of biofeedback researchers have been using techniques similar to EEG feedback for epilepsy to treat ADHD (for example, see Lubar, 1997). This EEG application has been referred to as *neurofeedback* by Lubar and others, and it is claimed that this type of feedback can improve attentive mechanisms. If it is established that EEG/BFT can improve behavioral and academic measures in those with ADHD, it could become an important treatment for the disorder, replacing the psychostimulants such as methylphenidate (Ritalin), which are currently the primary treatment modality for ADHD.

Lubar and Lubar (1984) reported on the successful treatment of six boys (ages 10–19) using EEG feedback designed to increase beta activity to enhance attention and arousal, and to decrease slow activity (4–8 Hz). Training was long-term, consisting of two sessions per week for 10 to 27 months. All six children showed improvement in school grades or achievement test scores. In a later study, it was found that young males diagnosed as ADHD (ages 9–12) had increased theta activity (4–7.75 Hz) activity and decreased beta1 (12.75 to 21 Hz) when compared with 27 controls matched for age and grade level (Mann, Lubar, Zimmerman, Miller, & Muenchen, 1992).

A strategy used by Lubar and colleagues in treating ADHD with neurofeedback has been to enhance beta activity (16–20 Hz) while simultaneously training suppression of theta waves (4–8 Hz). This approach was used in a 1995 study (Lubar, Swartwood, Swartwood, & O'Donnell) and found effective in the improvement of attention, behavior ratings, and intelligence test scores. The subjects were 23 children (8–19 years) who participated in a 2- to 3-month summer program of neurofeedback training. A comparison of EEG/BFT and medication on tests of inattention, impulsivity, and information processing was conducted by Rossiter and LaVaque (1995). One group of 23 ADHD individuals was given EEG/BFT while another 23 ADHD subjects were given a psychostimulant. The results indicated similar improved performance with both treatments. More importantly, they showed that EEG/BFT is an effective alternative to stimulants and could be the treatment of choice when medication is ineffective or has unwanted side effects. The investigators note that medication is effective only as long as the individual continues to take it and that there is evidence that EEG/BFT may have longer-term beneficial effects. Lubar and colleagues have reported that the increase in higher frequency activity and decrease in low-frequency EEG has resulted in long-term improvements in academic performance in both normals and individuals with ADHD (Rasey, Lubar, McIntyre, Zoffuto, & Abbot, 1996). In a controlled study of neurofeedback with 18 ADHD children, some of whom were learning disabled, random assignment was made to either an EEG/BFT group or to a wait-list control group (Linden, Habib, & Radojevic, 1996). Training was to enhance beta and suppress theta and was carried out over a 6-month period. The results indicated improvements in the experimental group that were not observed in the controls. These improvements included increases in IQ and attentive behavior.

Summary.   It has been reported that neurofeedback leading to production of fast brain wave activity (beta) while simultaneously suppressing slow wave activity (theta) results in both academic and behavioral improvements in individuals diagnosed with ADHD. However, although these results are promising, there is a need for more large scale, controlled studies, to convincingly demonstrate the value of neurofeedback training in ADHD. There is also a need for longitudinal studies to determine how this treatment helps children over the long term, and into adulthood.

Blood Pressure and BFT Applications

Application to Hypertension.   The cardiovascular abnormality known as high blood pressure, or *hypertension*, is estimated to occur in 5% to 10% of the population in the United States (Shapiro, Mainardi, & Surwit, 1977). One of the first studies to use BFT in an attempt to regulate hypertension via BFT was that of Benson, Shapiro, Tursky, and Schwartz (1971). They used BFT with hypertensive patients and reported decreases in systolic blood pressure, ranging from 16 to 34 mm Hg, in 71% of the patients. The effectiveness of the training in terms of transfer outside of the laboratory situation is not known, because no follow-up data were obtained.

Schwartz and Shapiro (1973) discussed general procedures, findings, and theoretical issues in the BFT of blood pressure regulation. They noted that a common training procedure is to provide "binary" feedback, that is, the subjects know with each heartbeat whether blood pressure has gone up or down. In the binary feedback–reward situation, the subject is provided with information regarding momentary fluctuations in blood pressure, and a reward is presented for a sustained (tonic) change in some direction (e.g., when systolic pressure has decreased by at least 5 mm Hg). They also pointed out that baseline blood pressure values may change either up or down over a session, independent of learning. For example, increases may occur if the stimuli used for feedback or reward are arousing, and decreases will be observed as subjects adapt to the experimental situation. Thus, researchers must be careful to control for these in order not to misinterpret changes from baseline as indicating a therapeutic effect.

Schwartz and Shapiro mentioned that the novelty of the experimental situation plus expectancy may operate as a placebo effect, thus making it difficult to assess the effects of BFT alone. However, the placebo effect should not be regarded negatively. Stroebel and Glueck

(1973) pointed out that the novelty of a BFT situation with its equipment, feedback displays, and the possibility for self-regulation of certain processes may produce a placebo effect that has good results, especially if it can help to produce a reduction in the blood pressure of hypertensives. However, there are difficulties associated with depending on placebo effects, because not enough is known about the conditions and types of persons in which they are operative. Hence, the utility of a placebo as a method of treatment is limited, because these unknowns make the control of this effect very difficult.

Motivation looms as an important factor in any learning situation, and is crucial in BFT. The problem of motivating hypertensive patients has been discussed by Schwartz and Shapiro (1973), who noted that, unlike the tension headache patient, individuals with high blood pressure typically have little or no discomfort from this condition. The rewarding effects of blood pressure reduction, therefore, are not readily recognized by the patient, and it is important to ensure that hypertensives are properly motivated in the BFT situation. Another problem is that it is easier to take a pill to control BP than to take time out to do a relaxation exercise or to monitor BP on a regular basis.

In a study conducted by Kristt and Engel (1975), a number of hypertensive patients were taught to reduce systolic BP. Pre-BFT readings were first compiled at home over a 7-week period. Then the patients were trained to raise, to lower, and to alternately raise and lower systolic BP. Finally, BP readings were taken at home during a 3-month follow-up period. Reductions in BP between 10% to 15% occurred between the pretraining period and the follow-up. Changes in diastolic and systolic BP were observed. The lowered pressures occurred in patients suffering from a variety of ailments, including heart arhythmias and cardiomegaly (enlarged heart).

Summary.   This brief review of direct BP biofeedback for treating hypertension indicates that it may have clinical value. However, feedback of other physiological measures, such as skin conductance level (SCL) and skin temperature, combined with relaxation techniques, have proven effective in lowering the BP of hypertensives. Skin temperature BFT, in particular, is more commonly used than any other approach in treating hypertension.

APPLICATIONS OF ELECTRODERMAL ACTIVITY (EDA)

Hypertension.   Several well-conducted studies of Patel and associates have illustrated the benefits of a treatment program in which biofeedback is only one element. Yoga exercises for complete mental and physical relaxation, combined with BFT of SCL, led to improved blood pressure levels in 16 of 20 hypertensive patients (Patel, 1973). Patel used SCL instead of continuous BP feedback, because she wanted to avoid entering an artery to obtain direct BP readings. (Other investigators mentioned in this section obtained indirect BP readings, i.e., with a noninvasive pressure cuff technique.) Patel attributed the beneficial effects to the control of SNS activity through yogic relaxation and through BFT influence over SCL (a response controlled by the SNS). The patients participated in $1/2$-hour sessions, three times a week, over a period of 3 months and showed average decreases of 25 mm Hg for systolic BP and 14 mm Hg for diastolic. In a second study, Patel (1975) found average decreases in systolic BP of 26 mm Hg to 28 mm Hg and 15 mm Hg to 16 mm Hg for diastolic. These improvements were maintained at follow-up 12 months later. In a well-controlled study, Patel and North (1975) shortened the procedure to 12 sessions over 6 weeks and again achieved lowered BP in hypertensives. This time, the experimental subjects were treated first and evidenced improvements. Later, the controls were treated and showed similar gains. Follow-ups at 4 and 7 months showed that improvements were still in evidence. Patel apparently developed an effective combination of feedback and relaxation training to achieve reduction of BP in hypertensives. An important aspect of her program is the practice of relaxation exercises at home. The continuance of relaxation exercises on a regular basis after the formal program has ended is essential if the gains realized are to continue. Although this puts demands on the patient, a positive aspect of this is that the relaxation techniques do not have side effects and are not as costly as medications that might otherwise have to be used.

Summary. The combination of skin conductance feedback and relaxation techniques has been used to good effect in treating hypertensives. The question of the specific contribution of the SCL feedback to the effects observed still remains unanswered. The next section discusses applications of skin temperature measurements in BFT, and one of these includes studies using ST feedback with hypertensives.

APPLICATIONS OF SKIN TEMPERATURE BFT

Skin Temperature BFT and Raynaud's Disease

Skin temperature has been found to be related to blood flow in skin tissue as measured by plethysmography (Sargent, Green, & Walters, 1972). Thus, increases or decreases in ST would be related to vasodilation and vasoconstriction of blood vessels. Because degree of vasoconstriction is under sympathetic control, ST is an indirect measure of SNS activity. The continuous measurement of ST involves low cost and portable instrumentation with sensors that can be conveniently applied to fingers or toes. This makes ST especially attractive as a measure in ailments that involve changes in ST or SNS activity.

Feedback of ST has been described in the treatment of patients suffering from Raynaud's disease by Surwit, Pilon, and Fenton (1977) and by Taub (1977). Raynaud's symptoms include intermittent constriction of arteries or arterioles of the hands and feet (vasospastic attacks). During an episode, the affected extremities (fingers or toes) undergo sequential color changes: from white to deep blue to bright red. The fingers become cold and numb, and pain can be severe and debilitating. The symptoms are elicited by cold and/or emotional stress. One postulated mechanism for Raynaud's is a hyperactive SNS, and one treatment has been *sympathectomy*, a surgical procedure in which connections between the SNS (spinal nerves) and blood vessels are severed. According to Sedlacek (1979), many patients remain untreated because they have been told there is little that can be done about the disorder. The disease affects four times as many women as men.

Thirty patients with Raynaud's were trained to control finger ST with a combination of feedback and autogenic relaxation, or autogenic relaxation alone (Surwit et al., 1977). Autogenic relaxation requires that the patient repeat certain phrases presented on a tape recording. The phrases consist of suggestions about "heaviness and warmth" in various body areas, for example, "my hands feel heavy and warm." In the study by Surwit and colleagues, patients were trained either at home or in the laboratory. All were able to maintain finger skin temperature in a cold environment (exposure to temperatures as low as 63°F for a period of 1 hr). In addition, the patients reported significant reductions in both frequency and intensity of attacks. There was no difference between the autogenic training alone, as compared to autogenic training plus feedback. These researchers suggested that other forms of relaxation (including meditation, progressive muscle relaxation, or various forms of yoga) be investigated as possible aids in the treatment of Raynaud's.

The training of three Raynaud's patients to self-regulate increases in hand temperature was reported by Taub (1977). At times, patients began sessions with hand temperatures at or only slightly above room temperature. For example, at a room temperature of 70°F, a patient might have a hand ST of only 70°F to 72°F. At the same room temperature, a normal person would have a ST of about 85°F to 90°F. With training, the patients were able to increase hand temperature into the normal range. After 20 training sessions, 2 patients reported decreases in the number and severity of attacks and the ability to prevent them by using, without feedback, techniques learned in the laboratory. The third patient, also trained in the winter, avoided the cold, and training effects could not be evaluated. Sedlacek (1979) reported that 80% of Raynaud's patients in his private practice successfully learned self-regulation of symptoms caused by vascular spasms. Patients practiced home exercises for 15 min two times a day. If patients stop home practice or are overstressed, symptoms often return. Follow-ups at 12 to 36 months showed all but two of the successful patients in control of the symptoms. Freedman, Lynn, Ianni, and Hale (1981) used ST feedback in the treatment of six patients with Raynaud's disease and four with Raynaud's phenomenon. The distinction is that Raynaud's disease cannot be explained by known pathology, but Raynaud's phenomenon is due to some known disorder, for example, rheumatoid arthritis. Twelve sessions of ST feedback alone allowed all 10 patients to decrease their symptoms to 7.5% of the original frequencies, and to maintain improvement throughout a full year of climatic changes. The results cited so far, although clinically impressive, were obtained in the absence of untreated control groups.

A controlled study of ST biofeedback with Raynaud's patients was conducted by Guglielmi, Roberts, and Patterson (1982). Thirty-six patients were assigned to the following three groups of 12 each: (a) a ST increase group, (b) an EMG relaxation group, and (c) a no-treatment control group. Patients in the training groups had 20 sessions, and all 36 kept records of their symptoms throughout the study. Although all patients reported a marked improvement in symptoms, there were no statistically significant differences among the three groups in either frequency or duration of vasospastic attacks. The authors attributed the improvements to nonspecific factors, such as keeping records of symptoms and warming weather over the course of the study (January to June). However, examination of the results showed that the duration and frequency of attacks was lower for the two training groups, and raises the possibility that the lack of statistical significance was due to the small number of persons in each group.

Summary. Preliminary results are encouraging, but the data available are still insufficient to firmly establish the efficacy of BFT in treating Raynaud's. The promising clinical results warrant continued trials of BFT with Raynaud's, especially because a surgical alternative is a drastic measure and not always effective.

Skin Temperature BFT and Hypertension

Previously, we discussed the regulation of BP using feedback of systolic and diastolic pressure, mostly in operant conditioning paradigms. The question of whether feedback of other physiological responses can assist in lowering BP may be answered affirmatively with some caution. A report, by E. Green, A. Green, and Norris (1979), showed reductions of BP in hypertensives using ST to train foot warming. Six of seven patients originally on medication were able to remain unmedicated while maintaining BP below 140/90 mm Hg. Since then, the use of a program that combines feedback of ST, relaxation techniques, home monitoring of BP, and home practice of relaxation had been found effective in lowering BP of hypertensives by researchers at the Menninger Foundation (Fahrion, Norris, Green, Green, & Snarr, 1986) and at the State University of New York at Albany (Blanchard et al., 1987). For example, Fahrion and associates (1986) found significant reductions in systolic and diastolic BP and medication use in 77 patients with essential hypertension. A multimodal procedure was used, which included biofeedback-assisted training aimed at self-regulation of hand and foot ST. Most patients were able to discontinue medication while reducing BP by 15 mm Hg for systolic and 10 mm Hg for diastolic readings. Follow-up data on 61 patients over an average of 33 months indicated continuance of good control in 51% of patients and partial control in 41%. The remaining 8% were unsuccessful in lowering BP or medications to a clinically meaningful extent.

The effectiveness of thermal feedback in lowering BP was noted by Blanchard and McCoy (1984). These investigators used thermal feedback with 20 hypertensives over 16 sessions, and progressive muscle relaxation with another 22 patients over the same time period. The patients were classified as mildly to moderately hypertensive and were taking two medications for BP control at the beginning of the program. Biofeedback of finger ST was superior to relaxation training in reducing BP and maintaining it at the lower level after 3 months with only one of the original drugs. This represented a significant savings in money and also reduced the risk of side effects by reducing medication.

The importance of continued home practice of relaxation techniques in the maintenance of lowered BP was underscored in a study by Hoelscher (1987). Planned withdrawals of practice for periods of 3 and 10 weeks led to increased levels of BP, followed by decreases with resumption of practice. Cohen and Sedlacek (1983) divided 30 hypertensives into 3 groups: a waiting-list control (no treatment), a relaxation-only group, and a relaxation-plus-thermal and EMG-feedback group. The only significant BP reduction that occurred was for the relaxation-plus-feedback group at the end of the 20 sessions. This group showed average decreases of 13 mm Hg for systolic and 12 mm Hg for diastolic pressure.

Exaggerated cardiovascular reactivity has been suggested as a risk factor for heart disease, so it would be important to determine if amount of reactivity could be reduced through biofeedback or relaxation techniques. Some preliminary findings by Blanchard and associates have indicated very modest reductions in reactivity to a psychological stressor (mental arithmetic) but none at all to physical (cold pressor) stimulation. Blanchard, McCoy, and McCaffrey, et al. (1988) used thermal feedback and autogenic training, and Blanchard and colleagues (Blanchard, McCoy, & Wittrock, et al., 1988) employed progressive muscle relaxation. Individuals with high blood pressure were used in both studies.

Blanchard (1990) reported that thermal feedback combined with autogenic relaxation led to significant reductions in diastolic blood pressure in a cross-cultural comparison of American and Russian hypertensives. His recommendations for future research include: (1) techniques to maintain improvements over the long run, (2) identification of good and poor candidates for treatment and (3) model building to test and understand how thermal biofeedback works in affecting BP. An interesting aspect of the cross-cultural comparison was that at the end of 1 year, 75% of the treated Russian patients were still normotensive compared to only 24% of the American patients. One speculation was that continued home practice may have accounted for the differences.

Blanchard and colleagues (1996) noted that one of the problems with the thermal BFT/stress management approach to treating hypertension has been a lack of repetition of positive results from one evaluative study to the next. They pointed out that analysis of 12 federally funded controlled studies of stress management applied to hypertension revealed only a small benefit for DBP and no benefit for SBP (Kaufmann et al., 1988). This led to a pair of controlled studies by Blanchard et al. (1996) to evaluate thermal BFT as a treatment modality in unmedicated mild hypertensives. In a first study, 21 of these subjects completed 16 sessions of thermal BFT for hand and foot warming over 8 weeks, and 21 monitored BPs at home for 8 weeks. Although there was a trend for more of the treatment group to have DBPs less than 90 mm Hg (57%) it was not significant compared to the home monitoring group (33%). Sixteen of the 21 patients in the monitoring group were later treated, and analyses of treatment effects across all 37 patients showed a significant DBP decrease for females, but not for males.

A second study was designed to compare the effects of an intensive follow-up approach versus a conventional follow-up in maintaining lowered SBPs. Twenty-two of the treatment successes (DBP below 90 mm Hg) were divided randomly into an intensive group (monthly visits for 6 months, then every 2 months for a year) with emphasis on home practice with an electronic thermal feedback device supplied by the investigators. The conventional group only had follow-ups every 3 months for 1 year. Twelve of the 22 patients were still normotensive after 12 months, but there was no difference between the intensive–conventional follow-up groups even though the reported frequency of home practice was greater for the intensive group. Thus, home practice does not explain the earlier reported difference in the maintenance of BP improvements for Russian and American patients. Blanchard and colleagues could not explain the failure to replicate their earlier results in which there was a significant difference in DBP lowering for the treated patients compared to controls. They suggested that there may be many individual difference variables which could account for the results.

Summary.   A number of early studies had encouraging results regarding the use of skin temperature BFT with hypertensives. Most of these studies were not controlled. More recent controlled studies have not yielded significant effects in lowering BP. We are left with the sobering conclusion that more reliable results across samples of patients and across clinics need to be demonstrated before thermal feedback can be accepted as a treatment for hypertension. One encouraging outcome was the significant improvement shown for the treated female subjects as compared to controls. Clearly more work is needed on specific effects of skin temperature BFT, as well as the use of multimodal behavioral techniques (relaxation, stress management, exercise) for treating hypertension. The potential benefits are great considering that popular medications used for hypertension all have unpleasant side effects.

Skin Temperature BFT and Migraine

A combination of skin temperature BFT and autogenic phrases has been used to treat migraine headaches (Sargent, Green, & Walters, 1972; Sargent, Walters, & Green, 1973). Migraine is a severe form of headache often accompanied by nausea and blurring of vision, and usually confined to one side of the head. It is believed to be due to dilation in superficial cranial arteries (Dalessio, 1972), and during the headache phase, the pain is one-sided and throbbing, often resulting in a constant ache spreading over the scalp and head. Even worse, the pain may continue for several hours to several days. Sargent et al. (1972) treated 62 migraine patients using biofeedback training for hand-warming. Clinical ratings indicated that 74% of the migraine sufferers were improved. Sargent and colleagues (1973) reported that the combined hand-warming training and autogenic procedures produced improvement in 81% of 42 migraine patients who were followed for more than 150 days. These investigators believed that one mechanism operative in their approach is the voluntary relaxation of the portion of the SNS serving the hand, resulting in the increased flow of blood to that area. Presumably, the effect of SNS relaxation spreads to other body areas, including the superficial arteries of the head. However, the researchers did not investigate this possible spread of effects to other areas of the body, thus leaving the reasons for the beneficial effect rather uncertain. The lack of control groups and little attempt to identify nonspecific and placebo effects serve to weaken this early work. Nevertheless, it has led to a great deal of clinical work and research on the use of ST feedback with migraine.

Analyses of behavioral and drug approaches to treat migraine headaches in children have shown skin temperature biofeedback to be one of the most effective (Hermann, Kim, &

Blanchard, 1995). There is suggestive evidence indicating that treatment of pediatric migraine in clinics is superior to treatment based in the patient's homes where there is minimum contact with a therapist (Hermann, Blanchard, & Flor, 1997). In order to determine the influence of a child's adjustment, age, and family environment on the outcome of home-based treatment for pediatric migraine, Hermann et al. (1997) studied 32 child migraine patients, between the ages of 8 and 16. The home-based format involved four training sessions administered over 8 weeks by a therapist and 15 minutes of daily practice with a portable temperature device. The children recorded daily progress over the 8 weeks. There was a significant drop in headache activity (intensity, frequency, duration), a drop in days missed at school, and a 57% decrease in medication intake. An interesting and important finding was that treatment success was related to age, with younger children having better outcomes than the older ones. Family environment did not impact on treatment outcome.

A controlled investigation of ST feedback with migraine patients was conducted by Blanchard, Theobald, Williamson, Silver, and Brown (1978). Thirty patients were divided into three groups: (a) finger ST feedback with autogenic relaxation; (b) relaxation alone; or (c) no treatment. The treatment sessions were 2 times a week over a 6-week period. Both treatment groups were improved at the end of training, whereas the control patients were not. Gauthier, Lacroix, Cote, Koyon, and Drolet (1985) assigned patients to finger ST feedback, blood volume pulse feedback (BVP), and a control group. Both finger ST training and temporal artery BVP feedback were effective in treating migraine. The researchers did not find a relationship between therapeutic expectancy and migraine relief.

Encouraging results regarding the long-term benefits of combined thermal feedback and relaxation for migraine patients were reported by Holroyd et al. (1989). Patients successfully treated (50% or greater reduction in headache activity) were contacted for follow-up evaluation 3 years later. Those patients treated with feedback/relaxation were more likely to have maintained improvements without additional treatment than those treated with a drug (ergotamine).

A group of researchers led by Blanchard tested the hypothesis that hand-warming is not superior to hand-cooling or maintaining a stable hand temperature in treating migraine headache (Blanchard et al., 1997). In this study 70 patients with chronic migraine were randomly assigned to one of four groups: BFT for hand-warming, for hand-cooling, for stabilization of temperature, or BFT to suppress alpha in the EEG. Participants in each group believed in the potential benefit of the procedures they followed in terms of therapeutic benefit. Headache diaries were kept by all four groups for 4 weeks prior to treatment, during 6 weeks of treatment (two times per week) and 4 weeks after treatment. Three of the four groups showed significant improvements in headaches (hand warm, hand cool, and alpha supress) and two of the four showed significant decreases in medication use (hand warm and hand cool). Blanchard and colleagues point out that home practice of hand-warming between clinic sessions, a procedure usually followed in treatment for migraine, was omitted. However, the results raise questions regarding the specific effects of hand-warming for treatment of migraine headache and, obviously, further study is necessary.

Summary. The use of skin temperature BFT with migraine has yielded promising results, especially with children. There have been several controlled studies that demonstrated beneficial effects of biofeedback alone and in combination with relaxation. In order to establish the use of thermal feedback with migraine patients, additional controlled and long-term follow-up studies are required. The equivalent results for hand-warming and cooling as a treatment raises the question of whether it is the control of blood vessel diameter (not only vasodilation) that is crucial in producing beneficial effects with migraineurs. This intriguing question needs to be explored further.

BLOOD VOLUME BFT AND MIGRAINE

Feedback of a direct cephalic vasomotor response (CVMR) was used by Feuerstein, Adams, and Beiman (1976) and Friar and Beatty (1976) with migraine patients. Both sets of investigators used BFT to train self-regulation of vasoconstriction in superficial temporal arteries (located in the temporal region of the head above the ears). They reported success in treating migraine with BFT employing the CVMR.

Price and Tursky (1976) measured changes in temporal artery blood volume and finger blood volume in 40 migraine sufferers and 40 matched controls. The objective was to train vasodilation by providing feedback about increases in hand temperature. Ten subjects from each group were assigned to one of four treatments: (a) feedback, (b) false feedback, (c) relaxation induced by taped instructions, and (d) a neutral-tape control. Responses of migraine sufferers were very different from those of the controls. Normal subjects produced vasodilation in accordance with experimental demands, but the migraine patients tended to show constriction, or no change, in blood vessels. There were no significant differences in vasodilation and relaxation conditions. Both of these latter procedures were better than the irrelevant listening task in producing vasodilation. Price and Tursky suggested that migraine sufferers be studied to determine whether stressful stimuli produce temporal artery vasoconstriction, which in turn results in headaches. A further suggestion was that if this is the case, then migraine patients might be trained not to respond to such stimuli with vasoconstriction. Feuerstein and Adams (1977) investigated the use of CVMR and EMG (frontalis) BFT in two migraine and two tension-headache patients. Training consisted of six sessions of CVMR and six EMG biofeedback sessions for all patients. The CVMR training helped migraine patients, and EMG training helped tension-headache patients to reduce the frequency and duration of headaches.

The hypothesis that BFT producing temporal artery constriction would be superior to that producing dilation in alleviating migraine was proposed by Gauthier et al. (1983). Training patients to voluntarily constrict the temporal artery mimics the action of ergotamine, a drug used to treat migraine. Three groups of migraine patients were given feedback for temporal artery constriction, dilation, or served as wait-list controls. The BFT consisted of 15 sessions over 8 weeks. All patients completed 5 weeks of self-monitoring of headaches and medication use before and after the BFT period. To the surprise of these workers, and contrary to their hypothesis, both the vasoconstrict and vasodilate groups showed improvements in frequency, intensity, and duration of migraine attacks. The waiting-list controls showed no change. The researchers found evidence that reductions in migraine were associated with decreased variability in blood vessel constriction and dilation. This led them to suggest an alternate hypothesis that voluntary vasoconstriction and vasodilation were effective because they allowed greater regulation of vasomotor activity. Research to test this hypothesis would be designed to show that reductions in migraine headaches are caused by decreases in vasomotor variability.

This result by Gauthier and colleagues is similar to those reported by Blanchard et al. (1997) because both hand-warming (vasodilation) and cooling (vasoconstriction) reduced migraine headache activity in that study. The result also raises the interesting possibility that blood vessel diameter changes in the fingers are mirrored by similar changes in the temporal arteries of the head. This could be evaluated through simultaneously measuring blood volume or skin temperature in these two areas.

Summary.   Blood volume feedback for migraine sufferers seems promising with respect to alleviating symptoms and understanding more about the origins of migraine. However, as with the other measures, blood volume BFT requires further testing as a treatment for migraine headache.

Overall Conclusions Regarding Clinical Applications of BFT.   There is suggestive evidence that biofeedback can assist in the alleviation of certain disorders. The EMG applications are numerous. Positive results obtained with EMG feedback for tension headache seem as much due to nonspecific factors as the feedback itself. The nonspecific factors include the learning of relaxation techniques, therapist attention, home practice, monitoring of symptoms, changes in lifestyle, and other factors that have been mentioned in this chapter. The beneficial effects of EMG/BFT with stuttering are only suggestive, whereas its application to neuromuscular disorders is very promising. The lack of controlled studies of EMG feedback with anxiety patients makes this application preliminary at best. Biofeedback with asthmatics has advanced beyond an exploratory stage with some promising preliminary findings. Initial encouraging results with hyperactivity should set the stage for larger-scale studies with good control procedures. The continued use of EEG feedback with epileptics should be encouraged in order to follow up promising possibilities. The application of EEG/BFT (neurofeedback) to attention deficit hyperactivity disorder (ADHD) has shown some potential. Additional controlled studies and longitudinal evidence of continued improvement are needed to convince both the scientific community and third-party reimbursers (insurance companies) that neurofeedback is beyond the experimental stage. Investigations into the use of skin temperature feedback with hypertensives, although initially very promising, have recently revealed inconsistencies in findings that need to be resolved. Applications of thermal feedback to Raynaud's can still only be said to be preliminary. Skin temperature feedback with migraine patients appears to be very effective with young patients. The specific benefit of hand-warming procedures with adult migraine patients, however, has recently been questioned. The use of blood volume feedback with migraine patients is still at an early stage of development.

More good clinical research is needed on all of these applications of biofeedback to clinical disorders. Controlled studies that isolate the specific effects of biofeedback are also desirable. The adequate control procedure would be to expose both treatment and control groups to the same procedures, except for the physiological feedback provided for treatment groups. Thus, for example, the treatment and control groups would both have therapist attention, instructions in relaxation techniques, home practice, and be asked to monitor symptoms. Any differences between groups could not then be attributed to nonspecific or placebo effects.

If a multimodal treatment package (including self-regulation, relaxation techniques, stress management, and counseling) can be shown to be effective in alleviating certain physical disorders such as hypertension or migraine headache, the biofeedback practitioner would get little argument from the patient or insurance companies who benefit from reduced medical costs and fewer medication side effects. From a scientific standpoint, however, it is essential to know the contribution of each element in the treatment package to the improvement observed.

PSYCHONEUROIMMUNOLOGY
(BRAIN, BEHAVIOR, AND IMMUNITY)

The information contained in this section concerns the effects of stress on the immune system. Because there has been some effort to counteract stress effects through relaxation techniques, some of them involving BFT, this information is presented here. Researchers have been busy over the past 15 to 20 years studying the relationships among brain, behavior, and immunity. Investigations have documented the effects of stress-producing behavior on immunity, and are now also focusing on nervous system and immune system connections. A brief review of immune function will be followed by discussions of stress, personality factors, and attempts to overcome the detrimental effects of stress through relaxation and other behavioral techniques.

The Immune System.   This system protects the body from disease-causing microorganisms like viruses and bacteria, and also assists in eliminating tumor cells. Another function is to act against allergens that can be inhaled or swallowed. In general, there are two types of immune reactions. The first of these is referred to as a *humoral response system* because it consists of substances circulating throughout the body. The action of the humoral system is relatively rapid and involves the release of antibodies that bind to foreign bodies called *antigens*. Antigens stimulate the production of B lymphocytes and other lymphocytes (memory cells) that enable a more rapid response should the same antigen be encountered again. Also circulating are K lymphocytes (killer cells) that have the capacity to recognize antigen-bearing cells and bacteria, and to destroy them. The humoral component of the immune system contains five types of immunoglobulins (IgA, IgG, IgE, IGD, and IgM), which are released by white blood cells.

The second type of immune reaction is termed a *cell-mediated response*, and is a slower-reacting system primarily for defense against viruses and some bacteria, and it may defend against cancer cells. *Lymphocytes* are the primary components of the immune system at the cellular level (a variety of T cells). The T lymphocytes, so-called because they originate from the thymus gland, are responsible for the specificity of cell-mediated immunity. Other T lymphocytes, the cytotoxic T cells, directly kill target cells. A subset of T cells, termed *helper cells*, assists the B lymphocytes in the production of antibodies. Another type of T cell called *T-suppressor/cytotoxic cells* inhibits the production of antibodies by the B cells. This limits the immune response so that allergic reactions do not get out of hand (e.g., asthma and hay fever). The *natural killer* (NK) cell, monitors for, and destroys, tumor cells and virally infected cells. The activity of lymphocytes growing in tissue cultures can be evaluated. For example, the lymphocytes may be exposed to a specific stimulus (an antigen) or a nonspecific stimulus (a mitogen) and their production of antibodies can be measured.

Brain and Immunity.   A number of current researchers in the area of psychoneuroimmunology recognize the important interactions that take place among the brain, behavior, and the immune system (e.g., see Ader, Felten, & Cohen, 1990; Biondi & Kotzalidis, 1990). Ader et al. (1990) implicated the cortical and limbic forebrain regions as the major system of the CNS responding to immune signals and regulating CNS outflow to the immune system. Ader (1980) believed that many diseases are psychosomatic in the sense that they are ultimately subject to the regulatory influence of the brain as a sensor and interpreter of the psychosocial and physical environment. He cited a study by Holmes, Treuting, and Wolff (1951), who described a situation in which the presence of an antigen (pollen) alone was not sufficient to elicit symptoms in a subject with hay fever, but the combination of pollen and a threatening life situation did produce symptoms. Environmental influences have been observed to alter cellular immunity; stimuli that elevate adrenal cortical steroid levels are frequently immunosuppressive, but such effects depend on time of stimulation and dose level of antigens (Ader, 1980). Besedovsky, Felix, and Haas (1985) reported an increase in firing of ventromedial hypothalamic neurons (a limbic structure), which corresponded to peak antibody production in response to two different antigens.

Situational Stress and Immune Function.   There is evidence to indicate that situational stress, either prolonged or transient, can affect immunocompetency. There were hints in the medical literature as early as 1919 that psychological factors could influence resistance to disease. In that year, Ishigami (1919) reported on decreased phagocytic (foreign cell-destroying) activity of white blood cells during periods of emotional stress in tuberculosis patients. More recently, Bartrop, Lazarus, Luckhurst, Kiloh, and Penny (1977) observed that immune function of T cells was decreased in 26 persons mourning the death of a spouse. Responses of T and B cells to antigens were studied at 2 and 6 weeks after bereavement, with the significant differences between the bereaved and a control sample showing up only at the 6-week period. Schleifer, Keller, Camerino, Thornton, and Stein (1983) found highly significant suppression of lymphocyte activity (both T and B cells) during the first month after bereavement compared with responses before bereavement.

The hypothesis that stress can temporarily inhibit some facets of the immune response was confirmed in a study by Jemmott et al. (1983). The study examined rate of secretion of salivary IgA (Immunoglobulin A), one of the bodies' first lines of defense against germs, during two low-stress periods and three periods of high stress (major exams of 64 first-year dental students). Salivary IgA secretion was significantly lower in high stress periods compared to low stress periods.

Kiecolt-Glaser and colleagues studied effects of situational stress on immunocompetence in two investigations. In one study, they took blood samples from 75 first-year medical students 1 month before final exams and again on the first day of finals (Kiecolt-Glaser, Garner, et al., 1984). They also obtained data on stressful life events (Holmes–Rahe scale) and loneliness (UCLA scale). Natural killer cell activity (NKCA) declined significantly from the first to the second sample, showing the detrimental effects of stress on this component of the immune system. High scores on stressful life events and loneliness were related to significantly lower levels of NKCA. In another study, Kiecolt-Glaser, Speicher, Holliday, and Glaser (1984) observed the effects of examination stress and loneliness on immunocompetence in 42 medical students. Blood samples were analyzed 1 month before finals, on the first day of finals, and on return from summer vacation. The investigators placed Epstein–Barr virus (EBV) in cultures and found that the activity of B lymphocytes, stimulated by EBV, can be adversely affected by both stress and loneliness. Thus, there are data to indicate that stress produced in a variety of ways can interact with personality factors and have an adverse effect on the immune system.

The effects of a chronic stressor on immune function was examined by studying family caregivers of Alzheimer's patients (Kiecolt-Glaser, Glaser, et al., 1987). Alzheimer's is a long-term degenerative illness of the nervous system that takes its toll on caregivers, who often report an increase in depression and a decrease in life satisfaction. Kiecolt-Glaser and colleagues studied a group of 34 caregivers and 34 controls. Caregiving time ranged from 9 months to 16 years, with an average of 5.5 years. They found that caregivers had lower levels of total lymphocytes, lower percentages of T-helper cells, and greater antibody reactions to Epstein–Barr virus. Caregivers also reported more psychological distress and greater degrees of loneliness than controls.

An interesting link between immune response and cardiovascular reactivity was suggested in a study by Manuck, Cohen, Rabin, Muldoon, and Bachen (1991). Subjects performed laboratory tasks under both time pressure and distraction. The findings indicated that subjects who showed greater amounts of cardiovascular reactivity during the stressor (HR and systolic BP) also had a compromised immune reaction, as indicated by an increase in T suppressor/cytotoxic lymphoctyes and a decrease in T cell response to an antigen. The researchers suggested that the influences of psychological stress on the cellular immune function may be mediated by the sympathetic nervous system, which is responsible for cardiovascular reactivity. A similar finding was reported by Sgoutas-Emch et al. (1994) in that high HR reactors to acute psychological stress (mental arithmetic plus noise) also had higher NK cell and cortisol activity compared to low HR reactors. This type of result indicates interactions among the sympathetic nervous system, immune system, and endocrine system that may allow one to predict immune response, for example, from measures of cardiovascular reactivity.

Social isolation and loneliness may have implications for health if these factors affect immune response (Cacioppo et al., in press). In a study conducted to explore to effects of chronic loneliness on a variety of physiological responses, Cacioppo and colleagues found that chronic feelings of loneliness were associated with high levels of salivary cortisol (an index of lowered immune function), especially in evening hours. Studies in psychoneuroimmunology indicated that psychological stress delays the healing of wounds (Kiecolt-Glaser et al., 1998). Stress associated with exams affected healing of mucosal wounds in a group of dental students (Marucha et al., 1998). Healing of wounds placed 3 days before a major test took significantly longer than those made during summer vacation. Other research results indicate that greater fear and anxiety prior to surgery is associated with slower and more complicated postoperative recovery. In addition, it has been found that pain has adverse effects on immune function (Kiecolt-Glaser et al., 1998).

Effects of Relaxation on Immune Function.   Research suggests that stress management and relaxation techniques may enhance the immune response (Andreassi, 1993). In one study, Kiecolt-Glaser et al. (1985) reported that progressive relaxation, practiced three times a week for a month, led to increased NK cell activity in geriatric patients. In addition, Gruber, Hall, Hersh, and Dubois (1988) found increased immune reaction to antigens and an increase in NK cell activity, IgG, and IgM with relaxation techniques among cancer patients whose disease had spread. The patients engaged in relaxation and guided imagery exercises over a 1-year period while monthly blood samples were taken by a laboratory not involved with the study. It is possible that the subjects of both of these studies may have had compromised immune systems at the start of the relaxation training, but nevertheless they showed benefits from the stress management program. The effects of a 3-week program of daily relaxation exercises on concentrations of serum IgA, IgG, and IgM, and secretion of salivary IgA were examined by M. L. Green, R. G. Green, and Santoro (1988). Blood and saliva samples collected before and after supervised 20-min relaxation sessions showed increases in salivary IgA secretion and in serum IgA, IgG, and IgM. A longer-term practice effect was also observed in that all immunoglobulin levels were higher in the relaxation group after 3 weeks as compared to a wait-list control group practicing relaxation for the first time.

Acquired immunodeficiency syndrome (AIDS) is a disease that devastates the immune system. It is caused by the human immunodeficiency virus type 1 (HIV-1), which is known to be transmitted via body fluids (e.g., blood, semen). The HIV-1 virus affects cell-mediated (T cell), humoral (B cell), and natural (NK cell) immunity, even though the primary target of the virus is the T-helper cell. The HIV-1 infected person goes through several stages of progressive deterioration of immunologic function and becomes increasingly susceptible to a host of viral and bacterial infections.

A question arises as to whether the HIV-1 positive individual can be helped through behavioral interventions. This possibility has been investigated, and preliminary results indicate that behavioral techniques (such as stress management, relaxation techniques, and aerobic exercise) can help HIV-1 infected persons cope with their illness and perhaps slow the progression of the disease (Schneiderman, Antoni, Aronson, LaPerriere & Fletcher, 1992). In one study, 47 healthy gay men were randomly assigned to a stress management or a control group 5 weeks before being notified of a blood test that would tell them whether or not they were HIV-1 positive. Blood samples were taken 72 hr before and 1 week after they were given their results (Antoni et al., 1991). Those in the stress management group showed increases in immune function through increases in NK cell counts and T-helper cells. Control subjects showed slight decreases in cell counts from the pre- to postnotification period.

Beneficial effects of both aerobic exercise and stress management on immune responses of HIV-1 positive persons was also reported by Esterling et al. (1992). Subjects in an aerobic exercise condition met for three 45-min sessions per week over a 10-week period, whereas the cognitive behavioral stress management group met twice weekly (90-min sessions) for 10 weeks. The stress management group received training in relaxation (progressive muscle relaxation and guided imagery); in assertiveness skills; in behavioral change strategies; and received basic information on the psychological, social, and physiological effects of stress. Thus, there is some evidence suggesting that improved immunocompetence among HIV-1 infected persons can be produced by behavioral interventions. These encouraging results argue for the further application of research in this area. Some evidence indicating that imagery specifying mucosal immunity could alter salivary IgA levels was reported for individuals who had high levels of concentration skills (Gregerson, Roberts, & Amiri, 1996). Experimental conditions included a relaxation alone group, a vigilance task control group, and the relaxation with mucosal immune imagery group. Five milliliters of whole saliva was sampled before and after the 60-min task periods and showed the elevated salivary IgA, for the imagery group.

The questions raised at the beginning of this chapter have only been partially answered to date, and the process of investigating these and other questions related to BFT will keep both applied and basic researchers busy for years to come. We have now seen that a tremendous amount of information has been gathered by psychophysiologists. What has been presented thus far represents only a sample of the basic and applied research accomplished to date. The next chapter considers some of the major conceptual formulations that have been developed and used in attempts to integrate and explain some of the diverse findings in psychophysiology.

REFERENCES

Ader, R. (1980). Psychosomatic and psychoimmunologic research. *Psychosomatic Medicine, 42*, 307–321.

Ader, R., Felten, D., & Cohen, N. (1990). Interactions between the brain and the immune system. *Annual Review of Pharmacology and Toxicology, 30*, 561–602.

Allen, F., Pincus, H. A., & First, M. B. (Eds.) *Diagnostic and Statistical Manual of Mental Disorders* (4th ed., 1994). Washington, DC: American Psychiatric Association.

Andreassi, J. L. (1993). Psychophysiologists and the AIDS epidemic: Can we help? *International Journal of Psychophysiology, 14*, 99–101.

Antoni, M. H., Baggett, L., Ironson, G., LaPerriere, A., August, S., Klimas, N., Schneiderman, N., & Fletcher, M. (1991). Cognitive–behavioral stress management intervention buffers distress responses and immunologic changes following notification of HIV-1 seropositivity. *Journal of Consulting & Clinical Psychology, 59*, 906–915.

Bartrop, R. W., Lazarus, L., Luckhurst, E., Kiloh, L. G., & Penny, R. (1977). Depressed lymphocyte production after bereavement. *Lancet, 1*, 834–836.

Basmajian, J. V., & Hatch, J. P. (1979). Biofeedback and the modification of skeletal muscular dysfunctions. In R. J. Gatchel & K. P. Price (Eds.), *Clinical applications of biofeedback: Appraisal & status* (pp. 97–111). New York: Pergamon.

Basmajian, J. V., Kukulka, C. G., Narayan, M. G., & Takebe, K. (1975). Biofeedback treatment of foot-drop after stroke compared with standard rehabilitation technique: Effects on voluntary control and strength. *Archives of Physical Medicine and Rehabilitation, 56*, 231–236.

Basmajian, J. V., Regenos, E. M., & Baker, M. P. (1977, April). Rehabilitation biofeedback for stroke patients. Second Joint Conference on Stroke, American Heart Association, Miami, FL.

Bates, D. B., Macklem, P. T., & Christie, R. V. (1971). *Respiratory function in diseases*. Philadelphia: Saunders.

Benson, H., Shapiro, D., Tursky, B., & Schwartz, G. E. (1971). Decreased systolic blood pressure through operant conditioning techniques in patients with essential hypertension. *Science, 173*, 740–741.

Besedovsky, H., Sorkin, E., Felix, D., & Haas, H. (1985). Hypothalamic changes during the immune response. In S. Locke, R. Ader, H. Besedovsky, N. Hall, G. Solomon, & T. Strom (Eds.), *Foundations of psychoneuroimmunology*, (pp. 51–53). New York: Aldine.

Biondi, M., & Kotzalidis, G. D. (1990). Human psychoneuroimmunology today. *Journal of Clinical Laboratory Analysis, 4*, 22–38.

Birbaumer, N., Rockstroh, B., Elbert, T., Wolf, P., Duchting-Roth, A., Reker, M., Daum, I., Lutzenberger, W., & Dichgans, J. (1994). Biofeedback of slow cortical potentials in epilepsy. In J. G. Carlson, A. R. Seifert, & N. Birbaumer (Eds.), *Clinical applied psychophysiology* (pp. 29–42). New York: Plenum.

Black, A. H., & Cott, A. (1977). A perspective on biofeedback. In J. Beatty & H. Legewie (Eds.), *Biofeedback and behavior* (pp. 7–19). New York: Plenum.

Blanchard, E. B. (1990). Biofeedback treatments of essential hypertension. *Biofeedback & Self Regulation, 15*, 209–228.

Blanchard, E. B., Andrasik, F., Neff, D., Teders, S., Pallmeyer, T., Arena, J., Jurish, S., Saunders, N., & Ahles, T. (1982). Sequential comparisons of relaxation training and biofeedback in the treatment of three kinds of chronic headache or, the machines may be necessary some of the time. *Behavior Research & Therapy, 20,* 469–481.

Blanchard, E. B., Eisele, G., Vollmer, A., Payne, A., Gordon, M., Cornish, P., & Gilmore, L. (1996). Controlled evaluation of thermal biofeedback in treatment of elevated blood pressure in unmedicated mild hypertension. *Biofeedback and Self-Regulation, 21,* 167–190.

Blanchard, E. B., & McCoy, G. C. (1984). Preliminary results from a controlled evaluation of thermal biofeedback as a treatment for essential hypertension. *Biofeedback & Self-Regulation, 9,* 471–495.

Blanchard, E. B., McCoy, G. C., McCaffery, R. J., Berger, M., Musso, A. J., Wittrock, D. A., Gerardi, M. A., Halpern, M., & Pangburn, L. (1987). Evaluation of a minimal-therapist-contact thermal biofeedback treatment program for essential hypertension. *Biofeedback & Self-Regulation, 12,* 93–104.

Blanchard, E. B., McCoy, G. C., McCaffrey, R. J., Wittrock, D. A., Musso, A., Berger, M., Aivasyan, T. A., Khramelashvili, V. V., & Salenko, B. B. (1988). The effects of thermal biiofeedback and autogenic training on cardiovascular reactivity: The joint USSR–USA behavioral hypertension treatment project. *Biofeedback & Self-Regulation, 13,* 25–38.

Blanchard, E. B., McCoy, G. C., Wittrock, D., Musso, A. Gerardi, R. J., & Pangburn, L. (1988). A controlled comparison of thermal biofeedback and relaxation training in the treatment of essential hypertension: II. effects on cardiovascular reactivity. *Health Psychology, 7,* 19–33.

Blanchard, E. B., Peters, M. L., Hermann, C., Turner, S. M., Buckley, T. C., Barton, K., & Dentinger, M. P. (1997). Direction of temperature control in the thermal biiofeedback treatment of vascular headache. *Applied Psychophysiology & Biofeedback, 22,* 227–246.

Blanchard, E. B., Theobald, D. E., Williamson, D. A., Silver, B. V., & Brown, D. A. (1978). A controlled evaluation of temperature biofeedback in the treatment of migraine headaches. *Archives of General Psychiatry, 41,* 121–127.

Bogaards, M. C., & ter Kuile, M. M. (1994). Treatment of recurrent tension headache: A meta-analytic review. *The Clinical Journal of Pain, 10,* 174–190.

Braud, L. W. (1978). The effects of frontal EMG biofeedback and progressive relaxation upon hyperactivity and its behavioral concomitants. *Biofeedback & Self-Regulation, 3,* 69–89.

Brown, B. B. (1974). *New mind, new body.* New York: Harper & Row.

Budzynski, T., Stoyva, J., & Adler, C. S. (1970). Feedback-induced muscle relaxation: Application to tension headache. *Journal of Behavior Therapy & Experimental Psychiatry, 1,* 205–211.

Cacioppo, J. T., Ernst, J. M., Burleson, M. H., McClintock, M. K., Malarkey, W. B., Hawkley, L. C., Kowalewski, R. B., Paulsen, A., Hobson, J. A., Hugdahl, K., Spiegel, D., & Berntson, G. G. (in press). Lonely traits and concomitant physiological processes: The MacArthur social neurosciences studies. *International Journal of Psychophysiology.*

Canter, A., Kondo, C. Y., & Knott, J. R. (1975). A comparison of EMG feedback and progressive muscle relaxation training in anxiety neurosis. *British Journal of Psychiatry, 127,* 470–477.

Cleeland, C. S. (1973). Behavioral techniques in the modification of spasmodic torticollis. *Neurology, 23,* 1241–1247.

Cohen, J., & Sedlacek, K. (1983). Attention and autonomic self-regulation. *Psychosomatic Medicine, 45,* 243–257.

Coleman, J. C. (1976). *Abnormal psychology and modern life.* Dallas: Scott, Foresman.

Craig, A. R., & Cleary, P. J. (1982). Reduction of stuttering by young male stutterers using EMG feedback. *Biofeedback & Self-Regulation, 7,* 241–255.

Dalessio, D. (1972). *Wolff's headache and other head pain.* (3rd ed.). New York: Oxford University Press.

Denkowski, K. M., Denkowski, G. C., & Omizo, M. M. (1984). Predictors of success in the EMG biofeedback training of hyperactive male children. *Biofeedback & Self-Regulation, 9,* 253–264.

Engel, B. T., Nikoomanesh, P., & Schuster, M. M. (1974). Operant conditioning of rectosphincteric responses in the treatment of incontinence. *The New England Journal of Medicine, 290,* 646–649.

Engel-Sittenfeld, P. (1977). Biofeedback in the treatment of neuromuscular disorders. In J. Beatty & H. Legewie (Eds.), *Biofeedback and behavior.* (pp. 427–438). New York: Plenum.

Esterling, B. A., Antoni, N. H., Schneiderman, N., Carver, C. S., LaPerriere, A., Ironson, G., Klimas, N. G., & Fletcher, M. (1992). Psychosocial modulation of antibody to Epstein–Barr viral capsid antigen and human herpesvirus type-6 in HIV-1 infected and at-risk gay men. *Psychosomatic Medicine, 54,* 354–371.

Fahrion, S., Norris, P., Green, A., Green, E., & Snarr, C. (1986). Biobehavioral treatment of essential hypertension: A group outcome study. *Biofeedback & Self-Regulation, 11,* 257–277.

Feuerstein, M., & Adams, H. E. (1977). Cephalic vasomotor feedback in the modification of migraine headache. *Biofeedback & Self-Regulation, 2,* 241–254.

Feuerstein, M., Adams, H. E., & Beiman, I. (1976). Cephalic vasomotor and electromyographic feedback in the treatment of combined muscle contraction and migraine headaches in a geriatric case. *Headache, 16,* 232–237.

Flor, H., & Birbaumer, N. (1991). Comprehensive assessment and treatment of chronic back pain patients without physical disabilities. In M. Bond (Ed.), *Proceedings of the VIth World Congress on Pain* (pp. 229–234). Amsterdam: Elsevier.

Flor, H., Schugens, M. M., & Birbaumer, N. (1992). Discrimination of muscle tension in chronic pain patients and healthy controls. *Biofeedback & Self-Regulation, 17*, 165–177.

Freedman, R. R., Lynn, S. J., Ianni, P., & Hale, P. A. (1981). Biofeedback treatment of Raynaud's disease and phenomenon. *Biofeedback & Self-Regulation, 6*, 355–365.

Friar, R., & Beatty, J. (1976). Migraine: Management by trainer control of vasoconstriction. *Journal of Consulting & Clinical Psychology, 44*, 46–53.

Friedman, A. P., & Merritt, H. H. (1959). *Headache: Diagnosis and treatment.* Philadelphia: Davis.

Furedy, J. J. (1987). Specific versus placebo effects in biofeedback training: A critical lay perspective. *Biofeedback & Self-Regulation, 12*, 169–184.

Gatchel, R. J., Korman, M., Weis, C. B., Smith, D., & Clarke, L. (1978). A multiple response evaluation of EMG biofeedback performance during training and stress-induction conditions. *Psychophysiology, 15*, 253–258.

Gauthier, J., Doyon, J., Lacroix, R., & Drolet, M. (1983). Blood volume pulse biofeedback in the treatment of migraine headache: A controlled evaluation. *Biofeedback & Self-Regulation, 8*, 427–442.

Gauthier, J., Lacroix, R., Cote, A., Koyon, J., & Drolet, M. (1985). Biofeedback control of migraine headaches: A comparison of two approaches. *Biofeedback & Self-Regulation, 10*, 139–159.

Green, E., Green, A., & Norris, P. (1979). Preliminary report on a new non-drug method for the control of hypertension. *Journal of the South Carolina Medical Association, 75*, 575–582.

Green, M. L., Green, R. G., & Santoro, W. (1988). Daily relaxation modifies serum and salivary immunoglobulins and psychophysiologic symptom severity. *Biofeedback & Self-Regulation, 13*, 187–199.

Gregerson, M. B., Roberts, I. M., & Amiri, M. M. (1996). Absorption and imagery locate immune responses in the body. *Biofeedback and Self-Regulation, 21*, 149–165.

Gruber, B. L., Hall, N. R., Hersh, S. P., & Dubois, P. (1988). Immune system and psychological changes in metastatic cancer patients using relaxation and guided imagery: A pilot study. *Scandinavian Journal of Behaviour Therapy, 17*, 25–46.

Guglielmi, R. S., Roberts, A. H., & Patterson, R. (1982). Skin temperature biofeedback for Raynaud's disease: A double-blind study. *Biofeedback & Self-Regulation, 7*, 99–120.

Guitar, B. (1975). Reduction of stuttering frequency using analog electromyographic feedback. *Journal of Speech & Hearing Research, 18*, 672–685.

Haynes, S. N., Griffin, P., Mooney, D., & Parise, M. (1975). Electromyographic biofeedback and relaxation instructions in the treatment of muscle contraction headaches. *Behavior Therapy, 6*, 672–678.

Hermann, C., Blanchard, E. B., & Flor, H. (1997). Biofeedback treatment for pediatric migraine: Prediction of treatment outcome. *Journal of Consulting & Clinical Psychology, 65*, 611–616.

Hermann, C., Kim, M., & Blanchard, E. B. (1995). Behavioral and prophylactic pharmacological intervention studies of pediatric migraine: An exploratory meta-analysis. *Pain, 60*, 239–256.

Hoelscher, T. J. (1987). Maintenance of relaxation-induced blood pressure reductions: The importance of continued relaxation practice. *Biofeedback & Self-Regulation, 12*, 2–12.

Holmes, T. H., Treuting, T., & Wolff, H. G. (1951). Life situations, emotions and nasal disease: Evidence on summative effects exhibited in patients with hayfever. *Psychosomatic Medicine, 13*, 71–82.

Holroyd, K. A., Holm, J. F., Penzien, D., Cordingley, G. E., Hursey, K. G., Martin, N. J., & Theofanous, A. (1989). Long-term maintenance of improvements achieved with (abortive) pharmacological and nonpharmacological treatments for migraine: Preliminary findings. *Biofeedback & Self Regulation, 14*, 301–308.

Hutchings, D., & Reinking, R. H. (1976). Tension headaches: "What form of therapy is most effective?" *Biofeedback & Self-Regulation, 1*, 169–183.

Ishigami, T. (1985). The influence of psychic acts on the progress of pulmonary tuberculosis. In S. Locke, R. Ader, H. Besedovsky, N. Hall, G. Solomon, & T. Strom (Eds.), *Foundations of psychoneuroimmunology* (pp. 287–297). New York: Aldine.

Jemmott, J. B., Wilson, J., & McClelland, D. C. (1983, June). Academic stress, power motivation and decrease in salivary secretory immunoglobulin A. *Lancet, 25*, 1400–1402.

Kaufman, P. G., Jacob, R. G., Ewart, C. K., Chesney, M. A., Muenz, L. R., Doub, N., & Mercer, W. (1988). Hypertension intervention pooling project. *Health Psychology, 7*, 209–223.

Kiecolt-Glaser, J. K., Garner, W., Speicher, C., Penn, G. M., Holliday, J., & Glaser, R. (1984). Psychosocial modifiers of immunocompetence in medical students. *Psychosomatic Medicine, 46*, 7–14.

Kiecolt-Glaser, J. K., Glaser, R., Shuttleworth, E. C., Dyer, C. S., Ogrocki, P., & Speicher, C. E. (1987). Chronic stress and immunity in family caregivers of Alzheimer's disease victims. *Psychosomatic Medicine, 49*, 523–535.

Kiecolt-Glaser, J. K., Glaser, R., Williger, D., Stout, J., Messick, G., Sheppard, S., Ricker, D., Romisher, S. C., Briner, W., Bonnell, G., & Donnerberg, R. (1985). Psychosocial enhancement of immunocompetence in a geriatric population. *Health Psychology, 4*, 25–41.

Kiecolt-Glaser, J. K., Page, G. G., Marucha, P. T., MacCallum, R. C., & Glaser, R. (1998). Psychological influences on surgical recovery: Perspectives from psychoneuroimmunology. *American Psychologist, 53*, 1209–1218.

Kiecolt-Glaser, J. K., Speicher, C. E., Holliday, J. E., & Glaser, R. (1984). Stress and the transformation of lymphocytes by Epstein–Barr virus. *Journal of Behavioral Medicine, 7*, 1–12.

Kotses, H., & Glaus, K. D. (1981). Applications of biofeedback to the treatment of asthma: A critical review. *Biofeedback & Self-Regulation, 6*, 573–593.

Kotses, H., Glaus, K. D., Bricel, S. K., Edwards, J. E., & Crawford, P. L. (1978). Operant muscular reduction and peak expiratory flowrate in asthmatic children. *Journal of Psychosomatic Research, 22*, 17–23.

Kotses, H., Glaus, K. D., Crawford, P. L., Edwards, J. E., & Scherr, M. S. (1976). Operant reduction of frontalis EMG activity in the treatment of asthma in children. *Journal of Psychosomatic Research, 20*, 453–459.

Kotses, H., Harver, A., Segreto, J., Glaus, K. D., Creer, T. L., & Young, G. A. (1991). Long-term effects of biofeedback-induced facial relaxation on measures of asthma severity in children. *Biofeedback and Self Regulation, 16*, 1–21.

Kotses, H., Hindi-Alexander, M., & Creer, T. L. (1989). A reinterpretation of psychologically induced airways changes. *Journal of Asthma, 26*, 53–63.

Kristt, D. A., & Engel, B. T. (1975). Learned control of blood pressure in patients with high blood pressure. *Circulation, 51*, 370–378.

Kuhlman, W. N. (1978). Functional topography of the human mu rhythm. *Electroencephalography and Clinical Neurophysiology, 45*, 290–294.

Kuhlman, W. N., & Allison, T. (1977). EEG feedback training in the treatment of epilepsy: Some questions and some answers. *Pavlovian Journal of Biological Science, 12*, 112–122.

Lanyon, R. I. (1977). Effect of biofeedback-based relaxation on stuttering during reading and spontaneous speech. *Journal of Consulting & Clinical Psychology, 45*, 860–866.

Lanyon, R. I., Barrington, C. C., & Newman, A. C. (1976). Modification of stuttering through EMG biofeedback: A preliminary study. *Behavior Therapy, 7*, 96–103.

Lehrer, P., Carr, R. E., Smetankine, A., Vaschillo, E., Peper, E., Porges, S., Edelberg, R., Hamer, R., & Hochron, S. (1997). Respiratory sinus arrhythmia versus neck/trapezius EMG and incentive inspirometry biofeedback for asthma: A pilot study. *Applied Psychophysiology & Biofeedback, 22*, 95–109.

Lehrer, P., Generelli, P., & Hochron, S. (1997). The effect of facial and trapezius muscle tension on respiratory impedance in asthma. *Applied Psychophysiology & Biofeedback, 22*, 43–54.

Lehrer, P., Hochron, S. M., Mayne, T., Isenberg, S., Lasoski, A., Carlson, V., Gilchrist, J., & Porges, S. (1997c). Relationship between changes in EMG and respiratory sinus arrhythmia in a study of relaxation therapy for asthma. *Applied Psychophysiology & Biofeedback, 22*, 183–191.

Linden, M., Habib, T., & Radojevic, V. (1996). A controlled study of the effects of EEG biofeedback on cognition and behavior of children with attention deficit disorder and learning disabilities. *Biofeedback and Self-Regulation, 21*, 35–49.

Lubar, J. F. (1997). Neocortical dynamics: Implications for understanding the role of neurofeedback and related techniques for the enhancement of attention. *Applied Psychophysiology and Biofeedback, 22*, 111–126.

Lubar, J. F., & Bahler, W. W. (1976). Behavioral management of epileptic seizures following EEG biofeedback training of the sensorimotor rhythm. *Biofeedback & Self-Regulation, 1*, 77–104.

Lubar, J. O., & Lubar, J. F. (1984). Electroencephalographic biofeedback of SMR and beta for treatment of attention deficit disorders in a clinical setting. *Biofeedback and Self-Regulation, 9*, 1–23.

Lubar, J. F., Swartwood, M. O., Swartwood, J. N., & O'Donnell, P. H. (1995). Evaluation of the effectiveness of EEG neurofeedback training for ADHD in a clinical setting as measured by changes in T.O.V.A. scores, behavioral ratings, and WISC-R performance. *Biofeedback and Self-Regulation, 20*, 83–99.

Mann, C. A., Lubar, J. F., Zimmerman, A. W., Miller, C. A., & Muenchen, R. A. (1992). Quantitative analysis of EEG in boys with Attention-deficit-hyperactivity Disorder: Controlled study with clincial implications. *Pediatric Neurology, 8*, 30–36.

Manuck, S. B., Cohen, S., Rabin, B. S., Muldoon, M. F., & Bachen, E. A. (1991). Individual differences in cellular immune response to stress. *Psychological Science, 2*, 111–115.

Marucha, P. T., Kiecolt-Glaser, J. K., & Favagehi, M. (1998). Mucosal wound healing is imparied by examination stress. *Psychosomatic Medicine, 60*, 362–365.

Middaugh, S. (1977, October). *Comparison of voluntary muscle contraction with and without EMG feedback in persons with neuromuscular dysfunction.* Paper presented at the 17th annual meeting of the Society for Psychophysiological Research, Philadelphia, PA.

Middaugh, S., Whitehead, W. E., Burgio, K. L., & Engel, B. T. (1989). Biofeedback in treatment of urinary incontinence in stroke patients. *Biofeedback & Self-Regulation, 14*, 3–19.

Miller, N. E. (1974). Introduction. In N. E. Miller, T. X. Barber, L. V. DiCara, J. Kamiya, D. Shapiro, & J. Stoyva (Eds.), *Biofeedback and self-control 1973: An Aldine annual on the regulation of bodily processes and consciousness* (pp. 11–20). Chicago: Aldine.

Patel, C. H. (1973). Yoga and biofeedback in the treatment of hypertension. *Lancet, 1*, 1053–1055.

Patel, C. H. (1975). Twelve-month follow-up of yoga and biofeedback in the management of hypertension. *Lancet, 2*, 62–67.

Patel, C. H., & North, W. R. S. (1975). Randomized controlled trial of yoga and biofeedback in management of hypertension. *Lancet, 2*, 93–99.

Peper, E., & Tibbetts, V. (1992). Fifteen-month follow-up with asthmatics utilizing EMG/incentive inspirometer feedback. *Biofeedback & Self-Regulation, 17,* 143–151.

Price, K. P., & Tursky, B. (1976). Vascular reactivity of migraineurs and non-migraineurs: A comparison of responses to self-control procedures. *Headache, 16,* 210–217.

Rasey, H. W., Lubar, J. F., McIntyre, A., Zoffuto, A. C., & Abbot, P. L. (1996). EEG biofeedback for the enhancement of attentional processing in normal college students. *Journal of Neurotherapy, 1,* 15–31.

Raskin, M., Johnson, G., & Rondestvedt, J. W. (1973). Chronic anxiety treated by feedback-induced muscle relaxation. *Archives of General Psychiatry, 28,* 263–267.

Reinking, R. H., & Hutchings, D. (1981). Follow-up to: "Tension headaches: What form of therapy is most effective?" *Biofeedback & Self-Regulation, 6,* 57–62.

Rokicki, L. A., Holroyd, K. A., France, C. R., Lipchik, G. L., France, J. L., & Kvaal, S. A. (1997). Change mechanisms associated with combined relaxation/EMG biofeedback training for chronic tension headache. *Applied Psychophysiology & Biofeedback, 22,* 21–41.

Rossiter, T. R., & LaVaque, T. J. (1995). A comparison of EEG biofeedback and psychostimulants in treating attention deficit hyperactivity disorders. *Journal of Neurotherapy,* 48–59.

Santee, J. L., Keister, M. E., & Kleinman, K. M. (1980). Incentives to enhance the effects of electromyographic feedback training in stroke patients. *Biofeedback & Self-Regulation, 5,* 51–56.

Sargent, J. D., Green, E. E., & Walters, E. D. (1972). The use of autogenic feedback training in a pilot study of migraine and tension headaches. *Headache, 12,* 120–124.

Sargent, J. D., Walters, E. D., & Green, E. E. (1973). Psychosomatic self-regulation of migraine headaches. *Seminars in Psychiatry, 5,* 415–428.

Schellenberger, R., & Green, J. (1987). Specific effects and biofeedback versus biofeedback-assisted self-regulation training. *Biofeedback & Self-Regulation, 12,* 185–210.

Schleifer, S. J., Keller, S. E., Camerino, M., Thornton, J. C., & Stein, M. (1983). Suppression of lymphocyte stimulation following bereavement. *Journal of the American Medical Association, 250,* 374–377.

Schneiderman, N., Antoni, M. H., Aronson, G., LaPerriere, A., & Fletcher, M. (1992). Applied psychological science and HIV-1 spectrum disease. *Applied & Preventive Psychology, 1,* 67–82.

Schwartz, G. E., & Shapiro, D. (1973). Biofeedback and essential hypertension: Current findings and theoretical concerns. *Seminars in Psychiatry, 5,* 493–503.

Sedlacek, K. (1979). Biofeedback for Raynaud's disease. *Psychosomatics, 20,* No. 8, 21–25.

Seifert, R. R., & Lubar, J. F. (1975). Reduction of epileptic seizures through EEG biofeedback training. *Biological Psychology, 3,* 157–184.

Sgoutas-Emch, S. A., Cacioppo, J. T., Uchino, B. N., Malarkey, W., Pearl, D., Kiecolt-Glaser, J. K., & Glaser, R. (1994). The effects of an acute psychological stressor on cardiovascular, endocrine, and cellular immune response: A prospective study of individuals high and low in heart rate reactivity. *Psychophysiology, 31,* 264–271.

Shapiro, D., Mainardi, J. A., & Surwit, R. S. (1977). Biofeedback and self-regulation in essential hypertension. In G. E. Schwartz & J. Beatty (Eds.), *Biofeedback: Theory and research* (pp. 313–347). New York: Academic Press.

Sterman, M. B. (1973). Neurophysiologic and clinical studies of sensorimotor EEG biofeedback training: Some effects on epilepsy. *Seminars in Psychiatry, 5,* 507–524.

Sterman, M. B. (1984). The role of sensorimotor rhythmic EEG activity in the etiology and treatment of generalized motor seizures. In T. Elbert, B. Rockstroh, W. Lutzenberger, & N. Birbaumer (Eds.), *Self-regulation of the brain and behavior* (pp. 42–54). Heidelberg: Springer.

Sterman, M. B., & Friar, L. (1972). Suppression of seizures in an epileptic following EEG feedback traiing. *Electroencephalography and Clinical Neurophysiology, 33,* 89–95.

Sterman, M. B., MacDonald, L. R., & Stone, R. K. (1974). Biofeedback training of the sensorimotor EEG rhythm in man: Effects on epilepsy. *Epilepsia, 15,* 395–416.

Stroebel, C. F., & Glueck, B. C. (1973). Biofeedback treatment in medicine and psychiatry: An ultimate placebo? *Seminars in Psychiatry, 5,* 379–393.

Surwit, R. S., Pilon, R. N., & Fenton, C. H. (1977, October). *Behavioral treatment of Raynaud's disease.* Paper presented at the 17th Annual Meeting of the Society for Psychophysiological Research, Philadelphia, PA.

Takebe, K., & Basmajian, J. V. (1976). Gait analysis in stroke patients to assess treatment of footdrop. *Archives of Physical Medicine and Rehabilitation, 57,* 305–310.

Taub, E. (1977). Self-regulation of human tissue temperature. In G. E. Schwartz & J. Beatty (Eds.), *Biofeedback: Theory and research* (pp. 265–270). New York: Academic Press.

Weinman, M. L., Semchuk, K. M., Gaebe, G., & Mathew, R. J. (1983). The effect of stressful life events on EMG biofeedback and relaxation training in the treatment of anxiety. *Biofeedback & Self-Regulation, 8,* 191–205.

Whitsett, S. F., Lubar, J. F., Holder, G. S., Pamplin, W. E., & Shabsin, H. S. (1982). A double-blind investigation of the relationship between seizure activity and the sleep EEG following EEG biofeedback training. *Biofeedback & Self-Regulation, 7,* 193–209.

18

Concepts in Psychophysiology

Explanatory concepts enable scientists to categorize and understand large amounts of data. They also suggest hypotheses to be tested and questions to be asked by investigators of various phenomena and, thus, help to guide the researcher. The answers obtained through experimental study may suggest modification or elaboration of existing concepts, or a relationship with other formulations. Within the field of psychophysiology, the most elaborate of the concepts deal with cardiovascular or autonomic activity in one form or another. Concepts concerning brain responses are as numerous, but not as well-developed. In addition, there are formulations regarding electrodermal response and muscle activity. Thus, the field of psychophysiology does not have an all-inclusive conceptual framework within which most of the collected data may be tested, integrated, and interpreted. Instead, there are a number of concepts that have relevance for the interpretation of experimental findings. Some of these concepts, at least in part, contradict one another. Perhaps one day, the various concepts may be reconciled and subsumed within one or a few theoretical frameworks that will account for most of the existing data. This is probably an overly optimistic goal, but one for which scientists in diverse areas, including psychophysiology, constantly strive.

Scientific concepts and theories enable isolated findings and information to be bound together into a meaningful pattern. They provide a basis for the interpretation of past and present information and act as stimulators for future investigations. The very experiments that are suggested by a given scientific concept may be responsible for the modification or elimination of the concept. The development of concepts includes the sharpening of predictive value and modifications to accommodate an increasing number of new facts. The development of these kinds of concepts is one sign of a maturing science. The concepts discussed in this chapter are the law of initial values, autonomic balance, activation, stimulus response specificity, individual response specificity, cardiac–somatic coupling, adaptation, rebound, the orienting response, and defensive responses. In addition, conceptual approaches in the areas of social psychophysiology and event-related brain potentials are considered.

THE LAW OF INITIAL VALUES

The law of initial values (LIV) states that a particular physiological response to a given stimulus or situation depends on the prestimulus level of the system being measured (e.g., see Wilder, 1957, 1967, 1976). More specifically, the law says that the higher the initial level, the smaller the increase in physiological response to a given stimulus. On the other hand, the higher the level, the larger the decrease produced by stimuli normally capable of producing decreases. How might the LIV predict a change in HR in a given situation? It has been found that subjects who are fearful of mutilation show an acceleration in HR to slides of accident victims (Klorman, Weisenfield, & Austin, 1975). The LIV would predict that if HR is higher than usual for these persons, HR acceleration would not be as pronounced as it would be for a lower prestimulus rate. Thus, a *ceiling effect* of sorts would operate for HR increases. Suppose, further, that the prestimulus rate was higher than usual for individuals who customarily show HR deceleration to mutilation slides. In effect, these subjects would now have more room for a downward change in HR and a greater than usual decrease would be observed. Although this test has not actually been carried out, it is an example of a procedure that could be used to test the predictive power of the LIV.

Wilder (1967) considered the LIV to apply to all responses under the control of the autonomic nervous system. His purpose in proposing the LIV was to describe the effects of activating drugs on autonomic variables, recognizing that higher initial levels led to smaller increases with activation. However, experimental results indicate that not all physiological responses are subject to effects of prestimulus level. For example, Hord, Johnson, and Lubin (1964) found that the LIV operated as predicted for HR and respiration rate responses, but not for skin conductance or skin temperature. The experimental paradigm they used tested the LIV with respect to the part that predicts smaller upward changes in a given function with higher prestimulus levels of that activity. The physiological responses of 105 persons were measured to experimental stimuli that included sounds, lights, and mental arithmetic. When the prestimulus level of each physiological function was compared with poststimulus levels, the results led Hord et al. to conclude that the LIV does not hold for skin conductance or skin temperature.

Libby, Lacey, and Lacey (1973) predicted that pupil dilation and HR deceleration would occur as a characteristic response of subjects to interesting pictorial stimuli. Their predictions were confirmed based on the analysis of responses of 34 males. Incidental to their main analysis was the observation that the magnitude of change in the two physiological variables was related to prestimulus level in both, thus supporting the LIV. They cautioned, however, that experience revealed wide variations in the relationship between prestimulus levels and responsivity, depending on the experimental conditions, the stimulus situation, and even the subjects used. Thus, further restrictions are imposed on the applicability of the LIV, and a need to delineate the extent of its limitation is emphasized. Caution is advised by Jamieson and Howk (1992), who used a computer model to show that measurement errors, the "ceiling/floor" effect (LIV), reactivity, and a skewed (nonnormal) distribution of scores all act to influence the LIV. For example, positively skewed distributions act against the LIV effect, whereas those that are negatively skewed exaggerate the LIV effect. In a follow-up simulation Jamieson (1993) added a fifth factor, variance, and illustrated its effects on the LIV. He demonstrated that decreased variance enhanced the LIV effect, whereas increased variance attenuated the LIV effect. These influences on calculations of LIV may account for some of the discrepancies found in empirical studies; for example, the puzzle concerning predictive ability for LIV with vascular activity, but not for skin conductance.

Results for finger vascular activity consistent with the LIV were obtained by Lovallo and Zeiner (1975). The cold pressor (CP) test was used as the stimulus. The CP is a procedure that involves the immersion of an extremity, in this case the left foot, in a bucket of ice water. It is often used to test degree of vasoconstriction on stimulation, because blood vessels of the skin become narrowed when exposed to cold temperatures. The researchers predicted that when vasoconstriction was maximal, the CP (severe cold) would produce vasodilation; when vasodilation was high, substantial vasoconstriction would result. Room temperature was used to manipulate the prestimulus state of the peripheral vasculature. A room temperature of 12°C (54°F) produced prestimulus vasoconstriction, and a temperature of 32°C (90°F) resulted in vasodilation. The subjects were also tested at a room temperature of 22°C (72°F). The results of the CP were in line with their predictions because the response magnitude was not only dependent on the stimulus, but was related to the initial level of vascular tonus (i.e., vasoconstriction or vasodilation). Figure 18.1 depicts a portion of the results from the Lovallo and Zeiner study.

White (1977) reviewed a number of studies, using salivation as a measure, to determine whether response magnitude was related to prestimulus level. The studies used different methods, subjects, and stimuli. White concluded that, in general, the LIV did not hold for salivation. In addition, Scher, Furedy, and Heslegrave (1985) found that LIV was not confirmed for two cardiovascular variables (HR and T-wave amplitude) when a between-subjects design was used. However, the LIV did hold for these same variables when a within-subjects design was used, that is, a procedure where subjects served as their own control. When exceptions to the LIV occur, they are more likely to be observed for between-subjects designs than within-subjects analyses.

Peripheral blood flow underlies finger skin temperature, and it has been noted that right-handed persons frequently have higher skin temperature in their right hand than in their left hands (Jamieson, 1987). The LIV was shown to operate for finger skin temperature as subjects responded to cognitive stressors, for example, counting backward by 17s. Jamieson (1987) reported that, in keeping with LIV, persons whose right hands were initially warmer responded with a greater temperature decrease of the right hand.

Summary.   The LIV is a concept that focuses on the level of prestimulus activity for a physiological measure in determining magnitude of response. Experimental investigations suggest that certain physiological variables change in a way predicted by the law (e.g., respiration and vascular tonus). Other measures (e.g., skin conductance and salivation) show changes that do not appear to be consistent with the LIV. Furedy and Scher (1989) argued that the LIV should be considered as an empirical generalization that requires further testing to specify its boundaries, and it should not yet be "enshrined" as a methodological rule. Thus, it

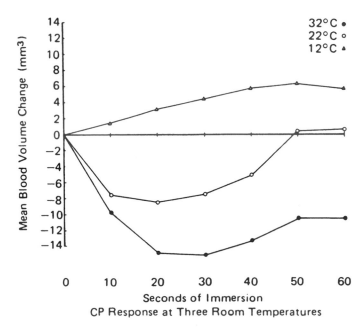

FIG. 18.1. Three curves showing an increase in blood volume to cold pressor for subjects tested under 12° C room temperature and increasingly large decreases in blood volume for those tested at 22° C and 32° C.

should be viewed as a "principle" and not a "law." Jamieson (1993) further questioned the value of LIV for psychophysiological research in view of the fact that it can be influenced by so many variables. Although these caveats are important, it is also true that the LIV has alerted investigators to the possible influence of prestimulus physiological activity on reactions to stimuli.

AUTONOMIC BALANCE

The concept of autonomic balance examines human performance and behavior in the context of autonomic nervous system imbalance—that is, the extent to which the sympathetic nervous system (SNS) or the parasympathetic nervous system (PNS) is dominant in an individual. This dominance operates at both tonic (long term) and phasic (short term) levels. The name most prominently associated with this concept is that of Wenger and associates (Wenger, 1941, 1948, 1966; Wenger & Cullen, 1972). Wenger and co-workers proposed that, in a given individual, either the SNS or the PNS may be dominant. The degree to which one or the other is dominant may be estimated by an empirically determined weighted score called $\bar{A}$ (autonomic balance). The person's $\bar{A}$ is derived from a number of autonomically innervated functions, which include palmar skin conductance, respiration rate, heart period, salivation, systolic and diastolic blood pressure, forearm skin conductance, pulse pressure, and red dermographia (persistence of skin after stroking with a stimulator). The value for each variable (e.g., skin conductance level or heart period) is converted to T scores and included in an equation. High $\bar{A}$ scores indicate PNS dominance, whereas low $\bar{A}$ scores reflect relative SNS dominance. The predominance of this autonomic factor for an individual remains constant from year to year (tonic level) but may show phasic changes to current external or internal stimuli. The central tendency of these estimates of the autonomic factor are what Wenger meant by autonomic balance (Wenger & Cullen, 1972).

Wenger (1941) proposed that the distribution of $\bar{A}$ scores should be approximately normal (i.e., bell shaped, see Fig. 18.2) for a large random sample of individuals. In fact, Wenger

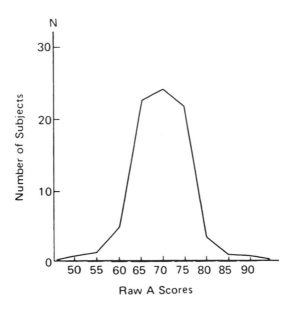

FIG. 18.2. The frequency distribution of the mean $\bar{A}$ scores (estimates of autonomic balance) for 87 children, ages 6 to 12.

found such a distribution for samples of children (1941) and adults (1948). Figure 18.2 depicts an average $\bar{A}$ of 70. Thus, individuals who score below this value would be SNS dominant and those above reflect PNS dominance, in relation to other persons in the sample. The amount by which the $\bar{A}$ score differs from the central value would indicate increasing degrees of imbalance. The procedure to obtain $\bar{A}$ scores is described by Wenger and Cullen (1972).

Wenger and his associates conducted many large-scale studies to determine the nature of the $\bar{A}$ scores in different samples of individuals. For example, Wenger (1948) studied autonomic balance in 225 military persons hospitalized for "operational fatigue" and 90 Air Force personnel diagnosed as "psychoneurosis-anxiety state." An example of their findings was that neurotic individuals had faster respiration, higher blood pressure, and lower finger temperature than persons suffering from fatigue. This trend would indicate greater SNS activity for anxiety neurotics. A sample of 448 Air Force cadets provided a normal distribution of $\bar{A}$ scores with an average of 69, very similar to that of the sample of children tested in 1941. Wenger, Engel, and Clemens (1957) concluded that autonomic factor scores are related to certain personality patterns and diagnostic categories such as anxiety psychoneurosis, battle fatigue, and asthma. They also hypothesized in 1957 that differences in autonomic response patterns, supplemented by differences in autonomic balance could be used to predict which persons will not react favorably to psychological stress and those who might develop psychosomatic disorders. In a study designed to test the hypothesis that patients with different psychosomatic disorders would show different response patterns for variables under ANS control, Wenger, Clemens, and Cullen (1962) tested the responses of 100 hospitalized males under controlled resting states and with the CP test. The patients included 31 with stomach ulcers, 36 with gastritis, and 33 with skin disorders (17 with neurodermatitis). The variables measured included HR, respiration rate, skin conductance, finger pulse volume, blood pressure, and skin temperature. One finding was that the resting $\bar{A}$ score of each patient group indicated greater SNS activity than a group of 93 normal subjects. There was no significant difference in reactivity to CP among the patient groups. Patients with gastritis, however, seemed more different from normals than other patient groups. In general, the results did not support the hypothesis, but did show differences in $\bar{A}$ score for patients and nonpatients.

Smith and Wenger (1965) estimated $\bar{A}$ for 11 graduate students under phasic anxiety (immediately before taking an oral examination for the Ph.D. degree) and under relatively relaxed conditions, either 1 month later (eight persons) or 1 month earlier. The hypothesis that $\bar{A}$ would significantly decrease during anxiety—thus indicating SNS dominance—was confirmed. For example, on the day of the examination, the subjects had less salivary output, higher blood pressure, shorter heart period, and higher sublingual (under tongue) temperature. Lovallo and Zeiner (1975) reviewed a number of studies in which the CP test was used to determine patterns of physiological responsivity. They viewed the results of these studies as useful in understanding homeostatic mechanisms, especially in relation to the concepts of LIV and autonomic balance. (*Homeostasis* is the term coined by W. B. Cannon to describe the tendency of the body to maintain a state of equilibrium in the face of external and internal changes.) Lovallo and Zeiner provided support for the use of LIV in understanding the magnitude and direction of responses to stimuli, as well as interactions between base levels of activity and task performance under stress. They also emphasized the interaction between initial values and autonomic balance in determining an individual's response to a given stimulus. Thus, we see a possible complementarity between LIV and autonomic balance in understanding physiological responsivity. Berntson and Colleagues have advanced the concept of "autonomic space" to refer to research indicating that there are times when the SNS and PNS may be active simultaneously and others when one may be active and the other silent (Berntson, Cacioppo, Quigley, & Fabro, 1994). They do this in order to point out that in certain situations the two systems do not only act in a reciprocal fashion, in which one increases activity of a certain target organ while the other decreases it, as we often see with control of heart rate.

Summary.   The concept of autonomic balance, and the Ā score, appears to provide a useful mechanism through which the relative dominance of the PNS or SNS of an individual may be established. However, relatively few studies to test and expand this concept have been performed, despite the fact that it has existed for some time. Most of the studies conducted to date have been performed by Wenger and his associates. Its value as a conceptual model would be enhanced if further studies testing its applicability (e.g., in understanding psychosomatic disorders, were performed by other investigators. The recent work of Berntson and associates, who introduced the concept of autonomic space, is a step towards rejuvenating research in this area.

ACTIVATION

The concept of activation attempts to explain the relationship between variations in level of physiological activity and changes in behavior. According to Duffy (1972), the description of behavior at any particular instant requires consideration of the goal toward which it is directed and the intensity of the behavior. The intensity of behavior is most commonly called "activation" or "arousal" and can be reflected in the level of responsivity in a number of physiological variables. For example, increasing levels of HR, blood pressure, muscle potentials, skin conductance, and EEG desynchronization are related to increased activation, whereas decreased levels of these same variables would indicate lowered activity. Various formulations of this concept are found in the writings of Duffy (1934, 1957, 1962, 1972), Hebb (1955), Lindsley (1951), and Malmo (1959, 1962).

The basic idea of a relationship between level of stimulation and performance arose from studies of discrimination learning in the mouse conducted by Yerkes and Dodson in 1908. They used a paradigm in which incorrect choices were followed by different intensities of electric shock, and found that a medium intensity shock led to more efficient learning than either a weak or strong shock. In a second experiment three levels of discrimination difficulty were used. For an easy discrimination, strength of electric shock did not affect learning speed. However, for both the medium and difficult discriminations moderate shock led to best performance. Thus, this seminal experiment showed that intensity of stimulation, as well as task difficulty, must be taken into account in studying the influence of external stimulation on performance. Later experiments by psychophysiologists added physiological measures to experiments with human subjects and developed the concept of activation.

A consistent idea in the writings of those who support the activation concept is that level of performance rises with increases in physiological activity of an organism up to a point that is optimal for a given task, and beyond this point, further increases cause a drop in performance. Thus, this concept proposes that performance is optimal at some intermediate level of physiological activation, and the relation between the two can be described by an inverted-U-shaped curve (see Fig. 18.3). Figure 18.3 is based on a discussion by Malmo (1962). An important role is given to the ascending reticular activating system (ARAS) by Malmo in regulating level of cortical excitability and, hence, performance.

Let us examine how arousal might operate in an everyday situation. Suppose that a person is very sleepy or drowsy early in the morning. The level of activation as reflected in various physiological measures would be low, and performance (e.g., in a RT task) would be poor. Later on in the day, when the physiological variables register at some intermediate level for this individual, performance would be best. If, at some other time, the individuals' perform-

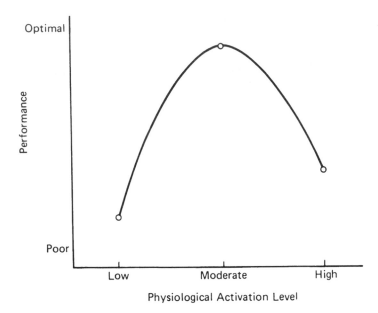

FIG. 18.3. The hypothetical inverted-U relationship indicates that performance is best at some moderate level of physiological activation. Malmo (1962) attributes the upturn in the curve to effects of nonspecific stimuli that influence the cortex through the ARAS. Activity in a circulating chain of neurons is said to be facilitated by impulses arriving at the cortex. Overstimulation, on the other hand, causes neurons in the chain to be less excitable and produces the downturn in the curve observed at high activation levels.

ance and physiological responses are measured when they are in a state of panic, or very high excitement, efficiency would be low and activation would be extremely high. This last situation would produce the downturn in the curve, thus producing the inverted-U-shaped function.

Empirical support for the activation concept is derived mainly from studies in which levels of physiological activity are manipulated and performance measures are taken, and from neurophysiological findings regarding the arousal functions of the reticular formation of the brain. In the first category of studies, which offer empirical support for an inverted-U-shape relation between activation and performance, are the many investigations of induced muscle tension (IMT) effects on task efficiency. An early example is a study by Courts (1939), who investigated the effects of six IMT levels on verbal learning. He found that an IMT level of one fourth of maximum was optimal for learning. Higher degrees of tension were also superior to the no-tension condition. However, at a level of three-fourths maximum IMT, learning efficiency fell below the no-tension condition, thus yielding an inverted-U-shape relationship between level of muscle tension and performance. In a review by Courts (1942), it was noted that performance in a wide variety of tasks had been improved with IMT. Tasks for which detrimental effects were noted involved motor adjustments, for example, tossing balls at a target. Moderate levels of IMT have been found to facilitate perception of strings of numbers (Shaw, 1956) and recognition of forms (Smock & Small, 1962). Malmo (1959) contended that muscle tension induction is one way to systematically increase overall physical activation. This contention is supported by studies of Freeman and Simpson (1938), who found that skin conductance increased with increased IMT, and those of Malmo and Davis (1956), who found high relationships between skeletal muscle activity and two autonomic measures (heart rate and blood pressure). In addition, Pinneo (1961) measured forearm EMG, SCL, EEG, HR, and respiration rate while six levels of IMT were produced by a dynamometer in the right hand. Pinneo reported that all of these physiological responses showed regular and continuous rises as a function of IMT level. Thus, there is good evidence that IMT is related to changes in activation.

One study frequently cited in support of the activation concept is Freeman's (1940). This investigator measured skin conductance and RT of a single subject over a series of 100 experimental sessions. The observations were made at various times of the day, over a number of days, when the subject varied widely in levels of alertness. Freeman found a curvilinear, inverted-U-shape relationship, between skin conductance and RT, in which RTs were slower at high and low conductance levels and fastest at the middle levels. Stennett (1957) manipulated activation level through the use of incentive and found an inverted-U relation between tracking performance and two measures of physiological arousal (skin conductance and EMG). However, an inverted-U was not found by Schlosberg and Kling (1959), who attempted to repeat the Freeman (1940) study with a larger number of subjects. Nor was it indicated in a study by Kennedy and Travis (1948), who investigated the relationship between frontalis muscle tension, reaction time, and level of performance in a continuous tracking task. Kennedy and Travis found a linear relationship between EMG level and performance—that is, tracking and RT were poor at low EMG levels and better at the higher levels of muscle tension. A similar finding was reported by Andreassi (1966) for the relationship between skin conductance and RT in a continuous monitoring task in which subjects had to respond to infrequent and random auditory signals. Andreassi found that RT was fast when SCL was high and slow when SCL was low. Intermediate SCL was not associated with best RT performance. It was suggested that an inverted-U-shaped function will be observed only when levels of activation are purposely manipulated to produce very high and low levels of physiological activity.

Puposeful manipulation of SCL to between 6.5 and 8.5 μmhos, on both hands, was related to optimal performance of children in processing visual and auditory stimuli (Mangina & Beuzeron-Mangina, 1988). Physiological underactivation was defined as bilateral SCLs lower than 5.01 μmhos, and overactivation was indicated by an SCL of 10.1 μmho or more, both when processing cognitive information. When SCL fell below 6.49 μmho, an alerting tone was presented automatically to increase SCL. If the SCL continued to drop, light flashes and postural manipulations (stand up-sit down) were used. Relaxation techniques were used when SCL was considered to be too high. According to these investigators, these "optimal" activation strategies have implications for helping the learning disabled to improve school performance. In another study, relaxation exercises were used to decrease levels of physiological activity just before teacher candidates were about to be tested on their teaching ability by a panel of judges (Helin & Hanninen, 1987). Compared to controls, the individuals who listened to an 18-min relaxation tape just prior to the test had better scores and lower systolic BP during the examination. In addition, males showed decreased trapezius EMG during the test, whereas females had reduced heart rates. Complex interactions among gender, personality, and physiological response make it difficult to interpret the Helin and Hanninen results simply in terms of the activation concept.

The neurophysiological bases for the activation concept are found in studies of the reticular formation. Moruzzi and Magoun (1949) discovered that electrical stimulation of the brain stem reticular formation (BSRF) of anesthetized cats shifted the EEG recorded at the cortex from high voltage slow waves to low voltage fast waves. The cat's EEG showed the signs of a normal arousal from sleep. The excitable area included the central core of the brain stem extending from the medulla up to the hypothalamus (see Fig. 18.4). Moruzzi and Magoun concluded that the reticular formation acted as a general alarm mechanism that aroused the cortex, and they referred to it as the reticular activating system (RAS). Further work by these investigators, and others who studied the behavioral and physiological effects of stimulation and lesions in the RAS, led to the recognition of this system's importance in maintaining

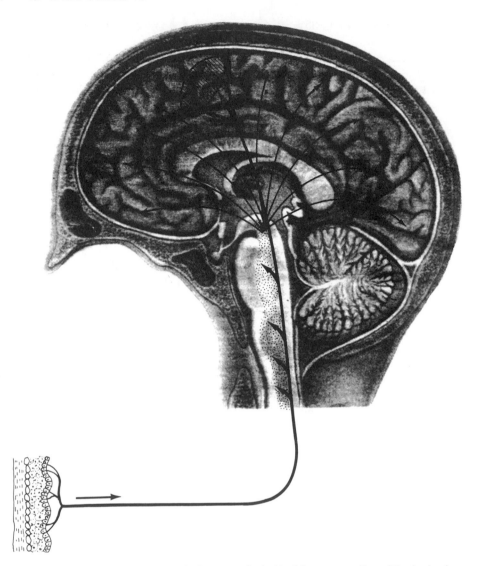

FIG. 18.4. The reticular formation is the area stippled in this cross section of the brain. A sense organ (lower left) is connected to a sensory area in the brain by a pathway extending up the spinal cord. This pathway branches into the reticular formation. When a stimulus travels along the pathway, the reticular formation may "awaken" the entire brain (arrows).

wakefulness and producing arousal of cortical areas under appropriate stimulus conditions. Lindsley (1951) reviewed evidence that lesions in the ARAS (ascending reticular activating system) abolished the activation pattern of the EEG and produced a behavioral picture of apathy and somnolence. Lindsley (1956) noted that the ARAS projects fibers to, and receives projections from, the cerebral cortex, indicating mechanisms for interaction between these two areas of the brain. Thus, the central location and connections to and from the ARAS point to its potential as a mechanism for regulating and integrating input to other levels of the CNS. Fuster (1958) provided evidence that moderate electrical stimulation of the ARAS can facilitate visual perception and RT in monkeys. High intensity stimulation of the ARAS led to a decrement in performance, as would be predicted by proponents of the activation concept.

Duffy (1972) reviewed many studies that lend support to the activation concept. One criticism of the concept (J. I. Lacey, 1967) is that autonomic, central (electrocortical), and behavioral activation are different forms of arousal, each with its own complexities. Thus, for example, increased cardiac activity is not necessarily related to elevated cortical activity, and, in fact, is accompanied by decreased brain activation. The Laceys' concepts are discussed more fully later in this chapter. However, Eason and Dudley (1971) provided an example of a situation where various physiological responses do vary simultaneously in the same direction. Three levels of activation were produced by manipulating experimental conditions as follows: (a) Subjects were told that they would be shocked if they did not respond quickly to light flashes ("high activation"), or (b) they were merely instructed to react as quickly as possible to the flashes ("moderate activation"), or (c) they were told not to observe the light flashes without responding ("low activation"). All the physiological variables measured (HR, SCL, EMG, and visual–cortical-evoked potentials) increased with higher levels of activation. Although HR deceleration was observed just prior to the response signal at all levels of activation, the major trend showed a generalized activation that was similar for cortical, somatic, and autonomic variables.

Summary.   There is a good deal of empirical support for an activation/arousal concept relating level of physiological activity to behavioral intensity. The support stems mainly from studies in which the level of physiological activity is purposely manipulated and from neurophysiological evidence regarding the importance of the reticular formation in regulating levels of alertness. One weakness of the concept has been its lack of precision in specifying an a priori optimal physiological level for a given group of individuals performing a task under conditions in which level of activation has not been purposely manipulated. This may be difficult because of large individual differences in any index of physiological activation that may be used. Another weakness has been the failure of its proponents to consider different patterning of physiological responses in different situations. Thus, there are instances when one physiological measure increases (e.g., SCL) while another decreases (e.g., HR) simultaneously. J. I. Lacey (1959) called this effect *directional fractionation*. An example of a situation where this type of divergent response can be observed is the vigilance task in which an individual is attuned to the occurrence of some critical signal. Here a decrease in HR is related to increased attentiveness at the same time that an increase in skin conductance occurs. Barry (1996) has suggested that there are different kinds of arousal, and that we can observe simultaneous cardiac, electrodermal or EEG arousal with a defensive response and a divergence in these same measures during an orienting response. The way in which Barry integrates activation/arousal and the orienting reflex is briefly discussed later in this chapter.

Another difficulty for activation theory is dealing with stimulus–response specificity (Stern & Sison, 1990) or the pattern of physiological responsivity that may occur in a particular situation. For example, if one suddenly notices that something of value is missing, then there might be an increase in muscle tension and SCL, but a decrease in respiration rate and HR. Thus, there is not merely an increase or decrease along some unidimensional activation continuum. Nevertheless, the concept has stimulated a great deal of research and can predict changes in physiological activity and performance under straightforward conditions of physical manipulation (e.g., IMT) and some psychological manipulations (e.g., Eason & Dudley, 1971) and remains as a useful, though limited, construct in psychophysiology.

STIMULUS–RESPONSE (SR) SPECIFICITY

The concept of stimulus–response specificity refers to a patterning of physiological responses according to the particular stimulus situation. It has been discussed in the writings of Ax (1953); J. I. Lacey, Bateman, and Van Lehn (1953); J. I. Lacey, Kagan, B. C. Lacey, and Moss

(1963); and Engel (1972), among others. The concept states that an individual's pattern of physiological activity (e.g., HR, EMG, SCL, respiration, and blood pressure) will be similar in a given situation, and that the pattern may vary when the situation is different. One basic question here is whether the pattern of physiological response will indicate the nature of an emotion being experienced by an individual. Or, to put it another way, what is the pattern of response in happiness versus sadness, or in anger versus fear, or in disgust versus surprise?

One of the first investigators to study this experimentally was Ax (1953), who induced fear in his 43 subjects with a bumbling experimenter who gave them "accidental" shocks. Anger was produced in the same persons through insults and criticism delivered by an "arrogant" and "incompetent" assistant. Ax found greater increases in respiration rate and SCL in fear than in anger. However, greater increases in EMG, diastolic blood pressure, and greater decreases in HR were observed in anger as compared to fear. There were higher intercorrelations among the physiological reactions for anger than fear, indicating to Ax that there was greater coordination of response during anger. Studies by Dimberg (e.g., Dimberg, 1990) and other psychophysiologists, mentioned in chapter 8, indicate that specific muscle groups are active when subject experience different emotions. For example, the finding that increased corrugator muscle activity is associated with angry feelings, whereas zygomatic muscle activity is related to pleasant emotions supports the notion of stimulus–response specificity.

Additional evidence that patterning of physiological response can differentiate emotional states comes from a study by Ekman, Levenson, and Friesen (1983). These researchers studied six emotions (surprise, disgust, sadness, anger, fear, and happiness) produced through two tasks: *directed facial action* and *relived emotion*. In the directed action condition, subjects produced different facial muscle patterns, whereas the other condition required them to reexperience particular emotional events. Heart rate increased more in anger and fear than in happiness, and skin temperature increased more in anger than happiness. Sadness produced larger skin conductance responses than fear, anger, and disgust. These intriguing findings require additional follow-up and confirmation, but to date, to this writer's knowledge, they have not been repeated.

Variations in the stimulus situation produced different patterns in physiological responding, as reported by J. I. Lacey (1959). He gave examples of situations in which HR showed a decrease while SCL increased, and instances in which they changed in the same direction (see Fig. 18.5). Lacey referred to the divergent response of these two measures as "directional fractionation of response." This term describes stimulus situations in which direction of change in physiological activity is contrary to the view that ANS responses must co-vary simultaneously, up or down, in a given situation.

Lacey (1959) also presented evidence that tasks involving cognitive functioning (e.g., mental arithmetic) are accompanied by increases in HR, whereas those emphasizing perceptual activities (e.g., attention to visual stimuli) led to HR deceleration. He suggested that cardiac deceleration facilitated "intake" of environmental stimuli, whereas acceleration was associated with attempts to exclude or "reject" those stimuli that would be disruptive to the performance of some cognitive function. Lacey et al. (1963) observed that cognitive activities were accompanied by HR increases, whereas primarily perceptual functions led to cardiac deceleration.

Directional fractionation of response has also been reported by Andreassi, Rapisardi, and Whalen (1969) and Hare (1972). Andreassi and colleagues found HR to be significantly higher when subjects were required to respond to an irregular pattern of signals than with a fixed interval. In contrast, SCL and SCRs were elevated for the fixed intervals, as compared to the variable presentations. The variable pattern was likened to a cognitive task, because it required more mental effort to anticipate signals when they occurred at irregular intervals. Thus, HR acceleration occurred, as would be predicted by Lacey et al. (1963) for cognitive

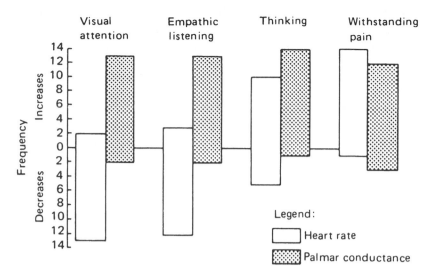

FIG. 18.5. The "directional fractionation of response" according to the nature of the subjects' tasks. For the 15 subjects whose responses are shown here, all four stimulus conditions produced increases in palmar conductance, but visual and auditory attending resulted in heart rate decreases, while the other tasks involving "rejection" of input resulted in heart rate increases.

tasks. On the other hand, relatively lower HR levels were observed with regular intervals, presumably because simple attention was involved in performing the task. Hare (1972) measured HR, SCL, and vasomotor activity (finger and cephalic vasoconstriction) while subjects viewed slides of homicide victims. One group was instructed to rate the slides on a 7-point scale of unpleasantness (raters), whereas the other group merely viewed the slides (nonraters). The nonraters showed directional fractionation, which included cardiac deceleration, increased SCL, digital vasoconstriction, and cephalic vasodilation. However, the raters did not display fractionation, because they showed HR acceleration, an increase in SCL, and both digital and cephalic vasoconstriction. The results for raters were interpreted as being consistent with the hypothesis that HR increases are associated with cognitive activity. The rise in SCL was attributed to the fact that increased requirements for evaluation caused the subjects to notice more disturbing aspects of the slides.

Libby et al. (1973) found that pupil dilation was greater to unpleasant stimuli, and cardiac slowing was related to pleasantness. Pictures rated as pleasant produced greater HR deceleration than those rated as unpleasant. These results are a further example of directional fractionation and stimulus-response specificity. Evidence for stimulus-response specificity and directional fractionation were obtained in a study using impedance cardiography (Wilson, Albright, Steiner, & Andreassi, 1991). Stimulus–response specificity was evidenced by greater changes in systolic and diastolic blood pressure, HR, stroke volume, total peripheral resistance, and peripheral skin temperature when comparing cold pressor test to IQ quiz reactivity. Directional fractionation was shown in myocardial contractility and cardiac output, because they decreased during cold pressor and increased during the IQ quiz.

Cardiac deceleration has been assigned an important role in the regulation of brain function and performance in later refinements of the "intake–rejection" hypothesis. For example, J. I. Lacey (1967) argued that changes in HR and blood pressure can influence cortical activity and thereby affect sensitivity to stimuli. A decrease in HR would be sensed by baroreceptors in the carotid and aortic arteries, resulting in decreased visceral feedback to cortical areas, thus causing increased cortical activity. This is partially based on neurophysiological evidence from animal studies that have shown that level of cardiovascular activity can affect EEG frequency (Bonvallet, Dell, & Hiebel, 1954). Cardiovascular feedback has been shown to inhibit the rage response in cats (Baccelli, Guazzi, Libretti, & Zanchetta, 1965; Bartorelli, Bizzi, Libretti, & Zanchetta, 1960). In addition, Galin and J. I. Lacey (1972) recorded HR, respiration, EEG, and RT in cats under conditions in which the midbrain reticular formation was either stimulated or not stimulated. They reported that HR deceleration sometimes accompanied reticular stimulation, indicating that HR slowing and CNS arousal could occur simultaneously.

B. C. Lacey and J. I. Lacey (1978) discussed some neurophysiological findings strongly supporting the notion that sensory and motor functions can be inhibited by increases in baroreceptor activity (Coleridge, Coleridge, & Rosenthal, 1976; Gahery & Vigier, 1974). For example, Coleridge et al. (1976) found that stimulation of carotid baroreceptors inhibited the activity of single neurons in the motor cortex. The Laceys observed that, by inference, sensory and motor functions may be facilitated by decreased baroreceptor afferent activity. For example, an association among a measure of brain activity (CNV), HR deceleration, and RT efficiency has been reported by J. I. Lacey and B. C. Lacey (1970). They found that the greater the HR deceleration during the foreperiod of a RT task, the greater was the CNV, and both of these were related to quicker RTs. Higher CNV amplitudes and greater HR decelerations were accompanied by faster RTs. In a later study, B. C. Lacey and J. I. Lacey (1977) reported that magnitude of HR deceleration was differentially affected during a single cardiac cycle, depending on when a signal to respond occurred within that cycle. This latter study was more fully discussed in chapter 12. The Laceys' hypothesis concerning cardiovascular feedback effects on attention has been criticized by Elliott (1972) and Hahn (1973). The criticisms generally called for clarification of terms such as "attention," and less reliance on HR alone as a dependent measure of cortical effects.

Summary.   The studies of the Laceys and others have indicated support for stimulus or situational response specificity. That is, a consistent pattern of physiological responses will occur in a given situation. In addition, "directional fractionation," in which different physiological variables show different directions of response, has been reported in a number of investigations, particularly those that require subjects to note and detect environmental events. The "intake–rejection" hypothesis has developed into a concept concerning interactions between cardiovascular activity and the brain and its effects on behavior, especially sensorimotor performance.

Available neurophysiological and psychophysiological data have prompted the Laceys to propose that decreases in cardiovascular activity facilitate sensorimotor performance and attentional processes by increasing brain activity. According to their formulation, the increased brain activity is produced by afferent feedback from baroreceptors. Conversely, increased cardiovascular activity (e.g., HR and blood pressure) decreases efficiency in the same types of activities, because increased afferent feedback from the same baroreceptors inhibits cortical and subcortical activity. There is some evidence for improvement in behavioral efficiency during periods of lowered HR (Sandman, McCanne, Kaiser, & Diamond, 1977), and for the influence of the cardiovascular system on brain activity (Sandman, 1984; Walker & Walker, 1983). Criticisms of the Lacey's concepts regarding the significance of heart rate changes for behavior were made by Carroll and Anastasiades (1978). This thoughtful critique focuses on the nature of the intake–rejection environment in cardiac dynamics and the role of cardiovascular dynamics and cardiovascular changes in regulating brain attentional activities. Regardless of criticisms, concepts advanced by the Laceys have stimulated research on brain–autonomic interactions in behavior, and have highlighted the significance of cardiovascular dynamics for behavior.

INDIVIDUAL RESPONSE (IR) SPECIFICITY

In the previous section, we saw that the concept of stimulus response specificity referred to the characteristics of the stimuli that produced a typical response from most subjects. In contrast, the concept of individual response specificity says that a particular subject has characteristic responses to most stimuli. These two concepts may seem to be contradictory at first glance, but they are not (Engel, 1972; Sternbach, 1966). The concept of stimulus response (SR) specificity refers to a similar pattern of physiological response of most persons to a given stimulus situation, whereas individual response (IR) specificity involves consistency of an individual's response hierarchy in a variety of stimulus situations.

The concept of IR specificity has had an interesting historical development (see Sternbach, 1966). Briefly, it had been reported by Malmo and Shagass (1949) that psychiatric patients with a history of cardiovascular problems and those with headaches and neck complaints responded differently to pain stimuli. For example, those with the cardiovascular symptoms showed elevated HR, yet those with headaches and neck pains had higher EMG in response to pain. Malmo and associates proposed the principle of "sympton specificity" to describe situations in which psychiatric patients respond to stressful stimuli according to the physiological mechanism underlying the symptom. This principle was applied to normals by J. I. Lacey, Bateman, and Van Lehn (1953) and formulated as "autonomic response specificity," or what is now called "individual response specificity." The notion that individuals would respond maximally with a certain physiological system was confirmed in Lacey et al. (1953). They measured SCL, HR, and HR variability under four "stressful" conditions: cold pressor, mental arithmetic, letter association, and hyperventilation. Evidence was found for maximal response in the same physiological variable under different stress conditions. Further, they concluded that some people responded to different stimuli with a fixed pattern—for example, the greatest response change might be HR, followed by SCL, and then HR variability.

An example of this response patterning to various stimulating conditions was provided by J. I. Lacey (1959). He obtained results indicating similar response patterns to the CP test, mental arithmetic, and word fluency within a given subject. For example, diastolic blood pressure decreased for one subject, whereas it consistently increased for a different subject under the conditions just mentioned. Engel (1960) measured a number of physiological variables in a group of young women while they were presented with a variety of stimulus conditions—including mental arithmetic, proverbs, cold pressor, exercise, and loud auditory stimuli. The data indicated the simultaneous occurrence of SR specificity and IR specificity for these subjects. For example, blood pressure, respiration, skin conductance, HR, finger ST, HR variabililty, and face temperature showed similar hierarchies of response, but the response of a given physiological system was influenced by the individual's tendency to respond with that system.

Moos and Engel (1962) reported that hypertensive subjects showed more blood pressure changes in reacting to stressors than did arthritic patients. However, those with arthritis showed more EMG increases in muscles overlying the arthritic joints than did hypertensives. Hodapp, Weyer, and Becker (1975) reported that 20 hypertensives responded to landscape slides with a greater rise in systolic blood pressure than did a group of 31 matched normal control subjects. Thus, the concept of IR specificity may have implications for studying certain psychosomatic reactions, as initially suggested by Malmo and Shagass (1949).

Findings having relevance to the concepts of IR specificity and activation were obtained by Schnore (1959). A group of male subjects had a number of physiological measures taken (including forearm EMG, HR, systolic blood pressure, and respiration rate) while they perfomed tracking or arithmetic tasks under conditions designed to produce low or high arousal. For example, under high arousal conditions for tracking, subjects performed under the threat of an electric shock, whereas in the low arousal condition, tracking trials were presented as though they were not part of the experiment proper. The results indicated that during the different stimulus situations, subjects showed highly individual response patterns (both somatic and autonomic), even when variations produced increases in the overall level of activation. These findings were interpreted as being in support of J. I. Lacey et al. (1953) and J. I. Lacey and B. C. Lacey (1958) with regard to IR specificity for autonomic variables. Further, Schnore reported that four of the measures (HR, blood pressure, respiration rate, and right forearm EMG) consistently differentiated between high and low arousal conditions. Schnore observed that, despite individual patterns of response, persons placed in an arousing situation showed an increase in most physiological functions. The increases were relative; for example, although an individual might have shown increases in both HR and EMG under arousal, the level of HR may have been high and EMG low in comparison with others.

There are limitations to the IR specificity concept. J. I. Lacey and B. C. Lacey (1958) pointed out that although most persons may have some tendency for IR specificity, quantitative differences exist. This point is illustrated in a study of Wenger and associates who found that only 8 of 30 male subjects (27%) showed complete IR specificity (Wenger, Clemens, Coleman, Cullen, & Engel, 1961). A tendency toward a stable hierarchy in autonomic response pattern to different stimuli was found in 22 of the subjects (73%). Sternbach (1966) presented several studies indicating that IR specificity is unstable over time, especially as the number of stimulus and physiological response variables are increased. The possible role of explicit sets to respond by the subject (e.g., instructions) and implicit ones (e.g., preconceived ideas) as possible factors affecting IR specificity have also been discussed by Sternbach (1966).

Stern and Sison (1990) observed that a psychological factor related to IR specificity concerns the ability of individuals to detect changes in their own autonomic responses. For example, individuals who report a high degree of autonomic awareness also show a greater amount of autonomic reactivity than those with a low degree of awareness. There is also a tendency for the more aware to exaggerate the degree of their reactivity, whereas low awareness persons underestimate reactivity.

Summary.   There is evidence that most individuals respond with a characteristic hierarchy of physiological responses depending on the situation. This concept of IR specificity has implications for understanding psychosomatic disorders.

CARDIAC–SOMATIC CONCEPT

According to the cardiac–somatic concept, cardiac response changes are seen as facilitating the preparation for, and performance of, a behavioral response. For example, there is an association between cardiac response (e.g., HR deceleration) and the inhibition of ongoing somatic activity not relevant to performance of the task (Obrist, Webb, Sutterer, & Howard, 1970). Reductions in somatic and cardiac activity are viewed as biological manifestations of changes in attention (Obrist, Howard, Lawler, Galosy, Meyers, & Gaebelein, 1974). Further, HR deceleration is considered to reflect a central (brain) mechanism that adjusts cardiac activity to metabolic requirements. The major proponents of this view have been Obrist and his associates, who have emphasized that the "coupling" between cardiac–somatic responses occurs because both are reflections of brain processes concerned with preparatory activities.

Support for the concept is derived from a variety of studies by Obrist and colleagues (Obrist, Webb, & Sutterer, 1969; Obrist, Webb, Sutterer, & Howard, 1970; Webb and Obrist, 1970). For example, Obrist et al. (1970) measured somatic activity (chin EMG and eye blinks) and HR while subjects performed a simple RT task in which various foreperiods were used. In one group of 31 subjects, HR decreases were blocked by intravenous administrations of atropine, which inhibits the vagus nerve. Another 31 persons performed without the drug. When cardiac deceleration was not blocked, faster reaction times were associated with greater decreases in both heart and muscle activity. The cessation of eye movements and blinks was the most pronounced effect. Blocking cardiac deceleration, however, did not influence performance. The HR deceleration observed in the RT task was explained in terms of processes initiated in the brain that had effects on both heart rate and muscle responses. In another study, Obrist (1968) found that increases in somatic activity paralleled increases in HR. A classical aversive conditioning situation was employed in which EMG increases from the chin and jaw were accompanied by cardiac acceleration. This was interpreted as evidence for cardiac–somatic linkage.

The relationship among RT, HR, and measures of task-irrelevant somatic activity (e.g., eye movements and blinks) were studied by Obrist, Howard, Sutterer, Hennis, and Murrell (1973). The subjects were four groups of children (4-, 5-, 8-, and 10-years-old) and an adult reference population. It was reported, for all groups, that a decrease in HR and a drop in task-irrelevant somatic activities were coincident with making the relevant response.

It was suggested by Obrist and his colleagues (1974) that HR may be uncoupled for somatic activity under conditions of intense stress produced by a subject's uncertainties. Thus, they proposed that HR is coupled to somatic activity in behavioral situations involving minimal sympathetic influences on the heart (i.e., that are not stressful). To test this proposal, Lawler, Obrist, and Lawler (1976) measured HR and somatic activity of 25 male college students and 25 fifth-grade boys while they performed a choice RT task. Attention was manipulated by varying uncertainty and motivation. With respect to the cardiac–somatic relationship, variations in uncertainty produced systematic effects only on HR during the foreperiod, that is, HR accelerations increased as uncertainty increased. Variations in motivation were differentiated only by forearm EMG during the foreperiod; it increased with increases in motivation. However, increases in motivation increased the average level of both HR and forearm EMG. Thus, the variable of stimulus uncertainty resulted in cardiac–somatic uncoupling. Further, forearm EMG increases during the foreperiod were considered as relevant somatic activity and were contrasted to decreases in chin EMG.

Obrist (1976) argued that situations in which the individual is minimally involved, or relatively passive (e.g., simple RT), are those in which cardiac–somatic coupling is evident. That is, the emotional involvement is such that the cardiovascular system is minimally mobilized for a metabolic state that is not demanding. However, emotional states that evoke active coupling mechanisms mobilize the cardiovascular system for dealing with high metabolic requirements. B. C. Lacey and J. I. Lacey (1974) did not agree that the metabolic relationship between HR and somatic activity could explain decreased HR during the preparatory interval of a RT trial. They believed that the somatic changes reported by Obrist and associates for the RT paradigm are small and not metabolically significant. Haagh and Brunia (1984) examined cardiac–somatic coupling during the foreperiod of a simple RT task and found only partial support for the concept. In agreement with the hypothesis, they found HR, eye movements, and jaw EMG to be decreased at the end of the foreperiod and just prior to the response. However, contrary to the concept, there was no EMG decrease in a number of response-irrelevant muscles (e.g., soleus and tibialis). Haagh and Brunia concluded that the EMG changes observed facilitated response execution.

Some support for the idea that emotional involvement may mobilize the cardiovascular system comes from a study by Obrist, Gaebelein, et al. (1978). They studied the effects of varying the subject's opportunity to cope with stressors on tonic levels of HR carotid pulse wave and BP (diastolic and systolic). In a first experiment, persons who believed they could control an aversive stimulus (shock) maintained elevated levels of HR, carotid pulse wave, and systolic BP, as compared to those who believed they could not control the shock. In a second experiment, three stressors were used. The subjects had no control over two of these (CP and a sexually arousing pornographic movie), but did not have control over a third one (electric shock) that could be avoided by good performance. The subjects had significantly elevated levels of HR, carotid pulse, and systolic BP during the portion of the experiment where they could control the stressor. The effects of sympathetic innervation on responsivity during coping and no-coping conditions was examined in a third experiment. Sympathetic innervations were blocked with a beta-adrenergic blocking agent (propranolol, 4 mg intravenously). The results showed that when SNS influence on the heart and vasculature were blocked, the physiological response differences between coping and no-coping situations were abolished. The authors interpreted the results as evidence that providing a subject with an opportunity to cope with stressful events produces more appreciable sympathetic influences on the cardiovascular system than conditions where control is minimal (viewing an erotic movie) or not possible (inescapable shock).

Obrist and his colleagues noted in later work that the effects of coping and noncoping situations differ for individuals, with greater effects seen in what they termed *reactive subjects*. These reactive persons show greater cardiovascular response to any novel or challenging event, a tendency that reflects differences in adrenergic excitation. The Obrist team has noted that although reactive and nonreactive persons show little difference in HR during baseline conditions, the reactives show much larger increases in HR due to the cold pressor or shock avoidance tasks (e.g., as much as 48 bpm in shock avoidance). These reactivity differences in HR have led Obrist (1981) to include blood pressure in his studies, and he found that systolic BP also showed appreciable changes in the high "myocardial reactors." These observations about individual differences in HR and SBP reactivity in young adults raised the question as to whether the reactive persons are more likely to develop hypertension later in life. This intriguing question, with its important health implications, can only be answered by longitudal studies. Obrist and colleagues have provided evidence that young adults with hypertensive parents showed greater HR reactivity during shock avoidance than those with normotensive parents (Hastrup, Light, & Obrist, 1982). Similar, but less dramatic, findings were reported for SBP. This suggests a common factor that may relate to a predisposition to high cardiovascular reactivity and hypertension. The Obrist team continued to explore the influences of stressors on cardiovascular reactivity, as evidenced in Obrist, Light, James, and Strogatz (1987) and Light, Obrist, James, and Strogatz (1987).

Summary.   The cardiac–somatic concept has been fruitful with regard to suggesting experiments. Obrist and his colleagues expanded a great deal on the original approach, as evidenced by the coping–no coping paradigms and recent studies concerning the psychophysiology of hypertension. Those who have continued in Obrist's tradition have added important information regarding cardiovascular mechanisms in the control of blood pressure (e.g., see Lawler et al., 1998; Light, Kothandapani, & Allen, 1998; Sherwood & Turner, 1993; Turner, Sherwood, & Light, 1991).

Current and future research will determine the eventual form of the cardiac–somatic concept and hypotheses generated in explorations of the psychophysiology of stress. In this context it should be noted that none of the concepts presented in this chapter are completely fixed, and their forms may change as additional research findings foster new interpretations.

CONCEPTS AND SOCIAL PSYCHOPHYSIOLOGY

Social psychophysiology represents a relatively new area of research rather than a psychophysiological concept. However, it is included here because it is an area that is a potentially rich source of concepts that can be studied within the context of traditional psychophysiology. To paraphrase Cacioppo and Petty (1983), social psychology studies the behavioral effects of human interactions, whereas psychophysiology investigates relations between physiological events and behavior. Cacioppo, Petty, and Tassinary (1989) observed that, in the late 1960s and early 1970s, there were two articles about social psychophysiology (Shapiro & Crider, 1969; Shapiro & Schwartz, 1970). However, interest in social psychophysiology did not develop until more recently and was largely stimulated by the work of Cacioppo and Petty in the late 1970s and 1980s (e.g., see Cacioppo & Petty, 1982; 1986).

Theories in social psychology abound, and the objective techniques of psychophysiology can provide a means to validate some of these theories as well as to elucidate important aspects of human interaction. The social psychophysiological approach has been used in the study of attitudes, persuasion, sexual arousal, social facilitation, and dissonance. For example, in one study, heart rate and electrodermal activity were used to confirm the existence of tensions and their subsequent release in cognitive dissonance (Croyle & Cooper, 1983). The concept of cognitive dissonance was introduced by Festinger to describe the state produced when there is a discrepancy between individuals' attitudes and their behavior. In the Croyle and Cooper study, subjects were required to write essays in agreement or disagreement with preexisting attitudes. Those in the disagree (dissonant) condition showed greater arousal in the form of increased electrodermal activity than the agree subjects. Thus, the state of dissonance was reflected in physiological response, and the construct received some independent support.

An important role is attached to communication in social psychophysiology. An area of interest in this connection has been the communication of emotions through facial expressions. In chapter 8, studies of facial EMG in emotional expression were discussed. Researchers, such as Ekman and Schwartz have found different patterning of facial EMG in the enacting of various emotions. Eckman (1984) presented evidence for biologically based and evolved facial expressions of emotion from his studies of subjects from various cultures, including primitive New Guinean natives. Sackheim and Gur (1983) made a case for facial asymmetry in the communication of emotion based on findings that the left side of the face displays emotions more intensely than the right. This is presumably due to the influence of the right hemisphere in both the control of emotional responses and muscles on the left side of the face.

The effects of social affiliation on cardiovascular reactivity during a laboratory stressor were studied by Kamarck, Manuck, and Jennings (1990). Female subjects were asked to recruit a friend who could accompany them to a laboratory session during which they would be exposed to mild stressors involving mental performance (mental arithmetic and concept formation). In an "alone" condition they were asked to come without the recruited person, but in the "friend" condition they were accompanied by the friend throughout the experimental procedures. Cardiovascular reactivity (BP and HR) was significantly greater for the "alone" condition for both tasks. The study showed that social affiliation can produce clear reductions in cardiovascular response to a psychological challenge. One possible explanation is that the "friend" condition reduced the evaluation potential of a social setting, in this case the judgment of an experimenter in a laboratory. The effects of social interactions on cardiovascular responding could also have implications for health as well as empirical and conceptual value. Social psychophysiology is a welcome addition to conventional psychophysiological approaches. This area is now well established within traditional psychophysiology.

HABITUATION AND REBOUND

Habituation describes the decrease in physiological responsivity that occurs with repeated presentation of the same stimulus. For example, a change in skin conductance may be produced when a person's name is called out, but as the name is repeated over and over again, the novelty or unexpectedness wears off and the SCR may diminish until it is nonexistent. The psychological effect may be likened to boredom produced by the repetition of the same stimulus. Sternbach (1966) observed that although we do not know why habituation occurs, it might have survival value for the species. For example, it would be a waste of energy if a number of similar stimuli, occurring in rapid succession, produced the same magnitude of response as the initial one, especially if they were nonthreatening. On the other hand, it would be maladaptive if we quickly habituated to a potentially dangerous stimulus, like a truck approaching us as we started to cross a street. In general, habituation is less with very intense stimuli, important stimuli, more novel and complex stimuli.

The phenomenon of rebound may be observed when physiological variables return to values below those of prestimulus levels. If the SNS response to an intense stimulus, such as an electric shock or a pistol shot, is large in magnitude, then we may observe a poststimulus return of physiological variables to values below the level seen before the startling event. This overshooting of prestimulus levels in a direction opposite to that produced by an intense stimulus is called "rebound." Although rebound occurs in physiological systems innervated by both the SNS and PNS, Lang, Rice, Greenfield, and Sternbach (1972) pointed out that rebound is not due exclusively to antagonistic functions of the SNS and PNS, because it is observed to occur in systems mediated solely by the SNS (e.g., SCL). Sternbach (1966) noted that although we do not know why rebound occurs, it must be taken into account in the conduct of experimental investigations.

ORIENTING AND DEFENSIVE RESPONSES

Pavlov (1927) described a reflex that apparently enables animals to attend to novel and possibly biologically important stimuli. He noticed that a previously conditioned response failed to occur in a dog if an unusual stimulus (for example, a stranger entering the experimental area) was attended to by the animal. This attention to a novel stimulus was termed the "orienting," or "what is it?" reflex. Lynn (1966) outlined some of the physiological changes observed to occur when a novel stimulus is presented to humans. They include increased SCL, EMG, and pupil dilation, activation of the EEG pattern, a decrease in HR, vasoconstriction in the limbs, and vasodilation in blood vessels of the head. These physiological changes are said to be directed at facilitating the perception of, and possible responses to, new stimuli.

Another Russian psychologist distinguished between the orienting response and the defensive response (Sokolov, 1963). Whereas the OR occurred to novel stimuli, the DR was indicated as an accompaniment of intense, potentially painful stimuli. In addition, the OR habituates rapidly and the DR very slowly. The OR enhances perceptibility of stimuli, and the DR protects against the possible bad effects of intense stimulation. According to Sokolov the main factors producing the OR are novelty, intensity and significance of the stimulus. The novelty of a stimulus decreases with repeated presentations until it no longer produces a response (habituation). The intensity of a stimulus must be sufficiently above threshold to gain our attention. As it becomes progressively greater it can progress to a point where it is so intense that it produces pain, thus the OR changes to the DR. The significance of a stimulus may be natural, such as a response to one's own name; or it may be experimentally produced as with an instruction to note all the red items in a room. The hypothesized neural mechanism for the production of the OR has been outlined in chapter 9. Briefly, a neuronal model of a stimulus is developed in the cortex after a number of presentations. The difference between the model of the stimulus and the actual stimulus causes the OR. With repeated presentations the discrepancy decreases and the OR becomes smaller.

Graham and Clifton (1966) suggested that the OR would be accompanied by HR deceleration, but that HR acceleration would occur as a DR to stimuli of pre pain intensity. This suggestion was confirmed in a study by Raskin, Kotses, and Bever (1969), in which HR deceleration (OR) occurred with an 80-db (moderate) sound, whereas an increase in HR (DR) was produced by a 120-db (intense) sound. However, the dominant response in the blood vessels of the head was vasoconstriction. Hence, the cephalic vasomotor responses did not differentiate between ORs and DRs.

Hare (1973) reported HR of individuals who feared spiders and compared them to an equal number who were not fearful. The subjects viewed six spider slides and 24 slides of neutral objects (e.g., landscapes). The persons who feared spiders showed a DR in the form of accelerated HR, but those who were not afraid evidenced HR deceleration, especially when they found the slides to be interesting. There is a correspondence with the Laceys' intake–rejection hypothesis here. Namely, it appears that HR deceleration is associated with stimulus intake and the OR, whereas HR acceleration accompanies stimulus rejection and the DR. The OR–DR concept has obvious implications for psychophysiological research. However, Lang et al. (1972) noted several difficulties with Sokolov's conceptualization. For example, it does not explain selective attention or emotional specificity very well, and, in addition, it has proven difficult to obtain measures of the DR.

Bernstein (1979) and Maltzman (1979) have sought to expand OR theory as advanced by Sokolov, to include cognitive activity of the individual. Recall that Sokolov stressed the match–mismatch of stimuli to neuronal models as the critical factor favoring the appearance of the OR. Both Bernstein and Maltzman stress the importance of stimulus significance in the OR. Bernstein emphasizes that interactions between stimulus significance and uncertainty trigger the OR. Also, Maltzman believed that a "cortical set," present prior to the stimuli, influences the OR. Other researchers have contributed ideas regarding the nature of the OR, and these were presented in chapter 9, because they were in the context of electrodermal research (see Barry & O'Gorman, 1987). It is clear that Sokolov's OR theory has been heuristic and that additional research may lead to revisions to accommodate findings regarding influences of preexisting sets and cognitive activity on the OR. Barry and James (1981) examined the part of Sokolov's theory indicating that measures such as skin conductance, heart rate, respiratory pause and finger vasoconstriction would covary and show response decrement to stimulus repetition, recovery to a change in stimulus, dishabituation following the stimulus change, and an intensity effect with the larger stimuli. They reported that the only response showing this pattern was skin conductance. For example, with cardiac response, deceleration occurred in all conditions, even though skin conductance may have been increasing in some of them, thus indicating directional fractionation of response. Thus, response fractionation under these conditions argues against a unitary OR theory, just as it argued against unitary activation/arousal theory.

The consistency of response fractionation has led Barry (1996) to propose a "preliminary process theory" as an alternative to Sokolov's unitary OR theory. Preliminary process theory takes into account the fractionation of OR components and also recognizes that activation/arousal interacts with the OR. Thus, activation affects OR magnitude through its capacity to amplify responses, and the momentary OR affects activation level. Hence, what we observe is the interaction between an ongoing (tonic) level of physiological activation and a phasic change produced by the OR. Thus, responses may be fractionated over the short-term, against a certain tonic activation/arousal level.

CONCEPTUALIZATIONS CONCERNING EVENT-RELATED POTENTIALS

Researchers studying ERPs have borrowed concepts from other areas to help explain their findings. An example is the concept of "resource allocation" taken from theories of information processing to describe the effects of varying difficulty of a primary task on brain response to a stimulus related to some secondary task. Models of excitation–inhibition in the visual system have been used to explain relationships between visual masking and ERPs. The OR has also been used to explain results of certain ERP studies, as have attentional mechanisms and concepts regarding asymmetrical functions of the left and right hemispheres of the brain. Some of the theories have been simplistic and inadequate, such as the "neural efficiency hypothesis," which attempted to provide a rationale for a relation between intelligence and brain responses (see chapter 6). A search through chapters 6 and 7 of this book will reveal that a number of other concepts have been invoked to explain ERP results. Among these are the explanation of N400 as an attempt to reinterpret information, the recognition of the Nd wave as an early endogenous component related to attention and its distinction from the exogenous N1, and "mismatch negativity." This processing negativity has been related to a mismatch between a current stimulus and a "neuronal model" established by a previous stimulus, an idea reminiscent of the neuronal model proposed in Sokolov's OR theory. A concept of processing negativity has been proposed by Naatanen (see chapter 6). Additionally, an NA component occurring prior to N2 has been said to reflect an earlier stage of stimulus processing than N2 (see chapter 6).

Intentions to move and expectancies have been related to such slowly developing brain potentials as the readiness potential (RP) and contingent negative variation (CNV). The relative contributions of the psychological processes called distraction and attention were proposed as critical factors in CNV development (see chapter 7). The inverse relation that has been found between stimulus probability and P300 amplitude emphasized the endogenous–cognitive nature of this component. Additionally, P300 amplitude has been related to decision confidence and P300 latency to stimulus evaluation time. Researchers also proposed that P300 represents neural activity that occurs whenever a neuronal model of a stimulus must be updated (Donchin, 1981; Donchin & Coles, 1988). Further, whether the model will be updated depends on the surprise value and relevance of the stimuli. Thus, according to the context updating model, the P300 represents an information-processing "subroutine" in the brain.

Johnson (1986) suggested in his triarchic model that P300 amplitude can be accounted for by three dimensions of behavior: (a) subjective probability, (b) stimulus meaning, and (c) information transmission (see chapter 7). The classic P300 response has also been separated into P3a and P3b components based on behavioral and physiological data. In addition, the picture is made more complex by the identification of slow-wave components that overlap in time the appearance of P300, and outlast its disappearance by hundreds of milliseconds.

Thus, we have a situation in ERP research where there are many hypotheses and concepts to explain empirical findings, but they tend to be fragmentary. An integrating effort is needed that would help unify the various ERP constructs under several major concepts, rather than having dozens of explanatory devices. Integrating attempts—such as those of Johnson (1986) for P300; Nataanen and Picton (1987) for the N1 wave; and Rebert, Tecce, Marczynski, Pirch, and Thompson (1986) for relations among ERPs, neural anatomy, and brain chemistry—are the kinds of efforts that will help to consolidate masses of ERP data under fewer explanatory concepts. For example, in Johnson's triarchic model of P300 amplitude (1986), the effects of subjective probability and stimulus meaning are additive, and information transmission has a multiplicative consequence. This is expressed by the following equation:

$$P300 \text{ amplitude} = f\,[(T \times (1/P + M)]$$

That is, P300 is a function of information transmitted to the subject (T), multiplied by the summated effects of subjective probability (P), and stimulus meaning (M). The rationale for proposing an additive effect for probability and meaning is based on two kinds of empirical findings: (a) stimulus meaning effects are constant across probability levels and (b) probability effects are constant across variations in stimulus meaning. Johnson (1993) explained that the additive relations in his model suggest different neural generators for the meaning and probability factors. Different scalp distributions for P300 under different conditions supports the idea of P300 as a composite of activity arising from different brain processors or generators. Further, subcortical recordings of P300s and brain lesions in patients suggest multiple generator sites for P300. Johnson (1993) called for a major reassessment of P300, indicating that a current definition of P300 as "an endogenous positive component with a P_z–C_z maximum and a latency of between 280 and 1,000 msec" is not sufficient.

A brain theoretical approach to describe how assemblies of neurons enable learning, perception and cognition was proposed by Hebb (1949). Hebb theorized that cell assemblies, made up of groups of interconnected neurons both local and dispersed over distant cortical areas, are the basic elements for cognitive functions. The possible existence of cell assemblies with different organizations for nouns and verbs and for real and pseudowords have been supported by evidence from ERP and EEG studies according to Pulvermuller (1996). In his analysis Pulvermuller claims that three basic assumptions made by Hebb are supported by empirical evidence. These are: (1) cortical neurons strengthen their conections when they are frequently active at the same time; (2) the cerebral cortex is a structure in which synaptic strengthening can take place both on a local level and between neurons in distant cortical areas; and (3) strongly connected neurons will act together as a functional unit (assembly) even if only some of them are initially activated. Pulvermuller claims that this type of organization can explain language loss after focal brain damage in the left hemisphere, for example the inability to understand words due to lesions in Wernicke's area of the temporal lobe, and also the fact that widespread cortical activation occurs during various language tasks.

In one study, it was found that verbs produced ERP positivity over frontal lobes (motor), whereas nouns resulted in larger ERPs over occipital (visual) cortices (Preibl, Pulvermuller, Lutzenberger, & Birbaumer, 1995). The 50 verbs and 50 nouns used were matched for length, frequency of use, arousal ratings, and positive or negative arousal value (valence). They interpreted the results as indicating that processing of action verbs involves cell assemblies in motor cortices, whereas processing of visual words (nouns) affects assemblies of neurons in visual cortices. In another study it was found that 30-Hz EEG spectral responses (lower gamma range) to meaningful words was larger over the left hemisphere than to pseudowords (Pulvermuller, Preibl, Lutzenberger, & Birbaumer, 1995). This differential response was explained by assuming that cell assemblies generating high-frequency patterns are active during word processing, but do not operate when false words are presented. The use of Hebbian theory in an attempt to explain contemporary findings in brain electrophysiology is a welcome development that will stimulate further research in this area of cognitive neuroscience.

Summary.   A number of hypotheses and concepts have been generated by researchers involved in ERP investigations. Most of these ideas have been touched upon in the chapters devoted to ERPs and include formulations regarding processing negativity (Naatanen), attention-distraction in CNV development (Tecce), context updating (Donchin & Coles) and triarchic model (Johnson) to explain P300, and a recent resurrection of Hebb's classical cell assembly concepts to explain results in ERP and EEG research.

The concepts discussed in this chapter have been advanced by a relatively small number of workers in the field of psychophysiology. The field needs theories that help to integrate the various conceptual approaches. The concepts presented here have stimulated much research. Data collection in the field is currently proceeding at a rapid pace, and we may look forward to the confirmation and refinement of present concepts and the development of more inclusive new ones.

REFERENCES

Andreassi, J. L. (1966). Skin-conductance and reaction-time in a continuous auditory monitoring task. *The American Journal of Psychology, 79,* 470–474.

Andreassi, J. L., Rapisardi, S. C., & Whalen, P. M. (1969). Autonomic responsivity and reaction time under fixed and variable signal schedules. *Psychophysiology, 6,* 58–69.

Ax, A. A. (1953). The physiological differentiation between fear and anger in humans. *Psychosomatic Medicine, 15,* 422–433.

Baccelli, G., Guazzi M., Libretti, A., & Zanchetta, A. (1965). Pressoceptive and chemoceptive aortic reflexes in decorticate and decerebrate cats. *American Journal of Physiology, 208,* 708–714.

Barry, R. J. (1996). Preliminary process theory: Towards an integrated account of the psychophysiology of cognitive processes. *Acta Neurobiol. Exp., 56,* 469–484.

Barry, R. J., & James, A. L. (1981). Fractionation of phasic responses in a dishabituation paradigm. *Physiology and Behavior, 26,* 69–75.

Barry, R. J., & O'Gorman, J. G. (1987). Stimulus omission and the orienting response: Latency differences suggest different mechanisms. *Biological Psychology, 25,* 261–276.

Bartorelli, C., Bizzi, E., Libretti, A., & Zanchetta, A. (1960). Inhibitory control of sinocarotid pressoceptive afferents on hypothalamic autonomic activity and sham rage behavior. *Archives Italiennes de Biologie, 98,* 309–326.

Bernstcin, A. S. (1979). The orienting reflex as novelty and significance detector. *Psychophysiology, 16,* 263–273.

Berntson, G. G., Cacioppo, J. T., Quigley, K. S., & Fabro, V. T. (1994). Autonomic space and psychophysiological response. *Psychophysiology, 31,* 44–61.

Bonvallet, M., Dell, P., & Hiebel, G. (1954). Tonus sympathique et activite electrique corticale. *Electroencephalography and Clinical Neurophysiology, 6,* 119–144.

Cacioppo, J. T., & Petty, R. E. (1982). A biosocial model of attitude change: Signs, symptoms, and undetected physiological responses. In J. T. Cacioopo & R. E. Petty (Eds.), *Perspectives in cardiovascular psychophysiology* (pp. 151–188). New York: Guilford.

Cacioppo, J. T., & Petty, R. E. (1983). *Social psychophysiology.* New York: Guilford.

Cacioppo, J. T., & Petty, R. E. (1986). Social processes. In M. G. H. Coles, E. Donchin, & S. Porges (Eds.), *Psychophysiology: Systems, processes, and applications* (pp. 646–679). New York: Guilford.

Cacioppo, J. T., Petty, R. E., & Tassinary, L. G. (1989). Social psychophysiology: A new look. In J. T. Cacioppo, R. E. Petty, & L. G. Tassinary (Eds.), *Advances in social psychophysiology* (pp. 39–91). New York: Academic.

Carroll, D., & Anastasiades, P. (1978). The behavioral significance of heart rate: The Laceys' hypothesis. *Biological Psychology, 7,* 249–275.

Coleridge, H. M., Coleridge, J. C. G., & Rosenthal, R. (1976). Prolonged inactivation of cortical pyramidal tract neurons in cats by distension of the carotid sinus. *Journal of Physiology, 256,* 635–649.

Courts, F. A. (1939). Relation between experimentally induced muscle tension and memorization. *Journal of Experimental Psychology, 25,* 235–256.

Courts, F. A. (1942). Relation between muscular tension and performance. *Psychological Bulletin, 39,* 347–367.

Croyle, R. T., & Cooper, J. (1983). Dissonance arousal: Physiological evidence. *Journal of Personality and Social Psychology, 45,* 782–791.

Dimberg, U. (1990). Facial electromyograpy and emotional reactions. *Psychophysiology, 27,* 481–494.

Donchin, E. (1981). Surprise! . . . Surprise? *Psychophysiology, 18,* 493–513.

Donchin, E., & Coles, M. G. H. (1988). Is the P300 component a manifestation of context updating? *Behavioral and Brain Sciences, 11,* 357–372.

Duffy, E. (1934). Emotion: An example of the need for reorientation in psychology. *Psychological Review, 41,* 184–198.

Duffy, E. (1957). The psychological significance of the concept of "arousal" or "activation." *Psychological Review, 64,* 265–275.

Duffy, E. (1962). *Activation and behavior.* New York: Wiley.

Duffy, E. (1972). Activation. In N. S. Greenfield & R. A. Sternbach (Eds.), *Handbook of psychophysiology* (pp. 577–622). New York: Holt, Rinehart & Winston.

Eason, R. G., & Dudley, L. M. (1971). Physiological and behavioral indicants of activation. *Psychophysiology, 7,* 223–232.

Ekman, P. (1984). Expression and the nature of emotion. In K. Scherer & P. Ekman (Eds.), *Approaches to emotion* (pp. 319–343). Hillsdale, NJ: Lawrence Erlbaum Associates.

Ekman, P., Levenson, R. W., & Friesen, M. V. (1983). Autonomic nervous system activity distinguishes among emotions. *Science, 221,* 1208–1210.

Elliott, R. (1972). The significance of heart rate for behavior: A critique of Lacey's hypothesis. *Journal of Personality & Social Psychology, 22,* 398–409.

Engel, B. T. (1960). Stimulus–response and individual–response specificity. *Archives of General Psychiatry, 2*, 305–313.

Engel, B. T. (1972). Response specificity. In N. S. Greenfield & R. A. Sternbach (Eds.), *Handbook of psychophysiology* (pp. 571–576). New York: Holt, Rinehart & Winston.

Freeman, G. L. (1940). The relationship between performance level and bodily activity level. *Journal of Experimental Psychology, 26*, 602–608.

Freeman, G. L., & Simpson, R. M. (1938). The effect of experimentally induced muscular tension upon palmar skin resistance. *Journal of General Psychology, 18*, 319–326.

Furedy, J. J., & Scher, H. (1989). The law of Initial Values: Differential testing as an empirical generalization versus enshrinement as a methodological rule. *Psychophysiology, 26*, 120–122.

Fuster, J. M. (1958). Effects of stimulation of brain stem on tachistoscopic perception. *Science, 127*, 150.

Gahery, Y., & Vigier, D. (1974). Inhibitory effects in the cuneate nucleus produced by vago-aortic afferent fibers. *Brain Research, 75*, 241–246.

Galin, D., & Lacey, J. I. (1972). Reaction time and heart rate response pattern: Effects of mesencephalic reticular stimulation in cats. *Physiology & Behavior, 8*, 729–739.

Graham, F. K., & Clifton, R. K. (1966). Heart-rate change as a component of the orienting response. *Psychological Bulletin, 65*, 305–320.

Haagh, S. A. V. M., & Brunia, C. H. M. (1984). Cardiac–somatic coupling during the foreperiod in a simple reaction-time task. *Psychological Research, 46*, 3–13,

Hahn, W. W. (1973). Attention and heart rate: A critical appraisal of the hypothesis of Lacey and Lacey. *Psychological Bulletin, 79*, 59–70.

Hare, R. D. (1972). Response requirements and directional fractionation of autonomic response. *Psychophysiology, 9*, 419–427.

Hare, R. D. (1973). Orienting and defensive responses to visual stimuli. *Psychophysiology, 10*, 453–464.

Hastrup, J. L., Light, K. C., & Obrist, P. A. (1982). Parental hypertension and cardiovascular response to stress in healthy young adults. *Psychophysiology, 19*, 615–622.

Hebb, D. O. (1949). *The organization of behavior*. New York: Wiley.

Hebb, D. O. (1955). Drives and the C.N.S. (conceptual nervous system). *Psychological Review, 62*, 245–254.

Helin, P., & Hanninen, O. (1987). Relaxation training affects success and activiation on a teaching test. *International Journal of Psychophysiology, 5*, 275–287.

Hodapp, V., Weyer, G., & Becker, J. (1975). Situational stereotype in essential hypertension patients. *Journal of Psychosomatic Research, 19*, 113–121.

Hord, D. J., Johnson, L. C., & Lubin, A. (1964). Differential effect of the law of initial value (LIV) on autonomic variables. *Psychophysiology, 1*, 79–87.

Jamieson, J. (1987). Bilateral finger temperature and the law of initial values. *Psychophysiology, 24*, 666–669.

Jamieson, J. (1993). The law of initial values: Five factors or two? *International Journal of Psychophysiology, 14*, 233–240.

Jamieson, J., & Howk, S. (1992). The law of initial values: A four factor theory. *International Journal of Psychophysiology, 12*, 53–62.

Johnson, R., Jr. (1986). A triarchic model of P300 amplitude. *Psychophysiology, 23*, 367–384.

Johnson, R., Jr. (1993). On the neural generators of the P300 component of the Event-Related Potential. *Psychophysiology, 30*, 90–97.

Kamarck, T. W., Manuck, S. B., & Jennings, J. R. (1990). Social support reduces cardiovascular reactivity to psychological challenge: A laboratory model. *Psychosomatic Medicine, 52*, 42–58.

Kennedy, J. L., & Travis, R. C. (1948). Prediction and control of alertness. II: Continuous tracking. *Journal of Comparative & Physiological Psychology, 41*, 203–210.

Klorman, R., Weisenfeld, A. R., & Austin, M. L. (1975). Autonomic responses to affective visual stimuli. *Psychophysiology, 12*, 553–560.

Lacey, B. C., & Lacey, J. I. (1974). Studies of heart rate and other bodily processes in sensorimotor behavior. In P. A. Obrist, A. H. Black, J. Brener, & L. V. DiCara (Eds.), *Cardiovascular psychophysiology* (pp. 538–564). Chicago: Aldine.

Lacey, B. C., & Lacey, J. I. (1977). Change in heart period: A function of sensorimotor event timing within the cardiac cycle. *Physiological Psychology, 5*, 383–393.

Lacey, B. C., & Lacey, J. I. (1978). Two-way communication between the heart and the brain: Significance of time within the cardiac cycle. *American Psychologist, 33*, 99–113.

Lacey, J. I. (1959). Psychophysiological approaches to the evaluation of psychotherapeutic process and outcome. In E. A. Rubinstein & M. B. Parloff (Eds.), *Research in psychotherapy* (pp. 173–192). Washington, DC: American Psychological Association.

Lacey, J. I. (1967). Somatic response patterning and stress: Some revisions of activation theory. In M. H. Appley & R. Trumbull (Eds.), *Psychological stress: Issues in research* (pp. 14–42). New York: Appleton-Century-Crofts.

Lacey, J. I., Bateman, D. E., & Van Lehn, R. (1953). Autonomic response specificity: An experimental study. *Psychosomatic Medicine, 15*, 8–21.

Lacey, J. I., Kagan, J., Lacey, B. C., & Moss, H. A. (1963). The visceral level: Situational determinants and behavioral correlates of autonomic response patterns. In P. H. Knapp (Ed.), *Expression of the emotions in man* (pp. 122–155). New York: International Universities Press.

Lacey, J. I., & Lacey, B. C. (1958). Verification and extension of the principle of autonomic response stereotypy. *American Journal of Psychology, 71*, 50–73.

Lacey, J. I., & Lacey, B. C. (1970). Some autonomic–central nervous system interrelationships. In P. Black (Ed.), *Physiological correlates of emotion* (pp. 214–236). New York: Academic Press.

Lang, P. J., Rice, D. G., Greenfield, N. S., & Sternbach, R. A. (1972). The psychophysiology of emotion. In N. S. Greenfield & R. A. Sternbach (Eds.), *Handbook of psychophysiology* (pp. 623–643). New York: Holt, Rinehart & Winston.

Lawler, K. A., Kline, K., Seabrook, E., Krishnamoorthy, J., Anderson, S. F., Wilcox, Z. C., Craig, F., Adlin, R., & Thomas, S. (1998). Family history of hypertension: A psychophysiological analysis. *International Journal of Psychophysiology, 28*, 207–222.

Lawler, K. A., Obrist, P. A., & Lawler, J. E. (1976). Cardiac and somatic response patterns during reaction time task in children and adults. *Psychophysiology, 13*, 448–455.

Libby, W. L., Lacey, B. C., & Lacey, J. I. (1973). Pupillary and cardiac activity during visual attention. *Psychophysiology, 10*, 270–294.

Light, K. C., Kothandapani, R. V., & Allen, M. T. (1998). Enhanced cardiovascular and catecholamine responses in women with depressive symptoms. *International Journal of Psychophysiology, 28*, 157–166.

Light, K. C., Obrist, P. A., James, S. A., & Strogatz, D. S. (1987). Cardiovascular responses to stress: II. Relationships to aerobic exercise patterns. *Psychophysiology, 24*, 79–86.

Lindsley, D. B. (1951). Emotion. In S. S. Stevens (Ed.), *Handbook of experimental psychology* (pp. 473–516). New York: Wiley.

Lindsley, D. B. (1956). Physiological psychology. *Annual Review of Psychology, 7*, 323–348.

Lovallo, W., & Zeiner, A. R. (1975). Some factors influencing the vasomotor response to cold pressor stimulation. *Psychophysiology, 12*, 499–505.

Lynn, R. (1966). *Attention, arousal and the orientation reaction.* Oxford: Pergamon.

Malmo, R. B. (1959). Activation: A neurophysiological dimension. *Psychological Review, 66*, 367–386.

Malmo, R. B. (1962). Activation. In A. J. Bachrach (Ed.), *Experimental foundations of clinical psychology* (pp. 386–422). New York: Basic Books.

Malmo, R. B., & Davis, J. F. (1956). Physiological gradients as indicants of "arousal" in mirror tracing. *Canadian Journal of Psychology, 10*, 231–238.

Malmo, R. B., & Shagass, C. (1949). Physiologic study of symptom mechanisms in psychiatric patients under stress. *Psychosomatic Medicine, 11*, 25–29.

Maltzman, I. (1979). Orienting reflexes and significance: A reply to O'Gorman. *Psychophysiology, 16*, 274–282.

Mangina, C. A., & Beuzeron-Mangina, J. H. (1988). Learning abilities and disabilities: Effective diagnosis and treatment. *International Journal of Psychophysiology, 6*, 79–90.

Moos, R. H., & Engel, B. T. (1962). Psychophysiological reactions in hypertensive and arthritic patients. *Journal of Psychosomatic Research, 6*, 227–241.

Moruzzi, G., & Magoun, H. W. (1949). Brain stem reticular formation and activation of the EEG. *Electroencephalography and Clinical Neurophysiology, 1*, 455–473.

Naatanen, R., & Picton, T. W. (1987). The N1 wave of the human electric and magnetic response to sound: A review and an analysis of component structure. *Psychophysiology, 24*, 375–425.

Obrist, P. A. (1968). Heart rate and somatic-motor coupling during classical aversive conditioning in humans. *Journal of Experimental Psychology, 77*, 180–193.

Obrist, P. A. (1976). The cardiovascular–behavioral interaction as it appears today. *Psychophysiology, 13*, 95–107.

Obrist, P. A. (1981). *Cardiovascular psychophysiology: A perspective.* New York: Plenum.

Obrist, P. A., Gaebelein, C. J., Teller, E. S., Langer, A. W., Gringnolo, A., Light, K. C., & McCubbin, J. A. (1978). The relationship among heart rate, carotid dP/dt and blood pressure in humans as a function of the type of stress. *Psychophysiology, 15*, 102–115.

Obrist, P. A., Howard, J. L., Lawler, J. E., Galosy, R. A., Meyers, J. A., & Gaebelein, C. J. (1974). The cardiac somatic interaction. In P. A. Obrist, A. H. Black, J. Brener, & L. V. DiCara (Eds.), *Cardiovascular psychophysiology* (pp. 136–162). Chicago: Aldine.

Obrist, P. A., Howard, J. L., Sutterer, J. R., Hennis, R. S., & Murrell, D. J. (1973). Cardiac–somatic changes during a simple reaction time task: A developmental study. *Journal of Experimental Child Psychology, 16*, 346–362.

Obrist, P. A., Light, K. C., James, S. A., & Strogatz, D. S. (1987). Cardiovascular responses to stress: I. Measures of myocardial response and relationship to high resting systolic pressure and parental hypertension. *Psychophysiology, 24*, 65–78.

Obrist, P. A., Webb, R. A., & Sutterer, J. R. (1969). Heart rate and somatic changes during aversive conditioning and a simple reaction time task. *Psychophysiology, 5*, 696–722.

Obrist, P. A., Webb, R. A., Sutterer, J. R., & Howard, J. L. (1970). Cardiac deceleration and reaction time: An evaluation of two hypotheses. *Psychophysiology, 6*, 695–706.

Pavlov, I. P. (1927). *Conditioned reflexes: An investigation of the physiological activity of the cerebral cortex.* London: Oxford University Press.

Pinneo, L. R. (1961). The effects of induced muscle tension during tracking on level of activation and on performance. *Journal of Experimental Psychology, 62*, 523–531.

Preibl, H., Pulvermuller, F., Lutzenberger, W., & Birbaumer, N. (1995). Evoked potentials distinguish nouns from verbs. *Neuroscience Letters, 197*, 81–83.

Pulvermuller, F. (1996). Hebb's concept of cell assemblies and the psychophysiology of word processing. *Psychophysiology, 33*, 317–333.

Pulvermuller, F., Preibl, H., Lutzenberger, W., & Birbaumer, N. (1995b). Spectral responses in the gamma-band: Physiological signs of higher cognitive processes? *NeuroReport, 6*, 2057–2064.

Raskin, D. C., Kotses, H., & Bever, J. (1969). Cephalic vasomotor and heart rate measures of orienting and defensive reflexes. *Psychophysiology, 6*, 149–159.

Rebert, C. S., Tecce, J. J., Marczynski, T. J., Pirch, J. H., & Thompson, J. W. (1986). Neural anatomy, chemistry and event-related brain potentials: An approach to understanding the substrates of mind. In W. C. McCallum, R. Zappoli, & F. DeNoth (Eds.), *Cerebral psychophysiology: Studies in event-related potentials* (pp. 343–392). Amsterdam: Elsevier.

Sackheim, H. A., & Gur, R. C. (1983). Facial asymmetry and the communication of emotion. In J. T. Cacioppo & R. E. Petty (Eds.), *Social psychophysiology* (pp. 307–352). New York: Guilford.

Sandman, C. A. (1984). Augmentation of the auditory event-related potentials of the brain during diastole. *International Journal of Psychophysiology, 2*, 111–120.

Sandman, C. A., McCanne, T. R., Kaiser, D. N., & Diamond, B. (1977). Heart rate and cardiac phase influences on visual perception. *Journal of Comparative & Physiology Psychology, 91*, 189–202.

Scher, H., Furedy, J. J., & Heslegrave, R. J. (1985). Individual differences in phasic cardiac reactivity to psychological stress and the law of initial value. *Psychophysiology, 22*, 345–348.

Schlosberg, H., & Kling, J. W. (1959). The relationship between "tension" and efficiency. *Perceptual & Motor Skills, 9*, 395–397.

Schnore, M. M. (1959). Individual patterns of physiological activity as a function of task differences and degree of arousal. *Journal of Experimental Psychology, 58*, 117–128.

Shapiro, D., & Crider, A. (1969). Psychophysiological approaches to social psychology. In G. Lindzey & E. Aronson (Eds.), *The handbook of social psychology* (Vol. 3, 2nd ed.). Reading, MA: Addison-Wesley.

Shapiro, D., & Schwartz, G. E. (1970). Psychophysiological contributions to social psychology. *Annual Review of Psychology, 21*, 87–112.

Shaw, W. A. (1956). Facilitating effects of induced tension upon the perception span for digits. *Journal of Experimental Psychology, 51*, 113–117.

Sherwood, A., & Turner, J. R. (1993). Postural stability of hemodynamic responses during mental challenge. *Psychophysiology, 30*, 237–244.

Smith D. B., & Wenger, M. A. (1965). Changes in autonomic balance during phasic anxiety. *Psychophysiology, 1*, 267–271.

Smock, C. D., & Small, V. H. (1962). Efficiency of utilization of visual information as a function of induced muscular tension. *Perceptual & Motor Skills, 14*, 39–44.

Sokolov, E. N. (1963). *Perception and the conditioned reflex.* New York: MacMillan.

Stennett, R. G. (1957). The relationship of performance level to level of arousal. *Journal of Experimental Psychology, 54*, 54–61.

Stern, R. M., & Sison, C. E. E. (1990). Response patterning. In J. T. Cacioppo & L. G. Tassinary (Eds.), *Principles of psychophysiology: Physical, social, & inferential elements* (pp. 193–215). Cambridge: Cambridge University Press.

Sternbach, R. A. (1966). *Principles of psychophysiology.* New York: Academic Press.

Turner, J. R., Sherwood, A., & Light, K. C. (1991). Generalization of cardiovascular response: Supportive evidence for the reactivity hypothesis. *International Journal of Psychophysiology, 11*, 207–212.

Walker, B. B., & Walker, J. M. (1983). Phase relations between carotid pressure and ongoing electrocortical activity. *International Journal of Psychophysiology, 1*, 65–74.

Webb, R. A., & Obrist, P. A. (1970). The physiological concomitants of reaction time performance as a function of preparatory interval and preparatory interval series. *Psychophysiology, 6*, 389–403.

Wenger, M. A. (1941). The measurement of individual differences in autonomic balance. *Psychosomatic Medicine, 3*, 427–434.

Wenger, M. A. (1948). Studies of autonomic balance in Army Air Force personnel. *Comparative Psychology Monographs, 19*.

Wenger, M. A. (1966). Studies of autonomic balance: A summary. *Psychophysiology, 2*, 173–186.

Wenger, M. A., Clemens, T. L., Coleman, D. R., Cullen, T. D., & Engel, B. T. (1961). Autonomic response specificity. *Psychosomatic Medicine, 23*, 185–193.

Wenger, M. A., Clemens, T. L., & Cullen, T. D. (1962). Autonomic functions in patients with gastrointestinal and dermatological disorders. *Psychosomatic Medicine, 24*, 268–273.

Wenger, M. A., & Cullen, T. D. (1972). Studies of autonomic balance in children and adults. In N. S. Greenfield & R. A. Sternbach (Eds.), *Handbook of Psychophysiology* (pp. 535–569). New York: Holt, Rinehart & Winston.

Wenger, M. A., Engel, B. T., & Clemens, T. L. (1957). Studies of autonomic response patterns: Rationale and methods. *Behavioral Science, 2*, 216–221.

White, K. D. (1977). Salivation and the law of initial value. *Psychophysiology, 14*, 560–562.

Wilder, J. (1957). The law of initial values in neurology and psychiatry. *Journal of Nervous & Mental Disease, 125*, 73–86.

Wilder, J. (1967). *Stimulus and response: The law of initial value.* Bristol: J. Wright.

Wilder, J. (1976). The "law of initial values," a neglected biological law and its significance for research and practice. In S. W. Porges & M. G. H. Coles (Eds.), *Psychophysiology* (pp. 38–46). Stroudsberg: Dowden, Hutchinson & Row.

Wilson, B. L., Albright, G. L., Steiner, S. S., & Andreassi, J. L. (1991). Cardiodynamic response to psychological and cold pressor stress: Further evidence for stimulus response specificity and directional fractionation. *Biofeedback & Self-Regulation, 16*, 45–53.

Yerkes, R. M., & Dodson, J. D. (1908). The relation of strength of stimulus to rapidity of habit-formation. *Journal of Comparative Neurology and Psychology, 18*, 459–482.

19

Environmental Psychophysiology

This chapter underscores the increasing importance of understanding the effects of environmental factors in evaluating physiological responses of the behaving person. Most of the relevant environmental factors are internal (e.g., drugs, hormones) whereas a few are external (e.g., illumination). It is important to know about these effects not only for human welfare, but to consider them as possible influences in the conduct of research. Certain commonly used substances—such as coffee, tea, soft drinks, alcohol, nicotine, and prescribed and nonprescribed medications—can affect interpretations of psychophysiological data. Thus, investigators must be aware of these possible effects when carrying out studies in psychophysiology. Researchers can control for unwanted influences by asking participants to abstain from using certain substances for a suitable length of time before taking part in an experiment.

Some of the studies presented here may not be strictly psychophysiological in that they fail to use a behavioral manipulation. However, the influence of environmental factors must be considered because of the effects they exert on both behavioral and physiological responses. Our discussion of environmental effects starts with the EEG and continues in the same order in which the various measures are presented in earlier chapters. The material presented in the EEG section covers, for the most part, research performed subsequent to a review by Shagass (1972). In another comprehensive review, Stroebel (1972) discussed the behavioral and physiological effects of drugs and included sections on EEG and autonomic response patterns.

INTERNAL AND EXTERNAL ENVIRONMENTAL FACTORS AND THE ELECTROENCEPHALOGRAM

Drugs

The EEG is a valuable tool for objective assessments of psychoactive drugs that have either a psychologically depressing or stimulating effect. The EEG's usefulness is further enhanced when behavioral or performance tests, as well as blood samples to determine the amount of the drug in the bloodstream, are conducted. In addition, the use of drugs in EEG studies may help to understand some of the biochemical factors in the brain that are involved in the production of the EEG.

Table 19.1 is taken from Brown (1976) and provides a useful classification of some familiar drugs and their psychological effects. We will consider the effects on EEG of psychoactive drugs in the hallucinogen, opiate, and depressant categories.

The effects of drugs on behavior are by no means always clear-cut and understandable. There are many factors operating, including the *placebo effect*. The placebo effect refers to

TABLE 19.1
Drugs Commonly Employed for Mind Alteration

	Type	Examples
Experience expanding	Hallucinogens	LSD Mescaline Marijuana
	Stimulants	Amphetamines Cocaine Caffeine
Experience restricting	Opiates (narcotics)	Heroin Morphine Methadone
	Depressants	Barbiturates Alcohol Nicotine Tranquilizers Solvents Methaqualone

Source: From H. Brown, Brain and Behavior, Oxford University Press, 1976, p. 296.

the fact that the mere taking of a pill may have powerful suggestive effects on the person so as to influence either behavior, physiological response, or both. A *placebo* is an inert substance, such as lactose, which can be made into pill form and administered in experiments to separate real effects of an active drug from the suggestion effects of pill taking. Brown (1976) advised that correlations between drug actions and their consequences must be treated with caution. For example, alcohol may alter emotionality by depressing cortical inhibitory systems, whereas amphetamines produce a similar effect by stimulating subcortical facilitory areas. Let us now examine some studies of drugs and their effects on the EEG.

LSD. Lysergic acid diethylamide (LSD) is a known "psychotomimetic" drug that produces some symptoms of mental illness, such as hallucinations and changes in mood and behavior. At one time, it was thought that it could unlock some of the secrets of schizophrenia by producing symptoms of this disorder that could then be scientifically studied. Investigators who have measured brain activity after administration of LSD generally agree that EEG amplitude decreases, alpha rhythms disappear, and the tracings become low in voltage and high in frequency (Rodin & Luby, 1966). The LSD effects increase progressively over a period of 1 to 2 hrs following intravenous administration. Thus, the psychological effects may be related to faster brain activity, indicating a more aroused or hyperstimulated nervous system. The effects of LSD and several other psychoactive agents were studied by Fink, Itil, and Clyde (1966). Their computer analyses of the EEG spectrum indicated that beta activity was enhanced by LSD.

Marijuana. The effects of marijuana on EEG and psychological test performance were studied by Dornbush, Fink, and Freedman (1971). The subjects were male medical students who smoked cigarettes containing a high amount of marijuana (22.5 mg), a low amount (7.5 mg), or a placebo (the placebo was oregano, a spice that supposedly looks, smells, and tastes like "pot"). Measures of EEG, reaction time, short-term memory, and time estimation were taken under the different conditions. An increase in the percentage of time spent in alpha (8–13.5 Hz) activity and decreases in beta (18.5–24.5 Hz) and theta (4–7.5 Hz) activity occurred with the high dose, but not with the low dose or the placebo. In addition, RT was reliably slowed, and performance on a short-term memory task was inhibited by the high dose.

Accuracy of time estimation was not affected at any of the dose levels used. A similar result was obtained by Roth, Galanter, Weingartner, Vaughan, and Wyatt (1973), who tested the effects of smoking cigarettes containing marijuana or synthetic trans-tetrahydrocannabinol (THC) on EEGs of young chronic users. The amount of EEG alpha activity increased with the marijuana, but not with the placebo. The THC showed EEG effects that were in between the marijuana and the placebo, although both the THC and the marijuana cigarettes contained 10 mg of the drug. Thus, the amount of alpha activity, the brain wave associated with a relaxed waking state, increased with marijuana use in these two experiments.

Nicotine. It is the usual finding that smoking under resting conditions increases EEG frequency, with a decrease in alpha and theta and increases in beta activity (Cook et al., 1995). There is also some evidence to indicate that smoking under stressful conditions results in a lowering of EEG frequency (Houlihan, Pritchard, Krieble, Robinson, and Duke, 1996). In their study, Houlihan et al. recorded EEG while subjects were engaged in a RT task. The EEG was recorded presmoking, after smoking a .05mg nicotine cigarette (control), and after a 1.1 mg nicotine cigarette. Smoking the 1.1 mg cigarette quickened RT, and at the same time increased EEG activity in the beta2 band (18–28 Hz).

In another research paper, Cook et al. (1995) suggest that people smoke to either increase or decrease central nervous system arousal. This tendency is related to a presmoking state in which the individual may be in a "telic" (arousal avoidant) or "paratelic" (arousal seeking) mood. "In the telic state, low arousal is preferred and is experienced as relaxation, while high arousal is experienced as anxiety. In the paratelic state, high arousal is preferred and is experienced as excitement, while low arousal is experienced as boredom." (Cook et al., 1995, p. 248). In their study, Cook and colleagues recorded EEG from over left and right frontal and parietal cortices in smokers while they engaged in fake smoking for 5 min. and real smoking for 5 min. All subjects refrained from smoking for 4 hours prior to the experimental session and completed an Arousal Seeking Inventory to distinguish between telic and paratelic states. Expectations were confirmed since results indicated that telic subjects (low-arousal seeking) increased theta activity and paratelic individuals (high-arousal seeking) increased beta2 activity while smoking. Cook et al. suggest that one approach to improving success of smoking cessation programs would be to teach the ex-smoker to mimic the arousal altering effects of smoking. For example, the individual in the paratelic state could engage in activities of interest to avoid the boredom that might lead to smoking a cigarette, while those in the telic state could learn relaxation techniques to lower arousal level.

Heroin and Methadone. The short-term effects of heroin on the EEG and other physiological measures was investigated by Volavka, Levine, Feldstein, and Fink (1974). Detoxified (drug-free) male addicts received 25 mg of heroin intravenously, on two occasions, and a placebo, also intravenously, on two other occasions. Heroin produced a significant decrease in EEG frequency within the first 5 min after injection. The decrease peaked at 15 min postinjection and remained at peak level when the 30 min observation period ended. Respiration rate decreased from a mean of 18.5 cycles per minute before the injection to 7.6 cycles within 5 min after the administration of heroin. The authors suggested the possibility that some portion of the EEG decrease may have been caused by changes of blood chemistry resulting from decreased ventilation. An RT task indicated that responses of the subjects were significantly slower within 15 to 20 min after heroin injection than after the placebo.

The drug methadone is an analgesic that has widespread use as a detoxifying agent for narcotic addicts. Kay (1975) described the effects of methadone administration and withdrawal on the EEG of prison volunteers. The procedure involved the oral administration of 100 mg of methadone daily during a stabilization phase lasting 51 to 56 days. Then, an abstinence phase was instituted, which entailed a complete, abrupt withdrawal of methadone for a 5-month period. During the stabilization phase, significantly increased amounts of delta and theta activity and a slowing of alpha activity in the EEGs of the waking subjects were observed. The EEG activity returned to the normal control level after 10 weeks of the withdrawal period. The author pointed out that chronic administration of narcotic analgesics, such as methadone, may produce persistent functional changes in the nervous system. The appearance of delta waves in the EEG records of awake subjects is considered to be abnormal. The alpha changes (slowing) produced by the administration of methadone over a long period of time were similar to those obtained by Volavka et al. (1974) with the administration of a single dose of heroin. Both drugs had obvious CNS effects, as indicated by the records of brain activity.

Alcohol.   Murphree (1973) noted that 1 min after injection of a barbiturate (thiopental), fast frequency activity of 21 to 25 cps appeared in the EEG record. This curious phenomenon, in which activation of the EEG is produced by a substance that is supposed to be a depressant, is known as the "barbiturate buzz," and appears after relatively small doses of intravenously injected barbiturates (e.g., 1.5 mg/per kg of body weight, of thiopental). (Note: 1 kg is equal to 2.2 lbs.) The question that Murphree asked was whether such effects could be found after drinking an alcoholic beverage.

The EEG of a male subject was recorded for 10 min after drinking bourbon whiskey (1.00 ml/kg pure alcohol). This is equivalent to 6 oz of 80-proof whiskey for a 150-lb person. The EEG record showed a mixture of high amplitude alpha with a "buzz" in the beta range. The subject acted giddy and "high" before and after the recording. Results from this and other subjects led Murphree to conclude that alcohol can produce stimulant effects as well as being a depressant in other instances. He suggested that the fast EEG activity observed after ingestion of alcohol may be due in part to disinhibition in the CNS and in part to catecholamine release. Catecholamines have a sympathomimetic action; that is, they mimic the stimulating effects of SNS activity.

Although the short-term effect of alcohol may be to produce EEG activation, the longer-term effects produce a slowing of brain activity. This is illustrated in a study of "experimental hangover" performed by Sainio, Leino, Huttunen, and Ylikahri (1976). The EEGs of healthy male volunteers were recorded 14 to 16 hrs after they drank an amount of pure alcohol equivalent to drinking about 11 oz of 80-proof whiskey, for a 150-lb individual. (Individuals who weighed more or less were given proportionate amounts, based on body weight.) At the 14- to 16-hr interval, when hangover is supposed to peak, 5 of the subjects reported severe hangover, 21 mild hangover, and 1 reported no hangover at all. Analyses of the EEG at this time showed a decrease and slowing of alpha activity and an increase in theta activity (4–7 Hz). A significant increase in amount of 7- to 8-Hz activity was noted, as compared to the control condition in which subjects drank water. The researchers ruled out blood alcohol level, acidoses, hypoglycemia, or fatigue as a cause of the EEG change and concluded that the slowing of EEG during hangover was caused by the depressant action of alcohol, or its metabolites, on cortical function. Thus, the long-term effects of alcohol seem to be different in terms of EEG activity than short-term effects. No "barbiturate buzz" was reported by Sainio et al., but it must be noted that they recorded 14 to 16 hrs after alcohol ingestion, whereas Murphree recorded EEG immediately afterward.

A number of investigations have indicated that fast EEG activity is a distinctive characteristic of alcoholics, and that it may be genetically transmitted. Gabrielli et al. (1982) tested the hypothesis that 11- to 13-year-old sons of alcoholic fathers would show an excess of fast EEG activity. The EEGs of a sample of 27 children of alcoholics and 258 children of nonalcoholic parents were compared. The hypothesis was confirmed because male children at high risk for alcoholism themselves (25%–30%) showed faster EEG activity than male children at low risk. The authors speculated that drinking alcohol may be reinforced by the slower brain waves, and the more relaxed state, produced in those with a tendency towards fast brain activity. If such a relationship could be established, then perhaps a more acceptable way of slowing brain activity could be encouraged in persons at risk for becoming alcoholic (e.g., relaxation techniques or meditation).

In summary, the studies reviewed in this section indicate that marijuana and heroin both have depressant effects on brain activity and performance (methadone has effects similar to heroin). Administration of LSD resulted in low-amplitude, high-frequency brain waves. Nicotine, in general, has an activating effect on EEG activity. Some preliminary results suggest that whether EEG is activated or slowed may depend on the presmoking mood of the individual. Alcohol was seen to have short-term activating effects, but produced depressant effects after a longer period of time. Fast EEG activity (excess of beta, and deficient alpha, theta, and delta activity) characteristic of alcoholics, has also been found in sons of alcoholics, suggesting a biological factor that may be inherited.

Hormones

The endocrine system consists of ductless glands that secrete their chemicals (hormones) directly into the bloodstream. These hormones have profound influences over many body functions, and, in addition, their undersecretion or oversecretion may have behavioral effects. The endocrine system is regulated by the nervous system (primarily through connections between the hypothalamus and pituitary gland) and, therefore, the EEG may be able to reflect interactions between these systems. EEG activity has been found to be increased in cases of hyperthyroidism (excessive secretion of the hormone thyroxin) and decreased in hypothyroidism (Hermann & Quarton, 1964; Thiebaut, Rohmer, & Wackenheim, 1958). A lack of adrenal cortical hormones has been related to slow brain activity, which can be speeded up through administration of the hormone cortisone (Engel & Margolin, 1942).

The effects of hormonal changes on EEG changes during the menstrual cycle of 32 normal women, age 20 to 28, were studied by Creutzfeldt et al. (1976). The EEGs, blood hormone levels, and psychological test performance were measured for 16 spontaneously menstruating women and 16 women taking oral contraceptives. A significant increase in dominant alpha frequency occurred in the spontaneous group during the luteal phase of the cycle, and this increase in alpha was significantly correlated with an improvement in RT, simple arithmetic, and spatial orientation. (The luteal phase is that in which the hormone progesterone reaches a peak level, and it occurs shortly after ovulation.) No such acceleration of alpha frequency or performance improvement was observed in the oral contraceptive group. As a possible physiological mechanism for the increase in alpha frequency, the authors postulated a lessening of inhibitory postsynaptic potentials (IPSPs) in the thalamus during the luteal phase. They speculated that this decreased inhibition might also cause the improvement in RT and other tests. Another interesting suggestion by these authors is that the increased CNS activation may contribute to increased feelings of irritability noticed by some women at the end of the luteal phase, just prior to menstruation (premenstrual tension).

The studies reviewed indicate that hormones can affect EEG activity. Although these internal events may be difficult to control in the usual experimental situation, it is important that the psychophysiological investigator take them into account. However, the degree to which the cycle influences reactivity in psychophysiological studies seems minimal. For example, physiological reactivity of women in luteal and follicular phases of their menstrual cycle was examined by Stoney, Owens, Matthews, Davis, and Caggiula (1990). (The follicular is the phase during which follicles develop in preparation for ovulation.) They found that follicular and luteal phases did not change the HR or BP reactivity to three different laboratory stressors. They concluded that reports of menstrual cycle influences reported in the past may have been due to use of women with cycle irregularities, and/or a failure to adequately verify menstrual cycle phase.

Oxygen

The CNS is critically dependent on oxygen supply for its functioning. Hence, it would be logical to expect changes in oxygen supply, or factors that influence it, to be reflected in brain activity. Past studies have indicated that a lack of oxygen caused a slower frequency and higher amplitude EEG, whereas oxygen excess increased EEG frequency (Engel, 1945; Gibbs, Williams, & Gibbs, 1940). More recent studies show that factors causing oxygen deficit result in a slowing of EEG activity.

Radiation

An accident at a Russian nuclear power plant in April of 1986 led to the prenatal irradiation of many children whose pregnant mothers were in close vicinity to Chernobyl. Fifty of these prenatally exposed children were randomly selected and matched for age and gender with nonexposed children when they were between 6 and 8 years of age (Nyagu, Loganovsky, & Loganovskaja, 1998). Measures of EEG and intelligence were obtained and the groups compared. For the irradiated children, there was significantly greater amount of delta wave activity and significantly less theta, compared to controls, at left hemisphere sites. The authors also reported a significant increase in mental retardation (IQ < 70) and borderline IQ (70–90) as well as increased incidence of emotional disorders in children irradiated in utero. They hypothesized that the disorders observed were due to malfunction in left hemisphere limbic structures, especially in children exposed during a critical period of brain development (8 to 25 weeks).

Caffeine

Caffeine (150 mg), a 15 minute nap, or a placebo were given to subjects during a 30-min rest period between two 1-hr sessions of monotonous driving on an auto simulator (Horne & Reyner, 1996). The EEG and driving performance were monitored over the entire session. Alpha and theta activity were greater in the placebo condition than either the caffeine or nap condition. This EEG alerting was sustained throughout the second hour of driving. Simulator driving performance was best after drinking caffeine, next best after a nap, and worst after the placebo. Both caffeine and nap conditions were significantly superior to placebo, but not from each other. The authors suggested that caffeine intake may be more feasible in an actual driving situation, as not all individuals could nap for 15 min.

EFFECTS OF ENVIRONMENTAL FACTORS
ON EVENT-RELATED POTENTIALS (ERPs)

This section examines some studies dealing with the effects of drugs, hormones, and oxygen level on ERPs.

Drugs

There are numerous studies of the effects of pharmacologic agents on ERPs. Many of these were reviewed by Shagass (1972), who noted that various changes in ERPs occur as a result of drug action. For example, diazepam (Valium) has been found to reduce the amplitude of the visual ERP and somatosensory ERP. This would imply that beneficial effects with a psychiatric population are related to decreased cortical responsivity to sensory stimuli, and Shagass suggested that it may improve the functioning of central mechanisms by improving the balance between excitatory and inhibitory processes. Lithium has been frequently used in the treatment of manic-depressive patients in recent years. Manic-depressives show tremendously exaggerated mood swings, ranging from extreme excitement to immobilizing depression.

Tranquilizers and Barbiturates.   The commonly used antianxiety agent Valium (diazepam) has been found to decrease the amplitude of visual ERPs (Bergamasco, 1966). The effects of 7.5 to 10 mg of intravenously administered Valium on the visual and somatosensory ERPs of normal persons was investigated by Ebe, Meier-Ewert, and Broughton (1969). The amplitudes of both ERPs were reduced.

Saletu, Saletu, and Itil (1972) investigated the effects of chlorpromazine and diazepam on the somatosensory ERPs of healthy male subjects. Chlorpromazine is a powerful antipsychotic drug. Whereas the placebo did not effect the somatosensory ERP, 50 mg of chlorpromazine prolonged latencies of all components 2 hrs after administration. In addition, chlorpromazine resulted in decreased amplitudes of the late components of the somatosensory ERP (those occurring at 150 msec or later). Diazepam (5 mg) resulted in a decrease in somatosensory ERP amplitude. Thus it appears that both drugs suppress brain activity, but chlorpromazine has more potent effects as judged by its prolonged latency and amplitude changes.

The effects of bromazepam (antianxiety drug) on visual ERPs and vigilance performance were examined by van Leeuwen, Verbaten, Koelega, Kenemans, and Slangen (1992). The subjects were randomly assigned to one of three drug conditions (placebo, 6 mg, and 12 mg) in a double-blind experiment. Subjects performed a visual detection task for 30 min, 1 hr after capsule administration. Bromazepam caused an amplitude reduction in an early component (N1) of the visual ERP. The authors suggested that this reduction was due to the effects of bromazepam on brain stem reticular formation activity. The later P2–N2 amplitude was also reduced. With regard to performance, the drug group had faster motor responses, but more errors than the placebo group. This was attributed to a reduction in cautiousness while under the influence of the drug.

The CNV and RT of normal women was measured after they were given 50 mg of chlorpromazine or a placebo (Tecce, Cole, & Savignano-Bowman, 1975). The experimental paradigm was that of a constant foreperiod RT situation in which S1 was a light flash and S2 was a tone that occurred 1.5 sec after the light and was terminated by a key press. They found that this relatively small dose of chlorpromazine significantly reduced electrical brain activity (CNV) and lowered alertness (slower RTs) in the third hour after administration of the drug. Tecce et al. concluded that CNV amplitude appears to be an accurate indicator of drug-produced changes in alertness. Scopolamine is a commonly used ingredient in over-the-counter sleep preparations. The effects of scopolamine versus placebo on information processing and visual ERPs was studied by Brandeis, Naylor, Halliday, Callaway, and Yano (1992). Subjects participated under both drug and placebo conditions on two days in a double-blind experiment. Scopolamine slowed N1 latency (defined as a negative component occurring at 200 msec) in all four tasks used. It also slowed onset of the P300 component (latency 400 msec) in two of the four tasks.

In summary, the general pattern of results for tranquilizers is one in which brain activity is suppressed, and performance is detrimentally affected. The effects of a barbiturate on the visual ERP were illustrated by Bergamini and Bergamasco (1967). Thiopental was administered intravenously and was found to modify the ERP by decreasing its amplitude during initial stages of anesthesia. When barbiturate anesthesia was deeper (delta waves were present in the EEG), the early components of the visual ERP completely disappeared (those that normally occurred before 60 msec).

The effects of two barbiturates on CNV and attention were tested by Tecce, Cole, Mayer, and Lewis (1977). Thirty male subjects were randomly assigned to either pentobarbital (100 mg), phenobarbital (100 mg), or placebo groups. Pentobarbital has short duration effects, whereas those of phenobarbital are relatively long-lasting. The CNV was recorded from frontal (F_z), central (C_z), and parietal (P_z) scalp areas. The measure of attention was time to respond to a target letter in a series of letters. The only significant drug effect was a decrease in CNV amplitude recorded from P_z 2 hrs after administration of phenobarbital. This was accompanied by a decrement in attention performance.

Amphetamine is a CNS-stimulant and has been used as an antidepressant in psychiatric patients. Amphetamine had an unexpected effect on the CNV in the first hour after administration in a number of normal individuals (Tecce & Cole, 1974). Thirteen of 20 adults who were given 10 mg of dextroamphetamine evidenced lower CNV amplitudes and drowsiness during the first hour following administration of the drug. The other seven showed alertness and increased CNV amplitude. All subjects showed increased alertness and CNV amplitudes 2 and 3 hrs following administration of the drug. Tecce and Cole concluded that amphetamine is not a simple CNS stimulant, but can produce an early transient depression in brain activity, accompanied by feelings of lethargy in some persons.

Methylphenidate (brand name Ritalin) is a stimulant drug that, paradoxically, calms down hyperactive children with attention deficit disorder. This drug was used with normal young adults (Brumaghim, Klorman, Strauss, Levine, & Goldstein, 1987) performing the Sternberg task, which involves short-term memory and RT. These researchers found that P300 latency was shorter and RT was faster under the drug versus placebo condition. Hence, methylphenidate shortened the timing of motor processes and the duration of stimulus evaluation time (P300 latency). Some chlldren with attention deficit hyperactivity disorder (ADHD) fail to respond to methylphenidate treatment. These children are referred to as *nonresponders* and constitute between 15% and 30% of those with ADHD.

A comparison of ERPs between responders and nonresponders and control children was undertaken by Sunohara, Voros, Malone, and Taylor (1997). Response to methylphenidate was studied during a 4-week double-blind medication assessment period. When off medication, both responders and nonresponders had delayed P3b latencies compared to normal children. However, when both were on medication the nonresponders had longer P3b and N2 latencies than the responders. These results suggest that the ADHD responders and nonresponders have a different ERP response profile when taking methylphenidate.

It is known that acetylcholine and dopamine are neurotransmitters present in the visual system (Daniels, Harding, & Anderson, 1994). Alzheimer's disease has been linked to a deficit of acetylcholine in the brain and Parkinsonism is known to be related to deficiencies in brain dopamine levels. A study carried out by Daniels et al. sought to determine whether visual ERPs would be changed in Alzheimer's and Parkinson's patients compared to normals due to deficits in these neurotransmitters. Compared to controls, the P2 component of flash evoked visual ERPs was clearly delayed in patients with Alzheimer's disease. The authors suggested that the findings are consistent with a model suggesting that acetylcholine deficits in the superior colliculus–cortical association area pathway are responsible for the delay in the P2 component of the ERP produced by light flashes.

In summary, the general pattern of results for tranquilizers is one in which brain activity is suppressed, and performance is detrimentally affected. Barbiturates also suppress brain activity, and one suggestive study with amphetamine indicated that early effects may be stimulating or depressing, depending on the individual. Methylphenidate, a stimulant commonly used to treat ADHD, appears to shorten RT and speed up evaluation time in normal young adults. Persons with ADHD who respond to methylphenidate appear to have a different ERP profile and nonresponders (shorter P3b and N2 latencies). Suggestive evidence indicates that acetylcholine deficits may contribute to delays in a positive component of the visual ERP in Alzheimer's patients.

Effects of Marijuana on the ERP.   Lewis, Dustman, Peters, Straight, and Beck (1973) tested the effects of known oral doses of tetrahydrocannabinol (THC), the active ingredient in marijuana, on the visual ERPs and somatosensory ERPs of male and female subjects. They were divided into two groups: frequent smokers (three times a week) and infrequent smokers (two times a month). Three dosage levels (.2, .4, and .6 mg/kg of body weight) were administered to each subject on flavored sugar cubes. (These dosage levels are equivalent to about 10 mg, 20 mg, and 40 mg of THC for a 150-lb individual.) The highest dose (.6 mg/kg) produced delays in the appearance of the various wave components of the ERP. There was little effect on amplitude. All dose levels produced subjective "highs." The finding was interpreted in terms of decreased sensitivity of cortical and subcortical neurons due to the ingestion of THC, because visual responses were delayed after its administration.

Low, Klonoff, and Marcus (1973) measured visual and auditory ERPs and the CNV 45 min before and 45 min after smoking a marijuana cigarette containing high (9.1), low (4.8), or less than .01 mg of THC. Performance in a complex auditory discrimination task was simultaneously measured. High doses of marijuana resulted in longer auditory ERP latencies, and interfered with the discrimination task. The CNV amplitude increase was a consequence of marijuana smoking. Kopell, Tinklenberg, and Hollister (1972) also found enhancement of CNV with THC. Thus, marijuana appears to slow, and in one instance to reduce, the amplitude of sensory ERPs. However, the evidence suggests an enhancement of the CNV with marijuana. The enhancement has been interpreted by Kopell et al. (1972) as indicating that subjects who are intoxicated can better attend to relevant, simple stimuli as required in the CNV paradigm. These interesting marijuana effects on ERPs require further investigation.

Alcohol.   The effects of alcohol on ERPs have been studied by a number of investigators. For example, Gross, Begleiter, Tobin, and Kissin (1966) measured auditory ERPs of subjects after they drank either 100 cc of water with ice or 100 cc of 90-proof whiskey (about 3 oz) with ice. All components of the auditory ERP were reduced after ingestion of alcohol, with maximal effect noted 15 to 30 min after consumption. Similar results were found by Lewis, Dustman, and Beck (1970), who administered alcohol doses equivalent to about 1 and 3 oz for a 150-lb subject. Somatosensory and visual ERPs were measured after administration of either alcohol or water (placebo). The higher alcohol dose reduced amplitudes of late components of the visual and somatosensory ERPs. The smaller dose and placebo had no effect. Rhodes, Obitz, and Creel (1975) reported that alcohol reduced the amplitude of visual ERPs recorded from the central scalp.

Similar to earlier studies, it was the later components (60–200 msec) that were affected most by the alcohol. Salamy and Williams (1973) demonstrated that as the blood alcohol concentration (BAC) level of subjects increased, amplitude of the somatosensory ERP decreased. Again, the major effects were on later components of the ERPs. Salamy (1973) also found the somatosensory ERP amplitude to decrease with BAC. An illustration from Salamy (1973) is reproduced in Fig. 19.1 and shows a clear decrease in somatosensory ERP for one subject from Condition A (placebo) to B (low dose) to C (high dose). Thus, it is clear that alcohol has an effect on the neural processes reflected by the ERPs. Lewis et al.'s (1970) results led them

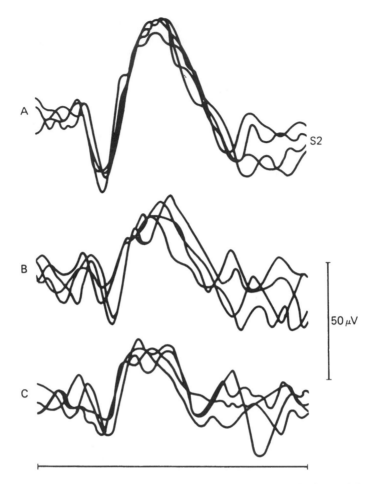

FIG. 19.1. Dose-response relationship between somatosensory evoked potential amplitude and blood alcohol concentration (BAC). Four superimposed single ERPs recorded from one subject under three alcohol treatments: A, placebo (BAC of 0 mg %); B, low dose (BAC of 50–65 mg %); C, high dose (BAC of 95–110 mg %).

to conclude that alcohol exerts a depressant effect on subcortical areas first (e.g., the reticular formation) and later on the cortex. It had previously been hypothesized that cortical effects appeared before subcortical ones.

Nicotine.   The effects of smoking withdrawal and resumption on the visual ERP were examined by Hall, Rappaport, Hopkins, and Griffin (1973). They measured visual ERPs of smokers (three quarters to three packs per day) to four intensities of light. The ERPs were taken during different baseline periods: before abstinence from smoking, after 12 and 36 hrs of abstinence, and finally after resumption of smoking (one cigarette). The results showed a decrease in ERP amplitude during the no-smoke period and an increase in amplitude when smoking was resumed. Hall and his associates suggested that the increased ERP amplitude indicated that the processing of sensory stimuli by the brain is changed when smokers use tobacco. Perhaps the withdrawal of nicotine for smokers is distracting, in which case it might result in lower ERPs. Distracting stimuli have been shown to reduce CNV amplitudes (e.g., see Tecce, 1972).

Neurotoxic Substances.   Neurotoxins are substances that are poisonous or destructive to nerve tissue. The damage may be produced selectively to certain areas of the brain or spinal cord. One of the most common sources of neurotoxins is industrial compounds. Among the metals recognized as neurotoxins are lead, mercury, and manganese. Chronic exposure to some industrial solvents may cause nerve damage with characteristic patterns. Some harmful solvents are n-Hexane, Methyl-n-Butyl Ketone (MBK), and Toluene. In addition, there are 39 separate compounds used as insecticides, which account for large numbers of poisonings among agricultural and industrial workers.

The effects of occupational exposure to mercury and lead on brain stem ERPs was examined by Discalzi, Fabbro, Meliga, Mocellini, and Capellaro (1993). They recorded the brain stem potentials from 22 workers exposed to lead, from 8 exposed to mercury, and from 2 control groups matched in age and sex to the workers, and who had never been exposed to neurotoxic substances. The mean durations of exposure were 9.3 and 11.7 years for lead and mercury, respectively. Both mercury and lead exposed workers showed a significant prolongation of Wave I-V of the brain stem potential (see chapter 16, Fig. 16.4). In addition, the prolongation was greatest in lead-exposed individuals whose blood lead concentration was greatest. Thus, the brain stem ERPs provide a sensitive index to detect subclinical neurotoxicity produced by lead and mercury. There is also evidence that lead and mercury exposure produce alterations in somatosensory (Langauer-Lewowicka & Kazibutowska, 1989) and visual ERPs (Araki, Murata, & Aono, 1987).

Aliphatic hydrocarbons, such as n-hexane, have the potential to be neurotoxic if fumes are breathed in for prolonged periods. To investigate the effects of n-hexane exposure, Seppalainen, Raitta, and Huuskanen (1979) studied visual ERPs to light flashes of 15 workers occupationally exposed to n-hexane for 5 to 21 yrs and compared their responses to 10 unexposed persons. The amplitudes of the ERP components were clearly smaller for n-hexane exposed persons. The changes were interpreted to indicate brain dysfunction, probably due to conduction blockage in axons. Previous studies had found n-hexane to cause axon damage in both experimental animals and humans, and the ERP results indicate that the visual systems of industrial workers are susceptible to its toxic effects.

Volatile solvents are not only used in factories but can be found in the home in glues, paints, thinners, and cleaning products. Solvents such as trichloroethylene and styrene are known to damage the auditory system of rats. Exposure to styrene and trichloroethylene was produced to assess the effects of combined exposure to these solvents on the brain stem responses of rats (Rebert et al., 1993). The animals were exposed 8 hrs/day to vapors produced by various concentrations of the two solvents. Decreases in brain stem response amplitude, indicative of hearing loss, was correlated with blood levels of total solvent. The greater the concentration, the greater the ERP decrease. Figure 19.2 shows the brain stem responses (BAERs) in normal rats and those exposed to styrene. The deficits can be seen as the decreased brain stem auditory evoked responses to the styrene exposed group at all sound intensity levels, ranging from 25 dB to 95 dB.

In summary, the drug studies reviewed here indicate that tranquilizers have depressant effects on ERPs. Alcohol, marijuana, and barbiturates also have depressant effects, but the effects of marijuana are different from the other two in that they are sometimes manifested as delays in ERP components rather than as decreases in amplitude. There is nothing in the results of ERP studies to contradict the generally accepted belief that the effects of depressant drugs are mainly on the reticular formation (ARAS). Abstinence from cigarette smoking seems to depress visual ERPs to original levels. This finding could be important in terms of the possible physiological mechanisms that cause certain individuals to become heavy smokers (i.e., does it activate their physiology to more effective levels?), or it may only reflect a distracting effect of nicotine withdrawal for these periods. More work is needed to settle this question.

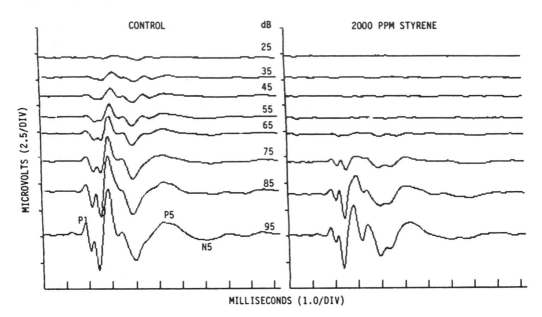

FIG. 19.2. Examples of group-averaged BAERs in normal (left tracings) and those exposed to 2000 ppm (parts per min.) styrene. Intensities range (lower-to-upper) in 10 dB increments from 95 to 25 dB (machine setting). Recording epoch = 10ms; 2.5 μV per division. Note clear response at 35 dB in normal rats, but the absence of a discernible response below 65 dB sound level for rats exposed to styrene. (Photo courtesy of Dr. C. S. Rebert.)

Exposure to neurotoxins produces changes in ERPs of both humans and animals. Occupational exposure to a single substance such as lead can lead to changes in the brain stem potential in persons who show no evidence of symptoms. Exposure to neurotoxins can also compromise visual and somatosensory ERPs in man. Experiments with animals show a dose-response relationship such that the greater the concentration of neurotoxin to which the animal is exposed, the greater the effect on ERP amplitude. This is an important area of research having implications for the health of persons exposed to even low levels of neurotoxins.

Effects of Hormones on the ERP

The undersecretion of the hormone thyroxin by the thyroid gland can have serious psychological effects in both infants and adults. A condition know as *myxedema* develops in adults with thyroxin deficiency (hypothyroidism) and is characterized by apathy and mental sluggishness, among other effects. The ERPs of patients with hypothyroidism were studied before and after administration of thyroid hormone (Nishitani & Kooi, 1968). The general results for the thyroid hormone correlate an excess with greater ERP amplitudes and deficiencies with lower amplitudes. This may mean that the CNS is differentially sensitive to stimuli when levels of this hormone are either high or low.

A number of investigators have reported that women have larger amplitude ERPs than men (e.g., see Shagass, 1972). Buchsbaum, Henkin, and Christiansen (1974) conducted an experiment to determine possible reasons for the noted sex differences. Visual and auditory ERPs of 166 normal males and females, age 6 to 60, and 10 females with gonadal dysgenesis (lacking in estrogen or progesterone production) were measured. The 10 female patients were compared with normal women. The role of gonadal hormones in producing the sex differences in amplitude were ruled out on two counts: (a) females had larger ERPs than males at all ages (prepuberty and postmenopause), and (b) ERPs of gonadal dysgenesis females did not differ from those of normals. Greater auditory ERP amplitudes to 1,000-Hz tones were obtained for women and girls as compared to men and boys in a study by Martineau, Tanguay, Garreau, Roux, and Lelord (1984). These differences were obtained at both Cz and Oz recording sites. One possible explanation for the difference was mentioned by Martineau and colleagues, and this was that male-female differences may be related to shorter anatomical distances in the sensory pathways and between generators and brain surface in females because of smaller average head and brain size. Another possibility (Shagass, 1972) is that females have thinner skulls. The issue remains unresolved.

ENVIRONMENTAL FACTORS AND THE ELECTROMYOGRAM (EMG)

Drugs

Complaints of muscle weakness have been noted in manic-depressive patients undergoing long-term lithium treatment (Girke, Krebs, & Muller-Oerlinghausen, 1975). To test the hypothesis that this was due to a disturbance in peripheral neuromuscular function, they measured EMGs of seven healthy volunteers before, during, and after lithium administration. The EMG was recorded from the extensor digitorum brevis muscle of the right foot. They found that the duration of potentials was increased and nerve conduction velocity was decreased after 1 week of lithium intake. Both muscle potential duration and nerve conduction returned to near prelithium levels 1 week after administration of the drug was discontinued. The authors hypothesized that lithium exerts its effect by influencing magnesium metabolism, which, in turn, affects the regulation of enzymes, such as ATP, that are important in muscle function.

Caffeine is one of the most widely used psychoactive substances, because it is present in common beverages such as coffee, tea and soft drinks. Those who habitually consume large amounts of caffeine each day (equivalent to 5 cups or more of coffee) suffer from withdrawal symptoms when intake is terminated. The symptoms include increased muscle tension, headache, muscle aches, anxiety, irritability, and drowsiness (Rizzo, Stamps, & Fehr, 1988; White, Lincoln, Pearce, Reeb, & Vaida, 1980). In a study by White et al. (1980), high consumers of caffeine had elevated forearm EMG after 3 hrs of abstinence, whereas low users stayed at the same level. Administration of caffeine speeded reaction times of both high and low user groups. Withdrawal of caffeine led to elevated scores on a measure of anxiety (State–Trait Anxiety Inventory) for the heavy users.

Exercise

Milner-Brown, Stein, and Lee (1975) reported that the degree to which firing of motor units in one muscle are synchronized is affected by the use of the muscle in physical exercise. That is, the impulses from two or more motor units coincide in time more frequently than would be expected for unrelated firings. Recordings from the first dorsal interosseus muscle of the hand in seven weightlifters showed significantly more synchronization than in seven control subjects. Further, records from four additional subjects before and after 6 weeks of exercise involving the same hand muscle showed a significant increase in the level of motor unit synchronization. The authors suggested that the different firing patterns of exercised versus nonexercised muscles may be due to enhancement of connections from motor cortex to spinal motoneurons to produce synchronization of motor units during steady, voluntary contractions. One may wonder whether synchronization of motor units occurs in the development of a skilled motor performance, such as touch-typing or piano playing.

ENVIRONMENTAL FACTORS
AND ELECTRODERMAL ACTIVITY

Hormones and Drugs

Venables and Christie (1973) discussed the possibility of hormonal influences on EDA. For example, they pointed out that progesterone has been found to decrease eccrine gland sweat output and that ACTH has similar effects. Presumably, then, these hormones have the potential to affect EDA. In fact, a decrease in resting SCL was found during the luteal phase in the menstrual cycle of 12 female subjects (Little & Zahn, 1974). Progesterone level reaches its peak during the luteal phase. Further, Little and Zahn found significant increases in SCR during the ovulatory portion of the menstrual cycle, the time when estrogen reaches peak levels in the body.

The effects of preanesthetic doses of diazepam on SCRs obtained under thiopental sodium induction was investigated by Williams, Jones, and Williams (1975). The subjects were physiologically normal young female patients about to undergo operations. One half received 10 mg of diazepam or 10 mg of a placebo intravenously. The diazepam subject required significantly less thiopental sodium (44%) to reach the point at which spontaneous SCRs abruptly ceased, compared to the placebo group. Corsico, Moiziszowica, Bursuck, and Rovaro (1976) compared the effects of two CNS stimulants, dextroamphetamine (5 mg) and etifoxine (300 mg) on SCRs and pursuit–rotor performance as compared to a placebo condition. A double-blind procedure was used and it was found that 2 hrs after administration both drugs led to improved motor performance and reductions in SCR magnitudes. These differences disappeared 6 hrs after the administration of the three treatments.

Alcohol

The effects of a moderate dose of alcohol on electrodermal indices of the orienting reflex (OR) were examined by Lyvers and Maltzman (1991). Social drinkers drank either tonic water alone, or tonic water plus enough vodka to raise blood alcohol content level to about .05%. Following an absorption period, subjects were asked to press a pedal whenever they heard an odd stimulus in a series of tones. Alcohol increased the number of spontaneous SCRs as well as the number of incorrect responses. It also enhanced the SCR to signal tones (the odd stimulus). Thus, alcohol had a disinhibiting effect on behavior as well as enhancing the signal-evoked OR. This effect is likely due to a selective depression of frontal cortex inhibitory functions, according to the researchers.

In summary, although the amount of data is scanty, hormones, drugs, and alcohol have been observed to affect EDA. Thus, investigators of electrodermal phenomena should be aware of these possible influences and gather appropriate information from subjects so that these factors may be accounted for in the design of their experiments.

ENVIRONMENTAL FACTORS, PUPIL SIZE,
AND EYE MOVEMENTS

Effects of Drugs on Pupil Size

The narcotic analgesic morphine produces pupillary constriction through its CNS effects (Goth, 1964). Pupillometry was used by Robinson, Howe, Varni, Ream, and Hegge (1974) to study pupil size of heroin users during the first 6 days of withdrawal. Control subjects were used for comparison purposes. In the acute heroin intoxication state, the pupils of patients were significantly constricted relative to controls, with average diameters of 3.5 mm and 5.0 mm, respectively. Ten hours after the last dose of heroin, there was no difference between patients and controls. As withdrawal progressed, the pupils of patients continued to dilate until, at the end of the 6-day periiod, the patients had significantly larger pupils than controls. The authors concluded that pupil diameter is a good differential indicator of heroin intoxication and withdrawal.

Another drug that produces pupillary constriction is pilocarpine. It can produce this action if applied to the surface of the eye in a 1% solution. Pupillary dilation is produced by the drug atropine. In ophthalmologic and research settings, it is applied to the eye as a 0.5% to 1.5% solution. Homatropine is preferable to atropine because it is much shorter in duration of action (Goth, 1964). Pupillary dilation can also be caused by neosynephrine (Hansmann, Semmlow, & Stark, 1974).

The usual pupil response to an intense light stimulus is constriction (called the light reflex). It has been observed that threat of electric shock will increase pupil diameter and at the same time reduce the usual pupillary constriction to a light stimulus (Bitsios, Szabadi, & Bradshaw, 1996). Thus, the emotional response (dilation due to SNS) can override the light reflex. Compared to a placebo, two dose levels of the anxiety-reducing drug diazepam attenuated this inhibition of the light reflex when electric shock was threatened (Bitsios, Szabadi, & Bradshaw, 1998). Thus, diazepam allowed the light reflex to occur, presumably because it reduced the anxiety associated with anticipation of an electric shock. The authors believe that this fear-inhibited light reflex can serve as a useful laboratory model of human anxiety.

Effects of Drugs on Eye Movements

Holzman (1975) measured the effects of three different drugs on the pursuit eye movements of normal adult males. The subjects were asked to follow a moving pendulum with their eyes for a 30-sec period while horizontal eye movements of both eyes were measured. Deviations from smooth-pursuit movements were quantified as velocity arrests (the number of times pursuit was interrupted when the eyes should have been tracking). The drugs diazepam and chlorpromazine had no significant effects on pursuit movements. However, sodium secobarbital (Seconal, 100 mg) affects the ability the follow the target with smooth-pursuit eye movements. Prolonged testing of Seconal effects (130 mg) with one subject showed that this barbiturate produced eye-tracking and eye-movement disruptions that lasted for 24 hrs.

The effects of diazepam on the reading eye movements of male college students was studied by Stern, Bremer, and McClure (1974). The administration of diazepam, as compared to a placebo, produced an increased frequency of long fixation pauses, and increased duration of fixations, and a decreased velocity of saccadic eye movements during line shifts. These changes were correlated with a decrease in the amount of material read.

ENVIRONMENTAL FACTORS AND HEART ACTIVITY

Drugs

A number of drugs are known to affect heart activity. Among them are those used for therapeutic purposes. For instance, the drug digitalis increases the contractility of cardiac muscle, or its capacity to do work. Nitroglycerin acts to increase blood flow to the heart by producing vasodilation (Goth, 1964).

Nicotine.   The effects of cigarette smoking on heart rate were studied by Elliott and Thysell (1968). The HR of 18 habitual smokers (one to two packs per day) were measured under three conditions:

1. Dragging on an unlit cigarette every 30 sec for 5 min. (sham smoking)
2. Deep breathing every 30 sec for 5 min.
3. Inhaling cigarette smoke every 30 sec for 5 min.

The researchers found that neither sham smoking (unlit cigarette) nor deep breathing influenced HR. However, actual smoking raised HR by 20 bpm, on the average, over resting levels. Fifteen minutes after actual smoking ceased, the HR was still 11 bpm over resting levels. The authors interpreted the increased HR in terms of the increased heart activity required to overcome the vasoconstrictive effects of smoking. In other words, HR speeded up to compensate for reduced blood flow. An interesting follow-up would be to observe the effects of secondhand smoke on the heart activity of nonsmokers in a controlled setting.

The effects of rapid and normal cigarette smoking on HR, as compared to sham smoking, were investigated by Danaher, Lichtenstein, and Sullivan (1976). The rapid smoking condition consisted of inhaling every 6 sec on a cigarette, whereas regular smoking involved inhaling a cigarette at a normal rate. The sham smoking condition was accomplished by inhaling on an unlit cigarette every 6 sec. Rapid smoking of cigarettes produced significantly higher HR than regular smoking, and regular smoking resulted in HR that was significantly elevated over the sham smoking condition.

MacDougall (1983) found that cigarette smoking plus stress effects produced greater cardiovascular changes than either one alone. The stressor involved playing difficult video games under challenging conditions. Subjects who smoked under no stress averaged a 15 bpm incnrease in HR, a 12 mm Hg increase in systolic BP, and a 9 mm Hg increase in diastolic BP. The individuals who smoked while engaged in the stressful task showed increases that approximately doubled these cardiovascular changes. The authors suggested that stress and smoking might combine to increase the risk of coronary heart disease.

The influence of nicotine on HR seem to be rather consistent; that is, a significant elevation occurs. Also, smoking while engaged in stressful tasks potentiates the effect.

Marijuana.   Clark, Greene, Karr, MacCannell, and Milstein (1974) tested the effects of marijuana on heart activity of 28 sujects, half of whom were experienced users. The drug was inhaled through a filtered breathing apparatus. The most consistent effect was an increase in HR. Clark (1975) reviewed a number of studies of marijuana effects on heart rate. Increases in HR from 18% to 51% over control levels have been reported with administration of synthetic (▲9 THC) or real marijuana. Some researchers suggest that marijuana produces its effect on heart activity through increased SNS activity mediated by epinephrine release. Others propose that marijuana may have its effects on HR by inhibiting vagus nerve activity, thus allowing HR to increase. The exact mechanism of the effect still remain to be elucidated.

Cocaine.   Cocaine was administered intravenously, in doses ranging from 4 to 32 mg, to nine adult males (Fischman et al., 1976). Mean HR was 74 bpm predrug, 100 bpm after 16 mg of cocaine, and 112 bpm after 32 mg. In general, HR peaked at 10 min, regardless of dose level, and returned to predrug baseline after 46 min. Control injections of saline solution had no effects on HR.

In summary, both marijuana and cocaine act to acelerate HR. The mechanisms by which this increase is produced remain obscure.

Caffeine. Caffeine at high doses resulted in overall increases in ANS activity, as reported by Zahn and Rapoport (1987). The investigators used a range of caffeine levels, including a placebo, with both users and nonusers. Regardless of prior caffeine use, administration of caffeine produced increased HR, EDA, and systolic BP. Decreases in skin temperature also occurred and were attributed to peripheral vasoconstriction. They found that caffeine did not improve RT or increase ANS activity during the RT task, as they had found in another study with children. Ceiling effects might have been operative because ANS arousal levels were already high and less likely to influence psychomotor performance.

Rizzo et al. (1988) examined effects of caffeine withdrawal on HR deceleration during a variable foreperiod RT task. Their data indicated that nonusers improved their RTs in a second session 1 week later. These faster RTs were related to an increase in the degree of HR deceleration during the foreperiod. On the other hand, the users showed neither an improvement in RT nor a change in HR deceleration from the first to the second session. The user group was required to abstain from caffeine for 2 days prior to the second session. The authors suggested that the effects of caffeine withdrawal may have negated RT practice effects and resulted in a lowered level of attention in the user group.

There is evidence that the effects of caffeine and stress on cardiovascular response are additive (France & Ditto, 1988, 1992; Lovallo et al., 1991). In the France and Ditto (1988) study, cardiovascular measures were taken while caffeine (250 mg) and placebo groups participated in a mental arithmetic task. A significant cumulative increase in diastolic BP was produced by caffeine in the resting and task conditions. Elevations in HR and systolic blood pressure also occurred, but they were not statistically significant. A more elaborate experiment by France and Ditto (1992) examined the combined effects of caffeine and three different stressors (mental arithmetic, cold pressor, and exercise). The physiological measures were HR, BP, forearm blood flow, finger skin temperature, and respiratory sinus arrhythmia. Caffeine plus stress had additive effects, which the authors interpreted as resulting from a combination of cardiovascular adjustments. These adjustments included an increase in cardiac output (HR X stroke volume), a decrease in vascular resistance in the large muscles (i.e., increased forearm blood flow), and increases in vascular resistance in other tissues (e.g., decreased finger skin temperature, indicative of vasoconstriction). In the Lovallo et al. (1991) study, the combined effects of caffeine and a demanding psychomotor task were examined. The subjects were 19 men at low risk for developing hypertension (no family history, low-normal resting BP) and 20 men at high risk (family history, high-normal resting BP). All subjects participated on 2 days under a placebo or caffeine (3.3 mg/kg body weight) condition. The two groups reacted differently. In the low risk group, BP was elevated by increased cardiac activity alone. In the high-risk men, the elevated BP in the task-caffeine condition was due to a combination of increased cardiac activity and greater systemic vascular resistance. The authors concluded that caffeine use during behavioral stress may produce elevated BP levels among those who are at high risk for developing hypertension.

ENVIRONMENTAL FACTORS AND BLOOD PRESSURE

Drugs

A number of drugs are known to affect blood pressure levels. For example, reserpine and pentobarbital sodium are known to lower blood pressure, whereas epinephrine increases it (Goth, 1964). The blood pressure of 79 healthy male students was measured 2 months before and on the day before final examinations (Ruttkay-Nedecky & Lagan, 1969). Subjects were administered either a barbiturate (10 mg of phenobarbital) or a placebo (double blind) on both occasions. Both the placebo and the barbiturate produced significant decreases in systolic and diastolic blood pressure measures.

The effects of two drugs (imipramine and methylphenidate) and a placebo on the blood pressure and pulse rate of 47 hyperactive children was studied by Greenberg and Yellin (1975). The children ranged in age from 6 to 13 years and completed an 8-week double-blind study in which of the patients received one of the drugs followed by a placebo, whereas the other half received the placebo first. Imipramine was found to produce significant increases in blood pressure (both systolic and diastolic) and pulse rate. Methylphenidate did not affect either of these variables. The authors recommended caution in using imipramine to treat hyperactive children.

Caffeine, Alcohol, and Nicotine.   Caffeine affects both systolic and diastolic blood pressure. The effect of caffeine is to raise SBP by 7 to 10 mmHg and DBP by 4 to 6 mmHg (Lane, 1983). The effects become noticeable about 30 min. after ingestion, reach a maximum at 60 min. and last about 3 hr. Alcohol also has effects on blood pressure. It has been recommended that subjects in psychophysiological studies do not consume alcohol for 12 hr prior to having BP measured in laboratory or real-life situations (Shapiro et al., 1996). Nicotine increases BP within the first few minutes of smoking and the effects last for an hour or more. Therefore, smokers should abstain for at least 2 hours prior to participation in psychophysiological studies. Other substances that can influence BP include cold remedies (vasoconstrictive), insulin, and anti-hypertensive medication. Tranquilizers and other psychotropic medications can also affect blood pressure. All of this suggests that subjects should be screened carefully for these substances prior to participating in psychophysiology research. The fact that these substances affect blood pressure suggests that they may also influence other commonly researched physiological responses.

Exercise and Blood Pressure

Buccola and Stone (1974) studied a number of physiological variables of 36 elderly men before and after they participated in a 14-week exercise program. The men ranged in age from 60 to 79 and participated in either a cycling program (20 subjects) or in a walk-jog program (16 subjects). The two groups trained for 25 to 50 min a day, 3 days a week. Both groups showed significant reductions in blood pressure and weight. Systolic pressure dropped from an average of 147 mm Hg to 141 mm Hg (4.1%), and diastolic decreased from 79 mm Hg to 72 mm Hg (8.9%). Thus, the subjects tested benefited physiologically from regular light exercise.

Hormones.   The luteal phase of the menstrual cycle is accompanied by elevated levels of estrogen and progesterone. The luteal phase occurs shortly after ovulation. Blood pressure and sensitivity to ischemic pain were tested at two phases of the menstrual cycle, early follicular (days 4 to 9) and mid-to-late luteal (5–10 days after ovulation) by a group of researchers (Pfleeger, Straneva, Fillingim, Maixner, & Girdler, 1997). Measures of systolic, diastolic and mean arterial presssure (MAP) were also obtained at all testing times. Ischemic pain was induced by occluding the upper arm with a blood pressure cuff and having subjects squeeze hand grips at the same time. The findings were that pain tolerance was significantly less during the luteal phase compared to the follicular. Also, there were positive correlations between pain tolerance and DBP and MAP, indicating that tolerance to pain increased with increased blood pressure levels. Thus, the study indicates cycle (hormonal) differences in pain sensitivity and relationships between arterial BP and pain sensitivity in women. Further research is needed to pinpoint the mechanisms involved in modulation of pain by hormones and blood pressure.

To summarize, various drugs and other commonly available substances can influence blood pressure. Regulated physical exercise appears to have beneficial effects on BP measures in elderly persons. There is preliminary evidence to indicate that pain tolerance in women is influenced by phase of menstrual cycle (hormones) and blood pressure levels.

REFERENCES

Araki, S., Murata, K., & Aono, H. (1987). Central and peripheral nervous system dysfunction in workers exposed to lead, zinc, and copper. *International Archives of Occupational Environment & Health, 59*, 177–187.

Bergamasco, B. (1966). Studio delle modificazioni della responsivita corticale nell' uomo indotte de farmaci ad azione sul SNC. *Sistema Nervoso, 18*, 155–164.

Bergamini, L., & Bergamasco, B. (1967). *Cortical evoked potentials in man.* Springfield: C. C. Thomas.

Bitsios, P., Szabadi, E., & Bradshaw, C. M. (1996). The inhibition of the pupillary light reflex by the threat of an electric shock: A potential laboratory model of human anxiety. *Journal of Psychopharmacology, 10*, 279–287.

Bitsios, P., Szabadi, E., & Bradshaw, C. M. (1998). Sensitivity of the fear-inhibited light reflex to diazepam. *Psychopharmacology, 135*, 93–98.

Brandeis, D., Naylor, H., Halliday, R., Callaway, E., & Yano, L. (1992). Scopolamine effects on visual information processing, attention, and event-related potential map latencies. *Psychophysiology, 29*, 315–336.

Brown, H. (1976). *Brain and behavior.* New York: Oxford.

Brumaghim, J. T., Klorman, R., Strauss, J., Levine, J. D., & Goldstein, M. G. (1987). Does methylphenidate affect information processing? Findings from two studies on performance and P3b latency. *Psychophysiology, 24*, 361–372.

Buccola, V. A., & Stone, W. J. (1974). Effects of jogging and cycling programs on physiological and personality variables in aged men. *The Research Quarterly, 46*, 134–139.

Buchsbaum, M. S., Henkin, R. I., & Christiansen, R. L. (1974). Age and sex differences in averaged evoked responses in a normal population, with observations on patients with gonadal dysgenesis. *Electroencephalography and Clinical Neurophysiology, 37*, 137–144.

Clark, S. C. (1975). Marijuana and the cardiovascular system. *Pharmacology, Biochemistry & Behavior, 3*, 299–306.

Clark, S. C., Greene, C., Karr, G. W., MacCannell, K. L., & Milstein, S. L. (1974). Cardiovascular effects of marijuana in man. *Canadian Journal of Physiology, and Pharmacology, 52*, 706–719.

Cook, M. R., Gerkovich, M. M., Hoffman, S. J., McClernon, F. J., Cohen, H. D., Oakleaf, K. L., & O'Connell, K. A. (1995). Smoking and EEG power spectra: Effects of differences in arousal seeking. *International Journal of Psychophysiology, 19*, 247–256.

Corsico, R., Moiziszowica, J., Bursuck, L., & Rovaro, E. (1976). Evaluation of the psychotropic effect of etifoxine through pursuit rotor performance and GSR. *Psychopharmacologia, 45*, 301–303.

Creutzfeldt, O. D., Arnold, P. M., Becker, D., Langenstein, S., Tirsch, W., Wilhelm, H., & Wuttke, W. (1976). EEG changes during spontaneous and controlled menstrual cycles and their correlation with psychological performance. *Electroencephalography and Clinical Neurophysiology, 40*, 113–131.

Danaher, B. G., Lichtenstein, E., & Sullivan, J. M. (1976). Comparative effects of rapid and normal smoking on heart rate and carboxyhemoglobin. *Journal of Consulting & Clinical Psychology, 44*, 556–563.

Daniels, R., Harding, G. F. A., & Anderson, S. J. (1994). Effect of dopamine and acetylcholine on the visual evoked potential. *International Journal of Psychophysiology, 16*, 251–261.

Discalzi, G., Fabbro, D., Meliga, F., Mocellini, A., & Capellaro, F. (1993). Effects of occupational exposure to mercury and lead on brainstem auditory evoked potentials. *International Journal of Psychophysiology, 14*, 21–25.

Dornbush, R. L., Fink, M., & Freedman, A. M. (1971). Marijuana, memory and perception. *American Journal of Psychiatry, 128*, 194–197.

Ebe, M., Meier-Ewart, K., & Broughton, R. (1969). Effects of intravenous diazepam (Valium) upon evoked potentials of photosensitive epileptic and normal subjects. *Electroencephalography and Clinical Neurophysiology, 27*, 429–435.

Elliott, R., & Thysell, R. (1968). A note on smoking and heart rate. *Psychophysiology, 5*, 280–283.

Engel, G. L. (1945). Mechanisms of fainting. *Journal of Mt. Sinai Hospital, New York, 12*, 170–190.

Engel, G. L., & Margolin, S. G. (1942). Neuropsychiatric disturbances in internal disease: Metabolic factors and electroencephalographic correlations. *Archives of Internal Medicine, 70*, 236–259.

Fink, M., Itil, T., & Clyde, D. (1966). The classification of psychoses by quantitative EEG measures. *Recent Advances in Biological Psychiatry, 8*, 305–312.

Fischman, M. W., Schuster, C. R., Resnekov, L., Shick, J. F. E., Krasnesor, N. A., Fennell, W., & Freedman, D. X. (1976). Cardiovascular and subjective effects of intravenous cocaine administration in humans. *Archives of General Psychiatry, 33*, 938–989.

France, C., & Ditto, B. (1988). Caffeine effects on several indices of cardiovascular activity at rest and during stress. *Journal of Behavioral Medicine, 11*, 473–482.

France, C., & Ditto, B. (1992). Cardiovascular responses to the combination of caffeine and mental arithmetic, cold pressor, and static exercise stressors. *Psychophysiology, 29*, 272–282.

Gabrielli, W. F., Mednick, S. A., Volavka, J., Pollock, V. E., Schuylsinger, F., & Itil, T. M. (1982). Electroencephalograms in children of alcoholic fathers. *Psychophysiology, 19*, 404–407.

Gibbs, F. A., Willliams, D., & Gibbs, E. L. (1940). Modification of the cortical frequency spectrum by changes in CO_2, blood sugar and O_2. *Journal of Neurophysiology, 3*, 49–58.

Girke, W., Krebs, F. A., & Muller-Oerlinghausen, B. (1975). Effects of lithium on electromyographic recordings in man. *International Pharmacopsychiatry, 10*, 24–36.

Goth, A. (1964). *Medical pharmacology*. St. Louis: Mosby.

Greenberg, L. M., & Yellin, A. M. (1975). Blood pressure and pulse changes in hyperactive children treated with imipramine and methylphenidate. *American Journal of Psychiatry, 132*, 1325–1326.

Gross, M. M., Begleiter, H., Tobin, M., & Kissin, B. (1966). Changes in auditory evoked response induced by alcohol. *The Journal of Nervous and Mental Disease, 143*, 152–156.

Hall, R. A., Rappaport, M., Hopkins, H. K., & Griffin, R. (1973). Tobacco and evoked potential. *Science, 180*, 212–214.

Hansmann, D., Semmlow, J., & Stark, L. (1974). A physiological basis for pupillary dynamics. In M. P. Janisse (Ed.), *Pupillary dynamics and behavior* (pp. 53–74). New York: Plenum.

Hermann, H. T., & Quarton, C. G. (1964). Changes in alpha frequency with change in thyroid hormone level. *Electroencephalography and Clinical Neurophysiology, 16*, 515–518.

Holzman, P. S. (1975). Smooth-pursuit eye movements, and diazcpam, LPZ, and secobarbital. *Psychopharmacologia, 44*, 111–115.

Horne, J. A., & Reyner, L. A. (1996). Counteracting driver sleepiness: Effects of napping, caffeine, and placebo. *Psychophysiology, 33*, 306–309.

Houlihan, M. E., Pritchard, W. S., Krieble, K. K., Robinson, J. H., & Duke, D. W. (1996). Effects of cigarette smoking on EEG spectral-band power, dimensional complexity, and nonlinearity during reaction-time task performance. *Psychophysiology, 33*, 740–746.

Kay, D. C. (1975). Human sleep and EEG through a cycle of methadone dependence. *Electroencephalography and Clinical Neurophysiology, 38*, 35–44.

Koppell, B. S., Tinklenberg, J. R., & Hollister, L. E. (1972). Contingent negative variation amplitudes, marijuana and ethanol. *Archives of General Psychiatry, 27*, 809–811.

Lane, J. D. (1983). Caffeine and cardiovascular responses to stress. *Psychosomatic Medicine, 45*, 447–451.

Langauer-Lewowicka, H., & Kazibutowska, Z. (1989). Multimodality evoked potentials in occupational exposure to metallic mercury vapour. *Polish Journal of Occupational Medicine, 2*, 192–199.

Lewis, E. G., Dustman, R. E., & Beck, E. C. (1970). The effects of alcohol on visual and somatosensory evoked responses. *Electroencephalography and Clinical Neurophysiology, 28*, 202–205.

Lewis, E. G., Dustman, R. E., Peters, B. A., Straight, R. C., & Beck, E. C. (1973). The effects of varying doses of 9-Tetrahydrocannabinol on the human visual and somatosensory evoked respnse. *Electroencephalography and Clinical Neurophysiology, 28*, 202–205.

Little, B. C., & Zahn, T. P. (1974). Changes in mood and autonomic functioning during the menstrual cycle. *Psychophysiology, 11*, 579–590.

Lovallo, W. R., Pincomb, G. A., Sung, B. H., Everson, S. A., Passey, R. B., & Wilson, M. F. (1991). Hypertension risk and caffeine's effect on cardiovascular activity during mental stress in young men. *Health Psychology, 10*, 236–243.

Low, M. D., Klonoff, H., & Marcus, A. (1973). The neurophysiological basis of the marijuana experience. *Canadian Medical Association Journal, 108*, 157–164.

Lyvers, M., & Maltzman, I. (1991). Selective effects of alcohol on electrodermal indices of orienting reflexes to signal and nonsignal stimuli. *Psychophysiology, 28*, 559–569.

MacDougall, J. M. (1983). Selective cardiovascular effects of stress and cigarette smoking. *Journal of Human Stress, 9*, 13–21.

Martineau, J., Tanguay, P., Garreau, B., Roux, S., & Lelord, G. (1984). Are there sex differences in averaged evoked responses produced by coupling sound and light in children and adults? *International Journal of Psychophysiology, 2*, 177–184.

Milner-Brown, H. S., Stein, R. B., & Lee, R. G. (1975). Synchronization of human motor units: Possible roles of exercise and surpaspinal reflexes. *Electroencephalography and Clinical Neurophysiology, 38*, 245–254.

Murphree, H. B. (1973). EEG and other evidence for mixed depressant and stimulant actions of alcoholic beverages. *Annals of the New York Academy of Sciences, 215*, 325–331.

Nishitani, H., & Kooi, K. A. (1968). Cerebral evoked responses in hypothyroidism. *Electroencephalography and Clinical Neurophysiology, 24*, 554–560.

Nyagu, A. I., Loganovsky, K. N., & Loganovskaja, T. K. (1998). Psychophysiologic after effects of prenatal irradiation. *International Journal of Psychophysiology, 30*, 303–311.

Pfleeger, M., Straneva, P. A., Fillingim, R. B., Maixner, W., & Girdler, S. S. (1997). Menstrual cycle, blood pressure and ischemic pain sensitivity in women: A preliminary investigation. *International Journal of Psychophysiology, 27*, 161–166.

Rebert, C. S., Boyes, W. K., Pryor, G. T., Svensgaard, D. J., Kassay, K. M., Gordon, G. R., & Shinsky, N. (1993). Combined effects of solvents on the rat's auditory system: Styrene and trichloroethylene. *International Journal of Psychophysiology, 14*, 49–60.

Rhodes, L. E., Obitz, F. W., & Creel, D. (1975). Effect of alcohol and task on hemispheric asymmetry of visually evoked potentials in man. *Electroencephalography and Clinical Neurophysiology, 38*, 561–568.

Rizzo, A. A., Stamps, L. E., & Fehr, L. A. (1988). Effects of caffeine withdrawal on motor performance and heart rate changes. *International Journal of Psychophysiology, 6*, 9–14.

Robinson, M. G., Howe, R. C., Varni, J. G., Ream, N. W., & Hegge, F. W. (1974). Assessment of pupil size during acute heroin withdrawal in Viet Nam. *Neurology, 24*, 729–732.

Rodin, E., & Luby, E. (1966). Effects of LSD-25 on the EEG and photic evoked responses. *Archives of General Psychiatry, 14*, 435–441.

Roth, W. T., Galanter, M., Weingartner, H., Vaughan, T. B., & Wyatt, R. J. (1973). Marijuana and synthetic-trans-tetrahydrocannobinol: Some effects on the auditory evoked response and background EEG in humans. *Biological Psychiatry, 6*, 221–233.

Ruttkay-Nedecky, I., & Lagan, S. (1969). Blood pressure of students the day before examination: A double-blind study of the effects of barbiturate and placebo. *Psychotherapy and Psychosomatics, 17*, 196–200.

Sainio, K., Leino, T., Huttunen, M. O., & Ylikahri, R. H. (1976). EEG changes during experimental hangover. *Electroencephalography and Clinical Neurophysiology, 40*, 535–538.

Salamy, A. (1973). The effects of alcohol on the variabililty of the human evoked potential. *Neuropharmacology, 12*, 1103–1107.

Salamy, A., & Williams, H. (1973). The effects of alcohol on sensory evoked and spontaneous cerebral potentials in man. *Electroencephalography and Clinical Neurophysiology, 35*, 3–11.

Saletu, B., Saletu, M., & Itil, T. (1972). Effect of minor and major tranquilizers on somatosensory evoked potentials. *Psychopharmacologia, 24*, 347–358.

Seppalainen, A., Raitta, C., & Huuskanen, M. S. (1979). n-Hexane-induced changes in visual evoked potentials and electroretinograms of industrial workers. *Electroencephalography and Clinical Neurophysiology, 47*, 492–498.

Shagass, C. (1972). Electrical activity of the brain. In N. S. Greenfield & R. A. Sternbach (Eds.), *Handbook of psychophysiology* (pp. 263–328). New York: Holt, Rinehart & Winston.

Shapiro, D., Jamner, L. D., Lane, J. D., Light, K. C., Myrtek, M., Sawada, Y., & Steptoe, A. (1996). Blood pressure publication guidelines. *Psychophysiology, 33*, 1–12.

Stern, J. A., Bremer, D. A., & McClure, J. (1974). Analysis of eye movements and blinks during reading: Effects of Valium. *Psychopharmacologia, 40*(2), 171–175.

Stoney, C. M., Owens, J. F., Matthews, K. A., Davis, M. C., & Caggiula, A. (1990). Influences of the normal menstrual cycle on physiologic functioning during behavioral stress. *Psychophysiology, 27*, 125–135.

Stroebel, C. F. (1972). Psychophysiological pharmacology. In N. S. Greenfield & R. A. Sternbach (Eds.), *Handbook of psychophysiology* (pp. 787–838). New York: Holt, Rinehart & Winston.

Sunohara, G. A., Voros, J. G., Malone, M. A., & Taylor, M. J. 1997). Effects of methylphenidate in children with attention deficit hyperactivity disorder: a comparison of event-related potentials between medication responders and non-responders. *International Journal of Psychophysiology, 27*, 9–14.

Tecce, J. J. (1972). Contingent negative variation (CNV) and psychological processes in man. *Psychological Bulletin, 77*, 73–108.

Tecce, J. J., & Cole, J. O. (1974). Amphetamine effects in man: Paradoxical drowsiness and lowered electrical brain activity (CNV). *Science, 185*, 451–453.

Tecce, J. J., Cole, J. O., Mayer, J., & Lewis, D. C. (1977). Barbiturate effects on brain functioning (CNV) and attention performance in normal men. *Psychopharmacology Bulletin, 13*, 64–66.

Tecce, J. J., Cole, J. O., & Savignano-Bowman, J. (1975). Chlorpromazine effects on brain activity (contingent negative variation) and reaction time in normal women. *Psychopharmacologia, 43*, 293–295.

Thiebaut, F., Rohmer, F., & Wackenheim, A. (1958). Contribution a l'etude electroencepahlographique des syndromes endocriniens. *Electroencephalography and Clinical Neurophysiology, 10*, 1–30.

van Leeuwen, T. H., Verbaten, M. N., Koelega, H. S., Kenemans, J. L., & Slangen, J. L. (1992). Effects of bromazepam on single-trial event-related potentials in a visual vigilance task. *Psychopharmacology, 106*, 555–564.

Vaughan, H. G. (1969). The relationship of brain activity to scalp recordings of event-related potentials. In E. Donchin & D. B. Lindsley (Eds.), *Averaged evoked potentials* (pp. 45–94). Washington, DC: NASA.

Venables, P. H., & Christie, M. J. (1973). Mechanisms, instrumentation, recording techniques and quantificantions of responses. In W. F. Prokasy & D. C. Raskin (Eds.), *Electrodermal activity in psychological research* (pp. 41–73). New York: Academic Press.

Volavka, J., Levine, R., Feldstein, S., & Fink, M. (1974). Short term effects of heroin in man: Is EEG related to behavior? *Archives of General Psychiatry, 30*, 677–681.

White, B. C., Lincoln, C. A., Pearce, N. W., Reeb, R., & Vaida, C. (1980). Anxiety and muscle tension as consequences of caffeine withdrawal. *Science, 209*, 1547–1548.

Williams, J. G., Jones, J. R., & Williams, B. (1975). The chemical control of preoperative anxiety. *Psychophysiology, 12*, 46–49.

Zahn, T. P., & Rapoport, J. L. (1987). Autonomic nervous system effects of acute doses of caffeine in caffeine users and abstainers. *International Journal of Psychophysiology, 5*, 33–41.

Appendix:
Laboratory Safety

Laboratories that use physiological recorders should take proper precautions to protect human subjects or patients from possible electric shocks or burns. If an accidentally high electric current passes through the skin, it can produce pain or tissue damage. If it is very high and flows across the body, it could interfere with heart activity. Ventricular fibrillation of the heart is the most frequent cause of death in fatal electrical accidents.

PROTECTION AGAINST ELECTRIC SHOCK

Modern physiological recorders use various techniques to protect subjects from shock. For example, many of them use transistor circuits (in the first stage amplifiers connected to the electrodes) to isolate subjects from high-voltage circuits. However, even though the probability of shock is very low, additional precautions must be taken. One approach is to fuse each electrode lead to prevent shocks through inadvertent shorts between the electrodes and associated circuitry. A 5-mA (milliAmp) fuse would limit electric current flow to a safe level in the event of a malfunction. This would be especially important when making recordings that require the placement of electrodes on either side of the body, as is commonly done in measuring heart activity. For example, electrodes might be placed on the right and left arms for heart rate recordings. Another approach would be to connect each electrode to ground through voltage-limiting diodes. (A diode is a device that limits current flow to one direction.)

Because electric current passed across the body is more dangerous than current limited to one side, the use of one-sided measurement is preferred where feasible. For example, skin conductance measures should be made from the same hand, rather than using two hands. Similarly, ground electrodes should be placed on the same side of the body as active electrodes whenever possible.

METHODS OF ACCIDENT PREVENTION

A number of techniques to prevent or minimize the probability of occurrence of an electrical shock have been outlined by Cromwell et al. (1976).

Grounding

Grounding may be achieved by connecting the metal equipment case to ground by a wire or by using three-pronged plugs in which the ground connection is established by the round con-

445

tact in the plug. In the event of an electrical short, the current will flow through the case and be shunted off to ground.

Use of Low Voltage

The use of low voltage requires the operation of equipment at lower voltages than that provided by electrical outlets (they commonly provide 115 V). One way of doing this is to operate equipment from batteries. Another method is to use a small transformer that reduces the power reequirement for operating the equipment (e.g., from 115 V to 6 V).

Isolation of Subject-Connected Parts

Isolation requires the use of amplifiers that are completely isolated from ground.

Ground-Fault Interrupter

Interrupters involve the use of a circuit that is designed to automatically interrupt power, like a circuit breaker, when a person touches a defective piece of equipment and current returns to ground through his or her body.

DO'S AND DON'TS

In their book, Cromwell et al. (1976) have provided a list of "do's and don'ts" with respect to making the operation of electrical equipment as safe as possible. These lists are summarized here:

Do's

1. Familiarize yourself with the equipment by studying its proper usage as explained in the operating manuals.
2. Always follow correct operating procedures.
3. Report any irregularities of equipment function to appropriate personnel. For example, intermittent operation, slight electric shocks, or loose controls should be brought to the attention of an electronics technician or engineer or maintenance personnel employed by the equipment manufacturer.

Don'ts

1. Don't remove plugs from outlets by pulling the line cord. This can break or loosen the ground wire.
2. Don't use "adapter" plugs, that is, two-pronged plugs that enable you to plug a three pronged equipment plug into an ungrounded outlet. The wiring should be redone to accomodate three-pronged plugs; otherwise, grounding is not possible.
3. Don't use extension cords. If absolutely necessary, use heavy-duty, three-wire cords that provide for ground connections.
4. Don't run carts over, or step on electrical cables or connectors. This can cause breaks in the ground wire.
5. Don't operate any piece of electrical equipment without being thoroughly familar with its operation and possible shock hazards.

ADDITIONAL SAFETY

In a section on laboratory saftey, Stern, Ray, and Davis (1980) suggested that plans for a medical emergency be made whenever a subject is under your supervision in a psychophysiology laboratory. There should be a prepared course of action for contacting appropriate emergency medical personnel or an ambulance, as needed. It is also suggested that the psychophysiological researcher, whether it be student or professional, does not unecessarily alarm a subject whose physiological responses appear abnormal. For instance, if a subject's EKG appears to have abnormal characteristics, this should be confirmed on another occasion before suggesting to the subject that perhaps an EKG be done by a cardiologist.

Stern et al. (1980) also pointed out the importance of adhering to ethical standards in carrying out any type of experimentation with human subjects. Some considerations include whether the procedure involves physical stress or anxiety, shame, or embarrassment to the subject. Provisions for supplying information about the study and answering questions before and after data collection should be made. Assurances about confidentiality of personal data and task performance should be given. Coercion should never be used, either prior to or after experimentation, and subjects must be allowed to terminate their participation in the study at any time they wish. In other words, informed consent should be obtained from the participant prior to the experiment, the consent form should be dated and witnessed and cannot be given by anyone under 18 years of age without the cosignature of a guardian. Detailed guidelines for conducting experimentation with human subjects is contained in a manual entitled "Ethical Principles in the Conduct of Research with Human Participants" and can be obtained from the American Psychological Association, 1200 17th Street, N.W., Washington, D.C 20036.

REDUCING RISK OF DISEASE TRANSMISSION

Infectious Diseases

Concern over the spread of disease, such as acquired immunodeficiency syndrome (AIDS) has led to the preparation of guidelines by a committee set up by the Society for Psychophysiological Research (Putnam, Johnson, & Roth, 1992). The guidelines identify factors that contribute to the risk of transmitting blood-borne diseases to subjects in laboratories or to experimenters and technicians. They also recommend procedures to minimize such risk. The following account is a summary of the article by Putnam et al., 1992. The reader is encouraged to read the original.

Risk Factors in Psychophysiological Research

Low Risk.   The lowest risk is associated with items of laboratory equipment that touch the intact skin. These include surface electrodes, stethoscopes, and photoplethysmographs and, although they require cleaning before reuse, they do not need disinfection.

Moderate Risk.   Items that are applied to skin that has been purposely abraded, or skin that is not intact because of scratches or cuts, require disinfection. Laboratory personnel can reduce risk of disease transmission by wearing rubber gloves or by care in preparation of the skin.

High Risk.   These items include any subdermal recording electrodes or any needles or lancets used in skin abrasion. They must be sterile at the time of use and require careful handling to prevent accidental punctures of the skin.

Risk Reduction Procedures

AIDS is not the only blood-borne disease that is potentially transmissible in the laboratory. Others are Hepatitis B and Creutzfeldt–Jacob Disease. Putnam et al. (1992) point out that the Center for Disease Control in the United States recommends that all subjects or patients be considered carriers of the AIDS virus to encourage proper precautions.

Wearing Sterile Gloves.   It is recommended that sterile surgical gloves be worn during skin abrasion and cleaning as well as during electrode preparation, application, and removal. This would be for any experimenter or technician whose hands will be in contact with the abraded skin surface, the electrode, or the electrolyte. Gloves are especially important if either the technician or subject has breaks in their skin. Hand washing should be faithfully practiced before and after working with a subject. Gloves should be disposed of after use.

Skin Preparation.   Only use disinfected or sterile instruments to abrade the skin. Abrade the skin only if absolutely necessary to achieve an acceptable recording. Sharp instruments should be avoided in skin abrasion because they can easily penetrate a rubber glove. Needles and lancets should be disposed of after use and placed in puncture proof containers.

Electrode Preparation.   Use disposable electrodes where possible. Although these will not require disinfection they should be considered contaminated and disposed of immediately. If reusable electrodes are employed, then use disinfectants. The AIDS virus can be inactivated by common disinfectants, such as sodium hypochlorite (household bleach) or hydrogen peroxide. High-level disinfection for gold, zinc, and platinum electrodes involves soaking for more than 20 min in a 1:25 dilution of 1 part bleach to 24 parts tap water. For silver/silver chloride type electrodes soaking in Cidex (2% Glutaraldehyde) for over 20 min is required for high-level disinfection, and sterilization requires soaking for about 10 hours. (For more detail see Table 1 in Putnam et al., 1992 and recommendations of the electrode manufacturer).

After each use, reusable electrodes should be cleaned with soap and water, rinsed thoroughly, and disinfected or sterilized. Before use on nonintact skin, surface electrodes should be subjected to levels of disinfection sufficient to inactivate the AIDS virus and the more hardy hepatitis-B virus.

Subdermal electrodes enter body tissue (e.g., muscle) and must be sterile at the time of use. Because they are exposed to blood, these electrodes offer substantial risk for disease transmission in the psychophysiology laboratory. They must be handled carefully to avoid accidental punctures and must be sterilized immediately after use if the intent is to reuse them.

Putnam and colleagues wrote that the risk of disease transmission in the psychophysiology laboratory is small, but it can be further minimized by following the procedures outlined above: use of gloves, careful skin preparation, and disinfecting or disposing of electrodes. They list a variety of germicides as possible disinfecting agents and point out that the procedures recommended for preventing the transmission of the hardier and more infectious hepatitis B virus will also minimize the risk of transmitting AIDS. However, even more stringent precautions are called for if the patient is suspected of having Creutzfeldt–Jacob disease. Some published guidelines also call for more strict precautions in patients known to be infected by AIDS or hepatitis B (American Association of Electromyography and Electrodiagnostics, 1986).

REFERENCES

American Association of Electromyography and Electrodiagnosis (1986). Suggested infection control guidelines for performing electrodiagnostic studies in HTLV-III positive patients. *Muscle Nerve, 9*, 762–763.

Cromwell, L., Arditti, M., Weibell, F. J., Pfeiffer, E. A., Steele, B., & Labok, J. A. (1976). *Medical instrumentation for health care*. Englewood Cliffs, NJ: Prentice-Hall.

Putnam, L. E., Johnson, R., Jr., & Roth, W. T. (1992). Guidelines for reducing the risk of disease transmission in the psychophysiology laboratory. *Psychophysiology, 29*, 127–141.

Stern, R. M., Ray, W. J., & Davis, C. M. (1980). *Psychophysiological recording*. New York: Oxford University Press.

Subject Index

A

$\bar{A}$, *see* Autonomic balance score $\bar{A}$
Acetylcholine, 16, 18
Action potential of neuron, 17, 20–21
  negative after potential, 20
  positive after potential, 20
  spike potential, 17, 20
Activation theory, 401–405
  ascending reticular activating system (ARAS),
    24, 401, 403–404
  induced muscle tension (IMT), 402–403
  inverted U-shaped curve, 402
  neurophysiological bases, 403–404
Adenosine diphosphate (ADP), 168
Adenosine triphosphate (ATP), 168
Affective states, *see* Pupillary response
Afferent feedback, *see* stimulus response
  specificity
All-or-none principle of neuronal firing, 15
Alpha wave, 26
Amino acids, 16–17
Anger, *see* Heart activity
Anxiety,
  autonomic balance score, 400
  EMG biofeedback and, 373
Aristotle, 4
Arteries, 302–303
Ascending reticular activation system (ARAS),
  see activation theory
Asthma, *see* Biofeedback applications
Attention contingent negative variation, 137–143
  EEG, 61–62,
  ERPs, 120–124
  heart rate, 267
  orienting response, 414–415
Attitude, *see* Pupillary response
Auditory evoked potential (AEP), 87–88

Auditory system testing, *see* sensory system
  testing, evoked potential audiometry
Autonomic balance, 399–401
  anxiety, 400
  cold pressor (CP), 397–398
  homeostasis, 400
  menstruation, 427–428
  PNS dominance, 399–400
  psychosomatic disorders, 400
  SNS dominance, 399–400
Autonomic balance score $\bar{A}$, 399–400
Autonomic nervous system (ANS), 35–39
Autonomic response specificity, 405–408
Average evoked potential, *see* Event-related
  potentials
Avicenna, 6–7
Axon, 13–16

B

Baroreceptors, 260, 303–304
Behavioral disorders, 354–359
  agoraphobia, 358
  anxiety neurosis, 357
  panic disorder, 358
  psychiatric diagnosis and brain ERPs,
    354–356
  psychopathy, 356
  psychopathy and EDA, 357–358
  schizophrenia and CNV, 299
  schizophrenia and P300, 355
  schizophrenia and EDA, 357
  schizophrenia and the EEG, 356–357
  schizophrenia and HR, 358
  schizophrenia and sensory ERPs, 354–356
Beta wave, *see* Electroencephalogram
Biofeedback, 365–395
  blood pressure, 379–380
  blood volume, 386